Discourse Networks, 1800 / 1900

Friedrich A. Kittler

Discourse Networks
1800 / 1900

TRANSLATED BY MICHAEL METTEER, WITH CHRIS CULLENS

FOREWORD BY DAVID E. WELLBERY

STANFORD UNIVERSITY PRESS, STANFORD, CALIFORNIA

Assistance for the translation was provided by Inter Nationes

Discourse Networks, 1800/1900 was originally published in German in 1985 as
Aufschreibesysteme 1800/1900, © 1985, 1987 Wilhelm Fink Verlag.
The Foreword has been prepared specially for this edition by David E. Wellbery.

Stanford University Press, Stanford, California
© 1990 by the Board of Trustees of the Leland Stanford Junior University
Printed in the United States of America

Original printing 1990

Last figure below indicates year of this printing:
09   08   07   06   05   04   03   02   01

CIP data appear at the end of the book

Contents

Foreword

DAVID E. WELLBERY

Post-Hermeneutic Criticism

Fashion, Georg Simmel once remarked, is distinguished from history by the fact that its changes are without substance. Whether ties are thick or thin, collars loose or buttoned down, sets no preconditions for subsequent development except for the empty or nonsubstantial one that what follows be different. Alterations of fashion are without consequence, mere signals of the new, empty of emergence. The remark is a sort of ideological crystal that assembles the tacit axiology of our fashion talk—surface versus depth, sign versus meaning, semblance versus seriousness, repetition versus growth—into symmetrically juxtaposed facets. It miniaturizes a code, reduces the already said, the already thought, the always already known, to the bounded framework of a sentence. Hence its evidentiary force, its effect of perceptual immediacy.

The axiology at work in Simmel's aperçu has recently become audible in the discussion of post-structuralism within American criticism. With increasing frequency one hears or reads the claim: the fashion of post-structuralism has worn thin (like last year's coat), has lost its appeal, is no longer in. This diagnosis betrays, I believe, a good deal about the present state of critical discussion in the United States. The claim that post-structuralism is going out of style serves to contain, in the tactical sense of the term, the disruptive and transformative potential of post-structuralist thought, to render it inconsequential. The prognosis of demise is a wish-fulfillment fantasy: the wish, precisely, that post-structuralism made (and makes) no real difference, that its intervention on the American critical

scene was as ephemeral as last year's Paris designs. At last we can exchange this vocabulary for a new one, and keep on doing—what else?—
what we were doing all along.

Of course, even where the instruments and strategies of post-structuralist
thought have been enthusiastically adopted, they have often served as a
modish disguise. Thus the reception and broad dissemination of Derrida
in the United States has taken shape as a blending of New-Critical immanent interpretation, on the one hand, with a negative theology of the literary work in which texts figure as the hopefully hopeless allegory of
their own failure, on the other. The difficult term *deconstruction* has become a laxly used synonym for negative critique. Advocacy of this sort,
held in thrall to fascination, is merely the inverse of the accusation of
fashionableness. Information, according to Gregory Bateson's definition,
is a difference that makes a difference. By consigning post-structuralism
to the realm of fashion, American literary criticism has systematically refused to be informed.

A literary criticism informed by post-structuralism: what would be its
protocols, its theoretical objects, its aims? The American critical debate
has refused to work through this question in any practical way. By keeping
post-structuralism at a distance, by assigning it the status of an exotic fashion, American criticism has avoided the experience of post-
structuralism, in Hegel's sense of experience as a transformative sufferance in which not merely consciousness changes, but also its objects
and its criteria of truth. For this reason, the American publication of
Friedrich Kittler's book *Discourse Networks, 1800/1900* is particularly
propitious. What distinguishes this book above all is that it is thoroughly
informed by post-structuralism; it has suffered through the difference that
post-structuralism makes. Kittler's book is not about post-structuralism,
does not take post-structuralism as its theme. Rather, it presupposes
post-structuralist thought, makes that thought the operating equipment,
the hardware, with which it sets out to accomplish its own research program. In *Discourse Networks*, post-structuralism becomes a working vocabulary, a set of instruments productive of knowledge.

That this transformation should occur in Germany is not without its
paradoxes. On occasion the resistance to post-structuralism within the
German discussion has been organized around the fashion topos mentioned above, echoing with phrases such as "the Parisian philosophy à la
mode" (Manfred Frank) cultural anxieties and animosities that go back
at least to the eighteenth century. But far more significant as a barrier to
authentic engagement with post-structuralist thought has been the predominant role of hermeneutics in defining research agendas within the
so-called "sciences of the spirit" (*Geisteswissenschaften*). Hermeneutics,

of course, is no German monopoly, as the distinguished work of Paul Ricoeur and Emilio Betti demonstrates, but nowhere, I think, has it so exclusively set the framework for discussion as in the Federal Republic, where, since the publication of Hans-Georg Gadamer's monumental *Truth and Method* in 1960, hermeneutic terminology has become the koine of intellectual work. Within literary studies the Constance School of reception theory has been the most influential tributary of Gadamer's work, but literary sociology, as in the case of Peter Bürger's institutional theory, has also drawn on hermeneutic motifs. Even the neo-Marxist Frankfurt School, in its redaction as a theory of communication and understanding (in, for example, the work of Jürgen Habermas), has adopted major presuppositions of the hermeneutic position. This breadth of appeal, moreover, is built into hermeneutic theory itself, which conceives of interpretation as our stance in being: we cannot but interpret, we are what we are by virtue of acts of interpretation. Hence the "universality claim" (*Universalitätsanspruch*) of hermeneutics, its claim to the position of queen of the sciences.

Given this hermeneutic hegemony, one might naturally expect that the importation of post-structuralism into the German context would elicit attempts at ameliorative appropriation. Precisely this occurs, for example, in Manfred Frank's book on Friedrich Schleiermacher (*The Individual Universal*, 1977), which purports to rediscover major tenets of Derrida's thought in the work of the father of Romantic hermeneutics. But a second type of response is equally imaginable, a response that actualizes aspects of post-structuralist thought incommensurate with the hermeneutic paradigm, and this is the direction that Kittler's book takes. Thus, *Discourse Networks* reveals more clearly than has been the case in the American discussion up to now that a literary criticism informed by post-structuralism is, in fact, a post-hermeneutic criticism. It abandons the language game and form of life defined by the hermeneutic canons of justification and enters into domains of inquiry inaccessible to acts of appropriative understanding. Post-hermeneutic criticism, to put the matter briefly, stops making sense.

Nietzsche once punned on Schleiermacher's name by literalizing it: the father of hermeneutics, he asserted, was really a veil maker (*Schleier-Macher*). Kittler, attending no less intensely than Nietzsche to the power of the letter, tears the veil away from hermeneutics and dispels its aura, its shimmering suggestion of sacral authority. This dismantling of hermeneutics follows two tightly interwoven strands of argument, the first of which is historical or, more accurately, genealogical—in the Nietzschean sense of the term. Under the optic of genealogical analysis, the universality claim of hermeneutics evaporates and hermeneutics is exposed in its situational boundedness, its particularity. Hermeneutic understanding is not at all what human beings always do with written or spoken texts, it is not a foundational condition for the processing of significant marks. Rather, it is a contingent phenomenon within the evolution of discursive practices in Europe; it rests on a host of preconditions such as alphabetization, the expansion of book production, the organization of the modern university, the emergence of the civil service; it presupposes specific forms of socialization to which in turn it contributes; and it is linked with other, equally contingent discourses such as those of pedagogy and poetry (*Dichtung*). Finally, hermeneutics draws on and ratifies a specific rendering of linguistic materiality, the myth of the silent inner voice that Derrida has described as foundational for the modern philosophy of the subject. In Kittler's analysis, however, this myth appears less as a philosophical hallucination than as a function of instructional practices and technologies. Far from being our natural or human condition, hermeneutics merely results from a specifically trained coordination of children's eyes, ears, and vocal organs. It is a discipline of the body.

The genealogy of hermeneutics cannot itself be written in the hermeneutic manner; it cannot stylize itself (as hermeneutics inevitably does) as a resuscitation of the living spirit from the tomb of the letter. Rather than eliminating the truth of hermeneutics, Kittler describes it from the outside, as an observer of the system and not as its interpreter. What distinguishes his account of the emergence and functioning of hermeneutics from all the narratives constructed on hermeneutic presuppositions, in other words, is that it is the story of a finitude. At the end of the introduction to his *Lectures on the Philosophy of History*, Hegel writes that there is really no historical past: everything that was true and substantial in history lives in an eternal present, which is the element of historical-philosophical thought. Kittler's historiography rejects precisely this claim. The discourse network of 1800 within which hermeneutics comes into being is a passing phenomenon, radically finite, and it contains no truth or substance that would preserve it from the erosion of time. Man, Foucault writes at the end of *The Order of Things*, is a figure inscribed in the sand at the ocean's edge, destined to be effaced by the waves of the future. Kittler's analysis provides the corollary of this claim: hermeneutic humanism is a finite and contingent inscription, written on the background of a granular noise and powerless against time's turbulence.

Despite this theoretical acceptance of finitude, however, Kittler's genealogy of hermeneutics is nonetheless a history of the present, a narrative of how our current practices of academic literary study came to be. For there can be no doubt that our entire system of literary education and scholarship continues to be defined by the hermeneutic language game and by the form of life within which that language game functions. This applies to Anglo-American literary culture as well as to the German context, even though the former has relied less on an explicitly formulated hermeneutic theory. On both sides of the Atlantic the presupposition of sense remains intact, the heyday of meaning (Ian Hacking) continues, and the task of literary education is still the formation of the individual universal that the discourse network of 1800 called into being. The thrust of Kittler's analysis is to show that as long as we continue to operate within the hermeneutic paradigm we are paying homage to a form of language processing long since deceased. Gadamer's *Truth and Method* is indeed a monument, a kind of memorial that holds the present in thrall to an ancient (but really not so ancient) law. Rather than breaking new ground, the hermeneutic turn of the 1960's appears from Kittler's perspective to be a restabilization, a defensive shield that protects the inherited discourse network against social and cultural mutations threatening to render hermeneutics obsolete. Moreover, it is not the first such apotropaic maneuver: already at the turn of the century Wilhelm Dilthey had erected a hermeneutics of vital expressivity that succeeded in barring the forces of modernity—those forces Kittler describes in the second section of his book (1900)—from the temple of the history of spirit (*Geistesgeschichte*). It is no accident that Dilthey's defensive action, as recent research has shown, is accomplished by suppressing Nietzsche, a suppression that continues in Gadamer and Habermas. Hermeneutics maintains its ghostly afterlife by refusing to hear the verdict pronounced upon it by the solitary of Sils-Maria.

Kittler's genealogy of hermeneutics is intertwined, as I mentioned, with a second strand of argumentation. One might call this the properly theoretical dimension of Kittler's book were it not for the fact that theory here has so thoroughly passed over into practice that it is hardly distinguishable as a separate component. Nevertheless, one can abstract from Kittler's text certain theoretical presuppositions that serve to enable his critical enterprise. These premises represent a remarkable condensation of the theoretical work accomplished by the post-structuralists, especially Derrida, Foucault, and Lacan. Indeed, one of the most striking features of Kittler's book compared with even the finest American adaptations of post-structuralist thought as well as with the work of the post-structuralists themselves is the absence of partisanship and schoolishness that characterizes its theoretical stance. It is as if the three variants of post-structuralist thinking had shed here the contentiousness of their individual articulations and entered into the anonymity of an episteme. Kittler's work cannot be classified as Derridean, Foucauldian, or Lacanian; rather, it grounds itself on what might be termed the joint achievement of the three. Perhaps this is the major methodological innovation of Kittler's book. By eliciting from the divergent elaborations of post-structuralist thought a collective epistemological apparatus, Kittler establishes a positive research program for a post-hermeneutic criticism.

The first component of this program—the premise that determines its overall perspective—might be termed the "presupposition of exteriority." The task of Kittler's critical investigation, in other words, is not to reabsorb the scattered utterances and inscriptions of the past into an inwardness that would endow them with meaning, be this inwardness the reflexivity of the subject as in Romantic hermeneutics or the reflexivity of language itself as in Gadamer. Rather, he practices what Foucault, in an early essay on Maurice Blanchot, called the "thinking of the outside," the thinking of language as a domain recalcitrant to internalization. Later in his career, Foucault named this domain "discourse" and set out to develop a lexicon of exteriority—series, event, discontinuity, materiality—with which to describe it. Kittler's discourse analysis follows the Foucauldian lead in that it seeks to delineate the apparatuses of power, storage, transmission, training, reproduction, and so forth that make up the conditions of factual discursive occurrences. The object of study is not what is said or written but the fact—the brute and often brutal fact—that it is said, that this and not rather something else is inscribed.

Inscription, in its contingent facticity and exteriority, is the irreducible given of Kittler's analysis, as the original German title of his book—*Aufschreibesysteme*—makes evident. That title, a neologism invented by Dr. Schreber, can be most literally translated as "systems of writing down" or "notation systems." It refers to a level of material deployment that is prior to questions of meaning. At stake here are the constraints that select an array of marks from the noisy reservoir of all possible written constellations, paths and media of transmission, or mechanisms of memory. A notation system or, as we have chosen to translate, a discourse network has the exterior character—the outsideness—of a technology. In Kittler's view, such technologies are not mere instruments with which "man" produces his meanings; they cannot be grounded in a philosophical anthropology. Rather, they set the framework within which something like "meaning," indeed, something like "man," become possible at all.

Writing (or arche-writing) as the condition of possibility of metaphysical conceptuality: this, of course, is a major tenet of Derrida's work. In Lacan, the cognate notion is that our existence is a function of our relation to the signifier. Kittler concretizes this post-structuralist theme by situating his analysis not at the level of writing or the signifier in general, but rather at the level of the historically specific machineries—scriptural and otherwise—that in their various arrangements organize information processing. His post-hermeneutic criticism, in other words, renders explicit and productive the tendency toward a radical historicism that is in fact immanent to the work of all the post-structuralist thinkers. To be sure, this historicism is no longer the narrative of a subject—a hero of knowledge, labor, or liberty—in the manner of the master plots of modernity; nor is it a particularist anamnesis of the lived past such as the so-called new historicism pursues. Like Foucault's, Kittler's historiography has a systematic thrust, tends toward the delineation of types. These types, denoted simply by the dates 1800 and 1900, are the discourse networks—the linkages of power, technologies, signifying marks, and bodies—that have orchestrated European culture for the past two hundred years.

The presupposition of exteriority, I claimed, determines the overall perspective of Kittler's post-hermeneutic criticism. The field within which that criticism operates, its domain of inquiry, is carved out by a second major premise, which I shall call the "presupposition of mediality." Here too Kittler develops insights that emerged within post-structuralism, for instance, in the investigations of the cinematic apparatus carried out by Christian Metz and Jean-Louis Baudry, investigations themselves strongly influenced by the Lacanian notion of the unconscious as a machine. Of course, the studies of Metz and Baudry are concerned with the medium of film alone, and it is principally in the area of film studies that, in both Europe and the United States, the concept of medium is broadly employed. The decisive methodological step undertaken by Kittler is to generalize the concept of medium, to apply it to all domains of cultural exchange. Whatever the historical field we are dealing with, in Kittler's view, we are dealing with media as determined by the technological possibilities of the epoch in question. Mediality is the general condition within which, under specific circumstances, something like "poetry" or "literature" can take shape. Post-hermeneutic literary history (or criticism), therefore, becomes a sub-branch of media studies.

This reclassification of literary criticism necessarily elicits a rethinking of its object of study. First and most obviously, if literature is medially constituted—that is, if it is a means for the processing, storage, and transmission of data—then its character will change historically according to the material and technical resources at its disposal. And it will likewise change historically according to the alternative medial possibilities with which it competes. In this regard, too, Kittler's work leads to a radical historicism that finally dissolves the universality of the concept of literature. Moreover, this dissolution does not bear merely on distant epochs such as the medieval period, where the question of orality versus literacy has long been a focus of research. It operates in our own historical back-yard, severing, as Kittler shows, Romantic "poetry" (produced under the monopoly of print and universal alphabetization) from modern "litera-ture" (where writing enters into competition with the technical media of phonograph and film). From this perspective, the typewriter, still a com-ponent of our historical a priori, can be seen to initiate a fundamental mutation in the mode of existence of language.

But the notion of mediality recasts our notion of literature in another sense. As soon as we conceive of literature as medially instantiated, then we must view its meaning as the product of a selection and rarefaction. All media of transmission require a material channel, and the characteris-tic of every material channel is that, beyond—and, as it were, against—the information it carries, it produces noise and nonsense. What we call literature, in other words, stands in an essential (and again, historically variable) relation to a non-meaning, which it must exclude. It is defined not by what it means, but by the difference between meaning and non-meaning, information and noise, that its medial possibilities set into place. This difference, obviously, is inaccessible to hermeneutics. It is the privileged locus, however, of post-hermeneutic thought.

A criticism oriented by the presuppositions of exteriority and medi-ality has no place for creative human subjects, allows no room to psy-chology and its internalizations, refuses to anchor itself in a notion of universal human being. This non-anthropological bent of Kittler's work will seem disturbing to many readers of the book, who will rightly ask: What is the interest that motivates this critical enterprise? Where are its bonds of solidarity? An answer to these questions, I believe, is implied by the third premise of post-hermeneutic criticism, the premise that defines not its analytical perspective (exteriority), nor its domain of study (medi-ality), but rather its point of reference and focus of concern. I call this premise the "presupposition of corporeality."

The reason that the concept of corporeality defines the point of refer-ence for post-hermeneutic criticism is clear. The body is the site upon which the various technologies of our culture inscribe themselves, the connecting link to which and from which our medial means of process-ing, storage, and transmission run. Indeed, in its nervous system, the body itself is a medial apparatus and an elaborate technology. But it is also radically historical in the sense that it is shaped and reshaped by the networks to which it is conjoined. The forerunner of this thinking in terms of corporeality, of course, is Nietzsche, whose philosophy follows, as he put it, the body's guiding thread and whose aesthetics, as he often insisted, is a physiology. Among the post-structuralists, Foucault cleaves most closely to this aspect of the Nietzschean program, especially in his work on the history of punishment and on sexuality. But in Lacan, too, for whom subject formation takes place at the intersection of the body and the signifier, and in Derrida, whose reading of Freud focuses on the question of intra-psychic inscription, the theme of corporeality is insistent. One widespread reading of post-structuralism claims that it eliminates the concept of the subject. It would be more accurate to say that it replaces that concept with that of the body, a transformation which disperses (bodies are multiple), complexifies (bodies are layered systems), and historicizes (bodies are finite and contingent products) subjectivity rather than exchanging it for a simple absence.

The presupposition of corporeality has two major methodological consequences for post-hermeneutic criticism. The first is that the question of agency recedes into the background. The body is not first and foremost an agent or actor, and in order to become one it must suffer a restriction of its possibilities: the attribution of agency is a reduction of complexity. As a result, culture is no longer viewed as a drama in which actors carry out their various projects. Rather, the focus of analysis shifts to the processes that make that drama possible: to the writing of the script, the rehearsals and memorizations, the orders that emanate from the directorial authority. This (in my view) important conceptual shift can be formulated somewhat less metaphorically as follows: post-hermeneutic criticism replaces the foundational notion of praxis (the materialist version of subjective agency) with that of training. Culture is just that: the regimen that bodies pass through; the reduction of randomness, impulse, forgetfulness; the domestication of an animal, as Nietzsche claimed, to the point where it can make, and hold to, a promise.

The second methodological consequence of the presupposition of corporeality is that the sufferance of the body, its essential pathos, becomes a privileged locus for the analysis of discourse networks in terms of both their systematic character and their effectivity. In other words, the point at which discourse networks reveal most sharply their specific impress is in the pathologies they produce. Just as post-hermeneutic criticism focuses on the difference between information and noise, sense and nonsense, that defines every medium, so too it attends to the difference between normal behavior and aberrance (including madness) that lends every cultural formation its identity. The victims who people Kittler's book—the Bettinas, the Günderodes, the Nietzsches, the Schrebers— speak the truth of the culture they suffer. Whoever would look for the bonds of solidarity that orient Kittler's investigation will find them here: in its unmistakable compassion for the pathos of the body in pain. Hermeneutics would appropriate this corporeal singularity in the construction of a meaning. Post-hermeneutic criticism, however, draws its responsibility precisely from the unassimilable otherness of the singular and mortal body. This is the ethical reason it stops making sense.

Romanticism

—Ach, ich bin des Treibens müde.   Goethe

German literary historiography normally distinguishes between Classicism (*Klassik*) and Romanticism (*Romantik*) as two differently oriented movements in literary and cultural history around the turn of the nineteenth century. The former term is more restricted in its temporal scope and cast of players insofar as it refers principally to the joint endeavors of Goethe, Friedrich Schiller, Wilhelm von Humboldt, and a few other figures during the last decade of the eighteenth century, whereas Romanticism extends well into the nineteenth century and includes a large number of writers, from Friedrich and August Wilhelm Schlegel, Novalis, Ludwig Tieck, and the philosophers Johann Gottlieb Fichte and Friedrich Schelling to Joseph von Eichendorff, Clemens Brentano, and E. T. A. Hoffmann, to mention only some of the major names. In Hegel, the two movements are sometimes thought to converge, or find their dialectical synthesis. Since the lives and works of most of the writers mentioned fall within Goethe's life span (1749–1832), and since Goethe's cultural esteem came to exceed that of all his contemporaries, the entire period is often called the Age of Goethe.

In Anglo-American historiography, however, such distinctions are unknown. The entire period in question is simply called Romanticism, and Goethe, insofar as he is acknowledged, is viewed not merely as a contemporary, but as an affine poet and intellect to Wordsworth. For this reason, the first part of Kittler's book fits well with the scholarship produced in the English-speaking world. Beneath the title "1800" it collectively treats most of the Classical and Romantic writers mentioned as participating in a common enterprise, or rather a common discourse network. It is a study—although it doesn't employ the term—of the German variant of European Romanticism.

What is the view of Romanticism that emerges from Kittler's posthermeneutic reading? To answer this question let us first imagine another sort of reading, let us imagine, in fact, a book about Romanticism that carries the title *The Ideology of Romanticism*. This book would be a critical study of Romanticism in the sense that it doesn't—as indeed Kittler's book doesn't—consider as fundamentally true the tenets of Romantic writing. Rather, as its title indicates, it sets out to demonstrate that these tenets involve an ideological mystification, that they cover up something, that they are delusions from which we must free ourselves. According to our fictional book, the center of the Romantic ideology is the extravagant view of art it propagates: the view that art is an autonomous sphere in which, above and beyond the social and political clashes of historical reality, something like a totalization of human experience occurs. The Romantic doctrine of artistic autonomy, together with cognate notions such as genius, organic form, creative imagination, is a flight from reality, a denial of the social functions of art, a sublimated projection unaware of the rifted world from which it springs.

Of course, no such book exists that argues its case quite this simply, but the caricature I have sketched can nevertheless be applied to a number of studies published during the seventies in Germany (when the question of artistic autonomy was intensely discussed) and no doubt to certain works produced within Anglo-American scholarship as well. The point of my little fiction, however, was not to open a discussion of research on Romanticism, but to provide a reasonably recognizable contrasting image to the critical approach charted in Kittler's reading. The first feature that emerges in this regard is that Kittler nowhere employs the notion of ideology. He dismisses the rather complicated apparatus that notion implies: the opposition between reality and its distorted representation, the theory of ideational sublimation, the distinction between mental and material production, the notions of expression and projection. His theory of Romanticism is not that of an alternate world that exists alongside the authentic world of social forces and forms of organization, and adamantly not that of a superstructural configuration produced by and yet dissimulating the nature of its infrastructure. On the contrary, he takes the Romantic texts he analyzes quite literally, he reads them as a certain technology of the letter. There are no hidden truths to be uncovered here, no depths beneath the texts that it is our task to appropriate. Everything lies on the surface, precisely because this surface materiality of the texts themselves—their inscription within a discourse network—is the site of their historical efficacy.

Another way of marking this difference between traditional ideological analysis and Kittler's discourse analysis is to say that in the latter the concept of the social function of literature undergoes a fundamental transformation. As in the sociological theory of Niklas Luhmann, the notion of society itself is abandoned in favor of an investigation of interacting subsystems endowed with their particular technologies and protocols. This shift in focus from a totalizing concept of society to an analysis of specific subsystems brings with it a tremendous gain in analytical precision and concreteness. Indeed, one might even claim that the old talk of "society" and "social function" in literary criticism did no cognitive work at all. "Society" was simply the marker of correct political sentiment, the membership card to a particular discursive fellowship. Be this as it may, the decisive methodological point is clear enough: for Kittler there is no longer any totalizing term—say, "bourgeois society"—that can serve as an explanans for individual and local cultural phenomena. These are, quite positivistically, what they are: data selected and steered by their commands and addresses. Kittler's innovation is to replace the traditional causal-expressive model of sociological explanation with a cybernetic one.

Romanticism, then, is a certain technology of the letter. What limits this technology and therefore renders it historically describable is the documented existence of other technologies, most notably that of modernism, described in the second section of Kittler's book. The differences between the two discourse networks (1800/1900) provide the epistemological lever that enables each to be viewed from the outside. Of course, this systemic comparison is burdened by the linearity of the medium "book" in which it is carried out: in order to see the various functions described in the first part of the book as functions—that is, as variable and substitutable—the reader should ideally have read the second part, and vice versa. Kittler solves this problem in two ways. First, his description of the Romantic discourse network is interlaced with comparative remarks that anticipate the findings of the modernism section. Secondly, he develops his analysis of Romanticism through an implicit juxtaposition with an anterior system, which he calls the Republic of Scholars.

This prior discourse network does not receive a full and detailed characterization, but its contours should be relatively familiar to the reader. We are dealing here with the system of learning that developed in early modern Europe in the wake of printing, a system in which knowledge was defined in terms of authority and erudition, in which the doctrine of rhetoric governed discursive production, in which patterns of communication followed the lines of social stratification, in which books circulated in a process of limitless citation, variation, and translation, in which universities were not yet state institutions and the learned constituted a special (often itinerant) class with unique privileges, and in which the concept of literature embraced virtually all of what was written. The breakdown of this system occurred gradually, beginning with Descartes' rejection of erudition and rhetoric and his simultaneous grounding of the truth of discourse in the inwardness of the ego in the *Discourse on Method*; and it extended across the first three-quarters of the eighteenth century that are generally referred to as the Enlightenment. Kittler, for economic reasons, leaves this period of disintegration and reorganization out of his account and draws his retrospective comparisons solely between Romanticism and the old res publica litteraria.

The strategy of periodization leads us to a second comparison, for the book most similar to Kittler's *Discourse Networks*, the paradigm of its genre, is clearly Foucault's archaeology of the human sciences, *The Order of Things*. In that study, Foucault contrasts three successive epistemic systems within which European culture has thought the domains of life, labor, and language. At the close of his study, Foucault speculates on the end of the third of these epistemes (which he calls "modern"), an end that coincides with the end of "man" as the central figure of knowledge. What I referred to above as the Enlightenment is discussed in detail by Foucault under the rubric of the "classical" episteme, a system of knowledge preceded in his account by the "Renaissance." Thus, Kittler's vaguely sketched Republic of Scholars correlates to Foucault's Renaissance and classical epistemes, his "1800" to Foucault's modern system, and his "1900" to Foucault's roughly sketched postmodernism. Where Foucault develops a rigorous analysis of two distinct "premodern" configurations of knowledge, Kittler operates with a nebulous, but generally accessible characterization of the older discursive formation. By contrast, where Foucault leaves things in a speculative haze, Kittler unfolds a detailed investigation. For the latter, in other words, the "postmodern" period (my term of convenience, not Foucault's or Kittler's) is not a future about to break in upon us, it has already occurred—during the thirty or so years surrounding the turn of the twentieth century. Foucault's and Kittler's periodizations exactly coincide (and this overlap is legible in Kittler's references to Foucault's work) with regard to the phase the former calls "modern" and the latter—without connotational baggage—"1800." This is likewise the phase traditional literary historiography refers to as Romanticism.

Further comparisons of Foucault's investigation of the Romantic period with that developed in Kittler's *Discourse Networks* would not be very fruitful here. Their respective inquiries into this period evidently bear on different objects and employ divergent modes of analysis. Foucault discusses cleanly circumscribed scientific disciplines; his orientation is principally semantic in character. Kittler, taking "literary" texts as his point of departure, considers a wider array of discourses and pursues a more pragmatic line of inquiry. But the general methodological tenet they hold in common nevertheless deserves emphasis. In both Foucault and Kittler, the Romantic period is delimited not genetically, not in terms of what it came from and what it developed into, but rather systemically, that is to say, in terms of differences that set it off from other historically describable systems. Romanticism, in the work of both writers, is a model, a product of analytic construction. Historiography here, even as it accounts for diachrony, sheds its traditional dependence on narrative linearity.

Beyond the matter of periodization, however, Foucault and Kittler share a further strategy—a strategy for the presentation of their respective arguments—that can lead us back to the specifics of Kittler's description of the Romantic technology of the letter. No reader of *The Order of Things* will forget the discussion of *Las Meninas* with which the book opens. There Foucault uses the painting as a kind of paradigmatic scene in terms of which to outline the various parameters of the classical episteme. It is as if Velasquez's masterpiece condensed all the elements and relations that Foucault's meticulous analysis of classical representation later unfolds across some hundred pages. Kittler begins his discussion of Romanticism with a similar primal scene, the "Scholar's Tragedy" that opens Goethe's *Faust*. In his construction, the drama played out across Faust's series of readings and writings—the Nostradamus manuscript, the evocation of the Earth Spirit, the translation from the Gospel of John, and finally Faust's signing the pact with Mephistopheles—enacts nothing other than the collapse of the Republic of Scholars and the emergence, out of this obsolete system, of the Romantic discourse network. Perhaps it was for the sake of this example that Kittler chose to use the older system of erudition, the res publica litteraria, rather than the classical episteme of transparent representation as the contrasting configuration to Romanticism. For Goethe sets his drama in the distant past of humanism and reformation; Faust is a contemporary of Luther, whose translation of the Bible he repeats. As Kittler shows, however, this repetition occurs with a difference: Luther's interpretive dictum of "sola scriptura" is displaced by a hermeneutics that moves beyond, beneath, and before the letter in order to seize the seminal act—the pure movement of origination—that produced the Word.

One of Kittler's many allusions can reveal the profile of the strategy organizing his reading of *Faust*. In the famous introductory sentences to the *Critique of Pure Reason*, Kant delimits his project by distinguishing between "beginnings" (chronological and empirical) and "origins" (achronological and transcendental). The latter, designated by the German verb *entspringen* ("originate"), turn out to have their own ultimate origin in the free act of auto-constitution that characterizes the transcendental ego, the sheerly active *Ich* that becomes the central philosopheme of post-Kantian Romantic thought. Faust arrives at this pure act prior to all language and externality in his translation of John, when he finally writes: "In the beginning was the Act." Faust's free translation, in other words, replaces, as does Idealist philosophy in general, the divine institution of the Word and the Law with the freedom of originary, generative subjectivity. The reason this complex is important to Kittler's analysis becomes clear when we consider the other element (which is also the element of the Other) in Kant's enabling opposition. To designate beginnings in the domain of empiricity—a domain that from the transcendental perspective is secondary and derivative—Kant uses the verb *anheben* ("commence" or "begin"). Precisely this word, today somewhat antiquated and therefore conspicuous as an allusion, determines the predicate of Kittler's first sentence, which opens his reading of the Faustian primal scene: "Die Deutsche Dichtung hebt an mit einem Seufzer." ("German Poetry begins with a sigh.") This citation of the Kantian verb does not merely signal that the analysis to follow is empirical and historical as opposed to transcendental in orientation. That would merely confirm the Kantian opposition and leave intact the hermeneutics resting on that opposition. What Kittler's reading shows, rather, is that the scene in which the origin is imagined is not an origin at all. The origin—the pristine moment of auto-constitution—itself derives from a non-origin, from a beginning that is intrinsically plural, empirical, and other. This beginning is the system of forces and relations that make up the Romantic discourse network.

The Romantic reverie of the origin—one variant of which is hermeneutics—is not a universal dream. It does not emerge from the inwardness of an unconscious whose actants (say Mother, Father, Child) are everywhere the same. Nor does it play out the drama of an ahistorical subject's initiation into an equally ahistorical "language" or regime of the signifier. Rather, it is a function of historically specific discursive technologies. This is the point where Kittler's reading of Romanticism departs from psychoanalysis, with which it nevertheless shares several motifs. In order to conceptualize this difference I would offer the following hypothesis. While Kittler accepts the Lacanian dictum that the unconscious is the discourse of the Other, he reads this formula from the standpoint of Foucault. That is to say, the term *discourse* no longer refers, as in Lacan's rendering, to the linguistic and therefore abstract notion of extended speech, but rather to positive modes of existence of language as shaped by institutions of pedagogy, technical means of reproduction, storage and transfer, available strategies of interpretation, and so on. Likewise the Lacanian Other is for Kittler not the general and sovereign instance of the one Law, but rather (and again, with Foucault) the network of forces and resistances, commands and addresses, that constitute historically specific configurations of domination. If the Romantic dream conforms in several of its features to the psychoanalytic family scenario, then, it is merely because the psychoanalytic script itself was written in reference to this historical field.

To see how this methodological fusion of Foucault and Lacan is worked out concretely, let us return to the primal scene of Romantic writing.

Faust's translation of John, his hermeneutic reappropriation of the origin, is a compensatory action. It fills a "lack" or "deficiency" (Goethe's word is *Mangel*), which itself is figured in liquid terms ("thirst"; a "drying up" of the "stream" that "springs forth" within his own "breast"). The desire, the inner trouble and turbulence that propels his writing and that will find its satisfaction and consolation (*getrost*) in the inscription of the originary deed preceding all language, is nothing other than Faust's separation from Nature herself. Romantic writing returns to the lost natural origin by translating Nature's wordless speech. Furthermore, as the semantics of "liquidity" reveals, this Nature is itself a figuration of the Mother. Faust's quest for the transcendental signified, the originary act and meaning from which language springs, follows a beckoning maternal imago. As Kittler points out, this logic of Faustian desire provides the link to the "Gretchen Tragedy" that in *Faust I* succeeds upon the "Scholar's Tragedy": Faust's singular beloved Gretchen is Mother and Madonna in one, another representative of the natural-maternal source. And *Faust II* remains faithful to this paradigm, culminating as it does in the apotheosis of the "Eternal Feminine" that orients our striving. To begin with the Faustian primal scene, as Kittler does, is to broach a reading of Romantic desire and writing as fixation on the imago of the Mother.

Kittler's elaboration of this reading across the first part of *Discourse Networks*, however, does not abide within the confines of psychoanalytic literary theory. He rejects a strictly psychoanalytic reading of the Romantic complex on the grounds that it would be hermeneutic and tautological. That is to say, insofar as it endeavors to return the text to its origin in the phantasm of the mother-child dyad, and insofar as it conceives this phantasm as the latent meaning of the text, the psychoanalytic interpretation of Romanticism repeats the fundamental gesture of hermeneutics. Moreover, a hermeneutic reading of texts that institute hermeneutic reading (as does the Faustian primal scene) is merely a tautological rewriting of those texts. Psychoanalysis, with its insistence on the Mother as a primary interpretive datum, remains immanent within the Romantic discourse system, remains, let us say, applied Romanticism. Indeed, the claim that the Mother is the origin repeats Romanticism's own most insistent asseveration. The methodological task, then, is to take up a position external to psychoanalysis while accounting for the (semantic) pertinence of a psychoanalytic reading.

Such a step to the outside is accomplished through the above-mentioned fusion of Lacan and Foucault. By bending the Lacanian concepts of discourse and Other in the direction of a Foucauldian "thinking of the outside," Kittler arrives at a thesis on Romanticism that avoids the trap of hermeneutic tautology. With all due precautions regarding oversimplification, I would formulate this thesis as follows: Romanticism is the discursive production of the Mother as the source of discursive production. Before the phantasm of the Mother and before the attachment of desire to this phantasm, in other words, there is a discursive network, and both phantasm and desire are functions of and within this network. The Romantic (and psychoanalytic) origin derives from a beginning, from a network of technologies themselves empirical, historical and other.

Romanticism is the discursive production of the Mother as the source of discursive production. The demonstration and concretization of this thesis in the first part of *Discourse Networks* takes us into regions entirely foreign to traditional literary criticism. Kittler begins with the new pedagogy of the late eighteenth century, a discourse that addressed itself to mothers and thereby constituted the Mother as the agency of primary socialization. It is the Mother who manages the child's initiation into the cultural techniques of reading and writing, and in doing so invests this initiation with an aura of erotic pleasure. This pleasure clings especially to the maternal voice, a kind of aural envelope that binds the mother-child dyad in a pre-articulate unity. Hence the Romantic fascination for a primary orality, for an inner voice, for a speechless transcendental speech. But orality is not merely a dream, it is a technological reality: the reforms initiated by the Bavarian school official Heinrich Stephani (1761–1850) produced this orality as an effect of didactic procedures. Stephani's method of teaching children reading and writing by teaching them the sounds the letters mark, however self-evident it may seem to us today, was in fact a discursive event of major proportions. It produced not merely a new conception, but a new and effective organization of linguistic materiality. Romanticism, it has long been held, rests on a revolution. For Kittler this is also the case. The revolution in question, however, is no longer the French one so dear to the hermeneutics of liberty, but rather the revolution of the European alphabet that occurred with its oralization around 1800.

Primary orality, the Mother, the self-presence of the origin: these are not merely sublimations or philosophical hallucinations, they are discursive facts, nodal points in a positive and empirical discursive network, functions in a system of relays and commands that has no center or origin. As such they do not disguise a reality that is anterior to them and from which they would spring; they produce reality by linking bodies (e.g., the eyes and ears and hands of children) to the letter and to instances of power. Soon this system develops its own theory (a linguistics of the root and the verb), its own imaginary (Poetry as translation of the language of nature), its own protocols of reading (the Romantic hermeneutics of the signified). It realizes itself across institutional reforms (from primary schools to university lecture halls), it is codified in laws (the Universal Prussian Law of 1794 mandates both authorial copyright and maternal breast feeding), it shapes careers (as the new genre of the Bildungsroman reveals). These aspects of the Romantic discourse network are described in great detail in Kittler's study: the ABC books that lead children from primal sounds (*ma*) to primal signifieds (*Mama*), the university reforms that institute Faustian hermeneutics, and especially the literary texts at once programmed by the discourse network in which they are written and programming their readers as subjects of that discourse. All of these subsystems, in their specific dispersion and paths of connection, are what is meant by the thesis: Romanticism is the discursive production of the Mother as the source of discourse.

I have stressed the "maternal" strand in Kittler's reading of Romanticism in order to highlight the specifics of his method. As the reader of *Discourse Networks* will soon discover, however, the thesis I have summarized is in fact only one component in a much more complicated construction. Romanticism is also the institutionalization of authorship, the emergence of a pragmatics of universal poetic address, the monopoly of writing as a medium for the storage and transfer of kinaesthetic data. In particular, my discussion has ignored the commands so central to Kittler's reading, that area in which his Foucauldian reworking of the Lacanian Other assumes prominence. After all, Faust's translation is guided not only by his yearning for the Mother, but also by the poodle present in his chamber. This poodle soon reveals himself as Mephistopheles, the spirit (*Geist*) with whom Faust joins in the infernal pact that determines the remainder of the drama. Starting from this pact, and in particular from the signature that makes it binding, Kittler unfolds an analysis of the imperatives and obligations that the discourse network of 1800 dispenses. The Romantic subject is not merely a subject tethered to the imago of the Mother, it is a subject functioning within a specific constellation of powers. It is a bureaucratic subject, a civil servant (state-employed teacher, university professor, jurist, secretary, etc.), and, as such, a subject engaged in particular ways with the production and interpretation of written material. Romanticism is the discursive production of the Mother as the source of discursive production, to be sure; but it is also the discursive production and distribution of bureaucratic governance. Furthermore, these two aspects, even as they mark off exclusive realms, are fully solidary with one another and mutually sustaining. Romanticism is a discourse network organized as a productive tension between Mother and State.

Everything begins with Goethe's *Faust*, and there too everything ends. Gretchen, pressed into service as maternal imago, murders her mother and child. This crime (against motherhood) earns her madness and, according to the judgment of Mephistopheles, who speaks for the State, execution. Faust, who had found in her the source of his desire and aspirations, goes on to a magical invocation of classical Greece and a philological-poetic marriage to Helen of Troy. In Kittler's reading, this is not a fiction, but a program. His study of Romanticism closes with the case of Karoline von Günderode, the beloved of the classical philologist Friedrich Creuzer. For Creuzer, she was the inner voice that guided his researches, the secret addressee of his translations from the classical sources. Pressed into service as maternal imago—a discursive impress that bars her from speech—Karoline drowns herself in the Rhine. The Rhine, it is often said, is the most Romantic of German rivers.

Modernism

Sehen Sie, mein Herr, ein Komma!   *Hölderlin*

Styles are necessarily various. There is, as Derrida showed in his study of Nietzsche (*Spurs*), no one style, but inevitably many. Derived from the notion of stylus, or writing instrument, the concept of style designates a labor of differential inscription that is both prior and irreducible to meaning.

This point marks a difficulty for the English reader of *Discourse Networks*. In order to register stylistic effects, a reader must be in a position to note differences from other styles. For the German reader of Kittler's book this is an easy task. His or her reading eye and inner ear have been trained to follow the syntactic-rhetorical ductus of German intellectual writing. Such writing is characterizable (I am simplifying, of course) as Hegelian suada: elaborate grammatical constructions, antithetical periods, conceptual reversals, nominalized adjectives—in short, dialectical resolutions. Above all, what distinguishes this style (which both Schopenhauer and Nietzsche derided in vain) is a certain superior distance from the language of everyday life. The brevity and choppiness of mundane talk, as well as its factual references and concreteness, are dissolved in a nimbus of generality. From Dryden to the present, by contrast, English prose has maintained a closeness to the patois of mundane social intercourse. The English intellectual style is inflected more by conversational affability than by the constraints of philosophical abstraction; its home is the practical sphere of commerce rather than the isolated study. For this reason, the difference that Kittler's style makes is lost in translation. His prose is written against the language of dialectical resolution. It is characterized by syntactic concision, by a certain "hardness" and concreteness of diction; it has the literalness sometimes of "lower" (or informal) colloquial exchange, sometimes of the technical language of engineers; its sentences often attain the compactness of a telegram message, or a command. Rendered in English, this stylistic profile necessarily loses its sharpness and tends to disappear in a sea of ordinary talk.

What won't disappear, however, is the stylization of the book as a whole, its precision and symmetry. Two sections, entitled only by dates. Two epigraphs, both mathematical equations. (The first of these, by the way, can be interpreted as an algorithm of "growth," the movement of progressive augmentation that characterizes the discourse network of 1800. The second formalizes the pulse of differential alternation that permeates the modernist discourse network.) Part I begins with a primal writing scene, Faust in his study destroying the discourse system of the Republic of Scholars and inventing Romantic hermeneutics. Part II likewise opens with a primal writing scene, but this time it is Nietzsche with pen (and later typewriter) in hand, and this time it is the Romantic discourse network that crashes to the ground in order to make room for the intransitive scriptural practice of modernism. At the same time, the Faustian opening of Part I points forward to the conclusion of the entire book, the "systematic reversal" of Romantic writing in Valéry's redaction of Goethe, 'My Faust.' With regard to their internal articulation, the two parts are also strictly correlated: in both cases an introit (Faust versus Nietzsche) followed by three large, symmetrically divided subsections. In short, the design of the book is so deliberate as to suggest mathematical formalization or musical seriality. The musical analogy holds for Kittler's style of argumentation as well, which deploys across its linearity a system of recurring leitmotifs (e.g., the sigh "oh" [German "ach"]). *Discourse Networks* is a constructivist assemblage, a model for a chess game, a machine diagram. This compositional strategy suits well the book's posthermeneutic critical practice.

And it suits equally well Kittler's allegiance with modernism, an allegiance that derives not from uncritical advocacy, but rather from the sober recognition that modernism—the discourse network of 1900—has defined the state of the art(s) as it exists today. What Kittler's analysis of modernism reveals, in other words, is that the thirty or so years that revolve around the axis 1900 have decisively altered our epistemological situation (perhaps by rendering it post-epistemological); that intellectual work today, in its most advanced inquiries, has its roots in the modernist transformation of discourse; that we are postmodern in the sense that the modernist intervention is irrevocable. This also is the indirect lesson of post-structuralism: Foucault develops his genealogical method through a reading of Nietzsche, Derrida his theory of arche-writing through a reading of Saussure, and Lacan his version of psychoanalysis through a reading—an endless reading—of Freud. Nietzsche, Saussure, and Freud all play a significant role in Kittler's discussion of modernism as well, but not (and this is decisive) as authors and authorities. In *Discourse Networks* the three figures of the Modernist theoretical triumvirate lose their individuality and are reabsorbed into a circumambient system. Our historiography of post-structuralism has been up till now mere intellectual history, a story of thinkers and their ideas. Kittler's book is the first to break with this antiquated paradigm and to reveal the discursive beginnings of our contemporaneity.

Our contemporaneity: the possessive here is meant to refer to Anglo-American readers of the 1990's, who will find in the modernism section of Kittler's book much more that is recognizably their "own" than in the 1800 portion. The first part of the book, I said, is a study of the German variant of European Romanticism, and with few exceptions the textual examples there come from the German-speaking lands. This means that a considerable labor of translation and transposition will be required of the reader who wants to think through, for instance, the implications of Kittler's investigation for English Romanticism. How does the English history of pedagogy compare with the German developments described by Kittler? Does the somewhat earlier establishment of copyright in England inflect the concept of authorship differently than in Germany? Is there an English process analogous to the German statification of the university? Of course, research on English Romanticism has long stressed German influences (especially with regard to Coleridge). Perhaps Kittler's book will incite a rereading of those borrowings and adaptations in terms of specific discursive conditions. Perhaps too it will prompt the so-called new historicists, who are increasingly turning to Romanticism after having plowed the fields of Renaissance and eighteenth-century research, to ask themselves what their object of study actually is.

The fact that the modernism section of *Discourse Networks* is more international in its range than the first section derives from the nature (or non-nature) of the modernist discourse network it describes. At one point Kittler cites the dissertation of the postal inspector and expressionist poet August Stramm on the "empirical law of the production of correspondence according to which every letter sent from one country to a second elicits a similar mailing from the second to the first." Stramm is writing about the economy of the world postal system, which, by the beginning of the twentieth century, had a real institutional existence, with codified agreements bearing, for example, on rate equivalences. In other words, the exponential explosion and acceleration of international communication Stramm's remark documents is a defining historical feature of modernist discourse. (In *Ulysse grammaphone*, a book written after *Dis-*

course Networks and, as it were, in its wake, Derrida demonstrates the effects of this discursive fact on Joyce's novel.) It is no accident, then, that Kittler's investigation of modernism ranges across national borders, that its onomastic repertoire includes Mallarmé, Villiers de l'Isle-Adam, and Proust in addition to Nietzsche, Benn, and Kafka; Edison, James, and Stein in addition to Lumière, Bergson, and Salomé; Rilke along with Valéry. Communication in Romanticism, of course, also had its international aspect, but it was not technically and institutionally international in the same way as with modernism: its framework remained that defined by the nation state. Hence the Romantic cultivation of national literary tradition; hence the modernist inmixing of traditions and languages (e.g., in Pound). The general point here is not unimportant for comparatist studies: the reference of the term *international* is a function of historically variable technologies of postal transport. As Goethe already recognized, "world literature" (*Weltliteratur*, the late Goethean coinage often thought to be the forerunner of "comparative literature") has its condition of possibility in *Verkehr*, in commerce, exchange, communication.

The noise of all those letters and telegrams noted by Stramm is the same noise K., the protagonist-letter of Kafka's novel, hears in the telephone lines when he attempts to call the castle. It is (technically, not metaphorically speaking) the noise of modernism. Romantic discourse had its "origin" in the pure inwardness of the maternal voice, a voice created by pedagogical reforms such as Stephani's oralization of the alphabet. The modernist exchange of letters likewise has its technical coupling between body and signifier, a coupling produced not by philanthropic pedagogues, but by the science of psychophysics (which soon found its pedagogical application). Hermann Ebbinghaus's memory experiments of the 1880's, in which the new discipline emerges, mark, in Kittler's analysis, a discursive event, a mutation of linguistic materiality. Readers of *Discourse Networks* will encounter here perhaps the most indigestible aspect of Kittler's argument, insofar as the inherited conception of literary modernism has systematically excluded a serious engagement with the historical accomplishments of positivism. Kittler's demonstration, however, is so compelling that one is led to suspect that the traditional exclusion (and even scapegoating) of positivism was in fact an attempt to save Romantic-hermeneutic discourse from the cultural forces that were dismantling it. What better way to do this than by making modernism itself a matter of ideas and worldviews? I have already mentioned Dilthey's suppression of Nietzsche in this connection, of the Nietzsche, that is, who devoted the little reading time his near-blindness allowed him to treatises in physiology and whose theory of violent memory inscription becomes, as Kittler shows, an experimental reality in the work of Ebbinghaus. The "literary" or "humanist" reading of Freud, which inevitably accentuates his transcendence of biologism, is likewise relevant here. Psychoanalysis has its conditions of possibility in the discursive field opened up in psychophysics. The unified and unifying *Geist* of Hegel has long been replaced by the functional multiplicity of Broca's brain and maintains its ghostly afterlife only in hermeneutic philosophy and literary criticism.

Ebbinghaus's experiment, in its basic outlines, is quite simple. In order to measure memory he lets pass before his eye a series of nonsense syllables and counts the number of passes required for the memorization of combinations of these syllables. In this procedure Kittler discloses the complexity of a discursive beginning. There is first of all the body of the experimental subject: stripped of the cultural equipment of subjectivity, it has become a physiological surface upon which the syllables—once, twice, or several times—are inscribed. Secondly, there is the source from which the syllables emerge: not books, not the maternal voice, but a mechanism for the production of random configurations. Having passed across Ebbinghaus's field of vision, having engendered there their instantaneous shocks, these syllables return to a storage mechanism of similar construction. Finally, there is the form of language the system employs, a language without syntactic coherence or semantic content, mere letters in their materiality and in the differential pulse of their alternation. The experiment, in short, institutes language as writing, a system of inscribed differences emerging as a selection from a reservoir of nonsense, etching their differences on the body's surface, and returning to the murmur of the source. The situation of Postal Inspector Stramm is no different: the noise of letters and telegrams out of which some few pass across his desk in order to be reabsorbed in the turbulent sea of communication from which they had come. And neither the postal nor the experimental observer is there to interpret, but merely to count and quantify, to measure either for economic or scientific purposes, the differential values of the selections that confront him. According to Nietzsche, qualities are in fact quantitative differences of force. This is the view that Ebbinghaus's experiment proves.

Psychophysics takes language to a point where it stops making sense, or rather, it shows that all sense making has its frontiers (and therefore its definition) in domains of nonsense and in automatized operations that no longer belong to a subjective authority. On the margins of language use there proliferate a host of breakdowns: dyslexias, aphasias, agraphisms, asymbolisms; the strict division between normal and pathological is transformed into a gradient of standards; intentional agency is dispersed in a system of organic and nervous functions. Speech no longer has its norm in the meaningful utterance of an authorial subject. It has become a selection and rarefaction embodying what cyberneticians call the order-from-noise principle. In short, the modernist discourse network unravels language, reduces its wholeness and centeredness to a tangle of nervous, sensory-motor threads, to a scatter of differential marks.

The precondition of this unweaving is the minimal experimental condition of psychophysics: that writing, as writing, be written down. In order for this detachment of writing from subjectivity to occur, however, inscription had to become mechanized, and this happens with the typewriter. The typewriter, Heidegger noted, alters our relationship to being: it takes language away from the hand, which—and here Heidegger is faithful, as so often, to Aristotle—distinguishes "man." Kittler, without sharing the philosopher's nostalgia, renders this Heideggerian intuition historically concrete. The typewriter frees writing from the control of the eye and of consciousness; it institutes spacing as the precondition of differentiation; it stores a reservoir of signifiers that strike the page much as Ebbinghaus's syllables strike the body's sensory surface. Nietzsche's notion of moral inscription is modeled on the typewriter, one of the earliest versions of which he owned and used. Saussure's linguistics, in Derrida's reading a linguistics of arche-writing, has its technological correlate in the typewriter. Freud's psychic apparatus, as he called it, is a writing machine. Moreover, as Kittler shows, the literacy production of the era is no less dependent, in conception and practice, on the new technology of the letter. Mallarmé calls for the disappearance of the elocutionary subject and derives poetry from the 26 letters of the alphabet and the spaces between them. Kafka's instruments of torture are writing machines. Morgenstern develops a poetics of autonomous punctuation. Like psychophysics (for which it is a technological precondition as well), the typewriter alters the status of discourse and repositions literature, science, and theory. The end of "man" postulated by Foucault is brought on by a mechanism that writes writing.

One way of formulating the discursive effect of psychophysics and the typewriter is to say that only with them does language become perceptible as a medium. But it is not the medial technology of the typewriter alone that makes this perception possible. The development of this technology around 1900 is co-emergent with other medial technologies, in particular the gramophone and film, both of which figure centrally in the Modernism section of *Discourse Networks*. Note the structural similarity of the three: just as the typewriter allows for the processing of scriptural differences that pass beneath the threshold of consciousness, so too film records data of the visual unconscious (as Benjamin noted) in discrete frames that cannot themselves be perceived in the film image; and so too the gramophone records and renders reproducible differences of vibrational frequency that escape conscious audition. The technological dissolution of the noematic world (the world of intentionality) in each of the three media has its counterpart, moreover, in the distribution of the possibilities of information processing among them. Kittler's thesis in this regard is especially provocative. In his view, the three Lacanian registers—the symbolic, the imaginary, and the real—are effects of medial specialization. Writing conveys the differences of the symbolic order; film, with its simulation of visual presence, transmits imaginary contents; and the phonograph allows for the technical recording of the real. The writers who around 1900 transformed literature into an intransitive practice of writing (quite literally "literature") had systematic rather than thematic reasons for doing so. In the modernist landscape of medial specialization, writing is one medium among others, with its own limitations and possibilities, and the writer a media specialist, a professional of the letter.

Kittler's argument regarding the medial constellation of modernism deserves accentuation. The emergence of technological media around 1900 represents a decisive historical and discursive caesura that alters the structure, placement, and function of cultural production. The only critic or theoretician I know who views the historical significance of the media in a similarly radical way is Walter Benjamin. In his brief and rightfully famous essay, "The Work of Art in the Age of Mechanical Reproduction," Benjamin argues that modernism is the destruction of aura, that is, of the sacral distance and otherness of the art work stemming from its singularity. With film, a mode of artistic creation comes into being that, from the beginning, is fashioned as reproducible. The film knows no authentic singular instance, has no original, and for this reason it marks the historical emancipation of art from its mythic-religious roots.

Readers familiar with Benjamin's essay (and with his Baudelaire studies that deal with related issues) will recognize the similarities between his work and Kittler's *Discourse Networks*. To cite merely two examples: both critics strongly emphasize the importance of "shocks," of unforeseeable and instantaneous perturbations, as a key component of experience in modernism; both stress the connection between film, the distracted form of attention it elicits, and the "popularity" or "mass-oriented" nature of its contents. Of course, a detailed comparison between Benjamin and Kittler would have to distinguish these points of similarity more sharply (by asking, for example, what the specific source of the "shocks" in each case is) and develop others as well (e.g., the link in both writers between media and the unconscious). I shall leave this task to the reader, however, and emphasize here merely one major difference between Benjamin and Kittler that strikes me as methodologically crucial. There is in Kittler's analysis of the emergence and significance of technical media no sense of an overriding narrative that event would instantiate. Like Benjamin, Kittler sees the modernist intervention as a break or rupture, but he refuses to invest this transformation with the historico-philosophical meaning of "emancipation." Benjamin's end-of-art thesis, in other words, rests on a diegetic scaffold that remains essentially Hegelian. Kittler is an evolutionist in the sense that he attributes no a priori directionality to historical change. The medialization of modernist discourse is a contingent event, an historical clinamen, not the realization of a project unfolding across the centuries.

In my discussion of the Romanticism section of *Discourse Networks*, I focused on the thesis that Romanticism is the discursive production of the Mother as the source of discursive production. Here too I have restricted my remarks to a single thread of Kittler's construction, the question of linguistic materiality and mediality. Much more than this, however, awaits the reader: for example, a discussion of the emergence of singularity (contra Benjamin) as a recordable datum, of the symmetrical and competitive positions of psychoanalysis and literature within the modernist discourse network, of the impossibility of translation and the constraints of medial transposition. As I mentioned, the *Las Meninas* of Kittler's construction is the Nietzschean writing scene that opens the 1900 section and which leads into a reading of Nietzsche's entire work as a paradigm of modernism.

I shall let these aspects of Kittler's analysis stand without commentary in order to mention briefly one final point. The discursive production of the Mother in Romantic discourse subsumed women in the prototype of the one Woman, the infinitely productive silence that is the source and ideal recipient of male poetic speech. One could speak here of a mono-sexualization of gender: the one Woman—the Mother—is essentially a narcissistic prop for male identity formation. The modernist discourse network institutes a linguistic materiality no longer grounded in the maternal voice and thereby makes possible what Romantic discourse could only acknowledge as an empirical deficiency: the plurality of women. Modernism, in other words, fundamentally restructures the triangular relation among men, women, and language, and therefore the relations between women and men. Especially revealing in this regard is Kittler's discussion of the emergence of the secretary/typist, of the medial mediation of writers' amorous attachments, of the modernist rediscovery of premodern women writers, of the role of women in psychoanalysis. But perhaps the most intriguing aspect of his analysis is this: whereas the Romantic discourse network monosexualizes gender, modernist discourse discloses a sexual difference that resists homogenization. The relation between the sexes, Nietzsche wrote, is essentially agonistic. This agon, in Kittler's view, is an effect of the discourse network that defines our contemporaneity.

Berlin
September 1989

I

1800

$$e^{ix} = \cos x + i \sin x \qquad \textit{Leonhard Euler}$$

The Scholar's Tragedy:
Prelude in the Theater

German Poetry begins with a sigh.

> Habe nun, ach! Philosophie,
> Juristerei und Medizin,
> Und leider auch Theologie
> Durchaus studiert, mit heißem Bemühn.

> Have, oh! studied philosophy,
> Jurisprudence and medicine, too,
> And, worst of all, theology
> With keen endeavor, through and through—[1]

If this is not the sigh of a nameless self—no self appears in the sentence—
it is certainly not the sigh of any known author. What moves through the
cadence of old German *Knittel*-verse is a pure soul. The verses of the
other German Classical Poet confirm this: the sigh "oh!" [*ach*!] is the sign
of the unique entity (the soul) that, if it were to utter another signifier
or (because signifiers exist only in the plural) any signifier whatsoever,
would immediately become its own sigh of self-lament; for then it would
have ceased to be soul and would have become "Language" instead. (The
title of Schiller's distich is unambiguous.)

> Warum kann der lebendige Geist dem Geist nicht erscheinen?
> *Spricht* die Seele, so spricht, ach! schon die *Seele* nicht mehr.

> Why cannot the living Spirit manifest itself to the Spirit?
> Once the soul *speaks*, then, oh!, it is no longer the *soul* that
>   speaks.[2]

Where speaking takes place, there the Other of the soul begins: academic titles and pedagogical deceit.

> Da steh' ich nun, ich armer Tor!
> Und bin so klug als wie zuvor;
> Heiße Magister, heiße Doktor gar,
> Und ziehe schon an die zehen Jahr
> Herauf, herab und quer und krumm
> Meine Schüler an der Nase herum.
>
> And here I am, for all my lore,
> The wretched fool I was before.
> Called Master of Arts, and Doctor to boot,
> For ten years almost I confute
> And up and down, wherever it goes,
> I drag my students by the nose.   (358–63)

Thus the university discourse of all four faculties brings forth the sigh—in the historical formation known as the *res publica litteraria*. The Republic of Scholars systematically prevents the fortunate occurrence that a living Spirit could manifest itself to another Spirit. It unilaterally instructs all its members—these "doctors, and teachers, and scribes, and Christers" (or, more exactly, physicians, philosophers, jurists, and theologians) to go "rummaging in phrases," for as long as life or reading lasts, in a heap of books "gnawed by worms, covered with dust" ("Doktoren, Magister, Schreiber und Pfaffen," 367; "in Worten kramen," 385; "Den Würme nagen, Staub bedeckt," 403). Faust, M.A.—indeed, Ph.D. to boot—sits in a library without new acquisitions, reads, makes extracts, and writes commentaries, in order then to dictate to his students in lecture what old books have dictated to him. The Republic of Scholars is endless circulation, a discourse network without producers or consumers, which simply heaves words around. Faust's raid on his stacks locates no one who could be the writer, creator, or author of a book—no one, then, who could understand, digest, or process any of these books. In a word: the old Republic of Scholars cheats Man of Man.

German Poetry thus begins with the Faustian experiment of trying to insert Man into the empty slots of an obsolete discourse network.

The first test in the series introduces into the anonymous junk heap of books the product of an author with a name.

> Und dies geheimnisvolle Buch
> Von Nostradamus' eigner Hand,
> Ist es dir nicht Geleit genug?
> Erkennest dann der Sterne Lauf,
> Und wenn Natur dich unterweist,
> Dann geht die Seelenkraft dir auf,

Wie spricht ein Geist zum andern Geist.
Umsonst, daß trocknes Sinnen hier
Die heil'gen Zeichen dir erklärt:
Ihr schwebt, ihr Geister neben mir;
Antwortet mir, wenn ihr mich hört!

And this book full of mystery,
Written in Nostradamus' hand—
Is it not ample company?
Stars' orbits you will know; and bold,
You learn what nature has to teach;
Your soul is freed, and you behold
The spirits' words, the spirits' speech.
Though dry reflection might expound
These holy symbols, it is dreary:
You float, oh spirits, all around;
Respond to me, if you can hear me.   (419–29)

To take a book by an author—his autograph manuscript, moreover—out of the dusty pile is to put a stop to the endless circulation of words. Among the copies of copies that fill the libraries of scholars, the author Nostradamus (who, not accidentally, is also a magician) manifests himself in the inimitable character of his manuscript. His imaginary presence makes scholarly brooding on signs as superfluous as the voice does writing. Everything takes its course as if his book were no longer a book. Described or designated signs are supposed to be able to hear the reader, and thus a virtual orality emerges. What the distich identifies as impossible happens: a Spirit manifests itself to another (as Schiller writes) or (as Faust says) speaks. Insofar as impossibility never ceases not to write itself,[3] this invocation of Nostradamus, through which something ceases not to write itself in order to assume instead the name of Spirit or Soul, is the contingency that since then has been called German classical literature.

If only the author Nostradamus had not written. "Was it a God that wrote these signs?" ("War es ein Gott, der diese Zeichen schrieb," 434) is Faust's first ecstatic question as he glimpses the symbol of the macrocosmos among the magic ideograms. But this supposed God—a magnified image of the authorship—manifests himself only for an instant, in the apprehension of his act of writing. Once what has been written has been seen and is known, authors withdraw behind their signs like God behind his Creation. The signs lead the reader, to whom they designate pure "creative Nature" ("Die wirkende Natur," 441) away from the producer to the product. Consequently, the macrocosmos ideogram represents how "all weaves itself into the whole" ("Wie alles sich zum Ganzen webt," 447) and thus how the designated cosmos has the texture of the sign that designates it. In this "continuum of representation and being," this "being as expressed in the presence of representation," there is no absence and no gap[4] except that the divine act of writing and creating is lacking. Hence Faust the interpreter of signs is once more robbed of what his experiment meant to introduce into the configuration of early modern knowledge: Man standing behind and above all bookish rubbish. With a return of the primordial sigh, a failed experiment breaks off. "What a spectacle!, but oh!, only a spectacle!" ("Welch Schauspiel! Aber, ach, ein Schauspiel nur!" 454).

The second test takes the opposite path: the consuming reader, rather than a productive author, is introduced as Man into the heap of books. For once, Faust does not just glimpse and gaze at signs. The first unperformable stage direction in European theatrical history declares that "he seizes the book and mysteriously pronounces the sign of the spirit" (at 481). "Mysteriously" indeed. This event, speaking out loud, is possible for books composed of letters, but not for a collection of magic ideograms, especially when the ideograms combine unsayable figures and equally unsayable Hebrew letters. Magical signs exist to be copied under the midnight moon, not to be spoken out loud. But the Faustian experiment consists in turning the semiological treasury of signifiers into the oral reserves of a reader.

Therefore the designated Earth Spirit becomes a voice, which calls both itself and Faust voices as well:

> Du flehst eratmend, mich zu schaun,
> Meine Stimme zu hören, mein Antlitz zu sehn. . . .
> Wo bist du, Faust, des Stimme mir erklang?
>
> You have implored me to appear,
> Make known my voice, reveal my face; . . .
> Where are you, Faust, whose voice pierced my domain?   (486–87,
>   494)

One who has become a vocalizing reader, and hence breath, also experiences written signs as the breath of a mouth. Where the Republic of Scholars knew only pre-given externalities, a virtual and supplementary sensuality emerges. Faust no longer transforms the sign of a sign into the representation of an absent author (as in the case of the macrocosmos) but into its effect on him, the reader.

> Wie anders wirkt dies Zeichen auf mich ein!
> Du, Geist der Erde, bist mir näher;
> Schon fühl' ich meine Kräfte höher,
> Schon glüh' ich wie von neuem Wein. . . .
> Ich fühl's, du schwebst um mich, erflehter Geist.

> How different is the power of this sign!
> You, spirit of the earth, seem close to mine:
> I look and feel my powers growing,
> As if I'd drunk new wine I'm glowing. . . .
> I feel you near me, spirit I implored. (460–63, 475)

It is no longer a question of the author's sacred power to create signs, but rather of the magic power of signs to liberate sensual and intoxicating powers in the reader once the signs have disappeared into the fluid medium of their signified—a voice. The chain of these forces climaxes in a moment of consumption: the reader Faust, whose mouth can drink signs-become-oral like young wine, replaces the author Nostradamus. This fulfills his wish no longer to experience mere spectacles but rather by an act of reading to suck on "breasts" or "Wells that sustain all life" ("Quellen alles Lebens," 456)—an elementary and infantile form of consumption.

But one cannot invoke the Mother by her metaphors with impunity. Faust's drinking of signs is an ecstasy and production that exceeds his powers. Instead of remaining master of the conjured sign, the reader disappears into the weave or textum of the signified. The Earth Spirit, who weaves "at the roaring loom of the ages" ("am sausenden Webstuhl der Zeit," 508) literally on the text of history, reduces Faust again to nothingness.

These two failed experiments delimit the borders within which the third takes place. The third test concerns neither the production of a foreign author, who disappears behind the representative signs, nor the consumption of signs to the point of intoxication, then drowning in the inexhaustible text. Faust gives up wanting to liquefy archaic ideograms with his alphabetical orality. First, he opens a book composed of quite ordinary Greek letters, which has always been there to be read. The book has authors with names, but Faust does not name them. Furthermore, the book has a reader, Faust himself, but this reader remains forgotten and is bypassed because he is involved only as Man. The third test puts in the place of the productive author and the consuming reader a single authority, which thus represents the enthroning of Man. A new return of the primordial sign finally leads to success.

> Aber ach! schon fühl' ich, bei dem besten Willen,
> Befriedigung nicht mehr aus dem Busen quillen.
> Aber warum muß der Strom so bald versiegen,
> Und wir wieder im Durste liegen?
> Davon hab' ich so viel Erfahrung.
> Doch dieser Mangel läßt sich ersetzen,
> Wir lernen das Überirdische schätzen,

Wir sehnen uns nach Offenbarung,
Die nirgends würd'ger und schöner brennt
Als in dem Neuen Testament.
Mich drängt's, den Grundtext aufzuschlagen,
Mit redlichem Gefühl einmal
Das heilige Original
In mein geliebtes Deutsch zu übertragen.

But oh! Even now, however, though I tried my best,
Contentment flows no longer through my breast.
Why does the river rest so soon, and dry up, and
Leave us to languish in the sand?
How well I know frustration!
This want, however, we can overwhelm.
We turn to the supernatural realm,
We long for the light of revelation
Which is nowhere more magnificent
Than in our New Testament.
I would for once like to determine—
Because I am sincerely perplexed—
How the sacred original text
Could be translated into my beloved German.   (1210–23)

This feasible job is the continuation and translation of an unquenchable longing. Faust opens the Bible in order to overcome a shortcoming, which always drove him "oh! to the source of life" ("Ach, nach des Lebens Quelle," 1201) in order to slake a thirst—and which after two failed tests makes even the poisonous brown juice of phiole look good. But in the meantime he has grown more modest. Gratification no longer needs to stream into that lack from the unique Source but rather from a text, which substitutes for it. Instead of the absolute and fatal consumption of the Earth Spirit, which is the essence of life itself, or of the phiole, which is termed the essence of all blissfully intoxicating juices, he consumes a surrogate. In its verbal form, to be sure, the surrogate has the value of an original, its opposite; but it remains a surrogate, because even the Primary Text is a text like all others in the heap of books. For once, Faust seems not to transgress the limits and restrictions of the university discourse; he translates "the source of life" in good humanistic fashion as bibliophile *ad fontes* and takes a book as a voice of nature. But this limitation assures that the third test will be successful. German Poetry does not begin with the magic testing of unalphabetical signs, nor does it renounce the themes and texts that were stored in the great archive of the Republic of Scholars; it merely gives up the manner of dealing with texts prescribed in that Republic. Faust translates, like innumerable scholars before and after him, from papers handed down from antiquity. The fact that he does not write Latin does not yet speak against "the proper

guild-scholarly character of his historical world."[5] What turns the ex-
M.A. into an anachronism and hence into the founding hero of an incipient, a transcendental Knowledge, is something else. Translation becomes hermeneutics.

> Geschrieben steht: „Im Anfang war das *Wort!*"
> Hier stock' ich schon! Wer hilft mir weiter fort?
> Ich kann das *Wort* so hoch unmöglich schätzen,
> Ich muß es anders übersetzen,
> Wenn ich vom Geiste recht erleuchtet bin.
> Geschrieben steht: Im Anfang war der *Sinn.*
> Bedenke wohl die erste Zeile,
> Daß deine Feder sich nicht übereile!
> Ist es der *Sinn,* der alles wirkt und schafft?
> Es sollte stehn: Im Anfang war die *Kraft!*
> Doch auch indem ich dieses niederschreibe,
> Schon warnt mich was, daß ich dabei nicht bleibe.
> Mir hilft der Geist! auf einmal seh' ich Rat
> Und schreibe getrost: Im Anfang war die *Tat.*

> It says: "In the beginning was the *Word.*"
> Already I am stopped. It seems absurd.
> The *Word* does not deserve the highest prize,
> I must translate it otherwise
> If I am well inspired and not blind.
> It says: In the beginning was the *Mind.*
> Ponder that first line, wait and see,
> Lest you should write too hastily.
> Is mind the all-creating source?
> It ought to say: In the beginning there was *Force.*
> Yet something warns me as I grasp the pen,
> That my translation must be changed again.
> The Spirit helps me. Now it is exact.
> I write: In the beginning was the *Act.*   (1224–37)

Saying (in words) that he cannot possibly value words or even (as the secret eavesdropper of this private conversation will paraphrase it) "thinks
the word so beggarly" ("das Wort so sehr verachtet," 1328) Faust takes
his exit from the Republic of Scholars. The rules decreed by Humanism
and the Reformation for dealing with books were becoming obsolete.
Humanism proceeded as philological activity, and philology means love
of the word. Luther's belief in and translation of the Bible were obedient
to the rule of *sola scriptura* and meant in a quite practical sense that students in the catechumenical schools that arose along with the Reformation had to be able to learn sacred texts by heart and "recount" them
"word for word."[6] If the Primary Text were, for example, the Decalogue,
then the *Little Catechism* (in contradistinction to the later *Analytical*) programmed a learning by heart not only of that law but also—although with

the question "What is that?" it was supposed to mediate between law and persons—of Luther's explanations.[7] Incontrovertible word sounds as re-duplication of an incontrovertible wording—that was true scriptural faith.

"Someone has been found who all day long speaks only the words: 'The Bible is in my head, my head is in the Bible.'"[8] No words could better express the early modern order of words. But in 1778, the year they were recorded, their speaker was in an insane asylum. Two hundred years of inscribed faithfulness to Scripture suddenly sounded pathological to the new sciences of man. There was now every reason to exchange the wording for what should have been written if the translator had had his way. Faust's Germanicization of a sacred original solely on the basis of sincere feeling is an epistemological break. "The slightest alteration in the relation between man and the signifier, in this case in the procedures of exegesis, changes the whole course of history by modifying the moorings that anchor his being."[9]

The beginning of the Gospel according to Saint John is a unique weave or textum of words, which with complete autonymity calls the Word the Beginning. The beginning with the word *word*, this beginning in its un-speakable replication—which all discourses, because they are themselves composed of words, cannot overtake—gave rise, until the early modern period in Europe, to the form of the commentary.

The language of the sixteenth century—understood not as an episode in the his-tory of any one tongue, but as a global cultural experience—found itself caught, no doubt, between these interacting elements, in the interstice occurring between the primal Text and the infinity of Interpretation. One speaks upon the basis of a writing that is part of the fabric of the world; one speaks about it to infinity, and each of its signs becomes in turn written matter for further discourse; but each of these stages of discourse is addressed to that primal written word whose return it simultaneously promises and postpones.[10]

A teachable form of such commentary, in practical and scholastic relation to canonical or sacred texts, constituted the rhetoric of the technique of tossing words back and forth between two Words:

The first mute, indecipherable, fully present to itself, and absolute; the other, gar-rulous, had only to voice this first speech according to forms, operations, and conjunctions whose space measured its distance from the first and inaudible text. For finite creatures and for men who would die, Rhetoric ceaselessly repeated the speech of the Infinite that would never come to an end.[11]

In the new space of the scholar's tragedy, such industrious humility does credit only to the famulus Wagner, this bookworm with his critical zeal, his learned hunt for sources, and his dream of rhetorical persuasion.

Faust, by contrast, ostracizes rhetoric and rhetoricians with the same rhetorical question:

> Das Pergament, ist das der heil'ge Bronnen,
> Woraus ein Trunk den Durst auf ewig stillt?
> Erquickung hast du nicht gewonnen,
> Wenn sie dir nicht aus eigner Seele quillt.

> Parchment—is that the sacred fount
> From which you drink to still your thirst forever?
> If your refreshment does not mount
> From your own soul, you gain it never.   (566–69)

He wants, not to leave thirst and desire open, as do philologists and rhetoricians, but to quench them so thoroughly that they are extinguished. The name of the death of desire, however, is soul. Therefore the new refreshment, when applied to the Gospels, consists in translating from one's own soul and honest feeling. Certainly, feeling and soul are also only translations, a nominalizing paraphrase of the sigh *oh!* as the unique signifier that is not a signifier. But they make possible another beginning and alter the function of all rhetoric. One who no longer wants to know about parchments and the letters on them does not simply give up reading and explicating, rhetorical variations and mutations. Even the lonely scholar works with paper, which he fills up, like the teachers and students of old-European universities and Latin schools when they imitated classic or sacred texts, that is, wrote paraphrases. On Faust's writing paper, too, "word" is paraphrased and replaced successively by "mind," "force," "act." But in the speeches that comment on this writing, the transcription is not described as a rhetorical procedure. The paraphrases are no longer understood as drawn from a treasury of tropes and figures; they are assigned the inverse function of denoting the true and authentic meaning of a word. This word turns out to be the word *word*. It is not one word or signified among others; it is the word as signifier submitted to the primacy of the signified. By means of rhetorical variation Faust undertakes a semantic quest for the transcendental signified.[12]

The transcendental signified, however remote from language it may seem, arises technically or grammatologically from a sequence of reiterated crossings-out. As soon as Faust writes down a word (*niederschreibe*, 1234), a strange Something pulls him and his pen up short. This Other, though called "Spirit," is not too supersensory to have eyes. A gaze reads along with what the hand writes down and by so doing makes sure that the pen does not run away with itself ("Feder sich nicht übereile!," 1231). Indeed it is characteristic of manual writing under normal circumstances—in sun or lamplight, and given eyesight—that one can watch one's hand in the present moment of writing and, where necessary, make corrections. In the lucid words of Angelo Beyerlen, the typewriter engineer: "In writing by hand the eye must continually observe the place where the writing goes and this place only. It must supervise the emergence of every written sign, must measure, keep in line, in short, lead and guide the hand in the execution of every movement."[13] By contrast, the eyes of theatergoers cannot look over the shoulders of the heroes of Scholarly Tragedies. We must resort to a hypothetical reconstruction. The sheet of paper on which Faust wrote must have looked something like this:

the Act.
the ~~Force~~.

In the Beginning was

the ~~Mind~~.
the ~~Word~~.

These crossings-out distinguish hermeneutical translation from rhetorical paraphrase. With the revocation of the first and absolute Word disappears the free play of the many varying and verbose words that can represent each other in one and the same syntactical position. The logic of signifiers is a logic of substitution; the logic of signifieds, a fantasy according to which one irreplaceable signified replaces all replaceable signifiers. If three of them were not crossed out, the words on Faust's page would form a paradigm of signifiers in Saussure's sense. They do not because in his freedom the translator does not perceive their coherence (what indeed is called a system). Faust hesitates, but not because no one can pronounce simultaneously all the exclusive elements of a paradigm. He hesitates because he seeks the one and only meaning lying outside all differentiality and therefore no longer sees words that have already been crossed out.

If he had seen them, it would have been readily apparent that all his trial runs are the vain efforts of a German to exhaust the polysemy of the Greek word for "word." Had Faust consulted his Greek dictionaries,[14] he would have noticed that he, Faust of the honest feeling, does not undertake the substitutions, but rather that already speaking in advance of him is the entire tradition that successively translated the *logos* as scholastic *sensus*, Leibnitzean force, and transcendental philosophical act, in so many epochs in the history of being. But this Occidental "series of substitutions of center for center" in which "successively, and in a regulated fashion, the center receives different forms or names"[15] and hence becomes endlessly further inscribed and denied, is already a matter of no consequence for the translator, because he himself is stepping out to found a new and irrevocable center. Faust characterizes in the "history of the sign" the moment without "paradigmatic consciousness."[16]

Faust's syntagmatic consciousness isn't much better. For sheer love of semantics the word sequences of the primary text are left unchanged or simply ignored. Faust is far from orienting his search for signifieds along the contextual lines of John. He does not hunt around in his heap of books for a commentary on parallel passages. His pen already balks at the first line; no glance falls on the following lines or on the text as a whole, which would illuminate the mysterious word via its concordances. The barking and howling of a dog is enough to prevent Faust on that day and forever from reading further.

Signs are found in three formal relations. If the two outer relations of the sign—to its immediate neighbors in what precedes and what follows in the discourse and to its virtual substitutes in the treasury of language—are both excluded, then there remains only the inner or imaginary relation between signifier and signified. This relation is what, particularly since Goethe's aesthetics, is "commonly called a symbol." [17] For a century the Faustian coup suspended the attribution of the sign to the group of which it is an element. This loss has very pragmatic grounds, for the relation to the signified is the sole one that does not attend to the discourse of the Other. To observe textual recurrences would mean to submit the translation to a superior author or work worthy of imitation. To observe paradigmatic columns, as Faust's pen inconsequentially piles them up, means to submit translation not to honest feelings but to the rules of a language.

But Faust is alone. He writes without consulting books, outside any discursive network. No one ordered a Bible translation from him, no one is going to get one dedicated to him or receive it as due—not his nearest colleague and not the nearest publisher. They, however, are the control mechanisms of scholarship, and they alone hold scholars to the observance of the formal relations of the sign. In dictionaries dwell the paradigms, in grammars the syntagms. As a student of philology, Nietzsche described how his guild would have had to scrutinize or rap the knuckles of this ex-M.A.:

> Whenever such types deign to practice philology, we are in our rights to raise our eyebrows a little and scrutinize attentively these strange workers. How they are accustomed to do things in philological matters Goethe told us in the mirror of his Faust. We recall the hair-raising methods by which Faust treats the beginning of the John Prologue and confess the feeling worthy of a Wagner that for us Faust is utterly ruined, as a philologist at any rate. [18]

Faust's deed is a free translation. Not only semantically, in that the word *word* is not repeated in the wording of the text, but above all pragmatically: because it does not attend to any external discursive controls. A hair-raising discursive practice only fills in what the many negations of the introductory monologue have already sketched out:

Mich plagen keine Skrupel noch Zweifel,
Fürchte mich weder vor Hölle noch Teufel—
Dafür ist mir auch alle Freud' entrissen,
Bilde mir nicht ein, was Rechts zu wissen,
Bilde mir nicht ein, ich könnte was lehren,
Die Menschen zu bessern und zu bekehren.

No scruple nor doubt could make me ill,
I am not afraid of the Devil or hell—
But therefore I also lack all delight,
Do not fancy that I know anything right,
Do not fancy that I could teach or assert
What would better mankind or what might convert.   (369–74)

The renunciation of impossible teaching made possible a free writing, which exceeds philological or indeed theological scruples. Free writing has no definite function for definite addressees and therefore does not lead students about by the nose. It finds no place in the discourse network from which Faust derives, because it itself begins a new discourse network. Having reached the zero point, Faust rejects along with traditional knowledge Knowledge itself, without (like his many successors) proclaiming free writing as the new science that more than any other would harbor the conceit of bettering and converting human beings, indeed, of making them for the first time into human beings.

Knowledge and ignorance, new doctrine and free act: in the zero hour of transcendental knowledge, these still lie side by side. "The explication that Faust attempts, the opposition of word and meaning, of deed and force, is—despite the reference to Fichte—neither philosophically clear nor purely poetic; it is, therefore, one of those places where philosophy and poetry are disinclined to join together in a complete unity."[19] This nonclosure characterizes the new beginning. In free translation poetic and philosophic discourse conspire in a fashion that henceforth will be called German Classicism. Schiller reads Kant for three years in order to be read himself for a century from the standpoint of Kant. Hegel reads and interprets poetry until his philosophy of art enters into relationship with poetic imagination.[20] Thus an oscillation comes into being between poetry and thought, which do not join together in complete unity because the two discourses are not even close to being able to write down the points where they cross one another.

Faust's *Act* is the fleeting act of writing itself. To write "In the Beginning was the *Act*" truly marks the end. First, the translation comes to an end because it has at last found the beginning itself. Second, the translation comes to the conclusion that the sought-after transcendental signified of *logos* lies in the search itself. Faust's crossings-out and substitutions receive a name, which gives a brand name as well to the authentic meaning of what has been crossed out, in Greek as well as in German. The translator, who so despises words, nonetheless does nothing but make words. No acts other than that of writing are seen in the quiet study in which the poodle no longer barks and has yet to bark again. Consequently the free translation ends as anonymously as the Gospels had begun. On the one hand there is the Word, from which all words stem, even those of the Gospel writers—on the other is the act, which is all that writing is, even the writing of the translator. A writer who writes around the sentence "I am writing," however, fulfills the modern conception of authorship. Free writing has brought Faust back to his first test. The author Nostradamus, whose manuscript momentarily guarantees his presence for the reader, is replaced by the author Faust, whose handwriting is the act of his own self-presence. Other translations of *logos* could justify themselves by counting out an average of common connotations between the primary text and the translation; translation as "act" is itself the act of writing off the wording (or casting it to the winds) instead of further copying it (or passing it down to posterity).

An act, in actuality, neither philosophical nor poetic. Before the Faustian revolution, poetry had a lot to do with the written and nothing with the strange, fugitive act of writing. The order of representations excluded the representability of the act of production. What philosophy had to say in the classical age, when it explicated Holy Scripture, is in accord with the outcome of Faust's gesture, but not with the gesture itself. Spinoza's *Tractatus Logico-Politicus*, which was certainly before the eyes of the author of the Scholar's Tragedy, justified Faust's high-handed treatment of the Bible by anticipating his contempt of words, but did not go so far as to make a new and free translation of those incriminated written words.

I only maintain that the meaning by which alone an utterance is entitled to be called Divine, has come down to us uncorrupted, even though the original wording may have been more often changed than we suppose. Such alterations . . . detract nothing from the Divinity of the Bible, for the Bible would have been no less Divine had it been written in different words or a different language. That the Divine law has in this sense come down to us uncorrupted, is an assertion which admits of no dispute.[21]

The difference between German Poetry and classical philosophy is produced by the words of the philosopher themselves. They are and remain commentaries, no longer upon the text but upon its pragmatic and semantic aspects. Therefore they dare to voice the scandalous suspicion that others could have changed or falsified the text of the Bible, but they keep silent about their own systematic falsification. Faust, by contrast, does not say whether or that he falsifies; when he does something, he

does it. Hence the philosopher replaces "discourse" and "word" semantically with "meaning," the poet pragmatically with "act." That it is an
intrusion and a falsification to understand the words of the Apostle "and
I think also that I have the Spirit of God" as "by the Spirit of God the
Apostle here refers to his mind, as we may see from the context," [22] Spinoza
had prudently not mentioned. Only poetry, a century later, first lifted the
veil and publicly translated the spirit of God as its own.

In the classical period representations or (to put it plainly) deceit and
masquerade went that far. Earlier, the *Tractatus* had insisted that no one
could doubt the divinity of scripture, while its own "scripture" did nothing
else; but this was done, for reasons of security, to deceive readers and students. Faust's farewell to his M.A. status, which only led students around
by the nose, announces to this strategy and this art of writing, which arise
from within and against persecution,[23] that he is quitting. Poetic free writing exits from the discourse of the Other. At the precise place where the
name MAster turns into "empty sound and smoke," Faust's authorship
begins. And as always, when someone tries not to deceive others, only
self-deception remains.

Faust lays claim to the beginning as an act this side of all representations, an act that is first of all his own.[24] And yet he does not write with
complete freedom. In the quest for the signified of a Something that
λόγος means, without its yet being the verbal meaning, hence like "the
symbol which is the thing, without being the thing, and yet the thing" [25]—
Faust has a method. Words, which could not possibly mean λόγος, no
matter in what language game or in what professional jargon, are excluded. German Poetry in its foundational act is not so free as to write in
place of Ἐν ἀρχῇ ἦν ὁ λόγος, let us say:

> In the beginning was blabla

There are grounds for the omission. No discourse, not even the freest
possible translation, can manage without authorized controls. In no culture is the dice throw of discourse not steered and curbed, checked and
organized. For the ex-M.A., it is true that all controls that circumscribed
the traditional European universities by means of estates and guilds fall
by the wayside. But even in his lonely study Faust does not remain alone.
For one thing, there is the poodle, whose barking triggers the translation
attempt and later puts a stop to it. That Faust orders the poodle (in vain,
incidentally) to "Stop howling so!" ("Pudel so laß das Heulen," 1239) so

he can search in peace for the Word instead of the word already betrays an authorized control, which is to some extent universal. It orders human beings to distinguish between human language, animal howling, and inhuman blabla. And at the other end there is "the Spirit," whose counsel enables the translation attempt to be completed. The fact that Faust twice justifies his unheard-of Germanizing as the input of "the Spirit" points to a second authorized control, whose emergence in turn can be precisely dated.

An anonymous Spirit, which has little to do with the Biblical λόγος but bears a close relation to Spinoza's bold conjecture about the passage from Paul, curbs his freedom. Faust translates according to the spirit and not the letter, but he does translate. A privately-shouldered obligation has replaced the professional one vis-à-vis the proper academic addressees and overseers. That does not alter the fact of discourse control. The Spirit does just what the good and evil spirits of the Republic of Scholars did: it can "illuminate" and "warn"; it brakes the quick tempo of writing. Its "reservations" help ensure that German Poetry does not start out with howling or blabla.

The lonely study, too, is therefore a scenario and therefore always already destined for the stage. "The 'subject' of writing does not exist if we mean by that some sovereign solitude of the author."[26] Aside from the mysterious poodle, a writer and a speaker act together in the playlet. "The Spirit" does not write but rather speaks. The translator writes, but when he reflects on what has been written, "the Spirit" is the agent. At times it becomes unclear which of the two speaks: whether, for example, in the command of "I" to his pen as "your [deine]" pen (1231) Faust has the floor or whether it is "the Spirit" who uses the familiar form of address.[27]

As so often in dialogues, the name of "the Spirit" remains unstated. Instead, something simply happens on stage. Out of the poodle comes, aroused by vexatious biblical words, a Spirit. The mask drops—Mephisto was seconding the entire scene of writing. Indeed, there cannot be more than one Spirit in the same room. The scene of the Logos has never been read literally enough: it describes the birth of German Poetry out of the Spirit of Hell.

Faust's first question to the Spirit after its unmasking reads: "What is your name?" ("Wie nennst du dich?" 1327). That is a hard question to answer when posed of someone who "holds semblance in disrepute / And craves only reality" ("weit entfernt von allem Schein, / Nur in der Wesen Tiefe trachtet," 1329–30), of someone, that is, who embodies sheer contempt of language. Thus Mephisto can continue to conceal his name. But

there are indices, nonetheless. A Spirit who, like the contemporary directors of the *Gymnasien*, becomes restless and displeased when someone
still practices reading and translating the Bible; a Spirit who can offer all
earthly joys and in exchange wants only the soul; a Spirit, too, whose
royal self in the *Tragedy: Part Two* invents paper money—that can only
be the "new idol," [28] which Nietzsche finally called by its true name. The
lectures "On the Future of Our Educational Institutions" describe with
an outlaw's keen sight a lecturing procedure that corresponds point by
point with Faust's writing procedure, at the end of which the idol removes
his mask.

The student listens to lectures. When he speaks, when he sees, when he is being
social, when he is practicing the arts, in short, when he lives, he is independent,
that is to say, independent of the educational institution. Very often the student
writes at the same time he listens to lectures. These are the moments when he
dangles from the umbilical cord of the university. He can choose what lectures he
wants to listen to, he does not have to believe what he hears, he can close his ears
when he is not in the mood to listen. This is the "acroamatic" theory of teaching.
    The teacher, however, speaks to the students who attend his lectures. What-
ever else he thinks and does is cut off by a monumental divide from the consciousness of his students. Often the professor reads while he lectures. In general, he
wants as many students as possible; if need be, he is satisfied with a few, almost
never with just one. A speaking mouth and many, many ears, with half as many
writing hands: that is the external apparatus of the academy; set in motion, that is
the educational machinery of the university. Moreover, the possessor of this
mouth is cut off and independent from the possessors of the many ears: and this
double independence is celebrated with lofty pathos as "academic freedom."
Moreover, the individual—to raise this freedom a notch higher—can say more or
less what he wants, the others can hear more or less what they want: only, standing at a modest distance behind both groups, with a certain tense, supervisory
mien, is the state, there in order to make clear from time to time that *it* is the
purpose, goal, and essence of this odd speaking and listening procedure.[29]

Faust's free translation is clearly a special instance of state-permitted
academic freedom. The two licenses—for the student to hear more or less
what he wants and for the professor to say more or less what he wants—
come together to produce the Faustian scene of writing. As students do
not have to believe what they hear, so Faust can hear the message of the
Easter bells without conviction and translate the Prologue to Saint John
without mentioning the words the *Word* or the *Son*.[30] As professors say
more or less what they want, so Faust does not read what is written but
what should be written. As students write while they are listening, so the
translation follows the dictates of the Spirit, who does not write but
speaks. And finally, as professors read while they speak, so the Faustian
new beginning rests on a read text. Accordingly, within the poetic freedom that is Faust's act appears, as its precondition, the academic freedom
of the new state universities. But Faust, whose first words already an-

nounce to the old university system that he is quitting, does not yet know this and cannot know yet how well a professorship in the new system would suit him. Of course, he does not plan a "reform of the universities,"[31] but he triggers one. After 1800, professors, especially in chairs of philosophy, made a career of free translation—of *Faust* in particular. In the course offerings of nineteenth-century universities (in the words of their best specialist), "the old expression *tradere* continued to be used, but even the youngest of lecturers—indeed perhaps he the most—would have seen in this an insult were it to be taken at face value."[32]

Academic freedom and poetic freedom (not to be confused with poetic license) are both guaranteed by the state. To pose the act in place of the word is above all a political act. In enlightened Prussia in 1794, one and the same code, the *Allgemeines Landrecht*, granted a copyright to books (which made the act of their authors inalienable) and a new statute to institutions of learning, which "separated them from the organs of churchly administration dependent on tradition":[33] "Schools and universities are institutions of the state."[34]

In their alliance the two legal acts founded the "alliance between the state and the educated," which not only led to the "transformation of the form of rule and government"[35] but for a century bore along German Poetry. The Spirit in Faust's study is no solitary. Everywhere reformers, appointed and protected by the articles of the *Landrecht*, visited the studies and educational institutions of the Republic of Scholars, in order to write down everything about them that required reform. The *Gymnasium* director Minister Gedike pilloried it as an "absurdity"

that today in a number of *trivium* schools even the *Bible*, sometimes as a whole, sometimes in pieces, is degraded to the level of a reader. . . . Just recently in a school with a great many students, I heard children of five and six reading from Isaiah 15: "The burden of Moab. Because in the night Ar of Moab is laid waste, and brought to silence; because in the night Kir of Moab is laid waste, and brought to silence; He is gone up to Bajith, and to Dibon, the high places, to weep: Moab shall howl over Nebo, and over Medeba . . . And Heshbon shall cry, and Elealeh: their voice shall be heard even unto Jahaz." All throughout this the teacher was completely unembarrassed, and it had probably never occurred to him in the simplicity of his heart to ask: Do you yourself understand what you are reading? . . . It is not hard to believe that it was his deliberate intention to make the Bible, which was being degraded to a common reader, an inferior and indifferent object to the children. And yet whoever, in justified zeal for the honor of the Bible, would dare to tear from the hands of this teacher the Bible he was profaning, or at least to advise him to have his pupils read only what they can understand or what he himself understands, would run the risk of being labeled an iconoclast and a heretic by him.[36]

Such school visitors were all the rage circa 1800. Jean Paul Richter called it "one of the greatest pedagogical errors" that "religious books are turned into reading machines";[37] the *Journal of Empirical Psychology* relaxed its customary discretion to castigate by name a living teacher whose "literal method" (as the word already indicates) in New Testament instruction required students to begin by "noting" "the name," then to write on the blackboard names and other curious features as abbreviated initial letters, and finally to learn them by heart. For the empirical psychologist, an alarming question was raised: "To what extent would such a dreadfully one-sided development of so subordinate an intellectual power as memory derange human reason?"[38]

Thus one and the same Spirit growls at the reading of the Bible like the poodle and furnishes inspired readings of the Bible like "the Spirit." Ar, Moab, Bajith, Dibon, Nebo, Medeba, Heshbon, Elealeh, Zoar, Luhith, Horonaim—so read the words to which Faust too cannot pay much heed and whose memorization[39] is dismissed in the act of writing *act* for *word*. The discourse network of 1800 revokes Luther's commandment to "recount from word to word." This is replaced by the new commandment to have only that read which students and teachers "understand." It is formulated clearly enough and, as the "only" indicates, enforces a selection and control of discourse like all others, even if hermeneutics owes its victory to having initially masqueraded as the opposite of that control. But people did not fall for it right from the start. Like Faust's thesis—namely, that his translation into his beloved German was at the same time a revelation of the sacred original—the project of the reformers, of replacing the Bible with primers simply to preserve its sanctity, was a transparent strategy. "The question was put as follows: Is it not sacrilege toward the books of religion to use them to teach children to read? Whereupon a general Yes! resounded. Really the question was meant as follows: Isn't it time to do away with or limit the old instructional materials?"[40] And "Understanding" was meant as it was understood. In 1776 a new *ABC Speller and Reader* for Nassau-Weilberg, which appeared without the Ten Commandments, Articles of Faith, and Lord's Prayer, aroused armed resistance. "No longer secure in his residence, the Prince sought help from the Palatine. Eight thousand Palatine troops marched in to pacify the popular uprisings."[41] A *Kulturkampf*, therefore, a century *avant la lettre*.[42]

Doing away with old instructional materials, even in literal ABC wars, marks the birth of the new. Instead of the word, the act enters, and instead of the Bible, Poetry: from the primer to the National Classic or from Friedrich Eberhard von Rochow's *The Child's Friend* to *Faust I*; from the sigh "oh!," which "the creative child breathes out in artless song" to "the greatest system of art, itself containing several systems more";[43] or from Bettina Brentano's love letters to *Faust: Part Two*.

Poetry is at once the means and goal of understanding, as demanded by the reformers in office, hence the correlative (and not the object) of the new human science: hermeneutics. Its distinction lies in linking together all the information channels participating in understanding. First, poetry itself functions as understanding, that is, as the transmission of words into pure meanings; second, it allows understanding, that is, a reading that does not have to struggle with the verbal monsters of Isaiah 15. Finally, it can understand others and other things *and* be understood by others—otherwise. The discourse network of 1800 has in essence been accounted for once this three-part schema is filled in with appropriate names and terms.

First, however, we must emphasize that power stands over the entire relation. The discursive net called understanding has to be knotted. There is such a thing as understanding and being understood only once a new type of discourse control has learned to practice its "modest distance" in order merely to point out from time to time that the state is the "purpose, goal, and essence of this odd speaking and listening procedure." Over the free space of hermeneutics there stands, as above every language game, an "order-word."[44] This command is the unique knot that itself will not and cannot be understood. The state remains closed off to every hermeneutic. Because understanding, despite its claim to universality, is one speech act among others, it cannot get behind the speech act that instituted it. Texts that are part of the hermeneutic net allow the power that governs them to come to light only in a masked fashion. The translator Faust is watched over by a devil in poodle's garb.

The only texts that are unmasked are those that exist not to be read and understood. In the drama, Faust's academic freedom remains as mysterious as it does in its innumerable interpretations; no one can say whether the free writing has addressees or who they are.[45] The *Code Napoléon*, by contrast, names naked necessity as the origin of the desire to understand; it is the first law book that punishes judges if they refuse hermeneutics: "The judge who shall refuse to judge, under the pretext of silence, obscurity, or the inadequacy of the law, can be pursued as guilty of the denial of justice."[46] Words of power, and only they, are what make necessary—that is, make a matter of life and death—the search for a transcendental signified even where (according to judges) there is no empirical signified or where (according to Faust) there is only a word. A new law decrees hermeneutics and with it readers/writers who apply it in all its senselessness, and in so doing surround it with a cloud of meaning. The judge must apply the law because otherwise he would fall outside it. The poet must apply interpretations because otherwise—Faust's translation in the presence of that poodle being in the last resort an apotropaic act—he'd go to the devil. The cloud of meaning legitimating the judge's activity is the illusion that, despite its incomprehensible nature, the law nevertheless validly applies to a referent, a punishable body. The nebulous legitimation of literature is that texts appear to be hermeneutically intelligible and not, rather, a matter of what has been programmed and programs in turn.

There is evidence of this in the Scholar's Tragedy. Only its hero can believe that texts and signs are all designed to be understood and to correspond to understanding (in the way he reproaches the junkpile of books for making understanding impossible, attributes understanding to the signs of Nostradamus and the Word of John, and finally puts understanding into practice in his own translating). This belief in meaning—with which the Scholar's Tragedy ends—encounters its truth. The devil is merely Faust's confrontation with a text that cannot understand nor be understood but is power itself. Mephisto demands Faust's signature.

Signatures, like law books, program people without taking the detour of understanding. The pact scene is therefore the opposite of free translation. In the latter we have the poetic or academic freedom of paraphrase; in the former, the bureaucratic act of signing one's name, which henceforth founds between the devil and the ex-M.A. "not a mere contractual relation based on deed and reciprocal deed but rather a unique relation of service and power and at the same time a relation of trust. . . . It is, if not indissoluble, nonetheless on principle and in fact of life-long duration." [47] This relation—as will not be hard to guess—is that between civil servants and the state.

When Goethe was named privy minister of the Duchy of Saxony-Weimar, obligations to which he was bound until death were "read out loud and put before" the author of the Scholar's Tragedy.[48] So too ought Faust's "spoken word" be "sufficient warrant" to commit his days "eternally" ("Ist's nicht genug, daß mein gesprochenes Wort / Auf ewig soll mit meinen Tagen schalten?" 1718–19). Among the young duke's overtures to reform were "suggestions for simplifying the forms and flourishes on decrees—for example the full array of titles and offices cited on even the simplest documents."[49] But this paper campaign foundered on the resistance of his minister Goethe, whose memorandum concludes: "A Chancellory does not have anything to do with material things; for him who is concerned only with observing and drawing up formalities, a little pedantry is necessary. Indeed, even if the 'By God's Grace' should be retained only as an exercise in official script by the chancellors, there would be some sense in it."[50] In the Tragedy, the same word, *pedant*, characterizes the devil, who, as if there were no such thing as spoken words, demands from Faust "for life's sake, or death's . . . a line or two" ("Um

Lebens oder Sterbens willen . . . ein paar Zeilen," 1714–15). In this perverse world where privy ministers are more bureaucratic than their duke,
Mephisto figures as the official and Faust as the poet. This doubling, for
its part, simply duplicates the double life with which German Poetry begins. "In contrast to his poetic style, Goethe's files are marked by their
elaborate, stilted bureaucratic style. With justice he could say in this respect: 'two souls dwell, oh! in my breast'—the bureaucrat and the poet." [51]

The object of exchange in the devil's pact is the soul. A stroke of the
pen transfers ownership to the devil for life and thereafter. Thus the soul,
instead of merely forming "the reactivated remnants of an ideology," is
"the present correlative of a certain technology of power," as central Europe conceives of it circa 1800.

It is not that a real man, the object of knowledge, philosophical reflection, or
technical invention, has been substituted for the soul, the illusion of the theologians. The man described for us, whom we are invited to free, is already in himself the effect of a subjection much more profound than himself. A "soul" in-
habits him and brings him to existence, which is itself a factor in the mastery that
power exercises over the body. The soul is the effect and instrument of a political
anatomy; the soul is the prison of the body. [52]

It is no wonder that Faust shrinks back from the demand for a signature
as from a spook. The facility of the kind of writing that understands gives
way to a symbolic bonding—poetry gives way to power. In signatures
there is nothing to interpret or to quibble about. The "Act" that took
place in free translating could play about or paraphrase the naked fact of
writing: the "Act" was and remained "in the beginning," or in the past
tense. The act of signing, by contrast, knows only the pure present and
the precise future of its fatality. In his striving Faust attains a status that is
certainly the loftiest of all but that, in its ever-binding fatality, is also the
most burdensome.

It is *sublime* and *honorable*, for the unique goal of his public and private striving
is humanity unified into a commonality of citizens; it is *burdensome*, for the
learned professor bears the responsibility of living only for the state, of devoting
every moment of his existence to the latter's purposes, of devoting himself to it
with everything he calls his higher or his baser possessions, of regarding his entire
sensibility, thought, and action, his physical, moral, and rational being, all his
powers, drives, and talents, not as his but rather as the property of the state, so
that no moment of his activity is thinkable, which does not belong to the state. [53]

The "pact" that educational bureaucrats concluded with the state
circa 1800 was to this extent "extravagantly extensive" in its "substantial
and formal content." [54] Faust, because he cares little for the beyond promised to him by the Bible, signs in this world and for this world so as to
assure it and his contractual opposite "That all my striving I unloose / Is

the whole purpose of the pact" ("Das Streben meiner ganzen Kraft / Ist grade das, was ich verspreche"; 1742–43). Transcendental knowledge sets up a new beginning, which bursts open solitary studies. Faust, the man who writes, vanishes in order to become the myth of German educational bureaucrats and of literary criticism; Faust, the man who is consigned to the devil, steps onto the stage.

Henceforth there is no further mention in *The Tragedy, Part I* of writing and reading. "Faust's writing skills attested to in literature aren't worth much": they are "exhausted in the five words of the Bible translation" and the "signing of the pact."[55] He who from a limited academic has become Universal Man, after a brief detour into the cellar of academic freedom, takes a path that his interpreters call the way to nature. But it is much more plainly a way of speaking and listening. After the last writing scene, the devil's pact (which is never mentioned again), only voices are heard. Power remains modestly in the background in order to make room for the impossible: a "natural" discourse. In higher education, M.A.'s conversed with their assistants; devils disguised as Ph.D.'s, with their pupils—it was a matter of males and only males. Whoever is fed up with this art of deceit has to go back beyond writing and reading. Genuine nature can only be conveyed through channels that are fundamentally excluded from the discourse of the university. Taking one step back, the ex-M.A. Faust discovers the Other, the female Other who in the discourse network of 1800 calls forth Poetry.

The Mother's Mouth

Nature, in the discourse network of 1800, is The Woman.[1] Her function consists in getting people—that is, men—to speak. Given these premises, which are not accidentally Freudian, two sentences that in the Age of Goethe went under Goethe's name and a century later led Freud to the invention of psychoanalysis take on precise meaning. The grammatical subject of each sentence is Nature.

> Sie saumet, daß man sie verlange; sie eilt, daß man sie nicht satt werde.
> Sie hat keine Sprache noch Rede; aber sie schafft Zungen und Herzen, durch die sie fühlt und spricht.

> She tarries, so that one calls out for her; she hurries, so that one never tires of her.
> She has neither language nor speech; but she creates tongues and hearts, through which she feels and speaks.[2]

Such is the definition of an infinite beloved. Infinite, because nature cunningly assures that the longing for her never dies. Infinite, too, because this desire exists only in the language and speech of her lovers, whereas she remains mute and mysterious. Nature therefore accomplishes a PRODUCTION OF DISCOURSES. She creates—since the text names only tongues and hearts, but no hands for writing or eyes for reading—a primary orality. In doing so she liberates herself from the Word of God. Instead of sighing until she rests in the Name of the Father, she creates human speech organs, which pursue self-enjoyment in her place. The origin of language, once a creation ex nihilo, becomes maternal gestation. Because

this mother presents herself as a lover to her human children and translators alike, she meets all the psychoanalytic criteria of Woman.

If the libido is simply masculine, it is only from there, the only place where she is
everything (which, of course, is the place from which man sees her), that the dear
woman can have an unconscious. And what good does that do her? It allows her,
as everyone knows, to make the speaking being, which we confine here to man,
speak; in other words—I don't know if you have noted this in psychoanalytic
theory—it allows her to exist only as mother.[3]

The discourse that the mother in the discourse network of 1800 creates but cannot pronounce is called Poetry. Mother Nature is silent so
that others can speak of and for her. She exists as the singular behind the
plurality of discourses. This is demonstrated in the relationship between
Gretchen and Faust, who, like all of Goethe's wanderers, finds in his lover
a Mother and nature madonna.[4] Whereas the original Dr. Faustus of the
Historia was for sound satanological reasons allowed, even required, to
have affairs with many women,[5] in the Tragedy there is only the One, and
"without the assistance of the Devil in person the great scholar could not
have brought [her seduction] about."[6] Of course, Faust has always rum-
maged through books and signs in search of a life source, but only beyond the libraries and their fraternities does his longing find fulfillment:
Gretchen represents, for her lover no less than for the little sister she cares
for, the milk-giving Mother. Masculine discourse responds thankfully
to the stream of milk. Gretchen's "curtness and brevity" ("kurz ange-
bunden"; 2617) become material for endless interpretation. Her old-
fashioned, catechizing question gives rise to the most famous declaration
of belief and love in the German language (3426–58). Woman's mandate
to make men speak just is that strong. Faust answers with a speech that,
like the new anticatechismal school curriculum,[7] evades all theological
commitment and instead understands the religion in question as the
poetico-erotic inner life of the questioner herself. Faust "responds to
Margaret's question about his religious convictions with her love for
him."[8] Thus, having put writing behind him in that last and horrible act
in which he signs the devil's contract, Faust becomes the hermeneutic interpreter of Woman's soul. As if to confirm Schleiermacher's extension of
hermeneutics to orality,[9] the traditional exegesis of Scripture shifts to an
exegesis of Woman. The spirit that suggested to Faust the transcendental
signified of λόγος is joined by the "motherly spirit" that "daily instructs"
Gretchen's nature ("mütterliche Geist," "täglich unterweist"; 2702–4).

The mother as primary instructor is, quite literally, an invention of
1800. "My, but what this century has invented!" cries the cool and conservative Brandes in mock astonishment; he then denounces in particular

the new "relationship between parents and children," above all the use of the familiar form of address between them, as a "great harm done by mothers." [10] The lengthy process of reshaping the population of central Europe into modern nuclear families was directed by paternal figures only during its first phase—in Germany, up to Lessing's time. Daughters, to whom even the titles of Lessing's plays were devoted, grew up under and were subject to the instruction of their fathers. In a second phase, which coincided with the Age of Goethe, "the Lord of Creation loses his place." [11] Mothers stepped into the position previously held by fathers—juridically, in an essay competition sponsored by the Academy of Berlin that in 1785 requested a reevaluation of maternal authority,[12] and poetically, in the rewriting that turned *Wilhelm Meister's Theatrical Career* into *Wilhelm Meister's Apprenticeship*. With that a transition took place in the materiality of acculturative speech. The word of the father came to young men and virgins as articulated doctrine; the motherly spirit that daily instructs Gretchen, being a construct of her lover, has little to do with her real mother. It doesn't speak, it only "murmurs" ("säuseln"; 2703). The maternal gift is language in a nascent state, pure breath as a limit value from which the articulated speech of others begins. Once again the psychoanalytic definition of woman applies exactly, but only within the boundaries of a specific historical field.

Learning to Read in 1800

Maternal instruction, in its positivity, was the input component of elementary acculturation techniques. Around 1800 a new type of book began to appear, one that delegated to mothers first the physical and mental education of their children, then their alphabetization. The list of such books is long: Friedrich Wilhelm Wedag, *Handbook of Early Moral Education, Intended Primarily for Use by Mothers, in Epistolary Form* (1795); Samuel Hahnemann, *Handbook for Mothers, or Rules for the Early Education of Children (after the Principles of J. J. Rousseau)* (1796); Christoph Wilhelm Hufeland, *Good Advice for Mothers on the Most Important Points of Physical Education in the First Years* (1799); Johann Heinrich Pestalozzi, *How Gertrude Teaches Her Children, an Attempt to Provide Guidance for Mothers in the Self-Instruction of Their Children* (1801); *The Mother's Book, or Guidelines for Mothers in Teaching Children to Observe and Speak* (1803); Christian Friedrich Wolke, *Instructions for Mothers and Child Instructors on the Teaching of the Rudiments of Language and Knowledge from Birth to the Age of Learning to Read* (1805); Heinrich Stephani, *Primer for Children of Noble Educa-*

tion, Including a Description of My Method for Mothers Who Wish to Grant Themselves the Pleasure of Speedily Teaching Their Children to Read (1807).

The titles speak for themselves. They leave little doubt about the identity of the instructor recommended; they emphasize that it is only by conferring elementary acculturation techniques on mothers that the Self of this identity has been found. In fact, by addressing themselves to mothers the pedagogical tracts and primers shortcircuited existing official channels. Everything that people in Europe before 1800 had had to learn—behavior and knowledge, reading and writing—had been passed on within differentiated groups and classes. There was no central locus of acculturation that could claim legitimacy in Nature; in particular, the treasure of formal knowledge reached children via a long path and many representative authorities. The first attempt to base a method of elementary instruction on mothers failed to make its way through the circuit. This occurred when Austrian priests preached Johann Ignatz von Felbiger's instruction method to nuns in order to enable them to teach mothers to become teachers and better mothers.[1]

But in 1800 the system of equivalents Woman = Nature = Mother allowed acculturation to begin from an absolute origin. A culture established on this basis speaks differently about language, writes differently about writing. Briefly put, it has Poetry. For only when phonetics and the alphabet shortcircuit the official route from a natural source to those on the receiving end can a kind of speech arise that can be thought of as an ideal of Nature. This placing of mothers at the origin of discourse was the condition of production for Classical poetry, and the Mother was the first Other to be understood by poetical hermeneutics. Here, the analysis will remain at an elementary level: that of the materiality of language. "When a new ABC book is invented for whole regions to read, the minor details that accompanied its birth in the guise of mothers and midwives take on great significance."[2] Because small changes in the play of letters and paper have changed the course of the so-called world, psychological introspection is superfluous. What is important are not biographical mothers with their comedies and tragedies, but the mothers and midwives of a completely new ABC book; not the transformation of dreams or desires, but a new technique of transcription that determines writing. "In the beginning" was, not the Act, but the ABC book.[3]

The primers of 1800 were written for and given to mothers in order for them to do the same violence to letters that Faust did to words. The project was to replace rote learning with "understanding." In this, mothers assumed strategic positions. The word embedded in a sentence easily allows paraphrases that translate according to the spirit and not the letter. The simple letter, however, on which centuries of reading and writing in the Near Eastern and European domain rest, is the cliff against which hermeneutics can be dashed. Letters have no meaning. Letters are not like sounds, related by the voice to the body and to Nature. The consequences drawn from this basic deficiency differentiate discourse networks. This deficiency is foundational for the age of representation and for the age of the signifier. The old primer wisdom, according to which "pictures like that / in which both pieces / namely sound and figure / are equal to the letters / won't be found in nature,"[4] coincides with the fundamental principle of psychoanalysis: "letters . . . do not occur in nature."[5]

The whole of primary education circa 1800, however, attempted the impossible proof for which the writer Carl Philipp Moritz was known, namely, "that letters are not arbitrary, but grounded in human nature and native to all the distinct regions of inner consciousness."[6] In a first phase at the turn of the century, this naturalization of the alphabet was mediated by supplementary sensory stimuli. In a second and decisive phase, all arbitrariness disappeared in an inner sense called the Mother's voice.

The introductory verse of Carl Friedrich Splittegarb's *New ABC Pictures* provides the motto of the first phase:

> HOLDES KIND! von welcher Wonne
> Wird dein junges Herz gerührt,
> Wenn bey sanfter Frühlingssonne
> Vater ⎫
> Mutter ⎭ dich ins Freye führt.
> Ha! da winket deinen Blicken
> Bald ein Blümchen, bald ein Stein,
> Bald erfüllt ein Vögelein
> Dich mit innigem Entzücken;
> Bald ein Lämmchen auf der Weide . . .
> Just so, unter lauter Freude,
> Ohne Schwierigkeit und Schmerz,
> Dich in unsre Bücherwelt,
> Die so manchen Schatz enthält,
> Angenehm hineinzuführen,
> Und dein weiches, zartes Herz
> Früh mit Tugenden zu zieren:
> Dieses Glück sey meinem Leben
> Oft durch dieses Buch gegeben!
>
> DARLING CHILD! what delight
> Will fill your young heart,
> When in the soft spring light
> Father ⎫
> Mother ⎭ walks you in the park

Ha! there you will see
A flower, there again a rock,
And here is a buzzing bee
And a little lamb that walks
On the meadow; what joy . . .
Just so, my little girl, my boy,
Without difficulty, with pleasure
To our world of books
I'll lead you, a world of treasure.
Your heart young and tender
Will learn beauty and virtue:
Such happiness to see,
This book, in life, oft gives to me.[7]

This very broad comparison merges the world of spring and the world of books, nature and culture. An imagined walk with mother and father makes the coercive act of alphabetizing seem pleasurable. It is not yet clear, however, from whom the young Faust, who is supposed to discover the source of life and nature in books, will acquire this ability to translate; were it otherwise, Splittegarb would not have to leave the pragmatics of his primer typographically open. The names *father* and *mother*, written in a column, enlist unspecified parents in a task that Splittegarb's primer is as yet unable to accomplish methodologically.

This vacant post is where the philanthropists began. In an area where after millennia of alphabetizing there would seem to be nothing more "to *discover* and *invent*," their invention consisted in drawing the method out of the children themselves and thus in becoming "the counsel of the current and of all future generations of children."[8] Because the child is supposedly absorbed in natural pleasures, Johann Heinrich Campe promises, in his *New Method of Easy and Enjoyable Reading Instruction* (1778), to present the alphabet as "candy."[9] Because such pleasures are to be thought as natural as possible, Johann Bernhard Basedow's *Elementary Instruction* provides a "letter game": Franz, not yet two years old, is allowed to figure out first letters, then syllables, and finally such pleasure-promising words as "pud-ding—cook-ies—rai-sins—straw-ber-ries."[10] At the end of his stay in Dessau, Basedow, much to the distress of his colleagues and readers,[11] hit upon a non-metaphoric truth that today survives only in vestiges (as garnish for soup, decoration for Christmas trees): he had edible letters baked for use in his curriculum. Philanthropic alphabetization aimed at a culinary orality for which the unspoken, riddle-solving word was *Mother*.

Encyclopedists and artists were the first to find this password. Nowhere, writes August Hermann Niemeyer, should "instruction, especially private instruction, be more like *play*" than in reading and writing—from which it follows "that *Mothers* would perhaps make the best teach-

ers."[12] And Basedow's *Elementary Instruction* displays (not in the text, which leaves the direction of the letter game to older children and head-masters, but in Daniel Chodowiecki's plate xxvɪb) an ideal of the nuclear family: the older sons map and study the course of the sun; the father abides in "silent meditation and consciousness of his self"[13] (which, how-ever, has the appearance of an absence and an after-dinner nap); and the mother teaches her youngest child to read.

The second phase of reform transformed this ideal into institution and method. The acquisition of language became the mother's prerogative. Friedrich Schleiermacher (in order first to confirm the statistical gener-ality of the phenomenon) rejected all school reading-instruction methods because "in the educated classes reading begins before entry to public schools" and because "household reading usually proceeds under the di-rection of mothers."[14] Hoping to ground child discourse completely in the elementary and oral dispensation of mothers, which leads directly from natural sounds to language,[15] Pestalozzi cursed schools with their grammars and ABC books,[16] yet failed to produce a substitute.[17] But at the cutting edge of progess was the royal Bavarian church and school minister Heinrich Stephani, who dispensed with sugarcoating and curses alike by liquidating letters in their inmost domain. He produced a primer that mobilized play, motherliness, and orality. It could even explain why it was new, that is, why mothers "have hitherto not cared to concern themselves in these matters" and instead left them to such improper authorities as fathers and schools.[18] The reason is simple: as long as reading was a function of writing, it excluded women. Stephani, however, revolutionized the material basis of letters by christening a purely phonetic method, like that Franz Xaver Hoffmann had attempted in 1780, but failed to produce.[19] As Stephani explained the method to mothers:

There are actually only two other methods of instruction besides the phonetic method: the *syllabic* and *spelling* methods. All others are merely variations of these and their deviations often consist only in extraneous helpful measures. The syllabic method shows children syllables and their pronunciation and has them repeat these. Through much practice children then learn syllables and words *in the entire outline* of their forms, as well as their pronunciation. But you will understand how difficult this procedure is, and children, if they have not been fortunate enough to notice for themselves the sound of letters, always run into trouble when they encounter syllables and words of unfamiliar composition.—

The *spelling method* proceeds from the mistaken assumption that the name of the letter is also its sound, and that therefore it is necessary to precede the pronunciation of every syllable with spelling (the naming of each letter). To grasp the uselessness of this method, take, for example, the word *ship* and mentally spell it out for a child: *es ach i pe*. Can you imagine that a child would know how the *sounds* of the first two letters are spoken together after having repeated the *names* of the letters? We do not connect names when we pronounce a word (translate *visual language* into *audible language*), but rather sounds. And in this method children remain completely ignorant of the sounds. But if you teach your child to pronounce the *sounds* of these two letters, first individually and then together, the child will have completely learned how to read the word.[20]

The revolution of the European alphabet was it oralization. Simple primers contributed to the epistemological shift from a general grammar to the science of language.

With Rask, Grimm, and Bopp language is treated for the first time . . . as a totality of phonetic elements. . . . A whole mystique is being born: that of the verb, of the pure poetic flash that disappears without trace, leaving nothing behind it but a vibration suspended in the air for one brief moment. By means of the ephemeral and profound sound it produces, the spoken word accedes to sovereignty. And its secret powers, drawing new life from the breath of the prophets, rise up in fundamental opposition . . . to the esoteric nature of writing, which . . . presupposes some secret permanently lurking at the centre of its visual labyrinths. Language is no longer to the same extent that sign—more or less distant, similar, and arbitrary—for which the *Logique de Port-Royal* proposed as an immediate and evident model the portrait of a man, or a map. It has acquired a vibratory nature which has separated it from the visible sign and made it more nearly proximate to the note in music.[21]

Stephani's concept of "pronunciation" marks the shift exactly. The alphabet is learnable only as "visual language" translated to "audible language." The syllabic method had left this rather Faustian translation to children; the spelling method made it impossible for them. The former consisted in rote learning of the links between optical and acoustic syllabic images; the latter, in rote learning of simple words, the names of letters, the ridiculousness of which is shown in Stephani's technique of transcription *es ach i pe*—even in this mockery the advocate of contemporary children.[22] Spontaneous readability was excluded in both cases. The new method opposed all rote learning and exteriority with an inner voice, which made letters (as if to illustrate the epistemological break) into "nothing but notes." Stephani advised mothers:

In order to provide you with a correct view [of my method], I must ask you from now on to consider *our mouth* with its different constituent parts *as an instrument upon which we are able to play certain meaningful tones* that together we call language. Like any other instrument, this one can be played with or without notes. We practice the former when we speak, the latter when we read. (*Note*: from this point of view writing could be considered as a kind of composition for the mouth instrument.) Reading then consists in the art of playing our language instrument from the page of notes before us. You will now easily guess what it is that letters represent from this point of view. They are really nothing but the notes invented for this purpose.[23]

The phonetic method culminated in the description or prescription of a new body. This body has eyes and ears only in order to be a large mouth. The mouth transforms all the letters that assault the eyes and ears into ringing sounds. This was not a new concept as regards the ear, but in relation to the eyes and letters it was a revolution. In losing their names, letters also lost their status. No tradition has defined writing as composition for the mouth instrument because letters are and remain graphic articulations (even if, since Aristotle, they have been defined as the signs for spoken sounds). There is, after all, a physiological reason for this: the difficulty of distinctly pronouncing together many single consonants, which of course take their names from the act of being "sounded with" one another. Ferdinand Olivier, Basedow's assistant, to whom the invention of the pure phonetic method is still occasionally attributed, also sacrificed purity on account of this difficulty. To Stephani's annoyance he had "in his method, which became known at the same time as mine, letters followed with a long *e*, and he *names* them *she, me, be*."[24] This crutch, which was called *schwa* and was used from the publication of the *New Berlin School Book* (1760) until the time of Basedow and Campe,[25] remained faithful, even in its name, to the consonantal and written character of the first, that is, Hebraic alphabet. When Stephani discarded the schwa, pure phonetics was established for the first time. He granted that vowels are untroublesome only in one aspect—namely, not because they can be pronounced in isolation, but because of the accidental fact that "their sounds have also become their names."[26] Therefore the practicing mouth instrument does indeed begin with *a ä e i o ö u ü*, a "natural scale that ascends from the lowest to highest note"; those who are more advanced, however, can produce single and isolated consonants with just as much virtuosity. One need only have intimately experienced one's own oral cavity, ranging over all the folds and hollows, in a sensual phonetics that develops all sounds out of one another. An example is the continuum between *m*, *n*, and *l*:

Did you know, ladies, that you can close the oral cavity without any help from the lips, simply by firmly pressing the forward part of the tongue tightly against the gums and thereby forcing the same original voice sound to travel also through the nasal passage? If you try this you will find that you have made a voice sound different from the previous ones, which is designated *n* in our speech notation system. Now try it again, but with the slight change of allowing a little of the original voice sound to escape on either side of the tongue. The sound that you now hear is the sound of the letter *l*.[27]

A primer for children had unexpectedly produced a (not accidentally contemporaneous) *Finishing Manual*, by Karl Czerny, for musical women and mothers without a piano. Where earlier analphabetics learned to read, mothers now first learned to know their own mouths. Autoexperimental phonetic practice first established the mother's mouth with its passages, hollows, and depths. And children, instead of attending to books or philanthropic letter games, were all eyes and ears for the instrumental presentations of this mouth. If later in life they should happen to speak what She spoke before them in earliest childhood, they would have the feeling that "often still [they] watched her lips and repeated her words."[28]

The Mother's Mouth thus freed children from books. Her voice substituted sounds for letters, just as in the course of his Scholar's Tragedy Faust substituted meanings for words. The phonetic experiment gave rise to a psychology or psychagogy that made possible the complete consuming of texts. Only the mother's pointing finger retained any relation to the optic form of the letter. And when later in life children picked up a book, they would not see letters but hear, with irrepressible longing, a voice between the lines.[29]

This voice works unheard wonders. It does not speak a word, let alone a sentence. The educational goal of children in reading is to speak out the written discourses of others, but this is not their mothers' goal. Once more, Lacan's definition of Woman exactly fits or (if historians would rather read it) so does Johann Christoph Tobler's definition of Nature. She doesn't speak, she makes others speak. Mothers learn something else. First, they relieve their children of all practice in optical discernment of letters (pattern recognition), and thus pretend that for them an alphabet can exist without writing. Given the hidden premise that the mothers have learned to coordinate eye and mouth under the old-fashioned method, they are capable of moving their mouths to notes and do not mistake a *u* for an *x*. (Behind the phonetic method is the discourse of the Other, which it repudiates.)

Second, mothers learn articulation under the guise of teaching children to read. Stephani's method for mothers is their "self-education as teachers" and belongs to the great program of education for educators that had been in progress since Lessing and Kant.[30] Self-education dismissed imitative learning and produced pure pronunciation for its motherly teachers through a methodical exploration of the oral cavity. All of Stephani's reading- and writing-instruction books declare war on the copying of empirical, and therefore imitative, models. Because in "previous methods children always imitated the pronunciation of their teachers, which of course always has provincial aspects,"[31] mothers' mouths are made to practice until *ü* no longer sounds like *i* and *g* no longer sounds like *ch*. The discourse of others, those who mistook *i* for *ü*, is thus eradicated: words like *Vergnügen* lose all Saxon accent.[32] The mother's pleasure is at once the methodical production *and* the methodical purification of sounds. An accomplished Mother's Mouth at the end of its self-education no longer works in an empirico-dialectical manner, but becomes the mouthpiece of an "original voice sound" that generates all others. The transcendental signified in Faust corresponds to the transcendental voice of Stephani. For the first time in history it teaches how "to pronounce words the way that language would have them pronounced, that is, so that their pronunciation is everywhere the same. It is therefore also the nation's means of gradually suppressing all the different dialects and replacing them with a completely pure pronunciation."[33]

With this measure, however, the phonetic method guaranteed that all discourses inscribed in the discourse network of 1800 would be homogeneous. Only through "suppressing" or "banning" all "provincialisms" and "deficient dialects" could German become High German.

Human language might have originated in a lengthy process of listening—an unconscious imitation as well as familiarity with certain signs—this is the language that the child learns from its parents, with all the deficiencies and imperfections that they naturally have; it is also the way in which most people learn to speak. But human language, in its particular and general aspects, can also be considered as a plenitude of artfully formed signs, determined by exact rules and fully adequate to *thought*. *This* type of human language is the product of a careful development of the instruments of language and understanding. Among Germans this is the *pure, High German idiom.*[34]

The basic differentiation in transcendental knowledge between copying and development, imitation and methodologically purified production, applied also to speech. As in other fields of knowledge, a norm appeared that redefined the many regional usages as pathologies[35] and called, under the name of the high idiom, for a parousia of pure signifieds or "thoughts." The norm was eloquent and effective enough to call its reign a power. Stephani wanted a language "as language wants it"; in his *Monologue* Novalis called the will to speak an imperative that followed only the workings "of language" and that constituted his dignity as poet.[36] The norm was thus universal enough to apply to everything from the babbling of children to the poetizing of poets. Because the norm worked in an "artful" manner, it became the vital element of German Poetry.

This preparation of a general, purified, homogenous medium was something new. Until the time of Johann Bodmer and Johann Breitinger, who sent their manuscripts to Leipzig for proofreading, the standard of High German was empirical rather than transcendental: the Meissen idiom (which was later to become the norm) functioned as one among many and was distinguished only by use and respect. The Mother's Mouth, by contrast, assured that the high and literary idiom would consist in the very absence of dialect. The young Goethe had only the beloved dialect of his native region to counter the "pedantic regime" of Saxony.[37] With the planned normalization of speech circa 1800, a campaign against all dialects began. In 1779 the Academy of Sciences in St. Petersburg offered prizes to mechanical engineers and organ builders for constructing an automaton that would be capable of purely pronouncing the five vowels. Antoine de Rivarol, not coincidentally the author of *A Treatise on the Universality of the French Language*, praised one of the machines subsequently developed and predicted that it would terrify all Gascon and Swiss language teachers and cause them to lose their jobs, because exact reproducibility would henceforth protect vowels from any idiomatic or historical denaturation.[38] Traditional language acquisition was thereby held to be denaturing because it merely handed the language on. Tradition produces copies of copies of copies and so on endlessly, until even the concept of the original is lost. A transcendental Mother's Voice, however, is inalienably identical with its oral experience, just as an automaton is the distortion-free identity of its mechanism.

Under the technical conditions of 1800, when automatons were mechanical rather than electrical or electronic, the Mother's Voice assumed the task of establishing Rivarol's dream of the purity and universality of standardized high idioms. Because the phonetic method did away with the rules of traditional acquisition, it was not merely a speech system but a writing system. It guaranteed iteration in a pedagogic (not technical) manner, thus assuring a structural transcribability of sound. Ferdinand Olivier, who in his philanthropic work in Dessau was himself one of Rivarol's despised Swiss French teachers, promised that his half-hearted phonetic method for fathers and mothers "would succeed eventually and with near necessity in unifying all dialects of a given language into, as their accepted foundation, the finest and purest idiom."[39] Through "The Theory and Analysis of Speech Sounds," "the sounds of language will be taken from their indefinite and fluid condition, in which they have been held by an incomprehensible prejudice, and, under a new relationship, will be defined almost as they once were in their visible form through the invention of writing."[40] To speak plainly, phonetic reading instruction is thus a writing system and not merely a method of speech. Only as such, through the regulation of pronunciation according to a hypothetically "accepted" norm, could it teach children orthography prior to any instruction in penmanship.[41] The phonetic method, a revolutionary development equalled only by the invention of writing itself, and therefore of high culture generally, would have been a worthy recipient of the St. Petersburg Academy prize.

In Germany the methodological purification of speech began with Johann Gottfried von Herder. In the context of his secondary school reform, Herder, a head consistorial counselor, delivered a speech entitled "On the Education of Students in Language and Speech," which for a century was again and again hailed as the founding document of German as a school subject[42] and which constructed the image of the new subject's enemy:

When we come into the world we are of course able to scream and cry, but not to talk or speak; we emit only animal sounds. These animal sounds remain with some people and races throughout their entire lives. One has only to stand at a distance from which the sound of the voice and accent can be heard without the meaning of the words being conveyed: in some people one will hear the turkey, the goose, the duck; in many speakers it will be the peacock, the bittern; in pretentious dandies it will be the canary; it will be anything but the human voice. Thuringia has many good things, but fine-sounding speech is not one of them. One realizes this when one hears sounds, sounds mixed together, but does not understand the meaning of what is said. Youths who have acquired this unpleasant dialect of merely animal sounds, whether they come from the cities or the country, should make every effort in school to acquire a human, natural speech possessed of character and soul and to rid themselves of their peasant or shrieking back-alley dialects. They should leave off the barking and yelping, the clucking and cawing, the swallowing and dragging together of words and syllables and speak human rather than animal language. Happy is the child, the boy, who from his first years onward hears understandable, human, lovely sounds that unnoticeably mold his tongue and the sound of his speech. Happy is the child whose caretaker, mother, older siblings, relatives, friends, and finally first teachers speak to him in their bearing and speech with reason, decorum, and grace.[43]

The dichotomy of norm and deviance is so powerful that dialects are no longer conceptually considered human and are instead relegated to the animal realm. Nonetheless, the school reformer knew of no measures against animalization besides his own speeches and fortunate childhood contingencies. So school reform created a gap that the pure phonetic method would fill. Stephani turned Herder's fortunate contingencies into a systematic semiotechnique. The irreplaceable Mother replaced all the various caretakers, siblings, friends, and teachers. She separated the child from everything animal because she did not speak or did not speak to anyone at all; rather, she practiced vowels and consonants. A concept like communication is inadequate for grasping the production conditions of literature, which included machines that generated presignificant sounds. What matters in the discourse network of 1800 is the difference that language, in order to become a high idiom and thus the medium of Poetry, opened between itself and animal sounds. "Language" became a mythical being at the very moment when its anthropological grounding burdened the scapegoat animal with the old-European techniques of language instruction and sent it out into the desert.[44]

What Herder celebrated as the specific difference of the ζῷον λόγον ἔχον ("animal that possesses language"), this language without barking and yelping, clucking and cawing, was simply a new alphabetization. Friedrich Herrmann's *New Primer* warned, in one of the rare sentences not to be spoken by the child itself, that the child should not be an animal.[45] Stephani's primer instituted this difference even in the most minute of its methodological steps. From the purified Mother's Mouth the child learns, besides vowels, some noisy consonantal combinations, such as *bl*, *br*, *pf*, *pr*, *fl*, *dr*; although they create the "greatest difficulty while reading," the child "can play them with the greatest ease on his mouth instrument."[46] The *rk* in *bark* and the *lp* in *yelp* no longer reminded one of animals. Although it could be overcome, the difficulty was so great that one primer, which introduced Stephani's Bavarian state-approved method to Baden, joined the ranks of the most heroic lipograms. It contained, in spite of its piety, "in the whole book not just *one syllable* words, but only words beginning with a *single* consonant"; so, for example, the multiple-consonant word "Jesus Christ" occurs only in an "afterword" for teachers.[47]

The first German-language primers, during the Reformation, introduced consonants and consonantal combinations very differently. Grüssbeutel's *Little Voice Book* presented *ss* as a hissing snake, *pf* as a snarling cat being barked at by dogs.[48] Peter Jordan's *Lay Book* gave these rules of pronunciation: "The *l* as the ox lows. The *m* as the cow moos. The *r* as the dog growls. The *s* as the young doves whistle and coo." [49] Finally, Valentin Ickelsamer, whose *German Grammar* was the source of such animal voice catalogs, hoped that they would provide exactly what Stephani sought from mothers: substitution of the sounds designated by letters for the traditional letter names. In this, however, he was as far from being the precursor of the pure phonetic method as the animals are from being the mother.[50] The sixteenth-century conception of language directed children toward the many languages of creation, toward the materiality and opacity of signs.[51] With Stephani's phonetic exercises, mothers become aware of the musicality of their mouths.

The dog that distracted the translator Faust in 1799 disturbed earlier readers so little that he could figure as one of the models for reading. Some sound or other could be usefully extracted from his barking.[52] The secondary-school students who terrified Head Consistorial Counselor Herder in 1796 with their Saxon animal sounds were not the mythic wolf children of the new anthropology of language, but simply parrots of their primers or house pets of their teachers. Even the Prussian King Frederick was said to have learned to read from epoch-making primers like the *Little Voice Book*.[53] Herder's belief that "our spirit secretly accommodates all dialects of the mother tongue" [54] applied initially only to the spirit of his school reform and of maternal phonetics. But there have been times when, to the contrary, language accommodated dialects and dialects accommodated the creatures of the earth.[55] In the discourse network of 1800, however, the place of the many animals—dogs, cats, oxen, cows, doves, snakes—became that of Woman.

This happened quite explicitly. The founding document of the anthropology of language, Herder's *Treatise on the Origin of Language*, has the human language of human beings, that necessary Other to the connatural baby crying or student alley dialects, proceed from naming an animal. The target of this act is a "white, soft, woolly" lamb, which (as these attributes suggest) could better be called a ewe. According to Herder, in order for man, this creature of lack and uncertain instincts, to arrive at the freedom of name giving, he must lack the instinct of a bloodthirsty lion, even that of an ardent ram, both of which might "throw themselves over" the lamb [56]—which would be perverse if a child or a neuter were concerned.

If the lamb stands for Woman, then the instinctual lack posited in Herder's anthropology is simply the cessation of male desire. A desire ceases and the capacity to speak emerges. The first name bestowed articulates this difference. The difference is in the name itself—between the natural-language bleating of the lamb or ewe and its "onomatopoeic" repetition.[57] "The sheep comes again. White, soft, woolly—the soul sees, touches, remembers, seeks a distinguishing mark—the sheep bleats, and the soul recognizes it. And it feels inside, 'Yes, you are that which bleats.'"[58] Such repetition, which at once displaces and differentiates, so that natural language is displaced onto human language and a human-animal difference is opened up, could perhaps be read in light of Derrida's *différance*.[59] But what is ignored in such a reading is that repetition and displacement are themselves a displacement of sexual difference. The explicit distinction between ram and man is not the first sign of this. Herder's initial thesis that "while still an animal, man already has language" projects a whole language of crying and weeping, of exhausted breaths and half sighs, that mocks alphabetization and transcription.[60] Herder leaves open the question of who speaks this language, but Mephisto makes it clear. To the keen-eared devil, "the dull 'ach!'" and "the fiery 'oh!'"—all the sounds of nature that Herder writes down as untranscribable[61]—are well-known symptoms of women, "to be cured in *one* way."

But the cure does not take place. An incest barrier separates Stephani's child from the mother and her natural sounds. An instinctual lack separates Herder's human beings from the ewe, and the barrier of centuries separates them from the language of Nature, which is not accidentally called the "original wild mother" of all discourses.[62] In both cases an unbridgeable distance makes them speak. Mephisto's advice remains unheeded so that sound can become language. Mother and Woman are agents of discourse production.

As the product of its Other, articulated and transcribable discourse is never a pure beginning. Herder does not make the "absolutely absurd" mistake of denying that a kind of language is the precondition for the first forming of names.[63] The hypothetical "baah" of the ewe *is* this precondition. It enters her human name in the same way that the natural sounds of the "feelings" and "passions" (however great the distortion) enter the "roots" of the earliest languages.[64] Thus prior to any discourse lies another, a dark and unarticulated discourse that stands to the articulated and articulating signifiers as their signified. The discourse network of 1800 measures the space of this difference under the title "Language":

> Why cannot the living Spirit manifest itself to the Spirit?
> Once the soul *speaks*, then, oh! it is no longer the *soul* that speaks.

When "language" is defined within the system, the outcome is at once not (yet) language and the sole signified of language. Herder's essay denies the transcribability of this discourse prior to language, and Schiller's distich denies its speakability. And yet "the soul" speaks/writes itself. After the caesura in the pentameter—that is, precisely where the line's heaviest accent falls—one hears/reads a pure sound of nature. The "soul" pushes toward language so forcefully that even lines of poetry, in which the unfulfillable character of the soul's wish becomes language, grant the wish and write down an autonymic signifier of the soul. This "oh!" is at once a word and not a word; it speaks and contradicts language; it constitutes the beginning of language yet is subsequently betrayed by all speaking. The discourse network of 1800 rests on a signifier that remains the network's limit value, because all articulated signifiers refer to it as their signified.

The Courses of Life as an Ascending Line, by Theodor Hippel, institutes that signifier in an abyss that separates it from all others. "Don't call *sighs, half-uttered* 'oh's' dead words, you wordhacks! They count for more than all your sad songs and condolences. In 'oh,' the Spirit releases the muted body and rushes forward to speak for it, but the Spirit alone speaks. There are unspeakable 'oh's'!"[65]

In the name of the unspeakable, then, Hippel set an explicit limit to discourse. Thereafter, it was forbidden to say that the one and only signifier reputed to be free of materiality and body (as if sighs were not expressions in which the body replaces the mute spirit) was merely one signifier among others. This rule of language had far-reaching consequences.

Gretchen opposes the exchange value of gold, which like discourse sets in motion an endless circulation, with the cry, "Oh! we poor!" ("Ach, wir Armen!"; 2804).

After it becomes clear to what vagaries love's desire will be exposed by seemingly straightforward yet nonetheless so misusable proper names, Alcmene ends the tragicomedy of Kleist's *Amphitrion* with her simple "oh"—only to remain mute in the unwritten tragedy of her further marriage.[66]

And when in Hoffmann's "The Sandman" a student is driven into paranoia and even his fiancée can offer no help beyond "profound philosophical letters,"[67] he suddenly and decisively falls in love with another, who gives him less or more than theory.

He sat beside Olympia, her hand in his, and with fervor and passion he spoke of his love in words that no one could understand, neither he nor Olympia. But perhaps she did, for she sat with her eyes fixed upon his, sighing again and again, "Oh, oh, oh!" Whereupon Nathanael answered: "Oh, you magnificent and heavenly woman! You ray shining from the promised land of love! You deep soul, in which my whole being is reflected," and more of the same. But Olympia did nothing but continue to sigh, "Oh, oh!"[68]

Nathanael's rejection of Clara, who has been all too alphabetized, follows the new language regulation word for word. Only a beloved given totally to "oh"-saying can fulfill the wish that language (mathematically put) should have no greater power than the soul, that it should really and exclusively "portray man's inner life."[69] Olympia is the soul that, instead of speaking, makes her lover speak and speak exactly that inner life. The promised beyond of language, also called love, ensures that Nathanael talks and talks until all the women "vanish from his memory" and only Woman remains.[70] Her unique signifier brings about a complete individualization of speech. It does the impossible: not only to designate but also to signify an individual. And to make the impossible as true as it is reproducible, one had only to construct an automaton according to St. Petersburg specifications for producing vowel sighs. Nathanael's beloved Olympia is the mechanical doll built to Spallanzani's specifications, and Woman, a mechanical effect of discourse. Her name (Gretchen, Alcmene, Olympia) is irrelevant.

The mechanical program allows discourses to be decomposed into the most basic elements, which can function as "natural as well as intentional signs," as "feeling and speech sounds."[71] Herder's bleating sheep did this for the first time, and Schiller's distich "Language" did it with admirable economy. As Joseph Heselhaus has observed, the sustaining opposition of the verse, the contra-diction between the title and the tone-setting signifier, is implied in the materiality of language, prior to any authorial intention whatsoever. In the graphics and/or phonics of the title word *Sprache* dwells the syntagma *ach*.

The decomposition *Spr - ach - e* represents the basic mechanical operation in the discourse network of 1800. It defines that machine precisely because it never occurs as a mechanical decomposition, being instead rewritten and reproduced by women and texts. Every culture has different techniques and standards to govern the concrete manipulation of language. The threshold that determines the possible extent and usefulness of analyses differentiates discourse networks from one another. In 1800 the threshold was drawn at the minimal element of significant sounds and sound combinations. This means two things. First, the decompositions possible in what murmurs and gleams from all sides did not stop at the word, which is scorned by Faust, Herder, Hippel, and Nathanael. Second, the decompositions did not cross the threshold beyond which the great Kingdom of Nonsense would begin. In 1800 the "love of the word" or "philology" applied neither to the word nor to those asignificative elements known as phonemes or letters. Instead it was devoted entirely to the Spirit or signified of language, through whose working "every *word* expresses a form, every usage a grouping, every choice of words a nuance of the picture" and (this is decisive) "the syllable also becomes meaningful."[72] With its meaningful syllable this definition named the limit and goal of all language analysis: a minimal element that unifies sound and meaning, Nature and Spirit. It is at once the ground and summit of language: a ground insofar as scientific analysis "seeks the particular significance of every vowel and consonant, for their more abstract aspects (lip movements, gum and tongue movements), and then for their combination;"[73] a summit insofar as at the end of a sequence of iterated decompositions the minimal signified equaled Poetry. "The finest poem consists of nothing but verses; the verses of words; the words of syllables; the syllables of single sounds."[74]

There is a world of difference between this minimal signified and the language elements that would be generated in the discourse network of 1900. Only the ahistoricism that afflicts literary histories of Modernism could allow A. W. Schlegel's definition of poetry to be set beside the "word-in-itself-poetry" of Ivan Goll or Hugo von Hofmannsthal's phrase "The material of poetry is words."[75] The phoneticism of syllables and sounds blocks such an equation. They had nothing of the literal, written character of the literary word and instead remained "pure poetic flash that disappears without a trace, leaving behind it but a vibration suspended in the air for one brief moment."[76] Philosophy in 1800 made this claim, and linguistics set about empirically confirming it. Thus Hegel called tone "the fulfilment of the expressiveness by which inwardness makes itself known" because it is "determinate being within *time*," and therefore "determinate being which disappears in that it has being."[77] August Bernhardi's grandiose and monomaniacal *On Language* was occupied with the thought that the whole of Nature sounded in minimal signifieds; man imitates these sounds and finally, in his perfection as poet, by abrogating all vestiges of writing returns to the original sounds.[78] In Herder's words: language in 1800 "was . . . full of living sounds."[79]

There were, moreover, explicit sanctions against equating the minimal signified with graphic signs. Whoever dared to count the sigh "oh!" as one signifier among others would be one of Hippel's despised wordhacks. Of meanings in the original language, Herder wrote: "In their living contexts, in the total picture of pulsating nature, accompanied by so many other phenomena, they are moving and sufficient unto themselves. Severed from everything else, torn away, deprived of their life, they are, to be sure, no more than ciphers." After the forbidden decomposition nothing would remain of the "voice of nature" but "an arbitrarily penciled letter."[80]

In 1800 linguistic analysis was not allowed to approach the two forbidden borders of the word and the letter. Instead, analysis was confined within the concept of the root, as instituted by a new science of language. Roots lead whole words back to an original historical significance that binds all Indo-European languages in a proper nuclear-family affection and makes them daughters of one mother. At the sight of "several samples of handwriting in Sanskrit," the hero in Ferdinand von Loeben's novel *Guido* says, "Languages have always seemed to me to be lost holy children who cover the whole world in search of their mother."[81] This mother, once found, could not be further analyzed. The indivisibility of Sanskrit roots promised the origin of all meaning. This thought would lead Jakob Grimm audaciously to extend a minimal but present meaning beyond the roots of words to morphemes, such as the series of graded vowels *a, i, u.*[82]

The combinatory rules of a given discourse network correspond to its rules of decomposition. Thus a nonproblematic and symmetrical procedure led linguistic science in 1800 from isolated elements back to words. "If one goes back in history to the origin of all languages, one finds that out of simple, unarticulated sounds increasingly articulated, complex combinations of words arose—this process is the way of nature."[83] This historical-systematic observation was transferred to instruction in language and reading. Olivier, for example, explains his phonetic method:

The means that my method of instruction, like the old spelling method, will employ in preparing the reader's competence are nothing but the entirely natural dissolution of the language's every word into actual, distinctly audible components, into the completely pure, simplest sounds or elements. To comprehend this analysis, one need only hear it, as the child is prepared in advance to do by its linguistic capacity. Hence the one thing that the child must accomplish in this preparatory exercise is to learn the technique of taking the more or less completely dissolved whole—that is, the dissolved word—and putting it back together, thus restoring it to its recognizable form. This technique is almost mechanical and therefore very easy.[84]

Because the analysis obeys the most natural Nature, the recombination is as good as accomplished. The postulate of the minimal meaning drastically limits combinatory possibilities: all assembly is excluded. (By *assembly* I mean first the three types of mathematical combinatorics—permutation, combination, and variation—and second aleatory possibilities, for example, those produced in a crossword puzzle between the columns and series of letters.) Products of assembly are as little constrained to make sense as the corresponding method of decomposition is to return always to signifieds: this is the simple secret of every *characteristica universalis* and is addressed in a satire by Christian Liscov.

The miserable scribes write books. A book is actually nothing but a lot of leaves covered with letters. If there is some agreement among these letters, then the book they make up is a genuine book. There is agreement among the letters if and only if they are combined in such a way that comprehensible words result. These words can be combined and recombined in all languages countless numbers of times, without any harm to the so-necessary agreement of the manifold, and so it is left to anyone's whim how the words of the language in which he writes will be mixed together.[85]

Decomposition and composition in the age of representation had followed the rules of a combinatory system that played on all levels of language at once and that was immortalized in Swift's Lagado Academy. In the writing system of 1800, by contrast, nonsense letter and word permutations were not even worthy of being ignored. In it, augmentation as a combinatory technique corresponded to implication as a technique of decomposition. Just as *ach* was contained in *Sprache*, so *Sprache*, theoretically and literally, proceeded from *ach*. Augmentation led from meaning to meaning; it came into play where minimal signifieds grow into meanings and so conformed to the organic model in which elements not fortuitously named roots grow whole words.

Assembly and augmentation as historically different manipulations of language stand to one another as do fugue and sonata, contrapuntal line and thematic-motivic work. The fugue contained no continual expansion and acceleration of its themes, only the whole-number amplification and diminution of note values. Furthermore, its technique of construction took into account the column and the series to which each tone belonged. Finally, the rules for the formation of crab motion, retrograde, and mirror crab were textbook examples of mathematical combinatorics. By contrast, the themes of the classical-romantic sonatas consisted of motifs that were at once minimal musical materiality and elementary meaning. In the opening motif of his C Minor Symphony, Beethoven, whose notebooks demonstrate an obsession with the smallest possible motifs, exemplified how a maximum of meaning can be drawn from a minimum of note value. Finally, thematic-motivic work proceeds by extensions and variations according to the combinatory rules of continual augmentation. Out of minimal meanings grew symphonies that culminate in the brotherly embrace of humanity.

In the primers of 1800 one can read how the changeover from one combinatory technique to another was effected. They intentionally eliminated very old combinatory games that had been brought to Germany in primers of the Reformation period. Combinations appeared first in the primer of Jacob Grüssbeutel (1534);[86] in that of Ickelsamer (1534) appeared the first column-and-series crosses, assembly techniques that led at most marginally to the output of meaningful words.[87]

ba	ab
be	eb
bi	ib
bo	ob
bu	ub

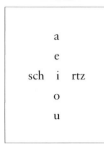

In 1800 a children's crusade was mobilized against the kind of nonsense generated by assembly techniques. Several of the early reform primers still included the Babylonian *ba be bi*,[88] but it became "almost a point of honor for the authors of primers . . . to include only meaningful words."[89] In 1796, August Niemeyer signaled some of the first opposition to the assembly method. "In teaching syllables one should not choose the meaningless *ab, eb, ib, etz, quau, quay*, and so on, but rather one-syllable words to which meanings can be attached: *bath, board, yard, pond, tooth, corn, hat, town*, etc."[90] Language instruction thus would do away with nonsense, latent as a threat or possibility in the material and combinatory character of all alphabetical writing. Thus a search began for "meanings" or signifieds inherent in the smallest sound combinations. In all their German holiness, Faust's words *mind, force, act*—all monosyllabic and shorter than the word they are supposed to translate—function like a word-example hodgepodge of the same type as *bath, board, yard*.

Ernst Tillich first introduced into pedagogy the genetic-methodological, and so truly augmentative merging of such minimal meanings. For Niemeyer and Faust the monosyllabic meanings fall from heaven as "whole impressions,"[91] whereas for Tillich they arise in a sliding transition out of single sounds. Without any introduction, the *First Reader for Children* begins with the sequence:[92]

a	*A*	*Aah*	*h*						
ab	ba	ap	pa	ma	am	Ad	da	at	ta
An	na	ak	ka	ag	ga	af	fa	va	wa
as	sa	ass	ssa	asch	scha	Ach	cha		

The beginning of science thus creates, as in Hegel's *Logic*, an unconditional immediacy: the primal sound, pure, undisturbed, uncolored. Just as Being is not anything intuited, but rather pure, empty intuition itself, so *a* is not an element of any given language, but pronunciation itself.[93] In the beginning, in other words, is the sound and not the letter *a*; from the ancient beginning symbol alpha there could be no path leading to *Aah*, for such a path can only be made by a voice's distortion, coloration, and extension of the unconditional—by an augmentation. Karl Philipp Moritz described this kind of elongation and even provided guidelines to syllabic "meaning" in his *German Prosody*, which enabled Goethe to versify his *Iphigenia*.[94] In Tillich a few old-fashioned variations follow, but only to bring the voice from pure sound to minimal meaning: to the *ach* (the sigh *oh*), which is, as we have seen, the language of Nature. With that, one has already run the entire course that Tillich's massive tome opens up. Eight pages later, the *Ach* that has been created by augmenting *a* undergoes its own augmentation:

ach   n   ach   r   ach   pr   ach   spr   ach

The language of culture (*sprach*) springs suddenly out of the language of Nature without the children noting the slightest differential step. With magnificent autoreferentiality, Tillich's *First Reader* magically draws the name of speaking out of the minimal signified *ach*. If the soul sp-o-ke, then, "oh," the soul almost spoke. Here this is demonstrated in reverse; the structure of material implication that is the secret of Schiller's distich is technically proved. In an illustration of the logic of pedagogical writing techniques, Tillich, after hundreds of pages in which sounds give rise to syllables, syllables to words, words to sentences, and sentences to stories, ends his first edition (1803) with a story called simply "Growth."[95] This story follows the same rules of construction as "the finest poem" (in the words of the elder Schlegel) and gives augmentation, that gradual formation of discourse from the Mother's Mouth, its proper name in German.

Biological time and its measurement became part of the pedagogical movement. They were used to calculate norms applicable not merely to ranking classes in schools but to minute steps in a child's lessons and progress in learning.[96] The steps outlined in the primers were not guided by the experimental approach to child measurement developed in the discourse network of 1900, but by a pseudobiology of language development based on pedagogical assumptions. Pestalozzi provided the commentary for what Tillich accomplished rigorously and without any commentary at all.

I tirelessly put together rows of syllables and numbers and filled whole books with them. I tried in every way to make the introduction to spelling and figuring as simple as possible; furthermore, I tried to put the introduction into a psychologically sophisticated form so that the child would be led gradually from the first step to the second, and then, on the basis of a firm understanding of the second step, to the third and fourth steps with rapid, certain progress.[97]

But this way of planning the first step, which was to provide the effortless, sliding transition from Nature to culture, did not entirely guard Pestalozzi against lapses. Letter combinations such as *eph, ephra, ephraim / buc, buce, bucephal / ul, ult, ultra, ultram, ultramontanisch* are indeed minimal steps in learning, but rather than proceeding through the continuum of the voice (like Tillich's "*a Aah*"), they merely move across discrete quanta of letters.[98] Pestalozzi reverts from augmentation to whole-numbered rhetorical amplification.

Herder, in his *Alphabet and Reading Book*, argued against the mistake of beginning with such artificial sound combinations as *ultramontanisch* (or *artifiziell*). His primer instead used imperceptible grammatical exercises with minimal signifieds, such as *I am / you are*, whereas previously "the most difficult words, *geheiliget, Benedicite*, and so on, stood on the first pages," so that "children did not understand anything of what they were spelling and reading."[99] The comment could apply to Pestalozzi's *ephraim* or to "the difficult Biblical names, such as *Nebuchadnezzar, Abednego*, etc.," that mystified Anton Reiser when he was learning to read.[100] Such references constituted not only a vocabulary of old-fashioned, yard-long words but a particular discourse, the theological. The "freeing of school governance from church governance" was simple:[101] the new primers depose Christianity by banning its key words.

This is not to say that gods or goddesses faced extinction: that simply doesn't happen. Herder's imperceptible grammatical exercise *I am / you are* was not an empty recitation but offered a saying different from the command *Benedicite*. It constituted training in an elementary speech situation. Where previously the Many had called upon One God, henceforth One Child spoke to the first You. The minimal signifieds of the new primers were the autonyms of primary education. A benediction of the nuclear family superseded praise of God. "The stability of religion derives from the fact that meaning is always religious."[102]

To make meaning is, of course, the definition and the cunning of minimal signifieds. A professor of psychology who inaugurated the systematic observation of infants, beginning with his own newborn son, and who thus became not a father but the father of child psychology, heard his son "purposefully articulate and repeat sounds" on March 14, 1782.[103] At this, the person whom the psychologist, Dieterich Tiedemann, designated as "mother"—with proper scientificity or infantilism—rather than as his wife "pronounced the syllable *ma*" for the baby. The experiment was a success, for on November 27 the child "speaks a few words clearly and also knows their exact meaning: namely, Papa and Mama."[104]

The case indicates the stringent logic of minimal signifieds. Unlike Nathan the Wise (the eponymous hero of Lessing's play), who provided his child with instruction, that is, with articulated doctrine, this father retreated to writing articulated essays about the child. He left uttering the syllable, the hesitant beginning of articulation and signification, to a "mother" who did not even continue to speak—she made the child speak. The syllable became a name only when repeated in the child's mouth, which in a fitting autonym called out the very one from whom all language learning proceeded. In Herder's essay, man translated the ewe's "baah" by onomatopoeic repetition; Tiedemann's son translated his mother's "ma" by a reduplicating repetition in language: both are textbook cases of augmentation. Thus arose a "clear pronunciation" and a "meaning" that was clearer still: it had no referent. Young Tiedemann employed his "'Mama' not in order to call the person, but almost arbitrarily, without wanting to say anything,"[105] and therefore proved that there is no empirical place at which the Mother could be addressed.

Mama or *ma* functioned as the most distinguished minimal signified in the writing system of 1800. It was the earliest one to be discussed, archived, and fed back into the system. *Mama* did not indicate, as it would a century later, the existence of a children's language beyond any national language, which could contribute to a general linguistics.[106] Instead, it was pronounced by parents only so that it might recur in children's mouths—as a signature for the new education. What occurred, then, was true programming, which could thus be continued by automatons. The Baron of Kempelen boasted that his automaton of 1778 could say, aside from a few other words, *mama* and *papa*. These two words constituted the entire vocabulary of the patented doll that Johann Maelzel exhibited in Paris in 1823.[107]

The pedagogic movement took the curiosities and ephemera of contemporary technology (because pedagogy could manipulate phonetics and the pragmatic linguistics of the minimal signified) and from them fashioned a functioning feedback-control system. Stephani's *Primer* promises in its subtitle to give mothers the pleasure of speedily teaching their own children to read and then begins, after briefly introducing the single syllables to be practiced in the mother's mouth, with a syllable list:

> ju jo ja jö jä je jü ji jau
>
> mu mo ma mö mä me mu mi
>
> mei mai mau mäu Ma-Ma

In what follows the same vowels are combined with the consonants *h b p d t k f*, from which the words *Bu-be* and *Pa-pa* arise as quickly and naturally as did the primal word *Ma-ma*.[108] Thus after three run-throughs of sounds and sound combinations, the phonetic method led to the signification and benediction of the nuclear family (not accidentally from the perspective of the "Bu-be," the boy). The holy triad was named. But in the beginning was and remained *Ma-ma*, the minimal signified that, as in the example of young Tiedemann, produced by augmentation an entire so-called world of meaning.

Acculturation in 1800 shortcircuited the circuit of discourse. In teaching their children, above all their sons, to speak and read, mothers taught them the transition from natural sounds and mouth exercises to calling the mothers' own names.

As soon as the child's awareness has developed sufficiently, sometime in its second year, it will hear its mother speak each time she gives it something: "Look what Mother has for you." Later, or as soon as it has a better understanding of language: "You're hungry, you want to eat; it wouldn't feel good to go a few more hours without food, or if no one were here when you're hungry, if no one loved you and wanted to help you. Don't worry my child! Your mother is here!"[109]

This eloquent doubling of the mother-child relation—a doubling that makes the relation possible in the first place—is the subject of the engraving that appears as the frontispiece to Stephani's book.

The engraving can also be used for this purpose. Your children should love and respect you as their educator rather than merely as their mother. If you have taught your children to read, show them the picture and lead them into a conversation about how much these children love their mother because of the burden she assumed in teaching them to read and about how pleased this mother was to instruct her children because she felt they would owe her twice as much love.[110]

A picture presented and introduced the mother as *Bildnerin*, or "cultivator." *Bildung*, that key word of 1800, arose by folding an empirical learning situation onto one that was ideal and programmed. When reform pedagogy merged the two situations, the core of the nuclear family became doubly erotic. The engravings, which both Stephani and Daniel

Doubly honor the mother who at once loves and instructs [*bildet*] you.

Chodowiecki used to present a mother and child with the image of a mother and child engaged in the task of *Bildung*, accomplished the doubling: they presented an image of both the Arcadian beginning and the Elysian end of the new alphabetization. Only in a picture can the child really be initiated "without difficulty, with pleasure to our world of books," as Karl Splittegarb promised in a pure paradox. In order to be receptive to written consolation, the child must already have been acculturated; the consolation is always too late. But the engravings and the maternal discussions they prompted were different. They accomplished the aim of the phonetic method: the effortless glide from *ma* to *Mama*, Nature to culture, sound to language. Pictures and orality tucked writing into the kind of love that the original maternal cultivator displayed and deserved. Stephani's advice to mothers programmed an infinite intensification of their image. An alphabetization in which all real work was taken on by the mother ceased to be an incision or pain; the latter, the forceable violation required to mark human beings with a storage or memory capacity, had always been forgotten because it was the precondition of memory itself. The discourse network of 1800 reversed this and made possible memories that reached back to a fully affectionate, maternal alphabetization.

Rousseau, a matricide at birth, was thrust at the age of five or six by the unconsolable widower, his father, into the explicit place of the one they had lost: at night he would read aloud to his father the novels that previously had been held and read by his mother. Not until this erotically charged cache of books had been used up did the two of them have recourse, by day, to the father's library in the Republic of Scholars. Violence and a chance event, then, brought a child and the ability to read together in the place of the child's mother. The author of the *Confessions* was therefore unable to recall how he learned to read around 1717. He could recall only his "first reading experiences and their effects," which naturally amounted to a solitary eroticization.[111]

In 1800 the chance event became an institutionalized program and the violence became love. Probably the first document supporting a gentle, maternal experience of learning to read was provided by the *Memoirs* of Karl Heinrich von Lang. But what Lang called "very tiresome and silly"[112] soon revealed itself to be a pervasive, portentous pleasure. Rousseau and Christoph Martin Wieland were taught to read by their fathers, but Friedrich Schleiermacher, Friedrich Jahn, Johann Tieck, Friedrich von Raumer, and the brothers Grimm were taught by their mothers.[113] Only for such as them, in contrast to Rousseau, do memories of the earliest alphabetizing become possible, because along with reading the mother taught that her gift of love was unforgettable—as a great range of resulting nineteenth-century autobiographies confirm.[114]

Such capacity for recollection could be augmented further. In 1809 a certain primer nostalgia appeared, one that via Karl Hobreker infected Walter Benjamin.[115] Friedrich Hempel, a judge and government official stricken with insomnia by the sufferings of those condemned by the laws, but not by his own feelings, found his sole consolation in conjuring up his first primer and its alphabet, then devoting himself to a phantasmal, book-length commentary.

Yes! It was you, my beloved ABC book, you who rescued me from this hellish ordeal, this torture chamber, and took me back to the charming fields of my youth. You healed the sufferings of my soul with the balm you poured from the nectar cup of memory! I wandered through the paradisiacal meadow of my springtime and was seized with a longing like the thought of a lost lover.[116]

This inspired comment neglects only one thing: like comedy and tragedy for Aristotle, the beloved ABC book and the disdained law statutes consist of exactly the same letters. The truth may have tortured government-appointed judges to a degree equaled only by the fate of their victims; nonetheless, judges learned to read only to be able to decipher and apply the laws. The functions of memory and storage on which the law is based dominate the phantasm of a "recollection," which in spite of its name was evoked to make the truth forgettable. As such, the recollection is bathed in the paradisiacal glow of an always-lost childhood lover.

For Tieck, the mother-beloved who instructed his alphabetical imagination and gave him memory of alphabetization was his real mother. He told his first biographer that he "learned to recognize letters on mother's lap, and the learning went quickly when imagination came into play. The letters seemed to be alive; they turned into droll figures of all kinds." One who learned to read at an age of "barely four years" and at the same time learned to recollect it pleasurably for a lifetime was all but predestined to become the romantic poet of droll figures.[117] He was able to write an artist's fairy tale in which the heroine recalls how as a child she ran away from a tyrannical stepfather and was taken in by a wise woman who lived in a forest; there she learned to read and found it "a source of unending pleasure."[118]

Writing about learning to read and write constituted a large feedback loop. It returned to the place from which all acculturation proceeded in order to retrieve it from forgetfulness. As Nature *and* Ideal, the Mother oriented the entire writing system of 1800. The various discourses whose regulated interplay constituted the system can be differentiated only in pragmatic respects. Each one of them operated as a return to the source by different paths and detours.

Motherliness and Civil Service

A simple and direct shortcircuit characterized pedagogical discourse. Educational tracts and primers written explicitly for mothers obliterated their own textuality for the sake of their addressees. Books disappeared in a Mother's Mouth whose original self-exploratory experience had been instituted by those very books. Stephani's *Primer* was a model of this disappearance. The phonetic method—in other words, the pretense of uncoupling learning to read from the discourse of the Other—substituted for the textuality of the book and alphabet a Voice that neither read aloud nor imitated, but instead spontaneously created the pure sounds of the high idiom or mother tongue. The inexplicable difficulty was how mothers who had not already learned to read before reading Stephani could know the pronunciation of certain black squiggles on white paper. They would have been unable to decipher even the primers designed for their use. For the sake of the Mother, a book would forget being a book.

Pestalozzi made this shortcircuit explicit in his joyful exclamation, "The book is not yet there, and already I see it disappearing again through its effects!"[1] The preface to his *The Mother's Book* assured each and every mother of its intention to place its pedagogical contents "most perfectly into your soul and into the soul of your child" and went on to remark:

I know that these are just forms, but as forms they are the containers of a power that will bring intelligence and life to you and your child. Mother! The spirit and power of perfection lie within you, and for the sake of your child you should develop them into *your* spirit and *your* power. You can and should do this, otherwise you are worth nothing, nothing at all. I will speak the truth and speak it plainly: you, friends and foes of the method, test it on this one characteristic, and then accept or reject it according to the results. Let me say it plainly right away: the method is worthless if it does not allow every reasonable mother who has practiced it carefully and sufficiently to rise to the point where, with psychological certainty, she can put the books aside as superfluous and proceed independently with the tasks they contain.[2]

There could hardly be stranger standards for the fitness or unfitness of scientific method. Pestalozzi delivered a mere form that was or was not given materiality only by mothers' use of it.[3] A man's book counted only when it disappeared as a book. Pestalozzi's book announced the emergence of a new pedagogy that would proceed with psychological certainty to derive all pedagogy from the mother's inherent educational gifts, in order, finally, to be swept aside with the same psychological certainty and be declared superfluous before those inherent educational gifts.

The Mother, or source of all discourse, was at the same time the abyss into which everything written vanished, only to emerge as pure Spirit and Voice. Not just lyrical literary lullabies, starting with "The Traveler's Night Song," were called forth, then consumed by Mother Nature;[4] sciences were no more resistant. The elimination of books was proclaimed in all the titles of pedagogical treatises. It made literal truth of Faust's turn from dusty books to the life source: the phylogenetic source of discourses reabsorbed those that had hardened into books. No wonder *The Mother's Book* was never finished.

Instead, the German states went to the source. Saxony dispatched high officials of education to Pestalozzi's school at Ifferten,[5] and Prussia, more advanced, "in order to view all aspects of the improved method of public education and to benefit from every experience offered by the contemporary state of educational science," sent young people there, with the declared intention of "having exceptionally apt and well-prepared subjects" (in the lexical sense of *subject*, namely, civil servants) "upon their return."[6] In place of a disappearing book that never appeared, one had the state. Nietzsche's diagnosis of the educational institutions of his century was thus quite accurate: "The mother actually dictates, the evil or false one, the one whom the teacher, as a bureaucrat of the state, cannot help but simulate. She pulls strings in the form of an umbilical cord attached to the paternal belly of the state. All movements proceed from the body of the father, who represents the alma mater."[7]

The alma mater or Mother, the addressee Pestalozzi apostrophized with every device that could be borrowed from the sublime, became concretized in a bureaucratic and therefore textual apparatus that was at once its caricature and its serial continuation. Pedagogical discourses disappeared into the Mother's Mouth only to reappear multiplied in the form of a bureaucratic administration. Indeed, such a process corresponded to the structure of address in a book in which the singular "Mother!" stood next to the multiplicative address "friends and foes of the method" as a means of inviting the "critique" of official experts. The Prussian reformers—Heinrich vom Stein, Johann Fichte, Wilhelm von Humboldt[8] needed only to take the invitation seriously and actually inspect, as desired, all aspects of Pestalozzi's improved method of public education. The method was approved and thus consumed a second time. First the Mother drank, then the civil servants lined up.

This by no means resulted in the state's disrupting the shortcircuit between the maternal producer of discourses and pedagogical discourse. The state could not usurp the rights of an authority deemed by Nature—in other words, by itself—to be responsible for primary education. What Faust called a life source became institutionalized. The mother "must be an educator" because "the child sucks in its first ideas with the mother's milk."[9]

In 1800 the state acted in accord with such maxims. Napoleon, the master of cannon fodder, directed Madame de Campan, headmistress of a boarding school for the daughters of indigent officers of the Legion of Honor, to provide him with mothers.[10] German administrations, in their circuitous yet ultimately more efficient manner, instituted this master's order. In the discourse network of 1800 political theory declares that the most sacred duty of the state is:

To do everything possible to educate the daughters of our age and make them into better mothers, so that the state will be able to place its future citizens into good hands rather than simply abandoning many of them, as it is now forced to do. Therefore let me repeat that I view the problem of women's education as one of the most sacred duties of the state and I would charge all those who neglect this problem, the ministers of education departments, consistorial presidents and advisors, school inspectors, and whatever other titles those responsible for public education may have, with crimes against suffering humanity.[11]

It became a duty to produce authoritative producers of discourse. The state of *Bildung* turned biological reproduction, that bare recurrence of the same, into cultural production. There came to be more and more mothers who were more and more motherly.

Historically, this was a new "determination of woman." A book published in 1802 described this determination in terms of "higher intellectual development." Amalie Holst hardly intended, by providing women with higher education, to redress a previous state of powerlessness and submission; she has nothing but scorn for old-European patriarchal fantasies of potency. "The more a husband brags about dominance, the less he has it." [12] Another woman provided an even more succinct justification for the necessity of state-supported schools and colleges of education for women: "Whether men care to face it or not, women rule the world." [13] Accordingly, higher education was not compensation for powerlessness, it was a mutation of power.

We are no longer satisfied with this form of power; we have awakened from a slumber and will now cast away the invisible threads with which we have hitherto, from behind the scene, directed all the action on the great stage of the world. We do this because it is beneath our dignity as human beings to continue to disguise ourselves and pursue our ends with deceit and force. [14]

The old puppet theater is very well suited for staging strategic-political scripts of victories in the war between the sexes. But such victories are disdained for the sake of a more important form of power. When the old-European pedagogues took into account the cultural influence of women, they always thought exclusively in terms of its impact on the surrounding world of men. [15] They therefore lacked, politically and erotically, the pre-programmed power of expansion that was invented in 1800 by exchanging the world of men for the world of children. [16] Amalie Holst wanted first to provide women with higher education and then to add authority over "the primary education of both sexes." The third step would be to secure an "influence that we consider to be infinitely more important than that exercised by people in state revolutions, in that we consider our influence to be the basis for the future character of individuals and so to have an effect on the whole." [17]

Thus a woman who explicitly rejected the role of revolutionary was able to outdo any revolution. The dispensation of the new gender determination called motherhood was a psychological power that subsumed all power. In the shift from "worldly woman" to "mother," [18] status to development, leisure to education, the recoding of women transformed them into the Truth. Only Truth, of course, can effortlessly transform agglomerates into wholes, make human beings "human beings in the noblest sense of the word," [19] and achieve its victory nakedly, without deception. Mother and Truth became synonymous. Anyone who could determine the very possibilities of being human by controlling the primary education of children had attained a transcendental power surpassing all empirical and political conditions.

The state could never control such an authority; it could only accommodate it. The state relinquished aspects of its judicial, bureaucratic, and political power in certain areas and instead instituted the function of Motherhood. An example was the Louise School in Berlin, an educational institution for daughters of the educated classes founded in 1811 and aptly named for the Prussian queen whom Novalis celebrated for having familialized political power and to whom Amalie Holst dedicated her book.[20] According to its program this institution was not to be a school so much as "a large family." "The principal would be called *father*, the headmistress and her assistants *mothers*."[21] And "every state, every municipality is to have" such "maiden houses" in which "everything is completely regulated according to familial relations" because they created mothers in the image of The Mother.[22]

A constantly swelling current of discourse, one held to be pure Truth, flowed between instructing mothers, girls educated to be mothers, and finally children. It traversed political currents and took its power from the separation between women and the state that it achieved. Pestalozzi demonstrated this separation quite clearly when he addressed his pedagogical discourse first and most importantly to mothers, then second and more distantly to educational theorists and civil servants. With the single, perhaps ironic exception of Theodor Hippel, who hoped that female civil servants would lead to *An Improvement in the Status of Women*,[23] reformers of both sexes agreed that "such a total change in the public order" would only "create havoc."[24] "The woman" must remain "continually distant from any direct service to the state" because "her condition, which was dictated exclusively by nature, would often come into conflict with the functions of a state office."[25] From today's standpoint, Hippel may well have spoken the truth. But he was far from the truth of his epoch's discourse.

The exclusion of women from state power and its bureaucratic discourses did not leave the determination of women vague or their achievements unused. The very exclusion of women from offices summons women to their official capacity, as mothers, to elicit discourses generally and magically to transmute them into Nature. Because they "are connected to the state, church, public, and so on, only through their husbands," women live "in an actual condition of nature."[26] Only the separation between the state and civil servants on one side, and families and mothers on the other, guaranteed that the function of Motherhood would not be empirically corrupted. If, as Hippel had wished, "female doctors, judges, preachers, etc." had been produced, then "children would be left to grow wild, corrupt."[27] The exclusion was not an excommunication; it contributed to a relationship of productive complementarity between the new determination of women and a civil service that was becoming the very foundation of the state. In the Mother the state found its Other, without whom it could not exist—as evidence, consider the passionate appeals to ministers, consistorial councilors, and school inspectors (in other words, to all the heads and members of the educational bureaucracy) to place the function of Motherhood above all political considerations.

The German classical philosophy of the sexes made this complementarity explicit. When the pedagogue of *The Elective Affinities* wanted "to sum up the whole task of education in a few words," he formulated it as follows: "Let the boys be raised as servants and the girls as mothers, then all will be well."[28] Philosophers had only to provide a theoretical basis for this practical maxim. Karl Heydenreich demonstrated in his *Man and Woman* that nature had created a sex that was bound "to found, order, govern, and administer the state" because "it is only in the state that mankind can be raised to the greatest possible enlightenment" and reaches its zenith in the pedagogic civil servant or "instructor of mankind."[29] But because human beings, in contrast to animals, can only be biologically reproductive when they are culturally productive and perfectible, nature also devised a sex different from men. This sex is excluded from bureaucratic careers for the most sacred reasons: women, "as mothers of helpless children, constitute, I should say, an end in itself in the state, without ever having to become, like men, a means for the state." Because with species-specific "progress in civilizing and culture" the administration of the state becomes progressively more complicated,[30] the historical role of men is an endless bureaucratization undergone solely to create the possibility of The Mother, the only end in itself that exists in the world.

The official role for men, civil service, entered a new phase in 1800. The German territorial princes of the early modern period had, in part by authority delegated to territorial churches, informally bound certain educated classes and the institutions that produced them to their lands: first judges and theologians, then in 1700 physicians. When the new idol replaced the prince, or civil servants replaced courtiers,[31] the old order of estates became a universal order: "Every citizen of the state is a civil servant," as a poet cum civil servant concisely put it.[32] Any attempt to derive the modern system of forming bureaucrats from medieval or early-modern procedures runs into a barrier at this juncture.[33] Only since 1800 have there been created universal bureaucrats, to whom mankind and even humanness are subordinated.

Heinrich, Freiherr vom Stein complained that the old-Prussian courtiers knew no science and that for them "participation in literary life was as good as forbidden."[34] Humboldt responded by recruiting civil servants via a general system of examinations based on revolutionary standards. "Nothing is as important in a high-level official of the state as the complete conception he has of mankind—how he conceives its dignity and its ideals as a whole—and as the degree of intellectual clarity with which he ponders these questions and responds to them emotionally. There is nothing so important as his interpretation of the idea of *Bildung*."[35] Spirit, Man, *Bildung*—such standards are absurd for the territorial state judge or church minister. But active civil servants who had had a literary-philosophical education and who were "charged with improving the inner condition of man" were indeed, according to Heydenreich's fine expression, instructors of mankind, or in Stephani's neologism, "education officers."[36] The new status of the German servant of the state in 1800 rested on the claim that "along with the preexisting spheres of law and legal scholarship, medical science and medicine, the henceforth equally justified modern system of education must take its place."[37] In 1787 Friedrich August Wolf obtained an administrative mandate "to establish a philosophical seminar as a center for the development of teachers in scholarly institutions," a mandate that was given "more than twenty years before the institutionalization of a separate class of teachers" and that produced scholars who were independent of the church.[38] In 1794 the *General Provincial Law [Allgemeines Landrecht]* declared all professors and secondary-school teachers to be civil servants.[39] In 1817, at the end of this founding period, when the Prussian Ministry of Culture declared the state itself to be an "institution of education writ large," the circle closed.[40] A state that reaches beyond its own laws and punishments to grasp the modern possibility of universal discipline must necessarily form a pact with that most universal and "indispensable class of civil servants" known as teachers. At the conclusion of a document entitled *A Defense of Rights and Claims Based on the Highest National Purpose of Scholar-Teachers*, the teachers addressed an apostrophe to their state in words that provided a straightforward description as well as the terms for a pact. "You must recognize that without us you have no moral value and will not be able to achieve any, just as our profession would be completely devoid of substance without you."[41]

"In the developing constitutional state of the early nineteenth century, the educated class . . . through the conception of the unity of the ideas of state and culture" advanced to a dominant position."[42] Official educators came to control the complex functions of reading and writing indispensable for all other administrative and state officials. "We cannot govern without reading and writing."[43] The identity established between being human and being alphabetized became a simple necessity,[44] at a time of "thoroughgoing implementation of bureaucratic principles in the authority structure of administrative departments and in the professional civil service."[45]

The system would be left with a central gap, however, if it could not provide for the production of civil servants who made other civil servants out of men or human beings out of civil servants. It needed an authority to educate the education officer and to teach reading and writing to the administrators of reading and writing. This elementary prerequisite of disciplinary power was as necessary as it was unwritten because it constituted the center of the system. Constitutional law and administrative method provided only the nexus between the state and the civil service, just as pedagogues provided the nexus between mother and child.[46] The two threads came together between the lines in poetry. When a servant of the state named Homburg impetuously disobeyed tactical commands of the elector and was condemned to death, he took leave of his beloved by requesting that she search in the mountains along the Main until she found a child with blond hair like his own, that she hold the child against her bosom, and that she teach it to stammer the one word "Mother!"[47] So goes recruitment for the civil service.

Thus different discourses, like the dismembered limbs of a phantasm, indicated their empty crossing point: the nexus between Motherhood and the educational bureaucracy. That nexus was unwritten and unavoidable, as was shown by all determinations of Woman. Only the Mother administered early childhood alphabetizing. Only she raised men who were solely and completely human. The Mother was the origin of pedagogic discourse, which returned and disappeared into her to be resurrected in officially educationalized form.

Social history interprets the fact that in 1800 women suddenly were no longer simply subordinate to the father of a household but were defined as standing in a polar and complementary relation to the other sex as a result of increasing bureaucratization, principally because the new definition arose within the administrative, educated middle class. As befits its emphasis on the grand scale of history, it views the macrosocial processes as causes, the gender processes as effects.[48] Jacques Donzelot was able to show, however, that the transformation did not occur "without the active participation of women," who acted in a "privileged alliance" as the partners of doctors and teachers.[49] The situation was therefore at once simpler and more complex: it consisted of interlocking circuits rather than simple causes. In order to generate universal civil servants, the Mother was generated, who in turn generated . . . and so forth. The educational state did not simply fall from the sky, and "the Creator ex nihilo [is] an absurdity."[50]

That the polar arrangement of the sexes can nonetheless appear to be a cover for a persisting patriarchy requires a different explanation. The Woman does not exist. This is one way of saying that the educational state, as a dance of innumerable civil servants around the alma mater, necessarily excluded women as a plurality. In the reorganization of the system of higher education in 1800, which was explicitly devoted to the induction of civil servants,[51] a number of interlocking decrees achieved this exclusion. First, the university as alma mater lost one of its corporate rights: an informal, occasional procedure for admitting students (e.g., after a conversation concerning admittance). A written examination [*das Abitur*] took the place of such spoken occasions. In 1788 Prussia introduced the examination with the declared intent of regulating, by a single act and document, graduation from secondary schools and admittance to universities. In 1834 matriculation was refused without prior examination, a step that accomplished what the secondary-school committee, above all Friedrich Gedike, had been demanding since 1787.[52] As a well-known back-room decision maker put it, the *Abitur* "would allow the state from the moment of the exam to look closely at those who would be its higher servants and to inform itself about their qualities."[53] Man, the individualized universal, came into being under recruiting inspection. The Latin schools to which the state delegated its inspecting eye became the modern secondary schools, whereas other schools lost access to the university.

Second, the course of university studies for the new educational civil servant was regulated. A Prussian edict of 1810 replaced the countless old-European certificates of qualification, some of which were academic, others ecclesiastical, with the examination *pro facultate docendi*, our well-known state exam for teachers.[54] A "circuit of legitimation"[55] with its sub-station in the secondary school for boys thus created a formal, inescapable linkage between the universities and the administrative state. "The 'connection' of 'official agency' and 'individual,' this objective bond between the knowledge of the state and the knowledge of civil society, the *state exam* is nothing other than the *bureaucratic baptism of knowledge*."[56]

Because girls' schools were created to create mothers, the intrusion of the state meant the opposite of what it did at boys' schools and universities. According to one teacher, official "public duty" was "neither healthy nor desirable for a woman."[57] Such a desire would unlink a chain of legitimation. The Louise School, for instance, designed its program so that "instruction will take the form more of family life than that of school . . . without ever having public examinations."[58] The fatal results of ignorance in old-fashioned girls' schools that broke this rule became a theme of the highest literature. In Goethe's *Elective Affinities* Ottilie embodies a silent inwardness and fails in a public examination, only to prove in life and death that she could superbly pass another examination, namely whether domesticity and ideal motherhood constituted the determination of woman. That too was a baptism or induction, albeit an unbureaucratic one: in the boarding school Ottilie learned "not as student, but as a future teacher" [59] and with that met, a year *avant la lettre*, Betty Gleim's demand for boarding-school teachers who would be essentially mothers. [60] Ottilie's antipode Luciane passed the same public examination with flying colors, only to suffer the bitter fate of being entrapped in worldly appearances. Without intending to comment on the latter's fate, Goethe's pedagogical friend Niethammer deduced the same result from the essence of Woman.

How will our daughters react to the quiet of the household when in raising them we ourselves involve them from infancy in every public pastime? We are not merely ruining them for domestic life; we harm virtue much more by making our daughters' education so public that they cannot learn or produce anything that cannot be shown off. How is a spoiled girl to enjoy the quiet tasks of housework, which remain unknown to the public? [61]

Luciane is not an Ideal Mother like Ottilie, and rather than discourse-productive silence she commands speech—she also disappears from the novel without a trace. [62] Likewise, women as a plurality were excluded from the discourse network of 1800. An *Abitur* in inwardness would be unthinkable. Educational reformers and most historians of education have suppressed this by-product of the chain of legitimation that forcibly linked boys' secondary schools, universities, and the state apparatus. When the system of higher education assumed a leading position in the state, women became that which never ceases not to write itself—Lacan's definition of impossibility.

The impossible Luciane isn't dumb and is not without curiosity in theoretical matters. She elicits specialized or professional knowledge from every man that appears. Her existence would have been possible before the establishment of the function of Motherhood. Certainly, statutes that forbade women in public office had long been in existence, [63] but none barred women from the public or the Republic of Scholars. As late as 1742, Dorothea Christina Leporin could justify her recent academic accomplishments with famous examples, a preface by her father, and a striking argument. "If a woman intends to achieve a doctoral degree, possesses as a candidate the requisite knowledge, and passes the examination of the respective faculty, then a degree in law, medicine, or philosophy cannot be refused her, unless there is a constitution to forbid it." [64] For the same reasons life stories in the eighteenth century could be played out in ways that read like word-for-word productions of Lessing's plays. One father who was as wise as Nathan tutored his daughter, providing her with knowledge sufficient to allow her, in the domestic setting of another professor, to pass her matriculation examination and to appear a few years later—dressed as a bride, as per the wishes of none other than her father—before the academic public to receive her master's and doctoral degrees. These events occurred in 1787 and resulted in the second doctoral cap in German women's history.[65]

But whatever scholarly women undertook became impracticable when the system of higher education was coupled with the state and became an instrument of gender differentiation. Women were no longer daughters, that is, brides of their (in fortunate circumstances, enlightening or professorial) fathers; they became incipient-mother daughters of their mothers. In Stephani's newly invented science of state education, to which we owe such fine school subjects as social studies and political education,[66] a strict division separated academic discourse, the autoproductive system for civil servants, from women's education, the self-regulative feedback loop of primary education.[67]

What the manifestos of the bureaucratic and human sciences left unsaid was that a strict division was also the closest correlation. There was no place, in a system of polar sexual difference, where the two sides of the system could both be written down. They remained separated by the abyss that divides writing from the voice. Civil servants wrote (not just anything, but the determination of Mankind); the Mother did not write, she made men speak. This double determination endows the human being with universality and so it can be written only at the price of universalization, or in other words, only as philosophy. Philosophy could formulate the discursive network of the two sexes, but in so doing it named the mother "Woman" and the civil servant the "human being." This led to the necessary contradiction of writing man as double and directing the definition of the human race to two addressees. Friedrich Schlegel addressed his treatise *On Philosophy* to his beloved and to the public.

Perhaps you would prefer a conversation. But I am wholly and thoroughly a writer. The written word has an elusive magic for me, which perhaps comes from the dawning of eternity that surrounds it. Indeed I must confess that I often marvel at the hidden power that lies in these lifeless marks; the simplest expressions, which seem to be nothing more than accurate and correct, can be so meaningful that they seem to gaze at one out of clear eyes, and as expressive as the unembellished accents from the inmost soul. One seems to hear what one is merely reading, and yet someone who reads such beautiful passages aloud can do nothing more than attempt not to spoil them. The silent marks of writing seem to me to be more fitting vessels for the deepest, most immediate expressions of the spirit than the noise of the lips. I would go almost as far as to say in the somewhat mystical language of our H. that life is writing: the sole determination of man is to inscribe, with the stylus of the imaginative spirit, the thoughts of the divinity into the tablets of nature. But as far as you are concerned, I think that your role in this determination of the human race can be perfectly fulfilled if you continue to sing as before, outwardly and inwardly, in an ordinary and symbolic sense; you should be less silent, and read now and then divine writing with reverence rather than have others read aloud for you and tell you stories. But above all you must appreciate the sacredness of words more than you have in the past. Otherwise my prospects would not look good. For of course I have nothing to give you, and must expressly stipulate that you expect nothing from me but words, expressions for what you have long felt and known, although not in as clear and orderly a way.[68]

Schlegel's letter, written in 1799, proclaimed a new century. All the definitions of the human species that had been transmitted from the Greeks and Romans, according to which man is the animal that possesses language or reason, were replaced by the written sentence "He is the writer." Only as an author is man free from the constraint of being also that which he is not; as author he fully and completely assumes his essence. This overflowing identity remains irrefutable to the degree that it stands written on the page. And yet it is not divine. For the writer has an office, whose givenness or authority separates him from the identity of I = I, and with the office he acquires a superior. "The civil servant class has always been an annex of the ruling warrior or priestly classes; it is their appendage, their tool, their corps of assistants or servants." This holds also in Germany, which "like China in Asia or Egypt in antiquity" is "the classic bureaucratic country of Europe."[69] The secondary-school principal Hegel described philosophic logic as "the exposition of God as he is in his eternal essence before the creation of nature and a finite mind."[70] The writer Schlegel described philosophic writing as inscribing the thoughts of the divinity on the tablets of nature with the stylus of the imaginative spirit. The educated class attained leadership by conflating conceptions of the state and of culture. The discourse of the university therefore flowed from the discourse of a master, and the doctrine of being (of the concept or of man) obeyed the imperative of a signifier. Philosophy was never any different.[71]

But just where its despotic signifier appeared, philosophy in the discourse network of 1800 executed a new maneuver. The very Nature that the philosopher's stylus uses as a writing surface for inscribing divine thoughts is at the same time, but in direct contradiction, the source of all writing. Not God, but a tranquil, immediate Nature guides the pen from the depths of the soul through clear eyes. Written translation of Nature is necessary because its speech remains transcendental, not because Nature is a tabula rasa. The silent or even dead marks of writing accomplish what the sound of the lips—the colloquial, animal, or at any rate empirical play of voices and mouths—is unable to do: writing reproduces unembellished accents from the profoundest regions of the soul as clearly as direct speech would sound. The minimal signified as the murmuring source of language remains merely itself as long as it does not speak; the stylus comes to its aid.

One thus has a metaphysics of silent reading, whose prerequisite was the alphabetization of central Europe. The jealous philosopher attacked those who read aloud and thus gave pleasure to Dorothea Veit; methodologically, he wanted to annihilate any others who read aloud because every letter presented them with a small puzzle to solve. Hegel was determined that silent reading should be schooled by habit, for only then would reading return to the "ground of inwardness," or to authoritative discourse production.

The achieved habit [of silent reading] eliminates the peculiar quality of alphabetical writing, which is that in the interest of seeing it appears as a detour through audibility to the signified representations, and transforms the alphabet for us into a hieroglyphic writing so that we do not require a conscious mediation through sounds when using it; by contrast, people who are hardly used to reading pronounce what they read out loud in order to understand it in sounds.[72]

Schlegel was well advised, then, to bind to her own reading a beloved who so enjoyed listening to stories. Only silent reading makes a habit of inwardness. And only silent reading prevents language from responding to the discourse of the Other, which it had done in old Europe as it wandered from one generation to the next, "with all its deficiencies and imperfections . . . through the unconscious imitation and the habituation of certain thought signs."[73] Everything changed when language acquisition began to occur through learning to read. Various inwardnesses gave rise to the language of the classical-romantic texts, a language no mouth had ever spoken. For one who wanted to be "wholly and absolutely an author," there was reason enough to sweeten the new technique of discourse with every word of his letter.

Instead of hearing the factual occurrence of speech, "one seems to hear what one is merely reading." A voice, as pure as it is transcendental, rises from between the lines. When the written lines become so "meaningful that they seem to gaze at one out of clear eyes," the hallucination becomes optical as well as auditory. The reader is no longer reading; in his joy he encounters a phantasmagorical Nature-body. It is not hard to say to whom it belongs. The only alphabetization technique in which one seems to hear what has been read is the phonetic method from the Mother's Mouth. Writing as a philosophical function thus obeys a master and a mistress. In its complexity the text transmits the understandably complex thoughts of God to Nature. In its elementary status of being written rather than spoken, however, the text is an expression of Nature, a fixing of its unembellished accents and minimal signifieds, and the only reproduction that Nature does not betray to language. If minimal signifieds, according to Olivier, are themselves fixations, a writing rather than a speech system of the transcendental Voice, then the transition of that voice into philosophical writing follows as a matter of course.

With a master signifier above and nature as signified below, philosophy in the writing system of 1800 was the effacement of sexual difference. It mediated the two authorities, state and Mother, that otherwise remained unwritten in its discursive network. When educational officials administer the complex functions of writing and mothers administer the elementary function of alphabetizing, the resulting writer, upheld by both authorities, is a true human being—because he "attempts to moderate and find a counterweight for the character of the sex, rather than exaggerating it, for after all that character is an inborn, natural endowment," until his "humanity" finds itself "at home" "in the middle" between male and female.[74] With that, however, the author of the letter had proved what he set out to prove: that writers like himself simply fulfilled the human condition. He could sign his letter and send it to Dorothea Veit.

This determination of the human race, however, was not the determination of the two sexes that constitute so-called humanity. The letter was forced to continue because all the rights of man proclaimed in 1800 were—as Marie Olympe de Gouges recognized—rights for men. Schlegel doubly inscribed the phallic stylus: first in the register *of* sex and then in the register of *a* sex. There remained the determination of that other sex, to which the addressee belonged. But that was no trouble for the pen. "It doesn't take a lot to discover that the female organization is directed completely and exclusively toward the beautiful purpose of motherhood."[75] Women play their "role in this determination of the human race perfectly" by remaining voices without writing, either outwardly and empirically or inwardly and transcendentally. The difference between the sexes therefore coincided in a mathematically exact way with the dichotomy between writing and authorhood on the one hand, and with that between the voice and motherhood on the other. The difference allowed the Woman as the Mother's Mouth every right to be a Voice, but no right to have one. Schlegel found it out of the question "to allow Nature a vote and voice in the law-giving council of Reason,"[76] and Ernst Brandes held that "the exclusion of women from the deliberative bodies in the state" was "very wise."[77] This did not mean that philosophical discourse would simply provide ideological backing for the discourse of administrative method. The two very similar exclusions were not identical, but congruent, as in geometry. Voices of pure song that are never spoken or written remain excluded, first from the state civil service, second from the discourse of the university—that is, from the two subsystems connected by the circuit of legitimation. A university within whose departments the philosophical faculty in 1800 had risen from the lowest ranking to the highest because of the necessity of forming universal educators before state clergymen, judges, and artists, designated itself "the law-giving council of Reason." That philosophy happened to exclude the daughter of an Enlightenment philosopher marked the whole difference between Dorothea, née Mendelssohn, and the doctoral women of the Republic of Scholars.

In its mandate to write down the whole, philosophical discourse went the discourse of administrative method one better. It formulated a relationship between the sexes. Not, to be sure, as a relationship of power between state and alma mater, as Nietzsche would mercilessly note, but as the normative relationship between the bureaucracy of writers and women. It was a twofold relationship between production and distribution *and* between distribution and consumption.

Through their mandate to represent The Mother, women made authors write. The Mother neither speaks nor writes, but from the depths of her soul arise the unembellished accents that the author rescues by writing. According to Schlegel, all the *words* that made up his letter—addressed to his beloved, the mother of two children—were "expressions for what you have long felt and known." There would be every reason for the letter *On Philosophy* to conclude like *The Mothers' Book*: namely, by announcing that all the words placed across the pages of writing paper were to be consumed once more by the Mother's Mouth. But the philosophical discourse was not pedagogical; inasmuch as it proclaimed the destiny of man to be authorhood, it created the need for another type of reception. Women stood at the origin of discourse only insofar as they represented the Mother; insofar as they existed as a plurality, they were charged with reading. Although everything written was only an augmentation of maternal feeling, Dorothea was requested to "appreciate the sacredness of words more than you have in the past. Otherwise my prospects would not look good."

Schlegel's letter inscribed each of the two sexes twice into the discourse network of 1800. Whereas men constituted the human being in general *and* the male, women played the role of absolute precondition for discourse *and* a facilitative function in establishing real discourses. Schlegel concluded his letter:

I have surprised myself, and now I am aware that it has actually been *you* who have introduced *me* to philosophy. I wanted to impart philosophy only to you; the genuine desire rewarded itself, and friendship has taught me to find a way of joining philosophy with life and humanity. In the process I have in a certain sense imparted philosophy to myself; it will no longer remain isolated in my mind, but will spread its enthusiasm to all regions of my being. And what one learns to communicate outwardly through this inner conviviality, will become, through such general communication, that much more our own.

In thankfulness for this, I will, if you have no objections, soon have this letter published.[78]

To the author's surprise, his words have not been his at all. It is as if they had been whispered by a prompter who in turn had them from the Woman or Nature. "I did not speak of her. No, it was she who said everything, the true and the false"—this was already clear in the *Fragment on Nature*.[79] And yet Dorothea Veit's leading voice counted only insofar as it could be exploited. The discourse she prompted has underscored its written character—the sacredness of the words and the erection of the stylus—much too passionately to be able to return and cross it out. Not only in Schlegel's philosophy but also in his profession as a writer *written* discourse was the difference that maintained the separation of the two sexes. As a text written by a man, *On Philosophy* remained "touched with the dawn of eternity," and so too much for Mothers' Mouths to swallow. This gave rise to a second reader beside the addressee: the former or apparent author himself, who *by* writing has unconsciously transmitted the prompted philosophy to himself. In order to become aware of this, Schlegel had to read the letter another time before he could understand it. His "inner conviviality" was a doubling of the functions of author and reader and so circulated the origin for the first time. It had the effect of technical amplification and therefore always had more readers in view. In spite of the greatest intimacy between the writer and the addressee, the letter went to press. Finally, then, Schlegel did attain the eternity to which writings have been eternally addressed. He said of his complicated eroticism: "I don't know if I could pray to the universe with the whole of my soul if I had never loved a woman. But then, the *universe* is and remains my watchword."[80]

Philosophy, the love of wisdom or Sophia, becomes possible only through the love of women as they exist in plurality. But after love has become writing, it returns to the world with its eternity, its generality, its universality, and—the university. The author Schlegel forged his way to a career as a professor of philosophy with published love letters.

Writing and publication, insofar as they were not just used but emphasized and taken into account in the very act of writing, distinguished such discourses from pedagogical discourse. In place of the negative feedback that returned pedagogic output to be devoured at its origin, supplementary couplings were inserted between authors and readers to achieve a programmed circulation that involved others besides The Mother. These others could only be: (1) the author, insofar as he could acquire *Bildung* by rereading his texts; (2) other women, insofar as they had and became mothers; and (3) other men, insofar as their destiny dictated their becoming authors through independent reading. Schlegel's letter *On Philosophy* developed only the schematics of such circulation. Its realization was the mandate of poets.

Language Channels

The output of Poets in the discourse network of 1800 constituted a DIS-
TRIBUTION OF DISCOURSES. It provided discourse with a maximum number of addressees. Schlegel's *Fragment on a Characteristic of the German
Classic* noted in praise of the classical writer Georg Forster that "conviv-
ial communication" was "one of the ideas he was most fond of, one that
presented itself to his spirit frequently and in the most varied forms." In
this the writer was not far from the merchant. Just as the latter "principally provides for the exchange of material goods," the writer makes possible the "interchange of intellectual goods and creations."[1] Thus an end
was set to the limited economy of circulating texts in the Republic of
Scholars and to the "annoying" prejudice by which "the sciences are
there only for certain classes, and are not to be seen as a store for all mankind."[2] Forster and Schlegel saw in the "interweaving and connecting of
the most varied insights" and in their "more widespread distribution . . .
the most characteristic advantage of our century."[3] Writing was granted
literally universalizing and literally textualizing functions: it wove a discourse that encompassed or generated mankind as a whole. "The fine arts
are the bond that holds men together."[4]

The Im-possibility of Translations

A simple precondition had to be met before authors could become
"spiritual economists":[1] there had to be a general equivalent for the texts
they would spin out. Otherwise the business transaction could not take
place. Reformed alphabetization provided this general equivalent. It was

the signified, the element that first had been subtracted from letters or signifiers and then had taken a superordinate position. "Just as the exchange of goods is regulated by money as a general equivalent, the exchange of knowledge is regulated by concepts."[2]

To base a discourse on signifieds, however, means to make it translatable. "Translations" are the discursive "market, to which the most distant merchants come with their wares."[3] The poet who led his Bible-translating tragic hero to the threshold of the new poetry had to guarantee fully the possibility of translation. Goethe saw the translatability of all discourses, even of the most sacred and formal, as ensured by the primacy of content (*Gehalt*) over the effects of the signifier.

I value both rhythm and rhyme, whereby poetry first becomes poetry; but what is really, deeply, and fundamentally effective, what is really permanent, is what remains of the poet when he is translated into prose. Then the pure, perfect substance remains. . . . I will only, in support of my position, mention Luther's translation of the Bible, for the fact that this excellent man handed down a work composed in the most different styles and gave us its poetical, historical, commanding didactic tone in our mother tongue, as if all were cast in *one* mold, has done more to advance religion than if he had attempted to imitate, in detail, the peculiarities of the original.[4]

The existence of untranslatable elements in the signifiers of any language was not denied, but it was discounted. The general equivalent came out as the precipitate of a "remainder": the "pure, perfect substance," or signified. Its effects were necessarily somewhat flattening: as in Wilhelm Meister's Mignon translation, "disconnected" material was "joined together."[5] Exemplary translations like Luther's Bible molded the most varied discourses (poetical, historical, pedagogical), according to Goethe's assessment of the Book of (many) Books, into a single and coherent style.

In the discourse network of 1800, the general equivalent was a basal construct that allowed for modifications. Herder's theory of national poetry allowed for the existence of untranslatable idioms (like the Johannine λόγος); in practice, however, Herder germanized folk songs from the most distant languages and cultures. Hegel, in his capacity as principal of a new humanistic secondary school—for transparent reasons, in other words—stressed the untranslatability of the Greek;[6] his aesthetics, however, the first such work based on contents or signifieds, made do largely without citations from the Greek and asserted that a poetic work could be translated "into other languages without essential detriment to its value."[7] Only the new linguistics in the discourse network of 1800 had the option of dealing with the untranslatable. August Ferdinand Bernhardi declared that poetry was untranslatable, "because the identity"—namely, the identity of signifieds—"must be represented by rhyme."[8] Above all, however, "grammatical composition has regularities which are not transparent to the signification of the discourse. Moreover, since signification can be transformed, practically unimpaired, from one language to another, these regularities allow us to characterize the individuality of a particular language."[9] Linguistics in 1800 stood at one extreme of a logic of the signified: at the other extreme was Poetry. In its striving to be truly educative and ennobling, Poetry embraced the general equivalent and with it inherent meaning, which is always religious, whether in Luther or Faust. "In the end all Poetry is translation."[10]

Of course, the new writing still embraced the myth of Babel whenever it declared its intention of "reuniting all essentially interrelated sciences, despite their current divided and fragmentary state."[11] A discursive original unity could not have existed before the invention of the general equivalent. Printing alone did not guarantee "an integrating and interrelating that is anything but innocent."[12] German poetry was not a reunification: instead, it was an unprecedented introduction of discursive unities. The "*one* mold" or style unified syntactically; the primacy of the signified unified semantically; and this was accomplished pragmatically by the receiver to which all translations from 1800 on were sent: humanity, the reader, and "general world trade."[13]

In 1798 Novalis began his *Allgemeines Brouillon*. The adjective in the title signaled unification and universalization, whereas the substantive indicated how one would go about making a single discourse out of the most varied scientific discourses—by mixing and shaking. The *Brouillon*'s method was to translate particular data from the sciences (ranging from poetics to physics) out of one vocabulary into another via systematic analogies. Of course, as a poet Novalis was even better equipped for a trouble-free poetization of the sciences.[14] In the novel *Heinrich von Ofterdingen*, general translatability is not achieved by any technical procedure; it simply comes into being via the ear of the Poet. True to Novalis's statement that "to translate is to write poetry as much as creating one's own works,"[15] the hero sets off on a journey in pursuit of *Bildung* during which practically nothing happens except that nearly all forms of knowledge and practice are present themselves in speech. Pure listening to economic, historical, archeological, religious, poetic, and mythological discourses is necessary and sufficient to form the archetypical Poet, who at the conclusion of the novel will be able to set everything he has heard into his own words and works. Ofterdingen made systematic truth of the proposition that poetic translation in 1800 had acceded to the status of art.[16]

Only one discourse remained untranslatable—for the simple reason that it did not occur. Businessmen, poets, monks, knights, miners—all explain the signifieds of their activity to the novel's hero, with the one exception of the girl who loves him. Instead, the girl's father speaks of this subject: "Just consider love. Nowhere else is the necessity of poesy for the continuation of mankind so clear. Love is mute; only poetry can give it voice. Or love is the highest form of natural poesy." [17] The constitutive exception to universal translatability is erotic discourse. Of course, love guarantees its basic translatability by being Nature's most sublime *Poetry*; but as the most sublime Poetry of *Nature* it is inaccessible to the articulated word. In order to be, then, love needs intercessors, or mouthpieces, or translators. Because Mathilda, who is the novel's allegory of speechless Love, cannot even express her speechlessness, her father speaks up for her. And because Love makes men speak, Heinrich, the novel's allegory of Poetry, translates Mathilda's speechless love and so becomes a poet. This relationship between Love and Poetry, which determines the novel, reproduces exactly a relationship defined by Herder: "Nature, the whole world of passion and action that lay within the poet, and which he attempts to externalize through language—this nature is expressive. Language is only a channel, the true poet only a translator, or, more characteristically, he is the one who brings Nature into the heart and soul of his brothers." [18]

Nature, Love, Woman—the terms were synonymous in the discourse network of 1800. They produced an originary discourse that Poets tore from speechlessness and translated. It is technically exact to say that language in such a function can only be a channel. If language had its own density and materiality, its own dead spots and transmission lapses, there would be no question of an all-encompassing translatability. Though Herder's proposition would sound scandalous in the realm of *poésie pure*, it was very much at home in the discourse network of 1800, which was not at all "defined in terms of language as language," but which leads through language on to something else." [19] The very fact that discourses have no intrinsic worth ennobles the soul/love/woman/nature, which, when it speaks, is already no longer the one speaking. The authority of discourse production traversed translations and the circulation of discourse in a manner that historically and technically divided the scholarly republican from the poetic means of distribution. Without the invention of a speechless and withdrawn origin, universal translation would have been confined to the surface of representation. Only when the untranslatable also became the task of the poetic translator could circulation without authors and consumers cease. Ofterdingen does not simply prolong talking about the sciences and professions; he couples them to an origin and aim of discourse: Love and Poetry. Poetry in 1800 was a doubled, simultaneous movement: first, it translated heterogeneous discourses that were still stored within Faust's "beloved German" or Luther's "mother tongue"; second, it translated the originary discourse that never transpires—in other words, it translated *out of* the mother tongue.

When the prepositional phrase is read as a subjective genitive, "the love of the mother tongue" constitutes the object; when the phrase is read as an objective genitive, it constitutes the subject of poetical translation.

Translating into the mother tongue is something that can be taught, something that can be transmitted in new-style humanistic preparatory schools to every future civil servant.[20] Translating out of the mother tongue was and remains a paradox, whose overcoming distinguished those who were Poets from those who were not. The discourse network that introduced the rule that no one could be taught to be a Poet simultaneously envisioned an exceptional rite of individual initiation for the rising generation of poets.[21] The test question was whether the initiate could become, in the course of his alphabetization, "the transmitter of Nature to the heart and soul of his brothers." The *Bildungsromane* were the proving ground for this test.

For seven years the child Anton Reiser was "always sad and alone." Finally, in the eighth year his father took pity on his son—instructing mothers had not yet been invented—and bought him two books: one was *Instruction in Spelling* and the other, a *Treatise Against Spelling*. Reiser chose the first book; in the second he might have encountered a forerunner of the phonetic method. Having made his choice, he was stuck with the tiresome spelling of yard-long Biblical names ("Nebuchadnezzar, Abednego, etc."), until he made a discovery: "However, as soon as he noticed that it was indeed possible to express reasonable ideas through the combination of letters, his desire to learn to read grew stronger by the day. Even now he recalled fondly the joy he experienced when, with effort and a great deal of spelling, he managed to make sense of the first few lines that contained something he could think about."[22] Reiser's discovery led to signifieds or ideas, the general equivalent of words. Compared with the alphabetical hodgepodge of the Biblical names, which are pure signifiers without translation, ideas were as enticing as Basedow's *rai-sins* or *straw-ber-ries*. This had several consequences. First, signifieds sweetened the pain and violence of alphabetization to such a degree that the hero Reiser, the artistic creation of a man who also wrote *Memories from the Earliest Years of Childhood*,[23] unlike Rousseau has no difficulty remembering how he learned to read. Second, the signifieds awaken such an intense desire to read that Reiser soon spends days living on nothing but air and signifieds, without taking a bite to eat—reading, as "an opiate," outdoes his hunger.[24] Third, signifieds secure the translatability of writing and orality.

> But he could not understand how it was possible that other people could read as quickly as they spoke; at that time he despaired of ever making this much progress. His amazement and joy were so much greater when, after a few weeks, he had progressed that far.
>
> Apparently this also earned him some respect from his parents, and even more from his relatives.[25]

When the new reader, still wet behind the ears, manages to dodge the time lag inherent in the language channel of writing, reading becomes equivalent to speaking. At a time when it was common to mumble half out loud while deciphering letters on the page, people took note. Reiser—and this translation into the mother tongue is the first precondition for the Poet—can consume written texts as if he were speaking them; in later years he was to practice this extensively with theological, dramatic, and narrative texts. But the true test of the poetic profession is still to come. Under the title "The Sorrows of Poetry," one reads:

> When the fascination of poetry suddenly seized him, there first arose a painful sensation in his soul, and he had a thought of something in which he lost himself, against which everything that he had ever heard, read, or thought was also lost, and whose existence, could he but portray it in some way, would produce a pleasure surpassing anything he had ever felt or known. . . . In such moments of blissful premonition, it was all his tongue could do to stammer out a few sounds; it was somewhat like certain odes by Klopstock, in which a gap between words was filled in with a series of periods.
>
> These isolated sounds, however, always designated a general feeling of what was splendid, noble, of tears of bliss and what not.—It would last until the feeling collapsed back into itself, without, however, having given birth to even a few reasonable lines as a beginning of something definite.[26]

This is the stillbirth of poetry out of the spirit of reading. The pleasant-painful feeling that refuses to become lines of poetry results from the leveling of all signifiers; the feeling traverses the reader and, because he has attained the fluency of speech, can only leave vague generality in its wake. Thinking and thought are the effects of a disembodiment of language. If it were otherwise, whatever had been thought would not be capable of surpassing all the oral and written discourses that have ever transpired. It surpasses them, however, in the joy of its positive namelessness. Reiser's antipathy for words, the return of his disdain for letters in his childhood, reaches the point where he calls words "a wooden wall" in front of, or "an impenetrable covering" over, pure thought; he "at times tortured himself for hours in the attempt to see if it were possible to think without words."[27]

Such experimental conditions for an attempt to write poetry allow only stammered, isolated syllables to appear, but no words. Writing poetry tests the possibility of voicing a thought consisting in pure signifieds. Therefore it begins, like the phonetic method, with minimal signifieds—interjections and sighs, which since Klopstock could be written with punctuation marks that had acquired an "expressive" function rather than "an exclusively discriminative function."[28]

But the pure reader's soul, which desires to write, remains as empty as Olympia's "ah!" All particularity is lost in the quid pro quo of the most individual and most general, and so Reiser must conclude: "It was certainly a sure sign that one had no calling to be a poet when a mere vague feeling was all that moved one to write, and when the particular scene one wanted to write did not precede that feeling or at least did not occur with it simultaneously."[29] The translation of the untranslatable fails because it would have required the ability to write down pure feeling. By the end of the *Bildungsroman*, the hero, who in the meantime has moved to a university, stands amid the ruins of his theatrical and poetic plans. A double displacement takes the place of the poetry Anton Reiser failed to write: the educational bureaucracy and the authorship of Karl Philipp Moritz. Instead of becoming a poet by translating from the Mother's Mouth, Moritz worked in central control stations—a military orphanage, secondary schools in Berlin and Neukölln—for the reform of higher education in Prussia. His program of reforms included the interpretation of German poets rather than instruction in rhetorical eloquence,[30] and the thorough investigation of student psychology rather than the violence of catechizing; as the prefaces to *Anton Reiser* make clear, the novel recapitulated, documented, and announced this program to a whole world of readers. Thus the official educator, as the metamorphosis of the failed poet, in turn metamorphoses the practice of reading poets.

Of course the novel does not tell us any of this. Because "the end of such apprenticeship consists in this, that the subject sows his wild oats" and enters into the "rationality" of reality or of the state,[31] the *Bildungsroman* can only lead as far as the threshold of that bureaucracy. Such novels say nothing of the institutions that have made possible writing as a reasoned (say, psychological) analysis of youthful errors. The hero renounces his poetic or theatrical dream; the novelist as civil servant (whether his name be Moritz or Goethe or finally Gottfried Keller) followed him only as far as his complete accommodation to the "rational order." What came later, public service as a dance around the new idol represented by the alma mater, remains a "blind spot."[32]

Here, however, the institution of Motherhood that was established in 1800 created another possibility. The romantic *Bildungsromane* did not necessarily let their artist-heroes fail. Anton Reiser had to discover on his own that poetry could only be written as translation from the Mother's Mouth, for his mother, who very early had resigned herself to marriage, did not love him and did not alphabetize him. Her only passive intervention in his reading instruction was to let Anton read the novels that his father had forbidden rather than the Pietist tracts his father propagated, for Anton's mother (like Rousseau's mother) had "once found intense pleasure" in reading them.[33]

But the new mothers were different; they dreamed of poetic careers for their sons.

I heard Johann Kriesler tell a story of how the madness of a mother led to the most devout education of her son as poet.—The woman believed herself to be the Virgin Mary and her son the unrecognized Christ, and whereas he walked on earth, drank coffee, and played billiards, the time would soon come when he would gather the community of the faithful and lead them straight to heaven. The son's lively imagination found an indication of his higher calling in his mother's madness.[34]

Although this is a spoof of Zacharias Werner, it is also the autobiography of E. T. A. Hoffmann, who grew up without a father and whose mother was nearly psychotic. Monomaniacal mother love made possible a double life divided between poetry and prose, the earth and ascension, Dresden and Atlantis. Thus the judicial civil servant Hoffmann found a poetic discourse capable of measuring the entire field, from Mother's Mouth to educational bureaucracy, from untranslatable origin to the universal circulation of discourses. Where the failed artists of the *Bildungsromane* fell silent, "a modern fairy tale," as Hoffmann's "The Golden Pot" is subtitled, still has something to say. With that the impossible poetic career became reality and the translation of the unspeakable was realized.

"The Golden Pot"

The hero of this modern fairy tale is a student by the name of Anselmus, though what he is studying remains unspecified. However, Anselmus's "schoolmasterish air,"[1] as well as his friends—a registrar, a dean and philologist of ancient languages, and soon a privy archivist—indicate that he is planning a career in the educational or administrative bureaucracy. He also "has a splendid classical education, which is the basis for everything."[2] In spite of or because of this, all his dreams center on a poetic career. His ability "to write very neatly" is useful in both professions: the poetic career and the "writing service"[3] projected for him by Dean Paulmann.

On Ascension Day, which "had invariably been a family celebration for him," Anselmus is initiated under the blossoming elder tree—in one of the places, that is, where mother goddesses dwelt before Christian colonization.

> Then a whispering and a lisping began, and it seemed as if the sound of little crystal bells were coming from the blossoms. Anselmus listened and listened. Then—he himself knew not how—the whispering and the lisping and the tinkling turned into half-heard words: "Betwixt, between, betwixt the branches, between the blossoms, shooting, twisting, twirling we come! Sister, sister, swing in the shimmer—quickly, quickly, in and out. Rays of sunset, whispering wind of evening, sounds of dew, singing blossoms—we sing with the branches and the blossoms; stars soon to sparkle—we must descend; betwixt, twisting, turning, twirling, sisters we!"[4]

Nature poetry begins with lisping, whispering, and tinkling. Such sounds of feeling came to Anton Reiser in his poetic dreaming, although he, and consequently the narrator of his story, were unable to write them down. Here, however, they ring clearly for the hero, narrator, and reader. Even the punctuation to which Reiser wanted to commit the unsayable between the isolated and unconnected sounds has been written. Anselmus's initiation is an auditory hallucination of the Mother's Mouth.

What the nameless sisters are singing—Wagner, in his admiration of Hoffmann, would later compose it as the sound of the Beginning[5]—sounds like one of the alphabetizing exercises of Stephani or Tillich. Three women move their tongues under the elder tree; the result is an exercise in the consonantal combinations *schl*, *sch*, and *zw* [in German, the sisters sing: "Zwischen durch—zwischen ein—zwischen Zweigen, zwischen schwellender Blüten, schwingen, schlängeln, schlingen wir uns—Schwesterlein—Schwesterlein, schwinge dich im Schimmer—schnell, schnell herauf—herab—"], or, for Wagner's three Rhine maidens, an exercise in *w*.[6] Tillich conjured the following sequence with the end syllable *gen*:[7]

klin gen   sprin gen   rin gen   drin gen   schwin gen   schlin gen

Hoffmann simply reverses the beginnings and endings of a similar verb series. In this way meanings come into being on the border between sound and word through the augmentation of minimal signifieds. The rhymes and assonances of the little round dance miraculously produce the identity of the signified, in conformity with the romantic conception of language. The instructional goal of all primers is realized. In spite or because of this, the event remains an enigma for the alphabetized listener. Anselmus has no idea how meaningful words could come out of sounds, nor does he have a clue as to the referent of their meanings. Nature poetry no longer reveals who is designated by the "we" and the "sisters."

Only when Anselmus hears "a chord of pure crystal bells" over his head—Wagner would expand and intensify this chord through the 137 measures of the prelude to the *Rheingold*, thus transposing the hallucinatory effects of romantic poesie into the technologically real—only then, "in the twinkling of an eye," do intuition and reference become possible: Anselmus "glanced up and saw three little snakes, glistening green and gold, which had twisted around the branches." The consonantal combination *schl* is an autonym for singing snakes [*Schlangen*], as *ma* is for speech-eliciting mamas. Just as the primers of the Reformation had conjured up the image of a snake as a creaturely example to accompany the letters s and *sch*, whereas the new phonetic method left all complications of pronunciation to a purified Mother's Mouth, so the little snakes begin by oscillating between being sounds of nature and daughters of a matrilineal family. Anselmus hesitates, unsure whether "the evening wind" is suddenly "whispering distinct words," or whether the longed-for girls at a family celebration are speaking to him.

The first clarification comes when the ringing chord makes the sisters visible, or when the auditory hallucination yields vision. At the chord a single sister emerges from the nameless, undifferentiated dance of the sisters. From women in the plural comes—as had been preprogrammed by the epoch-making dream of the blue flower in Novalis's *Heinrich von Ofterdingen*—the Woman. Two "marvelous blue eyes looked down at him with unspeakable desire, so that an unknown feeling of both supreme bliss and deepest sorrow seemed to tear his heart apart."[8]

By the time this gaze has been met by a hallucinatory gaze, the enigma under the elder tree has clearly become a reprise of Schlegel's letter *On Philosophy*. Once more things "can be so meaningful that they seem to gaze at one out of clear eyes, and as expressive as the unembellished accents from the inmost soul." Voice and gaze—an expression and window of the soul—are revealed. Wherever possible, the voices of the snakes remain "half-heard words" in order not to prostitute such souls with speech, given that they can store only the silent marks of writing rather than any talent for reading aloud.

Voice and gaze, acoustical and optical presence—the figure of the ideal beloved arises out of the originary play between sounds and speech. Anton Reiser poetically despaired because what was "vague" in emotion was never accompanied or anticipated by a vision of "the particular scene he wanted to write." But Anselmus, in his ecstasy beneath the elder tree, is given a vision by two dark blue eyes that entirely determines his future career. He can become the beloved of that gaze and therefore a Poet.

For one who has learned to read from yard-long biblical names, there is no bridge between signs and feelings. But one who has been from the beginning alphabetized with meaningful words is always in a scene that encompasses him and the Mother. He still needs to learn how the voice that was originally Nature can be made into a book, without having the vision collapse into letters. Anselmus, who is all eyes and ears under the elder tree, has a poetic path before him that will finally enable him to read and write the visionary moment of his own initiation. The agent of this sliding, pedagogical transition is a father. Anselmus hears from several of his bureaucratic friends that a mysterious privy archivist named Lindhorst wants to employ him as a scribe. Before beginning his secretarial duties, Anselmus learns from Lindhorst that "the three gold-green snakes" are Lindhorst's daughters and that his own love has been drawn to "the blue eyes of the youngest, named Serpentina."[9] A father's word, then, finally transforms the undifferentiated hallucination of nameless voices, which already had become one figure, into a name and therefore a love object. "On n'est jamais amoureux que d'un nom," as Lacan said.

The discourse of the father is interpretation: interpretation, but not enlightenment. Far from reducing the voices under the elder tree to the whispering wind, as earlier the father's words translated the Elfking's daughters into the mere rustling of leaves,[10] Lindhorst augments the minimal signifieds supplied by the voices into a positive and genealogical discourse. After the event it is revealed that the half-heard words, bright gaze, and tangled bodies of the snakes all embody the name *Serpentina*. So out of the "very unchristian name"[11] (as is immediately apparent to the fine ear of the citizens of Dresden) come the minimal signifieds under the elder tree. The new humanists say *Serpentina*; the eyes say *Schläng-lein*; and the ears say only *schl*. Such is translation into the mother tongue or Mother's Mouth. In order to complete the poetical translation cycle, Anselmus will only have to translate out of the mother tongue as well. And if in 1800 letters were consistently thought to be unnatural, becoming a Poet was a matter of perceiving what was written as a Voice.

Initially the father's word translates the elder-tree voices into writing. Lindhorst is not an archivist for nothing. Genealogies exist only as texts because the chain of signifiers known as filiation presupposes the death of the persons signified. Lindhorst can, of course, orally name his daughters "daughters," but the encompassing web of filiation, in which the archivist is also archived, necessarily is written. In Lindhorst's library is a roll of parchment that contains the mythic genealogy of his family back to the beginning of the world. Secretary Anselmus is supposed to copy it.

A written initiation by the father follows upon the spoken initiation by the daughters. Before taking up his position, Anselmus must first produce samples of his calligraphy. But even "writing in the finest English style," that is, "English cursive script," fails to impress Lindhorst.[12] Like a good educator-bureaucrat, he forces Anselmus to judge and condemn his own writing.

When Anselmus saw his handwriting, he felt as if a thunderbolt had struck him. The script was unspeakably wretched. The curves were not rounded, the hair-stroke failed to appear where it should have been; capital and small letters could not be distinguished; in truth, the messy scratchings of a schoolboy intruded, frequently ruining the best drawn lines. "Also," Archivarius Lindhorst continued, "your ink is not permanent." Dipping his finger into a glass of water, he ran his finger over the lines and they disappeared, leaving not a trace behind.[13]

This annihilating criticism, transmitted from the archivist to his secretary, finally purges the future poet or "child" of the old alphabetical method.[14] The criticism thus stands in the spot where other romantic fairy tales typically indict the dark figure of a scribe. In the tale of Klingsohr contained in *Heinrich von Ofterdingen*, a magic water dissolves the manuscripts of "the Scribe," who as a representative of writing and reason must yield to the singing child (of Poetry).[15] In the same way another child, a stranger who appears in the title of one of Hoffmann's fairy tales, teaches earthly children by means of poetry to escape the alphabetical method of their writing master.[16] But "The Golden Pot," the explicitly modern fairy tale, combines the magical annihilation with exact technical criticism. In this it contributed to the reform of writing instruction that Stephani, building on the earlier work of Heinrich Müller and Johann Paul Pöhlmann, was able to complete.[17] Such was the solidarity of poetry and the schools in 1800.

A year after the publication of Hoffmann's fairy tale, Stephani published the *Complete Description of the Genetic Writing Method for Public Elementary Schools*. The book attempted to abolish (as did his phonetic reading method) an old cultural technique of imitation in order to transform it into psychologically motivated, self-initiated activity.

As in most subjects, writing teachers were accustomed to using only the most mechanical teaching techniques and did not have the slightest inkling that writing instruction should be employed as *material for the autonomous development of intelligence and imagination*. . . . Up to now the usual procedure consisted in constraining students to copy and recopy examples until they developed a *me-*

chanical skill that allowed them *to copy correctly.* Although they practice for nearly six years, most students progress only to the point of being able to produce a decent copy as long as the model is at hand. Very few students are able to master the style so thoroughly that they can continue writing without the model and develop fine handwriting.[18]

Addressed to the old schools, the passage reiterates the charge against using an empirical standard rather than the general norm of a "national script."[19] Like sounds and sound combinations, letters and their combinations are henceforth to arise (as in the book's title) genetically out of the pure ego. But given a long-established repertoire of signs, a magical emergence of writing cannot occur of itself. First, the method had to break down all letters transmitted by tradition into basic elements. In Stephani these elements took the form of a vertical line, a half-circle to the right or to the left, a half-oval to the left—in other words, the basic elements were primal geometrical phenomena in which the "roundness" desired by Lindhorst predominated. Stephani's predecessor in Erlangen, Pöhlmann, had come up with a much larger number of basic elements, and because these were intended "to make the student as fully conscious as possible not only of what was to be done, but also of exactly how it was to be done,"[20] his method was more time consuming and correspondingly took up more of one's life.

Second, the reunifying of the analytically acquired basic elements had to be practiced (provided there was enough instructional time), not with mere assembly or combinatory techniques, but via an aesthetic that would guarantee their "combination into a true whole." "There is nothing more offensive to the aesthetic sense of the eye than the sight of something divided that should have the inmost connection."[21] Numbers constituted an exception to this inwardness: they must remain apart "so that one number cannot be so easily changed into another number, a circumstance that could lead to serious deception in bourgeois life."[22] Letters followed an inverse pattern. Although they must remain distinguishable, they were to be interrelated, not by the differentiality of the grapheme, but in the same manner as the sounds of the phonetic method, namely, by their family relatedness and transitiveness. Mothers demonstrated how one speech tone moved into another by a minimal change in the position of the mouth; teachers demonstrated the same technique with letters and handwriting motions. Wherever there was no threat of economic deception, then, an organically coherent handwriting (read: bourgeois individual) could arise.

The third step in the process was to transform the newly reconstituted letters into the elements of words. The guiding principle is again the individual or simply indivisible connection, the goal being "easily flowing" handwriting rather than writing that "often breaks off."[23] The point was to be repeated hundreds of times between the children (c) and the teacher (T) until the last and dullest had been individualized:

T: (*who has accurately and in proper style written the word* centner *on the board*): Which word have I just written on the board?
c: *Centner.*
T: Is the first *e* separated from the preceding *C* or not?
c: It is not separated.
T: So the two letters belong together. Which letter of this word is separated from the others?
c: No letter is separate.
T: What can one then say about all the letters of this word?
c: That they all go together.
T: There is no error in the way this word is written. Now, if you were to write this word and left every letter separate from every other, would that be the right way to write it?
c: No.
T: How do you know that?
c: Because if it were right, you would have written it that way.
T: To be sure.[24]

The common goal, then, after Rossberg's *Systematic Instruction in Fine Penmanship* (1796–1811) did away with the old, disconnected Fraktur handwriting, was a new aesthetic of "fine and accurate" connection.[25] Whoever wrote in block letters would not be an in-dividual. (This indivisible being therefore did not survive the typewritten typescripts and aleatory writings of 1900.) The great metaphysical unities invented in the age of Goethe—the developmental process of *Bildung*, autobiography, world history—could be seen as the flow of the continuous and the organic simply because they were supported by flowing, cursive handwriting—as Gerhard Rühm's concrete poem ironically indicates.[26] The continuous connection of writing and/or the individual was of such importance in 1800 that Stephani found it necessary to include in his lessons, which were designed to promote "the simple and pleasing connection of every letter with every other," exercises for connecting capital and small letters, given that the former could hinder the ideal flow of writing just as consonantal combinations could break the flow of the voice.[27]

Finally, as a fourth step following the progression through the augmentative continuum between the elements and connections of writing, there were exercises aimed at achieving an aesthetic balance of bold and thin lines, of shading and light, and of degrees of pressure by the pen. They underscored once more that writing is something that flows and connects: pressure is applied to the elements of letters; it is diminished on the connecting curves. Individual and independent handwriting was born in the interplay between "drawing" (i.e., connecting exercises) and "painting" (i.e., pen or calligraphic exercises).[28] Individuality was not a product of any particularities that would allow graphologist character-experts or police handwriting-experts to make identifications; rather, the organic continuity of the writing materialized the biographical-organic continuity of the educated individual in a literal, that is, letter-by-letter manner. "Thus, then, if at first the specific nature and innate peculiarity of the individual along with what these become as the result of cultivation and development are regarded as the inner reality, as the essence of action and of fate, this inner being finds its appearance in external fashion to begin with in his mouth, hand, voice, handwriting."[29]

To develop handwriting formed as out of one mold means to produce individuals. The norm-setting writings of Pöhlmann or Stephani were foundational script systems for the discourse network of 1800. Before Anselmus can join the system in his glory as Poet, he must first submit to writing instruction that will bring his handwriting up to the ideal norm. Stephani's letter elements correct the lack of "roundness" that Lindhorst faulted in his secretary, because "the angular form" would "insult the eye."[30] The "messy scratchings," which "frequently ruin the best lines," interrupt the fluid continuum of writing. Anselmus has also not mastered the relation between "capital and small letters" or proper pressure and its diminution; in other words, he has perfected neither "drawing" nor "painting." It follows that his handwriting is not a self-sufficient expression of his individuality, but rather the botched effort of a schoolboy. So much for "a splendid classical education" when judged by the reform pedagogue.

The new goal is presented directly after this annihilating criticism. Rather than imitating deceptive models, Anselmus must learn to bring forth letters as only the genetic writing method can. The ideal father Lindhorst directs this "learning to learn"[31] and so appears in the guise of the reformer of writing instruction. In contrast to the new reading methods (all but written into the bodies of mothers), writing instruction remains even in the titles of relevant treatises a domain of fathers and teachers. No reformer defied Schlegel's prescription, by which writing, though the determination of the entire human race, applied to only one sex, whereas the other was charged with developing orality, from inner singing to reading and reading instruction. "One must learn speaking from women, writing from men."[32] Therefore in literature after *Wilhelm*

Meister's Apprenticeship the father of writing stood next to the mother of speech.[33]

Lindhorst is an incarnation of this ideal father. When old-European teachers taught writing, they wrote; by so doing, however, they had their students copy their own imperfect copies. By contrast, Lindhorst does not write; he makes someone else write—just as the Mother makes others speak.[34] The development of a continuously flowing handwriting is left to the initiate. The decisive test occurs after Anselmus has successfully completed an exercise in Arabic script. Lindhorst gives his secretary the task of copying a roll of parchment, but the signs it contains are unlike all traditional types of letters. They represent the mythic origin of writing itself. With extraordinary abruptness, then, the student finds himself faced with the question of whether he can produce letters "genetically" from their origin. "Anselmus was more than a little struck by these singular intertwined characters, and as he studied the numerous points, strokes, dashes, and twirls in the manuscript, which sometimes represented plants or mosses or animals, he almost despaired of ever copying them accurately."[35]

The originary text, the mythic beginning of all writing, can be identified because it is not (yet) written. No one could write or read this text, this "writing without alphabet, in which signs, signifiers, and signifieds are identical."[36] Nature is convolution. And yet Lindhorst has said that the plant- and animal-hieroglyphics that he placed before his despairing secretary are the work of the "*Bhagavad-Gita*'s masters"[37] and so constitute a text in Sanskrit. His parchment consequently has the same status as the handwritten text of Nostradamus in *Faust*, which is a foreign-language text *and* a revelation of Nature. In fact, all poetically described texts in 1800 are characterized by an oscillation between a foreign culture and a foreign Nature. Novalis called the "great cipher-text" of nature "real Sanskrit."[38] Von Loeben has "flower petals" become "leaves of parchment full of writing and painting," which a woman then "binds together into a book."[39] The rhetorician's metonymy, "leaf/leaf," was taken literally in the writing system of 1800.

Because it oscillates between Nature and culture, the originary text is very difficult to reproduce (as Anselmus complains); at the same time, the text can be reproduced (as Stephani insists). The text eliminates the compulsion that would otherwise force one to receive the form of the European alphabet as something positive and real; the signs in the original text might be of the utmost complexity, but they are nonetheless related to familiar forms of Nature. In this the poetically described text realized something that would be "much more advantageous" in the school curriculum. The reformer Friedrich Gedike demanded "that instruction and practice in drawing precede exercises in calligraphy. Drawing is infinitely more pleasant for a child than writing. Drawing the delicate outline of any object familiar to the child—for example, that of a flower—incontestably gives the child more pleasure than drawing the very uninteresting form of a letter."[40]

The genetic writing-method is fulfilled by viewing the original text as the genesis of writing from Nature. The impossible, namely the presence of letters in Nature, is then realized. The originary text thus occupies the same position in the field of writing that the Mother's Voice, as the natural origin, occupies in the field of speaking and reading. But because the voice is the material reality of language, linked to the body through the oral and respiratory cavities, the discourse network of 1800 has a much easier time with orality. The construct of the originary text, which has no basis in the real, can be possible only through a parasitic relation to the Mother's Mouth. A fine illustration of this is provided by a parallel text to the plants and mosses in "The Golden Pot": "I stole out to my favorite stone, upon which mosses and lichens formed the strangest images and which I never tired of contemplating. I often believed that I could understand these signs, and it seemed to me that I could see in them the most wondrous stories, such as those that my mother had told me."[41] This passage from "Johann Kreisler's Certificate of Apprenticeship" provides technical instructions for the construction of the original text. In order for the signs to be comprehensible rather than simply readable, they must first be endowed with the figural quality of images drawn from nature, then these images must be animated by the hallucinated Mother's Voice. As in the phonetic method, optical signs are surrounded with the echo of maternal orality. The result is that instead of signifiers one has signifieds that can be "seen," as if the text were a film.

The copyist Anselmus has the same parasitic relation to the imaginary being of The Woman. The beloved Serpentina appears constantly between or behind the lines presented by Lindhorst. His first exercises with Arabic are accomplished as follows:

In truth, he could not understand the speed and the ease with which he was able to transcribe the convoluted strokes of these foreign characters. It was as if, deep within him, he could hear a whispering voice: "Ah! could you really work so well if you were not thinking of *her*, if you did not believe in *her* and in her love?" Then, throughout the room, whispers floated, as in low undulating crystal tones: "I am near, near, near! I am helping you. Be brave. Be steadfast, dear Anselmus! I am working with you so that you may be mine!" And as soon as Anselmus heard these sounds with inner rapture, the unfamiliar characters grew ever clearer to him, and he hardly needed to look at the original script at all; in fact, it seemed as if the characters were already outlined on the parchment in pale ink and there was nothing more for him to do but fill them in with black. Thus he worked on, surrounded by those precious, inspiring sounds, that soft, sweet breath.[42]

The pure signifiers—convoluted, foreign, incomprehensible—become readable and comprehensible through the agency of an obsessionally cursivized *her*: The Woman. She comes in response to a voice from the depth of feeling, which in turn emits the "Ah!" of the beloved's passion, here and everywhere else in the fairy tale a reprise of what was heard under the elder tree.[43] The imaginary presence of The Woman can then also arise as a voice. As if to confirm Herder's ascription of the origin of all discourse to the breathing spirit, Serpentina is speech before any articulation, whispering, singing, breathing, blowing; an inspiration in the etymological sense thus surpasses the mechanics of copying. Indeed, the inspiration explains its own power. For it is not Anselmus, but a voice from his inmost soul that tells how the spoken word can make written work possible and delightful.

Splittegarb's *New Child's ABC* promised to introduce children "without difficulty, with pleasure into our world of books," just as parents show them the pictorial beauty of nature. In "The Golden Pot" the Woman's Voice both makes and fulfills this promise, because both promises come from the same place. A pedagogical reformer wrote the primer that speaks to children in its own right and transforms books into nature. And a father and bureaucrat instituted the beloved voice that helps Anselmus in his copying. All the encouragement that Anselmus feels rising from his inmost soul actually comes from the complete opposite: that Serpentina exists and is called Serpentina, that she will appear to him as long as he "continues to work industriously," indeed that it all happens because she "loves" him—the student would know nothing of this if Serpentina's father had not spoken about it.[44] Over and above the imaginary presence of the Voice stands the discourse of the Other, which has no legitimation beyond its very occurrence.[45] As always, the inmost soul simply repeats this discourse.

Lindhorst thus directs the whole scene of writing and Serpentina is the appointed representative of the state or state bureaucrat, who after 1800 remains at a modest distance. That is why Lindhorst has substituted self-initiated activity for copying and extended the promise of erotic satisfaction to make sure that Anselmus "could not understand the speed and the ease" of his hand as it guided the pen—attributes that read like direct quotes from Olivier's promise to cathect reading and writing instruction "with wondrous speed and ease compared to all our previous experience, and what is of greater and inestimable importance in the matter, with the strangest pleasure, indeed with near incomprehensible desire."[46] If it seems to Anselmus that the characters are already outlined on the parchment in pale ink and need only to be blackened in,[47] that is because Lindhorst has magically accomplished a recommendation of Basedow's

Elementary Exercises: "whole words can be written in pencil, which the student will go over in ink."[48]

Such smooth transition confirms Basedow's title and makes writing an elementary exercise. First, the lightly prepared words blur the binary opposition of white and black, paper background and letter, which always carries the impact or shock of an event. Circa 1800 it was fashionable to print books "with *gray* rather than black ink (because it is softer and stands out more pleasantly on white paper)."[49] Second, the unbroken transition makes it unnecessary "to look at the original." Anselmus copies, as he is paid to do, and yet he does not copy. There is no immutable model to guide his writing, and this is in keeping with Lindhorst's or Stephani's "higher purpose" of letting students "teach themselves good handwriting."[50] Such freedom opens up an area of play in which the discourse of the teacher and the voice of the inmost soul become interchangeable. The unconscious of which Hoffmann is the reputed storyteller is a secondary effect of pedagogy. When fathers and teachers abandon their "positions as lords of creation,"[51] their place is filled by the state-instituted Mother, who rises to it from an abyss of inwardness. The voice of the soul glides without transition into the voice that breathed onto Anselmus under the elder tree. There in the middle of Lindhorst's library, as Anselmus is copying Arabic script, "whispers floated, as in low undulating crystal tones." A mother goddess emerges from the cultic merging of teachers and students, the manifest secret of the bureaucratic system.

The third vigil of "The Golden Pot" begins with a mythical genealogy. As in other modern fairy tales circa 1800, the narrative breaks a basic rule of specified reference and speaks even at first mention of "the spirit" and "the mother," rather than of a spirit or mother.[52] It thus begins like an absolute quote, which only later can be identified as the first-person narrative of the archivist. In retrospect it becomes apparent that Lindhorst has been telling his bureaucratic colleagues in Dresden the story of his own genealogy as a cosmogonic myth.

It is a genealogy in the precise, double sense of the word, as the story of a family and as history—just as Nietzsche's genealogy of the scholar would be.[53] Because the kinship terms are employed without singularized reference, the family story and history of the bureaucrat Lindhorst have a simple structure. In each generation of the cosmogony a male fire spirit mates with a female earth spirit; the latter perishes in the mating, like Semele, but not without giving birth to a virgin who again becomes the mother.[54] Lindhorst belongs to the fiery race of spirit princes, and his own marriage "with the green snake" produced "three daughters, which appear to men in the shape of their mother."[55] The romantic myth of the bureaucrat's genealogy could hardly be told less romantically. With proper administrative method women are determined as the endless reproduction of a single Mother, whereas men are determined as the endless (re-) discovery of the Mother. So Anselmus, when Serpentina appears to him, becomes the representative of the third-mentioned generation of men to meet with the "great-great-great-great grandmother." [56]

As a rebirth of "the green snake," Serpentina is a snake in the diminutive. It is all-important to maintain this miniaturization. Anselmus and a bureaucrat's daughter by the name of Veronica, who is in love with the boy, know all too well what can happen when a little snake suddenly becomes a snake in earnest, for in addition to Lindhorst, the good spirit prince and wise man, there is also an old and wise woman [57] whom Veronica recognizes as her childhood nanny. The old woman now appears to be an adherent of black magic, however, and on the day that Anselmus is to begin his secretarial duties she appears to him in the form of a demonic snake, which had been a simple bell rope.

Horror possessed Anselmus and thrilled through his limbs. The bell rope reached downward and changed into a white, diaphanous, enormous serpent, which encircled and crushed him, its coils squeezing him more and more tightly until his fragile and paralyzed limbs cracked into pieces and his blood gushed from his veins into the transparent body of the serpent, dyeing it red. "Kill me! Kill me!" he tried to scream in his terrible agony, but the scream was only a muffled groan. The serpent lifted its head and placed its long, pointed tongue of glistening brass on Anselmus's chest; then a cutting pain pierced the artery of life, and he lost consciousness. [58]

Clearly, Serpentina is the diminutive of an enormous serpent, one that is insane or causes insanity. As the virgin rebirth of the Mother, she stands as an apotropaic figure before the nightmarish vision of an enormous woman who is not *the*, but *a* mother, or not a mother at all, but one of the midwives of old Europe. As in "The Sandman," where her frightening stories unleash phantasms of dismembered bodies, [59] the nanny overwhelms the coherent individual until he can only wish to die.

The entire genealogy of the race of salamanders, or bureaucrats, narrated immediately after Anselmus regains consciousness, functions to bury that woman in the Orcus of prehistory. To call this female figure phallic would be euphemistic. Women as they exist in plurality, more real and threatening, appear in the form of nannies and break into a discourse that legitimizes only a single Mother. The European reform of child raising began by systematically repressing midwives, wet nurses, and nannies, and replacing them with civil servants and middle-class, educated mothers. [60] Lindhorst's myth, which repositions the green snake as the primal mother of spirit princes and spirit bureaucrats, *is* this repression.

Only the nanny remembers that Lindhorst, the bureaucrat, and she, the hag, are a dark, unspeakable pair.[61] "It seems that he is the wise man, but I am the wise woman."

Old Mrs. Rauerin is excommunicated because her troublesome spirit impedes the progress of alphabetization. She is Lindhorst's enemy because she takes pleasure, in her last encounter with Anselmus, in tearing the pages out of folios.[62] When the dean's daughter Veronica, already in love with Anselmus, goes to meet with her for the first time, Veronica has heard that the old woman has the power to make reading and writing unnecessary. The information came from a friend of Veronica's, who had heard nothing from her fiancé (a soldier away on a campaign) in months; Mrs. Rauerin was able to read in a magic mirror that the fiancé was "prevented from writing by a deep but by no means serious wound in his right arm, inflicted upon him by the sword of a French Hussar."[63] Such divination is not difficult; one has only to take signifiers as signifiers (the officer in question is named Victor). But such practice was inopportune in a writing system whose technicians were engaged in setting up the first optical telegraphic connections between major cities and correlated battle fields,[64] and whose educational bureaucrats esteemed the one signified above all signifiers. When women's knowledge can replace wounded officers' arms that are no longer able to write and can lame the arms of educational bureaucrats just as they are about to assume their duties, the whole alphabetical improvement of central Europe threatens to go down the tubes. In the modern fairy tale, therefore, the wise man and his mother/daughter must triumph over the wise woman.[65] Serpentina, Lindhorst's messenger to Anselmus, is the slim, diminutive snake that makes writing possible and necessary where the enormous serpent intends to make it unnecessary.

After Anselmus has successfully completed the test of Arabic script, he advances (as is customary in *Bildungsromane*) to his apprentice work: copying the *Bhagavad Gita*, or originary text. Faced with this task, with the "singular intertwined characters," alone in Lindhorst's library, Anselmus at first experiences something like an officer's wound. But he summons courage and begins to study "the exotic characters contained on the roll of parchment," in however unacademic a manner.

He heard strange music coming from the garden, and he was surrounded by sweet and lovely fragrances. . . . At times it also seemed to him that the emerald leaves of the palm trees were rustling and that the clear crystal tones he had heard under the elder tree that eventful Ascension Day were dancing and flitting through the room. Marvelously strengthened by this sparkling and tinkling, Anselmus ever more intensely focused his eyes and thoughts on the writings on the roll of parchment, and before long, almost as in a vision, he realized that the characters therein could represent only these words: "About the marriage of the salamander and the green snake." Then the air reverberated with a strong chord of clear crystal bells; the words "Anselmus, dear Anselmus!" floated down to him from the leaves; and—wonder of wonders!—the green snake glided down the palm-tree trunk. "Serpentina, lovely Serpentina!" Anselmus cried in a madness of absolute bliss.[66]

Critics have overlooked the fact that Hoffmann's admirably plain text constitutes a contract for a new type of the fantastic in literature. Foucault called this a "fantasia of the library":

Possibly, Flaubert was responding to an experience of the fantastic which was singularly modern and relatively unknown before his time, to the discovery of a new imaginative space in the nineteenth century. This domain of phantasms is no longer the night, the sleep of reason, or the uncertain void that stands before desire, but, on the contrary, wakefulness, untiring attention, zealous erudition, and constant vigilance. Henceforth, the visionary experience arises from the black and white surface of printed signs, from the closed and dusty volume that opens with a flight of forgotten words; fantasies are carefully deployed in the hushed library, with its columns of books, with its titles aligned on shelves to form a tight enclosure, but within confines that also liberate impossible worlds. The imaginary now resides between the book and the lamp.[67]

The new fantastic is, first, an endless oscillating from Nature to books back to Nature. Before the enchantment of the solitary reader begins, Lindhorst takes hold of one of the palm leaves in his library "and Anselmus perceived that the leaf was, in fact, a roll of parchment, which the Archivarius unfolded and spread out on the table before the student."[68] As in Loeben's *Guido*, the wordplay leaf/leaf first moves from Nature to culture, from palms to libraries. As one of the first histories of German literature puts it, "Over and against the lush vegetation of the south, the north brings forth an immeasurable world of books. There nature flourishes, here the spirit, in an ever-changing play of the most wondrous creations."[69] But to assure that bookworms and literary historians will not abandon their northern haunts to wander under palm trees, the story then moves in the reverse direction: sufficient absorption in the written page leads back to the palm and its hamadryad. The emerald-green leaves turn into Serpentina, "the green snake." The law that says daughters of the Great Mother will appear to men as their mother is strictly enforced.

Second, the new fantastic is identical with a technology. Whoever limits his field of vision to the space between book and lamp does not follow Nature. The literary criticism that constantly stresses the two realities in Hoffmann (the bourgeois and the Serapion brothers, the empirical and the fantastical) has overlooked this, probably because it still obeys the same technology. The image of a woman as beautiful as Serpentina would never have appeared in the leaves and lines of a text if the student concerned had not chosen the new university curriculum. But with the founding of seminars on philology, which around 1800 began to drive out the lecture, or *Vorlesung* (literally, the "reading before" an audience),[70] academic freedom moved into reading as well.

For Friedrich August Wolf, who as a student took the freedom of enrolling, in 1777, in the unheard-of discipline of philology, and then as a professor was permitted to found the first department of philology,

> The most important thing is that students get a sense of the whole instead of merely reading words. An introduction and perhaps also a synopsis of the content are useful in this regard. If it is impossible to complete a whole text in the original, students should be given a translation. . . . Wolf did not think much of studying grammar. When Klöden, a geographer, wanted to take up Greek and asked Wolf about the best book on Greek grammar, he replied that "he didn't know, that he didn't bother with grammar much and that Klöden would also be better off not worrying about it . . . of course, one did have to learn to decline and conjugate, but that wasn't difficult and could be learned by someone who hadn't studied any Greek, because one could use German words instead. For example, Wolf took the word *machen* ["to make, do"] and put it in the form μαχειν; from that the forms μαχω, μαχεις, μαχει, followed pretty much naturally, and all the other forms could be derived from them."[71]

This fine autonym, in which the word *to make* is used to make up one's own pidgin Greek, invited imitation. It is an amusing illustration of the general translatability of languages circa 1800. When professors are this free with translations, Anselmus has no need to study the primal mother tongue, Sanskrit. He can go to work unarmed—without grammars, dictionaries, or inventories of written characters—as long as he grasps the essence of individual reading and so concentrates his attention on the obscure roll of parchment in front of him. He is thus a heightened Faust, though Faust could still read Greek. The honest concern for accuracy that thoroughly informed the standard of scholarly knowledge became in the established discourse network a "feeling as of the inmost soul": a feeling of glorious autarchy and ignorance.

The page on which the student has concentrated his attention soon sends back his echo: the meaning and thoughts of the text. Academic freedom finds what it had read into the material. Anselmus, may God help him, stands in the mighty fortress of his inwardness before a free translation inspired by feelings that have floated through him as in a dream. The meaning and thoughts of the text are his translation into a pure signified: a book title in German. Whereas old Mrs. Rauerin still found signifiers in a magic mirror, the student of Lindhorst finds "meanings" as meanings.

Anselmus is indeed Lindhorst's student. When the privy archivist and salamander tells his bureaucratic colleagues gathered in a cafe the story of the genealogy of bureaucracy, everyone bursts out laughing except the future bureaucrat Anselmus, who could not listen "without shuddering internally in a way he himself could not comprehend."[72] Only he has heard the truth in its structure as fiction. Lindhorst's genealogical tale breaks off in that laughter before it can make good the promise of designating the place in the kinship system of the one who, after the father and mother, is referred to by ethnologists as "ego." But the text "About the marriage of the salamander and the green snake" is the seamless continuation of the genealogy, and the salamander is Lindhorst himself. Anselmus again reproduces with his inmost soul the discourse of the Other, Lindhorst's unspoken continuation of the genealogy. And no wonder: if the new freedom of academic bureaucrats allows them to say more or less whatever they like, there will necessarily be favorite students who, by free translation of any text, will have overheard exactly what their teachers wanted to say. No doubt the teacher would appear as the hero and son of an alma mater in such texts.

Marriages with green snakes tend to bring more green snakes into the world. The translator Anselmus rediscovers this third generation as well. This time, however, it does not occur in, but between, the lines of the text. The Sanskrit text has just been translated into the mother tongue when the fruit of the sacred marriage it announced appears: Serpentina in person. "Strangely convoluted" and, according to the story, unreadable characters release their incarnation. The scene under the elder tree has already constructed the augmentative word bridge from *schl* to *schling* to *Schlange*. Consequently, when she slithers her way down the trunk of the palm tree, Serpentina is and designates simply the winding curves of the well-rounded ideal handwriting of 1800. She spirits through the lines like the erotic, that is, speech-producing phantom of the library. So any student of Stephani would have been able to say what she was up to with Lindhorst's student.

She sat down on the same chair with Anselmus, clasped him in her arms, and pressed him to her so that he could feel the breath coming from her lips and the electric warmth of her body as it touched his. "Dear Anselmus," Serpentina began, "now you will be completely mine" . . . Anselmus felt as if he were so completely in the grasp of the gentle and lovely form that he could neither move nor live without her, and as if her beating pulse throbbed within him. He listened to every word she uttered until it resounded in his heart and then, like a burning ray, kindled divine bliss within him. He had put his arms around her very dainty waist, but the strange, ever-changing cloth of her robe was so smooth and slippery that it seemed as though she might writhe out of his arms at any moment and, like a snake, glide away. The thought make him tremble. "Oh, do not leave me, lovely Serpentina!" he cried involuntarily. "You alone are my life!" "Not now," said Serpentina, "not until I have told you all that you, because of your love for me, will be able to understand: dearest one, know then that my father is of the marvelous race of salamanders . . ."[73]

And so on and so forth for several pages, until Lindhorst's genealogical tale reaches the narrative present, that is, until the slippery little genealogist mentions herself. Of course nothing is as consistently slippery as self-referential erotic speech.

Chodowiecki's engraving in Basedow's *Elementary Exercises* shows a mother and child snuggled together over reading lessons at a table. One can see the same thing in an engraving in Stephani's *Primer*, but with commentary as well. Serpentina is just as close to Anselmus when she tells him about Serpentina and Anselmus. Self-referential coupling assures that the eroticism will become ever more erotic. Anselmus must also feel that he is bound to love Serpentina twice as much for her trouble and instruction.[74] Her speech is not just a story of the past, it is also an appeal that warns of the dangers posed to the race of salamanders by evil spirits and wise women: consequently it ends with the plea "Stay true! Stay true to me!" Anselmus can only answer by pledging his eternal love.[75]

This eternal love is known as hermeneutics. Anselmus is among the marvelous beings who can interpret the uninterpretable and read what has never been written. They came into the world at the beginning of the nineteenth century.[76] In Hoffmann, for example, a library contains an unreadable parchment, which in turn contains script of serpentine characters; before the parchment sits a solitary student, who is charged with copying it into serpentine handwriting. But the student does not copy; he understands. Similarly, in Nietzsche's cynical appraisal, hermeneutical reading consists in effacing the specificity of particular wordings.[77] Instead of looking at the text, Anselmus is all ears, all attention for a mouth that will make him palatable for other purposes. He was only able, in a rather strange way, to make sense of the title, "About the marriage of the salamander and the green snake"; Serpentina's voice substitutes for, or reproduces, the text that follows. First she gives the student a spoken introduction, as Wolf recommends, and probably she includes an overview of the content of the parchment. Then she allows for the comprehension of the whole, again in accordance with Wolf, by providing a seamless continuation of the genealogy that her father left as a fragment. In short, Serpentina teaches reading in the sense of that word in the discourse network of 1800. She is the Mother's Mouth.

The mothers who put into effect Stephani's method presented their children with sounds in an auditory field rather than with visual graphemes. A mother's voice substituted for and reproduced letters just as Nature was to substitute for and reproduce the artificial. Her phonetic method created a methodically purified high-idiom tone in place of the animal pictures in the Reformation primers; with Serpentina, a spoken love story replaced characters "which sometimes represented plants or mosses or animals." Hermeneutic reading makes this displacement of media possible. Instead of solving a puzzle of letters, Anselmus listens to meaning between the lines; instead of seeing signs, Anselmus sees a beloved appear to him in the shape of The Mother.

The coupling of alphabetization and erotic orality was not without consequences. Georg Lichtenberg notes: "Our young people certainly read much too much, and one should write against reading, as one would against—self-abuse." [78] In fact, a practice of solitary reading that is above the law of the letter (as draconian as it is arbitrary) and a sexuality that is no longer constrained by the laws of kinship and the incest taboo come to the same thing. [79] The great children's crusade against onanism, begun in 1760 with the publication of Simon Tissot's *Onanism; or, A Treatise on the Illnesses Produced by Masturbation*, held that among the principal causes of the vice was the all too early social and literary education of children. Johann Friedrich Oest and Joachim Campe, in their large *Revised Pedagogy*, had the following recommendation: "One should select with the greatest care the few books to be given to children, and reject not only those that contain suggestive or seductive passages, but also those that excite the imagination of children. . . . All books of poetry and prose whose subject is love, which can powerfully arouse children's imagination, should be forever banned from children's homes and classrooms." [80] Even if Serpentina were to speak of less fiery lovers' embraces than those habitually practiced by salamanders, Anselmus would still not be protected from the solitary vice. Serpentina herself remains as ever changing and slippery as the cloth of her robe. A fantastic spirit of the library, who arises out of convoluted lines in order to incarnate all readers' fantasies, who sits on the copyist's bench to whisper about salamander eroticism— such a being never stops seducing. Whatever the content of what is read, reading instruction from the Mother's Mouth is erotic from the beginning.

The pedagogical therapies for children's vice suffered from their own logic. A discourse network that subordinated discourses to the signified made its own pragmatics easily forgettable. Not love as a subject matter in the sense that Oest and Campe banned it from children's books, but love as the situation of instruction led to the early, all too early literary education of children in 1800. The coupling of reading oneself and satisfying oneself became unbreakable: because the children's crusade against both wandered into a "labyrinth of paradox," arming itself with weapons that in turn had to be read, [81] and, more generally, because a culture that sweetened acculturation with culinary or motherly orality provoked the very transgressions against which it invented so many words. [82] Historians of sexuality currently tend to assume that the ritual claim, often heard around 1800, of an unheard-of increase of masturbation is a self-serving lie covering increased repression. But perhaps it reflects a certain reality: namely, the effect on children of an environment insulated against nannies, domestic girls, and neighbors, and locked into mother love and education.

In Lindhorst's story of his mythic prehistory, the eroticism of the salamanders is simply genital. Fiery couplings give birth to new generations. The eroticism between Anselmus and Serpentina consists of his hearing her words, feeling her breath, melting at the beating of her heart, and in the end praising her in a language that is simultaneously "glance," "word," and "song."[83] Thus the situation of reading instruction is intensified by mutual stimulation, plus oral and kinesthetic pleasures: sensing and praising of the One who makes men speak.

According to Jean Paul Richter, Fixlein's "advantage" is being able to tell his story to a living mother. "Joy flows into another heart and rushes out again with twice the strength. . . . There is a greater intimacy of hearts, as of sound, than that of the echo: the greatest intimacy joins sound and *echo* together in a *resonance.*"[84]

Resonating systems cut off their relation to others. Between mother and child arises an eroticism of the "greatest intimacy," which is no longer fed by previous generations or directed toward future ones. Instead of creating children as his spiritual father did, Anselmus remains a child. Pleasures other than the oral or kinesthetic would deprive the function of motherliness only of its educative effects. In order to invent language, man in Herder's essay must never be allowed to mount Mother Nature.

Childhood sexuality thus became functionalized. The very educators who complained about too early and too frequent reading did more to propagate the practice than anyone else; moreover, they did so by creating a systematic double bind rather than, say, by advancing two different and contradictory levels of theory.[85] The path that led through hermeneutic reading was the most elegant method of recruiting poetical writers. The appearance of a dream lover—the first act of a masturbatory fantasy—leads immediately (and this is the second act) to a new dexterity.

A kiss was burning on his lips. He awoke as if from a deep dream. Serpentina had vanished. The hour of six was striking, and he felt oppressed because he had not copied a single letter. Deeply troubled, fearful of the reproaches of Archivarius Lindhorst, he looked at the sheet before him—Oh wonder!—the copy of the mysterious manuscript was perfectly complete, and when he examined the letters more closely, they spelled out the story Serpentina had told about her father, who was the favorite of Phosphorus, the Prince of the Spirits of Atlantis, the Kingdom of Marvels. Archivarius Lindhorst entered the room now . . . he looked at the parchment on which Anselmus had been working, allowed himself a hefty pinch of snuff, and with a smile said, "Exactly as I thought! Well, Herr Anselmus, here is your silver taler." [86]

The fingers have been busily writing, then, and the head has simply not noticed. By giving Anselmus the taler, Lindhorst confirms that the copy flows as beautifully as Serpentina's nature and official instructions dictate. The entire erotically charged scene is at once bureaucratic entry examination, performance of duty, and source of income—with the decided advantage of not appearing to resemble such activities. Such wonders are made possible by the new childhood sexuality, which is smilingly overseen by the teachers/fathers concerned. Reading and writing have been slipped into or hidden in listening to an eroticizing voice, via the magical transformation of the most complicated of the three, namely writing, "with its materials, muscular gymnastics, and manual technique," [87] into the easier reading, and reading in turn into pure listening. A continuum has been established between Serpentina's preverbal breathing and her actual writing, and with that the goal of the augmentation technique and the new anthropology of language has been reached.

Once again Hoffmann's fairy tale has put a simple school program into practice. The instructional practices of his time aimed to link listening, reading, and writing in what was then called the writing-reading method. Olivier's project, to be accomplished by pure pronunciation, is announced in the title of his book, *The Art of Learning to Read and Write Reduced to the One True, Simplest, Surest Principle*. Its bold definition of letters as "the simple signs for sounds," [88] or alternatively as "notes for the mouth instrument," [89] already encoded letters as aspects of spoken language. But a psychologically effective primary instruction explicitly coupled different modes or media of discourse. In order "to combine as many purposes as possible in one lesson," Niemeyer gave children "nothing to read or write that they cannot understand." [90] Ernst Christian Trapp intended "to combine learning to write with learning to read from the very beginning." [91] Johann Baptist Graser's *Reading Instruction Methods*, published in 1819, though not "the first book based on the unity of reading and writing," [92] was the first to advance the grandiose theoretical argument that the forms of letters are primitive images of corresponding positions of the mouth.

If writing proceeds from reading and reading proceeds from listening, then all writing is translation. And if Anselmus unconsciously writes down what he consciously encounters as original sound, then he accomplishes a translation from the Mother's Mouth. The impossible task by which Poets prove themselves and Anton Reiser fails is solved via the writing-reading method. Through continued hermeneutic absorption, in which Anselmus reads his own copy rather than the original text, Serpentina's spoken story has been perfectly written down and lies waiting on the table. There is no longer a foreign language or text "written in exotic letters that belong to no known language"[93]—the *Bhagavad Gita*, believe it or not, lies there in the mother tongue. This is the effect of a discourse network that traces Indo-European languages back to their mother, Sanskrit, and elder-tree maidens back to The Mother.

The textual issue of the Mother's Mouth in the discourse network of 1800 is called Poetry—both the substance of Poetry and Poetry as an act of writing. The concluding sentences of the fairy tale explicitly equate Anselmus's written description of life in the marvelous land of Atlantis with a life in Poetry.[94] But he has already proven his identity as Poet by writing down the story, not as a mere copy of a text in a foreign language, but in German as a story identical to Hoffmann's text. To be inspired by the heavy breathing of love in the library, to write with unconscious dexterity what attention and thought have divined—such feats are possible only for Poets. "To understand completely a work of art means, in a certain sense, to create it."[95]

The creation of texts translated into and out of the Mother's Mouth is also the self-creation of an author. Anselmus rides the crest of his hermeneutics and has forever left the backwater of the copyist's office. Stephani called his "improved," and, in Bavaria's teaching program, "adopted writing method" a victory over the "delusion" (current among the "unkempt masses") that instruction in copying would also provide one "with the ability *properly to express one's thoughts in writing*, which belongs to the higher art of writing alone."[96] Anselmus is therefore the living reply to Stephani's rhetorical question, "Are we diligently instituting writing instruction in all public schools merely to deliver one or two good copyists to our official departments?"[97]

Lindhorst's pedagogy saved from such secretarial humiliation a student with a "schoolmasterish air" for whom his friend the dean could project at best a career in the bureaucratic "writing service," although "there is a great deal in him . . . a privy secretary or even a court councilor."[98] After the initiation that Anselmus passed, like his poet-creator, "with the most distinguished skill" and "exemplary performance,"[99] Anselmus is allowed, unlike his poet, to give up the official departments for the sake of a higher writing destiny. Bureaucrats and poets are thus two complementary sides of a single coin. They are divided only by a small but decisive difference.

Every once in a while Anselmus has certain fits, and not only in front of the *Bhagavad Gita* or Serpentina, which make others fear for his sanity. Because his bureaucratic friends consider Anselmus "mentally ill," they recommend him, "in an attempt to divert his thoughts," for the copying job with Lindhorst.[100] They plan a psychiatric cure true to the method of Thomas Willis, Johann Christoph Hoffbauer, and Johann Christian Reil for psychiatry in 1800 sought its so-called psychic cures primarily by distraction.[101] The lowly bureaucrats could have no idea that Anselmus and Lindhorst would sacrifice the simple "copying of manu-scripts"—healing insanity by mechanical work[102]—to a higher art of writing. Instead, it is for them that the mechanics of the alphabet is fate. Heerbrand, already promoted to registrar, defends Anselmus from the charge of insanity and folly with foolish words:

And, dearest mademoiselle, worthy dean! . . . is it not possible for one to sink sometimes into a kind of dreamy state even while awake? I have myself had such an experience; for instance, one afternoon while at coffee, in the kind of mood produced by that special time of salutary physical and spiritual digestion, I sud-denly remembered, as if by inspiration, where a misplaced manuscript lay—and only last night a magnificent, large Latin paper came dancing before my open eyes in the very same way.[103]

This apology for fits of poetic inspiration demonstrates that the bu-reaucrat is the parody of the Poet. Heerbrand attributes what he calls in-spiration to coffee rather than to Serpentina; thus it is rationality rather than inspiration.[104] Whether he restores order to the archives and honor to his position as registrar or hallucinates letters with typographic preci-sion, Heerbrand deals only with the dead letter that no voice animates. That type of delirium may have been a matter of course in the Republic of Scholars, but in a discourse network whose center was Poetry, it became the very madness it was intended to dispute. A certain Klockenbring, a high official in the police department of Hanover, entered the Georgen-thal sanitarium in 1793 with symptoms of mania and the baffling ability to combine bits and pieces of poetry that he had learned by heart into poems—as if Klockenbring, "although he possessed not a single book" in the sanitarium, could see writing before his eyes like Heerbrand.[105]

Foucault described the fantasia of the library—that invention of the nineteenth century—with reference to Flaubert's *Temptation of Saint Anthony*, as the dance of black letters on white paper. But it could not attain such a technical definition until the turn of the century. The limit-ing and defining shadow that would fall across Poetry, the shadow of the technological media, had not been cast in 1800. Within the medium of writing there was only the opposition between Heerbrand's "angular and pointed" Fraktur and the "fine, graceful curves" of Anselmus's roman script.[106] Bureaucrats had to continue writing the empty phrase *By God's Grace*, if only, as Goethe put it, "as practice in Fraktur and in official writing for the officials." But men and poets were forbidden anything that might lead to the dance of black letters on white paper: from baroque typographical poetry to what one learned by heart in elementary school. "To learn words without thinking is like a destructive opiate for the soul, one that first might provide a pleasant dream, a dance of syllables and images, . . . but later, as with ordinary opium, one begins to sense the bad consequences of these word dreams."[107] Whereas the caffeine-drunk bureaucrat Heerbrand beheld dancing Fraktur letters and the insane Klockenbring hallucinated the syllables and images of absent books, the Poet Anselmus hears only a single Voice whose flow makes his roman letters rounded, individualized, and—the distinguishing feature—unconscious. Poetry in 1800 did not, like literature in 1900, place "the never-articulated sentence *I am writing*" at the basis of all writing.[108] Poetry wrote around that sentence, attributing a spoken quality to it, one taken from the earliest memories of learning to write. "Maternal dictation fixates—orally—in the scene of writing and in the written sign, what constitutes the psychological structure of childhood, the mode of existence of what is remembered in the individual." From this imaginary but insistently conjured spoken quality comes not the textual, but rather the "virtually textual nature of the bourgeois" and his poetry.[109]

Not that poetry would vanish again into the Mother's Mouth. Unlike pedagogical discourse, poetry possessed a barrier preventing such a shortcircuit: the description of writing itself. But writing was not pressed to its senseless and material extreme, where it becomes mere scribbling. It simply flows quickly, lightly, and dexterously from the hand. Thanks to his higher art of writing, the Poet Anselmus can write down effortlessly, completely, and unconsciously whatever a Mother's Mouth dictates—in contrast to other educated people, friends of Hoffbauer, who have not been won for the world of books and who "can read letters or books without moving a lip, but when they want to write something, even just a few lines, have to dictate it to themselves."[110]

Only the caricature of the working or dreaming bureaucrat—its very existence is an indication of a constantly threatening, buffoonish proximity—is overrun with typefaces; poetic justice pursues the bureaucrat whose written sentences pursue and harass people. By contrast the ideal of the Poet reaches the same people through the same channel, without molesting them with typefaces. The Poet addresses their souls with the pure, vocal signified, before which all signifiers are reduced to translations, just as the imaginary lover addressed the poet. Poetry in the discourse network of 1800 had the fundamental function of establishing connecting circuits between the system and the population.

The separation of poetic from bureaucratic writing in Hoffmann's text explicitly secured this phatic function. A counter test for inspired writing shows that when Poets act like bureaucrats in their offices, the soul-to-

soul connections are immediately broken. After completing the unconscious transcription from the Mother's Mouth, Anselmus is invited by his
bureaucratic friends to a social evening with punch; by the end of the evening, when all are thoroughly drunk, the student, dean, and registrar yell
out the mythic secrets of the salamander while Veronica is listening. Anselmus participates even though, or because, "it seemed obvious to him
that he had always thought of no one but Veronica; indeed the shape that
had appeared before him yesterday in the blue room had been none other
than Veronica, and that wild story of the marriage between the salamander and the green snake had simply been copied by him from the
manuscript and was not at all related to what he had heard." [111] The scene
thus becomes negative proof of Schlegel's philosophy. Anselmus momentarily forgets that writing is supposed to reproduce unembellished accents
from the depths of the soul as clearly as they exist in their original state.
Instead he reduces The Woman to a woman, Serpentina to Veronica, with
the result that even his writing is reduced to mere writing. Such canceling
of the constitutive spoken quality of poetry tempts Anselmus to say out
loud, indeed to yell, what Serpentina had whispered as a story. The highest punishment follows upon such noisiness. Although he has a severe
hangover the next morning, Anselmus nonetheless tries to continue copying the original text.

But he saw so many strange, crabbed strokes and twirls all twisted together in
inexplicable confusion, perplexing the eye, that it seemed to him to be almost impossible to transcribe this exactly; indeed, looking it over one might have thought
that the parchment was a piece of thickly veined marble, or a stone sprinkled with
mosses. He nevertheless resolved to do his very best and boldly dipped his pen in
the ink; but regardless of what he tried, the ink would not flow. He impatiently
flicked the point of his pen and—O heavens!—a huge blot fell on the outspread
original! . . . The golden trunks of the palm trees changed into gigantic snakes,
which knocked their frightful heads together with a piercing metallic clang and
wound their bodies around the distracted student. "Madman! Now you must suffer the punishment for that which you have done in your bold irreverence!" [112]

Any copyist who does not hear a voice and consequently can neither
read hermeneutically nor write with a fine, serpentine script must encounter the enormous serpent rather than the little snake. She punishes a
madness and blasphemy that amount to nothing more than an honest attempt at copying and demonstrate the undeniable materiality of the signs.
(One has to be very well brought up to regard handwriting as anything
other than blobs of ink.) A bureaucracy that forgets the secret orality
leads directly to the spot of ink that destroys the beautiful, voice-supported
flow of handwriting inspired by Serpentina.

In 1787 Lichtenberg came up with a plan for a "family archive" that
would store every child's earliest attempts at writing as so many "signa-

tures that the progress of the mind has left behind." Thanks to such pa-rental love, there would come to be a writing system for the most material effects of writing. "If I had a son, he would never be given any paper ex-cept bound paper, and if he tore it or made a mess of it, I would write next to it with paternal pride: my son made this mess on the X day of year X."[113] This curiosity, archived in Lichtenberg's *Scribble Book*, obviously occupies Father Lindhorst, who from the beginning (as if to provoke the transgression) warned of the terrible consequences that would follow if the copyist allowed any spot of ink to fall on the original. A spot of ink is the necessary outpouring of any reading that materializes ideal women, and it literally links what Lichtenberg had linked in a merely analogous way: reading and "self-pollution." Anselmus's reduction of Serpentina to Veronica goes back to a dream that had evoked Veronica in an erotically charged fashion. His spot of ink is as obscene as the noise of lips betray-ing the secrets of the soul or Serpentina, which can only be written.

The spot of ink opposes the ideal of the finely rounded, continuous, and thus individual handwriting with a metaphor of pollution. It desig-nates the trace of a desire that, instead of wandering through the many channels, connections, and detours of the world of language and books, shoots through them like an arcing current. When Charlotte, in the *Elec-tive Affinities*, adds an approving note to her husband's invitation to the captain, "she wrote with an easy flow of the pen, expressing herself affa-bly and politely"; however, "she finally smudged the paper with a blot of ink, to her great annoyance; and the blot only became larger when she tried to dry it up."[114] From this growing spot will later come, on his ma-ternal side, little Otto.

The captain is a bureaucrat and Veronica, one of Hoffmann's cunning daughters of bureaucrats, who singlemindedly intends that Anselmus should become Herr Court Councilor and she Frau Court Councilor.[115] Eroticism and the materiality of writing were intertwined in 1800. Ac-cording to the rule that whatever is foreclosed from symbolization appear in the real and therefore the impossible, they are present only in delirium or hallucination.[116] A spot of ink, we recall, means nothing less than mad-ness. And the party that gathered to drink alcoholic punch concludes with the paradoxical shout of Dean Paulmann: "But I must be in a lunatic asylum. Have I gone crazy myself? What kind of gibberish am I uttering? Yes, I am mad, I am also insane!"[117] The thread of madness in his speech is apparent in that he affirms himself with every word he speaks, and yet every word he speaks cancels out his own words. The delirious speech of the drunken bureaucrat parodies the poetical speech of Serpentina, just as the delirious writing of a drunken bureaucrat parodies the self-forgetful writing of Poet Anselmus. The two elementary, never written sentences "I am writing" and "I am delirious," which will support literature in 1900,[118] are the impossible real and the shadow of Poetry in the discourse network of 1800. The sentence "I am writing" appears, but only in Heerbrand's daydream; the sentence "I am delirious" appears, but only in Paulmann's drunkenness. Both appear, then, in order to restore to poetic writing its own nature, which would assure that such writing passes from voice to voice, and prohibit it from becoming literal and taking the form of bureaucratic madness.

The modern fairy tale is consistent enough to develop the difficult relationship between Poetry and a bureaucratic position in the figure of its lord and master himself. Lindhorst, at once the privy archivist and poet prince of Atlantis, indicates that these functions can and can't be unified. The lowly bureaucrats may represent nonunity for the student-poet, but the highest and most pedagogical bureaucrat in the text knows better. He leads a double life. A double life in itself causes no difficulty, but to publish it is another matter. The fact that a poet's life and a bureaucrat's position cannot be unified comes to our awareness only when poets break a gag rule and talk about the unity of both. This is the subject of the correspondence between the writer and the master of the modern fairy tale. Hoffmann appears under his own name in the last vigil and explains that his bureaucratic duties and bureaucrat's prose have kept him from finishing "The Golden Pot." He is rescued from this dilemma by a note, written in the finest German bureaucratese, from Lindhorst.

Respected Sir: I am familiar with the fact that you have, in eleven vigils, written about the extraordinary fate of my good son-in-law, Anselmus, erstwhile student, now poet, and that you are at present most sorely tormenting yourself so that in the twelfth and final vigil you may write something about his happy life in Atlantis, where he now lives with my daughter on a pleasant estate which I own in that country. Now, notwithstanding my great regret that my own singular nature is hereby revealed to the reading public (seeing that this may expose me to a thousand inconveniences in my office as privy archivarius; indeed, it may even, in the collegium, provoke the question of how far a salamander may justly bind himself through an oath, as a state servant) . . . notwithstanding all of this, I say, it is my intention to help you complete your work.[119]

With this offer of assistance to a poet-bureaucrat, the poet-bureaucrat Lindhorst betrays his trade secrets. These are summed up in the title of a then-current work, *The State Civil Servant as Writer or the Writer as State Civil Servant: A Documentary Account.* Max Friedrich Grävell's tract posed the very questions that preoccupy Lindhorst and his colleagues: "To what extent are the privileges of the writer limited by the duties of a servant of the state? To what extent can both roles be unified?

Who decides when one does something as a writer or servant of the state?"[120]

There is no doubt about Lindhorst's reply. His letter provides documentary evidence, in such phrases as "erstwhile student, now poet," for the unity of both roles. Bureaucrats can be poets and poets bureaucrats. The matter becomes delicate only when the double life is not merely confided to official yet confidential letters, but seizes an entire world of poetic readers, which includes bureaucratic colleagues. Lindhorst is not worried about the characteristically nonprivate title of privy archivist, but he is concerned about the essentially public title of Poet. States demand a commitment from their servants that forbids poetizing and fictionalizing. Once more the Faustian free speech called Poetry encounters a pact that makes discourses the basis of the state and itself becomes a discursive event in the bureaucratic oath. To keep secret the "deliberations of the collegium" and all other affairs of state requires—in the words of Hoffmann's appointment as a state judge—"his oath of duty in his new capacity."[121] This is the reason the lowly bureaucrat Heerbrand sees letters as letters, and this is the reason the lowly bureaucrat Paulmann is horrified to hear his own insane words about his own insanity.

And yet the oath of office and the life of poetry remain disunited in only one of the two discourse formations: Lindhorst's collegium. In the other, the opposite holds. "Whatever a state civil servant does as a writer is not done in his capacity as civil servant, but is sanctioned by universal freedom and specific civil rights."[122] Hoffmann and Friedrich von Hardenberg, Goethe and Schiller—all knew the possibility and the secret of a double life. And when isolated poets, such as Hölderlin or Kleist, fail at the transition from tutor to educational bureaucrat or from solitary crusader to adjunct to the king because they know nothing of a double life, the end comes in a tower in Tübingen or on the shore of the Wannsee.*

Poetry and bureaucracy can be depicted in Poetry as united because the description of this unity recruits more poet-bureaucrats. This is the reason Lindhorst pardons the writer of the fairy tale for exposing Lindhorst's double life. "It is my intention to help you complete the work, since much good of me and my dear married daughter (if only the other two were also off my hands!) has been said therein."[123] This "somewhat abrupt" but deeply felt sigh longs for the return of the Golden Age. "Not before" he has found husbands for all three of his daughters will the Poet in Lindhorst be permitted to throw off "his earthly burden" of bureaucracy and resume his leadership of Atlantis. But the advertisement for

---

* Hölderlin spent his last, insane years in a Tübingen tower; Kleist committed suicide on the banks of the Wannsee near Berlin. [Trans.]

more sons-in-law with "childlike poetic natures"[124] can only go out as poetry. Hoffmann reads this between the lines in Lindhorst's letter.

> He was here offering me a helping hand to complete my work. And I might, from
> this, fairly conclude that he was at heart not opposed to having his wondrous
> existence in the world of spirits revealed through the printed word. It may be, I
> thought, that through this means he perhaps expects to get his two other daugh-
> ters married sooner. Who knows but that a spark may fall in the heart of this or
> that young man and therein kindle a desire for another green snake—whom he
> will immediately seek out and discover on Ascension Day, under the elder tree.[125]

The function of initiation that Lindhorst supervised for the fairy tale's
hero is thus transferred for all future readers to the writer of the fairy tale.
His writing is publicity, and in a technical sense of the word he is a multiplier who transmits the wishes of his lord and master Lindhorst. "The
Golden Pot" and the Golden Age become possible because Lindhorst's
letter gives poetry, until then the despairing expression of an inwardness,
a function in the nexus of discourses. It becomes an advertisement for
advertisers. It must therefore fall into the externality of publication. As
Lindhorst is at once a poet prince and sworn archivist of the state, so his
ambassador Hoffmann is at once a dreamer and media technician. One
formulates his wish in the finest bureaucratic form, and the other is
charged with translating it into poetic gems and passing it along. That is
why poetry wrote around its written character rather than obliterating it,
as pedagogy did. If poetry were not published, it would not be possible to
recruit the sons-in-law necessary for the poetic project of redemption. If
the stories of the salamanders were to appear as sheer texts, they would
be as inaccessible to readers as Registrar Heerbrand's lost documents.
But because Lindhorst leads Hoffmann to substitute a poetical archive for
Lindhorst's bureaucratic one, the whole technology of storage is transformed into psychology. Readers can then take the circumscribed, written quality of poetry to heart and translate it back into speech or into the
childhood sexuality of a phantom lover.

The poetic texts of 1800 were devised with such backward-moving
translation in mind. The story of the poet princes and poets that we have
from the pens of the fairy tale's hero and writer need not refer to the two
other sisters of Serpentina as single, individual figures. Because the sisters
all appear to men in the shape of their mother, it is enough to elevate
Serpentina as the one signified. Readers can provide the referent for the
signified; indeed, readers' longing for the green snake or mother guarantees a successful reception. "One starts out by seeking the girl in one's
favorite novels—and in the end no one fails to find what he was looking
for."[126]

It is a particular pleasure to introduce the empirical proof for the preceding argument. Hoffmann's readers will inevitably find the two other daughters of Lindhorst because both resemble Serpentina, who in turn resembles The Mother or snake. The snake, again like Serpentina, was an element of contemporary ideal handwriting, and therefore was capable of being copied. "When snakes crawl they never move in a straight line. Instead they move in a series of curves, so that, if one were to crawl across fine sand, it would leave behind a line like this (Fig. 19 [in orig.; see the reproduction, below]). Therefore we call a line that curves up and down a *snake line*. Anyone who wants to learn to write well will have to master the drawing of such a line." [127] We can now for the first time publish a picture of Serpentina. Behold in Pöhlmann's Figure 19 the ideal form in which Hoffmann's readers can easily recognize Lindhorst's daughters:

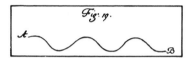

The poetic effect of multiplication thus proceeds quite elegantly through the logic of the signified. In poetry the word does not need to have any reference, it only needs meaning. It need not carry any responsibility, like an oath of office or a pact with the devil; it need only have a textuality that can be translated back, while one reads or writes, into the image and the whispering of the green snake.

The *Fairy Tales of the Modern Age* are word-for-word realizations of Herder's definition of poetry. The poet brings Nature or the Mother into the hearts and souls of his brothers. His addressees are men who read, and they are rightfully called brothers because all their love is devoted to the alma mater. Writing and speech are merely channels that flow from childhood sexuality to childhood sexuality. In front of or behind the channeling network stands a secret bureaucrat who hopes that it will allow his release.

What a state civil servant does as a writer is not done as a bureaucrat, but is sanctioned by universal freedom. At the end of the fairy tale, Lindhorst makes his double life into a division of labor between himself and Hoffmann. Of course, he must return to the collegium and sit through the discussion of his fitness for the oath of office, but no one can forbid his appointing another private secretary to take the place of Anselmus. Lindhorst's letter invites Hoffmann into the poetical office in which he initiates his spiritual sons into poetry. The story that Anselmus was writing until he was interrupted by the fatal spot of ink, the story that the narrator was writing until the pressure of his everyday life became too great—this single and yet doubled story is finally completed. The inner knowledge called poetry receives its bureaucratic baptism (as Marx would later call the state examination) in Lindhorst's archive. Only this baptism gives it discursive reality.

Hoffmann writes and writes because Lindhorst has set the central symbol of the fairy tale, a gold pot full of arrack, on the writing table.[128] As Hoffmann drinks he falls into a hallucination in which everything that is unimaginable under the conditions of prose is given sensual certainty. As if confronted with a magic lantern that could project images to all five senses, he sees Anselmus and Serpentina, finally united at the fairy tale's end in the land of Poetry. The hallucination begins with tactile and olfactory stimuli, which barely cross the writer's perceptual threshold,[129] and culminates in optical and auditory manifestations of love, which could be taken either as "glances" or as "song."[130]

The alcoholic intoxication of the fairy tale's writer achieves the same end as the romantic intoxication of the fairy tale's hero: both make possible a writing so hallucinatory that it never reaches consciousness. Finally Hoffmann discovers the secret of Lindhorst's double life. In retrospect he is able to figure out that it was all just another fantasy of the library. "For the vision in which I now beheld Anselmus bodily in his freehold of Atlantis I stand indebted to the arts of the salamander, and it was fortunate that when everything had dissolved in air, I found a paper lying on the violet table with the foregoing account written beautifully and distinctly by my own hand."[131] Such are some of the pleasures of the double life: in the shortcircuiting of hallucination and writing, intoxication and duty, the writer of the fairy tale becomes the return of his *semblable*, the hero of the fairy tale. He is also the counterpart of the lowly bureaucrats, who under the influence of alcohol merely hallucinate that they are hallucinating, or in daydreams see the dance of Fraktur letters. By contrast, poetic daydreams are a hallucinatory, multimedia love scene; and poetic inebriation, instead of forfeiting the word, is the neat but unconscious inscription of such scenes.

It is a joy of writing that only the lowly bureaucrats seem to ignore. The reform-minded pedagogues praised it and, indeed, held themselves up as examples. One has, for instance, Peter Villaume's *Method for Aiding Young People to Acquire the Skill of Expressing Their Thoughts in Writing*. "I do not know if it happens to other writers, but whenever I write the image of my subject is always present, and even in the most abstract matters I see a kind of phantom, my subject, whatever it may be. And I simply write, without thinking of words or rules. The words take care of themselves; I am hardly aware of them. When this occurs the writer puts down what is fitting and nothing more."[132] In just this way Hoffmann acquires the ability to write down the phantom Serpentina.

His automatic writing has no rules or consciousness of words and is thus in need of historical legitimation.[133] Lindhorst appears once more because the writer of the fairy tale does not immediately understand that poetry *is* the doubling of happy intoxication and bureaucratic duty, vision and a written text. Hoffmann's sigh of regret at having sojourned only briefly in the fantasy of the library and not at all in Atlantis has no basis, and the highest official has the last word. "Be quiet, be quiet, my revered friend. Do not lament so! Were you not yourself just now in Atlantis, and do you not at least have there a lovely little farmstead as a poetic possession of your inner mind? Is the bliss of Anselmus anything else but life in Poetry, Poetry, where the sacred harmony of all things is revealed as the most profound secret of nature?"[134] Thoroughly consoled, the narrator can write, with Lindhorst's blessing, "The End of the Fairy Tale." His text has become a work and he has become an author.

Authors, Readers, Authors

Historians differentiate between two types of culture with regard to writing: a culture of the scribe, in which the ability to write is a privilege and thus a function of the ruling class; and a culture of the learned, in which reading and writing are coupled together and thus can be universalized.[1] In the European Middle Ages, for example, scribes, being purely copyists or calligraphers, had no need of being able to read what they were manually multiplying: the discourse of the Lord. Moreover, medieval readers had to dictate to a scribe their own commentaries or continuations of texts. The discourse network of 1800 was the opposite: a culture in which reading and writing were coupled and automatized. The purpose of this coupling was a universal education, and its prerequisite was an alphabetization that connected reading and writing by linking both back to a singular kind of listening.

This system of education did not simply continue the process begun by the printing trade and the Reformation. Instead, the realization that "Europe would surely sink into error or even into madness because of its public instruction," as long as it had its eyes "on the idolized new knowledge, which is limited to letters and books,"[2] created a caesura in the alphabetizing process. Reading and writing became common property in 1800 only under the condition of simulating a pure, nonalienated listening. As if to stage a confrontation between the two types of cultures, Anselmus finds himself in the predicament of having to copy unreadable characters that seem completely to exclude listening and understanding. But when Serpentina's voice reaches him, not only is this anachronistic situation avoided, but the reader is also promoted to Poet. And because Poetry, unlike wisdom or insight, regulations or the teachings of the gods, cannot exist without readers, the reader-poet Anselmus generates more and more reader-poets, beginning with his writer Hoffmann and moving on through him as relay station to many other poetic youths. In this way reading and writing became universal.

The continuous transition from authors to readers to authors was a kind of mobilization. Not only technical innovations, such as the invention of uncut rolls of paper, and not only social changes, such as the much-touted rise of the middle class, but rather mutations in the practice of discourse itself led to the proliferation of the book industry in 1800. The fact that belles-lettres led the statistics in publishing would be an accident if technological or social causes were brought in to account for the expansion. But belletristic texts themselves wrote the history of this singular occurrence. German poetry is so constituted that—beyond any particularities of content or philosophical differences of opinion—it programs its readers for the proliferation of Poetry.

There is thus no reason to peel away the endless layers of idealist systems of aesthetics in an attempt to arrive at the intentionality of words like *poetry, author,* or *work.* Simple narratives determine such words more elegantly. The end of the fairy tale "The Golden Pot" says it clearly. Poetry as a "possession of the inner mind" arises in erotic and alcoholic intoxication; authorship arises in rereading what had been unconsciously written in the delirium; poetic works, finally, are media for the hallucinatory substitution of realms of the senses. These three key concepts in the discourse network of 1800 are as many promises of happiness.

On its inner side—that turned toward the world of readers—the medium of writing constituted a psychology. It was to the latter that writing, a cold, age-old technology, owed its sudden universalization. What technically would be signifieds without referents became psychologically endogenous voices or images that created pleasure *and* authors. In Anselmus's romantic intoxication, as well as in his author's arrack intoxication, Serpentina shines—whereas Lindhorst's letter names her very referentially as "my dear married daughter"—as an audiovisual hallucination. She exists only as the inner possession of senses that are dead to the world. The precondition of marriage with and according to Serpentina is psychological: the "childlike poetic nature." No one who is adult and sober, then, believes that a beloved voice dwells among the pages of a book. Intoxication or mania is a necessary condition for the production of the transcendental signified in its empirical nonbeing.

The rule of the Serapion brotherhood, the group in which Hoffmann's stories were told, was to do ample justice to a bowl of punch and at the same time mimic the pseudo-Serapion, who could "quite clearly" see the towers of Alexandria while looking at the towers of Bamberg and who in the stories of his madness could even bring the best psychologically schooled listeners "with magical power as if in a dream" to hallucinate his words.[3] In the *Biographies of the Insane*, a love-sick reform economist needs only to see a vision of his dead mother to halt "the ever-turning wheel of the imagination, which like a magic lantern throws out images of the past and future across the soul." The vision of his mother became an "image that refused to move, that constantly occupied the mind and drove it to madness."[4] In Tieck's *Runenberg* a woman emerges from ruins and the night to present the hero, Christian, a tablet, "as an eternal remembrance," which is covered with wondrous, incomprehensible script, and with that she fixates once and for all his insane longing.[5]

In such examples poetry was at the cutting edge of its age. The new human sciences, with their medico-psychological investigations of insanity, discovered around 1800 among the countless manifestations of unreason a distinguished form that revealed the very nature of unreason. This was the *idée fixe*. "Since it is the nature of madness to fasten onto any given idea or concept, often to the exclusion of almost all others,"[6] the fixed idea moved into the center of nosological categories, etiological explanations, and psychic cures, which were directed above all toward distraction. But most importantly the fixed idea became the sole form of unreason to be accorded the rank of poetic dignity. "That *fixed idea* that at least periodically dominates every genius and enthusiast nobly separates men from the table and bed of the earth."[7] Thus Jean Paul's insignificant educational bureaucrat, a writer who cultivates the idée fixe in miniature, can only be called Fixlein.

Whereas the century of Wilhelm Lange-Eichbaum would discover a thousand crossings between genius and madness, the writing system of 1800 knew only one, special connection. It was not Tasso's mania or paranoia, but his erotic fixation on the image of the Woman that made him a possible subject for one of Goethe's tragedies. It was not sheer stupidity or flight of ideas, but the "fixed idea"[8] of taking on the role of the martyr Serapion while in full possession of logic and transcendental philosophy that made the hermit of Bamberg the ἥρως ἐπόνυμος of the poetry club. For only fixed ideas can realize empirically, in a psychology, what the magic mirror achieves in the modern fairy tale: it "throws everything back into its true form, destroys all illusion, and eternally holds the primeval image."[9] Offices of the registrar such as Heerbrand's or archives such as Lindhorst's become historically unnecessary when souls are capable of directly storing ideas. The eternally held primeval image in Christian Heinrich Spiess, Tieck, Hoffmann, Jean Paul, and Novalis was, of course, the Mother.

Hector Berlioz provided or suffered (with the time lag typical of France) the biographical evidence. The *Symphonie fantastique*, which carries the programmatic subtitle "Episode in the life of an artist," first smuggled into symphonic music a paradoxical motif that was removed from all thematic-motivic development. Its function was to fixate an idea that would be the programmatic-musical representation of the artist's lover as she appeared in an opium dream. Hardly had Berlioz married that lover several years later, than she became, in all the fullness of the body, the matron . . .

Once a hallucination has produced a fixed idea in the first act of poetic production, the second act begins as the pen does its fixating. For if a fixed idea is related to poetical and, as in the case of Anselmus, prelingual breathing, then all mechanical distraction therapies, such as those planned by Heerbrand and Paulmann, come to nothing. Only the touch of the spear that opened it can heal the wound of such madness. After sobering up, the hero and the writer of "The Golden Pot" find their fixed ideas written down by their own poet-hands.

Tiedemann's *Investigations into Man* reported the case of a "young man who had dedicated himself to poetry and could spend a whole day without writing one line," until somnambulism came to his aid. He "got up in the middle of the night, wrote, then read over what he had written and applauded himself by laughing loudly." [10] The *Life of Fibel* (or Primer) reports the opposite youthful exercises, in which Fibel "wrote for a long time without looking at the paper, not in order to show off any skill, but in order to have one in case he ever had to work in the dark." Such a case does occur during one night when a dream hen gives Fibel the letter *h* as the first letter of his primer. [11] The famous nocturnal outpourings of the youth Goethe had in fact little originality. Poetic writing in 1800 always meant letting oneself go; for "the time for rewriting, deleting, and polishing what needs to be polished can always be found." [12] Only upon returning from intoxication or dream and in rereading the unconscious handiwork does an ego appear, together with its narcissism. The young man applauds; Fibel reaches the goal he dreamed of; Hoffmann admires his beautifully and distinctly written text of "The Golden Pot"; and Goethe had "a particular reverence" for poems that were "unpremeditated effusions" and had to be "fix[ed] down at once" by "writ[ing] in the dark." [13] Thus the narcissistic pleasure of rereading one's unconscious poetic liberties gave birth to the "authorial function." [14] Authorship in the discourse network of 1800 is not a function simultaneous with the act of writing, but a deferred effect of rereading.

Empirical evidence for this also can be gained simply by turning the motion-picture camera—as an early literary screenplay recommended in

1913—onto the poets. Immediately we see someone "moving around nervously in a room. He writes a line on a piece of paper that has been folded in odd ways. He stands in front of the mirror and reads the line and admires himself. He lies down with evident satisfaction on a couch." [15]

Self-forgetful writing, mirror stage, authorship—these are the three technological steps to the poetic career. But in order to record them a medium beyond books is necessary, a medium that was lacking in the writing system of 1800. What the motion-picture camera would debase a century later, to the laughter of both sexes, shone in 1800 as the highest technological achievement in the medium. Central Europe entered—not in the statistical sense that concerns social historians, but in a programmatic sense that made the future—the condition of general alphabetization. Writing no longer required the virtues of vigilance and attention, the ascesis of a learned class. It could become a skill of the fingers, which would write on through dreams, drunkenness, or darkness. Without disturbance or channel interference, without delay or transmission losses, the medium of writing transported pure signifieds or—fixed ideas. Alphabetization in the flesh made possible an automatic writing that was not automatic writing. For only from 1896 on, when rereading was prohibited, would unconscious writing yield pure signifiers. In 1800, however, an act of writing as punctual as it was unambivalent stood between two universal poles that neutralized the act: before it was the signified that had to be translated, behind it was an authorship that could enjoy the work of independent fingers as its own possession.

Poetry established its technical standard as the rule in the discourse network of 1800. Jean Paul, for example, with his passion for facts, traced all the writing of his time, including the most renowned, back to a primal author, Fibel, whom "no one in the German nation knows by name," but whom everyone had read because Fibel's original primer "not only found millions of readers, but before that had made them into readers." [16] The aesthetic disquisitions of the philosophers also exemplified the process, in reverse. When defining Poetry they forgot, fundamentally, that the poetry in front of them had been written and printed. Fibel's forgotten and thus constantly imitated work made poetic writing so easy that philosophers could call it speaking. [17] The philosophers also forgot that speaking is a technique of the body. The Mother's Mouth had made speaking so easy that it could be called the representation of a representation, or the hallucination of a fixed idea.

August Wilhelm Schlegel, in his *Lectures on Literature and the Fine Arts*, addresses the question "What is poetry?" as follows:

The other arts possess, according to their limited modes or means of representation, a definite domain that is more or less susceptible to delimitation. The medium of poetry, however, happens to be identical with that through which the human spirit first attains consciousness, and through which its ideas obtain the power of voluntary connection and expression: language. Therefore poetry is not bound to any objects but rather creates its own; it is the most comprehensive of all arts and at the same time the universal spirit present in them all. That which in the portrayal of other arts lifts us above commonplace reality into an imaginary world, is what we call the poetic element in them.[18]

Hegel's *Aethestics*, on the theme of poetry, agrees:

That is to say, it works neither for contemplation by the *senses*, as the visual arts do, nor for purely ideal *feeling*, as music does, but on the contrary tries to present to *spiritual* imagination and contemplation the spiritual meanings which it has shaped within its own soul. For this reason the material through which it manifests itself retains for it only the value of a *means* (even if an artistically treated means) for the expression of spirit to spirit, and it has not the value of being a sensuous existent in which the spiritual content can find a corresponding reality. Amongst the means hitherto considered, the means here can only be sound as the sensuous material still relatively the most adequate to spirit.[19]

Poetry enjoyed a privileged place in the systems of aesthetics. The other arts were defined by their respective media (stone, color, building material, sound); the medium of poetry, however—language or tone, language as tone, but certainly never language as letters—disappears beneath its content so that, as with Nostradamus/Faust, the spirit can appear directly to the spirit. The concluding line of Stefan George's poem "The Word"—"Without the word no thing can be"—would have been impossible or sacrilegious in the writing system of 1800. First, all real languages can be translated into one another; second, language itself is merely a channel. So poetry can establish a direct connection between "the meanings of the spirit" (signifieds) and the world (the set of all reference), a connection that establishes and guarantees the general equivalent and the universal translatability of all sensuous media. "As for poetry's mode of configuration, poetry in this matter appears as the total art because, what is only relatively the case in painting and music, it repeats in its own field the modes of presentation characteristic of the other arts."[20] Of course, poetry cannot accomplish this materially, but that is not the point. It is precisely the translation of other arts into a nonmaterial and universal medium that constitutes poetry. This medium is variously labeled fantasy or imagination. Imagination generically defines all the arts, but it specifically defines one highest art. Only poetry can claim "the imagination itself, that universal foundation of all the particular art-forms and the individual arts" as its proper material.[21] Such definitional doubling guaranteed that poetry could not be derived from words or let-ters or written signs. Poetry can manage magically to transform the rush of events and the beauties of the world into products of culture only by being the art of the nonmaterial imagination. "The imagination is that marvelous sense that can *replace* all of our senses." [22]

Some have thought it strange that Goethe's periodical *Propyläen* called upon its readers to submit themes from poetry that they held to be appro-priate for painting. But this simply represented a reversal of his practice of translating images back into the general equivalent. In *Wilhelm Meis-ter's Years of Wandering*, not only has Saint Joseph the Second mastered this practice, but the entire art curriculum of the Pedagogical Province teaches its use. One of the masters stands before a statue and calls upon his students "to awaken the imagination with fitting words in the pres-ence of this stationary work, so that everything that appears fixed regains its fluidity without losing its character." [23] Again, poetic words are to liquidate material media. It was not enough that in their own domain the flow of sound rather than letters should dominate; poetic words would liquidate, that is, liquefy, stones and colors, sounds and building materi-als, all kinds of materialities and techniques of the body, until the Imagi-nation could replace all senses.

In Lessing's Laocoön the poet is instructed: "In this moment of illusion we should cease to be conscious of the means that the poet uses for this purpose, that is, his words." [24] As part of a formulation of basic differ-ences among the arts, such a phrase presupposed a readership for which words had not yet become simply fluid. Only a completed alphabetiza-tion would make Lessing's poetic effect into a pedagogically guaranteed automatism. Jean Paul once had to remind his readers (in the middle of an address to the reader) that what they were reading, without noticing it, was in printed type. One of the fantastic episodes in "The Golden Pot" is presented as the optical vision of the apostrophized reader. [25] And in "The Sandman" the inner image, as brought forth in hallucinations by "that remarkable species of author," is to be presented to the public in the full intensity of "its vivid colors, the light and the shade." [26] All such programs of poetic effects presupposed an ability to read pure signifieds. The philosophical imagination that in 1800 attained the status of the nonmediate medium of poetry is archeologically a simple effect of primers.

There is textual and empirical evidence for this assertion. Textual evi-dence is provided by the patron saint of Hoffmann's poets' club. Hun-dreds of pages after Serapion relates his fantastic fixed idea, his simple secret is told. He has—as a model for all future poets—"spun stories out of his inner self as he saw it all with his own eyes and not as he had read it." [27] The transformation of Bamberg into Alexandria has thus been a fantasy of the library, and the madness of fixed ideas an effect of reading.

Empirical evidence is provided by the reading experiences of Karl Friedrich von Klöden, who did not have to await Wolf's instruction to bridge the gap between two discourse networks. In 1793, at the age of seven, Klöden entered a school for the poor. He later reported being endlessly bored by the "*a, b, ab, a, ba*" and complained that the rote learning of passages from the Bible produced "no understanding," which he significantly qualified as "no representation, no picture." Not until Klöden's mother, who enjoyed reading, proceeded to "explain the meaning" rather than the letters did Klöden gradually come to understand what he was reading. Like Anselmus, however, Klöden did not learn the perfect reading technique—which reveals the poetic in poetry, namely, the substitute for all the pleasures of the senses—until he fell into a delirium. While febrile, Klöden received a copy of Campe's bowdlerized *Robinson Crusoe* from his mother, and this led to reading with "real craving," which "represented every scene plastically" and "painted every scene down to the smallest detail." [28]

Understanding, representation, hallucination—the phantasmagorical modality of hermeneutics could not be more solidly displayed. After alphabetization became (with Pestalozzi) instruction in seeing and (with Stephani) conversation with the Mother's Mouth, it supplemented all other media. Self-proclaimed drug experts acknowledged this by using a "metaphor that turned up with near-epidemic frequency on the eve of the French Revolution" and that called the no less epidemic reading of poetry an opiate. [29] Reading became a "need" that, in the view of one contemporary primer, presupposed and heightened itself. [30] This, however, is a clinical definition of addiction. Thus Anton Reiser describes his reading as a "need, such as opium perhaps is for the people of the Orient, who use it to produce a pleasant numbing of the senses." [31]

"Sublimation" and "internalization," two of today's current explanations for the new addiction, do not go far enough. [32] Lachrymose pity for a middle class supposedly alienated from its so-called drives remains psychology and thus obfuscates positive technical effects. Everything *but* sublimation had occurred. In the discourse network of 1800, the Book of Poetry became the first medium in the modern sense. Following McLuhan's law, according to which the content of a medium is always another medium, poetry supplemented the data of the senses in a way that was reproducible and multiplicatory. Atlantis, the secret of "The Golden Pot," is simply a written desire of the eyes and ears. But such writing must take place. There were no techniques in 1800 to record the singularity and seriality of a progression of sounds or images. Musical scores allowed for the serial storage of data, but not in its singularity. (The nineteenth century would therefore invent the orchestral director as a surrogate for the then-impossible reproduction of sound.) In painting and the plastic arts, the output of singular data always occurs in a parallel way. Mechanical apparatuses for recording sound, such as the vocal automatons of Wolfgang von Kempelen or Lazzaro Spallanzani, remained curiosities or ephemera; so did mechanical apparatuses for recording serial images: one had only the illusions of a movable camera obscura or those children's picture books that, when their pages are rapidly fanned, suggest a series of movements.[33]

Aside from mechanical automatons and toys, there was nothing. The discourse network of 1800 functioned without phonographs, gramophones, or cinematographs. Only books could provide serial storage of serial data. They had been reproducible since Gutenberg, but they became material for understanding and fantasy only when alphabetization had become ingrained. Books had previously been reproducible masses of letters; now they reproduced themselves. The scholarly republican heap of books in Faust's study became a psychedelic drug for everyone.

As long as the book remained without competition, people believed its impossible promise. But Wagner's monomaniacal anticipation of the gramophone and the movies, his *Artwork of the Future*, would be at once capable of and constrained to settle accounts with "the solitary art of poetry," which "suggested, without satisfying its own suggestions; urged to life, without itself attaining life; gave the catalog of a picture gallery, but not the paintings."[34]

Automatized reading is the art of leaping over the gulf that separates the catalog from the pictures. At the sight of a tablet full of the crystalline signs of an originary text, Tieck's "Runenberg" visitor Christian begins deciphering like a director, and the signs become a hallucinatory production, as if "the magic lantern of our imagination,"[35] which had been sequestered from madness in the fixed idea, had suddenly begun to turn again, the signs open up within Christian an "abyss of figures and melodies, of desire and voluptuousness,"[36] in other words, a multimedia show. The fixed idea and poetry are thus connected technologically (and not theologically),[37] like parallel input and serial output.

The new status of letters and books in 1800 produced books of more than the new poetry. Its retroactive power could alter texts that previously had belonged to the Gutenberg galaxy and the Republic of Scholars. The club members of *The Brothers of Serapion* go beyond phantom texts like the *Bhagavad Gita* and establish, according to the critic Peter von Matt, a "veritable *ars legendi*,"[38] which organizes the historical changes of real books. One of the brothers digs up Johann Christoph Wagenseil's *Nuremberg Chronicle* of 1697, but not in order to produce "an antiquarian, critical study."[39] A book that had been a classic among Gutenberg texts, that had reproduced pre-Gutenberg, that is, handwritten sagas of the Wartburg singers' contest, is hermeneutically reworked until it can reproduce its own sensuousness. The solitary reader Cyprian, "captured by the magic and mystery of the past," closes the book and begins to ponder what he has read. Empirical sights and sounds blur, and "an inner voice" begins to speak. The reader falls into a daydream in which the minnesingers named in the *Chronicle* appear in a charming landscape that does everything but call out the minnesingers' names, until Wagenseil himself appears and identifies the figures in his book. Indeed, "Wagenseil looked just as he did in the ornate baroque engraving at the front of the book."[40] Alphabetization could hardly accomplish a more elegant translation of Gutenbergiana into phantasmagoria. The writer of an old book becomes an inner voice; the frontispiece becomes an inner image; the list of characters becomes a scene; and the chronicle's cold medium becomes a time-series of sounds and sights—it is sound film avant la lettre.

Such sensuousness (and sensuality) stored in Poetry is characteristic of an age in which the medium of the book is first universal—for all realms of the senses and people—and second without competition from other sound and image media. Not until the emergence of a technical storage capacity, such as that which shaped the discourse network of 1900, would hallucinatory sensuousness be abandoned to the entertainment industry and serious literature renew its commitment to the ascesis that knows only black letters on white paper. Film historians alone have recognized that the high texts of 1800 were at an opposite extreme, wallowing in audiovisual sensuality.[41] But the pleasure that made the unheard-of boom in belle lettres possible would remain obscure for interpreters who continued to indulge in it themselves. For hallucinatory staging, which put voices and visions in between the lines of texts, was the transmission technique that made new authors out of readers. Poetic texts were on the technological cutting edge because more than any others they could speak to and exploit alphabetized bodies.[42] They operated on the threshold of response itself, where discursive powers paraded as the innocence of bodies and Nature. For this reason, there were more and more writers. "There are so many writers because these days"—1801—"reading and writing differ only by degrees."[43] First, "if one reads correctly"—that is, if one was taught to read correctly—"a real, visible world unfolds within us in the wake of the words."[44] Second, if inner worlds constitute the ground of possibility for authorship, it is sufficient to run through texts like films in order make readers into writers. As evidence for this stands out one of the canonical *Künstleromane* ("artist novels") of 1800.

On his educational journey to Augsburg, the future poet Heinrich von Ofterdingen happens into the cave of a hermit who, like Lindhorst, archives books. The hermit notices that Heinrich enjoys leafing through books and so detains him in the library while his fellow travelers wander off to look at other parts of the cave. Immediately the boy, who has been cunningly separated from the others, sinks into a vision "that can never have its fill of seeing. . . . They were old histories and poems. Heinrich leafed through the large, beautifully written pages; the short lines of verse, the headings, particular passages, and the sharply drawn pictures, which appeared here and there like embodied words in order to lend support to the reader's imagination, powerfully aroused his curiosity."[45] Here the historical remake reaches further back than with Cyprian, extending to pre-Gutenberg handwritten texts. But the medieval verses are set off typographically, as was normal only with the new editions of the eighteenth century; the old miniatures take on hallucinatory effects: they "open a fresh, endless area of play for the imagination, without which no one should read."[46] Heinrich is thus not reading in the time of his troubadour's contest, but in the discourse network of 1800. His adventure continues in that vein.

At length he came across a volume written in a foreign language that seemed to him to have some similarity to Latin and Italian. He wished most fervently to know the language, for the book pleased him exceedingly without his understanding a syllable of it. It had no title, but as he looked through it, he found several pictures. They seemed wonderfully familiar to him, and as he looked more sharply, he discovered a rather clear picture of himself among the figures. He was startled and thought he was dreaming, but after looking at it repeatedly, he could no longer doubt the complete similarity. He hardly trusted his senses when soon after he discovered in another picture the cave, the hermit, and the miner at his side. Gradually he found in other pictures Zulima, his parents, the landgrave and landgravine of Thuringia, his friend the court chaplain, and several other acquaintances of his; yet their clothes were altered and appeared to be those of another age. He could not name a great many figures, but they seemed to be familiar to him. He saw his own likeness in various situations. Towards the end he seemed larger and more noble. A guitar was resting on his arms, and the landgravine was handing him a wreath. He saw himself at the imperial court, on shipboard, in the confiding embrace of a slender, lovely girl, in battle with wild-looking men, and in friendly conversation with Saracens and Moors. A man of serious mien often appeared in his company. He felt a deep respect for this great figure and was happy to see himself arm in arm with him.

The last pictures in the book were dark and unintelligible; still, several figures of his dream struck him with deepest ecstasy; the end of the book seemed to be missing. Heinrich was greatly distressed and wished for nothing more fervently than to be able to read the book and to possess it altogether. He looked at the pictures over and over and was dismayed when he heard the company returning. A curious embarrassment seized him. As he did not dare to let them notice his discovery, he closed the book and merely asked the hermit casually about the title and language of the book and learned it was written in Provençal.

"It is a long time since I read it," the hermit said. "I can't exactly remember the contents anymore. As far as I know, it is a novel about the wondrous adventures of a poet, in which poesy is presented and praised in its manifold relations. The finale is missing in this manuscript, which I brought with me from Jerusalem." [47]

The text, once more handwritten, in a foreign language, and unreadable, strikes the imagination like a silent film. A long optical hallucination is played out according to the rule of continuous augmentation (it grows toward the end); the hallucinatory character of the whole is manifest when it coincides with a dream that Heinrich has already had. The imagination is simply the wonderful sense that can replace all our senses. As in "The Golden Pot," dream and speech, vision and book, become one. The one difference from Atlantis is that there are no acoustic data; even conversations are in some magical way seen rather than heard. The sequence remains a silent film because it is only a hermit who, as spiritual father, directs commerce with books; at the end of the novel a "mother's story" was to have gone over Heinrich's path to poetry and duplicated it in audio. [48]

Heinrich has good reason not to believe his senses. What he sees intersects everything visible, like the invisible seeing eye. The book's signified (given several displacements of the signifiers of "clothing") is the one who contemplates it. Heinrich's own past in Thuringia is unmistakably represented; the future yet to come is blurred; the present moment of leafing through the book can hardly be believed. A life is played out as in time-lapse photography, as a sequence of minimal signifieds in minimal intervals. [49] The images can be called minimal signifieds because they have no redundancy. They represent Heinrich's own figure reasonably well, but that is the limit of their accuracy. They are certainly not portraits, which would encompass an excess of meaningless detail and so would pass beyond the signifieds stored in one's own body image. Heinrich does not encounter any personal file or mug shots. The similarity between the picture and the one who contemplates it must remain within limits if the imagination is to have a fresh, endless area of play.

The manifest secret of a discourse network that places ultimate value in the individual is never to inscribe the individual. "There are no individuals. All individuals are also *genera*," declared Goethe. [50] Thus all the *Bildungsromane* and *Künstleromane* of 1800 only sketch the physical image of their heroes in general terms. No one knows what Wilhelm Meister or Heinrich Ofterdingen looks like. Yet, despite or because of this, doubles constantly appear, as in the count's castle in *Wilhelm Meister's Apprenticeship* and the hermit's book in *Ofterdingen*. In the end the hero and the double share only a "single trait" which for Goethe was a silk bathrobe and which for Freud was a sufficient and necessary condition of psychic identification.[51]

The tactic of the single trait is obvious. The engravings in Stephani's *Primer* accomplish the same thing as the miniatures in Novalis's text. While browsing, Heinrich "discovers a picture of the cave with the hermit and old man next to him"; on the frontispiece of the primer the mother and child learning to read will see a mother and child learning to read. In each case the book doubles the present moment of commerce with itself and reflects information back. In each case identification is anything but an accident. The ideal image, in spite or because of the fact that it cannot and must not have any of a portrait's individualized features, is supposed to engage a remote-control fantasy. The fact that a child learning to read experienced the honor of being included in and sustained by a discourse network has seduced many other child readers to take their places in the system.

Situations rather than particular marks or signs (as with Odysseus's scar, or, from 1880 on, with anthropometric data) make identification a possible, narcissistic happiness. More than any other, the visually doubled reading situation is suited to stimulate the growth of new writers. Thus there was a theory of literary effect in the poetics of 1800, but it minimized the response threshold. In technical terms, the output impedance of a work, already reduced by the sensuous embodiment of the words, is brought near zero by using surrogates that double for the senses.

With minimal output impedance the connection back into the system can and must provide a maximum retroactive effect. In the hermit's cave the feedback between the book and its consumer transforms the book's identity and makes the consumer into a producer. At first the handwritten manuscript had no ending nor (as was common in the medieval period) title, or author's name. It receives a title only when Heinrich asks about the book; it receives an author when Heinrich discovers his likeness. The two modifications go together because, located on the book's margin, the title and name of the author have the same function.[52] First, the title of the novel, *Of the Wondrous Adventures of a Poet*, does not designate just any hero, but a poet or author. Second, the title and name of the author function strictly to unify stacks of paper in the discourse network of 1800.

There is evidence for both points in a fragmentary novel that continues and completes *Heinrich von Ofterdingen*. After having told the poet and hero of von Loeben's *Guido* a fairy tale about a poet hero, a wise old man says:

Fairy tales are deceptive, and one can often read them ten times before one realizes it. But then suddenly it's clear, and now you know that you've really been taken in, that we have had to imagine ourselves a figure among the strange, confused appearances. In the end all such stories are connected like the individual chapters of a book from which the title is still missing.[53]

The title thus includes (as with the *Bhagavad Gita* and *Ofterdingen*) the reader as part of the book. Only the title can guarantee that all the stored discourses constitute a unity—indeed, a trinity, of hero, receiver, and poet. It amounts to a nice denial of the apparent fact that Guido, in listening to the fairy tale, has been led around by his nose.

Authorship is no different. Throughout the novel the poet-hero is in search of a mysterious original manuscript, which, as usual, is written on plant leaves and which is simultaneously promised and withheld by his spiritual fathers. At the glowing conclusion of the novel, Guido receives the manuscript and the realization of what remained a premonition for the aspiring poet Ofterdingen in the unfinished novel *Ofterdingen*. This realization is, quite simply, that any primer has always been written by someone named Primer.

They occupied themselves in searching out an endless number of passages and pictures in the book; the king [Guido] could no longer imagine that he had once believed that the book didn't stem from him. He was the poet of this immeasurable work; his deeds, his love were the content of the great poem; and in the pictures he found nothing but objects that had been effortlessly woven into his life. Possessing this poem made him supremely happy.[54]

A veritable paroxysm of authorship occurs here: the reader promoted to author forgets that there were days when he had forgotten his authorship. In the fresh forgetting of this forgetfulness, the book closes like a trap and the anthropology of language that derives words from man has another adept. As if to confirm the etymology of the word *text*, the words and illustrations "weave" people into the medium of poetry.

The greatest cunning of the anthropology of language is to place this conclusion at the very end of the novel and defer it as long as the title and author of the manuscript are missing. Otherwise, the thoroughly familiar and traditional relationship known as prefiguration would link the text with the biography of the reader—just as the Bible presents an anticipation and model of something to be accomplished through a lifetime of imitation.[55] In the discourse network of 1800, by contrast, the opposite tendency leads to filling the margins and empty spaces of the text with whatever has not been represented in it. Such is the meaning of Ofterdingen's reading adventure. That the final portion of the book—its end—happens to be missing guarantees that "life," in proper transcendental-philosophical fashion, "is not a novel given to us, but one made by us."[56] Because the front matter—the title and name of the author—are missing, the man who creates language and the novel is given a very definite task to fulfill. The poet Heinrich already is must verify the title, *Of the Wondrous Adventures of a Poet*; the author that the contemplator of the book has not yet become must proceed from recognizing himself in the hero of the book. Not for nothing does the hermit, who pretends to have already forgotten the book, speak such portentous words at their parting. He is cunning and denial through and through, and everything about him provokes a child's most passionate wish for alphabetization. Heinrich feels that the old man knows of his discovery (that he is the hero of the manuscript) and has obliquely referred to it.[57] Thus the spiritual father has kept the secret and, like Lindhorst, left the initiate to discover his own authorship. The contemplator-hero-author of the book can proceed to receive his identity-saturated title.[58]

> *Heinrich von Ofterdingen*
> Heinrich von Ofterdingen

Habent sua fata libelli. "There was a time when those texts which we now call 'literary' (stories, folk tales, epics, and tragedies) were accepted, circulated, and valorized without any question about the identity of their author. Their anonymity was ignored because their real or supposed age was a sufficient guarantee of their authenticity."[59] In the beginning, the novel lies in medieval simplicity, without title or author's name, in the hermit's cave. But an incipient poet arrives, opens the book, and the handwritten text suddenly finds itself in the discourse network of 1800. Between the end of the eighteenth century and the beginning of the nineteenth, laws were established to regulate the rights of authors, the relationship between authors and publishers, the rights of republication, and so forth.[60] This new judicial phase, like that of media technology, had retroactive power. Not only contemporary books with a claim to poetic worth had to have a title page with an author's name; earlier books were retrospectively altered. The rediscovered *Jena Song Manuscript* "preoccupied [Johann Christoph] Gottsched particularly with the question of who had written the book. But most of his efforts to find out failed." And when Bodmer published the *Nibelungenlied*, "he concentrated all of his efforts on discovering who the author of the book was. He clung above all to the name *Chuonrat* in the Lament. Bodmer believed until the end of his life that the *Song of the Niebelungen* had a single author."[61]

The transformation of books into poetry through the attribution of a single, named author is an obvious intrusion. Critics like Gottshed and Bodmer, contemplators of books like Ofterdingen and Guido, dream readers like Cyprian and Anselmus: under the appearance of simply transmitting a text they all generate further poetic producers. Whenever possible in fiction, in its superiority over the empirical fact of literary history, this producer becomes identical with the reader. Cyprian, the spell-bound reader of Wagenseil, betrays to his dearly beloved reader that the daydreamer whose fantasy of the library he is describing is "the one who is leading you even now among the masters"[62]—Cyprian himself as the author of that Serapion story. Friedrich Schlegel's progressive universal poetry thus constituted a real definition for poetry in 1800. Semantically it translated heterogeneous discourses into the single Mother's Mouth; pragmatically it set its readers among the masters or authors.

By altogether bypassing reading, which disappears into a hallucinatory modality, universal poetry celebrated its final victory. The authorial function, that phantom of universal alphabetization, is epitomized and confirmed in a truly spectral art. When a phantom whose library contains the complete works of a well-known composer can sight-read these works at the piano, even though, to the indescribable astonishment of the witness and listener, the book contains only empty pages, then and only then is that reader the author. Hoffmann, the narrator, has it from the specter's mouth: the dead Gluck "said in a hollow voice, while hastily turning more empty pages of the book, 'I wrote all this, my good sir, when I came from the kingdom of dreams.'"[63]

The Toast

Function: Feminine Reader . . .

"My good sir"—among men, and therefore among authors, it is no secret that only empty pages can be brought back from the kingdom of dreams. Whoever produces in the act of consumption has no real acquaintance with books. "Out of something dead, an object, . . . a thought that by being written has become a mere thing . . . subjectivity" immediately returns."[1] In order to have tangible existence in real books, Poetry in 1800 needed recourse to non-masculine bodies. These bodies were "not I's" to the cursive "I" of authorship and transcendental philosophy. They were women as women exist in plurality.

Let us return once more to Schlegel, philosophy, and Dorothea. "*I*, at least, live in the world as an author," wrote that author to his beloved.[2] From this a complementary function necessarily follows: that of a feminine reader. We recall that Dorothea Veit was advised to be less silent and to read divine texts with reverence, rather than having others read to her or tell her stories. It was particularly necessary that she respect the sacredness of words more than she had in the past. Otherwise the prospects of a certain "I" would not look good.

So it was that feminine readers saved an author from having written nothing at all. Only their cultic worship could secure a positive reality for printed matter. Prospects would not look good for writers if women were to remain in the great kingdom of murmuring and hearsay, of gossip and slander, in which no Gutenberg had distinguished certain elect types of speech from all the others.[3] Prospects would be even worse if the progressive universal Poetry encountered women who were just as progressive, that is, continuously writing feminine readers. A form of reading divided off from speaking and writing was the necessary and sufficient function of the other sex. Thus the very "reputation" of "literature in Germany"[4]— thus it is written—depended on a reading by the other sex performed as a spiritual interest in poeticizing men. In other words, literature depended on a pure CONSUMPTION OF DISCOURSES. The other sex is necessary because it possesses "taste" but not the "creative power of genius": "good taste comes to the serious, masculine character from the fair sex, and so it comes to society, and everyone benefits."[5]

In order to integrate women into this new function, the network had recourse to its most basic operations. What made women read was a Mother who raised mothers. "While I can scarcely allow Nature a seat and vote in the law-giving council of Reason, I am nonetheless convinced that there can be no truth that Nature has not already indicated in her beautiful hieroglyphics; indeed I believe that Nature itself has endowed women with the domestic spirit and leads them to religion."[6] Woman, insofar as she persists as One, remains at the originary ground of all discourse production and is thus excluded from the channels of distribution as these are administered by bureaucrats or authors. She remains this unapproachable ground in order to confine women, in their existence as plurality, to a domesticated reading, which, as reverence for divine texts, is indeed religion. In this respect the division of the sexes in the discourse network of 1800 was quite simple. Because the Mother produced authors as the unifying principle of poetic works, women had no access to any such unity. They remained a manifold grouped around the authorial lodestar.

A manifold, however, is a realm of accidents. Nothing hindered women from taking up the pen from time to time. Of course, there was also nothing to prevent each such exception from remaining an exception.[7] Statistical and stochastic processes could do nothing against a rule based on Nature itself.

Florentin: A Novel Published by Friedrich Schlegel reads the title of a story of an artist's development, one written not by the developing artist Friedrich Schlegel but by his companion, a woman excluded from writing. To be sure, this was done only "to procure him leisure, to earn our bread as a modest working woman, until *he* be capable of it."[8] That purpose was served by the title page: in an age when men went to press with such identity-drunk title pages as Fibels' *Life of Fibel* or Ofterdingen's *Ofterdingen*, the writer Dorothea Veit vanished to the greater glory of a man's name, even if he is figured merely as the "editor."[9] She "never had the ambition to be known as a writer, and never published under her own name. Her literary activity was not an end in itself, but stood completely in the service of the man whom she so blindly loved." [10]

Huber's Collected Stories, Continued by Therese Huber, née Heyne is the title of a four-volume work, and the title loses no time in separating the man and author from his wife and continuator. On the one hand stands the simple and dignified last name, the sufficient condition for individualization in the system of authorship; on the other hand, one has a first name and two last names, which are necessary for the individualization of women in a middle-class system of names. On the one hand, there is the collected work guaranteed by the name of the author, on the other hand, there is an apologetic foreword by Therese Huber, née Heyne.

A vivid and sharply drawn image of feminine charm and duty had from the beginning led me to view the profession of writing as *denaturing* and *distorting* for my sex. In my eyes each exception was—an exception! and now that I have striven for twenty-four years to be an exception, I am more than ever convinced of this truth. Huber discovered my ability to present my experiences and observations in the form of well-thought-out stories, and for devout reasons I was bound to exercise this talent. For ten years even our closest friends had no inkling of my part in my husband's creative work, and during these ten years even I was unaware that a portion of the praise, the honorable judgments pronounced by gladdened readers of stories my husband published, belonged to me. I was too deeply devoted to him, too immersed in my domestic duties, to call anything my own. [11]

Nature keeps strict watch over women and any possibility that they might distort their domesticity by authorship. If an author is defined simply by naming certain discourses his own, women by contrast are defined by being the author's "able housewives," those who do not name anything their own any more than they "inspire" a husband to do "creative work." [12] Even women who write constitute an innocent accident in this silenced and anonymous function. "The girl who can write a poem" by no means desires the status of author; she "should not take any more credit for it than she would for a well-prepared recipe." [13] Women take up the pen only by pretending that the age is still one of medieval anonymity.

My name was never published, and I guarded against its occurrence, for this silence was the last vestige of the pure, feminine relationship to writing that remained for me from the period of Huber's life. An announcement of my *Letters from Holland* in the *Morning Review* mentioned my name—so far as I know—for the first time. It was uncalled for, neither the author nor the public was served, and the "Th. H." set on the title page by the publisher gave the advertiser no right. Later, brave Gerhard Fleischer in Leipzig thought it would be expedient to publish my name beneath an insignificant piece in his journal *Minerva*, and from then on my incognito became a charade that conflicts with my feminine instinct as much as does authorship itself. [14]

If authorship, as a distinguishing feature of the human race, distinguishes only one of the two sexes, women who wrote circa 1800 remained essentially anonymous or pseudonymous.[15] A Mother dwelt within them who was the adversary of anything public. Only an accidental chain of events, set in motion by men, could lift the veiling incognito of feminine modesty.

There is, of course, nothing in the realm of accidents to hinder women from forgetting the topos of modesty deemed appropriate for them. "I feel that I could bring the whole world into the world with my mouth," wrote Bettina Brentano to her friend Karoline von Günderode (who wrote poetry under the male pseudonym Tian).[16] Her comments are the wild oscillations of an orality that stands the relationship between the world and what is in it on its head and in so doing appears to announce literary ambitions. But because Bettina Brentano is unable to provide her discourse with any basis of ownership or unifying principle, her high spirits remain as far from authorship as Therese Huber's modesty topos.

I'm so glad to be an unimportant person, there's no need to come up with any fine thoughts when I write you, I can just talk about things, though I used to think one couldn't write letters without putting in some moral content or something intelligent, the way one usually weighs down a letter, but now I don't care about chiseling out a thought or gluing one together, I'll leave that to others—if I had to do it I wouldn't be able to think any more.[17]

Do I understand myself?—Even I don't know.—I'm so sleepy my eyes have fallen shut with the thought that tomorrow morning I have to give this letter to the messenger, and besides my light is so dim, it's sure to go out, so good night, Letter! The moon is shining so brightly in my room that it seems to ring—the mountains across the way are so mighty, they steam fog into the moon. Meanwhile the light really wants to say goodbye, but I'd like to see if I can write by moonlight.[18]

Out of such enthusiasm comes a feminine *écriture automatique* that parodies the Poet's freedoms. Bettina Brentano too can write unconsciously and in the dark. But instead of rising to consciousness and authorship through rereading, she does not bother to read her moonlight delirium again. She "has to" let her letters "flutter away like sounds carried by the wind."[19] What the parody neglects, then, is the feedback between writing and reading, by which, according to poetics and the reading-writing method, one makes a well-formed work out of wild oscillations.

Bettina's brother the poet answered by becoming a reading-writing technician. Clemens Brentano recommended that the passionate letter writer not simply note down "broken off thoughts," which only the receiver can unify, but that, in the "interest of art," she "also write to herself," because only rereading leads to "full and concise expression."[20]

Above all, however, he recommends to his sister, because she is a woman, the reverse feedback loop: intensive reading, during which Bettina, whenever possible, should "write down her impressions during or after reading" and send them to her brother. By this account, skillful, professional writing has nothing to do with women other than to confirm the feminine reading function.

I would be glad if you read some history, but otherwise mostly Goethe and always Goethe, above all the seventh volume of his new works; his poems are a fitting antidote for extreme sensitivity. . . . In general I have been bothered by the fact that you write nothing to me concerning your own inner development, that you don't ask me what you should be reading, and so on. What good can come of your restless love for me, when it simply repeats again and again what is already the case, namely, that we have affection for one another, as is proper with siblings. It would be better if you put your trust in me to some use, if you granted me some influence on your education, if you asked for my advice in all matters of reading.[21]

Since Reinhold Steig's discovery of the original of this letter, no one can claim any longer that the published version in *Clemens Brentano's Spring Wreath*, is one of Bettina's pretty forgeries, nor should anyone continue to overlook the reasons why Germany has classical writers. The name *Goethe* (like the Name-of-the-Father in other cultures) combines all the controls that the discourse network of 1800 needed. If Bettina would only listen to her brother, the network-appropriate division of the two sexes would be achieved. Men move up into the function of authorship by rereading their own writing; women move into the complementary reading function by describing what they read. On the one hand struts the primal author Goethe, setting the norm of Poetry as he published his collected writings. On the other hand, there are women, who, rather than externally repeat an amorous automatic writing, read mostly Goethe and always Goethe, until in gathering the fruits of their reading they secure the reputation of German Poetry. Here we have the production of books that dream-interpret unreadable originary texts or inaudible Mother's Voices; there we have the duty of intensive rereading, which a Faust, Anselmus, or Cyprian would never have taken to heart.

What remains in doubt is whether pure discourse consumption can, as promised, provide the antidote to feminine hysteria. Because Brentano's required reading is the "poet of femininity,"[22] a woman's reading of Goethe cannot be without consequences. There is a close connection between heroines and female readers. Brentano's sending his sister *Wilhelm Meister* began the most famous romantic reading affair of amorous sensibility. Bettina Brentano took the book to bed like a beloved and discovered in the child sweetheart of the hero her own likeness.[23] Indeed, her ostensibly so passive sensibility was bold enough to make its way from the book to its author. Bettina took her brother's advice all too literally, for not only did she write down her feelings during or after her reading, she sent her notes as letters to Weimar. The result was *Goethe's Correspondence with a Young Girl.*

To write to an author and tell him that, first, he loves the women that his fictional heroes love,[24] and second, that the undersigned is very much like these women—such writing up of one's own reading takes the feminine reading function to an extreme. All the transcendental signifieds of Poetry suddenly acquire referents: Woman becomes a woman, the hero becomes the author, and the author becomes a man. Thus a strict application of the new hermeneutics can only lead to escalating love. A book that had recently appeared, *The Art of Reading, Including Information on Books and Authors,* advised as a first step that one "fan the fires of the imagination in order to breathe life into the notions one reads." Bettina Brentano does this when she supplies referents to notions such as the hero and heroine. Faithful to his subtitle, Johann Adam Bergk comes right out and asks "not only that we love the books, but that we extend our love to the person of the author as well."[25] Bettina Brentano does this when she admits that all her acts of hermeneutical insertion are a declaration of love, and then follows her own letters to Weimar. "To see personally those authors whose works have made a great impression on one," is, of course, under the conditions of authorship, "*natural* to women."[26]

The authorial function, like any divinity, is supported by a certain Real. In this case it is women's pleasure. "What they were attempting to do at the end of the last century, during Freud's early years, what all those good people in Charcot's circle and others were looking for, was a way to reduce mysticism to sex. If you consider the matter carefully, it becomes clear they had it all wrong. For this *jouissance* that one experiences and knows nothing of, does it not start us off on the path of ex-istence? And why not interpret one aspect of the Other, that of God, as what is supported by feminine *jouissance?*"[27]

Feminine readers, too, knew this pleasure that is experienced and not known. As Dorothea Schlegel said of November 14, 1799, the day of her first encounter with Goethe: "To know that this god was so visible, in human form, near to me, and was directly concerned with me, that was a great, everlasting moment!"[28] Rahel Varnhagen said of August 20, 1815, the day of her second encounter with Goethe: "My knees, my limbs trembled for more than half an hour. And I thanked God, I said it out loud to his evening sun like someone gone mad . . . my own dear eyes *saw* him: I *love* them!"[29]

The author becomes God because women's pleasure supports him. Women's bodies are experienced because they experience the god and are capable, in the logic of the minimal signified, of "interpreting every word, every syllable, every 'ah'" that falls from his mouth.[30] A hermeneutic-erotic circle encloses feminine readers and the author; it regulates both reading and love. "One," that is, a woman, "cannot love without loving Goethe."[31] All equations of hero with author, heroine with women who read, serve this love. But because women's reading and love have already been inscribed in the works women read, it is the author who encounters, when this reading and love coincide in him, his truth.

> Es ist sehr billig, daß die Frauen dir
> Aufs freundlichste begegnen: es verherrlicht
> Dein Lied auf manche Weise ihr Geschlecht,
>
> It is quite proper that we women should
> Be well disposed towards you; for your poem
> In many ways has glorified our sex.[32]

says the Princess in Goethe's *Tasso* to her Poet, who is therefore a "poet of femininity" as much as is his author. The woman who speaks knows better than anyone what cordiality and glorification signify. When, spending her youthful years without health, without a beloved, without a husband, until her one pleasure, singing, was also finally forbidden by her doctors, the Princess "cradled all my pain and longing / and every wish in sweet and gentle tones" ("Schmerz und Sehnsucht / Und jeden Wunsch mit leisen Tönen eingewiegt"; 1808–9). For her, the diagnosis of hysterical sensitivity applied to Bettina Brentano would seem appropriate. And for the Princess, as well, a sickness of the soul is the best soil for transforming the appearance of the Poet into that of God. On her first meeting with Tasso, her experience is like that of Dorothea, Bettina, Rahel *e tutte quante* when they first saw Goethe.

> Ihn mußt' ich ehren, darum liebt' ich ihn;
> Ihn mußt' ich lieben, weil mit ihm mein Leben
> Zum Leben ward, wie ich es nie gekannt.
>
> I had to honor him, therefore I loved him;
> I had to love him, since with him my life
> Became a life, such as I'd never known.   (1887–89)

When the Poet glorifies the female sex, he makes women's "every mood more individual and charming through [his] loving understanding."[33] Only he can give them individual life, which consists in love for the author-individual. But the inverse question of whether the author, in his writing and love, has an individual woman in mind, must remain open. The discourse network of 1800 does not record particulars, whether particular names or unmistakable images. Women, as they exist in plurality, do not appear *in* Poetry because they fulfill the feminine reading function *for* Poetry. In place of women the Woman is written—"the model of every virtue, every beauty," according to Tasso, or (in Plato's "Greek") the ἰδέα τοῦ ἀγαθοῦ, which the author of *Tasso* perceived fundamentally as the form of woman. "A noteworthy self-reflection on Goethe's part: that he conceives of the Ideal in feminine form or in the form of woman. What a man's essence might be, he simply doesn't know."[34]

The Woman, the One who is written, is at once image and name, without, however, having an image or a name. Leonora Sanvitale, one of Tasso's feminine readers, recognizes that "he can enrich with multiple conceits / A single image in his many rhymes" ("mit mannigfalt'gem Geist ein einzig Bild in allen seinen Reimen verherrlicht"; 183–84) and that he "carries what he loves from every sphere / Down to a name the two of us share in common" ("was er liebt, aus allen Sphären auf einen Namen niederträgt"; 214–15). Tasso picked up this trick from Goethe, who observed it in old Zeuxis. So, for instance, the author of *Werther* granted himself "permission to model [his] Lotte on the figures and characteristics of several pretty young girls."[35] Single traits are combined and dissolved in order to construct the Woman out of women: a technique of poetic production corresponding to the aesthetic effects of the three daughters of Lindhorst and their one form. Thus the single image and one name in Tasso's verses have much the same influence as the Mother on future authors. The "plaintive euphony" ("die sel'ge Schwermut"; 195) with which he sings of his fair lady "Lures every ear, and every heart must follow" ("lockt ein jedes Ohr und jedes Herz muß nach"; 197).

What produces a glorious proliferation of discourse in a new crop of authors is not, however, without danger for feminine readers. Leonora and the Princess, as mouthpiece and ear for such poetic effects, are both within their domain of reference. They have women's ears and hearts. Consequently, the Princess attempts to limit Tasso's seductive power by coupling the model Woman with a singular referent. Not every woman's heart need fall to the poet, for

> Wenn er seinen Gegenstand benennt,
> so gibt er ihm den Namen Leonore.
>
> When he gives a name to his one theme
> That name, be sure of it, is Leonora.   (198–99)

But the one thus called by name has no trouble replying.

> Es ist dein Name, wie es meiner ist.
> Ich nähm' es übel, wenn's ein andrer wäre.
> Mich freut es, daß er sein Gefühl für dich
> In diesem Doppelsinn verbergen kann.

But that's your name, Princess, as well as mine.
And any other name I'd hold against him.
I'm pleased that in such ambiguity
He can conceal his feelings towards you.   (200–4)

The homonymy of the poetic image of Woman is thus, as one of the two
Leonoras clearly recognizes, neither accident nor exception. Poetry in the
discourse network of 1800 has by rights such double meaning. The fact
that Tasso breaks the rule of individualization in the middle-class system
of names is not a transgression; rather, according to Leonora, transgression would consist in compliance with the old rule. Authors and feminine
readers can play their two complementary roles only through the systematic polysemy of women's names and images in Poetry. Poets can write
their desire without setting it down inalterably; women in plurality can
become the desire of this desire. Polysemy produces discourse: it makes
men write and women decipher what is written. This too is an effect of an
anthropology of language that posits man and a soul at the origin of
speech.

The two women in *Tasso* indulge in a passion for riddles that at once
goads and rewards their reading. Either one Leonora encourages the
other by attributing the written name to her alone, or the other Leonora
reads the double meaning in the name as unambiguously her own. They
are, however, simply taking paths marked out by the creator of the homonym. God has given the author Tasso the ability to speak, poetically and
therefore polysemously, where man in his torment is dumb. But this gift,
far from inscribing desires in real areas of discourse, is itself torment. Because unambiguously naming a woman's name would be a transgression,
poetic homonyms preserve one from falling silent, but what the poet
Tasso envies in Antonio, the proto-bureaucrat, is a political practice forbidden to the poet, namely, the right to prepare treaties or contracts,
which are then put into action by the single, unambiguous signature of
the Prince. To achieve the same sort of definiteness for Poetry, by naming
or embracing a woman who is not merely the Woman, is Tasso's desire,
insofar as it is the desire of a desire. His relationship with the Princess is
transversed by all the anguish and bliss of an attempt to shed ambiguity.

The author of *Werther* not only granted himself "permission to model
[his] Lotte with the figures and characteristics of several pretty young
girls," but also, by contrast, borrowed "the main characteristics from the
most beloved." Correspondingly, Tasso explains to the Princess how little
generality there is in his general glorification of women.

Was auch in meinem Liede widerklingt,
Ich bin nur *einer, einer* alles schuldig!
Es schwebt kein geistig unbestimmtes Bild

Vor meiner Stirne, das der Seele bald
Sich überglänzend nahte, bald entzöge.
Das Urbild jeder Tugend, jeder Schöne;
Was ich nach ihm gebildet, das wird bleiben.
Und was hat mehr das Recht, Jahrhunderte
Zu bleiben und im stillen fortzuwirken,
Als das Geheimnis einer edlen Liebe,
Dem holden Lied bescheiden anvertraut?

Whatever in my poem may re-echo,
Only to one, to one I owe it all.
No vague and merely mental image hovers
Before me when I write, now brightly close,
Now dim again, withdrawing from my soul.
With my own eyes I've seen the prototype
Of every virtue, every loveliness;
What in that image I have made, will last . . .
And what is better fitted to live on
For centuries, effective, though in silence,
Than the kept secret of a noble love,
Humbly confided to the lilt of rhyme?   (1091–98, 1104–7)

The self-commentary that reduces the double meaning of the name
Leonora to a single referent and thus gives the author's own work the
function of revealing biographical secrets is as risky as it is authoritative.
(*Poets on Poetry* is not always gossip designed for literary seminars.)
Denying the Woman gives *one* woman a clear hint that can be answered
only by a similar gesture. The Princess takes Tasso's rhetorical question a
step further.

Und soll ich dir noch einen Vorzug sagen,
Den unvermerkt sich dieses Lied erschleicht?
Es lockt uns nach, und nach, wir hören zu,
Wir hören, und wir glauben zu verstehn,
Was wir verstehn, das können wir nicht tadeln,
Und so gewinnt uns dieses Lied zuletzt.

And shall I tell you one more rare distinction
That unremarked, your poem gains by stealth?
It draws us on, and on, we listen to it,
We listen and we think we understand,
What we do grasp of it we cannot censure,
And so we are won over in the end.   (1108–13)

The hermeneutic path from the ear to the heart, from a reading that
moves as automatically as listening to an understanding that discovers the
author in the text—one Leonora describes this as the path for feminine
readers in general; the other claims that it belongs to her alone. At the
limit of what she can allow herself to say, the Princess says that Tasso's

polysemy, rather than only praising the Woman, has "won" him a woman. And when the author of this understanding hears about understanding from a woman's mouth, when he for his part thinks he understands, then the erotic trap of the text has closed on him as well.[36] Erotomania and paranoia, the final stages of Tasso's psychopathological tragic drama, are not the endopsychic aberrations of an individual; they result from the very structure of address of Poetry. When the referent of the polysemous signifiers remains open for the sake of a transcendental signified, and when this signified remains an indelible fixed idea at the origin of Poetry, author and feminine readers succumb to a paranoia that attributes to every word and scrap of paper the unspeakable but also indelible truth.

Whereas Antonio prepares treaties for signature and sends off diplomatic dispatches, Tasso stumbles through a labyrinth of signs in which misplaced letters and lost papers reveal intention and betrayal. Poets and bureaucrats, these two fragments of "*one* man," (1705) are complementary. It makes little difference whether Tasso is in the right or is crazy; his paranoia demonstrates that people charged with social tasks connected with language and writing must often largely bear the symbolic discordances of their culture.[37] For the poet who harbors suspicions about misplaced letters and lost papers dispatches similar pieces of writing with near-professional industry. Like messages in bottles, Tasso's poems glorifying the one and doubled Leonora hang everywhere in the trees of the garden of paradise at Ferrara. Yet in all the lines that Poetry has the Poet and feminine readers say about Poetry, there is not a word about this dispersing of words. Only the subject of what is written (the poetic double meaning), not how it is written (its strategic function), becomes a theme. Tasso is finally wrecked upon, yet clings to, a cliff by the name of Antonio, where writing is sheer power. But the discourse network of 1800 would rather not know anything about it.

As with the author, so with his feminine readers. *Goethe's Correspondence with a Young Girl* realizes what *Tasso* had described or prescribed. Here, however, the feminine reader falls victim to the confusion between poetic and family names, poetic writing and letter writing, and, unlike the taciturn Princess, expresses her paranoia. Bettina Brentano, who even before reading Goethe endlessly repeated a declaration of love, finally obtained an answer that was not an answer. Instead of a declaration of love in reply, a sonnet arrived in Frankfurt, one that—according to the accompanying letter of the author, or hero of the epistolary romance, Goethe— should satisfy the girl. But the reply remained obscure, not only because Poetry had to sidestep any particular referent, but because it continued the game of names in the manner of Tasso's bottle messages in the garden of Ferrara. The sonnet was entitled "Charade," and to the infatuated feminine reader of Goethe it seemed an open invitation to tease her own name from the game. To speak with the Princess, it is a teleguided paranoia of attribution.

> Es lockt uns nach, und nach, wir hören zu,
> Wir hören, und wir glauben zu verstehn,
> Was wir verstehn, das können wir nicht tadeln,
> Und so gewinnt uns dieses Lied zuletzt.
>
> It draws us on, and on, we listen to it,
> We listen and we think we understand,
> What we do grasp of it we cannot censure,
> And so we are won over in the end.   (1110–13)

In keeping with this, "Charade" is about two words that the poet hopes to merge in one image and pronounce as the name of his beloved— very much Tasso's logic of woman's name and image. But Bettina Brentano, less or more fortunate than the two Leonoras, cannot discover the two disguised words of the charade and therefore her own name.

Who are the two? Who is my rival? In which image shall I mirror myself?—and with whom shall I melt in your embrace?—Ah, how many riddles are hidden in *one* riddle, and how my head spins. . . . You see, my friend, how you lead me on into an eternity of surmise; but the earthly word, which is the key to all, I am unable to find.

But you have achieved your purpose, that I should surmise and be satisfied, for in this I have divined my rights, my recognition, my reward, and the strengthening of our bond, and every day I will divine your love anew.[38]

The feminine reader believes the sonnet is a letter addressed to her. As Goethe had remarked, "Women understand everything *à la lettre* or *au pied de la lettre*."[39] Not contented with a transcendental signified, Bettina Brentano would like to see the "earthly word" in writing. But it eludes her, for good reason. *Herz* and *lieb*, the two solution words of the sonnet "Charade," are not only artfully disguised; if discovered and brought together, they would form the last name of another dream love of Goethe's: Minna Herzlieb. The author has fused poetic metaphors and middle-class names for women, nonreferential play and autobiographical confession. Because his sonnet makes exoteric sense, Goethe can send it to feminine readers who long for a reciprocal declaration of love, and because the esoteric meaning remains hidden between the lines, he can lead those readers around by the nose. Such is the cunning of literary works that also function as letters.

Because whether and who an author loves remains a mystery, feminine readers develop a hermeneutic love for his works. "Oh! one cannot love without loving Goethe," as Rahel Varnhagen recognized. The open secret of Poetry is to speak to women with a forked tongue. Whoever mails off a sonnet like "Charade" is not without love for his reader, and yet he dreams of someone else. There is always a remainder—one of those sweet images of a beloved woman that, following Keller, are not nurtured by the bitter earth. Beyond the eloquent women who write letters, there is always, taciturn and lapsing into silence, one "Herzlieb" or another.

After his ineffaceable vision of the Woman, the hero of Tieck's *Runenberg* attempts to achieve forgetfulness by marrying one of those who exist in plurality. But the fixed idea in his soul is more powerful. At the end of the fairy tale, Christian leaves his wife Elizabeth for the sake of the image, but not without imparting, in his last words to her, his duplicitously double-edged wish.

> "I know you very well, he said . . . you're Elizabeth." The woman started, afraid. "But how is it that you know my name?" she asked, trembling, as if she knew the answer already. "Dear God!" said the unfortunate, "I am Christian, who once met you as a hunter. Don't you recognize me?"
> In her fright and profound pity, Elizabeth could not think of anything to say. He embraced her and kissed her. . . . "Don't worry," he said, "I am as good as dead to you; out in the forest the beautiful, powerful one is waiting for me, the one with the golden veil." [40]

The hero of the fairy tale is obviously not without love for his wife, but another desire—the very waiting of the other woman—exiles him from the living. For someone to say between kisses that he is as good as dead to the one he is kissing demonstrates the paradoxical split between love and desire. And there the hero represents the author. Manfred, who narrates the story in the novella's frame and (as he emphasizes) invented it, observes at its end that his "listeners, particularly the women among them, had turned pale" (as if Elizabeth's fright were contagious). [41] Instead of heightening an erotic atmosphere among the men and women present by means of an erotic Poetry of men and women, and thus following the secular model of the *Decameron*, the romantic poet fascinates and seduces his feminine listeners by a different tack. He confronts them, in his storytelling as in his story, with another desire. On one hand, there is the proper love for one's wife and a family life; on the other, there is an insane desire for the signified, Woman. Afterwards, each one of the paled plurality can ask herself what she is to the storyteller: an Elizabeth or a powerful Beauty.

A text that describes writing and reading circa 1800 like no other could not have neglected the function of the feminine reader: let us return, then, to Hoffmann and "The Golden Pot." Tasso's two Leonoras, Goethe's two *Herzlieben*, and Christian's two women make clear this function in Hoffmann's tale. Aside from the One Woman in "The Golden

Pot," there is another woman who is simply one among many. Like the powerful Beauty, Serpentina possesses the gift of making the unreadable readable through her voice; she embodies the beloved muse who must precede all writing. An opposite position in the field of writing, however, is occupied by Veronica—a simple consumer who asks herself whether or not the fantasy of the library is a charade concerning the reciprocated love she desires.

When the dean and registrar touch upon Anselmus's prospects— which, thanks to Lindhorst's connections in the state, could include those of "a privy secretary or even court councilor"—the discussion leaves the bureaucrat's daughter Veronica with "a very special impression."[42] She immediately lapses into daydreaming. Whereas Gretchen could pluck the petals of an aster in the presence of her beloved ("he loves me, he loves me not"), her less fortunate sister has to guess about the absent Anselmus's affections. Of course, in daydream Veronica has no trouble retrieving one sure sign of love after another, until she finds herself Frau Court Councilor in an imagined future, living in a magnificent house on Dresden's Castle Street, or in New Market, or on Moritz Street and hearing every possible compliment from people on the street or from her husband Anselmus. The daydream culminates in an auditory hallucination, which— just as with Anselmus under the elder tree—unconsciously prompts her to speak aloud. This happens to be a classical symptom of mental disturbance, however.[43] "Are we having fits like Anselmus?" asks her father, the dean and philologist of ancient languages, who has been disturbed in his reading of Cicero. He says this without considering that he might be interrupting the composition of feminine nature poetry. But immediately the hallucination darkens; "it seemed as if a hostile figure was invading these beautiful visions" and spitefully insisting that Veronica would never become Frau Court Councilor, for Anselmus does not love her after all. "Tears almost welling in her eyes, she said aloud, 'Ah! it is only too true. He does not love me, and I shall never ever be Frau Court Councilor!' 'Romantic rot, romantic rot!' Dean Paulmann cried, and then, snatching up his hat and his cane, he indignantly and hurriedly left the house."[44]

On one hand, the "ah!," the minimal signified of poetic love; on the other hand, a repeated and more forceful disturbance of the bureaucrat's reading of Cicero, which finally enables that reader to say what, ah, happens to be true. When the sigh speaks nothing but its truth out loud, it is convicted of being an effect of reading. The clash is not between poetry and prose, a middle-class world and that of the Serapion brothers (whatever "world" might mean); rather, it is between two opposed techniques of reading in the same room. It is the simultaneity of the nonsimultaneous: the father (as if to confirm Rolf Engelsing's sociology of reading) practices

an intensive rereading, which educational officials semi-officially owe to
the treatise *De Officiis*; the daughter, meanwhile, reads the latest novels,
which in the discourse network of 1800 are written by "life."

It makes little difference whether someone like Anselmus reads his romance out of leaves that he cannot yet read, or whether someone like Veronica reads hers out of a romance that is still unwritten. By the end of
the fairy tale, at the latest, it will be available "written beautifully and
distinctly" by the narrator himself. Veronica prefigures Hoffmann's actual feminine readers much as the poet Anselmus prefigures Hoffmann. A
Poet and man might read about love without reading and speak out loud
without addressing any listener, but when a woman attains such spiritual
heights it is not the same. The difference lies in the unwholesome desire of
women to take everything *à la lettre* or *au pied de la lettre*. Veronica interprets the interpretive career that Lindhorst holds out to her beloved
quite literally as the prospect of a bureaucratic position. The old woman
Frau Rauerin used the same method to read in the name *Victor* (the fiancé of Veronica's friend) that man's imminent promotion to captain.[45]
The fact that such oracles tend to be accurate, given the new alliance concluded between the state and the educated class, makes this type of
woman's knowledge offensive. Instead of following hermeneutic detours,
it simply pronounces the name of the power they serve.

But Frau Rauerin reads in a magic mirror, whereas Veronica reads in
"The Golden Pot." The place of the old witch is taken by a young girl,
that of magic, by its historical, namely hysterical, parody.[46] When Anselmus, drunk with punch, roars "the green snake loves me for I have a
childlike nature and I have looked into Serpentina's eyes," Veronica is left
to sob "out her pain and sorrow on the sofa."[47] The woman's knowledge
in her has been demoted to the historically new feminine reading function; instead of conjuring and casting spells, it can only relive hysterically
the fantasies of the new authors. So Veronica fears she is not loved, "despite her blue eyes,"[48] despite the fact that it was blue eyes that individualized a Serpentina from the dance in the elder tree, and despite the fact
that Anselmus, faced with his spot of ink, has recognized that his library
muse is a phantasmagoric version of Veronica's voice. The real Veronica,
however, can only go on guessing what she is to Anselmus: a figure in a
double life in Dresden-Atlantis, or the dreary alternative to the Woman.
This riddle remains unsolvable, because by setting up the transcendental
signified, Woman, the polar definition of the sexes also distorts the signifier *man*. "What a man's essence might be, he simply doesn't know," as
Goethe knew. Thus men who read on their way to authorship have no
trouble locating a referent for any description of the Woman (they all
have a mother); but women who read cannot rediscover a man described

in the describing author. For "men, although they make the female sex the means and stuff of their speech," draw a veil over their own sex. Their sex remains "the one that writes and speaks and in so doing keeps silent about itself."[49]

Veronica will never learn whether Anselmus will have loved her or Serpentina and have become poet or bureaucrat—not even when, at the end of the fairy tale, Registrar Heerbrand appears and announces to Veronica that he has just been named court councilor and has the papers, *cum nomine et sigillo Principis*, in his pocket; or when, in consequence, he asks for her hand in marriage and so realizes her daydreams. For this ending (entirely appropriate to poetic ambiguity) makes two types of reading possible. According to one reading, which Veronica proposes, her beloved student Anselmus left her because of his love for the green snake Serpentina, who is "more beautiful and rich," leaving Veronica "to love and revere" the Councilor Heerbrand "as befits a true and faithful wife."[50] Just this type of reading would be recommended in text and illustration to elementary school students, a typical love story of the forked-tongued Poet of 1800.

The fairy tale's ending makes possible a second reading, proposed by Heerbrand. The fact that Anselmus left the foolish and shrewish Veronica because of his love for another writer's companion, a woman to whom his drunken images of women more readily applied, is "nothing but a poetic allegory, like a poem in which [Veronica] celebrates her final complete farewell to the student."[51] Anselmus is thus still present, but not as an idealized student-poet. With her renunciation, Veronica would have been simply taking to heart the second commandment in Schleiermacher's *Catechism of Reason for Noble Women*, which (as if to demonstrate the shift from Bible to primer) makes an erotic norm of the feminine reading function. "You should not create an ideal for yourself, neither an angel in heaven, nor a hero of a poem or novel, nor one dreamed-up or fantasized by yourself; rather you should love a man as he is. For Nature, your Mistress, is a strict divinity, one who will pursue the idle dreaming of young girls become women into the third or fourth generation of their feelings."[52]

To love a man as he is can only mean to love a state official. If Veronica's "romantic rot" has made the ideal author Anselmus out of a student, her withdrawal cure, prescribed by Nature, will make a student, as if by bureaucratic baptism, into a bureaucrat by the name of Heerbrand. According to Jochen Schmidt, the two men (like Tasso and Antonio) stand for *one* man.[53] In fact, if one adds a poetic first name without a last name, which would qualify one to be Serpentina's poet, to a middle-class family name without a first name, which would qualify one to be bureau-

In the first quarter [of Chodowiecki's Plate *L*] you see a well-educated young woman, who, with a mistrustful expression, refers her friend, a man who wanted to become her husband, to a passage in a letter, with stern criticism. A pair of finely bound books lie on the table. The man is a writer, and in a passage in his book he has described the advantageous qualities possessed by a certain person who resembles a young woman, their mutual friend, more than the man's sweetheart. The author has given a copy of the book to the friend a few hours earlier than he has to his sweetheart. The sweetheart has found out about this and becomes suspicious; she thinks the man loves her friend more than he does her, that he is carrying on a forbidden liaison with her, and that this passage in the book, which of course was written for the sake of the content, had been written in particular admiration of the friend. The man was wise enough to leave the foolish and shrewish woman. (Basedow, *Elementarwerk*, I: 149f.)

crat and bridegroom of Veronica, the sum would be the signifier *Anselmus Heerbrand*—just as a judge by the name of Ernst Theodor Wilhelm Hoffmann became, by baptizing himself, the poet Ernst Theodor Amadeus Hoffmann.

But the identity neither of A and A, Anselmus and Amadeus, nor of A. H. and A. H. are written down. Poets in the discourse network of 1800 write around their own writing; they do not write down the system itself. (When philosophers, by contrast, write the proposition of identity, A = A, it means merely, with the exclusion of all proper names, I = I.) The network produces linkages precisely at this empty slot. The empty slot does not point to extradiscursive facts, such as the much touted material basis; it simply programs the technical expansion of discourses. It does not arise because, as in the much-belabored philosophical argument, an autonym is always aporetic, but because it permits filling pages that for men remain fundamentally empty. The empty slot in poetic texts recruits feminine readers. The whole point of "The Golden Pot" is that its point, as discovered by Schmidt, transcends the text.

All the Veronicas who read Hoffmann's fairy tale could sharpen their hermeneutic skills on the puzzle of whether they would be a Serpentina or Veronica to Hoffmann. All the Ottilies who sought the "hidden" moral of *The Elective Affinities* were its ideal public.[54] To a man who criticized his novel for lacking any moral, Goethe replied that he hadn't written it for him; he had "written it for the young ladies."[55]

To write for the young ladies was a historical innovation. Richard Alewyn has shown how Klopstock's poetry, ignored by scholars, created a new public: the illiterate, the young, and above all women. Understanding, until then a specialized technique in the Republic of Scholars, became a psychic qualification that measured man in general and women in particular. "Not only is the ability to understand a poem now the criterion for a woman's value, but the effect of a poem on a woman reader or listener is also the criterion for a poem's value." In consequence, Klopstock, this *poète à femmes*, repeatedly read his own love story, which he had cunningly written into his *Messias*, to circles of charming, feminine Klopstock readers "surrounded at a distance by men."[56]

Gerhard Kaiser has argued that Tasso's tragedy is also that of his favorite feminine reader. "The modern dilemma of aesthetic existence seen in the Princess corresponds to the dilemma of the modern poet, the former being as much the cause as the effect of a vital weakness. In the Princess we see the rise of a new public for the new type of poet, a public that no longer looks to art for a transfiguration of what exists so much as it seeks the realization of what is nonexistent, the dawning of a utopia transcending the contradictions of reality."[57] Lacking a husband and child, the Princess seeks in Poetry a substitute for life; unlike Tasso, however, she does not transform this supplement into an objective work, she simply consumes it. "The Golden Pot" takes this hysterical trait in the feminine-reader function to an extreme, as its young lady sobs on the sofa. But this excess reveals the rule.

The discursive connections begun experimentally by founding figures like Klopstock and Goethe spread far and wide in 1800. In order to achieve "the most important reforms," or, in other words, "to work on a large scale," Poets would henceforth "educate and inspire young men and women."[58] Their texts, encoded so as to lead to the author, generated ever more authors-as-young-men, and, being written for young women, ever more feminine readers. The new crop of authors made the programmed move into the position of the author-hero; the feminine readers identified the author-hero with the author, and the ambiguous description of women with themselves. This bifurcation was necessary because the proliferation of authorship (as one of the first histories of German literature recognized) would mathematically eliminate male consumers. "We can assume that at present there are nearly fifty thousand men living in Germany who have written one book or more. If their number continues to increase at the same rate, it will be possible to prepare a register of all earlier and current German writers that would include more names than a register of all living readers." [59] More and more authors, however, pose a threat to the name of the author, which, unlike the personal pronoun, is supposed to anchor the referent to a man behind the discourse. The author's name would become as elusive as the shifter *I*. The threat was not limited to productive men, who always translated written texts back into subjectivity, that is, back into the shifter. The function of the feminine reader also labored under discursive conditions geared to an endless multiplication of authors. On the one hand, the god by the name of author was supported by the pleasure of women. But on the other hand, the more these names increased and substituted for life and love, the more vulnerable to substitution they became. One of the endings of "The Golden Pot" demonstrates this, as does the fact (somewhat more positively) that Goethe's *Correspondence with a Young Girl* breaks off immediately before the author Arnim's marriage to a young woman commenced.

The law that "governs both natures, in an intellectual sense as well as others," according to which "the woman puts to use what the man makes and procures," has a corollary: "Women, even the most educated, have more appetite than taste. They are attracted by whatever is new, and like to sample everything." [60] Thus a mode of consumption came into being that had disastrous consequences for the intended permanence of poetic writing and was an exact parody of the consumption practiced by aspiring poet-readers. Words that are merely sampled or merely devoured cannot endure. Unlike the works of elementary pedagogy, they are absorbed, not by the Mother's Mouth, but rather by small talk, gossip, and forgetfulness on the part of the many. This is the nosology of the much-discussed reading addiction circa 1800. Too-extensive reading robbed words of the stature necessary for a work to constitute an unshakable authority and have an unforgettable author. [61] Women were at the source of this danger, for they are "the half of the human race that by virtue of the duties consigned to them, have much more leisure than men, while their more lively spirit and active imagination only rarely and unwillingly dwell on serious matters."[62] Dean Paulmann therefore studies *De Officiis* for pedagogical purposes, while his daughter "fills her time reading such books as are suited to a woman's vivacity and more subtle feelings." In actuality, then, she reads novels that have yet to be written.

The symptoms of the feminine reading disease were clear, but therapeutic measures became delicate and controversial. Only the simplest measures assumed as a starting point that the new "automatic"[63] alphabetization would just as automatically cure the disorders it had brought about. "The reading mania is a foolish, damaging misuse of an otherwise good thing, a truly great evil which is as contagious as the yellow fever in Philadelphia. . . . It does nothing for the mind or the heart, because reading becomes mechanical. . . . One reads through everything without purpose, enjoys nothing and devours everything; there is no order to it, everything is read lightly and just as lightly forgotten, which is just as useful considering most of what is read."[64] The fact that fully mechanized reading makes the consumption of useless books forgettable is not enough to save the work of great authors. Thus the reading mania, a contagious evil and a parody of the programmed proliferation of Poetry, cannot be abandoned to natural healing powers. A whole new branch of physicians intervened as "friends and guardians of humanity";[65] as the title indicates, they were relatives of instructors of mankind and educational bureaucrats. Realizing that certain measures advocated by others (censorship, book banning, indexing of certain books and book channels)[66] would achieve nothing, because coercion only makes the addict mistrustful and fuels the addiction, the bureaucrats of discourse consumption found indirect and inconspicuous means more expedient. First, there was (to use Nietzsche's expression) an active forgetfulness rather than the merely natural, widespread variety. If all educated men, reviewers, and editors of literary periodicals would follow the "principle of *ignoring* bad products, they will not be read."[67] Second, (and this was decisive) was the contribution of hermeneutics.

Around 1800 there appeared, escalating the new primers' self-referentiality, the first books whose theme was the reading of books. Fichte, himself an early and painful case of reading mania,[68] planned off and on to publish "popular aids" intended to "make the art of understanding a work more accessible to the greater public."[69] Bergk did publish a more methodical work, *The Art of Reading, Including Information on Books and Authors*. A good Kantian, Bergk makes his therapeutic program the central concern of his book and mentions the conditions that caused him to write it only in passing at the end:[70] namely, the reading addiction in "Germany, where never has so much been read as now" and where women especially waste their time reading empty novels. Because "reading is dangerous if we bring to it a merely receptive rather than an active, productive mind,"[71] the philosophic aspect of the therapy (like reading and writing instruction) guards that productivity against all externality. "Our interiors must be the workshops in which we undertake all operations conducive to understanding a book. We must never lose sight of ourselves in order to maintain our presence of mind, lest we fall into distraction and from there into insanity."[72]

The insanity of distraction is thus driven out by that of a fixed idea: the reader-ego that must be able to accompany all my reading. The hero of the *Runenberg* is thus very up to date when he goes insane at the sight of a tablet covered with originary script. To ensure that all readers have his experience, hermeneutics needed only to add a technical rule to its philosophical principle. Thus, the fixation of the reader-ego is accompanied by a restriction to certain reading material.[73]

With that the art of reading is back where it started: the all-consuming reading mania. Bergk does concede that, particularly with "works of fine art, we can seldom bring ourselves to begin a second reading of a book whose content is known to us."[74] But because an autonomous ego and reading material can be distinguished only when an act of recognition or memory confronts the flow of appearances or newly appearing books, it is "of course better for us to read a work of art more than once."[75] Otherwise the sacred work of art could not exist.

Technically, then, the therapy for reading mania required intensive rereading, even under the conditions of an expanding book market. It was impossible to reread in the same way as before 1800, when people read and reread the Book of Books in the rhythm of the Church calendar. But one could reread in a new way, a way that replaced the Bible with Poetry and selected a loose group of classical works out of the flood of books in order to reread them until they became unforgettable. Hereafter, a multitude of common and thoughtless books produced according to the law of the marketplace will stand opposed to a few original and intelligent books, determined by the unity of the author and formed into the requisite unity of a work by autonomous, intensive rereading.

Possibly with these measures the art of reading overreached its therapeutic goals. The consumption of books is a danger if we bring to it a merely passive rather than autonomous mind. Yet, in a good Kantian manner, such receptivity is said to define women.[76] The sex most afflicted with the mania cannot be reached with the cure. Books on the correct method of reading even admit this. Jean Paul's *Lecture for and to the Reader*, more concerned with diagnosing the reader's "practical reading methods" than with therapy, addresses the reader directly, but the feminine reader indirectly, in its *Brief Afterword to the Foreword on Aesthetics.*

Dear reader, in order for you to make proper use of these priceless gifts, you need advice and instruction. Although you have been through preschool and after-school classes, through philosophic schools and royal academies, and have been in singing, dancing, and fencing lessons, a lesson in reading was never offered to you. . . . As for your wife, dear reader, namely, the feminine reader, her reading habits are ten times worse, but a hundred times less curable. Let us by all means leave her to do what she will—the silk scrap or thread may fall out of her book, or the open book on her lap may be turned upside down and shut by someone else, so that she won't know where she was. Or, for the sake of the story, she may begin with the Revelation of St. John and then read until she reaches Genesis and the creation—at least she will finish her book, and let that be sufficient for every-one. Indeed she will finish it sooner than a male reader, because she is not delayed by any sentences, to say nothing of words, that she doesn't understand; rather, more concerned with the whole, she will continue on. She owes this splendid habit at least in part to the conversation of men, where daily hundreds of tech-nical words from law and medicine and other areas fly by her, without anyone taking the time to explain them.[77]

For men and male readers, the failures of discourse-pedagogic institu-tions can be corrected. Jean Paul, a second Bergk, proceeds to open this reading school for them himself, a school that was entirely absent in the early modern system of corporeal training. But for feminine readers and women, there is only the knowing smile between the author and the reader. The feminine parody of hermeneutics is incurable, principally be-cause nothing written, not even Jean Paul's hermeneutics, can count as instruction for women. Open on the lap of a sleeping woman—in the dis-course network of 1800 that is the *degré zéro de l'écriture.*

Men are not entirely innocent in this merciless consumption of books by women, in this reading of the "whole" that is so complete no "sen-tences, to say nothing of words," survive. In this the afterschool aestheti-cian Jean Paul and the Bavarian school reformer Friedrich Immanuel Niethammer agree.

We have been persuaded to see education as knowledge itself, and imagine that a man is more educated to the degree that he has more knowledge in diverse areas. . . . Since then, polyhistory has become fashionable and so has placed an unavoidable demand on anyone who seeks to adopt the proper tone. The wisdom of the paperback book, the science of the magazine and journal have since be-come the order of the day: everywhere lectures for women and dilettantes are an-nounced; everyone reads and attends universities to become educated; and this love of education has become a national vice in the form of an insatiable lust for reading, which must always have something new to devour. . . . The pedantry of men used to be moderated by the natural and free spirit of women, but what hap-pens now? Are they not themselves in the grip of the worst possible pedantry, these feminine know-it-alls? Is it possible to escape the atmosphere of the study in their company? Are we still able to exchange our knowledge for the pure gold of natural feeling and unprejudiced judgment? Do they not pay us back now with our own paper currency? [78]

It makes little difference whether the women attending the new lectures held for them simply let the words fly by, as Jean Paul would have it, or devoured them, as Niethammer put it: their consumption first revealed that paper is only paper. The function of the feminine reader was thus coupled with the positive reality of texts in 1800. The proliferation of authorship had produced its own abuse. One might send women the latest paperbacks and almanach (as if to confirm Niethammer's argument), whose newness would stimulate the lust to read, and yet accompany such Greek gifts with a lecture for women (as if to ignore Niethammer) written against the misuse of reading.

Dearest Friend!
For some time I've had an almanach I meant to send to you lying on my desk, and now finally I'll forward it; I only hope that my delay will not have caused it to lose the charm of novelty. Yet this story is certainly good enough to be read from time to time, and in any case the beauty of a work of art is decided only by the pleasure of repeated contemplation—by the fact that one gladly returns to it. . . .
I don't know how it happens that I always find my way into generalized reflection on any topic; but you will forgive a man who once got a master's degree and has since dragged this title along with all its baggage, as if it were a messenger of Satan that pummeled him with its fists. . . .
Your sincere friend, Hegel [79]

If even the most reflective of philosophers succumbs to the pragmatic paradox of attempting to regulate a woman's reading by lecturing to her in magisterial style, then the therapy for women's reading addiction must have recourse to simpler and more direct measures. Hegel's demon drives him to make aesthetic reflections on the meaning of aesthetic reflection (the practice of intensive rereading as the technical method of constituting a work of art); the true M.A.'s, namely, the educational bureaucrats, came up with more elegant solutions. A teacher at a girls' school gladly gave those in his charge books to read, but only books he had selected. The reason was: "When those who write *for* women argue against *all* reading by women, they contradict themselves in the most ridiculous way—*their* writing ought to be read!" [80] Niethammer, a leading educational bureaucrat, was still more perspicacious in realizing that any attempt "to develop the *artistic sense* through the *theory of art*" would simply turn "art and the artistic sense into mere talking about art." [81] The necessary conclusion demanded that, prior to any aesthetic, anthologies of poetry be created to separate enduring works from the flood of books and to put a stop to the devouring reading mania. Anthologies present works in a manner that slakes any thirst forever. The canonization of German Poetry began with such didactic anthologies rather than with theories.

The anthology was invented as a didactic tool circa 1800. The "historical background of this didactic development," however, can only be attributed to "the rise of capitalistic mass production"[82] insofar as Poetry itself became alphabetically reproducible. Poetry anthologies only repeated in the repeatability of an institution, the new school, the command repeatedly to read "mostly Goethe and always Goethe," which Brentano gave to his sister. Women, instead of "eternally repeating what is already the case," which is called love, took their oaths by reading and rereading the German classics in secondary schools for girls. This was the reason for establishing the German classics. According to the most knowledgeable expert in the field, "the best of all available aesthetic readers"[83] was written by a teacher at a girls' school in Bremen. Betty Gleim was unsurpassed in deriving the basic theorems for her *Education and Instruction for the Female Sex* from Poets (Goethe, Schiller, Novalis). She was also unsurpassed in the degree to which her selection of poems, stories, and dramas adhered to the principle of "considering classicism especially, so that the experience of reading will also be one of forming taste."[84] And yet, as the rather sparse evidence available from girls' secondary schools suggests, Gleim's collection of classics represents a general tendency. In Caroline Rudolphi's school for women in Heidelberg, in the Hirschberg academy for women, in Blankenberg, in Goslar, and of course in Gleim's school for girls in Bremen, everywhere from 1792 to 1806 contemporary German poetry was put into the weekly lesson plan.[85] Tasso's Princess, the prototype of the new reading public, was mass produced. Countless girls followed the One Woman in the belief that Gleim's scholastic poetry reader transmitted to them: namely, that "only divine Poesy leads one into true, complete humanity. To view the world with poetic vision, to beautify life with ideal meaning and feeling, to carry the unearthly magic of the infinite into the prose of earthly life, this is what the educators of mankind should encourage."[86]

Not for nothing did Gleim's reader surpass all others in its adoration of Goethe. In the process of educating man- and also womankind, the Poet—particularly the poet who like no other "looked so deeply into woman's nature . . . as if the whole sex, from the most noble to the most common, had brought their confessions to him"[87]—returned to the source of his inspiration. A loop closed and the danger of the author's oblivion was banished. When educated young women read Goethe, they learned neither writing nor the talk about Poetry that horrified Niethammer—that is, they learned none of the discursive practices that would further multiply the multiplication of authors. The weekly lesson plan for Poetry, the canon of Poets, and the readers were geared exclusively to consumption. Even Rudolphi, a poetess, taught her girls none of the techniques of writing. She too limited her lessons in German to the reading, recitation, reception, and enjoyment of verse.[88] The discourse network of 1800 solved its "halting problem"[89] by having girls read in their classrooms.

As often happens with wishes, the young philosopher's wish—that his beloved should consider words more sacred than she had in the past and more often read with reverence in divine writings—was realized through institutionalization. Poets and thinkers could babble about the essence of Woman, while teachers at girls' schools would see that it was brought into existence. What "exalted poets always demand" is "for a start" only that "a woman go into a somnambulistic fit of delight over everything they say, that she sigh deeply, roll her eyes, and now and then have a little fainting spell, or perhaps go hysterically blind as a sign of the highest level of feminine femininity."[90] What the teachers at girls' schools do with this dream wish is assign the reading of Poets while forbidding any writing. "Once one recognizes the established difference between genius and taste, one will realize that practice in the fine arts should be recommended to girls for the formation of taste rather than for the creative power of genius."[91] With this philosophic-pedagogical insight, the schools would spend a century producing women who drank their fill of Poets' words with infinite enjoyment.

. . . and the Kingdom of God

The pleasure of women makes waves. In the year that Gleim's reader appeared, the Bavarian minister of education Immanuel Niethammer proposed to his superior *and* to his poet the project of creating not *a*, but *the* anthology. This was a megalomaniacal project, intended to cure the reading mania outright rather than begin the cure at specific institutions or with one sex; moreover, the cure was to be accomplished by committing Poetry entirely to pedagogy. "We have our national classics, but we do not know them; we read them, perhaps, but we do not learn them. The reading mania that has become a national vice of the Germans always demands something new, it devours the good with the bad."[1] The project was megalomaniacal because it pleaded for the absolute scholastic reader "just as we petition for the advent of the Kingdom of God."[2]

Indeed, the early romantics' lucid dreams of a unique historical opportunity to establish, following the state's dismissal of the Bible as an elementary reader, a new, but poetic Bible would have attained discursive reality in the One Reader of all German schools.[3] Niethammer, rather than Schlegel or Novalis, articulated this nexus. Only because "the Bible has ceased to be a unifying point for the education of all classes" and "can hardly be expected to attain that position again, given the kind of thinking now in ascendancy" was there "the need for a *National Book*."[4] The many anthologies that began to appear around 1800 were at once the scars and the bandages of this wound. How could people like Gleim, C. F. R. Vetterlein, or Friedrich Gottlieb Welcker save Germany? A poetic Bible cannot be assembled from "the abritrary choices and preferences" of individuals. The work must "be *classic as a collection* in order, by its inner value and external authority, to earn its position above all other arbitrarily produced collections," which means it must "unify the German nation in the use of the one classical collection either by free choice, or by an agreement that could easily be reached." In short, the poetic Bible would be "a gift of God."[5]

Therefore, God must write it. After recommending "only two men," Goethe and Johann Heinrich Voss, to his administration, Niethammer finally offered the project to Goethe alone. A reader that "is to attain classical authority can only be created by classical writers."[6] The school reformer had quite an exact understanding of private audiences in Weimar "on education and national culture, and in particular on the Bible and traditional books of the people"[7]—an understanding, that is, of the Faustian act. The age in which the unthinkable reduplication of the word *word* at the beginning of a gospel provided the ground and measure of all doctrine was past. An age had arrived in which the authorial act, that of writing *act* for *word*, placed the ground and measure of all doctrine in the unthinkable reduplication of authorship. If the one classical writer were to label his own works classics in the very personal act of selecting them for inclusion in the new poetic Bible, the etymology of the title *author* would become literal truth. The absolute "authority" required by Niethammer's pedagogy applied in 1800 only to words "accompanied by the name of an author."[8] A classical reader provided by the pen of a classical writer would not cease to inscribe/(ascribe) itself—the definition of necessity.

But the great deed failed. Goethe apparently did not understand Niethammer as profoundly as Niethammer understood him. His extensive preliminary work on the national book came down to two historical-empirical collections of texts rather than to a personal authorization of his own works; the collections, although quite substantial, fell short of the phantasm of the One Book.[9] In any case, "the episode" did more than demonstrate that "the prince of poets did not intend to stand before the school gates."[10] If he had entered with all due state-programmed ceremony and presented the secondary schools with the Kingdom of God, the discourse network of 1800 would have imploded. The institutionalized rereading by all students of "mostly Goethe and always Goethe," or the establishment of a litany to be memorized,[11] one that would be unquestionable because authorized by the master's word in the discourse of the master, would have eradicated all room for movement in the discourse of the university and the circuit of legitimation stretching to it from the secondary school.[12] Because the discourse network of 1800 existed through its hermeneutic recruitment of authors, even and especially a discourse of the masters must necessarily devolve on discretionary determinations of its selection, definition, and interpretation. The formation of a canon would have established a rigidly incontestable selection under Goethe's direction; under the direction of educational bureaucrats it became mere continuation. A number of different and uncertain canonizations appeared around the hole left by the non-appearance of one classic classical reader, and these became the constant, repeatedly renewed business of the schools.[13]

Thus Niethammer had to suffer and practice the arbitrariness that a gift from God was to have absolved. Not Goethe himself but the administrative chain of command put "Goethe's songs" as lyric poetry, *Hermann and Dorothea* as epic, and "Goethe's works" as drama into the lesson plans of the secondary schools in Bavaria.[14] Because these *General Norms* were contingent, despite their title, they could be removed at any time. By the time of Niethammer's successor in the educational bureaucracy, German classicism was no longer inscribed within the classrooms. Because the New High German texts (with the exception of the *Messias*) did not require the study required for older texts, Thiersch relegated the former to reading for the students' free time. With that Bavaria returned to a practice that was dominant in the other German states around 1800.[15]

While all young women at the higher schools had lessons in the reading, reception, recitation, and enjoyment of German poets, the young men in the gymnasiums became new humanists. It was deemed inappropriate for them "to dally with contemporary poets and writers during school time" and to enjoy German lessons "like a continuous holiday."[16] Future servants of the state were to be above pure consumption. Their free-time reading in German, encouraged and guided by newly founded school libraries, was to bear fruit. "The status of German in the lessons of the upper classes [was] significantly shifted" by the Prussian *Abitur*: the rhetorical circulation of texts in the old schools gave way to the "principal goal of a written essay prepared privately by the student."[17] This was the German essay. Johann Meierotto's plan in 1794 for a native-language canon of German writers for the secondary schools, though still titled a "Rhetoric," was designed to instill the ability "to prepare reports, deductions, legal opinions, and other documents" so necessary "to the administrative service of the state."[18] The *Abitur* essay of 1810 carried out this writing project. Gymnasium students who were to go on to universities "must be brought to the point where they can begin service as writers who command language."[19] From the time that "the state assumes the responsibility of ensuring that its citizens can write,"[20] the responsibility includes bureaucratic as well as poetic writing, Lindhorst as well as Anselmus. The topic of the German *Abitur* essay can be freely chosen and thus its theme can "never be merely factual," in that "the essay should give evidence of the development of the understanding and of the powers of fantasy."[21] Writing out fantasies puts "the whole individuality" of the student, "his innermost self, . . . into the hands of the teacher." Such is "the significance of the essay written in the mother tongue."[22]

German was not a central subject at the higher boys' schools, it was a surplus of the lesson plan. Gymnasium students—who sought out their native-language authors only in libraries during their free time, reflected on their private reading in personal reading journals (as they were encouraged to do),[23] and stored the imaginative power and individuality thereby produced until it could become productive in the *Abitur* essay— were doing their part in the discourse network of 1800. Because Goethe's anthology of Goethe texts did not exist, the individual student, through selection and interpretation, had to play the roles of reader, anthologist, and author in miniature.

None of the (old or new, laudatory or critical) statistics concerning curriculum planning since its invention circa 1800 have measured anything bearing on the difference between the sexes. The available, late figures do indicate, however, that the new subject German was at once the center of education for young women and the beyond for the education of bureaucrats. In the Prussian curriculum plan of 1810 for the gymnasium, German claimed "a quarter of [the time allotted to] ancient languages,"[24] 7 percent of language time in later plans at the gymnasium, and 10 percent of the course load in schools not aimed at preparing students for the university. The girls' schools, with 20 percent, included twice as much German.[25] The existence and reputation of German poetry may have owed a great deal to the other sex, but the publicly employed sex needed for its satisfaction an active mental life that reading could not offer, because public employment had come to include public writing.[26] In the pedagogically institutionalized difference between the sexes, girls' schools thus directed reading mania into the consumption of German classics by providing ample time in the lesson plan, whereas boys' schools directed reading into generalized essay writing by releasing it from the lesson plan. Humanistically educated future bureaucrats learned what works and authors are by studying the ancients.[27] German as a subject remained marginal in that, according to Schleiermacher, it transcended all school subjects. "Instruction in the German language is not merely language instruction but rather, in that the mother tongue is the immediate organ of the understanding and the general medium of the imagination, provides the occasion for everything the school can accomplish in the free and formal development of the mind, including all training for philosophy."[28]

In German as a subject in boys' schools, then, the philosophers of 1800 had what they wanted. German, like Poetry or the imagination a spiritual medium of all media, was in the gymnasium and yet beyond the gymnasium; it linked subject disciplines to private reading and to a science not taught at all in the gymnasium, but taught in universities. The chain of legitimation linked institutions of higher learning institutionally, and German linked them in particular subjects. Philosophers required of "Man" precisely such a process of augmentation from the gymnasium to the university. Bergk's art of reading educated readers in autonomous philosophical reflection; Friedrich Schlegel, the philosopher and artist, philosophized: "the artist should desire neither to rule nor to serve. He can educate and nothing more, and thus do nothing for the state but educate rulers and servants, nothing but raise politicians and economists to the level of artists."[29] And so it goes in German, when from a point beyond the state, where since Schiller neither rulers nor the ruled are supposed to exist, the free and formal development of the mind and the aesthetic education of mankind penetrate the future rulers and servants of precisely this state. For what philosophers called the raising of rulers and servants to the level of the artist was rewritten into entrance requirements by pedagogues like Niethammer. "It should become a legal requirement for entrance into the higher positions of state service, of administration, of legislation, of moral and religious education, and so forth—in short, of those positions directed toward the realm of ideas, that no one shall be admitted who has not been educated and legitimately certified in the domain of higher ideas."[30]

The old faculties in the Republic of Scholars became a civil-servant factory that produced, beyond the traditional elites of judges and priests, moral educators (in other words, teachers), who in turn formed elites, and so on. The new conditions of admittance made new qualification criteria necessary. Unlike the time when Faust, the ex-M.A., broke the cycle of reading, explication, and lecturing, the mere circulation of knowledge no longer constituted legitimation in the domain of higher ideas. Only by writing productively could one demonstrate that he was cultivated [gebildet] rather than simply erudite. One could not learn such writing from theory, however; it had to be learned from German Poetry, which had invented it in the first place. Johann Wilhelm Süvern's Prussian curriculum plan for the gymnasium placed "the study and development of great masterpieces of poetry and rhetoric" above all scholarship because such study promoted "the aesthetic sense and"—decisively—"the ability to present one's own thoughts."[31] Even more precise (and for that reason they read like a prophecy of today's state examination themes) were the questions that the state ideal of Bavaria put to its future crop of bureaucrats. "Is he capable of developing the spirit of any secular writer? Can he present his ideas clearly and completely in the mother tongue? What are his views of the writer? Can he analyze the writer philosophically and explain his relation to current philosophical trends? . . . How is his own style?"[32]

Present-day academic interpreters hardly notice the engima of a legitimation of *and* through literature.[33] They are still following rules decreed 170 years ago. Classical Poets achieve legitimation because they provide civil servants with the norm of their own legitimation, a "legitimation in the domain of higher ideas." It was a hermeneutic circle and a reciprocal means of establishing evidence.

The midpoint through which the two extremes, Poetry and the bureaucracy, had to pass in order to reach their respective conclusions was called philosophy. According to Schleiermacher, German breaks the boundaries of any subject matter because all preparation for philosophy enters into it. According to Süvern, the study of masterpieces in the gymnasium awakens philosophical spirits. Christian Daniel Voss argued in his *Essay on Education for the State as a Need of Our Time* that "every servant of the state ought to have achieved a thorough grounding and education in philosophy, in that he cannot be expected to find fulfillment, given his subordinate position, in the moral and cultural domain of the state; for every servant of the state has an essential need for spiritual freedom."[34]

The circuit of legitimation between German as school subject and philosophy at the university had institutional consequences. First, the philosophical faculty was emancipated: whereas earlier it had preceded the three important faculties as a simple propaedeutic, it now ranked as the highest faculty. "When, at the beginning of the nineteenth century, the preparation for all university studies was shifted to the gymnasium, the philosophical faculty, until then a general-education preparatory course for the three older faculties, attained an independent position. Along with the supervision of scholarly research, it had the particular responsibility of *preparing students for the teaching profession.*"[35]

Second, philosophy as a subject had to break the bonds of received ideas within its own faculty. Spirit became the new philosophical concern so that it could be freed in the new crop of bureaucrats. The philosopher H. F. W. Hinrichs could show, by direct reference to *Faust*, that universities served "state functions" and had their highest calling in a science that "cannot be considered a faculty in the ordinary sense, in that philosophy . . . is not limited to particulars, but rather raises what is particular in the subject matter of the other faculties to universality." [36] An explicit *Phenomenology of the Spirit* was not necessary for such spiritual emancipation and universalization. It was enough to alter philosophical discourse pragmatically, even if semantically it retained signifieds such as "I" and "knowledge." Fichte accomplished a reordering of rules of production and consumption in *The Foundation of the Complete Science of Knowledge*:

> The *Science of Knowledge* is so constituted that it cannot be communicated in any way by the mere letter, but must be imparted through the spirit; its fundamental ideas must be produced by the creative imagination of every person who studies it. It could not be otherwise in a science that returns to the very first foundations of human knowledge, in that the very enterprise of the human spirit proceeds from the imagination, and in that the imagination cannot be grasped except through the imagination. [37]

Faust sought "how one spirit speaks to another" ("Wie spricht ein Geist zum andern Geist"; 425) as he opened the manuscript by Nostradamus. Fichte's answer is that it occurs through the *Science of Knowledge*, or as philosophy. Out of the simple propaedeutic in the Republic of Scholars came, once the emphasis had been shifted to Spirit, a "matter [concerning] the whole of man," [38] infinitely noble, but also infinitely difficult. Anyone who simply writes using letters of the alphabet can no longer be considered a philosophical author, nor can anyone who simply reads receive philosophy. In the discourse network of 1800, what distinguished philosophy was its maximization of all the postulates of autonomy characteristic of the new art of reading and its establishment of alphabetization-made-flesh or "imagination" as an admissions requirement. Thus an inescapable, double-connection was established between Poetry and philosophy. On the institutional level, the chain of legitimation linking German as a school subject with philosophical study at the university corresponded to the reception of philosophical texts through the creative imagination as it was practiced on the basic level of reading. Thus Kleist, quite unfaithful to the letter of the scholarly-republican philosopher of Königsberg, read Kant until a crisis point that had very little to do with philosophy but much to do with narrative perspective. And thus Novalis, quite faithful to the letter of the letter-despising Fichte, read, excerpted, commentated upon, and finally by creative imagination so transformed the *Science of Knowledge* that reading philosophy veered into writing novels.[39] But according to Fichte himself precisely this path from the German essay to authorship is the only one worthy of man:

Always *to read*; to follow another's train of thought; to make one's mind the receptacle of nothing but foreign and not always similar thoughts; this can be tiring, it slackens the soul and lulls it with a certain indolence. But there is no happier way of interrupting the stagnation thus induced in the human spirit than the development of one's own thoughts. . . . There is certainly no greater spiritual pleasure for those capable of it than that which one experiences through, or during, writing itself, and which . . . would remain so even in a world where no one read or heard of anything read. One then returns to reading with a sharpened mind, puts oneself more confidently and subtly into the spirit of the author; one understands him more accurately and judges him more thoroughly, and one is no longer intimidated by the man whose nimbus fades and has become our own. Certainly no one can completely understand a writer and feel himself his equal who is not already in some sense a writer himself.[40]

The clear implication is that, in the writing of the *Science of Knowledge* as well, the imagination had surpassed all letters. For free writing that cannot be intimidated by any established author is, according to Schlegel, the very determination, and according to Fichte, the highest pleasure "of man." Not for nothing was the *Science of Knowledge* subtitled "manuscript" [*als Handschrift*]. It was at once the provisional arrangement and the triumph of a new type of thought production. Indeed Fichte, all too rapidly promoted from farm boy in Lausitz to tutor, then from tutor to professor, had nothing at all to present when his first lectures at the university in Jena were announced. At the time of the Republic of Scholars a lecture meant paraphrasing a standard text possessed by the professor and his students. "Even in the early eighteenth century a 'textbook' was still defined as a 'Classick Author written very wide by the Students, to give Room for an Interpretation dictated by the Master, &c., to be inserted in the Interlines' (O.E.D.)."[41] Such interpretation in the lexical sense, however, would be beneath the dignity of a philosopher who had oriented production and consumption to the creative imagination and productive writing. In full consciousness of the great historical moment, Fichte laughingly dismissed the old-European, endless circulation of books. "Now that there is no longer a single branch of science that is not represented in a surplus of books, one nonetheless still feels obligated *to republish* this whole world of books through the university, and to have professors *recite* what lies *printed* on the page for all to see."[42]

Whereas Kant, a transitional figure, played the double game of lecturing on an outdated ontology and writing its critique, the new philosophy shortcircuited production and consumption. Fichte accomplished an act as revolutionary as that of Faust. Realizing that reading and particularly lecturing can indeed be tiresome, Fichte did not base his first lecture source on a textbook or the work of other philosophers; rather, he lectured on his own book. There was, however, a small problem: because he had yet to make up his mind on all his deductions,[43] he had to produce his own textbook from hour to hour and have it appear at the same rate. "At least three sections" of the *Science of Knowledge* appeared each week during the semester and were given to Fichte's students—and to Goethe.[44]

Such was the provisional and triumphant beginning of a new epoch in philosophy: the literary. A lecturer who wrote the material on which his own lectures would be based became an author in the fullest sense of the word in 1800. A writer who published arguments without knowing quite how he would be able to support them in the next publication mimicked the new freedom of Poets, who could simply write on and wait until the moment of rereading to come to corrections, consciousness, and coherence.[45] Where previously the printing presses and professors simply republished the whole world of books, the author-ego (to use his favorite term) Fichte published himself. In the same year, 1795, his essay *On the Spirit and Letter in Philosophy* announced to the reading public that an aesthetic drive—an inner, molding, and shaping force—was by no means particular to Poets, but distinguished philosophers as well, who heeded the creative imagination rather than the mere letter.

There was thus something of a scramble for the central position in the discourse network of 1800, where the "whole man" wrote for the "whole man." Poetry claimed it and so did philosophy; a conflict resulting from the competition seemed unavoidable. One poet's initial reaction to Fichte's essay signalled the collision. As editor and publisher of the journal *The Horai* Schiller declined to publish *On the Spirit and Letter*, not only because the essay contradicted his own *The Aesthetic Education of Man*, but for the principal reason that philosophy must not compete with German Poetry. Schiller bluntly replied to Fichte's assessment of the reception they would both have from future readers:

One hundred or two hundred years from now, when new revolutions will have occurred in philosophic thinking, your writings will certainly be cited and judged according to their merit, but they will no longer be read; this is as much in accord with the nature of the matter as the fact that my writings . . . will not be *read* any *more frequently*, but certainly not any *less frequently* than they are at present. And what might be the reason for this? The reason is that writing that has its value only in the results it obtains for the understanding, as excellent as these results may be, becomes superfluous to the degree that the understanding eventually determines that the results are indifferent to it, or discovers a more expeditious path to the same results; but writing that produces effects independent of its logical content, and in which an individual gives living expression to himself, can never become superfluous, for it contains an ineradicable principle of life, in that each individual is single and therefore irreplaceable and inexhaustible.

Therefore, dear friend, as long as you provide nothing more in your writing than what can be attained by anyone who knows how to think, you can be sure that another will come after you and say it differently and better. . . . But this cannot occur with work produced by the imagination. I admit that now and in the future much, perhaps the best, of what I have written can be communicated only with difficulty, and to some not at all. . . . But it is equally certain that the greatest part of the effect produced by my writing (whether among the few or the many) is of an *aesthetic* nature, and thus the effect is secured for all following ages in which the language of the author is understood.[46]

This is one passionate reply to Fichte's proposition that spirit in philosophy and spirit in the fine arts are related like two species of a single genus.[47] According to the poet, only the aesthetic treatment of aesthetic themes, not the aesthetic treatment of speculative themes, guarantees immortality. Men of words secure their territory by such self-referentiality. Far from counting only on the higher levels of literary theory, the irreplaceable individuality of the author is a bone for which poets and philosophers contend on the battlefield of public reception. The historical moment's force lines are inscribed in this battlefield. The sorry fate that Schiller predicts for Fichte's reputation amounts to the observation that under the conditions of an expanding book market, someone who first publishes in a factual field in which others will continue to publish will easily be forgotten. The order of discourse euphemistically named "reading mania" by its contemporaries spelled failure for the philosophers' longing for authorial fame while promising success to the strategy of Poets. Thus Schiller attacked his rival with the latter's own arguments. For Fichte promised that only productive writing in the spirit of the German essay would lead to understanding of the author one was reading and beyond: namely, that the author from whom one's own writing proceeded would lose his nimbus and no longer intimidate. With the same logic the Poet prophesies that the Thinker will be forgotten in one or two hundred years.

The two hundred years are almost up, but among the remaining readers "Fichte" still intimidates just as much as "Schiller." The prophet overlooked something because he left something out: his own essay, with which Fichte was not allowed to compete in *The Horai*, was indebted to the *Science of Knowledge*, just as his poet's letter on the ephemerality of philosophers owed much to the philosopher Humboldt.[48] Given that philosophy circa 1800 had anything but a one-sided, parasitic relationship to Poetry, the two discourses did not cancel each other out. Fichte and Schiller soon put their conflict behind them. Fichte's demand that speculative and aesthetic writing be on an equal footing was withdrawn in a conciliatory gesture by Schelling and others, in that they had philosophy issue into Poetry and Nature only at the end of its worldwide odyssey. More fundamental than the momentary flare-up of 1795 was a systematic connivance of both discourses, a game of give and take in which each stabilized the other and both endowed one another with the desired "effect for all following ages."

> To the Absolute:
> A toast!
> With kindest regards,
> the Ur-Phenomenon.

In a greeting written in his own hand, inscribed in a copy of his *Theory of Colors* sent to Hegel,[49] Goethe celebrates that connivance. The indissolubility of poetic Ur-phenomena and the complete dissolution, referred to as the Absolute, do not coincide, but neither do they collide with one another; they are separated *and* linked as sender and receiver. The words with which the poet greeted the thinker were not accidentally accompanied by a drinking glass from Carlsbad, not just because the glass illustrated certain properties of color. Beyond any scientific study, goblets are for drinking. Goethe's toast, like grace before dinner, offers his own poetic corpus for consumption—a consumption quite different from that of reading-addicted women, of course, for it would respect or even heighten what was unthinkable or inexhaustible in Ur-phenomena. The toast invites the philosopher to interpretation, not reading.

When philosophy became literary around 1800, the event affected Poetry itself. In the "intellectual work of art," the "poetic work of art" acquired a new addressee.[50] Poetry did not cease to be written for young women and their directed reading. But because reading cannot sufficiently do justice to author-individuals, the distribution rules provided for another channel by which works could attain philosophical treatment and thus acquire a certificate of inexhaustibility.[51] The literary philosophy of 1800 became interpretation.

There is testimony, and not just any testimony, to this innovation. The tragedy *Faust*, which, upon completion, as if to put all the rules of poetic production into operation, would run from a starting point in the minimal signified "oh" to the transcendental signified of the Eternal Feminine, appeared in 1790 [as *Faust, ein Fragment*] to a rather cool reception. "The important philologist Heyne, Wieland, Schiller's childhood friend Huber, and Schiller in his prephilosophical period were critical and reserved."[52] The multiplication of authors programmed by a discourse network is, of course, not exactly the most favorable environment for singular works. For this reason a feedback link was added to the program.

Philosophers constituted its final control mechanism, and it converted authors like the mature Schiller to philosophy and *Faust*. Indeed,

all significant representatives of classical German philosophy, Fichte, Schelling,
and Hegel, received the [*Faust*] fragment enthusiastically and immediately recognized its importance as universal poem. And this reception was by no means limited to the leading figures of the philosophical revolution, for it soon spread
throughout the younger disciples of the movement. When Goethe talked with the
historian Luden in 1806, the latter talked about the feeling concerning the *Faust*
fragment that prevailed among those reading philosophy during his student
years. According to Luden the students of Fichte and Schelling would say things
such as the following: "In this tragedy, when it is finally completed, the spirit of
the whole of mankind will be portrayed; it will be a true image of the life of mankind, encompassing the past, present, and future. In Faust mankind is captured in
its essence; he is the representative of humanity.[53]

Georg Lukács has reason to applaud his forebears, for they founded
all the interpretive techniques that refer interwoven words to a single and
universal "man." When the production and consumption of philosophical books demand "the whole man," then the philosophical interpretation of works must also proceed toward this essence. Otherwise they
would remain philological critique, scholarly commentary, or subjective
judgments of taste—in other words, secondary texts of the old and outmoded variety. They would never be able to prove that *Faust* was the
"universal poem" or (what amounts to the same thing) "the one absolutely philosophical tragedy."[54]

Speculative extrapolation, which could discover the whole course of
history in a fragment and anticipate unwritten endings, led to the reciprocal stabilizing of Poetry and philosophy. In the *Aesthetic Lectures on
Goethe's Faust*, which Hinrichs, a student of Hegel and philosopher in
Heidelberg, held in the winter semester of 1821–22, the demonstration
that Goethe had written *the* philosophical tragedy provided at the same
time a *Contribution to the Scientific Judgment of Art*.[55] Hegelians could
thus hold out the goblet that justified their dipsomania to the enemies of
philosophic poetry consumption (which, as usual, was called science).

The fact that Goethe's fragment was received coolly by poets and enthusiastically by thinkers does demonstrate something. *Ulysses* was not
the first instance in which Poetry became "a production industry for a
reception industry" of equal professionalism.[56] Not only "borderline
cases," such as Schlegel or Novalis, contributed to the immediate contact
between Poetry and philosophy, whose proclamation of eternal truth is
justifiably questionable.[57] Rather, the discourse network of 1800 formed

the configuration that established in Western Europe a new relation among (say)
literary production, positive law, and the critical institutions of evaluation, preservation, archiving, and legitimation by founding and awarding titles—every-

thing, then, that has its particular place and form in the *universitas*. The model of the university, within whose borders we in the West work—more or less well for some time still—was . . . established in the moment of (or in relation to) the inscription of the fundamental rules that regulate the ownership of works, the rights of authors, of republication, translation, etc. . . . This event had an essential, inner, and decisive bearing upon what others would call the inmost inner production of literary and artistic forms in general.[58]

The configuration is as obvious as it is overlooked. An investigation entitled *The Origin of Art as a Middle-Class Institution*[59] considers it unworthy of mention. Court ceremony in Saxony-Weimar-Eisenach, the situation of the artisans, the Protestant rectory—all have been illuminated by the social historians of German Poetry. But the new universities, culminating in philosophy, are taboo. The temple in which they, too, continue to celebrate remains unnamed.

German idealism, with its social locus in "Germany's higher schools and universities,"[60] made German Poetry into universal and university Poetry. There was no media-technical divide in 1800 between "higher" and "lower" forms of literature, but *Rinaldo Rinaldini* was mentioned in diagnoses of reading mania, whereas *Faust* was the subject of philosophy lectures. Fichte wrote one of the essays that led to the codification of authors' copyrights; Schelling, as if to prepare the return of his philosophy to literature, came up with the antiquarian and speculative dates out of which—they were unavailable to lay readers and so could only be professionally decoded—came the "Classical Walpurgisnight";[61] Hegel furnished evidence for his dictum concerning the absolute philosophical tragedy. Philosophy, in the discourse network of 1800, was the title-founding and -awarding legitimation of Poetry. Goethe's toast was one of thanks.

The absolute Spirit raises the goblet to its lips—and "its infinity foams forth from the chalice of this realm of spirits."[62] It was a thirst that grew as it was quenched and a stream that became more inexhaustible as it was consumed: German Idealism found at once desire and fulfillment in German Poetry. When Hegel's absolute Knowledge, having come home at last to its philosophical beyond, looks back at all the phenomenal forms of Spirit that have carried it along on its ascending journey, it sees them as a "gallery of images" and the transversed "realm of spirits" as therefore an aesthetic realm. Thus when the god or philosopher wishes to express this highest knowledge, verses of German classical Poets come to mind. The verses that sign and seal *The Phenomenology of Spirit* are not cited, however, nor have they been looked up—"recollection, the *inwardizing* of that experience, has preserved" them.[63] Otherwise, it would read "chalice of the" realm of spirits rather than the "chalice of this realm of spirits" and the author's name "Schiller" would stand under the correct quotation from the poem "Friendship." Two minute deviations, but they are evidence enough that philosophy circa 1800 is based on completed alphabetization (which is why it "inwardizes" rather than reads Poets) and constitutes a free-interpretive continuation of texts (which is why the name of the author cannot intimidate).

The goblet that the Absolute receives from Poetry in order to drink itself into infinity does not contain mere water. According to a Poet, the *Foundation of the Complete Science of Knowledge* should have been called the *Complete Guide to Drinking*.[64] Hegel thanked Goethe with the promise that he would peer into the Ur-phenomenal only while drinking wine.[65] Like the animals Hegel mentions, thinkers are also initiates in the Eleusinian mysteries: given the supplementary sensuality offered them by poetry, "they fall to without ceremony and eat it up." Because philosophic truth is "the Bacchanalian revel in which no member is not drunk,"[66] hardly one among all the quotations in the *Phenomenology* taken from Goethe, Schiller, Diderot, and Lichtenberg remains true to the letter of the text. When Friedrich Schlegel describes to his brother his reading of Hamlet, how he had grasped the "spirit of the work" behind every "husk," the reason for the disloyalty to the letter comes out. "I have nothing more to say to you about Hamlet for now; of course there is much more to be said, but that would mean I would have to read it once more, and that would disturb me too much."[67]

An interpretation that seeks the Spirit or Man behind every word is not a reading. It remains unconstrained by the therapeutic requirement of rereading in order to become itself as free as its *interpretandum*. Faust's style of translating infected his descendants. That is why the system function of philosophical "re-collection" (so vastly different from memory) is so easy to overlook. If every discourse network fundamentally requires some means of storage, the network of 1800 invented an archive in which the data, instead of being solely accessible as such, as in ROMs (Read Only Memories), could always be altered. But precisely because it functioned as RAM (Random Access Memory), philosophy in 1800 was safe from the most acute of all threats: that of becoming superfluous. In a philosophical history of the whole world of books, one that made a rigorous distinction between a past epoch of scholarly feuilletons devoted to literature and an "age of the science of reason" that had just begun, Fichte explained how the science of reason altered the method of archiving scientific and poetic authors.

In order to demonstrate our necessity, we must do something that the other either has not been able to do, or has not been able to do without accomplishing a particular task of which we have relieved him. We cannot tell our reader for a second time what the author has already said once; the author has said it and the reader has many ways of finding this out from him. But what the author does not say, through which he arrives at all his writing, can be imparted to the reader. We must discover what an author himself *is* inwardly, for this can remain hidden from his gaze; we must discover the particular means by which he develops his style—in short, we must elicit the *Spirit* from the letter.[68]

Philosophy avoids becoming a superfluous leftover by swallowing up authorial leftovers, down to the last word. Random access also implies the absolute and arbitrary right to scan and select. A discourse would become superfluous only if (according to Fichte) it republished the whole world of books or if (according to Schiller) it merely provided results. But the individual irreplaceability that Poets claim becomes the *interpretandum*; a paraphrase as distant from the letter of the text as Faust's is "said" by the soul that the author cannot speak (because otherwise it would be simply language), which is nonetheless his "being," because it brought him to everything he says in his work. The noble question τί ἐστίν ("what is it?"), asked of the cosmos by the Greeks and of God by the monks, was asked in German Idealism of the author.

We return to Goethe and to *Faust*. What would an author of an absolute philosophical tragedy never have said? Only this: that Faust, rather than being simply a depressive scholar in the Republic of Scholars who was on the threshold of a new science of reason, represents Self-Consciousness outside all place and time. But that is exactly what Hegel's interpretation claims; for the first time in the history of philosophical evidence and proof, it raised a fictional hero to the same level as Robespierre or a slave owner of antiquity. In the tragedy, Mephisto characterizes his companion:

> Verachte nur Vernunft und Wissenschaft,
> Des Menschen allerhöchste Kraft,
> Laß nur in Blend- und Zauberwerken
> Dich von dem Lügengeist bestärken,
> So hab' ich dich schon unbedingt—
> Ihm hat das Schicksal einen Geist gegeben,
> Der ungebändigt immer vorwärts dringt. . . .
> Und hätt' er sich auch nicht dem Teufel übergeben,
> Er müßte doch zu Grunde gehn!

> Have but contempt for reason and for science,
> Man's noblest force spurn with defiance,
> Subscribe to magic and illusion,
> The Lord of Lies aids your confusion,
> And, pact or no, I hold you tight.—
> The spirit which he has received from fate

Sweeps ever onward with unbridled might, . . .
And were he not the Devil's mate
And had not signed, he still must perish. (1851–57, 1866–67)

In *The Phenomenology of the Spirit*, the Spirit elicited from the letter says, citing freely as always:

Es verachtet Verstand und Wissenschaft
des Menschen allerhöchste Gaben—
es hat dem Teufel sich ergeben
und muß zu Grunde gehn.

It despises intellect and science
The supreme gifts of man
It has given itself to the devil
And must perish.[69]

"It," namely "Self-Consciousness," and "he," namely Faust, M.A.—this is the difference between the Being and text of an author. German Idealism legitimized German Poetry by rewriting its phenomena as a λόγος and its heroes as a Spirit. Consequently all names disappear from the archive, *Faust* no less than *Goethe* or *Schiller*. What remains behind is only a gallery of pictures in which the portraits (the discourse network of 1800 does not write down individuals) all represent Man in his world-historical and "pedagogical" development.[70] It is the apotheosis of the educational bureaucrat.

Now the one particular incarnation of the one Educational Bureaucrat—who was otherwise known as Faust, but who in the Kingdom and gallery of God is henceforth "Self-Consciousness, which . . . knows itself to be *reality*"—makes the mistake of plunging into life. Disdaining science, Faust finds for himself the "ripe fruit" of a "natural consciousness or one developed into a system of laws," otherwise known as Gretchen. At which point philosophy can only note that "the pleasure enjoyed has indeed the positive meaning that self-consciousness has become objective *to itself*; but equally it has the negative one of having reduced *itself* to a moment."[71] In the orgasm, then, Hegel sees Mephisto's oracle of destruction fulfilled and substantiated. Orgasm is forbidden, so that philosophy may exist. The highest pleasure for children of the earth (contrary to Goethe) is still the personality and not its negation. Being, as always, one more negative experience the richer, the Spirit leaves its incarnation in Faust and proceeds to the next, whose bureaucratic ethos includes "the universal of law *immediately* within itself."[72]

It is no accident that this interpretation in terms of Spirit calls on an authority that is already Spirit. The name of Hegel's chief witness for Faust and Gretchen, *Pleasure and Necessity*, is Mephisto. But for a thinker who admittedly dragged his title as M.A. around with him like a demon, it matters little that this Spirit had characterized himself in the unquoted portion of the text. If Mephisto's autonym "spirit of deceit" had not been left out, the interpretation of Faust would stand in the dark shadow of the man from Crete who said that every Cretan lies. But a science that would turn disdain for science into pleasure, and pleasure into necessity, must cite cunningly. It must overlook its own name wherever it happens to appear.

Hegel lied. Of all the candidates that could stand in for "Self-Consciousness," not one perishes or is destroyed: not Faust or Mephisto any more than Goethe or Hegel. Their careers fill libraries. Only Gretchen goes down, in that she is merely "natural consciousness" and, in accordance with her "true concept," an "object of pleasure."[73] But what is the death of a woman in the world-historical-pedagogical path from sense certainty to philosophy, from alphabetizing elementary instruction to the highest faculty of universities? The *Phenomenology* does not close accidentally with the poem "Friendship" as a way for the god or philosopher to express his pleasure in the poets that preceded him. Like the relationship of Aristotelian friends, who love the good in one another insofar as they love God's highest goodness, the friendship between German Idealism and German Poetry is also homosexual. Sexual difference doesn't count.[74]

The evidence for this is provided by the most natural consciousness with which Knowledge starts out: sense-certainty. It poses for the *Phenomenology* its very first object or interpretive theme.

The question must therefore be considered whether in sense-certainty itself the object is in fact the kind of essence that sense-certainty proclaims it to be; whether this notion of it as the essence corresponds to the way it is present in sense-certainty. To this end, we have not to reflect on it and ponder what it might be in truth, but only to consider the way in which it is present in sense-certainty. It is, then, sense-certainty itself that must be asked: "What is the *This*?" If we take "This" in the twofold shape of its being, as "Now" and as "Here," the dialectic it has in it will receive a form as intelligible as the "This" itself is. To the question: "What is Now?", let us answer, e.g., "Now is Night." In order to test the truth of this sense-certainty a simple experiment will suffice. We write down this truth; a truth cannot lose anything by being written down, any more than it can lose anything through our preserving it. If *now, this noon*, we look again at the written truth we shall have to say that it has become stale.[75]

Knowledge, then, is sensual long before it is called Faust, and its object, long before it is called Gretchen, is night. All the truth on earth is put down on paper and reads

---
Now is Night

If we look at Hegel's example again, on this Monday before Lent, 1981, we will have to admit that it is not an example. Philosophy necessarily starts out during a night "in which all cows are black"[76] and in which all women are confounded. Before the law of truth is written down and so becomes the state, it is a νόμος ἄγραφος ("unwritten law"): a law that is not "above ground and in the light of day," but rather "in weakness and darkness." Because they are familiar with the subterranean regions, as Antigone is familiar with her grave, women rule on behalf of the law. Such is the care with which Hegel reads "the most magnificent and satisfying work of art,"[77] the Sophoclean tragedy, in order to be able to forget it again in writing his own tragedy. He neglects to mention that the night of the senses is also called woman. And yet the chapter on *Antigone* and ethics (with the subtitle *Man and Woman*) stands in a relation of rigorous homology to the chapter on sensuality. An unwritten word also marks the beginning of the unwritten scene of writing that is the whole *Phenomenology*. Sense-certainty, like women in Greece, also knows nothing but night. The night must be destroyed, as Antigone is by a decree of the state; but the decree, which begins all dialectical progress, is issued by philosophical writing itself.

A question of feigned innocence marks the beginning of the end of night. The philosopher (who, like his reform-pedagogical comrades in arms, wishes to lead no one around by the nose) poses the question of time. But the ontologist's lips magically transform "this" into "the This" and "now" into "the Now," so that the question "What is the Now?," impossible among ordinary speakers, must receive the equally impossible answer "The Now is Night." A more clever answer would have been no answer at all. But once Hegel is given an inch, he can proceed to his "simple experiment." Standing at a modest distance has paid off; the servant of the state now shows his concerned, overseer's face. The sentence spoken for the record is put into the record—but not without the formulaic concession that writing something down is an act without consequences for truth, or in other words is not an act at all. Such is the logic of a discourse network that never quite drops the pretense of not being a discourse network. But what sees the light of proverbial day twelve hours later is the fact that writing and archiving are concrete discursive practices and are fatal to truth. In RAM philosophy nothing that people have said is correct any more.

This is not because the night of sense-certainty—according to Hegel—is nonexistent, but because his own writing destroys something spoken. The night has done its duty, which consists in getting men to speak and philosophize; it can now dawn. Hippel's quip, that one should learn speaking from women and writing from men, became true. The ostensible observer, who wanted to let the subject and object of the senses *be*, throws off his mask and steps into the truth of his bedeviled M.A. degree: a teacher of reading and writing like Friedrich Eberhard von Rochow, Pöhlmann, Johann Christian Dolz, Stephani, and Lindhorst.

Rochow's *Child's Companion*, the first literary primer, tells its beginning readers the sad story of Farmer Hans. He lent money to a city slicker, but being illiterate he accepted meaningless scribbling instead of a proper receipt and therefore never saw his money again. Belatedly convinced of *The Usefulness of Reading and Writing*, Hans immediately sent his children to elementary school.[78]

At the beginning of the system of higher education—and *The Phenomenology of the Spirit*, as a preparation for philosophy, is nothing else—there thus stands a reprise or reflection of the system of elementary education.[79] The discourse network of 1800 centered on the question of how the most rustic, natural, or sensual consciousness could be made to see the importance of reading and writing. Anyone who only speaks or hears will necessarily be cheated—by those who can write, like middle-class citizens, or by hollow truths like the night. Thus only the reverse deceit will work. Anyone who learns to believe that writing and reading are innocent and necessary has already passed the point of no return and taken the first step into the Kingdom of God. Reading, as the stoic Zenon was once told by Pythia, reading means having intercourse with the dead.

Whereas Poetry, as midpoint in the classical discourse network, procured its medial pleasures or the leap into pure signifieds, the two extremes, elementary instruction and philosophy, dealt with writing in its materiality. The false receipt is effective as a signature, and the recorded sentence at the beginning of philosophy is effective as a date.[80] Thus both discourses played with the linking of writing and power. But because pedagogy spoke so vaguely about "*these children*" and "this *mother*,"[81] in order to trap all children, just as philosophy legitimized the translation of "this" into "the This," any possibility of the signature has already been sublated. After canceling speaking and dating, the *Phenomenology* can bring on the forms of Spirit like the successive pictures in a gallery, just as Poetry could let its film roll. All that remains of the conspiracy between writing and power is the fact of its having been brought about. The writer Hegel can forget it for that reason and thus go out after readers.

"The Now is Night" must be read twice to be falsified. The iteration does not involve the two moments of writing and of refutation. Of course, the law of the dark allows for writing, but not reading—as evidenced by the poetic freedom of 1800. Night, woman, and speaking go together like day, philosophy, and writing. Thus the night is not a mere example and the successive moments of reading and writing are irreversible. The recorded sentence produces its two possible readings only in the light. The first, insipid reading takes it as meaning simply a particular time marked by the adverbial "now," the other, speculative reading as determining the essence of the similarly named, but substantive category. In the first case the sentence is false during the day, but was once true; in the second case it is entirely false, because categories cannot be dated. They can only take predicates, which exceed the subject of the sentence in generality and in so doing "destroy" it. That is precisely Hegel's theorem of the speculative sentence and his practice in refuting the night.[82]

There is something very simple to both theory and practice here. What is true can no longer be inscribed in a single sentence, which can now figure only as an element in a larger speculative movement, or, in other words, in a book. Philosophy owes its raison d'être to the refuted night. At the same time, what is true can no longer be read in a single reading. As a network of speculative sentences filling a book, it escapes all reading mania and forgetfulness. Hegel's cunningly constructed requirement of "returning to the sentence and understanding it differently" is of course the reason "that in such circumstances, in order that the thought expounded might be fathomed, no advice can be given other than to read the book twice."[83] Consequently the writer of philosophy owes to the refuted everyday sentence his rescue from a danger clearly immanent in the discourse network of 1800: he, too, could be as gracelessly consumed and disposed of as the philosophy texts of old Europe were by a book of his own entitled the *Phenomenology*.[84] But philosophemes that contain two possible readings and thus must be read repeatedly become just as unforgettable as (according to Schiller) poetry alone.

The philosopher thus exults victorious after the final refutation of "thisness." Lovers of the sensual, no matter what their sex, will never be able to devour these sentences, in which Hegel gives them a piece of his mind.

They speak of the existence of *external* objects, which can be more precisely defined as *actual*, absolutely *singular*, *wholly personal*, *individual* things, each of them absolutely unlike anything else; this existence, they say, has absolute certainty and truth. They *mean* "this" bit of paper on which I am writing—or rather have written—"this"; but what they mean is not what they say. If they actually wanted to *say* "this" bit of paper which they mean, if they wanted to *say* it, then this is impossible, because the sensuous This that is meant *cannot be reached* by language, which belongs to consciousness, i.e., to that which is inherently universal. In the actual attempt to say it, it would therefore crumble away.[85]

After a mere piece of paper has registered and refuted the recorded sentence, it becomes a piece of dialectical evidence. In the process, however, the material of storage turns into the material of decay. Hegel's sentences rise above the stuff on which his handwritten first draft was recorded; a book that must be read again and again, that transcends all "Thisness" through technical means of reproducibility and reception—such a book can safely let its manuscript go the way of all trash. From night to book— the logic of the signified was never more brazen. It triumphs because the materiality of the signifiers becomes "beyond reach" for readers and opponents.

The demonstration of his being beyond reach encourages the philosopher to conclude with an even more deictic refutation of "deixis." Once he leafs back through his own manuscript "on which I write *this*, or rather have written it," he makes excessive use of the elementary power of the pen to underscore. And that real, absolutely singular, wholly personal, individual Being, which in keeping with or because of his sentences comes to nothing—that Being returns with Hegel's simple "I." For once the word *I*, otherwise used very unpoetically by philosophers as a neuter or substantive, appears in the first person. The strange fate of all shifters ("here, now, this, that, it, I, you" etc.) in the sciences is to be "usually taken as the occasion for repair or revision practices," which "clear up, translate, or interchange"[86] the shifters or even (as in the *Phenomenology*) charge them with absurdity. When Hegel makes an exception of his pen or even (as at the end of the book) brings it in, he repairs the reparation. Whereas in Schiller only "infinity" foams up out of "the chalice of the whole realm of spirits," the god or philosopher (of) Hegel enjoys "his infinity out of the chalice of this realm of spirits."

In the discourse network of 1800, the philosophical expurgation of discourses constitutes a purge in the political sense of the word. Every "thisness" disappeared in the face of the totalitarian "thisness" of the author. It began with women as they exist in plurality and proceeded as far as the devil, whose quoted speech in the *Phenomenology* had its shifters amputated. The mopping up thus did not stop with educational bureaucrats.

Consider Hegel's comments on Schelling's *System of Transcendental Idealism* and on the author of a critique of that work, Wilhelm Traugott Krug, later a professor of philosophy at Leipzig.

The *second* inconsistency Mr. Krug notices is that it was promised that the entire system of our representations was to be deduced; and although he himself had found a passage in the *System of Transcendental Idealism* that explicated the meaning of this promise, he nevertheless cannot keep himself from forgetting that it is a question here of philosophy in general. Mr. Krug cannot keep himself from treating the matter like the most common plebeian and demanding that every dog and cat, and even Mr. Krug's own writing quill, should be deduced; since this doesn't occur, he avers that his friend should be reminded of the mountain that gave birth to a mouse; *one* shouldn't have tried to give the impression that one could deduce the entire system of representations.[87]

The author foams at the mouth and pen when it seems to him or a one-time friend [Schelling] that for once there is no infinity foaming out of *his* spirit realm. Krug has the audacity to want to see the most unreachable of all unreachable "thisnesses" deduced: the pen that writes down his critique. Rather than study German Idealism in tireless rereadings and in so doing pay homage to the absolute pen, he writes his own replies. This merits the philosophic death sentence: banishment into "the rabble" and the declaration that all other "thisnesses" "have more to do with philosophy than Mr. Krug's pen and the works it has written."[88]

Dieter Henrich has shown that Hegel's "mocking and ostensibly superior polemical tone conceals uncertainty about the problem,"[89] an uncertainty inspires the *Phenomenology* to "this piece of paper," and the *Encyclopedia* to the promise that, after all other problems are resolved, one would be able "to give Mr. Krug hope for this achievement and respective glorification of *his* pen."[90] But all Hegelian critiques of Hegel remain glorifications of the totalitarian pen, just as they include Krug's exclusion. And yet the Saxon philosopher—if only in the beyond that gives his autobiography date and signature—unambiguously declared his pen-deduction wish. For Krug, as if to sign the death sentence Hegel issued, informs the "dear reader" that "I have already, as they say below, passed away, and am now sitting and writing up here in heaven; I will send this manuscript with the next express mail, that is, with the next comet that will touch the earth with its tail, to my friend the bookseller N. N., so that he can have it published."[91]

In his past days on earth, however, the autobiographer confesses that he had written less absolutely and with a pen much shorter than a comet's tail. A "brief report on his literary activity in Wittenberg," which is introduced by references to a mysterious sadness and "frequent, very frequent writing," cites as the seventh of Krug's early works the *Letters on Recent Idealism: Against Schelling*. Not until after the publication of this list of publications, only in the divine kingdom of completed alphabetization, where one "no longer blushes, because the ethereal bodies have no blood, at least not red blood," does Krug confess: "There was a third reason why I became such a copious writer. It was—can I admit this without blushing?—*love*."[92] It is always the same story in 1800. A "miserable adjunct of the philosophical faculty" strove "for literary fame" only because "his beloved was keen on writing, because she spoke with enthusiasm of well-known authors." But the future thinker did not think of marrying the woman. "I would have had to elope with her, and elopement was always abhorrent to me. It seemed so common to abscond with a woman." Deprived of his happiness by abhorrence of the rabble to which Hegel would consign him, poor Krug could only "cry like a child that has been torn from its mother's breast before it has quenched its thirst."[93] Such crying was synonymous with writing in 1800. Thus the pleasures of love turn once more into necessity. In place of the impossible sexual relation there arises, with an air of quiet grief, an educational bureaucrat, whose works incessantly implore other educational bureaucrats to deduce, along with the universe, this one, particular, irreplaceable pen. For only under the (admittedly improbable) condition that the educational bureaucrats could determine who had made him, Wilhelm Traugott Krug, cry and speak and write, "would he have no hesitation in signing his name to the whole system with his deduced pen."[94]

But there are no women in philosophical discourse; it remains in a neutered mode between friends or men. Krug revealed his motive for writing among the dead and the Poets; Hegel, because his experience was never very different,[95] never sought where he might have found. And thus philosophy forever lacks the signatures of those concerned. That is the difference between philosophy and poetry, and whereas the latter did not name any of the plurality of women, it did have the double-tongued, reference-as-you-like signified: Woman. In consequence, any number of feminine readers signed the Poet's text.

The difference was thus not determined by a doctrine of author-individual versus the results of thought (as Schiller put it). The difference occurs only at the level in which such talk deals with the origins of the different doctrines. Poets could claim singularity and thus love because they invoked the lost Woman who made them speak and write. Philosophic doctrine, having lost or destroyed women (whether named Gretchen or nameless like Krug's mother-beloved), remained limited to the male brotherhood of educational bureaucrats and returned only at the end, as to a thoroughly constructed ideal, back to Mother Nature.

There are advantages and disadvantages to both projects. The poetic project of translating out of and into the mother tongue constantly brings about an insanity to which philosophy is immune: philosophy does not know the unspeakable night except by writing, and can consider Reiser's or Franz Anton Mesmer's attempts "to think without words" only as "unreason."[96] That is precisely why Poets could leave the recruitment of readers to the ersatz modes of sensuality that came into being behind their words; the philosopher, however, who stored sense-certainties and spoken words only in written sentences, had to devise his own theory and practice of the speculative sentence in order to make a necessity of the repeated rereading of his work.

Poets and thinkers—the two remained separate even as the discourse network of 1800 brought about their conjunction. Goethe called philosophers "those whom I could never do without and with whom I could never come to terms." [97] In a system that first produced, second distributed, and third consumed discourses, the poetic profession of distribution was never very far from its productive abyss. The Poetry that in 1800, but no earlier, became the wine of the new aesthetics of content interposed itself between the consumption of philosophic discourse and the institutional authority in charge of its production. The Other—meaning always the other sex—is repressed in poetic discourse and foreclosed in philosophic.

Evidence for this is provided by a professor of philology, one whose efforts (in the fine phrase of a successor to the same chair) made philosophy out of what had once been philology. [98] Friedrich Creuzer, married to the widow of his doctoral adviser but in love with one of the impossible woman poets of the period, contributed to the bond of friendship between Poetry and Idealism through his work on mythology, though the myths in question had stood under a very different sign. But to reconceive *The Study of the Ancients as Preparation for Philosophy* had a price. [99] This was "an old, melancholy story" that "one could just as well forget" were it not "characteristic of the spiritual mood of the age in which dwell the finest memories in the history of German intellectual life." [100]

For Creuzer owed the inspiration that led him to works such as *Dionysus* or *Symbolism and Mythology of the Ancients* to Günderode, his beloved. Creuzer identified her, beyond all sexual difference, with the god in his treatises, who of course dissolved all differences; he also identified himself with her. The study *Dionysus* was to have "attained its purpose when you realize how much I wish to be *one* with you in spirit and in my work (where that is possible)." [101] Nothing is more necessary than "to harken to you in such research," and nothing is more logical than "to write for you" [102] a philosophical transposition of mythology. In an apparent exception, then, philosophy retracted its constitutive foreclosure; like Poetry, it invoked the feminine producer of discourse.

But letters are not lectures. Public speech among the latest crop of bureaucrats, and therefore men, required that the mystical union of Dionysus, poetess, and philosopher be expressed differently. Creuzer did not speak the name of the one who put words into his mouth.

I must tell Poesy the story of how I happened to quote some of her verse in a lecture lately. It was in ancient history, where I wanted to explain how after the death of Alexander the Great the ensuing wars . . . gave birth to a new world. Who was it that put these words into my mouth?

> Such powers, too, the universe requires
> and is never suited by standing at rest.

To which I added, quite properly and soberly, "as a new poet has said so well." Later I was happy about the event and had to smile, until my genius came sadly forward and spoke the Greek words: poetry brings you love at the *lectern* but never to your bed.[103]

The incident demonstrates what became of women's names in the discourse of the university. They vanished through a double substitution. The letter accomplished a first substitution in a manner homologous to that of poetry, in that the impossible author's name "Günderode" is replaced by "Poesy." Women could not write poetry because they *were* Poetry—and thus accidents like Sophie Mereau or Günderode could only be named the Woman or Poesy.[104] An Eternal Virgin remains a virgin even when one sleeps with her (though not in the marriage bed).[105] But that is not enough; the repression must be repressed until sex no longer counts. Properly sober, Creuzer moved toward foreclosure. Rather than "Poesy," which in turn stands for Caroline von Günderode, the students hear "a new poet." The homosexuality of philosophy and poetry has just destroyed another woman.

Whether publishing Günderode's dramas in his scholarly journal or dodging his wife's suspicion of love letters, Creuzer constantly gave Günderode masculine names. Thus she became, in word and deed, one of those boys who ultimately were the reason for the refusal of her constant plea to be allowed to live in the same city as her beloved. A pseudonymous Eusebio answers his (fe)male beloved:

Indeed, let it be said, for once I want to think selfishly only of Eusebio: his life's work is to open up the *silent* temple of antiquity for a number of boys. But where will he find the calm presence of mind necessary for the task, when he is driven, as if by malevolent spirits, back and forth through fruitless effort and storms of opposition against a bitter fate? Beloved, please understand! I owe you a great debt, a debt to be weighed against the value of life (because only you have given me a *life* worthy to be so named)—but you owe me *peace*, and *you will grant it to me*.[106]

Thus the ethos of educational bureaucracy in its relation to women: a Kingdom of God revealed to boys through the philosophic interpretation of antiquity has as little room for women's bodies as it does for their names. Any noise of the lips, whether it be speaking or kissing, disturbs the hermeneutic of silent temples. Only as long as women do not set foot in Heidelberg and remain instead the distant source of all philosophizing can the initiation ritual of the university be successful. One can lead students around by the nose for years with a new poet.

Six weeks after this letter the exchange was perfect. For his lifelong debt, Creuzer received peace: Günderode drowned herself—Winkel on the Rhine, July 26, 1806, irrefutable night.

The discourse network of 1800 closes like a trap on its victims. It rests on corpses. With that we close its book.

II

1900

$$y = (+a) + (-a) + (+a) + (-a) + \ldots \qquad \textit{Bolzano}$$

Nietzsche: Incipit Tragoedia

"My time extends only from the summer months in Sils-Maria (Nietzsche's 'Foreword to the Early Works') and in the foothills of Antibes, as Monet painted it, into this winter of damnation and nights of fire."[1] The historical adventures of speaking do not form a continuum and so do not constitute a history of ideas. They are marked by breaks that in a single stroke can consign entire discourse networks to oblivion, and they have plateaus that make one forget the advance of armies and hours even during the winters of world wars. What came to an end during the summers of Sils-Maria, those few summers of free writing, was everything "in the order of culture, scholarship, and science, of the familial and benevolent character that distinguished German literature of the nineteenth century in so many ways."[2] Thus Gottfried Benn, with characteristic exactness, selected and gathered up the particular functions that constituted the discourse network of 1800. The official locus of production for German Poetry was the nuclear family; scholars saw to its multiplication; and a science that claimed the title Science provided its justification. If, with Hofmannsthal, one claims that only this organization of discourse is legitimate, then everything that began with Nietzsche comes to nothing. In the empty space where one would wish to see a "new literature," there would be only "Goethe and beginnings."[3] But the break was so radical that those fascinated with Goethe had difficulty recognizing that the "literature" that developed in place of German Poetry was in fact literature. "Two men determine the German aesthetic of our time: Goethe and Nietzsche. One forms it, and the other destroys it."[4] When the one Mother gave way to a plurality of women, when the alphabetization-made-flesh gave way to technological media, and when philosophy gave way to the psychophysical or psychoanalytic decomposition of language, Poetry also disintegrated. In its place arose, whether German or not, an artistry in the full range of this Nietzschean term: from the magic of letters to a histrionics of media.

Over the beginning of literature circa 1900 stands a curse. "Whoever knows the reader will henceforth do nothing for the reader. Another century of readers—and the spirit itself will stink. That everyone may learn to read, in the long run corrupts not only writing but also thinking."[5] Zarathustra's curse strikes at the technological-material basis of the discourse network of 1800: universal alphabetization. Not content or message but the medium itself made the Spirit, the corpus composed of German Poetry and German Idealism, into a stinking cadaver. The murderer of the letter met its own death.

Nietzsche therefore described, although in a transvaluation of all values just what the reading and writing reformers of 1800 did. Except for the sign determining value, there is no difference between the two following descriptions of reading (the first published in 1786, the second in 1886).

With practice, everything should become a knack as natural as feeling, so that one can survey the whole easily and quickly without being conscious of every single detail, and then make one's choice. Knowledge of letters is not yet knowledge of reading, even though mechanical reading is nothing more than pronouncing letters. Only one who can take in whole words or even lines at a glance, without thinking of individual letters, knows how to read.[6]

Just as little as a reader today reads all of the individual words (let alone syllables) on a page—rather he picks about five words at random out of twenty and "guesses" at the meaning that probably belongs to these five words—just as little do we see a tree exactly and completely with reference to leaves, twigs, color, and form; it is so very much easier for us simply to improvise some approximation of a tree. . . . All this means: basically and from time immemorial we are—*accustomed to lying*. Or to put it more virtuously and hypocritically, in short, more pleasantly: one is much more of an artist than one knows.[7]

Nietzsche's description confirms the great extent to which the educational programs of 1800 had achieved statistical reality.[8] But a sobering period follows that triumph. Hermeneutic reading, once praised as knack or even feeling in order to make it palatable, is scorned and called a lie. When unfeelingly described as discursive manipulation rather than viewed from the inner perspective of its beneficiaries, universal alphabetization turns out to be the beginning of self-deception and, as such, of the proliferation of artists. Modern readers who arbitrarily hit upon five words out of twenty in order to get to the meaning as quickly as possible practice the same technique as writers and rewriters.

The most astonishing thing may come to pass—the host of the historically neutral is always there ready to supervise the author of it even while he is still far off. The echo is heard immediately: but always as a "critique," though the moment before the critic did not so much as dream of the possibility of what has been done. The work never produces an effect but only another "critique"; and the critique itself produces no effect either, but again only a further critique.[9]

From skipping over letters to surveying an author, from an elementary trick in reading to semi-official literary criticism—the method remains the same. According to Fichte, hermeneutics simply means writing anything about a work, with the exception of its actual text. Nietzsche's diagnosis of a pathological increase in the population of authors continues a complaint made when the malady had just begun;[10] but Nietzsche named the root of the evil. In *Human, All too Human*, one reads in the section entitled "The Name on the Title-Page":

That the name of the author should be inscribed on the book is now customary and almost a duty; yet it is one of the main reasons books produce so little effect. For if they are good, then, as the quintessence of the personality of their authors, they are worth more than these; but as soon as the author announces himself on the title-page, the reader at once dilutes the quintessence again with the personality, indeed with what is most personal, and thus thwarts the object of the book.[11]

Alphabetized reading, which would continue writing rather than recognize letters on the page, thus has a correlate in production: the function of authorship. From the same exterior position in which his irony revealed the arbitrary choice among twenty words, Nietzsche also scorns the new rule of discourse that embellishes title pages with names. The human, all too human or personal, indeed, most personal, which is attributed by the anthropology of language to all signs, burdens a reading that "at once looks beyond the work" and asks after "the history of its author. . . . in the previous and possible future progress of his development."[12]

Alphabetization, reading that continues writing or the name of the author—with the exception of the feminine reading function, Nietzsche's unsparing analysis brings together all the control loops of the classical discourse network. The summary results in a negative evaluation. Words have no effect because they are skipped over; reading issues only in writing; authors' names detract from the phenomenon of the book. In retrospect the discourse network of 1800 is a single machine designed to neutralize discursive effects and establish "our absurd world of educators"—"to the 'able servant of the state' this promises a regulating schema"—founded on the ruins of words.[13]

On the basis of this analytically very accomplished summation, Zarathustra can dare to call the Spirit a stinking cadaver.

Nietzsche knew what he was talking about. The former student of the royal academy truly owed "the totality of his education" to the discourse network of 1800; according to the rector, Pforta under Prussian occupation constituted "a self-contained educational state, which completely absorbed all aspects of the life of the individual."[14] In 1859, on the one-hundredth birthday of Schiller, students heard a teacher, who had been commissioned by Prussian authorities to write the first textbook on German literary history, deliver an address on the greatness of the Poet; they then spent the evening hours, after a celebratory dinner, in general, but private, reading of Schiller in the school library.[15] One spent the rest of one's school time attempting to deal with one's own person in the manner that Karl August Koberstein's literary history dealt with the classical writers. As Poet and Critic unified in one person, the schoolboy Nietzsche wrote, aside from poetic works, the corresponding poetic autobiographies, which, after conjuring the inexhaustible days of his childhood, regularly listed his private reading and writing. "My Life"; "Course of My Life"; "A Look Back"; "From My Life"; "My Literary and Musical Activity"—and so on runs the list that an author from the new crop by the name of Nietzsche added to the classical discourse network. Only much later, namely, at the university level of the same educational path, could he read the "autobiographical constructions, which were to have justified the contingency of his being"[16] for what they were: German essays, programmed by pedagogues and written by students in the royal academy. Looking longingly toward a different "Future of Our Educational Institutions," Nietzsche, the professor of philology, described their nineteenth century:

The last department in which the German teacher in a public school is at all active, which is also regarded as his sphere of highest activity, and is here and there even considered the pinnacle of public-school education, is the "German essay." Because the most gifted pupils almost always display the greatest eagerness in this department, it ought to have been made clear how dangerously stimulating, precisely here, the task of the teacher must be. The German essay is a call to the individual, and the more strongly a pupil is conscious of his distinguishing qualities, the more personally will he do his German essay. This "personal doing" is further encouraged at most schools by the choice of essay topics, and I find the strongest evidence of this in the lower grades, where pupils are given the non-pedagogical topic of describing their own life, their own development. . . . How often does someone's later literary work turn out to be the sad consequence of this pedagogical original sin against the spirit![17]

All the sins of the classical discourse network thus concentrate in the German essay. Alone, crying in the wilderness, Nietzsche discovered the material basis of any literary work and, in particular, of his own. The pamphlet *Our School Essay as a Disguised Dime Novelist* was soon to appear in mass editions; with affectionate stylistic criticism it demonstrated the identity between, on the one hand, Karl May, Buffalo Bill, and Texas Jack, and on the other hand, the 386 model essays on *Iphigenia* written by teachers.[18]

The Spirit stinks because of the pedagogic original sin against it. First the German essay generates productive literary men (more precisely, schoolboys); second, it generates the autobiographies of their production; third, it generates—because they so gladly make "obligatory" the "judgment of works of poetry"[19]—the literary-critical continuators, those who wrote "Letter to My Friend, in Which I Recommend the Reading of My Favorite Poet" and generally neutralized discursive effects.[20]

Even in dead-silent, solitary rooms, the gymnasium students of the nineteenth century were never alone; the "totality of their education" contained them as the German essay contained the literary industry. They could intend and understand everything that paper patiently took and gave—except the "influence of women," as Nietzsche later learned to his "astonishment."[21] They were very well prepared for a culture of universal alphabetization.

Thus the classical-romantic discourse network ended in megalomania and desperation. A fragment, not accidentally entitled "Euphorion," sets the courtly signature "F W v Nietzky, homme étudié en lettres" beneath a self-portrait of naked despair.

It is deathly still in the room—the one sound is the pen scratching across the paper—for I love to think by writing, given that the machine that could imprint our thoughts into some material without their being spoken or written has yet to be invented. In front of me is an inkwell in which I can drown the sorrows of my black heart, a pair of scissors to accustom me to the idea of slitting my throat, manuscripts with which I can wipe myself, and a chamber pot.[22]

This is a primal scene, less well known but no less fraught with consequences than the despair of Faust in and over his study in the Republic of Scholars. The scholar is replaced, however, by the very man of letters whom Faust made to appear magically as the redeemer from heaps of books. The one who signs himself "homme étudié en lettres" has experienced nothing beyond the formative education of the gymnasium, which as an "appeal to the individual" is the opposite of scholarly training. The scene of writing is therefore bare of all library props, and thus bare, too, of any enigma about how supposed texts are to be translated into Spirit and meaning. The solitary writer is a writer and nothing more: not a translator, scribe, or interpreter. Bare and impoverished, the scratching of the pen exposes a function that had never been described: writing in its materiality. There is no Bible to Germanize, no voice to transcribe, and so there are none of the miracles that in 1800 obscured that materiality. One no longer writes around the fact of writing—writing has become its own medium. Even in the clinic for nervous diseases in Jena, Nietzsche was "happy and in his element" as long as he had pencils.[23] But already the man of letters F W v Nietzky, in contrast to the schoolboy Wilhelm Friedrich Nietzsche, is through with putting literary works, literary auto-biographies, and discussions of literature on paper—beyond the act of writing there is nothing at all. Whether or not the star pupil of the Schulpforta Gymnasium would have had anything to say, had the ped-agogues left him alone, is unimportant. In the "Euphorion" fragment, in the countless notebooks that until the final day in Turin recorded thoughts and laundry receipts, possible book titles and headache reme-dies, to say nothing of the few scribbles from the insane asylum, which found their way back to the empty schema of the autobiographical Ger-man essay,[24] Nietzsche's papers record only the primal scene and its en-during enigma.

What is most disturbing in the posthumous fragments is the fact that they are not a collection of notes, but rather a collection of writing exercises, indeed rhetorical exercises in the sense of attempts at various styles, in which the ideas are then run through their declensions. Nietzsche finally achieved a lexicon in which words emptied of all context were brought back into phrases, or were idiomized, so to speak; it was a mute exercise, carried on without further commentary, between the vocabulary notebook, the translation guide, and the collection of stylistic howlers.[25]

When writing remains a writing exercise, a spare and dismal act with-out any extension into what is called book, work, or genre, there is no place for the "personal presentation and formation" so dear to the essay pedagogues. The "appeal to the individual" to become an individual and author comes to nothing precisely because the model pupil takes it liter-ally. For the one who takes up the pen and writes is no one; instead of serving an individual, the inkwell drowns a black heart; instead of aiding the process of revision and rereading, the technical premises of author-ship, the pair of scissors has a quite different task. And as with the indi-vidual, so too with his production—manuscripts destined for the cham-ber pot. Zarathustra's nose for Spirit or the stench of the writing culture thus comes from a scene of writing in which the props—pen, inkwell, scissors, chamber pot—have done away with the ego and its meanings. The author disappears, to say nothing of the readers he might address; in the "Euphorion" fragment writing produces refuse and feces rather than poetic works. Precisely because Nietzky is another Euphorion, who pos-sessed in his parents a complete classicism and romanticism, in that he had at his command every facility of the classical-romantic discourse net-work, the pedagogic promises and the literary training, there was no eu-phoria; he fell, true to his name until the end.

Modern texts would follow this downward trajectory in various ways. Nietzky-Nietzsche touched on the zero point on which literature in 1900 would build. It is intransitive writing that is not directed toward written truths or readers; rather, "all its threads converge upon the finest of points—singular, instantaneous, and yet absolutely universal—upon the simple act of writing"; it is writing that "breaks with the whole definition of *genres* as forms adapted to an order of representation" and that can be "a silent, cautious deposition of the word upon the whiteness of a piece of paper, where it can possess neither sound nor interlocutor."[26]

In the deathly still room, only the pen makes a sound. Neither sound nor phonetic method supports a writing that occurs without preliminary speech and so without a soul. If something precedes its materiality, it is only the materiality of sound itself. An isolated, early observation by Nietzsche records the deafening noise in this still scene of writing: "What I fear is not the horrible shape behind my chair but its voice: not the words, but the frighteningly inarticulate and inhuman tone of that shape. If only it would speak as people speak!"[27]

In its beginning German Poetry had shut out the animal sounds of a poodle and preferred, when translating prelinguistic feelings, to follow the advice of a Spirit that only later articulated its own name. An inarticulate tone defines the zero point of literature, a tone not only inhuman, but also not animal or demonic. The creaturely sounds that filled the language space of the sixteenth century were silenced when Man became aware of a beloved language or a woman's voice. The inhuman tone behind Nietzsche's back is not the speech at the beginning of articulation; it is not speech at all. All discourse is powerless against it because all discourses add to it and fall prey to it. Within the realm of all sounds and words, all organisms, white noise appears, the incessant and ineradicable background of information. For the very channels through which information must pass emit noise.

In 1800 simple, unarticulated tones were excommunicated. They fomented an insanity that, in contrast to the fixed idea, had no poetic value: that of the imbecile.[28] If one had no "ability to comprehend the speech of others," one was required to assume "the posture of reading aloud and slowly during an attack."[29] Writers like Faust or Anselmus were allowed to trust their inmost feeling only because it was supported by reading, which in turn was supported by a human language or voice.

Nietzsche, however, wrote before and after white noise. He took so literally the German essay's appeal "to listen to one's own thoughts and feelings" that thoughts and feelings turned into their opposites: the listener hears a "humming and roaring of the wild camps" within him, which fight an irreconcilable "civil war." Where there should have been a prelinguistic inwardness, susceptible to articulation and development, "a roar went through the air." [30]

The frightening, inarticulate tone that Nietzsche heard behind his back hums in the ears themselves. What does not speak as people speak would be called (if it could have a name) "Nietzsche." The autobiography demonstrates this for Nietzsche's own beginning: "At an absurdly early age, at seven, I already knew that no human word would ever reach me." [31] The medical records from Jena demonstrate it for his end: "Often screams inarticulately." [32] Everything began for him, then, when human or pedagogical encouragement was unable to cover over the noise at the basis of all information channels and instead merged with it. And everything ended when he left *The Will to Power* sitting on his desk, turned around in his chair, and dissolved into the noise that had horrified him for as long as he lived or wrote.

The woman's voice that made Anselmus write occupied the same chair he did: it exemplified the interlocking media network of speaking and writing, of the soul and Poetry. The voice that formed the ground for Nietzsche's writing exercises remained behind his chair, and he was unable ever to unlearn the horror it inspired. It halted all erotic exchange between orality and writing, reducing writing to pure materiality. "You should have sung, my soul," is a pathetic sentence—in that "there is no soul" and "aesthetics is nothing but a kind of applied physiology." [33] Henceforth, there exist only the two sides of an exclusion. Behind the chair there is white noise, that is, physiology; in front of the chair, there are the inkwell, the scissors, paper, and words as multiple as they are empty. For if the incessant noise can whisper anything to writers, its message can only be Nietzsche's sentence "I am a maker of words: what do words matter! what do I matter!" [34]

Writing and writers as accidental events in a noise that generates accidents and thus can never be overcome by its accidents: Nietzsche comes quite close to the poetics of Mallarmé. Faust's helpful Spirit diverted the act of writing toward a goal in the beyond, the transcendental signified of the word; Hippel's anathema excluded literary hacks from the realm of souls; makers of words, however, never escape the medium they institute. An anecdote concerning Mallarmé illustrates this. "Degas occasionally wrote verses, and some of those he left were delightful. But he often found great difficulty in this work accessory to his painting. . . . One day he said to Mallarmé: 'Yours is a hellish craft. I can't manage to say what I want, and yet I'm full of ideas. . . .' And Mallarmé answered: 'My dear Degas, one does not make poetry with ideas, but with *words.*'" [35] The last philosopher and the first modern poet agreed even in their choice of words. Mallarmé decomposes the phrase *maker of words* in a single sentence. For Nietzsche it became impossible to put his own thoughts and feelings on paper because all meaning was lost in noise. For Mallarmé meanings or ideas had been played out, so that there was no longer any translation from one medium, literature, to another, such as painting. There was nothing to makers of words (according to the word-maker Nietzsche); Mallarmé called his hellish profession the "elocutionary disappearance of the poet, who cedes the initiative to words." [36] Writing that can discover the basis of its rights neither in what is written nor in the writer has its message only in the medium it constitutes. In 1900, in direct descent from Nietzsche, "word art" became synonymous with literature. [37]

A professor who was no longer a professor and an educational bureaucrat who no longer wanted to be one stood at the threshold of a new discourse network. [38] Soon every child would learn that makers of words are not authors and that words are not ideas. The confusion between words and ideas that had supported an entire classicism did not end only in solitary rooms. On December 4, 1890, the emperor's irrefutable mouth issued an order placing German as a school subject at the center of all pedagogy and essay writing at the center of this center. [39] With that, German ceased to be beyond all school instruction, a realm where words were always bypassed for their meanings and thus for the university discipline of philosophy. Consequently, a decree of 1904 did away with the study of philosophy as an "obligatory part of the doctoral examination." [40] Indeed, the great experimental psychologist Hermann Ebbinghaus nearly succeeded in having philosophy replaced by physiological psychology in examinations for teaching positions. Schools also came close to teaching that aesthetics is nothing more than applied physiology.

But if writing came to be at the center of the center in school, physiology also found its way into the classroom, even without being included in examination regulations. The noise that grounded Nietzsche's writing was put down on paper. Free essays, advocated by the art-education movement beginning in 1904, contributed neither to unfolding the individuality of their authors nor to the ideality of their thoughts. At an extreme they simply led to writing down the droning in feverish children's heads. What Nietzsche already knew at the absurdly early age of seven years attained positive discursive reality. Art education gave up on reaching its pupils with human or pedagogical words. Instead, it emphasized how "productive the child is with its language," and complained that children should be "forced to produce in a foreign language, namely that of the adult." [41] Little makers of words were most free if their speaking and writing remained untouched by a mother's mouth. In 1900 linguists and psychologists claimed that even "the newborn child brings language, universal language, into the world: we do not teach it to speak, we only teach it our own language."[42] It thereby follows that there is no Mother's Mouth at the origin of human speech and masculine writing. Instead of the female Other, who with the minimal signified *ma* created the beginning of articulation and Poetry, there is an autarchic children's language, which cannot be formed by parents because it respects no national boundaries and spontaneously produces signifiers such as *Amme* or *Mama*.[43] Makers of words thereby lose the authority that had once made them authors. Ever since, there has been only deathly stillness and white noise in the writing room; no woman or muse offers her kiss.

The discourse network of 1900 could not build on the three functions of production, distribution, and consumption. Discursive practices are so historically variable that even elementary and apparently universal concepts are lacking in certain systems.[44] In 1900 no authority of production determines the inarticulate beginning of articulation. An inhuman noise is the Other of all signs and written works. No distribution can use language as a mere channel and thus attract ever more writers and readers. Like any medium in 1900, discourse is an irreducible fact that will not disappear in philosophical meaning or psychological effects. Therefore it cannot allow a consumption that would retranslate speech back to its origin.

This all constitutes a largely unwritten chapter in literary studies, and it still needs to be described in its technological and institutional aspects. But the hermit of Sils had already traversed this space, without institutions, almost without technologies, simply as his tragedy. Although he does not seem an imposing figure, a founder of a new discourse,[45] in his failed experiments Nietzsche was the victim offered up to a writing other than the classical-romantic.

The experiments began with a theory of language concerned, to quote the title of an essay, with "Truth and Falsehood in an Extramoral Sense." Considered apart from the ostensible truth-telling demands of moralistic or even educative voices, language is no longer the translation of prelinguistic meanings, but rather one medium among others. Media, however, exist only as arbitrary selections from a noise that denies all selection. Nietzsche absorbed the lesson of the scene of his writing so completely that "Nature" itself, rather than assuming human or maternal form became one with the frighteningly inarticulate tone. "She threw away the key: and woe to the fateful curiosity that once would look out and downward through a crack in the room of consciousness and would sense that man, in the indifference of his ignorance, rests on the merciless, the craving, the voracious, the murderous, and hangs in dreams on the back of a tiger."[46]

No medium of information can translate the terror that excludes consciousness and that consciousness in turn excludes. Falsehood, in an extramoral sense, is truth. A lie is only a lie of selection, which veils the terror or even, like someone at his desk, turns his back on it. Reading is one example, in that Nietzsche compares the actual text from which random selection was made to an unthinkably complex object of nature. But language itself does not function any differently.

A juxtaposition of different languages shows that words never have anything to do with truth or adequate expression: for otherwise there would not be so many different languages. The "thing in itself" (and that would be pure, inconsequential truth) is incomprehensible and utterly unworthy of effort for the creator of language as well. He designates only the relations of things to men and for their expression makes use of the most daring metaphors. First of all a nervous impulse is translated into an image. First metaphor. The image is again further formed into a sound! Second metaphor. And each time there is a complete leap, from one sphere into a completely different and new one.[47]

Whereas in the discourse network of 1800 an organic continuum extended from the inarticulate minimal signified to the meanings of factual languages, there is now a break. Language (as its plural suggests) is not the truth and consequently not any truth at all.[48] Though there is no nature of language for philosophers to uncover behind its bold metaphors,[49] another, physiological nature appears. Nietzsche's theory of language, like his aesthetics, proceeds from nervous impulses. Optical and acoustic responses to impulses, images and sounds, bring about the two aspects of language, as signified and signifier. Yet they remain as separated from one another as they are from the pure stochastic processes to which they respond. The break between the imaginal signified and the acoustic signifier cannot be bridged by continuous translation; only a metaphor or transposition can leap the gap. Separate sense media come together against the background of an omnipresent noise—as "completely different and new spheres." Instead of deriving media from a common source like the poetic imagination, Nietzsche divides optics and acoustics into a "world of sight" and "world of sound."[50]

Each of the two media repeats its common relation to an origin that, being a random generator, is not an origin. Nietzsche dreamed of a music that would not, like all German music, "fade away at the sight of the voluptuous blue sea and the brightness of the Mediterranean sky," music that "prevails even before the brown sunsets of the desert."[51] Only an audible world in which sound and color triumph over form and morality would remain, despite any process of selection, close to its inhuman background, one that (as we know) answers to the god's name Dionysus. But the optical medium of Apollo does not function any differently.

When after a forceful attempt to gaze on the sun we turn away blinded, we see dark-colored spots before our eyes, as a cure, as it were. Conversely, the bright image projections of the Sophoclean hero—in short, the Apollonian aspect of the mask—are necessary effects of a glance into the inside and terrors of nature; as it were, luminous spots to cure eyes damaged by gruesome night.[52]

Nietzsche's visual world is born in the eye itself. Entoptical visions heal *and* transpose pain in the eyes, which, in a reversal of all tradition, is not caused by a blinding sun but by a horrible night. This ground, against which colors and forms are only selections, is at once preserved (by pain) and metaphorically veiled (by the reversal of darkness into light). Apollonian art, too, fulfills a condition constitutive of technological media by meeting the "demand that it should not only be similar to the object, but should furnish the guarantee for this similarity by being, so to speak, a creation of the object itself, that is, by being mechanically produced by it."[53] No imagination can stand up to such demands; where psychological translation once sufficed, material transposition now becomes necessary.

Moving "images of light" by which the eye forms an image of its own retina have little to do with productions of Sophocles at Athenian festivals. Nietzsche's Apollonian art describes something quite different— the technological medium of film, which the Lumière brothers would make public on December 28, 1895. Nietzsche and the Lumières based Apollonian art and the movies on applied physiology: the entoptical after-image, or the illusion, created by afterimage and strobe effect, in which discrete images proceeding with sufficiently high frequency appear to form a continuum. And if the Apollonian hero is "in the last analysis nothing but a bright image projected on a dark wall, which means appearance through and through,"[54] then all the elements of film have come together: first, the black before each selection, which for Nietzsche was original night and in film is the protective concealment of the reel during transport; second, the optical or even entoptical hallucinatory effect; third, the projection screen, precisely the contribution of the Lumières, which made Edison's cinemascope of 1891 into the movies.[55]

A music that holds its own in the desert and a theater that is film *avant la lettre*[56]—by their physiological effects these innovations explode the limits of European art. They become media. As in Wagnerian opera, their heroic predecessor, media no longer speak "the language of the culture of a caste and in general no longer recognize any distinction between the cultivated and the uncultivated." [57] Only the ingrained alphabetization of 1800 made it possible to celebrate and understand the "philologist-poet" Goethe in the way that his Discourse of the Master understood understanding. An aesthetics of applied physiology, by contrast, required neither training nor elite culture.

But Nietzsche was not Wagner. For makers of words, even if they dream of music and movies, there remains only the paradoxical desire to break open the general medium of culture within and by means of its own structure. Therefore Nietzsche began by countermanding the Faustian revolution. Goethe's universality joined philological and poetic practice to create Spirit from letters and human happiness from study. When even as a student Nietzsche scolded Faust for his method of translation, he did so in the name of a philology that was still a particular competence of the Republic of Scholars. An old-fashioned professional ethic confronted universal alphabetization. Whereas "we moderns read nothing but thoughts" and distill Faustian meaning from five out of twenty words, Nietzsche praises the ascesis of the philologist who still reads words and understands "conjectural criticism" as "an activity of the kind employed in solving a rebus." [58]

All appearances to the contrary, Nietzsche made no serious attempt to rescind the historical fact that everyone was now able to learn to read. He did not plan an "imitation of the historical practices of communication" for their own sake; [59] they were only to provide him with the means of and weapons for his own writing project. Instead of practicing conjectural criticism to solve the rebus of purported texts, he invented riddle after riddle. Philological insights, for instance, that in Horace's poetry "this *minimum* in the extent and number of the signs" attains "the maximum . . . in the energy of the signs" in that "every word—as sound, as place, as concept, pours out its force right and left," [60] became for Nietzsche the writer a design for his own experiments. *Zarathustra* was a "play of every kind of symmetry" "down to the choice of vowels." [61]

In the guise of historical regression, Nietzsche pushed the structures of writing to an extreme. Faust's translation of λόγος marked a moment in the history of the sign when there was no awareness of the paradigmatic; by contrast, Nietzsche's writing, in its program and practice, established pure differentiality. A topology of the signifier, as Saussure would apply it to the paradigmatic and syntagmatic axes, orders the text and therefore its programmed reception as well. Nietzsche demanded an "art of interpretation" by which each sign was to be read together with contiguous signs as well as with those for which it was a substitute. In place of hermeneutic rereading he saw a simple, physiological "rumination—something for which one has almost to be a cow and in any case *not* a 'modern man.'"[62] All of Nietzsche's stylistic techniques embody this one command—including the sentence that issued it. His typographical accents were intended to keep the reader from "skipping over" the imperative and, being "held by the restrictive clause, to spell it."[63] Alphabetized fluency is throttled; the insistence of the signifier takes the paradigm *man/animal* apart syntagmatically (in a transvaluation of all connoted values). As cows, the readers (or rather the feminine readers) Nietzsche demanded became analphabetical. "He who knows the reader does nothing further for the reader"; but where nonreaders are being eliminated, style itself must enforce the difficult process—the old-European norm—of spelling out the text.

Ever since Nietzsche, the logic of the signifier has become a technique of sparseness and isolation, and minimum signs release maximum energy. Hermeneutic theories, with their notions of context, are inadequate to such a calculus. They are familiar only with organic relationships and with a continuous—that is, psychological or historical—narrative representation of them. The relative value of signifiers, by contrast, is given mathematically; its articulation is called counting.

To count words—in the days of romanticism this was the ridiculously outmoded fixed idea of a Fixlein with his kabala of the Bible;[64] in the age of media it becomes a primary and elementary necessity. Mallarmé derives the essence of literature from the fact that there are twenty-four letters.[65] In the opening line of a poem, Rilke raises his eyes "from the book, from the near, countable lines." What Nietzsche praises in Horace applies also to the "telegraphic style" of his own aphorisms.[66] For simple, economic reasons telegrams demand the paucity of words that for Nietzsche had a physiological basis in nearsightedness and lenses of fourteen diopters.

Where the hermit of Sils seems to retreat from universal alphabetization into the prehistorical, he is preparing the way for the rule of the enigmatic letter in the discourse network of 1900. The topology and economics of the signifier are a matter more for engineers than for Renaissance philologists. Only a very ordinary understanding of the *Sociological Foundations of Literary Expressionism in Germany* could see in August Stramm and Ferdinand Hardekopf "a certain disjunction between their avant-garde literary activity and their professions as postal official and parliamentary stenographer."[67] In reality there is no truer or more urgent juncture. Stramm's poems, with their six to eight lines of one to three words each, are the telegraphic style as literature. They are entirely appropriate from a postal inspector who, after thorough training in the postal and telegraphic services, wrote a doctoral thesis entitled "Historical, Critical, and Fiscal Policy Investigation of the World Postal System's Postage Rate and Its Basis" for the philosophical faculty of the University of Halle. Once there is a world postal system, signifiers have standardized prices that mock all meaning. Once there are telegrams and postcards, style is no longer the man, but an economy of signs.[68] What Horace meant to Nietzsche the philologist of ancient languages is for Stramm "the general business principle of obtaining the greatest possible value for the least expense." It was, of course, a principle that raised "exchange of information" and, in particular, expressionist poetry to the second power: the costs are "costs that do not immediately create value or raise values, but which make the creation of value possible."[69] They are discourses in the good Nietzschean manner, then, as a self-heightening of structures of mastery, which became ever more necessary under the conditions of standardized and mass produced information. Only the minimax of sign energy escapes the fate of incalculable masses of data, as in Nietzsche's inner civil war. From the "empirical law of correspondence production, according to which each letter posted from one country to another country elicits another letter from the second country to the first,"[70] there follows finally only noise.

In *The Wanderer and His Shadow*, Nietzsche first experiments with the telegraphic style. The conjectural critic had become so ill, his eyes so nearsighted, that each letter he read exacted its price. The professor from Basel had become so tired of his profession that the night in his eyes gave birth to a shadow, one beyond culture and the university.

My sickness also gave me the right to change all my habits completely; it permitted, it *commanded* me to forget; it bestowed on me the necessity of lying still, of leisure, of waiting and being patient.—But that means, of thinking.—My eyes alone put an end to all book wormishness—in brief, philology: I was delivered from the "book"; for years I did not read a thing—the greatest benefit I ever conferred on myself.—That nethermost self which had, as it were, been buried and grown silent under the continual pressure of having to listen to other selves (and that is after all what reading means) awakened slowly, shyly, dubiously—but eventually it spoke again.[71]

A physiological accident made Nietzsche's second experiment possible. Near-blindness released writing from being the productive continuation of reading it had been in 1800 or the commentary on a pile of books it had been in the Republic of Scholars. Though Nietzsche's method of philological spelling out governed his own work, he was no longer a scholar, one "who at bottom does little nowadays but thumb books—philologists, at a moderate estimate, about 200 a day."[72] At the point where the eyes or imagination of others see printed paper, night intervenes. Hegel's refutation of sense-certainty would do nothing for someone too blind to read. The absolute certainty of night and shadow put the cultural medium of the book on the same level as physiological media, which had their ground and countersupport in the desert, noise, and blinding darkness. In place of the uncounted words already written, in place of philologists' two hundred books per day (first counted by Nietzsche), an unconscious self appears, which in its refusal to do the required reading is as foreign and physiological as the voice behind the chair. What finally begins to speak is, of course, never reached by any word. Near blindness, more effective than the devouring of books by women ever was, grants forgetfulness.

But the accident of illness brought about merely the conditions that distinguish all signifiers. In order for a sign to exist, it must necessarily stand against a background that cannot be stored by any mechanism. For letters, this is empty white paper; in another case, the mirror-image transposition of writing, it is the empty black sky.

To write—
    The inkwell, crystal clear like a conscience, with its drop of darkness at the bottom, so that something may come out of it: then, set aside the lamp.
    You noticed, one does not write the alphabet of stars luminously, on a dark field, only, thus is it indicated, barely begun or interrupted; man pursues black on white.
    This fold of dark lace, that holds the infinite, its secret, woven by thousands, each one according to its own thread or unknown continuation, assembles distant interlaced ribbons where a luxury yet to be inventoried sleeps, vampire, knot, leaves and then present it.[73]

The inkwell, in whose darkness Nietzky would drown his black heart; the lamp set aside, which the half-blind hardly need anyway; the dark field on which stars are stars and where the afterimages of Apollonian visions ease pain—the materiality of signifiers rests on a chaos that defines them differentially. Nietzsche could call his styles, because of their "variety" or in spite of it, "the opposite of chaos."[74] A precondition for something to "come out," that is, to be written down, is a relation to the dark ground. The fact that writing reverses this relation of figure and ground (Max Wertheimer would soon study the physiology of perception involved) into dark marks against luminous space changes nothing in its logic. As a "fold of dark lace" that "assembles distant interlaced ribbons," letters are determined by the space between them.

The logic of chaos and intervals was implemented as a technology by the discourse network of 1900—through the invention of the typewriter.

When his eyes decreed an end to all bookwormishness, Nietzsche wrote that he had no idea how he would handle written material (letters and notes). He was thinking about getting a typewriter, and he had been in contact with its inventor, a Dane from Copenhagen.[75] Five months later, Paul Rée brought the machine, which cost 450 Reichsmark, to Genoa. It had "unfortunately been damaged during the trip. A mechanic was able to repair it within a week, but it soon completely ceased functioning."[76]

Nietzsche as typist—the experiment lasted for a couple of weeks and was broken off, yet it was a turning point in the organization of discourse. No other philosopher would have been proud to appear in the *Berlin Daily* as the owner of a strange new machine.[77] As far as one can reconstruct the unwritten literary history of the typewriter, only journalists and reporters, such as Mark Twain and Paul Lindau, threw away their pens in the pioneering days of 1880. The stinking Spirit, as it led its skimming readers, also made its move to a machine that, in contrast to the pen, was "capable of putting one's first thoughts, which are well known to be the best, onto paper."[78] Nietzsche's decision to buy a typewriter, before greater interest in the new technology arose in Europe around 1890, had a different motivation: his half-blindness. Indeed, the first typewriters (in contrast to the Remington of 1873) were made for those who were blind, and sometimes (as with Foucauld and Pierre) by those who were blind. Nietzsche's Dane from Copenhagen was Malling Hansen, pastor and teacher of the deaf and dumb, whose "writing ball" of 1865 or 1867 "was designed for use only by *the blind*," but by virtue of improved mechanics and working speed "was the first practical and usable typewriter."[79]

Nietzsche, who even as a school boy dreamed of a machine that would transcribe his thoughts, knew better than his biographer Kurt Paul Janz, who with feigned outspokenness (and probably out of respect for fabricators of munitions and buyers of typewriter patents like the Remingtons) flatly denied the Dane (whom he calls Hansun) any credit for the invention.[80] Nietzsche's choice, by contrast, as half-blind as it was certain, picked out a machine whose rounded keyboard could be used "exclusively through the sense of touch," because "on the surface of a sphere each spot is designated with complete certainty by its spatial position."[81]

Spatially designated and discrete signs—that, rather than increase in speed, was the real innovation of the typewriter. "In place of the image of the word [in handwriting] there appears a geometrical figure created by the spatial arrangement of the letter keys."[82] Indeed, a peculiar relationship to place defines the signifier: in contrast to everything in the Real, it can be and not be in its place.[83] As soon as the typewriter was ready to go into mass production, therefore, "a powerful movement in favor of intro-

ducing a universal keyboard got under way, and the 1888 congress in Toronto agreed on a standard one."[84]

```
Q   W   E   R   T   Y   U   I   O   P
  A   S   D   F   G   H   J   K   L
    Z   X   C   V   B   N   M
```

In an apparatus and its discrete letters, Toronto in 1888 realized (beyond Gutenberg) what Sils-Maria praised in Horace and his verse: that elements of a keyboard can be structured to the "right and left" and throughout the whole. In the play between signs and intervals, writing was no longer the handwritten, continuous transition from nature to culture. It became selection from a countable, spatialized supply. The equal size of each sign—a lofty, distant goal for the genetic method of writing instruction—came about of itself (if only, as in Hansen's typewriter, because the machine had nothing but capital letters). The only tasks in the transposition from keyboard to text remained the manipulations of permutation and combination. "Yes! With its 24 signs, this Literature precisely named Letters, as well as through its numerous fusions in the elaboration of sentences and then verse, a system arranged like a spiritual zodiac, contains its own doctrine, abstract and esoteric like a theology."[85]

In typewriting, spatiality determines not only the relations among signs but also their relation to the empty ground. Type hits paper, leaving an impression, or sometimes even a hole. Not for nothing was the typewriter born in the realm of blindness. Whereas handwriting is subject to the eye, a sense that works across distance, the typewriter uses a blind, tactile power. Before the introduction of John T. Underwood's "view typewriter" in 1898, all models (much to the disadvantage of their popularization) wrote invisible lines, which became visible only after the fact.[86] But Underwood's improvement did little to change the fundamental difference between handwriting and typescript. To quote Angelo Beyerlen's engineering expertise:

In writing by hand, the eye must constantly watch the written line and only that. It must attend to the creation of each written line, must measure, direct, and, in short, guide the hand through each movement. For this, the written line, particularly the line being written, must be visible. By contrast, after one presses down briefly on a key, the typewriter creates in the proper position on the paper a complete letter, which not only is untouched by the writer's hand but is also located in a place entirely apart from where the hands work. Why should the writer look at the paper when everything there occurs dependably and well as long as the keys on the fingerboard are used correctly?

The spot that one must constantly keep in view in order to write correctly by hand—namely, the spot where the next sign to be written *occurs*—and the process that makes the writer believe that the hand-written lines must be seen are precisely what, even with "view typewriters," *cannot* be seen. The only reasonable purpose of visibility is not fulfilled by the "view typewriters." The spot that must be seen is always visible, but not at the instant when visibility is believed to be required.[87]

Underwood's innovation unlinks hand, eye, and letter within the moment that was decisive for the age of Goethe. Not every discursive configuration rests on an originary production of signs. Circa 1900 several blindnesses—of the writer, of writing, of script—come together to guarantee an elementary blindness: the blind spot of the writing act. Instead of the play between Man the sign-setter and the writing surface, the philosopher as stylus and the tablet of Nature, there is the play between type and its Other, completely removed from subjects. Its name is inscription.

Instead of writing on his broken machine, Nietzsche continued to write about the typewriters that had made certain very forgetful "slaves of affect and desire" into so-called human beings. Out of technology comes science, but a science of techniques. "Our writing materials con- tribute their part to our thinking" reads one of Nietzsche's typed letters.[88] Five years later *The Genealogy of Morals* gathered a whole arsenal of martyrs, victims, maimings, pledges, and practices to which people, very tangibly, owe their memories: "perhaps indeed there was nothing more fearful and uncanny in the whole prehistory of man than his *mnemotech- nics.* 'If something is to stay in the memory it must be burned in: only that which never ceases to *hurt* stays in the memory.'"[89] This writing out of fire and pain, scars and wounds, is the opposite of alphabetization made flesh. It does not obey any voice and therefore forbids the leap to the sig- nified. It makes the transition from nature to culture a shock rather than a continuum. It is as little aimed at reading and consumption as the pain applied ceases not to cease. The signifier, by reason of its singular rela- tionship to place, becomes an inscription on the body. Understanding and interpretation are helpless before an unconscious writing that, rather than presenting the subject with something to be deciphered, makes the subject what it is. Mnemonic inscription is, like mechanical inscription, always invisible at the decisive moment. Its blindly chosen victims are "virtually compelled to invent gods and genii at all the heights and depths, in short, something that roams even in secret, hidden places, sees even in the dark, and will not easily let an interesting, painful spectacle pass unnoticed."[90]

Nietzsche's third experiment was to step into the place of such a god. If God is dead, then there is nothing to keep one from inventing gods. Dio- nysus (like Dracula several years later) is a typewriter myth. The mne- monic technique of inscription causes bodies so much pain that their la- menting, a Dionysian dithyramb in the most literal sense of the word, can and must invent the god Dionysus. Hardly anything distinguishes the drama described in the *Genealogy* from Nietzsche's dithyramb "Ariadne's Lament."[91] Tortured and martyred by an Invisible One who represents the naked power of inscription, Nietzsche's Ariadne puzzles over the desire of this Other. Such speech was not heard, indeed would have been unheard of, in the classical-romantic discourse network. It was first necessary to write with and about typewriters; the act of writing had first to become a blind incidence from and upon a formless ground before speech could be directed toward the unanswering conditions of speech itself. Ariadne speaks as the being who has been taught to speak by torture, as the animal whose forgetfulness has been driven out by mnemonic techniques; she talks about and to the terror that all media presuppose and veil. She became "the fateful curiosity that once would look out and downward through a crack in the room of consciousness and would sense that man . . . rests on the merciless, the craving, the voracious, the murderous."

But because language itself is a transposition, the desire of this Other remains unspoken. Ariadne says it.

> Stich weiter!
> Grausamster Stachel!
> Kein Hund—dein Wild nur bin ich,
> grausamster Jäger!
> deine stolzeste Gefangne,
> du Räuber hinter Wolken . . .
> Sprich endlich!
> Du Blitz-Verhüllter! Unbekannter! sprich!
> Was willst du, Wegelagerer, von mir?

> Stab further!
> Most cruel thorn!
> Not a dog—I am your trapped animal
> most cruel hunter!
> your proudest prisoner,
> you bandit behind clouds . . .
> Speak finally!
> You who hide in lightning! Stranger! speak!
> What do you want from me?, highwayman . . .

Dionysus, hidden in formlessness, stabs but does not speak. The torments and only they are his style. For that reason Ariadne, in contrast to women in the discourse network of 1800, knows nothing of authorship or love. She can only speak in monologues that can call the inscription "love" just as well as "hatred."

> Was willst du dir erhorchen?
> was willst du dir erfoltern,
> du Folterer
> du—Henker-Gott!
> Oder soll ich, dem Hunde gleich,
> vor dir mich wälzen?
> Hingebend, begeistert ausser mir
> dir Liebe—zuwedeln?

> What would you command?
> what would you extract,
> you torturer
> you—hangman-god!
> Or should I, like a dog,
> throw myself before you?
> Come wagging, devoted
> and beside myself—with love?[92]

It was as Nietzsche wrote: "Who besides me knows what *Ariadne* is!—For all such riddles nobody so far had any solution; I doubt that anybody even saw any riddles here."[93] When Friedrich Schlegel wrote *On*

Philosophy to his beloved, there was neither riddle nor solution. The man enjoyed his human determination, authorship; the woman remained the mute feminine reader of his love and of the confession that it was not he, but she who had introduced him to philosophy. With the "news" that far from docents and professors there was a "philosopher Dionysus," all the rules of the university discourse were reversed.[94] Ariadne and her "philosophic lover" conduct "famous dialogues on Naxos,"[95] where first and foremost a woman speaks and learns from her mute executioner-god that "love—in its means, [is] war, at bottom, the deathly hatred of the sexes."[96] The discovery of "how *foreign* man and woman are to one another"[97] does away with the possibility of placing the two sexes in polar or complementary relations within a discourse network. Henceforth there is no longer any discursive representation of one through the other, as Schlegel presupposed and practiced it. Because they are at war, Dionysus does not speak for Ariadne, and Ariadne certainly never speaks for Dionysus. The discourse network of 1900 codifies the rules that "one class cannot represent another" and "that it is much less possible for one sex to represent another."[98] Thus "a particular language" comes into being: "the woman's language."[99]

Another language follows immediately after the woman's language, after Ariadne's lament. Following the stage direction "Lightning. Dionysus appears in emerald beauty," the god speaks and thus materializes the logic of media. In his shroud of lightning Dionysus gives Ariadne's eyes the reversed afterimage effect that turns glimpsed darkness into light in order to protect the retina. Where earlier poetic hallucination had passed quietly over the reaction-time threshold of the senses, the lightning sends a dark and assaulting light, which transposes speech into its other medium.

> Sei klug, Ariadne! . . .
> Du hast kleine Ohren, du hast meine Ohren:
> steck ein kluges Wort hinein!—
> Muss man sich nicht erst hassen, wenn man sich lieben soll? . . .
> *Ich bin dein Labyrinth . . .*

> Be wise, Ariadne! . . .
> You have small ears, you have my ears:
> stick a wise word in!—
> Must we not first hate each other, if we are to love one another . . .
> *I am your labyrinth . . .*

The god does not answer or grant anything with his words, rather, he heightens the enigma. Rather than dissolve the ambiguity of light and darkness, love and hatred, he underscores it. A Dionysian "yes"—his wise word names the dark ground behind all words, even as he incarnates that ground. If Ariadne's lament was a glimpse out of the room of consciousness into the abyss, then Dionysus transgresses this transgression. With the line "*I am your labyrinth,*" the abyss of language declares that it is an abyss. Ariadne's lament remains unheard: "the ears of the god become smaller and more labyrinthine, and no word of lament finds the way through."[100] Something else happens instead. If, in contrast to the many he- and she-asses, Ariadne has small ears, if she sticks the wise word in, then what takes place is not elegy, monologue, or epiphany but, very suddenly and technically, dictation. The philosopher Dionysus, unlike his university-tamed predecessors, utters a Discourse of the Master, or despot. A dictate (in the double meaning of the word), however, is not to be understood or even read; its sense is literal.[101] "Stick a wise word in!" Ariadne's lament began with words about torture, stabbing, and inscription; it ends with a word that stabs.

Nietzsche, who was proud of his small ears just as Mallarmé was proud of his satyr's ears, thus wrote the program of his program. Rather than simply being thought as *The Genealogy of Morals,* typewriter became act in the dithyramb. The rhythm of the lyric has, of course, the "advantage" of "better impressing" words "into memory." (Human beings are that forgetful, and gods that hard of hearing.)[102] Hence, instead of declaring an ambiguous love to women with classical-romantic lyricism, Nietzsche stages a scene of torture. "If something is to stay in the memory it must be burned in: only that which never ceases to *hurt* stays in the memory." This fixed something is neither signified nor fixed idea; it is a dictated word. Nietzsche as lyric poet, or "How to Write Poetry with a Hammer."

The end of all women's laments is based on the historical fact that script, instead of continuing to be translation from a Mother's Mouth, has become an irreducible medium among media, has become the typewriter. This desexualization allows women access to writing. The following sentence applies literally to the discourse network of 1900: "The typewriter opened the way for the female sex into the office."[103] Nietzsche's Ariadne is not a myth.

In place of his broken Malling Hansen typewriter, the half-blind Nietzsche engaged secretaries—for *Beyond Good and Evil,* a Mrs. Röder-Wiederhold. She had such difficulty, however—as if in empirical demonstration of the title and of Nietzsche's dithyrambs—in tolerating the anti-democratic, anti-Christian master's discourse stuck into her ear that she "cried more often" than her dictator "cared for."[104] Ariadne's lament . . .

Women circa 1900 were no longer the Woman, who, without writing herself, made men speak, and they were no longer feminine consumers, who at best wrote down the fruits of their reading. A new wisdom gave them the word, even if it was for the dictation of a master's discourse.

Whenever the hermit of Sils went out among people, he consorted with emancipated women—that is, with women who wrote. For their part, from 1885 on they traveled to Engadine "only in order to make the acquaintance of Professor Nietzsche, who nonetheless seemed to them to be the most dangerous enemy of women." [105] The quiet mountain valley thus witnessed the future of our educational institutions. Whereas until 1908 Prussia's bureaucratic university held fast to its founding exclusion, Switzerland had long admitted women to the university.[106] Lou von Salomé is only the most well known among them; aside from her and other women students, at least three women Ph.D.'s appeared in Nietzsche's circle: Meta von Salis, Resa von Schirnhofer (to whom Nietzsche vainly recommended himself as a dissertation topic),[107] and one of the first women to earn a doctorate after the great historical turning point, Helene Druskowitz. Yet this context of Nietzsche's writing remains as unanalyzed as it is decisive.[108] With writing women as with writing machines, the man of many failed experiments was the first to use discursive innovations.

The text that Nietzsche first composed and then transferred into Ariadne's lament came from Lou Salomé. One has only to exchange "enigma" or "enigmatic life" for "Dionysus" in the "Hymn to Life," and the woman's verse "If you have no happiness left to give me, good then, you still have pain!" becomes Nietzsche-Ariadne's "No! Come back! *With* all your martyring!" The dithyramb (to say nothing of the rest of Nietzsche's relationship to Salomé) thus remains quite close to what suffragettes called "the language of woman." In a letter to his sister from Zurich, where Druskowitz was a student, Nietzsche reports:

This afternoon I took a long walk with my new friend Helene Druscowicz, who lives with her mother a few houses up from the Pension Neptune: of all the women I have come to know she has read my books with the most seriousness, and not for nothing. Look and see what you think of her latest writing (*Three English Poetesses*, among them Eliot, whom she greatly esteems, and a book on Shelley). . . . I would say she is a noble and honest creature, who does no harm to my "philosophy." [109]

A woman (Nietzsche's sister) is thus written that other women write—particularly about other women, who without disparagement are called "poetesses." She reads further that writing women are the most serious of Nietzsche's readers, without any doubt about their independence. There is no longer any talk about the ravages of feminine reading mania. Nietzsche learned with great care the negative lesson of the Pforta school, where pupils could become acquainted with everything but women. His "philosophy," therefore set between quotation marks, reversed the university discourse. Out of the exclusion of the other sex came, circa 1900, an inclusion. "*I am your labyrinth,*" says Dionysus to one who in the

Cretan cultic dance was herself the mistress of the labyrinth. Not only because Nietzsche exploded the interpretation rules of 1800 is it unnecessary to identify Ariadne with Cosima Wagner, as so often occurs. The enigma at the origin of all discourse has been played out; henceforth "women" count only insofar as they are known to Nietzsche and are acquainted with Nietzsche's writing.

Women are neither One nor all, but rather, like signifiers, a numbered multitude, or with Leporello, *mill'e tre*. Accordingly, their relation to Nietzsche's "philosophy" is ordered by selection. George's male circle, which would implement a reduction of books and book distribution, was not the first to put an end to the classical proliferation of texts. First, *Zarathustra* was already, in a direct reversal of the reception aesthetics of 1800, *A Book for Everyone and No One*. Second, *Zarathustra* concluded with a secret fourth part, carefully planned as a private edition. Third, Nietzsche dispatched this private edition with all the wiliness of a Dionysus, who passed his wiliness on only to certain women. One copy went to Helene Druskowitz, who, however, "took it to be a loan and soon returned the book to Köselitz's address, which made Nietzsche and Köselitz quite happy, for Nietzsche later—correctly—characterized his trust of her as 'stupidity.'"[110]

Whether knowledge of a stupidity or stupidity of a knowledge, there arises a type of book distribution that was not distribution at all. The public shrinks to private printings and private addresses, to books as loans, even misunderstood ones. In the war between the sexes, any means is justified to select women with small ears out of an open group. Only for a time did Druskowitz belong to the happy few who read Nietzsche without any harm to Nietzsche. Once she was called "my new friend," another time "that little literature-ninny Druscowitz," anything but "my pupil."[111] Dionysus, too, once praises Ariadne for her small ears; another time he asks her why she doesn't have larger ones.[112] Unstable circumstances, dictated by physiology and chance, confronted writing men and writing women circa 1900. The philosopher who had come up with provocative theses on woman as truth *and* untruth recommended to women (as if to realize as quickly as possible his well-known dream of chairs in Zarathustra studies) doctoral work on these theses. But when the women philosophers then—as in the books Druskowitz wrote after her dissertation—wrote about and against Zarathustra, Zarathustra's dispatcher had to wonder for once whether *he* were not the long-eared jackass. As long as women write books, there is no longer any guarantee that their torment and pleasure will consist in receiving wise words.

Druskowitz, when Nietzsche was in an insane asylum, rose in the titles of her books to "Doctor of World Wisdom" and (as if to parody F W v

Nietzky) into the aristocracy. But that was not enough: before she herself
vanished into an insane asylum, she also published only "for the freest
spirits." Thus was issued an answer to Dionysus and Zarathustra, who,
after all, approached women with declarations of war, whips, and torture. Druskowitz's last book deals with "the male as a logical and temporal impossibility and as the curse of the world":

> Throughout the entire organic world, the superiority claimed on behalf of the
> male sexual form has been lost by the human male in two senses: (1) as regards
> the more attractive part of the animal kingdom, (2) as regards his feminine com-
> panion. The she-goat and female ape would more deserve to be called his natural
> companions. For he is horribly made and carries the sign of his sex, in the shape
> of a sewer pump, before him like a criminal.[113]

The feminist, despite Nietzsche's denial, just might be a true pupil. "Must
we not first hate each other, if we are to love one another?" The polarity
of the sexes in 1800 unified mothers, writers, and feminine readers in
One Love, but now two scare tacticians, as hostile as they are equal, enter
the scene. The language of man and the language of woman deny one
another with the charge that everything said by one side is determined by
what is said by the other. Dissuasion includes "asking-behind," a phrase
coined by Nietzsche. Druskowitz sees in his philosophy only a dusty love
of the Greeks, determined by his neohumanist education; Nietzsche, perhaps because he recommends his philosophy to women as a dissertation
topic, sees in their books only a gymnasium-determined, stinking alpha-
betism. "For heaven's sake don't let us transmit our gymnasium education to girls! An education that so often takes spirited, knowledge-thirsty,
passionate young people and makes of them—images of their teachers!"[114]

"Asking-behind" can be precarious. No sooner has one traced certain
discourses of others to the Discourse of the Other, than the topic turns to
boys who are images of their teachers and who are thus precisely the Discourse of the Other in that they are also images of the star pupil who
writes. The escalation of scare tactics in the war between the two sexes
can thus only end in dithyrambic self-scorn.

> Ha! Herauf, Würde!
> Tugend-Würde! Europäer-Würde!
> Blase, blase wieder,
> Blasebalg der Tugend!
> Ha!
> Noch Ein Mal brüllen,
> Moralisch brüllen,
> Als moralischer Löwe
> Vor den Töchtern der Wüste brüllen!
> —Denn Tugend-Geheul,
> Ihr allerliebsten Mädchen,

Ist mehr als Alles
Europäer-Inbrunst, Europäer-Heisshunger!
Und da stehe ich schon,
Als Europäer,
Ich kann nicht anders, Gott helfe mir!
Amen!

Ha! Upward, dignity!
Virtue-dignity! The European's dignity!
blow, blow again
bellows of virtue!
Ha!
Roar once more,
the moral roar,
roar like a moral lion
before the daughters of the desert!
—For virtue-wailing,
you dearest girls,
is more than anything
the European's ardor, the European's craving!
And there I am,
as a European,
I have no choice, God help me!
Amen![115]

This was the riskiest of experiments, and therefore it remained on paper. Before the daughters of the desert, one prostitutes a discourse, which as the Discourse of the Other rules animals and can make them speak. What the Pforta school denied to its star pupil is realized in the desert: women appear, very different from gymnasium pupils and their emancipated copies. They neither speak nor write; a moralistic howling monkey, although he calls himself the labyrinth of women, finds that Dudu and Suleika, these "mute, ominous she-cats," "*resphinx*" him. The enigma of sexual difference, the phallus that Nietzsche transfigures into a Dionysian instrument of torture and that "Erna (Dr. Helene von Druskowitz)" proclaimed was a stigma in the shape of a sewer pump—in the desert its only invitation is to play.

Diese schönste Luft trinkend,
Mit Nüstern geschwellt gleich Bechern,
Ohne Zukunft, ohne Erinnerungen,
So sitze ich hier, ihr
Allerliebsten Freundinnen,
Und sehe der Palme zu,
Wie sie, einer Tänzerin gleich
Sich biegt und schmiegt und in der Hüfte wiegt
—man thut es mit, sieht man lange zu!
Einer Tänzerin gleich, die, wie mir scheinen will,

Zu lange schon, gefährlich lange
Immer, immer nur auf Einem Beine stand?
—Da vergass sie darob, wie mir scheinen will,
Das andre Bein?
Vergebens wenigstens
Suchte ich das vermisste
Zwillings-Kleinod
—nämlich das andre Bein—
In der heiligen Nähe
Ihres allerliebsten, allerzierlichsten
Fächer- und Flatter- und Flitterröckchens.

Drinking this finest air,
with nostrils filled like Chalices,
without future, without memories,
here I sit, you
dearest friends,
and watch the palm tree,
how like a dancer
she plays and sways her hip
—one dances along if one watches for long!
Like a dancer, who, it seems to me,
stands too long, dangerously long,
always, always only on One Leg?
—She forgot, it seems to me,
that other leg?
I at least
have looked in vain
for the missing twin jewel
—the other leg, namely—
in sacred nearness
to her dearest, most graceful
sparkling, fluttering, fanlike dress.

The phallus is missing or forgotten or there, where it is not: on women. The palm tree, instead of immediately becoming a piece of paper, as under the conditions of northern culture, dances the erection. Even the howling monkey, instead of merely learning to read and write from women as from palm trees, succumbs to the rhythmical imperative. The music that Nietzsche had vainly awaited from Wagner, Bizet, Köselitz, or Gast arises after all: a music equal to the brown sunsets of the desert. Women who are daughters of the desert, and therefore do not exist in the singular at all, place writing on the unmeasured ground without which signs and media would not exist. The despot's dream of being able to fix words as purely and simply as incessant pain would burn itself in evaporates in the emptiness that reduces words to small, amusing accidents. (The howling monkey himself mocks the word *resphinx* as a sin against language.) "Un coup de dés jamais n'abolira le hasard."

In the desert of chance there is neither future nor memory. Fixed ideas might once more excite the European's ardor, but circa 1900 an opposite symptom grounds the act of writing: the flight of ideas. Having become a lion or howling monkey, the philosopher can finally partake of the privilege of animals—an active forgetfulness, which does not merely forget this or that, but forgets forgetting itself.[116] Mnemonic technique, simply by being called technique rather than being, like memory, an inborn faculty, exists only as a resistance to the incessant and thought-fleeing innocence of speech.

The dithyrambic, flight-of-ideas wish to be out of Europe and in the desert, to lose one's head among its daughters, was not unfulfilled. In another desert, the institute for the cure and care of the insane in Jena, the ex-professor demonstrated this fulfillment in front of experts. What "came to" the psychiatrists writing the case report and listening to Nietzsche's speech was what always occurred to them circa 1900: "flight of ideas."[117]

The Great Lalulā

In the discourse network of 1900, discourse is produced by RANDOM GENERATORS. Psychophysics constructed such sources of noise; the new technological media stored their output.

Psychophysics

Two years before Nietzsche argued that mnemonic techniques were the genealogy of morals, a professor of psychology in Breslau, Hermann Ebbinghaus, published a short but revolutionary work entitled *On Memory*. Whereas the last philosopher ended the history of Western ethics by reducing history and ethics to machines, Ebbinghaus made a new, that is, technological contribution to knowledge of an age-old phenomenon. And whereas the philosopher and man of letters described the scene of writing with every line he wrote until such autoreferentiality issues in a megalomaniacal scream (or the book *Ecce Homo*) and brought psychiatrists into the picture, Ebbinghaus was quite reticent about the subject of his painful autoexperiment of memory quantification. This silence makes it possible to turn the great words of the ex-professor into science. Where the one had come to his end with psychiatrically defined flight of ideas, the other risked the same fate experimentally; his text, however, records only numbers, not a word of pain or pleasure. Yet numbers are the only kind of information that remains relevant beyond all minds, whether insane or professorial: as an inscription in the real.[1]

"During two periods, in the years 1879–80 and 1883–84," Ebbinghaus daily conducted autoexperiments, beginning at varied times of the day in the first period but using the early afternoon during the second. "Care was taken that the objective conditions of life during the period of the tests were so controlled as to eliminate too great changes or irregularities."[2] Who might have created such chaos—servants or wives, students or colleagues—remains unspecified. What matters is that a German professor modified his life during specified periods in order to be able to count something that was previously deemed common knowledge and therefore beneath notice: his own memory capacity.

How does the disappearance of the ability to reproduce, forgetfulness, depend upon the length of time during which no repetitions have taken place? What proportion does the increase in the certainty of reproduction bear to the number of repetitions? How do these relations vary with the greater or less intensity of the interest in the thing to be reproduced? These and similar questions no one can answer.

This inability does not arise from a chance neglect of investigation of these relations. We cannot say that tomorrow, or whenever we wish to take time, we can investigate these problems. On the contrary, this inability is inherent in the nature of the questions themselves. Although the conceptions in question— namely, degrees of forgetfulness, of certainty and interest—are quite correct, we have no means of establishing such degrees in our experience except at the extremes. We feel therefore that we are not at all in a condition to undertake the investigation. . . . For example, to express our ideas concerning their [memories'] physical basis we use different metaphors—stored-up ideas, engraved images, well-beaten paths. There is only one thing certain about these figures of speech and that is that they are not accurate.[3]

What seems most familiar to introspection here becomes an object of research. And the customary metaphors and images of psychology cannot be eradicated without mortification. Nietzsche had derived the most spiritual of memories from the body and its suffering; psychophysics approached the same enigma mathematically, with methods that H. L. F. von Helmholtz and G. T. Fechner had developed to measure perception.[4] A shift in paradigms occurred: Nietzsche and Ebbinghaus presupposed forgetfulness, rather than memory and its capacity, in order to place the medium of the soul against a background of emptiness or erosion. A zero value is required before acts of memory can be quantified. Ebbinghaus banned introspection and thus restored the primacy of forgetting on a theoretical level. On the one hand, there was Nietzsche's delirious joy at forgetting even his forgetfulness; on the other, there was a psychologist who forgot all of psychology in order to forge its algebraic formula. This is the relation of the Discourse of the Master to that of the university, of Nietzschean command to technological execution. Rather than give a philosophical description of mnemonic inscription and practice it in dithyrambs, Ebbinghaus took the place of Nietzsche's victim or experimental subject and then retroactively became the observer of his own experience in order to quantify what he had suffered.

Reading aloud at a tempo dictated by the ticking of his pocket watch, the professor spent years reading line after line of meaningless syllables, until he could recite them from memory. "His idea of using meaningless syllables as experimental material solved in a single stroke the introspectionist problem of finding meaning-free sensations."[5] From that point on, the bare relation of numbers could serve as a measure for the force of psychophysical inscription. Lines of seven syllables can be learned instantly, lines of twelve syllables have to be read sixteen times, and lines of twenty-six syllables have to be read fifty-five times before the mechanism of reproducible memorization clicks on. It was not always easy, however, to exclude self-fulfilling prophecies in the numerical results; the forgetting of forgetting remains as paradoxical as the effort "to rid oneself of a thought and by that very attempt foster that thought."[6] After three quarters of an hour of uninterrupted memory exercises, "occasionally exhaustion, headache, and other symptoms," set in, "which if continued would have complicated the conditions of the experiment."[7] Psychophysics is thus quite real, particularly for its inventor, for whom it (like all mnemonic techniques, according to Nietzsche) causes physical discomfort. It was known in the classical age that "such a dreadfully one-sided application of so subordinate a mental power as memory can derange human reason";[8] but for this reason Anselmus circumvented mechanical repetition through hermeneutics. In 1900 the opposite is necessary. A subordinate mental function becomes the most fundamental, because it is quantifiable.[9] For the sake of a few formulas, Ebbinghaus sacrificed (as Nietzsche did for the desert) his subject of knowledge.[10] Dizzy, numbed by all the syllables, his mind became a tabula rasa.[11]

The test's individual conditions all contributed to such emptiness. Language was artificially reduced to a raw state. First, Ebbinghaus did not allow "the meaningless syllables to be connected with any associated meanings, as is characteristic of certain mnemonic techniques."[12] Second, the empty page he had become was cleansed of memories and his native language. To isolate memory from all other cultural practices, Ebbinghaus eliminated signifieds from the beginning, because they might have provoked hermeneutic activity. "Associations tending in different directions, differing degrees of interest, the recollection of particularly striking or beautiful verses, etc.," all such ordinarily sanctioned mental activity amounted only to "disturbing influences."[13] With his head spinning, Ebbinghaus achieved an unthinkable distance where nothing, but nothing, means anything. He instituted the flight of ideas.

There is nothing exotic in distance, and the great kingdom of nonsense is no exception. In order to prove that recollecting meaningless material was the rule, Ebbinghaus conducted counter experiments. As if to test Nietzsche's thesis of the basic utility of metrics, Ebbinghaus memorized cantos from Byron's *Don Juan* under the same experimental conditions as before. Even he was surprised by the result. "From this point of view it almost seems as if the difference between sense and nonsense material were not nearly so great as one would be inclined *a priori* to imagine." [14] Thus the great doctrine bestowed by the discourse network of 1800 on its reformed primers is shaken: namely, the notion that readers would learn signifieds, because of their immanence in the mind, with much greater speed than they would learn signifiers by rote. To the contrary, pure nonsense reveals certain specific aspects of attention that hermeneutics could not even conceive. "The homogeneity of the series of syllables falls considerably short of what might be expected of it. The series exhibit very important and almost incomprehensible variations as to the ease or difficulty with which they are learned." [15] Just beyond the purpose of the test, then, there is something that no longer concerns Ebbinghaus but that will interest Freud and the writers; it is the differentiality that precedes all meaning: the naked, elementary existence of signifiers. If "from this point of view" the difference between sense and nonsense dwindles, then the kingdom of sense—that is, the entire discourse network of 1800—sinks to the level of a secondary and exceptional phenomenon. Neither understanding nor the previously fundamental capacity of "inwardizing" or recollection has any significant effect on the mechanics of memory.

If signifiers obey laws that are as fundamental as they are incomprehensible, it is essential to have the test material expressed in strict, statistical terms. Long before the expressionist "language eroticism" [*Spracherotik*] that "first must demolish language" and "establish the chaotic, originary condition, the absolute homogeneity of the material," [16] Ebbinghaus went to work on the same project. The nonsense that he spent hours, days, weeks, and years memorizing was never picked up from any native speakers in any locality. It was generated by a calculation at the beginning of every test series. Through an exhaustive combination of eleven vowels, nineteen beginning consonants, and (for the sake of pronunciation) only eleven end consonants, there came to be "ca. 2,300" or (as anyone might calculate) 2,299 tripthong syllables. [17] The random generator can not keep a few meaningful German words from appearing in a series, "*dosch päm feur lot . . .*" [18] These, however, are exceptions that can be read over (like *lot* five seconds ago) and that have little effect. "Among many thousand combinations there occur scarcely a few dozen that have a meaning and among these there are again only a few whose meaning was realized while they were being memorized."[19]

Never before had such passion been devoted to syllables. Of course, Reformation primers did, to the dismay of the classical age, play through single vowel-consonant combinations of the second order. But their *ab eb ib ob ub / ba be bi bo bu* was only an example; the goal was not a mathematically guaranteed completeness of assembly. The discourse network of 1900 was the first to establish a treasury of the signifier whose rules were entirely based on randomness and combinatorics.[20] It is not that, with Ebbinghaus's numbered sounds and sound combinations or Mallarmé's twenty-four letters, an old-European discursive practice returns from its repression circa 1800.[21] The fact that combinatory groups do not necessarily produce sense also applied to the letters and words of the miserable scribes of 1736. But not even Liscov's satire had the scribes systematically avoid "agreement among the letters" the way Ebbinghaus did. The difference between the polyphonic line and the twelve-tone technique is similar; the latter not only revives all contrapuntal-combinatory arts, but also avoids all accidental harmonic effects just as counterpoint had avoided all dissonance.

The homologies between dodecaphony and Ebbinghaus, who began a whole positivist movement, are so far-reaching that a search for factual cross-connections would be worthwhile (though it would not be merely the investigation into the ambience of Viennese coffee houses that Adorno's philosophy of modern music in all seriousness proposes). First, Ebbinghaus memorized the meaningless syllables in groups of seven to twenty-six, which, like Schönberg's twelve tones, are called series. Second, he eliminated the disturbing effects of easily learned syllables by putting aside the syllables from the available supply of 2,299 combinations that had already been memorized until all the other combinations had been gone through.[22] Dodecaphony proceeded in the same way with serial tones that had already been employed: these were taboo until the remaining eleven had been run through. Third, in order to refute the doctrine of free association taught in 1800, Ebbinghaus produced a very complicated demonstration showing that the interconnection of members of a row facilitates memorization; for example, if an already memorized series *dosch päm feur lot* . . . , is reordered into the series *lot päm feur dosch* . . . . Accordingly, "not only are the original terms associated with their immediate sequents," that is, those following in either direction, but "connections are also established between each term and those which follow it beyond several intervening members."[23] Schönberg proceeded in the same manner by bypassing certain notes in a melody and transferring them to parallel voices.[24] In both cases a combinatorics presented in the original material is subjected to a further combinatorics of the series and column.

Permutations of permutations eliminate any natural relation. Nonsense syllables or chromatic tones of equal value constitute media in the modern sense: material produced by random generation, selected and grouped into individual complexes. The fact that these materials always join discrete elements and do not develop in continuous genesis from an unarticulated nature distinguishes them from minimal signifieds. To Ebbinghaus the unique "oh" would simply be one among the 209 possible dipthong combinations. It would not take until the year 2407, as Christian Morgenstern's *Gingganz* announces, for "the great paper-shredding snow centrifuge of the American Nature Theater Company Ltd. of Brotherson & Sann" to take the place of organically grown snow crystals.[25]

If a syllable such as *ma* does not grow out of a mother-child love transcending words and then glide into the first word of the high idiom, *Mama*, but rather is thrown out like dice, it forfeits any ranking above the countless other syllables that are and remain meaningless. On the contrary, the effect of meaning, greeted by Tiedemann and Stephani as a revelation from beyond all language, becomes a disturbance that troubles the pure flight of ideas with memories and associations. Thinking and intending, however, are the imaginary acts that led the philosophers of 1800 to assert the primacy of the oral. In contrast to the technologies of the letter, only speaking—an externalization that immediately disappears—could figure as the frictionless unification of Spirit and Nature. But orality, together with thought, vanishes from randomly generated language material. Of course, Ebbinghaus worked with phonemes in order to be able to read aloud, but they were presented to him as writing. Syllable after syllable comes out of the random generator, onto the desk and into the file of worked-through alternatives, until all 2,299 have been used and output and input can begin again.

Memory tests in which the experimental subject necessarily thinks nothing and abandons the position of knowing subject have an equally subjectless observer, who is not as far from Nietzsche's new god as hasty distinctions between myth and positivism would have it. The two mechanical memories on either side of the tabula rasa Ebbinghaus—the one generating the syllables and the other recording them after they have passed before him—form a writing machine that forgets nothing and stores more nonsense than people ever could: 2,299 nonsense syllables. This is the necessary condition for a psychophysical investigation of memory: memory is taken from people and delegated to a material organization of discourse. The discourse network of 1800 played the game of not being a discourse network and pretended instead to be the in-wardness and voice of Man; in 1900 a type of writing assumes power that does not conform to traditional writing systems but rather radicalizes the technology of writing in general.[26]

The most radical extrapolation from a discourse network of writing is to write writing. "All letters that have ever been written by man count."[27] Given an assortment of letters and diacritical signs, like a typewriter key-board (even, after 1888, in its standardized form), then in principle it is possible to inscribe more and different sorts of things than any voice has ever spoken. Of course, such notations have no purpose beyond notation itself; they need not and cannot be dematerialized and consumed by a hermeneutics; their indelible and indigestible existence on the page is all that the page conveys.

THE GREAT LALULĀ

Kroklokwafzi? Seṁmemeṁi!
Seiokrontro—prafriplo:
Bifzi, bafzi; hulaleṁi:
quasti basti bo . . .
Lalu lalu lalu lalu la!

Hontraruru miromente
zasku zes rü rü?
Entepente, leiolente
klekwapufzi lü?
Lalu lalu lalu lalu la!

Simarar kos malzipempu
silzuzankunkrei (;)!
Marjomar dos: Quempu Lempu
Siri Suri Sei []!
Lalu lalu lalu lalu la!

Before Morgenstern's 1905 collection *Gallows Songs*, no poem had existed as a small discourse network. Literary historians have sought classical-romantic models for these poems and have found some non-sense verse here and there.[28] But even the "Wien ung quatsch, Ba nu, Ba nu n'am tsche fatsch," sung by a dark-skinned cook in Clemens Brentano's *Several Millers of Sorrow*, if it is not pidgin Rumanian, is at least speak-able.[29] No voice, however, can speak parentheses that enclose a semicolon (as specified in "The Great Lalulā") or even—to demonstrate once and for all what media are—brackets that surround an empty space. System-atic nonsense, which demands inhuman storage capacities, exists only in writing. The fact that Morgenstern's syllables owe their existence not to a combinatory method but, at first sight at least, to lovely chance doesn't make them all that different from Ebbinghaus's series. "The Great Lalulā" is also material without an author; the more chance enters, the more literally does the imperative in the motto of the *Gallows Songs* apply: "Let the molecules roar / whatever they dice together!"

Clearly, the discourse network of 1900 is a dice game with "serially ordered discrete unities,"[30] which in the lyric are called letters and punctuation signs, and to which writers since Mallarmé have ceded the initiative. More anarchic than Liscov's miserable scribes, who can at least discard a bad dice throw, less Faustian than all *poetae minores* of 1800, who produced quantities of meaning in inverse relation to their stature, literature throws out signifiers. "The Great Lalulā" says that, in the beginning and in the end, language is Blabla. "You can say what you like, people more often than not do nothing but—bark, cackle, crow, bleat, etc. Just listen for once to the animal conversations in a bar."[31]

What remains is the enigma of the signifiers' use. To write down script that is simply script had no appeal for hermeneutic interpreters or for philosophers, whose chief concern is "naturally the stress on the factor of meaning" and therefore "naturally" German Poetry.[32] "Lalulā" is more useful to cryptographers (of whom more will be said). But psychophysics would have the greatest use for such writing. There are people in whom Morgenstern's nonsense "lives on as a fount of citation"—the most certain "sign for what we call a classic poet"[33]—though one does not know how such mnemonic technique works. Because "new creation in language has something in common with the invention of undreamed-of physical phenomena,"[34] the "Lalulā" would be an occasion for readers to instigate autoexperiments in memory, especially since Ebbinghaus himself fudged things a bit. In order to measure eventual differences between sense and nonsense, the psychophysicist introduced verses by Byron and thus determinants supplementary to meaning: rhyme and meter. In "Lalulā," by contrast, only these two redundancies, with no meaning, restrict chance. As a missing link between the syllabic hodgepodge and the lyric form, "Lalulā" could bring experimental clarification to the controversial question whether rhyme and meter, in their mnemonically convenient conspicuousness, represent the identity of signifieds or are the effects of signifiers.[35] In this way one could distinguish those functions that, in Byron, remain clumped together as "unified strains of sense, rhythm, rhyme, and membership in a single language."[36] Nietzsche's doctrine of the utility of poetry, which stressed mnemonic technique and questioned rather than supported the possibility of the transmission of meaning, could be brought to bear on *The Scientific Foundations of Poetry* more materially through "The Great Lalulā" than the apostle of naturalism, Wilhelm Bölsche, had intended in his title.

Following the heroic autoexperiments of Ebbinghaus, breaking down discourses into single and discrete functions became the task of an entire psychophysics of complex cultural practices. These functions have nothing to do with one another or with any unity imposed by consciousness; they are automatic and autonomous. "We may sum up the experiment by saying that a large number of acts ordinarily called intelligent, such as reading, writing, etc., can go on quite automatically in ordinary people."[37] In 1900 speaking and hearing, writing and reading were put to the test as isolated functions, without any subject or thought as their shadowy supports. "Between finitude and infinity the word has ample room to be able to do without any help from thought."[38] Rather than the long genetic path of the word from its beginning in nature to its end in culture, what counts is the signifier's mechanism and how it runs under either normal or pathological circumstances. Psychophysics is not a pedagogy that takes necessary truths from Mother Nature for mothers and teachers; rather, it inventories previously unresearched particulars. Culture [*Bildung*], the great unity in which speaking, hearing, writing, and reading would achieve mutual transparency and relation to meaning, breaks apart. Even if schoolmen draw massive conclusions from the inventory, the experimenters are at the wheel. Pedagogic reforms are only applications; they apply to only one cultural practice; indeed, they tend to make instruction in reading or writing into a somewhat muddled order of research. Thus even in its own field, in the "psychology of reading," "the competence of pedagogy" ends.[39] Exit Stephani.

The victory of psychophysics is a paradigm shift. Instead of the classical question of what people would be capable of if they were adequately and affectionately "cultivated," one asks what people have always been capable of when autonomic functions are singly and thoroughly tested.[40] Because this capability is not a gift of productive nature, but as simple as either spelling or writing "Lalulā," it has no ideal completion or endpoint. There is no universal norm (inwardness, creative imagination, high idiom, Poetry) transcending the particular functions. Each has a standard only in relation to defined experimental subjects and conditions.

When ten pupils from each of ten gymnasium classes read aloud and as quickly as possible one hundred connected words from *Egmont*, the measured average reading time for those in the sixth class is 55 seconds, for those in the fifth class 43 seconds, and for those in the first class 23 seconds.[41] These standards mean nothing to educationally bureaucratized lovers of Goethe. Ebbinghaus adds to these numbers his own, namely 0.16 seconds per word of Goethe, thus leveling any distinction in rank between pupils and professors, empirical evidence and norm. To measure one's own reading pace as well as that of the sixth class means methodically disposing of culture [*Bildung*]. Thus Ebbinghaus does not announce any record, because "the numbers continue to diminish with further practice in reading."[42] So the transcendental norm falls into an endless series, at whose irreal end might be someone who could only speedread. If psychophysical standards had ideals rather than provisional records, those ideals would resemble the genius of Kafka's hunger artist. Indeed, the first German graphologist took such interest in cripples who wrote with their mouths or feet that he attempted to do so himself and reproduced facsimiles of his efforts.[43] Psychophysics ceased subjecting cultural practices to a dichotomy of the normal and pathological, the developed and underdeveloped. It investigated capabilities that in everyday life would have to be called superfluous, pathological, or obsolete.

Ebbinghaus, having been alphabetized, could read silently, without moving his mouth, but for test series he preferred the old-fashioned method of reading aloud at a tempo that could be mechanically directed.[44] Of course, typewriters that eliminated all the individuality of script had recently appeared,[45] but a psychophysical graphology arose in a counter movement and focused on the difference between standardized letters and unconscious-automatic hands that write. It was concerned with what under normal conditions would be considered a "superfluous addition to the letters."[46] If "it is emphasized—and rightly so—that a pupil should not learn material that is meaningless to him,"[47] each psychophysical experimental subject—from the infant to the psychology professor—is an exception to such pedagogical norms. All the abilities and inabilities despised in 1800 return, not as simple regressions from an erstwhile culture, but as objects of analysis and decomposition.

The cultural-technological standards do not represent Man and his Norm. They articulate or decompose bodies that are already dismembered. Nature does its own work before any experimenter arrives.[48] Apoplexy, bullet wounds to the head, and paralysis made possible the fundamental discoveries upon which every connection drawn between cultural practices and physiology is based. In 1861 Paul Broca traced motoric aphasia, or the inability to pronounce words despite unimpaired consciousness and hearing, to lesions in a circumscribed area of the cerebral cortex. In 1874 Karl Wernicke made the mirroring discovery that sensory aphasia, or the inability to hear words despite unimpaired speech capacity, corresponded to a deficit in other areas of the brain. The method of isolating and measuring cultural practices by reference to deficiencies led finally to the decomposition of discourse into single parameters.[49] Circa 1900 optical disturbances corresponding to the acoustical disturbances investigated by Broca and Wernicke, the alexias or agraphias, also became familiar. Further, a certain reversal in relation to linguistic reference and its agnosias was discovered, for there turned out to be an oral, and then a graphic asymbolia, or the inability "to find the verbal image of an object" even when the doctor would show it to the patient.[50] Diverse subroutines finally had to be distinguished within each cultural practice; for example, writing included "dictation, copying, written description, and spontaneous writing"[51]—and each of the subroutines might lead to different results. What we ordinarily call language is thus a complex linkage of brain centers through no less numerous direct and indirect nerve connections. As Nietzsche had prophesied and, as a paralytic, demonstrated to his psychiatrist Theodor Ziehen, language breaks down into individual elements: into optical, acoustical, sensory, and motoric nervous impulses and only then into signifier/signified/referent.

Research into aphasia marked a turning point in the adventures of speech. Disturbances in language no longer converged in the beautiful wordlessness of the romantic soul. If there are "as many sources of language disturbance as there are organs of speech wanting to speak,"[52] then the single "oh" becomes only an incidental case.[53] The Poetry that listened to or inspired that "oh" is replaced by sciences. Only on the basis of psychophysics does it make terminological sense for Saussure, in founding a new linguistics, to decompose the linguistic sign into the notion of a concept (signified) and an acoustic-sensory image (signifier),[54] or for Freud, more copied than understood by his students, similarly to divide "thing representation" [Sachvorstellung] from "word representation" [Wortvorstellung].[55]

The cultural goal of universal alphabetization fades away with the "oh" of the soul. The pedagogy of 1900, because it was applied physiology, was preoccupied with standardizing, individually and successively, the brain regions of its pupils. The center of concrete representations, the motoric and sensorial centers for speech and writing—all had to be approached separately. "The reading-writing method in no way corresponds to the state of contemporary science."[56] Because not every local center has direct nerve connections to every other, there is no unity of the transcendental signified capable of organically developing speaking and hearing, writing and reading out of one another. The pedagogical uncoupling of the cultural-technological subroutines simply followed cuts made by the scalpel. Children circa 1900 learned to read without understanding and to write without thinking. The investigation of aphasia is always already its production.

In 1913 Wassily Kandinsky published a volume of poems in German. He accompanied the title *Sounds* with some very practical tips. He meant not romantic primal sounds, but "inner sounds" that remain when one has repeated words until they become senseless—a proven and oft-employed means of simulating aphasia. Thus Kandinsky's poetry isolated the sound images of words physiologically with the exactness that his painting isolated colors and forms. That does not hinder Germanists from attacking him in the name of a linguistics that grew out of the same premises.[57] But alexia seems to haunt the books of its forgotten investigators . . .

In 1902 Hofmannsthal's *A Letter* appeared with a self-diagnosis of the sender.

And could I, if otherwise I am still the same person, have lost from my inscrutable self all traces and scars of this creation of my most intensive thinking—lost them so completely that in your letter now lying before me the title of my short treatise stares at me strange and cold? At first I could not comprehend it as the familiar image of conjoined words, but had to study it word by word, as though these Latin terms thus strung together were meeting my eye for the first time.[58]

One who writes that he is hardly able to read any more is virtually formulating a case of sensory and near-amnesiac alexia. But the person is Phillip Lord Chandos, and the pile of letters that refuses to coalesce into the images of words is the title of a Latin tract that Chandos has recently written. In the meantime he has not lost the ability to write (say letters). But he has lost a part of his ability to read, and he suffers from a thoroughly physiological "dullness" of the "brain."[59] Whereas Ofterdingen or Guido could give to even the most foreign books their own titles, the writer of 1902 can no longer even understand his own title. We can read "Chandos" in place of "the patient" when a great physiologist describes the symptoms of alexia:

The patient can see the letters sharply enough, he can write them spontaneously, eventually he can even copy them without error—and yet he is unable to read anything printed or written, even the words he had just clearly and correctly written (notes, short letters). . . . The alexic recognizes single letters or even syllables, but he cannot grasp them successively and retain them as complete words so as to arrive at an understanding of what he has read, even for single words.[60]

The solidarity of physiology and literature extends to concrete details. One isolates the symptoms to which the other attests. Nietzsche praised the half-blindness that kept him from reading and allowed only the writing of signifiers. Chandos experiences a similar blindness vis-à-vis signifieds, but he develops a new discourse out of alexia (just as sensory language disturbances often influence the motoric aspect of language):[61] he avoids "even pronouncing" signifieds, above all the transcendental ones ("Spirit, soul, or body"), and envisions instead "a language in which not one word is known to me, a language in which mute things speak to me."[62] In much the same way, pedagogues versed in psychophysics separated reading and writing, because neither should be confused with signifieds and referents, from wordless observational or practical instruction.[63] As if he were a pupil in their school, the Lord finds that "a dog in the sun, an old churchyard, a cripple" and so on are "sublime revelations" beyond all words.[64] This is not surprising in the cripple he himself is. Because they switch off medial operations of selection, aphasia and alexia necessarily present the nameless and formless. In aphasics, Nietzsche's terrible voice returns to the physiology of everyday life. "Speaking, whistling, clapping the hands, etc., everything is to their ears the same incomprehensible noise."[65]

Aphasia, alexia, agraphia, agnosia, asymbolia—in this long list of dysfunctionalities the noise that precedes every discourse becomes at once theme and method. The products of decomposed language observed in the experimental subjects are as usable as the material provided by the experimenters. What terrified Nietzsche and Chandos discovered as a wondrous, foreign realm can also be transmitted. Discursive manipulations in the discourse network of 1900 were quite extensive. Psychophysics transmits white noise through a certain filter so that what comes across is, say, pink noise; whatever the eyes and ears of the receiver make of this is then the experimental result.

Ebbinghaus further tested his nonsense syllables on others. But something remarkable occurred, for not all experimental subjects had his command of the flight of ideas. For some,

at least in the beginning, it is hardly possible to refrain from the learning aids of all sorts of memory supports, to perceive the syllables as mere letter combinations and memorize them in a purely mechanical fashion. Without any effort or volition on their part, all kinds of associated representations constantly fly toward them from individual syllables. Something occurs to them, indeed a motley of things: a syllabic assonance, relations among letters, similar sounding meaningful words or the names of persons, animals, and so forth, meanings in a foreign language, etc. . . . For example, *pek* is expanded to *Peking*, *chi* to *child*; *sep* recalls *Joseph*, *neis* the English word *nice*. . . . In the case of one subject, the syllables *faak neit* stimulated the idea "Fahrenheit," in another case, *jas dum* (via the French *jaser*) suggested the notion of stupid jabbering; the syllable sequence *dosch päm feur lot* was on one occasion joined together in the brief sentence: "The bread fire licks."[66]

Such is the countertest to aphasia. The farrago of syllables that aphasiacs produce from signifieds is put before normal speakers in order to see how they produce signifieds out of a syllabic hodgepodge and at the same time betray a sense-producing notion, which in the case of *jas dum* still means talking nonsense. In this way, the difference between *Hearing and Understanding* can be quantified. An experiment run under that title sent nonsense syllables, such as *paum* and *maum*, through telephone and phonograph channels; subjects (in spite or of because of the frequency band restriction) received "the more probable *baum* ['tree']," thus providing experimental verification of Nietzsche's oracles of language theory, or demonstrating that discourses are "eclectic combinations" of noise spectra.[67] "We find it much easier to fantasize an approximate tree. . . . We are artists more than we suspect."

Thus a physiological work entitled *The Brain and Language*, which reconstructs the path from the speechless patches of light and noise the infant perceives to the ordering of images and speech sounds, comes to the conclusion: "We proceed like poets."[68] But such poetic activity, rhyming *Baum* and *maum* or hitting upon *faak neit* / *Fahrenheit*, having been confirmed by Nietzschean brain researchers, no longer has any need of a muse. Even in the greatest authors, the unconscious functions of the brain are at work. A judgment on Anselmus's ecstasy beneath the elder tree, "made possible on the basis of a psychiatric and scientific contribution,"[69] led the psychiatrist Otto Klinke to conclude that Anselmus, in listening to the whispering of the three sisters, was clinically psychotic:

It can also happen, and with the mentally ill it does, that these sounds and words in a certain rhythm . . . are heard by the inner ear as occurring at a regular tempo and are projected to a spot in the person's own body or onto the environment. This rhythm, expanding to associations, alliterations, and even rhymes, is often brought about by noises in the ear that are synchronous with heart or pulse rates, but it can also be provoked and maintained by regular external sounds, such as marching to rhythm, or, recently, the regular rolling of train wheels. We see Anselmus in a similar situation at the beginning of the story.[70]

This conclusion abolishes the precondition for Poetry.[71] The noises that led Anselmus to the Mother's Mouth lose all human quality, while his interpretation of them, called Serpentina, loses any basis. But magic is not lost, as it was in the age of enlightened fathers, when the Elf King's whispering voice became rustling leaves. Psychophysics advances, beyond all attribution of meaning and its transparent arbitrariness, to the meaningless body, which is a machine among machines. A roaring in the ears and the roaring of trains are equally capable of providing disordered brains with assonances, alliterations, and rhymes. The fact that "Sister, sister, swing in the shimmer" was once written down as Poetry is no longer applauded by psychophysics.

It had hardly any occasion to applaud. Circa 1900 noise was everywhere. A psychotic in his cell constantly hears imbecilic voices that snap up words in the imbecility of his surroundings "which have the same or nearly the same *sound* as what they have to say or rattle off." Like the subjects in Ebbinghaus's experiment, the hallucinations rhyme "Santiago" with "Cathargo" or (in a somewhat Saxon accent) "Briefbeschwerer" with "Herr Prüfer schwört." [72] A psychiatric researcher drew the sad conclusion from his association tests that rhymes such as *Herz/Schmerz* or *Brust/Lust*, those honorable old warhorses of German Poetry, flood the inner ear "only in psychic disorders, that is, wherever so-called flight of ideas is the rule." Ziehen cites a manic patient who associates *Hund-Bund-Schund* [*dog-band-trash*], [73] and who thus calls the output of rhyming words by its proper name.

Decisively, trash and nonsense had been scientifically recorded in 1893, not only in 1928, as even an informed literary scholarship would admit. [74] Lyric poetry, too, would have to check over its jingles in the *Handbook of Physiological Psychology* (the title of Ziehen's book). "*Brust/Lust*" and "*Schmerz/Herz*" are among the examples presented by Arno Holz in his *Slimy Rhymes and the Nonsense of Rhymes in General.* The transition to modern free verse cannot always be described as an inherently literary innovation. When rhyme shows up in laboratories and madhouses, it must vanish from the printed page if poets and psychotics are not to be confused.

Yet free verse was only one historical option circa 1900. A second, paradoxical option was mimicry. If the clattering of trains could suggest rhymes to the mentally ill, the lyric poet could detect new rhymes in such poetry of the body. The railroad itself, rather than an author or High German, speaks in Detlev von Liliencron's "Rattattattat." [75] And if marching to rhythm has the same effect, then Liliencron's rhyme play of "Persian Shah" and "klingling, bumbum and tschingdada" logically follows.

A military-musical sound source transmits *tschingdada*; the experimental subjects are asked if any rhymes occur to them. Such was the procedure, in the year of the *Gallows Songs* (1905), of Narziss Ach, M.D. and Ph.D. His test consisted in meaningless syllables (excluding the syllable *ach*, unfortunately), to which subjects, under hypnosis and in a normal state, were to respond with meaningless rhymes or assonances. [76] Difficulties appear only if the permitted reactions, unlike Ach's test or "Lalulā," are to be exclusively meaningful words. Hermann Gutzmann's eclectic combination *maum/Baum* is harmless; *tschingdada* provokes foreign words; but things become truly aporetic with Stefan George. The inventor of so many unheard-of and nonetheless German rhymes has all discourse culminate in a syllabic hodgepodge that chokes off any reaction in the experimental subjects.

We were in that special region of unremitting punishments where the people are who had been unwilling to say, "O Lord!," and where the angels are who said, "We want." There in the place of their torment they blaspheme the eternal judge and pound their breasts; they claim to be greater than the blessed and despise their joys. But every third day a shrill voice calls from above: "Tiholu· Tiholu"—

a tangled confusion results· the damned fall silent; trembling, gnashing their teeth, they prostrate themselves on the ground or try to hide themselves in the glowing dark depths.[77]

The dream of "Tiholu" perverts George's lifelong inspiration for rhyme and translation: Dante's *Divine Comedy*. Dante inflicted on his damned every imaginable speech disturbance, whereas the blessed were with the Word and God in one and the same measure. George, however, has the damned speak, but only so long as that shrill voice, in its mechanically regular act every three days, does not deliver its catchphrase. Nonsense syllables are the divine punishment that reduces them to a chaos of bodies. People who did not want to call out to their Lord are answered by the Discourse of the Master with his own, very contemporary perversion: hell as a random generator.

In discussing his theory of memory and its inscription, Nietzsche once mentioned the "slogan and catchphrase" [*Schlag*- und *Stichwort*][78] and with that illustrated the process he was describing.* Psychophysical experiments impose slogans and catchphrases until the tortured disappear into glowing depths or render up the physiology of cultural practices. With patients like Chandos, whose disturbances allow them "to read correctly individual letters, but not to combine them into words," Ziehen recommends that one "spell a word for the patient and have him put it together, or, in reverse, present a word somehow and have the patient spell it."[79] These catchphrases were such hits that they reappear everywhere circa 1900.

Freud analyzed a female hysteric who "at nineteen, . . . lifted up a stone and found a toad under it, which made her lose her power of speech for hours afterwards." Emmy v. N. fled a psychiatrist "who had compelled her under hypnosis to spell out the word 't . . .·o . . . a . . . d.'" Before she would go to the couch, she made Freud "promise never to make her say it."[80] As if he had been a witness to the first psychiatrist's consultation, Malte Laurids Brigge overhears a doctor-patient conversation through the walls of the Salpêtrière, Jean Martin Charcot's great healing or breeding institution for hysterias:

But suddenly everything was still, and in the stillness a superior, self-complacent voice, which I thought I knew, said: "Riez!" A pause. "Riez! Mais riez, riez!" I was already laughing. It was inexplicable that the man on the other side of the partition didn't want to laugh. A machine rattled, but was immediately silent again, words were exchanged, then the same energetic voice rose again and ·

---

* The prefixes *Schlag* and *Stich* literally mean "blow," or "hit," and "stab." The German terms for "slogan," "catchphrase," and "header" thus retain violent overtones of forcible, abbreviated mnemonic impression less obvious in their English equivalents. [Trans.]

ordered: "Dites-nous le mot: avant." And spelling it: "A-v-a-n-t." Silence. "On n'entend rien. Encore une fois . . ."[81]

Even in its oral, imperative form, the slogan and catchphrase is inscription. Chopping and iteration reduce discourse to discrete unities, which as keyboard or store of signs immediately affect bodies. Instead of translating visual language into audible language, as the phonetic method did, breathing the beautiful inwardness of music into speech, psychophysics imposes the violence of spacing. Localization is the catchphrase of all aphasia research, spelling the psychiatrist's overheard command. It is only logical for the catchphrase technique to be applied to reading and writing.

Following the procedure of Helmholtz, who built device after device to measure reaction-time thresholds, the psychophysics of the nineties went to work measuring reading with kymographs, tachistoscopes, horopterscopes, and chronographs. There was intense competition among these machines to determine the smallest fraction of time in which reading could be measured in experimental subjects. Thus the physiology of the senses and aphasia research were joined: James McKeen Cattell calculated in milliseconds the time in which a letter, exposed to view for one lightning instant, traveled from one language area to the next. In other experiments, however, he (and later Benno Erdmann and Raymond Dodge) worked with tenths of seconds, which could measure subjects' eye movements and their backtracking to reread. By contrast, Wilhelm Wundt's experimental tachistoscope continuously diminished a letter's exposure time to the limit value of null. Only at 0.01 sec "can one be sure that any movement of the eye or wandering of attention is impossible."[82] Experimental subjects (who were once more also the professorial directors of the experiments) thus sat, chained so as to hinder or even prohibit movement, facing black viewing boxes out of which for the duration of a flash—a pioneer of reading research, Frans Cornelius Donders, actually used electrical induction sparks[83]—single letters shone out. This is modernity's allegory of the cave.

"Lightning. Dionysus appears in emerald beauty," said the dithyramb. A tachistoscopic trick—and letters appear for milliseconds in scriptual beauty. "Stick a wise word in," said Dionysus in Ariadne's ear. The device also writes signs, whether wise or meaningless, onto the retina, signs that can only be taken literally. After the elimination of rereading and the recognition of complete words, even the educated fall back on "the most primitive spelling" as the minimum *and* standard of all reading.[84] This was probably the first time that people in a writing culture were reduced to the naked recognition of signs. Writing ceased to wait, quiet and dead, on patient paper for its consumer; writing ceased to be sweetened by pastry baking and mothers' whispering—it now assaulted with the power of a shock. Catchphrases emerge from a store of signs to which they return with unimaginable speed, leaving behind in the subject inscriptions without ink or consciousness. The tachistoscope is a typewriter whose type hits the retina rather than paper. The mindless deciphering of such blindings can be called reading only by a complete uncoupling from orality, as if the madness of Heerbrand and his dancing Fraktur letters had become a standard. The helplessness of the experimental subjects before the tachistoscope ensures that all "processes" whose "uncommonly complex embodiment" is reading[85]—from the recognition of letters to that of words, from speed to error quota—will yield only measurable results.

Standards have nothing to do with Man. They are the criteria of media and psychophysics, which they abruptly link together. Writing, disconnected from all discursive technologies, is no longer based on an individual capable of imbuing it with coherence through connecting curves and the expressive pressure of the pen; it swells in an apparatus that cuts up individuals into test material. Tachistoscopes measure automatic responses, not synthetic judgments. But they thus restore the reputation of spelling, which had generally come to be viewed with contempt.

In 1803 the psychiatrist Hoffbauer neatly calculated the normally educated person's reading speed.

An average accomplished reader reads three signatures per hour, when the latter are of the type of the present volume and the subject of the book causes him no difficulty. On a rough estimate, he needs no more than one and a quarter minutes to read one page. There are thirty lines to the page, and every line contains thirty letters; thus in one and a quarter minutes or seventy-five seconds he must recognize and distinguish nine hundred letters. The recognition of a letter occurs as the result of an inference. Thus our reader makes twelve different inferences in a second. . . . If one assumes that the reader is following the writer, so that the latter's thoughts are transmitted to the soul of the reader, one is struck with amazement. Some have wanted to conclude from this and other examples that we perceive objects without being conscious of it. This does not seem to follow in the least.[86]

The mathematics of *Bildung* went this far and no further, if for no other reason than that numbers were written out. A reconstruction of completed alphabetization, from a whole signature back to a single letter, culminates in reverence for a consciousness that can make 12 inferences per second, inferences that certainly do not justify the conclusion that the consciousness that has to accompany all my reading (to adapt Kant's phrase) amounts to nothing. As long as reading transported thoughts from soul to soul and had its norm, as with Anton Reiser, in the tempo of speech, it was in fact recognition, and any notion of the unconscious, technically defined, was absurd.

The automatism of tachistoscopic word exposition is not designed to transport thoughts. But there are other reasons the 10 ms for entire words undercuts Hoffbauer's twelfth of a second per letter. An apparatus does not let alphabetization run its course, then applaud it afterwards. The apparatus itself, like Dionysus, dictates the tempo of exposition with lightning speed. Such procedures shed light on functions as foreign to the individual and consciousness as writing ultimately is. Psychophysics (and it thus made film and futurism possible) investigated "only the movements of matter, which are not subject to the laws of intelligence and for that reason are much more significant."[87] Cultural technologies could be attributed to Man only as long as they were marked off along the abscissa of biological time, whereas the time of the apparatus liquidates Man. Given the apparatus, Man in his unity decomposes, on the one hand, into illusions dangled in front of him by conscious abilities and faculties and, on the other hand, into unconscious automatisms that Hoffbauer hardly felt the need to dignify with a refutation.

It was illusion for the first typists to want to be able to see and read the text as it was being written, to want "view typewriters." Automatized hands work better when blind. It was illusion for educated subjects to be "certain" that they had "seen the 'whole'" in the tachistoscope. In the realm of milliseconds, unaffected by introspection, even the most trained reader's eye proceeds by successive spelling.[88] It was an illusion of "subjective judgment" that Fraktur was more readable than roman script. Precisely the "people who much prefer to read Fraktur and believe they can do so with greater ease are the ones who require more reading time."[89]

Hermann Bahr hit upon a succinct rule for all such illusion. Classical alphabetization had attempted to mediate between Man and World (while avoiding all discourses), but: "The experiment with man has failed. And the experiment with the world has failed. The experiment can now take place only where man and the world come together (sensation, impression."[90] All that remains of the real is a contact surface or skin, where something writes on something else. This is precisely the tachistoscopic effect planned by a literature intent on addressing "nerves" in order to "bring about certain moods" rather than "stammering about nonsensical pleasures."[91] It would thus assault the language centers in the brain individually and successively. Nietzsche's view that language first transposes nervous impulses into images and then images into sounds is the most exact characterization of literary language. Holz not only replaced rhyme with a number of acoustic effects; he also asked "why the eye should *not* have its particular pleasures in the printed type of a poem."[92] These pleasures are not miniature images of Man and World, but rather (as if they were calculated on the tachistoscope) ergonomically optimal uses of reading time. Beginning in 1897, Holz typographically centered the lines of his poetry for physiological reading ease. "If I left the axis at the beginning of the line, rather than in the middle, the eye would always be forced to travel twice as far."[93] What the verses have in view, then, are not readers and their understanding, but eyes and their psychophysics, in other words: "Movements of matter, which are not subject to the laws of intelligence and for that reason are much more significant." Holz's *Phantasus*, rather than addressing fantasy as the surrogate of all senses in the finest romantic manner, reckons with unconscious optokinetics (which Husserl's contemporaneous phenomenology thematized). The aesthetics of reception had become quite different circa 1900: instead of communication and its myth of two souls or consciousnesses, there are numerical relations between the materiality of writing and the physiology of the senses. Whether and how actual readers approve of their nerves having been saved such and such many milliseconds is of no concern to Holz the lyric poet. Whereas his predecessors had invited readers to pass over letters, he was concerned with technical calculations concerning the materiality of his medium. Spengler's desire that "men of the new generation devote themselves to technics instead of lyrics, the sea instead of the paint-brush, and politics instead of epistemology" came somewhat after the fact.[94] Since Nietzsche, "aesthetics is nothing but a kind of applied physiology."

The movements of matter had their greatest triumph in the field of writing. An experimental subject wrote in a test journal, after thirty-eight days devoted to typing practice, "To-day I found myself not infrequently striking letters before I was conscious of seeing them. They seem to have been perfecting themselves just below the level of consciousness."[95] Psychophysics investigated or generated unconscious automatisms in handwriting as well. *Ecriture automatique* appeared as early as 1850, but only among American spiritualists; it was not analyzed until the turn of the century.[96] After the theoretical work of F. W. H. Myers and William James, profane automatic writing arrived in the Harvard laboratory of the German psychologist and inventor of psychotechnology Hugo Münsterberg. In order to demonstrate the normality of hysterical automatisms, two students, who could be called normal according to a vague estimation of their introspective capacity (even if the young Gertrude Stein was one of them), participated in experiments that made them no less delirious than Ebbinghaus. Because reading runs more quickly and thus unconsciously than writing, experiments in automatic reading were included at the outset.

"This is a very pretty experiment because it is quite easy and the results are very satisfactory. The subject reads in a low voice, and preferably something comparatively uninteresting, while the operator reads to him an interesting story. If he does not go insane during the first few trials he will quickly learn to concentrate his attention fully on what is being read to him, yet go on reading just the same. The reading becomes completely unconscious for periods of as much as a page.[97]

It is a pretty experiment indeed, one made as if to dismiss hermeneutic reading. At one time our inner selves were supposed to be the workshop in which all reading operations were conducted; our ego was always to be kept in view because of the risk of insanity by distraction. But now the protocol calls for just what had scandalized Bergk, and once the rock of insanity has been circumnavigated, everything runs as unconsciously as it does normally. Rather than being rooted together in one voice from the inmost soul, the isolated routines of reading, listening, and speaking become automatic and impersonal: "the voice seemed as though that of another person." [98]

In a more advanced step, Leon Solomons and Gertrude Stein experimented with a coupling of automatic reading and writing. "For this purpose the person writing read aloud while the person dictating listened to the reading. In this way it not infrequently happened that, at interesting parts of the story, we would have the curious phenomenon of one person unconsciously dictating sentences which the other unconsciously wrote down; both persons meanwhile being absorbed in some thrilling story." [99] The division of the unity of Man can thus be accomplished by two readers or writers. While both consciousnesses are fed with signifieds, one unconscious takes dictation from the other—just as the psychoanalyst "must turn his own unconscious like a receptive organ towards the transmitting unconscious of the patient." [100] The deceptive proximity of this writing situation to the romantic fantasy of the library in fact marks the latter's total perversion. When Serpentina whispered their love story to the student Anselmus, his hand wrote along in unconscious dictation. But nothing could be less impersonal than a phantom-beloved capable of playing the Mother's Mouth for a man's soul. For that reason her voice never really uttered anything aloud; it arose as a utopian shadow thrown by very real but unreadable signs. Because the Woman does not exist and plural women had no place in the educational system, an imaginary woman's voice had simultaneously to remind young authors or bureaucrats of their writing duty and to transform it magically into infantile sexuality.

Circa 1900, however, experimentation dissolved the utopia.[101] Gertrude Stein, not for nothing Münsterberg's ideal student,[102] could study psychophysics like anyone else. While German universities still trembled at the thought of the chaos women students would provoke, the Harvard Psychological Laboratory had long been desexualized. In their test report, Solomons and Stein are referred to throughout as "he."[103] The scientific discourse gives only hints that during this strange cooperation the man dictated and the woman wrote. Gertrude Stein, for years employed as an academic secretary, was in the experiment similarly "the perfect blanc while someone practises on her as an automaton."[104] Nothing is said of why the two sexes were divided in that way. Two years later, however, with Solomons significantly absent, Stein continued her autoexperiments with others—with the explicit purpose of "comparison between male and female experimental subjects."[105] Such a question already reveals what supports the new scientific discourse. Real women, as they exist in plurality, had attained access to writing as practiced in university discourse. Their hysteria, rather than remaining out of the way as some idiosyncrasy like Brentano's sister, was experimentally simulated in order to make it a completely normal motoric automatism. As unconscious as she was obedient, Gertrude Stein took dictation from her fellow student.

With that, the positions of the sexes in the discourse network of 1800 were reversed. Into the place of the imaginary Mother's Mouth steps a man who dictates factually; into the complementary place of the unconscious author steps one of many women who have studied enough to be able to take dictation—Ariadne, Frau Röder-Wiederhold, Resa von Schirnhofer, Gertrude Stein, and so on. The fact that one of them became a writer is part of the logic of the experiment.[106]

The greatest triumph of psychotechnology was to have made dictated writing into spontaneous, automatic writing. After their practice experiments in reading and taking dictation, Solomons and Stein went to work. A woman's hand produced texts without knowing that or what it wrote. With this, psychophysics discovered the rules of literary automatic writing long before the surrealists. First, it is forbidden to reread anything written—precisely the act that made authors out of writing hands "stopped automatic writing."[107] Second, the annoying intrusions of an ego are to be put off by repeating prewritten sentences with an obstinacy that matches their meaninglessness. Thirty years later André Breton translated these two fundamental rules in his *Surrealist Manifesto*:

Write quickly, without any preconceived subject, fast enough so that you will not remember what you're writing and be tempted to reread what you have written. . . . Put your trust in the inexhaustible nature of the murmur. If silence threatens to settle in, if you should ever happen to make a mistake—a mistake, perhaps due to carelessness—break off without hesitation with an overly clear line. Following a word the origin of which seems suspicious to you, place any letter whatsoever, the letter "l" for example, always the letter "l."[108]

Having been educated as a psychiatrist, Breton cannot not have known where such rules of literary production came from. To give conscious, that is, distorting attention to repeated iterations of a sign reverses psychiatric diagnosis. The "senseless repetition of the same letter for a half or whole line, as in children's writing books," which psychiatrists call, in the mentally ill, "written verbigeration," that is, flight of ideas,[109] became, as *écriture automatique*, the duty of nothing more and nothing less than literature. As this scene of inscription reveals, automatic writing is anything but freedom. The alphabetization campaign of 1800 also intended to automatize cultural practices, but only in order "to found and purify the ground of inwardness in the subject."[110] When, by contrast, Gertrude Stein worked through a series of failed exercises and finally arrived at the experimental goal of "automatic writing by invention," precisely the freest invention conjured up inevitabilities as binding as the sentence, decades later, that a rose is a rose is a rose. The longest of the few examples cited by Solomons and Stein says this clearly: "Hence there is no possible way of avoiding what I have spoken of, and if this is not believed by the people of whom you have spoken, then it is not possible to prevent the people of whom you have spoken so glibly . . ."[111]

What speaks, when It speaks, is always fate. This was no news to Freud. The medium and the message coincide because even in grammar the repetition compulsion rules. Such discourse is unavoidable precisely because it is empty. Automatic writing says nothing of thought or inwardness, of intention or understanding; it speaks only of speech and glibness. Neither the inevitable nor the people it threatens exist except by hearsay. In the methodic isolation of her laboratory, cut off from all the classical determinations of woman and integrated into the new desexualized university, an ideal student speaks and writes as if the rejected truth of Western thought had returned. Psychophysics thus took the place of occult media (read: women). Alone and dazed, a Pythia sits on the tripod again, and men or priests whisper to her the secret fears of the people. But the mistress of the oracle cannot console. Whatever she says becomes unavoidable because she says it. No one is more tragic than Cassandra. Unconscious words transpire, and immediately the listeners harbor a suspicion close to a truth intolerable for philosophers: that discourses conjure up what they seem only to describe. Whether under the sign of myth or of positivism, the release of automatic speaking means that Cassandra will not be believed and will find no way to warn the people who have just been spoken of so glibly. Thus, literally and without commentary, the leading journal of American experimental psychology, volume 3, 1896: "Hence there is no possible way of avoiding what I have spoken of, and if this is not believed by the people of whom you have spoken, then it is not possible to prevent the people of whom you have spoken so glibly . . ."

Technological Media

A medium is a medium is a medium. As the sentence says, there is no difference between occult and technological media. Their truth is fatality, their field the unconscious. And because the unconscious never finds an illusory belief, the unconscious can only be stored.

In the discourse network of 1900, psychophysical experiments were incorporated as so many random generators that produce discourses without sense or thought. The ordinary, purposeful use of language— so-called communication with others—is excluded. Syllabic hodgepodge and automatic writing, the language of children and the insane—none of it is meant for understanding ears or eyes; all of it takes the quickest path from experimental conditions to data storage. Good, old-fashioned handwriting is the storage mechanism for automatic writing, with the slight modification that Gertrude Stein watches her hands like separate machines with a modicum of curiosity rather than commanding them to write particular signs.[1] In other cases, deposition into writing is impossible, because the random generators produce effects only at extremely high speeds. Automatic writing and reading already exhibit a tendency toward increasing speed: the tempo of dictation races ahead of the hands, that of reading exceeds the articulating organs.[2] Thus, in order to retain anything at all, psychophysics had to join with the new media that revolutionized optics and acoustics circa 1900. These, of course, are Edison's two great innovations: film and the gramophone.

The long process that culminated in the Lumières' cinematographs was dictated by the technical-industrial necessity of surpassing the human eye's limited capability to process single images. The birth of film was attended by Eadweard J. Muybridge's serial photographs, Etienne-Jules Marey and G. E. J. Demeny's photographic gun, and Johann Heinrich Ernemann's slow-motion photography. The gramophone also depended on being able to function at speeds slower than people can talk. It could not have been invented—contemporaries were wrong about this[3]—before Jean-Baptiste-Joseph Fourier's mathematical analyses of amplitude or Helmholtz's studies in physiological acoustics. The technical simulation of both optical and acoustical processes presupposed analyses made possible by the speed of the apparatuses themselves. Voice reproduction required a frequency band between 90 and 1,200 Hertz even for the fundamental tones; studies of body movements required illumination speeds in the realm of milliseconds.

The ability to record sense data technologically shifted the entire discourse network circa 1900. For the first time in history, writing ceased to be synonymous with the serial storage of data. The technological recording of the real entered into competition with the symbolic registration of the Symbolic. The wonderfully super-elevated Edison whom Philippe Villiers de l'Isle-Adam made the hero of his *Tomorrow's Eve* concisely formulated the new development. Musing among his devices and apparatuses, he begins a monologue, ignored by literary theorists, that will bring Lessing's *Laocoon* up to date in 1886.

The Word Made Flesh paid little attention to the exterior and sensible parts either of writing or of speech. He wrote on only one occasion, and then on the ground. No doubt He valued, in the speaking of a word, only the indefinable *beyondness* with which personal magnetism inspired by faith can fill a word the moment one pronounces it. Who knows if all the rest isn't trivial by comparison? . . . Still, the fact remains, He allowed men only to print his testament, not to put it on the phonograph. Otherwise, instead of saying, "Read the Holy Scriptures," we would be saying, "Listen to the Sacred Vibrations."[4]

Believers in the Book were prohibited in the name of their Lord from celebrating the exteriority and sensuality of the word and scripture. The permitted medium of printing made it possible to bypass signs for sense, the "beyond" of the senses. Only under the counter-command "Hear the sacred vibrations!" does the symbolic registration of the Symbolic lose its monopoly. Vibrations, even in God's voice, are frequencies far below the threshold of perception and notation for single movements. Neither the Bible nor the primer can record them. Therefore, phonograph's Papa, as Edison is known in the novel, rethinks the sacred itself. He dreams of ideal phonographs capable of registering the "oracles of Dodona" and "chants of the Sybils" (to say nothing of pure "noise") in indestructible recordings for "sonorous archives of copper."[5] The dreams of an American engineer dreamed by a French symbolist come quite close to the strange occurrences in Münsterberg's laboratory. What the student as medium could hardly note down for all her psychotechnical ecstasy is caught by the gramophone as medium—the murmuring and whispering of unconscious oracles.

But not all women of 1900, as oracles or students, were abreast of their age and technology. Among the Germans there were still feminine readers. Anna Pomke, "a timid, well brought-up girl," can only regret "that the phonograph was not invented in 1800." For, as she confesses to a favorite professor: "I would so much like to have heard Goethe's voice! He was said to have such a beautiful vocal organ, and everything he said was so meaningful. Oh, if only he had been able to speak into the gramophone! Oh! Oh!"[6] Among the believers in culture, holy vibrations are not sibylline whisperings but the tone and content of a voice that has long delighted feminine readers in the imaginary and that must now do so in the real. A loving professor, however, could not resist that sigh of longing and the wish to modernize a love of books. Abnossah Pschorr sneaks into the cemetery, makes a secret mold of Goethe's skeleton, reconstructs the larynx, wires it to a phonograph, and puts together this fine composite of physiology and technology in the office of the Goethe House. For "whenever Goethe spoke, his voice created vibrations," whose reverberations "become weaker with the passage of time, but which cannot actually cease." To filter the sound of Goethe's voice out of the noise of all the discourse that had occurred, one fed impulses into a "receiving organ" that simulated his larynx, with the help of an amplification device that was brand-new in 1916.[7] Accordingly, Salomo Friedlaender's story is called "Goethe Speaks into the Gramophone." The story has a sad and logical ending: no engineer can stand having women love not the invention itself but its output. In jealous competition between media, Professor Pschorr destroys the only recording of the beautiful, monstrous, and absent voice that in 1800 commanded an entire discourse network.

A roll capable of recording Dodonian oracles, a roll capable simply of recording the poet: those were the writer's dreams in 1900. The lyric poet and feuilletonist, bohemian and amateur, who came up with the technical principle of the phonograph in 1877, gathered all these dreams in verse under the significant title *Inscription*.

> Comme les traits dans les camées
> J'ai voulu que les voix aimées
> Soient un bien, qu'on garde à jamais,
> Et puissent répéter le rêve
> Musical de l'heure trop brève;
> Le temps veut fuir, je le soumets.
>
> Like the faces in cameos
> I wanted beloved voices
> To be a fortune which one keeps forever,
> And which can repeat the musical
> Dream of the too short hour;
> Time would flee, I subdue it.[8]

But Charles Cros, the writer, only pointed toward the phonograph and never built it. The deeds of Edison, the practical man, are more profane, less erotic, and more forgettable than writers' dreams or novelistic fantasies. Precisely that is their greatness. The phonograph and the typewriter exist for the same reason. Edison was nearly deaf, and the blind were foremost among the builders of typewriters. Media, like psychophysical experiments, begin with a physiological deficiency. The very first tin-foil roll to record a voice, on December 6, 1877, registered the shouts of its inventor, a voice that remained distant and unreachable to his actual ears. Edison roared "Mary Had a Little Lamb" into the phonograph's bell-mouth.[9]

The history of sound recording did not begin with oracles or poets, but with children's songs, though in the roar of a deaf and childish engineer. In 1888, however, when his gramophone had just gone into mass production, Edison began to market dolls in which the speech roll had been recorded by young girls.[10] Again one heard—the hit among twelve choices—"Mary Had a Little Lamb," but this time as a children's song sung by a child. When Villiers, with a symbolist's love of oracles and sibyls, had Edison listen via stereophonic recording and playback devices to his young daughter sing "ring-around-a-rosy" in front of the laboratory, he approached the engineer's profane illumination.[11]

Talking dolls also mark the turning point between two discourse networks. Kempelen's and Maelzel's mechanical children of 1778 and 1823 repeated the minimal signifieds of loving parents for those parents. Circa 1800 there was no children's language independent of pedagogical feedback. In the Edison talking doll, by contrast, real children sang children's songs about little Marys and their lambs. The century of the child began with such self-relatedness, unreachable by any Mama/Papa psychology.

According to Ellen Key, *The Century of the Child* brought an end to "soul murder" in school.[12] Instead of establishing pedagogical norms for what should be spoken by children, one gave free reign to language games. But these standards (in spite of all child's-century oracles) were technological from the beginning. There cannot be any children's language unfiltered through the language of adults until discourses can be recorded in their positive reality. The classical pedagogical dream of forming adults with analytic, slow-motion pronunciation—walking phoneme archives for their children—became obsolete. Edison's invention was not called a phonograph for nothing: it registers real sounds rather than translating them into phonemic equivalencies as an alphabet does. Emile Berliner's more modern device, which replaced rolls with records, was not called a gramophone for nothing: true to its name, it retains "the sounds of letters" and has a writing angel as its trademark.[13]

Technologically possible manipulations determine what in fact can become a discourse.[14] The phonograph and gramophone allow slow-motion studies of single sounds far below the perception threshold of even Stephani's ideal mothers. Though the frequency bandwidth possible circa 1900 could not match the entire speech spectrum and particularly distorted *s*-sounds (with frequencies up to 6kHz), this was not a handicap. The talking machine moved into laboratories and schools very soon after its invention. In laboratories its very distortions made it possible to measure hearing.[15] In schools it was useful because "it is essential for achieving an accurate impression of the most fleeting, unrepresentable, and yet so important, characteristic aspects of language, of line phonetics (speech melody) and of line rhythm," whereas (because of its accurate recording) it "is not suited for pure pronunciation practice."[16] Thus wrote Ernst Surkamp, publisher of a journal that is nearly impossible to locate today, *Instruction and Talking Machines*—as if any further demonstration that the epoch of High German phonetic norms is past were necessary. Of course, talking machines can create "a store of readily accessible language sounds in exemplary, faultless accent" and dictatorially inscribe schoolchildren with language sounds or universal keyboards.[17] But they can do more and different things. To the student Rilke, whose physics teacher had his students reconstruct and experiment with a phonograph that he had acquired as soon as the machine was on the market, the registered sounds opened "as it were, a new and infinitely delicate point in the texture of reality."[18] The fact that a purely empirical phonetics (in rigorous distinction to phonology) suddenly became possible led to storing real phenomena according to technical standards rather than to regulating them according to educational norms. One could record the wild army that Nietzsche despaired of ever getting down. Because "dialects in schools deserve every possible encouragement, the talking machine can be effective in that its undistorted oral presentations nourish one's delight in a native language."[19]

In the discourse network of 1900, media rehabilitated dialects, those of groups like those of children. Not the delight of the subjects but the delight of the researcher came to power. In the absence of normativization, this delight brought to light discourses that previously had never passed a recording threshold—"a new and infinitely delicate point in the texture of reality."

On the second German Art-Education Day in Herder's Weimar, a speaker dismissed the unified language that for a hundred years had ruled over teachers and students.

The school-age child brings his own language to school, his native language, his family language, the language of his playmates, his own naive, intuitive language: our task and our desire is to teach him our language, the language of our poets and thinkers. . . . But isn't it asking a great deal when we demand that children, from the first day of school, speak nothing but school language? . . . It is not long before the children will be overtaken by books and book language: a child learns to read. Reading, however, weakens and cuts across—it cannot be otherwise—the child's coherent, fluent speech, and book language begins more and more to influence and control school language; finally, in its often foreign and refined way, it creates a child who is now shy and monosyllabic.[20]

This speaker admits that book language represents a never-spoken exception and impedes actual speech. The most fluent speaker is the one who, like children or the writer of *Ecce Homo*, never reads a line. Therefore progressive pedagogues can only compete with the media. Like the bell of a recording phonograph, they absorb every freely flowing word, every naive pun of children's dialects.

Christian Morgenstern, the child of German letters, immediately recognized and exploited this development. Even if he was later to declare in mediocre verse that the gramophone was the work of the devil—before his master, Rudolf Steiner, said the same thing[21]—his heroes knew better.

> Korf und Palmström nehmen Lektionen,
> um das Wetter-Wendische zu lernen.
> Täglich pilgern sie zu den modernen
> Ollendorffschen Sprachlehrgrammophonen.
>
> Dort nun lassen sie mit vielen andern,
> welche gleichfalls steile Charaktere
> (gleich als obs ein Ziel für Edle wäre),
> sich im Wetter-Wendischen bewandern.
>
> Dies Idiom behebt den Geist der Schwere,
> macht sie unstet, launisch und cholerisch . . .
> Doch die Sache bleibt nur peripherisch.
> Und sie werden wieder—Charaktere.
>
> Korf and Palmström are taking lessons
> From Ollendorff's didactic gramophones;
> To learn Weather-Wendish's grammar and tone,
> They wander hence for daily sessions.
>
> There they put with all the rest,
> Who are stiff characters, too, it seems,
> (the place attracts elite esteem)
> Their Weather-Wendish to the test.
>
> The idiom tends to untie fetters,
> Make people moody, things look dismal,
> But still it all remains peripheral,
> and they revert once more—to characters.[22]

This poem, entitled "Language Studies," may be an exact description—except that Surkamp would be a more appropriate name than Ollendorff. Heinrich Ollendorff's method of language instruction emphasized conversation more than the rules of grammar, but Surkamp's company had at the time a near-monopoly on language-instructional gramophones and strongly encouraged dialects in the schools. In 1913 Korf and Palmström could choose among more than a thousand instructional records. The fact that they chose Weather-Wendish legitimately established the new status of dialects as an autonym of "naive and intuitive" children's language.* The play on ethnography and weather reports is like the children's puns and jokes that were recorded by the psychologist Stanley Hall.

Words, in connection with rhyme, rhythm, alliteration, cadence, etc., or even without these, simply as sound-pictures, often absorb the attention of children, and yield them a really aesthetic pleasure either quite independently of their meaning or to the utter bewilderment of it. They hear fancied words in noises and sounds of nature and animals, and are persistent punners. As butterflies make butter or eat it or give it by squeezing, so grasshoppers give grass, bees give beads and beans, kittens grow on the pussy-willow, and all honey is from honeysuckles, and even a poplin dress is made of poplar-trees.[23]

. . . and so on and so forth, until even the Wends speak Weather-Wendish. Their fantastical Slavic has its grave opposite in what the art-educators designated as the weakening, intimidating high idiom. Either there are characters, individuals, and the one norm, or gramophonics raises all the unstable, capricious changes in speech to the level of standards. Then "there is in fact no reason, as long as one recognizes Wendish as a language, that the same recognition should not be extended to Weather-Wendish."[24]

Korf and Palmström, of course, broke off their gramophone studies and became characters—that is, and not only in Greek, letters once more. Morgenstern's simulated children's language remained high idiom, written language, which quickly made its way into children's readers and dissertations.[25] Discourses that had previously never been able to cross a recording threshold were stored and returned; the gramophone had paid its debt.

But heroes in poems were not the only ones to discover the talking machine. Those who wrote poems were also tempted to give it a try. In 1897 the Wilhelmine poet laureate, Ernst von Wildenbruch, was probably the first German writer to record his voice on a wax roll. (His Kaiser had long since preceded him.) Wildenbruch wrote a poem expressly for the occasion, "For the Phonographic Recording of His Voice"; the history of its transmission says it all. The *Collected Works* did not collect it; Walter Bruch, who as the inventor of the PAL television system had access to archives of historical recordings, had to transcribe the verses from the roll. They will be quoted here in a form that will horrify poets, compositors, and Germanists.

* *Wendisch* is the language of the Wends, a Slavic group that once inhabited parts of eastern Germany. [Trans.]

Shapes can constrain the human visage, the eye be held fast in an image, only the
voice, born in breath, bodiless dies and flies off.

The fawning face can deceive the eye, the sound of the voice can never lie, thus
to me is the phonograph the soul's own true photograph,

which brings what is hidden to light and forces the past to speak. Hear then,
for in this sound you will look into the soul of Ernst von Wildenbruch.[26]

A copious writer, Wildenbruch did not always rhyme so poorly. But in
the moment he took leave of the Gutenberg galaxy, he was overcome by
written language. As if in Gertrude Stein's dark oracle, an inevitability
appears and does away with all poetic freedoms. Wildenbruch had to talk
into a black phonographic speaker, which stored pure sounds rather than
his words and notions. Of course, the voice did not cease being born in
breath; it retains the vibration fundamental to classical-romantic lyric
poetry; but—and this is too empirical or trivial a fact for Foucault's
grandly styled history of discourse—the voice can no longer be pure poetic breath that vanishes even as it is heard and leaves no trace. What once
necessarily escaped becomes inescapable; the bodiless becomes material.
The gramophone is not quite as volatile, capricious, and secondary as
Korf and Palmström thought. The lyric poet Wildenbruch reacted like a
rat in a test labyrinth. His musings on physiognomy and photography,
which allow their subjects cunning countermeasures and escape hatches,
circumscribe only the optical medium that he was familiar with: writing.
When the phonograph forces the hidden to speak, however, it sets a trap
for speakers. With it, speakers are not identified in the symbolic with a
name, or in the imaginary by hero-reader identifications, but in the real.
And that is not child's play. Wildenbruch alluded to the symbolic and
imaginary registers when he coupled the sound of the poem with his own
noble proper name and a look into his poetic soul in order not to speak of
the real, the speaking body.

Herder dreamed long before Anna Pomke of an improved "*reading
and notational system*" in which one "will probably also find a way of
designating the characteristic substance and tone of a lyric piece."[27] With
the gramophone's capacity to record lyric poetry, the dream becomes at
once reality and nightmare. It is one thing to write proudly about the
phonographic recording of all voices, as Charles Cros did; it is another
thing to write, as Wildenbruch did, "For the Phonographic Recording
of His Voice" and then to have to speak it. What good are the poetic
mnemonic techniques of rhyme and meter when wax rolls can store not
only substance and tone but real sounds? Like Alfred Döblin's defiant
motto, "Not phonography, but art,"[28] Wildenbruch's poetaster rhymes
bear witness to an embittered competition between poetry and technological media.

Sound is a complex of physiological data that are impossible to put into writing or to counterfeit. In the discourse network of 1900, psychophysics and media subvert the imaginary body image that individuals have of themselves and substitute a forthright positivity. The phonograph is called the true photograph of the soul; graphology is called the "X ray" of handwritten "indiscretions."[29]

Mocking the doctrine of psychological physiognomy in 1800, philosophers could joke: nothing more was required than a decision of the individual to make itself incomprehensible for centuries.[30] That is what Wildenbruch hoped to accomplish with his line about the fawning face deceiving the eyes of the physiognomist; but given a machine that dodges the tricks people use with one another, the laughter has died away after a century. Phonography means the death of the author; it stores a mortal voice rather than eternal thoughts and turns of phrase. The past that the phonograph forces to speak is only Wildenbruch's helpless euphemism for his singular body, which was posthumous even while he lived.

The death of man and the preservation of corporeal evidence are one. In a brilliant essay, Carlo Ginzburg has shown that around 1900 a new paradigm of knowledge gained ascendancy, one that operated only with unfakeable, that is, unconscious and meaningless, details—in aesthetics as well as in psychoanalysis and criminology.[31] Thus a writer in *Scientific American* said of the phonograph, which was just then going into mass production, "It can be used as a reliable witness in criminal investigations."[32] The individual of 1800, who was an individual universal, did not survive this fine-grained investigation. What one can know of a human being today has nothing to do with the 4,000 pages that Sartre, posing the same question, devoted to the psychology of Flaubert. One can record people's voices, their fingerprints, their parapraxes. Ginzburg also underestimates the modernity of these encroachments when he puts the origin of the gathering of evidence among prehistoric hunters and Renaissance physicians. The snow that helped trackers was an accident; Edison's tin-foil roll or Francis Galton's fingerprint archive were purposefully prepared recording surfaces for data that could be neither stored nor evaluated without machines.

Thus Wildenbruch's mediocre verse points out whom the phonograph benefits. A lyric poet immortalized in the grooves on a record enters, not the pantheon, but the archive of the new "deposition psychology." Under this name William Stern and others instituted a science based on the superiority of technical over literary storage devices. Whether for criminals or for the insane, the use of "stylized depositions often produces a false impression of the examination and obscures the psychological significance of individual statements." Because each answer "is, from the point of view of experimental psychology, a reaction to the operative stimulus in the question," experimenters and investigators provoke countertactics in their subjects as long as they use the bureaucratic medium of writing. If, however, one selects "the use of the phonograph as an ideal method,"[33] then, especially if the recording is done secretly, any parasitic feedback between the stimulus and the reaction will be prevented. Secrecy is "absolutely essential" with children in order to "guarantee the genuine innocence of their responses."[34]

As a photograph of the soul, the talking machine put an end to the innocent doctrine of innocence. Circa 1800 innocence was a historical-philosophical limit concept; it referred to a region it itself made impassible. "Once the soul speaks, then oh!, it is no longer the soul that speaks." Although this loss of the soul's identity with itself had been attributed to the progress of the human race or to the division of labor, it resulted, in the final analysis, simply from the technological impossibility of storing the newly discovered voice in any form except that of writing. Olympia's automatized "oh" would otherwise never have been so fascinating and terrifying. Circa 1900, by contrast, the builders of automatons had carried the day. There was no longer any innocence below the recording threshold; there was only the tactical rule of anticipating counter reactions while recording. But the innocence that comes into being where bodies and media technologies come into contact is called flight of ideas.

In order to investigate "glossophysical" disturbances, or those that, beyond alalia or aphasia, affect entire sequences of speech, the Viennese psychiatrist Erwin Stransky devised a new type of experimental procedure. After having "shut out as far as possible all extraneous sense stimuli," Stransky had his subjects "look and speak directly into the painted black tube" of a phonographic receiver for one minute.[35] The subjects were selected partly from among Stransky's psychiatric colleagues, partly from among his patients. The principal distinction between the cohorts, however, was that most of the patients reacted with fright to the intentionally stimulus-free (that is, black) field of the receiver, with the unfortunate result that their responses had to be recorded stenographically rather than phonographically.[36] But in the absence of any transcendental norm, psychiatrists and psychiatric patients exhibited the same speech behavior. After an initial trial period, they could produce nonsense for one minute (the recording time for one roll). The command to speak as much and as quickly as possible, together with a recorder capable of registering more material at a quicker pace than the alphabet, brought about an experimentally guaranteed hodgepodge of words. As in the experiments of Ebbinghaus, the initial difficulties resulted from the paradoxical imperative to bracket the operative imperatives of normal speech.

In the beginning, it was normal for subjects to get no further than the first few sentences; they would stall and claim that nothing occurred to them, that they could no longer speak. . . . We are ordinarily so accustomed to thinking under the direction of general concepts that we constantly fall back into this tendency whenever we are presented with a particular aim, even when this aim consists in shutting out all general concepts . . . Only when the subjects realized that *searching* for verbal ideas was completely unnecessary, that these ideas would come spontaneously and profusely to the foreground, did the initial stalling rapidly cease so we could proceed to the actual experiment.[37]

From a technological medium that records their voices without asking for hidden thoughts or ideas, experimental subjects learned "the release of linguistic expression from mental life" through their own bodies. In its "autonomy,"[38] language proceeds without any need to look for signifieds. Nietzsche announced long before Stransky that he learned to find once he grew weary of seeking; long after Stransky, Breton urged writers to trust the inexhaustible murmur.

The resultant output is all practically interchangeable. Automatic writing generates sentences reminiscent of "Rose is a rose is a rose." Stransky's phonograph records the sequence, "Hope, green belief, green, green, green, green is an emerald, an emerald is green, a sapphire is green, a—a sapphire is green, green is, that isn't right,"[39] etc. Henceforth speech knows only tautology and contradiction, the two empty, informationless extremes of truth values.[40] In identifying the new artistic age of technical reproduction with film, Benjamin singled out the movie screen as making the single image obsolete and therefore establishing the rule of distraction, rather than bourgeois concentration. But the principle applies more generally and rigorously. Film has no privileged position among the media that have revolutionized literature and art. All have brought about, in exact psychiatric terms, the flight of ideas; corresponding terms in cultural criticism, such as "distraction," remain euphemistic.

Stransky's phonograph did not record mere lapses in attention or moments of distraction; it registered disdain for political and pedagogical norms, norms that would not have endured for a day were it not for a normativized language.[41] The catatonic Heinrich H., for instance, responded to test questions concerning the nature of state and school regulations thus:

The state is many people living together, hour by hour, places separated by hours, bordered by mountains on four sides.

[School regulation] is that law over school-age children who are often in conditions of illness, when they stay home and when they should be working out on the land. Alternate daily, when they work for two days and go to school for two days, they change every week. When they work for a week and go to school for a week, all school-age children who are ill and have to stay home and save time, thus save time, stay home, perhaps to work, perhaps to cook, perhaps to wash carrots . . .[42]

Responses on the order of vegetable stew effectively dismantle the powers on which education had been based since 1800. Fritz Mauthner's prophecy that "the states will one day have to pay for making their schools into institutions in which the minds of children are systematically destroyed" was fulfilled before it was written.[43] What the technological media record is their own opposition to the state and school. People who are encouraged to speak more quickly than they think, that is, to outpace the controlling function, necessarily begin guerrilla warfare against disciplinary power. The one who not only forgets, but in a Nietzschean manner also forgets his forgetfulness, always delivers, like Kafka's drunken man, the *Description of a Struggle*:

Now the drunk jerked up his eyebrows so that a brightness appeared between them and his eyes, and he explained in fits and starts: "It's like this, you see—I'm sleepy, you see, so that's why I'm going to sleep.—You see, I've a brother-in-law on the Wenzelsplatz—that's where I'm going, for I live there, for that's where I have my bed—so I'll be off—. But I don't know his name, you see, or where he lives—seems I've forgotten—but never mind, for I don't even know if I have a brother-in-law at all.—But I'll be off now, you see—. Do you think I'll find him?"[44]

Stransky hoped that by using a neutral recording device he would avoid the psychophysical danger of producing mere "laboratory artifacts,"[45] or of programming the response into the stimulus; yet steno- and phonographic recording functions like alcohol in the passage from Kafka. It provokes the provocative responses that no self-respecting servant of the state or educational bureaucrat would have wanted to write down. As catchphrases pronounced by the experimenter, "state" and "school" can no longer be subsumed under any more general heading. Psychiatry also realized, then, that "enumerations"—catchphrases, inventories, address books, grammars—are themselves instances of the flight of ideas;[46] to which the pedagogy of learning impairments could respond that hyperactive children's flight of ideas was a result of enumerative textbooks.[47] Thus when Stransky stated that "the formation of general concepts" might have been inhibited for "pathological or experimental reasons,"[48] the "or" should be replaced by an equal sign.

The very fact that flight of ideas governed both sides of the experimental situation allowed it to be transposed into other media. By substituting ordinary writing materials for the phonograph and artificial laboratory artifacts for phonographic ones, one could achieve "the release of linguistic expression from mental life" in literature as well. The physician Gottfried Benn demonstrated this when he had his fellow physician Jef van Pameelen "enter the foyer of a hospital for prostitutes" and registered the associations of this his doppelgänger with phonographic fidelity. To be sure, nothing at all occurs to the subject Pameelen. In his "dread at his inability to experience anything" he sees only "an empty hall with a clock." But hardly have these words escaped him when a disembodied "voice" sounds above him. "An empty hall with a clock? Further! Extension! Yield! The doorman's apartment? The hairpins on the ground? The garden on the right? And so?" There are only disconnected catchphrases, but like "state" or "school regulations" they demand continuation, if only into ideational flight. Acting the part, as if to make things easier for his archivist, Pameelen consents to the flight of catchphrases:

> PAMEELEN (*acting the part*): I know a house very similar to the one you have just described, Herr Doctor! I entered it on a warm spring morning; first there was an empty hallway with a clock, the doorman's apartment was on the right, hairpins were lying on the ground, very funny, and on the right there was a small garden, a bed of roses in the middle, two wethers grazed tethered to the grass, probably the Aquarian goats.[49]

Truly an "epistemological drama" (as *The Survey Director* is subtitled): although it dutifully, indeed exhaustively runs through the catalogue of questions, Pameelen's answer confuses identity, the epistemological bedrock, with mere sameness.[50] Clearly drama (long before Peter Handke's *Kaspar*) is about speaking rather than action. Identity falls into simulacrum without any extradiscursive context. Empty words circulate between Pameelen and the voice with no figure behind it, words without points of view, address, or reference, determined and guided by the imperative of association.[51] The voice notes down Pameelen's venerealogical joke about the Aquarian goats as a "very good," namely, "distant association that plays on the meaning of hospital with a light, humorous touch." The medical profession does not exempt one from the status of experimental subject in drama any more than it does in a laboratory full of phonographs. The voice that directs Pameelen is anything but transcendental—he addresses it as "Herr Doctor!" This experimenter shares Stransky's insight that any search for verbal ideas is superfluous. Whenever "peripheral fatigue" or "cortical fading" in Pameelen's "brain" hinder the associations, the doctor cracks his whip and commands "further!"[52] Pameelen is obviously among the "worst cases" of imbecility who "already grow tired of the procedure by the 58th reaction."[53] With his whip, however, the doctor (like the phonograph) commands speech at a tempo that separates discourse from mental life or "experiential perspectives." Drama, once the genre of free subjects, becomes pathological "or" experimental.

This is because free subjects appear in books of philosophy, whereas experimental subjects appear in the field of psychophysics. "The *one* science that most strongly captures the world's attention throws its light and shadow across prose fiction as well. Since about 1860 this has been pathology, physiological and psychological."[54] Thus the enigma of the whip-brandishing Herr Doctor can be quickly clarified. One need only write out the previously quoted dramatic dialogue in the following manner:

VOICE	PAMEELEN
Hall with a clock?	first there was an empty hallway with a clock
Doorman's apartment	doorman's apartment on the right
Hairpins on the floor?	there were hairpins on the floor, very funny
A garden on the right	and to the right there was a small garden, a bed of roses in the middle

Next read one of many published pages of interviews that the psychiatrist Ziehen conducted with school children in Jena.

O. G., 12 years, 9 months. Father tailor. School performance quite variable, average. July 3, 1898. 9 A.M. Previously one hour of class (reading and explanation of a poem about the Pied Piper of Hamelin).

STIMULUS WORD	RESPONSE
Teacher	*Herr Stichling* (teacher, with whom he was just in class)
Father	*my father*
Snow	*some fell* (thought of yesterday's snowfall)
Blood	*when an animal is slaughtered* (thought of a cow he saw slaughtered the day before yesterday)
Rat	*how the rat catcher lures the rats into the trap*
Snow	*white* ("that's on the ground")[55]

Consider, finally, that Ziehen's *Idea Associations of the Child* aimed to "determine the speed of association," indeed "to determine the association process and its speed under special conditions (fatigue, etc.),"[56] and one will have also deduced the special condition of the whip. From this, it is only a step to recognizing that the head physician of the psychiatric intern Gottfried Benn was none other than Professor Theodor Ziehen.

It hardly matters whether the experimental subject is a child or a doctor, is O. G., J. v. P., or G. B. For the physician Werff Rönne, the hero of Benn's first novella, to practice random association without the whip of an experimenter, is merely a further transposition of psychophysical techniques into literature. But the only genre that can present an experimenter and an experimental subject as separate agents is the drama. The hero of Benn's novella, by contrast, stands under an order of association that functions despotically because it has transposed itself into flesh and blood. The laboratory artifact becomes absolute. No interpretation could recognize it. Only the schoolchildren in Jena with whom Ziehen experimented, while attending to his patient Nietzsche on the side, would have known why Rönne would intensify, in a continuous commentary that is also the narrative perspective, the mumbo jumbo he hears in the officers' mess over the strangely soft tropical fruit. He can do nothing else. "It was only a matter of transmission, all the particulars remained untouched; who was he to appropriate or oversee or, resisting, to create?"[57]

Verbal transmission as neurosis, without any basis in a transcendental or creative Poet's ego; medial selection without reference to the real, to the incomprehensible background of all media—even in his delirium, Rönne obeys orders. Pameelen has to transmit the doorman's apartment, hairpins, the hospital hallway, and goats, and Rönne has to transmit everything heard and said. What his acquaintances in the mess say, what they associate with this, what he himself says and associates with what is said and associated—it all becomes impossibly exhausting. "The struggle between associations, that's the final ego—he thought and walked back to the institute."[58]

Where else should one go, except into a catatonic stupor?[59] That at least allows Rönne to forget his forgetful project leader. But before final paralysis, the failed doctor extends his associations to their material basis, the brain itself. "I have to keep investigating what might have happened to me. What if the forceps had dug a little deeper into the skull at this point? What if I had been hit repeatedly on a particular spot on the head? What is it with brains, anyway?"[60] In an aporetic attempt to get behind his own thinking, that is, to localize it using his own medical knowledge, Rönne literally sacrifices his knowing subjectivity. The fact that he has words and associations at all becomes an improbable exception to the countless possible deficits and disturbances. Language ceases to be a bastion of inwardness; the gesture that simulates turning his brain inside out also reverses the condition of language into one of chance and exteriority.

Therefore Rönne (in direct descent from Nietzsche) never encounters a "word that reached me."[61] When blows to the head lead to aphasia in one instance, to associations and words in others, the preconditions of Poetry become one more casualty. The word that had always reached people operates at a certain psychic reaction threshold, which was called the discourse of nature and the nature of discourse. Psychophysics does away with both of them. Thus nothing remains for a psychiatrist who has become a psychiatric case, like Rönne, and who nonetheless wants to be reached by something, nothing remains but to undertake *The Journey* into other media.

He looked down the street and saw where to go.

He rushed into the twilight of a movie house, into the unconscious of the first floor. Reddish light stood in large calyxes of flat flowers up to hidden lamps. The sound of violins, nearby and warmly played, scraped over the curve of his brain, drawing out a truly sweet tone. Shoulders leaned against shoulders, in devotion: whispering, closing together, touching, happiness. A man came toward him, with wife and child, signaling familiarity, his mouth wide and laughing gaily. But Rönne no longer recognized him. He had entered into the film, into the sharp gestures, the mythic force.

Standing large before the sea, he wrapped himself in his coat, its skirts flapping in the fresh breeze; he attacked the air as he would an animal, and how the drink cooled the last of the tribe.

How he stamped, how vigorously he bent his knee. He wiped away the ashes, indifferent, as if possessed by great things that awaited him in the letter brought by the old servant, on whose knee the ancestor once sat.

The old man walked nobly up to the woman at the spring. How surprised the nanny was, as she put her handkerchief to her breast. What a lovely playmate! Like a deer among young bulls! What a silvery beard!

Rönne hardly breathed, careful not to break it.

Then it was done, it had come to pass.

The movement and spirit had come together over the ruins of the period of sickness, with nothing in between. The arm sailed clearly from an impulse; from light to the hip, a bright swing, from branch to branch.[62]

A movie theater in the suburbs of Brussels in 1916 is this Christological goal of all journeys. The novella makes what was accomplished in the film unambiguously clear. "Movement" can now be recorded in the technological real, no longer only in the imaginary.[63] Rönne, the man whom no word reaches, is not altogether beyond contact, but his reaction threshold functions physiologically rather than psychically. Film establishes immediate connections between technology and the body, stimulus and response, which make imaginary connections unnecessary. Reflexes, as in Pavlov's animals, occur with "nothing in between": they arc between sensory impulses and motoric reactions. This is true of the figures optically portrayed in the silent film; it is true of the accompanying music. The violins playing in the dark theater become an immediate presence for the physiologically schooled listener: just as in Schönberg's "Pierrot lunaire," they play on the curves of his brain.[64] For that reason the individual named *Rönne*, who in the medium of language had just renewed acquaintanceships, falls into a condition for which his contemporary psychiatrists had the fine word *asymbolia*: Rönne no longer recognizes anyone.

Psychiatry or no, asymbolia is the structure of the movies.[65] One autobiographer who (as the sad title of his book, *The Words*, already indicates) later became only a writer, wrote of his first visits to the movies: "We had the same mental age. I was seven years old and knew how to read, [the new art] was twelve years old and did not know how to talk."[66] The new medium, whether in Paris in 1912 or Brussels in 1916, presented language deficits as happiness. With his mother, who loved movies,

Sartre fled his grandfather, a man of letters, who like all the bourgeoisie went faithfully to the theater only to be able to go home "insidiously prepared for ceremonious destinies." The movies release Rönne from a discourse that is as incessant as it is empty. Two literary descriptions of film celebrate, in simple solidarity, "the unconscious of the first floor" and "the living night" of the projections as the end of the book's monopoly.[67] Film transposed into the technological real what Poetry had promised in the age of alphabetization and granted through the fantasy of the library. Both cineasts attribute the highest, that is, unconscious pleasure to the heroes and audience; both submerge themselves in a crowd that is bodily contact and not merely (as in *Faust*) a philosophic humanity; both blend into boundless identification with the phantasmagoria. One transfers words spoken at the Cross to film, the other writes more garrulously, but in the same vein.

All of this was one and the same: it was Destiny. The hero dismounted, put out the fuse, the traitor sprang at him, a duel with knives began: but the accidents of the duel likewise partook of the rigor of the musical development: they were fake accidents which ill concealed the universal order. What joy when the last knife stroke coincided with the last chord! I was utterly content, I had found the world in which I wanted to live, I touched the absolute.[68]

Habent sua fata libelli. There were times when the Absolute was manifest to people as a gallery of images of Spirit, that is, as poetic-philosophical writing. There are other times when it departs from the heaps of paper. Coherence, identification, universality—all the honorary titles conferred upon the book by universal alphabetization are transferred to the media, at least among the common people. Just as in 1800 the new fantasy of the library, despised by scholars, became the joy of women, children, and the uneducated, so too, a century later, did the apparatus of film, despised by library fantasts. A psychiatrist who has sunk to the level of a patient meets an acquaintance at the movies "with wife and child"; among the Sartres, mother and son go to the movies, whereas the writer and theater-goer grandfather can only ask stupid questions: "'Look here, Simonnot, you who are a serious man, do you understand it? My daughter takes my grandson to the cinema!' And M. Simonnot replied, in a conciliatory tone: 'I've never been, but my wife sometimes goes.'"[69]

As technological media, the gramophone and film store acoustical and optical data serially with superhuman precision. Invented at the same time by the same engineers, they launched a two-pronged attack on a monopoly that had not been granted to the book until the time of universal alphabetization: a monopoly on the storage of serial data. Circa 1900, the ersatz sensuality of Poetry could be replaced, not by Nature, but by technologies. The gramophone empties out words by bypassing their imaginary aspect (signifieds) for their real aspects (the physiology of the voice). Only a Wildenbruch could still believe that a device would be properly attentive to his soul, to the imaginary itself. Film devalues words by setting their referents, the necessary, transcendent, indeed absurd reference points for discourse, right before one's eyes. When Novalis read rightly, a real, visible world unfolded within him in the wake of the words. Rönne, struck with "mythic force" by the facticity of gestures and things in the silent film, no longer needs such magic.

Writers were justified in complaining that "the word is gradually losing credit" and "is already something somewhat too conspicuous and at the same time oddly undifferentiated for us today."[70] To use Lacan's methodological distinction between symbolic, real, and imaginary, two of these three functions, which constitute all information systems, became separable from writing circa 1900. The real of speaking took place in the gramophone; the imaginary produced in speaking or writing belonged to film. Hanns Heinz Ewers, author *and* screenplay writer of *The Student of Prague*, stated this distribution (though with a certain bias): "I hate *Thomas Alva Edison*, because we owe to him one of the most heinous of inventions: the *phonograph*! Yet I love him: he redeemed everything when he returned fantasy to the matter-of-fact world—in the movies!"[71]

While record grooves recorded bodies and their heinous waste material, the movies took over the fantastic or imaginary things that for a century had been called Poetry. Münsterberg, inventor in word and deed of psychotechnology, provided in 1916 the first historical theory of film in his demonstration that film techniques like projection and cutting, close-up and flashback, technically implement psychic processes such as hallucination and association, recollection and attention, rather than, like plays or novels, stimulating these processes descriptively with words.[72] As mechanized psychotechnology the "world of the movie" has "become synonymous with illusion and fantasy, turning society into what Joyce called an 'allnights newsery reel,' that substitutes a 'reel' world for reality. . . . His verdict on the 'automatic writing' that is photography was the *abnihilization of the etym*."[73]

In 1800 words went about their task of creating a real, visible world in such an undifferentiated way that visions and faces, which the book described for the purpose of recruiting authors, shared only one trait with their readers. Film exhibits its figures in such detail that "the realistic" is "raised into the realm of the fantastic," which sucks up every theme of imaginative literature.[74] Quite logically, early German silent films repeatedly took up the motif of the doppelgänger.[75] In *Golem*, in *The Other*, in *The Cabinet of Dr. Caligari*, in *The Student of Prague*—everywhere doppelgängers appear as metaphors for the screen and its aesthetic. A film trick demonstrates what happens to people when the new medium takes hold of them. These doppelgängers, instead of sharing a single trait with their originals, as in a book or screenplay, are the heroes of the films and therefore the focus of identification. With its guaranteed perfection in preserving evidence, film does not need, like the solitary hero of a romantic novel, to talk the reader into identification; what the moviegoer Rönne called his entry into film can occur automatically and wordlessly.

Movies thus took the place of the fantasy of the library. All the tricks that once magically transformed words into sequential hallucinations are recalled and surpassed. "In the movies," not just the "most beautiful" but also the "most common" is "miraculous."[76] Like any unconscious, the unconscious of the movie house is determined by the pleasure principle.

The schoolboy wants to see the prairies of his Westerns; he wants to see strange people in strange circumstances; he wants to see the lush, primitive banks of Asian rivers. The modest bureaucrat and the housewife locked into her household long for the shimmering celebrations of elegant society, for the far coasts and mountains to which they will never travel. . . . The working man in his everyday routine becomes a romantic as soon as he has some free time. He doesn't want to see anything realistic; rather, the realistic should be raised into an imaginary, fantastic realm. . . . One finds all this in the movies.[77]

To counter this triumphant competition, literature has two options. One easy option tends toward "trivializing mechanisms": namely, while underrating the technological media, to join them.[78] Since 1900 many writers have given up on getting their names into the poetic pantheon and, intentionally or not, have worked for the media. Whereas Wildenbruch summoned up pathos and spoke his name and soul into the phonograph, other lyric poets, preferring anonymity and success, produced texts for phonographic hits. The first screenplay writers also remained anonymous. When Heinrich Lautensack in 1913 published the written text of a screenplay after the film had been shot, the sensational use of his name demonstrated "that real poets, too, have written films, even if anonymously (how many might have done that, because of the money, over the years!)." Before Lautensack, "H. H. Ewers [was] probably the only known author whose name appeared with his films."[79]

Mass literature has been identified as non-value ever since hermeneutic reading guides distinguished between works and mass products, repeated rereading and reading mania. But when texts could be transposed to other media, the difference became one of method of production. The judgment that "the best novel and best drama are degraded into dime novels in the movies, full of sensationalism and make-believe" can be reversed.[80] Audiovisual sensuousness, also employed by high literary texts in 1800, became the speciality of books that aimed at hallucinatory effects with the methodical efficiency of digital-analog converters. Turn-of-the-century bestsellers were quickly made into films: historical novels like *Quo Vadis* (whose writer won the Nobel Prize), stories of doppel-gängers like *The Golem*, psychopathological thrillers like Paul Lindau's *The Other*, to say nothing of *Buddenbrooks*. For "the Paul Lindaus have their merits and their immortality." [81] They were there when the type-writer made the publishing process more economical; they knew what was going on when psychophysics reduced the mystery of the soul to fea-sibilities. Their books thus appeared where they belonged: on the movie screen. Lindau's "Other" is a district attorney; when a crime occurs in his house, he uses the best criminological methods to gather evidence, only to discover that he himself, as doppelgänger or schizophrenic like Jekyll and Hyde, was the perpetrator. A year earlier, Hallers, the district attorney, had had a riding accident and injured the occipital lobe, on which brain localization theories focus . . .

Of course, role inversion was characteristic of literary heroes like Rönne and literary techniques like automatic writing circa 1900, but only in film could hallucination become real and indices like a clock or por-trait bring about unambiguous identifications. Criminology and psycho-pathology work with the same technologies as the entertainment indus-try. [82] A district attorney who unconsciously (as his friend, a psychiatrist, explains to him) every night becomes his own other is a metaphor for the shift from bureaucracy to technology, from writing to media. In the un-conscious of the movie house, modest bureaucrats or women trapped in their households don't want to see symbolic or real servants of the state. What they want is imaginary reversal.

Literature's other option in relation to the media is to reject them, along with the imaginary and real aspects of discourse to which they cater, and which have become the province of popular writers. Because "kitsch will never be eliminated from humanity," one group of writers renounces it. [83] After 1900 a high literature develops in which "the word" becomes something "too conspicuous," that is, it becomes a purely differ-ential signifier. Once imaginary effects and real inscription have been re-nounced, what remains are the rituals of the symbolic. These rituals take into account neither the reaction thresholds of people nor the support of Nature. "Letters of the alphabet do not occur in nature." Words as literal anti-nature, literature as word art, the relation between both as material equality—this is their constellation in the purest art for art's sake and in the most daring games of the avant-garde. Since December 28, 1895, there has been one infallible criterion for high literature: it cannot be filmed.

When idealist aesthetics bound the various arts together as parts of a single system, sculpture, painting, music, and architecture were unambiguously determined by their respective materials—stone, sound, color, building material. Poetry, however, as the universal art, was permitted to reign over the universal medium of the imagination. It lost this special status circa 1900 in the interest of thorough equality among materials. Literature became word art put together by word producers. As if to confirm Lacan's theory of love, Kurt Schwitters was in love with his Anna because "her name [can be spelled] backwards as well as forwards: *a-n-n-a*." It is hardly controversial to make this claim with respect to the writers of experimental modernism. But even writers like Holz or Hofmannsthal, often seen as continuing the projects of Herder or Humboldt one hundred years after the fact, expressed concern to do justice to the material they worked with.[84] Hofmannsthal argued concisely that the basic concepts of classical-romantic Poetry were so much blabla in relation to its material, the word. "I wonder whether all the tiresome jabbering about individuality, style, character, mood, and so on has not made you lose sight of the fact that the material of poetry is words. . . . We should be allowed to be artists who work with words, just as others work with white or colored stone, shaped metal, purified tones or dance."[85]

Less concise, but astonishing in a direct descendant of Schleiermacher, is Dilthey's line that before any hermeneutics there are "sensually given signs": "stones, marble, musically formed sounds, gestures, words, and script."[86] No voice, then, no matter how traditional its idiom, can be heard locating Poetry in an immaterial imagination. It is simply wrong to assign "an abstraction from the realm of literary-historical media to the period" in which "the paradigms of media used in positivistic literary history were widened to include film, radio, and records."[87] What is here vaguely circumscribed as "abstraction" had long cemented the classical bond of friendship between poets and thinkers. But in 1900 film and the gramophone (radio would not appear until twenty-five years later) would lead to the very opposite result by isolating the word theoretically as well, leaving to the media its previous effects on the imagination. The rankings of the individual arts in a synchronic system inevitably shifted.[88] But historical derivations of modernist word literature, such as Günther Sasse's, are perhaps superfluous; by presupposing a "situation in need of clarification, namely, that not until one hundred years after the thematization of language in philosophy, did the same problem become central in literature,"[89] such an approach creates more problems than it solves. But because there was once a brief friendship between literature and philosophy, literary historians still read Humboldt's philosophy instead of test series.

All the evidence indicates that the high literature of 1900 gave up its symphilosophizing because other contemporary movements gained prominence. The new sciences and technologies made it necessary to renounce the imagination. Mallarmé stated this when he answered an inquiry *On the Illustrated Book* with a decided "No." "Why," he asked in response, "don't you go right to the cinematographs, for their sequence of images will replace, to great advantage, many books in image and text."[90] If reform primers and novels of artistic development cunningly used images to contribute to an imperceptible alphabetization and identification, high literature cut out everything available to the other media. For all his love of film, Kafka conveyed to his publisher his "horror" at the very thought that an illustrator of his *Metamorphosis* "might even want to draw the insect itself. Not that, please! I don't want to diminish the area of his authority, but issue my request only on behalf of my naturally better grasp of the story. The insect itself cannot be drawn. It cannot be drawn even from a great distance."[91] Literature thus occupies, with creatures or noncreatures that can only be found in words, the margin left to it by the other media. Illustrations outgrew their baby shoes, their contributory role, and learned to walk and wield power in the unconscious of the movie house; the symbolic remained, autonomous and imageless as once only God had been.

The literary ban on images allowed only two exceptions. One occurred when Stefan George wanted to document the fact that he was not a classical author and thus not for the young ladies. He gave his artist and book designer, Melchior Lechter, "a nonartistic task" that "leaves the realm of art" and ended any further collaboration between them.[92] The *Commemoration* for Maximin was to be prefaced, not by the hand-drawn portrait Lechter suggested, but by Maximilian Kronberger's photograph. Only the scandal of technological media in the midst of the ritual of letters could materialize the scandal of the master desiring a singular and real body.

The other exception was systematic. After 1900 letters were permitted to construct figures, because they had always been figures. This too directly reversed classical norms. Schleiermacher "completely" excluded from Poetry verses in dialect as well as those others "that look like an axe or bottle."[93] Ninety-eight years later, Apollinaire justified his *Calligrammes* by citing the competition of film and records.

It would have been strange if in an epoch when the popular art par excellence, the cinema, is a book of pictures, poets had not tried to compose pictures for meditative and refined minds that are not content with the crude imaginings of the makers of films. These last will become more perceptive, and one can predict the day when, the photograph and the cinema having become the only form of publication in use, the poet will have a freedom heretofore unknown. One should not be astonished if, with the means they now have at their disposal, poets set themselves to preparing this new art.[94]

Pictures made of letters remain in the cleared area, in the technological niche of literature, without suffering any material inequality vis-à-vis the other media that, Apollinaire prophesies, will soon be the only ones. Such pictures had been despised for a century, because any emphasis on the figural quality of letters would have made it more difficult to ignore them. To achieve the psychophysical insight, to see letters "as a great quantity of strange figures on a white background," or as calligrammes, "one has only to look at a newspaper page upside down."[95] The literality and materiality of the written can be realized only at the expense of readability and in limited experiments. Apollinaire and Mallarmé competed with the technological medium of film, whereas it would have seemed sufficient to distinguish letters and books from traditional painting. The call for a cult of typefaces issued by writers circa 1900 had nothing to do with fine writing, everything to do with machines. In the words of Anton Kaes: "The reform movement in literature that ran parallel to the rise of the movies as a mass medium took shape against the background of the new technological media."[96]

Research into the localization of language replicated the typewriter. The tachistoscope of the physiologists of reading was the twin of the movie projector, with the side effect of typographically optimizing the typewriter. Brain physiology did away with the illusion that language is more "than a play of mechanical equipment learned by practice," which "is set into ordered motion by ideas, just as one can operate a sewing, adding, writing, or talking machine without needing to be familiar with its construction."[97] Prior to consciousness, then, there are sensory and motor, acoustical and optic language centers linked by nerve paths just as the working parts of a typewriter are connected by levers and rods. As if taking Nietzsche's dictation style as a metaphor, brain physiology formulates the path from the sound image of the word to the hand that writes and to consciousness as an inaudible dictation, to which only autonomic reaction is appropriate at the level of consciousness.[98] To produce actual discourse, there must be impulses in the cerebral cortex "through which the word, as an acoustical and optical image, is transposed into its sensory sound parts on a sound clavier." All keyboards (including those that produce sounds), however, are spatial arrangements, or a sort of typewriter keyboard of language. A "cortical soundboard" virtually conjures up the lever system of the old Remingtons.[99]

As soon as one connects the brain physiology of language with the psychophysics of the senses via the tachistoscope, the hypothetical machine in the brain becomes a real machine in front of the retina. The letters and words presented for milliseconds by the tachistoscope are aleatory choices from prepared stores or vocabularies. The procedure is only apparently arbitrary and "peculiar to our experiments." For "as rich as the number of words in our civilized languages has gradually become, their number diminishes considerably in each language during a particular period, for a particular domain of literature, and for a particular author."[100] Periods, genres, authors—all play on unconscious word keyboards and even more unconscious letter keyboards. The philosopher become experimenter Erdmann says nothing of them; instead, he presents the basic rule that words are recognized in their "totality," that is, by those traits "in which the black marks of the letters contrast with the white background." In which case, "the surface areas of the white background are as essential for the whole configuration as the black ones are."[101]

Erdmann's followers and critics, however, were not philosophers or hermeneutic interpreters, and they limited their investigations to the materiality of letters. They turned the tachistoscopes to speeds higher than those at which reading can take place because only disturbances and deficiencies betray the fundamental secrets of letters and forms of script. The film projector's twin thus functions in an opposite manner. The projector, in the unconscious of the movie house, presents a continuum of the imaginary, generated through a sequence of single images so precisely chopped up by and then fed through the projector's mechanism that the illusion of seamless unity is produced. With the tachistoscope, in the darkened laboratory of the alphabetical elite, a cut-up image assaults as a cut in order to establish out of the torment and mistaken readings of victims the physiologically optimal forms of letters and script. As with the typewriter, which has its own key for spacing, intervals are built into the experimental procedure. But they also become the test result. The tachistoscope demonstrates that on the most basic level reading consists in perceiving not letters but the differences between them, and that word recognition proceeds by hitting upon discontinuous, single letters that literally stick out. Systematically evaluated misreadings indicate that letters at x-height (vowels and some consonants) are relatively undifferentiated, but that consonants with ascenders or descenders serve as typographic recognition signals.[102] According to Julius Zeitler, the historically renewed primacy of the letter is based on a "decomposition of the letter continuum into groups." "There are whole series of words, analogous in their letter composition, that run through heterogeneous meanings if one letter in the same position is changed. . . . If the new meaning of the word image that has been altered in this way is to be registered, the letter must be determined, that is, it must be spelled out. When this does not occur, the original word image is constantly reassimilated, as is the original meaning along with it." [103]

The letter-crosswords with which Reformation primers liked to play could therefore be resurrected. One theorist of elementary education illustrated Zeitler's theory for his deaf and dumb children with the following example: [104]

```
              r
              p
        ca    n
              t
```

One need only read this series as a column—and Saussure's theory of language as a combinatory system is born. As it says in the structuralist bible: [105]

In every such case the isolated sound, like every other unit, is chosen after a dual mental opposition. In the imaginary grouping *anma*, for instance, the sound *m* stands in syntagmatic opposition to its environing sounds and in associative opposition to all other sounds that may come to mind:

```
        a    n    m    a
                  v
                  d
```

But, as Derrida was the first to rediscover, [106] the modest letter researchers or grammatologists were more rigorous than linguistics' founding hero. Their tachistoscope locates pure differentiality not in "sounds," that is, in incorporeal sound images of words, but in the material signs of type. Thus the machine demonstrates *and* practices what structural linguistics accomplishes insofar as it writes down nonsense words such as *anma*, even though it stresses their use in speech. In order to engrave an example of the differentiality of phonemes into his own text, Saussure was forced to shift to the distinction between necessary and arbitrary, graphematic and graphic differences between letters.

The value of letters is purely negative and differential. The same person can write *t*, for instance, in different ways:

The only requirement is that the sign for *t* not be confused in his script with the signs used for *l*, *d*, etc.[107]

It is because the example of the three handwritten *t*'s does not constitute an example, but is rather a conclusive demonstration with which differences in sound could never compete, that structural linguistics and psychophysical positivism belong together. Instead of continuing in the line of Schleiermacher's hermeneutics,[108] Saussure systematized, at the price of a methodological phonocentrism, the countless scriptural facts that experiments circa 1900 produced and let stand in their facticity.

But the love of facts can also bear fruit. It might not produce a system, but it does produce typographies. Erdmann's measurement of the relation between letters and background, Zeitler's differentiation of letter recognition according to x-height, ascenders, and descenders, Oskar Messmer's calculation of the frequency of these three types in coherent texts, all culminated in a knowledge of differentiality that could become immediately practical. The secular war between Fraktur and roman scripts, for instance, no longer need be burdened with the imaginary values of Things German in opposition to the world. After simple tests with both types of script—with the tachistoscope, in low light, with beginning pupils and professors—the superiority of roman was a matter of fact. Semiotic positivism allowed Friedrich Soennecken to explain that roman consisted of two basic lines, whereas Fraktur consisted of "no less than sixty-six basic lines differing in form and size."[109] This sort of massive differential difference made decisions easy for researchers who published works such as *The Economy and Technology of Learning*:[110] "Anyone who has ever experimented with the tachistoscope knows that the simpler a type of script is, the easier it is to learn."[111]

Indeed, under the conditions of pure differentiality there is nothing simpler than the opposition that, in theory and praxis, determines the current century: binary opposition. If roman consists of only two "elements, the straight line and the half circle,"[112] then an ideal script has been found, one whose elements can be combined and analyzed quite differently from Pöhlmann's or Stephani's handwriting norms. An economy took the place of organic merging, one that (perhaps following the new standard of Morse code) technically optimized signs and the differences between them.

Thus differences appeared even in roman typeface, the very minimalization of difference. Saussure distinguished necessary and arbitrary differences among letters; embracing necessary difference, since 1900 the various roman typefaces that reject ornament have flourished and become as pervasive as chemically pure industrial design.[113] Forms to be filled out call for block letters; lower case and sans serif are the height of Manhattan advertising chic.

The call was answered. Because roman capital letters are what "the child first encounters at every turn"—"on street signs, street cars, post offices, train stations"[114]—the block letters of technological information channels found their way into elementary-school instruction. Rudolph von Larisch's students in Vienna learned from a manual *Instruction in Ornamental Script*; but they learned a surface art that rejected all "perspective and shadow effects" of the Stephani type of word painting. The goal, "in competition with other demands," was "a HIGHER degree of readability": "that the characteristic qualities of a letter be stressed with all possible force and the difference from similar letters be stressed."[115] Psychophysicists and structural linguists hardly say it more clearly. The medium of writing and paper no longer pretended to be a springboard to painted nature. Using uniformly thick lines, Eckmann and Peter Behrens,[116] Larisch and Soennecken drew block letters as block letters.

The decomposition of roman letters, as it confronts elementary binary opposition, is the mirror image of their composition. To write block letters is not to connect signs with other signs but to combine discrete elements piece by piece. In the age of engineers an armature construction set replaces the growth of plants and originary script.[117] Separate letters consisting of separate elements are based, in strict opposition to classical writing rules, on Saussure's most daring opposition: that between signs and emptiness, medium and background. "The beginner has to learn to look, not simply at the form of the letters, but constantly BETWEEN the letters; he must use all the power of his vision to grasp the surface forms that arise between the letters and to assess the effect of their optical mass."[118] A reversal of every habit or facility thus grants the "BETWEEN" the same status as the positive marks it separates. So Larisch knocked children over the head with the lesson that psychophysics produced with the tachistoscope and with newspapers turned upside down: the fact that letters are what they are only against and upon a white background. A "BETWEEN" in capital block letters is a sheer autonym. And if educators circa 1800 aimed at mitigating the shock of binary opposition by connecting lines and an attenuation of the black-white contrast, Larisch—as a student of William Morris—gave his students the "feeling of how poorly the softening halftone fits into a printed book," in that "simple, powerful outlines and the full contrast of black and white spaces have an appearance characteristic of printed type."[119]

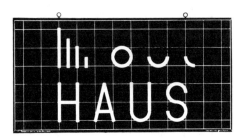

And yet—the implications of the tachistoscope and the economy of letters for literature and literary science become even more obscure, if possible, here on the page, for all its black and white space. One needs the whole power of one's vision to glimpse the overlooked visibility of texts. The black and white of texts seems so timeless that it never occurs to readers to think of the architects of that space. The forgotten technicians of 1900, however, revolutionized the page of poetry, from the most playful verses to the most ritualized. Morgenstern's *Gallows Songs* enact the derivation of what the Stefan George typeface practiced in mute solemnity.

> Es war einmal ein Lattenzaun
> mit Zwischenraum, hindurchzuschaun.
>
> Ein Architekt, der dieses sah,
> stand eines Abends plötzlich da—
>
> und nahm den Zwischenraum heraus
> und baute draus ein grosses Haus.
>
> Der Zaun indessen stand ganz dumm,
> mit Latten ohne was herum.
>
> Ein Anblick grässlich und gemein.
> Drum zog ihn der Senat auch ein.
>
> Der Architeckt jedoch entfloh
> nach Afri- od- Ameriko.
>
> There used to be a picket fence
> with space to gaze from hence to thence.

An architect who saw this sight
approached it suddenly one night,

removed the spaces from the fence
and built of them a residence.

The picket fence stood there dumbfounded
with pickets wholly unsurrounded,

a view so naked and obscene
the Senate had to intervene.

The architect, however, flew
to Afri- or Americoo.[120]

"The Picket Fence" is the fairy tale of a new age. Where Anselmus saw
the woven arabesques of handwritten letters, the cold eye of the architect
sees the opposite. One evening Larisch's imperative—to look constantly
BETWEEN the letters, to grasp the space outlined between them with all
one's strength—is realized word for word. In so doing, the architect does
not discover merely how indispensable concepts of relation are.[121] Something more tangible is at stake: the fact that the readability of signs is a
function of their spatiality. The architect's manipulation of space demonstrates that, when the lack is lacking and no empty spaces remain, media
disappear, "naked and obscene," into the chaos from which they were
derived.

Consider the final stanza of "The Picket Fence" in light of the architecture of block letters. Whereas "the alliteration of *Africa* and *America*
feigns an ending in *-(i)ca*,"[122] which also plays with the ending of *oder*
[the placement of "or"], a "between" appears in the realm of the grapheme: the space designated by the dash. The words of the poem, complete
autonyms in this sense, foreground their own intervals between stem and
ending. Morgenstern's constructed architect does not disappear into far-
off lands, but into the space between signs that he had usurped.

From this vanishing point called paper, it is only a step to "the ideal of
purely abstract, absolute poetry," an ideal of such brilliance "that it also
means the end of poetry; it can no longer be imitated or surpassed; it is
transcended only by the empty white page."[123] "The Picket Fence" describes the binary opposition between letters or pickets [*Lettern/Latten*]
and the space between them, but "Fish's Night Song" uniquely enacts this
opposition without any description at all.[124] In it, the reduction to straight
line and half curve that distinguishes roman from Fraktur scripts becomes textual event. Circumflex and dash, two signifiers that define
themselves through mutual opposition and relation, are the absolute
minimum economy of the signifier. Their binary opposition to each other,
canceled or articulated through the shared opposition of both to paper,

constitutes the poem that meets all the reading-psychological desiderata of its epoch. Period. For there is nothing more to write about a minimal signifier system.

Or there would be nothing more to write if the poem did not have a title composed in the very different, redundant, signifier system of the twenty-six letters. Through the title, one discourse network answers another across the turning point that divides them. "Fish's Night Song" is the cancellation of Goethe's "Wanderer's Night Song II." In the latter, a human voice outlasts the surrounding sounds of nature for one breath in order to express the promise that it, too, would find rest in the lap of Mother Nature. In the former, the text brings a mute fish not to speech, but into a typogram. It thus realizes Schleiermacher's nightmare: namely, that a real optics would render superfluous the imaginary, imaginal aspects that meaningful words suggest to alphabetized readers. As mute and dead as any script, the fish no longer needs the phonocentric consolation of a seamless transition between speech and nature. The signs on the page cannot be spoken by any voice—regardless of whether one reads them as fish scales or discrete elements of the roman typeface. Man and soul, in any case, no longer apply. With all the wanderers between day and night, Spirit and Nature, male and female, Man simply died around 1900. It was a death to which the much-discussed death of God is a footnote.

Stephani wrote that written letters provide notes for the mouth instrument. But a mute fish demonstrates that signs can mock all speech and nonetheless still be written signs. The half curve and dash, the two minimal signifieds of Soennecken and of the "Night Song," can be found on every universal keyboard. The first German monograph on the typewriter thus celebrated the fact that "with a little inventiveness one can produce very fine borders and flourishes" on Remingtons and Olivers.[125] It presented the prototype of modernist ideal poetry years before Morgenstern.

$$((—))   ((—))   ((—))$$

Not only is the human voice incapable of reproducing signs prior to and beyond alphabets, but writers, by prescribing their own alphabets, can remove their texts from hermeneutic consumption. The existence of a Stefan George script in the discourse network of 1900 demonstrates that "Fish's Night Song" is the signet of the whole system.

The Stefan George script, which Lechter fabricated and used throughout the first edition of George's *Collected Works*, was adapted from George's handwriting. But it was handwriting only in name. First, the single letters—beyond any supposed Carolingian reference—were based on a contemporary advertising grotesque.[126] Second, any handwriting that can be transposed into reusable typeface functions fundamentally as mechanized script.

Technology entered the scene in archaic dress. Larisch came up with "the ideal of a personal book" that would be "self-designed, -written, -ornamented, and -bound."[127] That is exactly what George did before Lechter and Georg Bondi made him aware of the possibility of technological reproduction. Under the pressure of media competition, high literature returned to the monastic copyists whom Gutenberg had rendered unnecessary and Anselmus had made to seem foolish. At the same time, however, the personal book (that oxymoron) was to be set in block letters that, "equal in their characteristics," have none of the redundant differences of individual handwritten letters. According to Larisch, the historic "moment" was "favorable" for old-fashioned, manually made books because "precisely now the use of typewriters is becoming widespread."[128]

The ascetics of handwork art, even when they played at being medieval, were in competition with the modern media. As soon as there were typewriters, there were fashioners of texts like Mark Twain or Paul Lindau, who had "the production means of the printing press at their disposal" on their desks. According to Marshall McLuhan, the fact that "the typewriter fuses composition and publication" brought about "an entirely new attitude to the written and printed word."[129] Like innovation, its effects surpassed its applications. When Larisch and George stylized their handwriting until it became a typeface, they achieved what Malling

Hansen and Nietzsche had been praised for: script "as beautiful and regular as print." [130] "Perfect lyrical creations and perfect technical objects are one and the same." [131]

The new relation to the printed word became printed reality in the layout of George's books. From the time of his break with Lechter, at the latest, his books constituted an imageless cult of letters. The cry of material equality extended from the single lyrical word to the entire alphabetical medium. If modern, Morris-inspired publications, such as *Goals of Internal Book Design*, state in tautological conclusion that "paper and type make up a book," the poets of the George circle were "more or less the first to realize that a book consists of paper and type." [132]

But it is not only the fact that books of the turn of the century "looked very booklike" that places them into technological contexts. [133] More important, the Stefan George script (as typeface, in the form of its letters, and in its orthography and punctuation) presupposed, maximized, and exploited experimentally obtained standards. In terms of the physiology of reading, it was evident that the "letters and other elements of the typeface" and "the capital and small letter should be as similar as possible." It follows that roman is by far "more efficient" than Fraktur, which would be "unthinkable as a typewriter typeface." [134] The Stefan George script met just these standards; in its new letter forms for *e*, *k*, and *t*, capital and lowercase letters were even more alike than in ordinary roman type. [135] George eliminated the ascenders from two of the twenty-six letters (*k* and *t*). This might seem a minimal innovation, but in combination with Grimm's orthography (the use of small letters for nouns, the elimination of *h* from many *th* combinations, and the use of *ss* rather than the *Eszett*), it had a significant cumulative effect. Whereas the physiologist Messmer counted 270 letters above or below x-height in an ordinary text a thousand letters long, I find in George an average of only 200 extended as opposed to 800 small letters. (The same passages in Duden orthography would contain nearly one hundred more ascenders and descenders.)

Messmer could show that words such as *physiological* or *psychological*, taken simply as collections of letters containing a high percentage of ascenders and descenders, do not convey the "unitary whole impression" that distinguishes words such as *wimmern*, *nennen*, or *weinen*. [136] Extended letters quicken the pace of tachistoscopic word recognition, but in a special script or cult of the letter intended to hinder any alphabetized skipping over of letters, material equality is everything and a gain in speed is nothing. Therefore masses of words like *wimmern*, *nennen*, and *weinen* fill the eighteen volumes of an oeuvre whose esotericism is physiologically guaranteed. In it, homologies, recognitions, and knowing smiles are exchanged between the most aristocratic of writers and the modest experimenters of 1900. The inventor of psychotechnology confirmed an esotericism in the inventor of the Stefan George script that—a first in the history of writing—could be measured. "The fact that the elimination of capital letters from the beginning of nouns constitutes a strong check against rapid absorption can be easily verified, should readers of Stefan George find it necessary, by psychological experiment in an easily measurable procedure." [137]

These lines are as true as they are prophetic. Whereas readers of Nietzsche stumbled only here and there over italicized introjections, readers of George have trouble with every letter. A perfect experimental procedure forestalls understanding in order to fix the eyes on signifiers as murky as the "Fish's Night Song." But the readers were fascinated and forgot they were experimental subjects. In opposition to the technological media, they conjured up a secondhand old Europe. Consider Gert Mattenklott's consideration of George: "The image of Stefan George appears finally as the sheer allegorical corpse. . . . Everything arbitrary and individual is transcribed into a meaningful universal, perhaps most clearly when George made his own handwriting resemble a typeface intended to replace the conventional one." [138] These lines are as false as they are Benjaminesque. Their writer is simply unaware of the technologies of his own century. The facts that the typewriter made it inevitable that handwriting should come to resemble type, that there was the project of a "world letter" to unburden memories,[139] and that the logic of the signifier explodes the "meaning" of the age of Goethe all fall victim here to an allegory of allegory. "Conventional handwriting" is a non-concept. If histories of the material basis of literature are to be possible, apparent conventions, especially in the elemental field of writing, must be dismantled and examined as feedback control loops and programs. George, whether a corpse or not, was evidence of an epochal innovation.

No appeal to timeless conventions could ever explain why a nameless artist (not George) changed his handwriting three times between 1877 and 1894, attracting the attention of psychiatrists with the third change and landing among them with the fourth. Above all, however, conventions cannot explain why science took precisely this patient at his word or pen and made facsimiles of his handwriting.[140] Only the assumption that the four writing experiments portray an upheaval, as if in time-lapse photography, can explain both acts of writing, that of the patient and that of the psychiatrists. Proceeding exactly as had George (who, of course, was not born writing block letters), the anonymous artist made the transition from the rounded and connected handwriting ideal of Stephani or Lindhorst to the cult of the letter. One of the first studies of its kind, entitled *Handwriting of the Insane*, noted that it was "in no way accidental" that patients' handwriting lost "the normal connecting lines between adjacent letters."[141] As if to demonstrate the explosive force of discursive events, the isolation of letters leads to the isolation of their writers.

In 1894, the *Encyclopedic Review* commissioned a young medical student to query writers about the recent appearance of graphology. Mallarmé's answer runs:

Yes, I think that writing is a clue; you say, like gesture and physiognomy, nothing more certain. Nevertheless, by profession or by taste, the writer *recopies* or sees first in the mirror of his mind, and then transcribes in writing once and for all, as if invariable. The immediate effect of his emotions is therefore not visible in his manuscript, but there one can judge his personality as a whole.[142]

This states the issue directly. While graphology was being developed to provide another type of evidence, literate people fell into two subclasses: on the one hand, those whose handwriting was a direct reflection of their unconscious and so could be evaluated psychologically or criminologically; on the other, the professional writers, who were writing machines* without handwriting. Among the latter, what appears to be the production of a soul is always only the reproduction on a keyboard of invariable letters. Writers' texts therefore could not be interpreted unless graphology made "major modifications." That is exactly what happened when Ludwig Klages studied an original manuscript of George (as was explic-

---

* Here and throughout this chapter, there is a play on the etymology of *Schreibmaschine* ("typewriter," but literally "writing machine"). [Trans.]

Stefan George

itly noted in George's *Works*):[143] "ornament," rather than the usual "expressive marks," necessarily became the object of interpretation.[144] Professional, intransitive writing barred the abyss of the unconscious and ruled out the techniques of gathering evidence. The remaining word specialists quickly learned the lesson that the phonograph taught foolhardy Wildenbruch. Mallarmé became an incomprehensible personality en bloc; George was practical enough, in his monthly dealings with the Deutsche Bank, to have his favorite disciple write the signature on his checks, *Stefan George*. "He said that Gundolf could sign his name in such a way that even he could not tell, at a later date, whether he or Gundolf had signed it."[145]

For all the disdain of words that made him the founding hero of *Bildung*, Faust still believed in and obeyed the binding power of his signature. Without the bureaucratic ethos, the pact between the humane disciplines and the state would not have come about. For all his cult of the word, George, the technician in spite of himself, played a little strategic game in his commerce with the bank. A signature that, like the graphologically dreaded "machinescript," avoids "every trait of intimacy" and thus can always be forged, can be found in print.[146] Although the technicians, on their side, soon discovered George's trick, he did demonstrate

DAS WORT

Wunder von ferne oder traum
Bracht ich an meines landes saum

Und harrte bis die graue norn
Den namen fand in ihrem born –

Drauf konnt ichs greifen dicht und stark
Nun blüht und glänzt es durch die mark ...

Einst langt ich an nach guter fahrt
Mit einem kleinod reich und zart

Sie suchte lang und gab mir kund:
›So schläft hier nichts auf tiefem grund‹

Worauf es meiner hand entrann
Und nie mein land den schatz gewann ...

So lernt ich traurig den verzicht:
Kein ding sei wo das wort gebricht.

something. Only as long as people believed in their inwardness did that inwardness exist. Man stands or falls with the signature of his signature. It is impossible to give exemplary status to Man and to Language in one and the same discourse network.[147]

Thus circa 1900 the universal bureaucratic ethos of the age of Goethe was replaced by professional ethics. In the competitive struggle of media everyone swears by a particular professionalism. It can mean nothing else when lyric poets after George prominently publish poems entitled "THE WORD."

THE WORD

I carried to my country's shore
Marvels and dreams, and waited for

The tall and twilit norn to tell
The names she found within the well.

Then I could grasp them, they were mine,
And here I see them bloom and shine . . .

Once I had made a happy haul
And won a rich and fragile jewel.

She peered and pondered: "Nothing lies
Below," she said, "to match your prize."

At this it glided from my hand
And never graced my native land.

And so I sadly came to see:
Without the word no thing can be.[148]

Rebus

Untranslatability and the Transposition of Media

A medium is a medium is a medium. Therefore it cannot be translated. To transfer messages from one medium to another always involves reshaping them to conform to new standards and materials. In a discourse network that requires an "awareness of the abysses which divide the one order of sense experience from the other,"[1] transposition necessarily takes the place of translation.[2] Whereas translation excludes all particularities in favor of a general equivalent, the transposition of media is accomplished serially, at discrete points. Given Medium A, organized as a denumerable collection of discrete elements $E_1^a \ldots E_n^a$, its transposition into Medium B will consist in reproducing the internal (syntagmatic and paradigmatic) relations between its elements in the collection $E_1^b \ldots E_m^b$. Because the number of elements n and m and the rules of association are hardly ever identical, every transposition is to a degree arbitrary, a manipulation. It can appeal to nothing universal and must, therefore, leave gaps. The elementary, unavoidable act of EXHAUSTION is an encounter with the limits of media.

The logic of media may be a truism in set theory or information theory, but for Poets it was the surprise of the century. Before they founded *The New Empire*, the kingdom of blank machine-written bodies of words, poets more than any other profession remained faithful to the classical discourse network. The translatability of all discourses into poetic signifieds endowed poets with such privilege that only bitter experience forced them to renounce their constitutive illusion. For an entire century poets had worked with language as if it were merely a channel.[3] Love and intoxication transported the author into hallucinations that he would later, as "marvels and dreams," have only to transcribe. Being the general equivalent of all the senses, the imagination guaranteed that every "jewel" would have no trouble finding a name. Because addicted masculine and feminine readers quickly read past these names, their effect was anything but equality among the various aesthetic materials: through backward-moving translation, discourses became once more a sensual Nature, one that "blooms and shines."

In 1919 the exchange broke down. The norn with whom a Poet bartered his imaginative visions for words is no longer a Mother, the one who, as the unarticulated beginning of articulation, guaranteed unlimited expression. The norn has only a bourn or treasury in which signifiers co-exist spatially as denumerable elements. Whatever jewels glow in other media need not necessarily have equivalents, even in Stefan George script. After a long and exhaustive search, the norn breaks this sensational news. Whereas poetic translation was led on by the constant promise of fulfill-ment, literature is a transposition of media; its structure is first revealed, in the best positivistic and consequently *Dasein*-analytic manner, by deficits.[4]

Experimenters with the tachistoscope and writers at the norn bourn agree that in every language "the number of words is limited at a particu-lar time, in a particular domain of literature, and for a particular author." An economy of the scarcity of signs replaced universal trade in 1900. George did not limit his economizing with words to his programmatic poem. He was also the "first modern German poet whose vocabulary is contained in a complete dictionary," which, however, does not make him into an "unfathomable spring."[5] It would have been better—aside from the exhaustibility of even the deepest norn bourns—to check at least once with the positivists. Poetic languages, like that of the symbo-lists, which "made it necessary to compile a special dictionary for their works (J. Plowert, *Petit glossaire pour servir à l'intelligence des auteurs décadents et symbolistes*)," thus identify themselves as "professional jargon."[6]

Consequently, George's final stanza celebrates The Word as the ethic of a media professional. In what sounds like resignation, Heidegger's un-erring art of reading deciphers something quite different.

His renunciation concerns the poetic relation to the word that he had cultivated until then. Renunciation is preparedness for another relation. If so, the "can be" in the line, "Without the word no thing can be," would grammatically speaking not be the subjunctive of "is," but a kind of imperative, a command which the poet follows, to keep it from then on. If so, the "may be" in the line, "Where word breaks off no thing may be," would mean: do not henceforth admit any thing as being where the word breaks off.[7]

An imperative issues from the realization that the transposition of media is always a manipulation and must leave gaps between one embodiment and another. This imperative does not deny that there are media other than writing; it rejects them. On the threshold of the Indian temple caves of Shiva, whose name, *Ellora*, George celebrates as he had the nonsense word *Tiholu*, are the lines:

> Pilger ihr erreicht die hürde.
> Mit den trümmern eitler bürde
> Werft die blumen werft die flöten·
> Rest von tröstlichem geflimme!
> Ton und farbe müsst ihr töten
> Trennen euch von licht und stimme
> An der schwelle von Ellora.

> Pilgrims, you have reached the gate
> With your pack of worthless freight.
> Leave the garland, leave the flute,
> Shreds of solace, shreds of show,
> Tints shall fade and sound be mute,
> Light and voices cease to flow
> On the threshold of Ellora.[8]

To deny the other media would be absurd, because color and sound, light and the voice have become recordable, become part of the general acceleration, "in the sense of the technical maximization of all velocities, in whose time-space modern technology and apparatus can alone be what they are."[9] Henceforth command will conflict with command, medium with medium. High literature circa 1900 became a despotic, indeed murderous command to limit data to what the medium of script could exhaust. Its spirit [*Geist*], according to Morgenstern's very serious play on words, ought to be named "It is called / It commands" [*Heisst*].[10] The spirit—or George—became a dictator giving dictation, followed by young men who killed off what was real in them and recorded by secretaries who derived a complete pedagogy from the recording threshold of Ellora.

At conferences of the art-education movement "the possibility of translation in the deepest sense" was rejected precisely in a figure who promoted translatability and world literature. Stephan Waetzoldt, an official in the Prussian Ministry of Culture, Education, and Church Affairs, experimented with native and foreign students to determine whether it was possible to translate Goethe's poem "Dedication." His results were:

It is no more possible for a Frenchman to become a German than it is to translate French into German or vice versa. Only where everyday matters, the banal, or the strictly mathematical are expressed, can there be any question of real translation. One can rethink or re-form something in another language, in another image of the world, but one can never actually translate. How could you ever translate Musset, and how could you ever translate Goethe![11]

The imaginary (the everyday) and the real (the mathematical) can thus be translated, but the symbolic allows only transpositions. Poems therefore provide the greatest inner resistance to translation. To demonstrate (again in opposition to Goethe) that the poetic effect is nearly lost in prose translations, despite his own doctrine of hermeneutic understanding, Dilthey cited Fechner, the inventor of psychophysics.[12] Reference to scientific studies was the innovation here. Magical or theological untranslatability was an ancient topos that became fashionable again circa 1900,[13] but no appeal to magical spells could hide the fact that psychotechnical untranslatability had been experimentally and recently established rather than miraculously found.

Magical spells or incantations are isolated, foreign bodies in actual languages; circa 1900, however, entire artificial languages were deliberately created. Referring to his contemporaries, Morgenstern claimed the right of "imaginative youths . . . *to invent* a tribe of Indians and all it entails, its language and national hymns" and, with reference to his "Lalulā," termed himself "one of the most enthusiastic Volapükists."[14] Around 1885, there was a fashionable project to construct "Ideal-Romanic" (reminiscent of the world language of Volapük) as an extract of the various forms of Vulgar Latin. Lott, Liptay, and Daniel Rosa contributed to this linguistically much "more solid edifice,"[15] as did (a little later) a student of Romance languages by the name of George, who invented his Lingua Romana in 1889.[16]

The Lingua Romana allowed George to anticipate Waetzoldt's experiments with students using his own Germanic and Romance-language medium: he wrote translations of Ideal-Romanic poems in German and vice versa. Since Champollion, the decoding of unknown languages had rested upon the foundation of a bilingual informant. But this was not so for the languages that George constructed at the age of seven or nine for himself and his friends, shortly before Morgenstern's Indian language game. His poem "Origins" presents a childhood on the pagan–Roman Rhine, which has come under the influence of the language of the Church—until George counters the traditional incantation *hosanna* with one of his own making.

> Auf diesen trümmern hob die kirche dann ihr haupt·
> Die freien nackten leiber hat sie streng gestaupt·
> Doch erbte sie die prächte die nur starrend schliefen
> Und übergab das maass der höhen und der tiefen
> Dem sinn der beim hosiannah über wolken blieb
> Und dann zerknirscht sich an den gräberplatten rieb.

Doch an dem flusse im schilfpalaste
Trieb uns der wollust erhabenster schwall:
In einem sange den keiner erfasste
Waren wir heischer und herrscher vom All.
Süss und befeuernd wie Attikas choros
Über die hügel und inseln klang:
CO BESOSO PASOJE PTOROS
CO ES ON HAMA PASOJE BOAŇ.

The Church then reared her head above these stones, and she
Grew stern and scourged the flesh she found too bare and free.
But she was heir to pomp, aflash in death-like sleeping,
And gave the standard set for height and depths in keeping
To minds that in Hosannahs wheeled above the clouds
And on the slabs of tombs in self-abasement bowed.

But near the stream in a palace of reed
On by the tide of our lust we were swirled,
Singing an anthem which no one could read,
We were the masters and lords of the world.
Sweet and inciting as Attica's chorus
Over the mountains and islands flung:
CO BESOSO PASOJE PTOROS
CO ES ON HAMA PASOJE BOAŇ.[17]

The poem enacts its theme. The secret language of the IMRI triumphs
because it remains a norn bourn. George would quote and allude to it
many times,[18] would even present it in conversation to a linguist and expert in secret languages, who immediately confirmed that it was a rare
example of wholly invented grammars and vocabularies[19]—but the greatest translator in the German language did not think of translating it as
well. When George's disciples discovered a handwritten translation of
portions of the *Odyssey* into the IMRI language among George's papers,
it was logical and not merely pious of them to destroy the single bilingual
document.

According to Nietzsche, language exists only because nature has
thrown away the keys to its secrets. George's quotation from his own language, in a poem entitled "Origins," shows that the writers of 1900
would yield nothing to nature. CO BESOSO PASOJE PTOROS / CO ES ON
HAMA PASOJE BOAŇ. How painfully trivial, then, is the "suspicion" of a
literary critic that "the content of those lines could be painfully trivial."[20]
Precisely because the IMRI undo the act with which the Church transferred the measure of heights and depths to meaning or the signified,
many worse things are possible: the two lines might not have any content
whatsoever.

Literature that simulates or is constructed out of secret languages and that thus always stands under the suspicion of being "a kind of nonsense,"[21] forces interpretation to rearrange its techniques. The classical path to origins in the soul or childhood of the author is gone; a "littérature à rébus" demands (not only with Dilthey) an objective interpretation on the model of cryptographic decoding techniques. The "new symbolism" employs "symbols in a completely different way" than was common in the classical-romantic lyric; it takes not "feeling itself" as its theme "but another and distant object" under the rules of the transposition of media.[22] Thus a technical, rather than a psychological-historical, understanding retransposes or decodes the transposition. Georg Simmel demonstrated this for poetic works as well as for black-box machines.

A creation of the mind that is intended to be understood can be compared to a problem or puzzle that the inventor has constructed with a code word. If someone attempting to solve the puzzle should find a second word, one that, objectively, solves the puzzle with equal logical and poetic success, the second word is as perfectly "correct" a solution as the one intended by the poet; indeed the latter has not the slightest priority over the former or over all the other, in principle unlimited, code words that might still be found.[23]

Interpretation is only a special instance of the general technique of transposing media. There is no psychological bridge between the encoding author and the decoding interpreter, but a technical contest. Each has at his disposal a norn bourn, so that with luck, which nothing and no one guarantees, the elements and associative rules of Medium A can be reproduced in the elements and associative rules of Medium B. When Bettina Brentano attempted to interpret Goethe's "Charade" as a reciprocal declaration of love, without being able to crack the *Herzlieb* code, she was unfortunately working in a different discourse network. Had she been able to attend Simmel's seminars in Strasbourg, as many women did around 1900, much would have been easier. An interpretive method without an author as idol obviates not only the vain effort of deciphering, but also the threat of discovering *Herzlieb* in the riddle after all.

Indeed, for short periods the transposition of media can be lifesaving. In 1902 Emil Strauss published a novel about a gymnasium student and born musician who is driven to suicide by the dust-covered new humanism of his teachers and their lesson plans. After having been forbidden to play his beloved violin, Heinrich Lindner spends every afternoon doing his homework.

During the first few days it was not so bad; indeed, he thought with slight bitterness: Everything is turning out well! But on the fourth day he suddenly caught himself not concentrating on the equation he was supposed to be solving but reading the letters as notes, and, without being aware of it, he had already hummed a whole page of the book.

"Good God!" he cried out laughing, "what nonsense!" But he could not resist looking at the page once more and consciously attempting to see if there might be, somewhere among the boring letters, a hidden musical combination. Soon, however, he was no longer laughing; he noticed that he could no longer concentrate on the mathematical value of the letters, and that the simplest sequence of letters would remind him of a musical phrase or suggest a motif.[24]

It is thus sheer mockery when the obtuse bureaucrats hermeneutically certify that their problem student, despite "very irregular reading," is capable of "penetrating the spirit of an author."[25] One who reads note values rather than algebraic variables (and also letters in other places), is proceeding neither irregularly nor according to an author's psychology. His reading is conceivably a precise transposition of media and can be interpreted and legitimized by Simmel's objective interpretation. It is no less radical an act in that Lindner is not alone. His contemporary Alban Berg transposed letters into notes (as a means of erotic disguise); for the hero of the novel, the same process is an unconscious and thus lifesaving compulsion, a special instance of alexia with the purpose of evading high school alphabetizing. In fact, research into speech deficits has uncovered cases (aside from the strategic simulation of aphasia) in which patients "lose words, but retain the meaning of notes."[26]

The *Trio for Piano, Violin, and Violincello by Heinrich Lindner, Opus 1*, is subsequently inspired by a train station. The composer manqué hears the stationmaster sing commands as melodies (like the "children who while playing give rhythm and alternation to their calls"). Shortly afterwards the concourse sounds in a confusion of voices, but this does nothing to disturb Lindner's musical dream, because all media circa 1900 presuppose white noise. The "confusion of voices, letting no single sound reach or disturb him," inspires the precocious and supposedly ungifted student to *Opus 1.*[27]

If the transposition of media can make musical notes out of letters and scores out of a confusion of voices, a decoding of the darkest and least translatable of texts is also possible and necessary. "The Great Lalulā" has, if not meaning, at least method, and not merely as "a more or less modulatory expression of an entirely definite and to the greatest extent exscene worldcomprehensivewordchildandartview."[28] For the decoding that Morgenstern himself produced, albeit as "Jeremias Mueller, Ph.D."— that is, with professional distance from his own wordchildandart—allows no modulation whatsoever.

THE GREAT LALULĀ

Too much has been attributed to this song so far. All it hides is simply— checkmate. No chess player will ever have understood it any other way. But in order to accommodate the layman and beginner, I will outline the position here.
Kroklokwafzi = K a 5 (white) king a 5. The question mark signifies some

question as to whether the position of the king might be stronger in another position. But let us proceed.

Sememeṁi! = S e 1 (black) knight e 1. The exclamation point signifies a strong position.[29]

And so on and so forth, until all the nonsense words are exhausted and a crazy checkmate position is left. The self-commentary, far from translating any life of the soul, is once again a transposition of media. The contents of the system of notation count only insofar as they equal a homonym in the second system. (Nothing in S e 1 explains the *m* and *i* of Sememeṁi.) Whether from algebraic variable to note values or from letters to chess abbreviations, every transposition leaves gaps. Most importantly, however, the result is never a surplus of meaning. "Too much has been attributed to this song so far"—that could be written on the gravestone of an entire literary criticism.

Attention to materials and the transposition of media are two sides of the same positivism. Only the methodologically rigorous isolation of individual groups of signs or cultural technologies can make such exact connections possible. Voice and gesture, lettering and ornament, picture and sound, letters and notes, Stefan George script and the "oral reading of poems"[30]—all of these connections presuppose technical analyses. There are odd and quite compelling indications of this.

When Morgenstern's late master invented a new type of dance, what had once been a parody of explication, as in "Lalulā," became dead serious. Eurythmy consisted in taking letter after letter, part of speech after part of speech, out of Goethe's poems and assigning to each particular signifier an iterable expressive gesture. Once these had been definitively established, the master, Rudolf Steiner, would simply command "faster, faster"—and the female disciples, whose "own, very wise head is somewhat out of it, help the essential power of the sound gain its autonomous effect."[31]

Whether or not such women were of flesh and blood has nothing to do with the parallel connection of media. The Edison of Villiers' novel constructs a mechanical Eve with a phonographic vocabulary of 2×7 hours playing time rather than human lungs and so-called linguistic competence. Because this vocabulary is denumerable, Edison is able to synchronize Eve's recorded speech capacity with her no less mechanical expressive movements.[32] What will and must strike the future beloved of the future woman as a coherent organism is actually technological eurythmy.

What happened in the novel also happened in reality, but with far-reaching sociohistorical effects. From the very beginning the silent film was coupled (either mechanically or through subaltern accompanists)[33] with recorded sound. The two separate media, picture without sound and sound without picture, allowed synchronization. The progressive literati Albert Ehrenstein, Walter Hasenclever, Else Lasker-Schüler, Kurt Pinthus, Franz Werfel, and Paul Zech were dismayed that "dismal background piano clinking" and (the scene is Dessau in 1913) "a narrator commenting on the action in a mighty Saxon accent" drowned out the film.[34] But their suggested improvements, all of which tended toward a media-true *l'art pour l'art* of the silent film, themselves coupled the movies and the professionalism of writers. The screenplays that Pinthus and his comrades offered to the industry as their *Movie Book* demonstrate with every word that the untranslatability of media is essential to the possibility of their coupling and transposition.

Psychoanalysis and Its Shadow

The transposition of media could be applied from jokes to mysticism to the culture industry. Moreover, it could be grounded methodologically, and so it became the paradigm of a new science. Freud's *Interpretation of Dreams*, in the date on its title page proudly and proleptically displaying the zero number of a new century, inaugurated the transposition of media as science.

Before there can be any interpretation of dreams, three secular fallacies need to be dismissed. The first is the philosophers' prejudice, which holds that dreams are without objective, reasonable connection and are unworthy of interpretation. As opposed to Hegel (whom, justifiably, he cites only indirectly),[1] Freud prefers to follow the lay opinion that assumes "a meaning, though a hidden one" in the dream. But popular dream interpretation has remained translation in two complementary ways: it makes the whole dream "symbolic" of global meanings, or it translates parts of a dream by "mechanically transferring" each part "into another sign having a known meaning, in accordance with a fixed key."[2] Both techniques, the analogical and the digital, presuppose that the two media, the dream and language, are either similar or coextensive. The new science rejects these two views as naive. In a well-known comparison, Freud defines his procedure of strict transposition of media.

The dream-thoughts and the dream-content are presented to us like two versions of the same subject-matter in two different languages. Or, more properly, the dream-content seems like a transcript of the dream-thoughts into another mode of expression, whose characters and syntactic laws it is our business to discover by comparing the original and the translation. The dream-thoughts are immediately comprehensible, as soon as we have learnt them. The dream-content, on the other hand, is expressed as it were in a pictographic script, the characters of which have to be transposed individually into the language of the dream thoughts. If we attempted to read these characters according to their pictoral value instead of according to their symbolic relation, we should clearly be led into error. Suppose I have a picture-puzzle, a rebus, in front of me. It depicts a house with a boat on its roof, a single letter of the alphabet, the figure of a running man whose head has been conjured away, and so on. Now I might be misled into raising objections and declaring that the picture as a whole and its component parts are nonsensical. A boat has no business to be on the roof of a house, and a headless man cannot run. Moreover, the man is bigger than the house; and if the whole picture is intended to represent a landscape, letters of the alphabet are out of place in it since such objects do not occur in nature. But obviously we can only form a proper judgement of the rebus if we put aside criticisms such as these of the whole composition and its parts and if, instead, we try to replace each separate element by a syllable or word that can be represented by that element in some way or other. The words which are put together in this way are no longer nonsensical but may form a poetical phrase of the greatest beauty and significance. A dream is a picture-puzzle of this sort and our predecessors in the field of dream-interpretation have made the mistake of treating the rebus as a pictorial composition: and as such it has seemed to them nonsensical and worthless.[3]

Interpretive techniques that treat texts as charades or dreams as picture puzzles have nothing to do with hermeneutics, because they do not translate. The translation of a rebus fails because letters do not occur in nature, the ultimate reference of all translation. In George's poem "The Word," the poetic imagination and the treasury of language are not co-extensive, just as in Freud's comparison the picture of the landscape is not coextensive with an alphabetic sign system. Negative findings such as these necessitated a new approach. In order to transpose the manifest content of dreams into latent dream thoughts, each of the two media must first be designated as defined sets of elements with defined rules of association (laws of articulation). If Faust marked the moment in the history of the sign in which there was no awareness of the paradigmatic axis, *The Interpretation of Dreams* conducts the analysis of signs solely according to the place values of discrete elements.[4] It does not establish the status of *a* symbol in the classical sense—in other words, a transcendental signified, which previously absorbed all words, above all the word *word*. In its place there are now separate subsystems of signifiers, in which the parts of the rebus must be tentatively placed until they fit in a subsystem. *Rebus* is the instrumental case of *res*: things can be used like words and words like things. Interpretation has everything to learn from "the linguistic tricks of children, who sometimes actually treat words as though they were objects, and moreover invent new languages and artificial syntactic forms."[5] Therefore every manipulation of letters and words is allowed within the framework of a determined language. Dreams, "impossible as a rule to translate into a foreign language,"[6] traverse all the associative domains of a given language. The transposition of media is thus an exact correlate of untranslatability.

Neither similar nor coextensive, dream-content and dream-thoughts relate to one another like "Lalulā" and checkmate in chess. Freud, "one of the most daring language adventurers and word mystics," is also "a brother of Morgenstern."[7] The decoded dream-content is no more poetry than chess notations are poems. Dreams could pass as Poetry only as long as optical and acoustical hallucinations were counted as part of the dream. Nothing remains of the beautiful appearance when the elements of a dream-content are transposed one by one into signifiers, even if the result is a poetical phrase of the greatest significance. Freud's irony is intended only for those who would see in the picture puzzle the substitutive sensuousness of a drawing or landscape. As true "syllabic chemistry"[8] with which the decoding method competes, the dream is already a piece of technique distant from nature and painted landscapes.

But this technique bears the stamp of its era. Bahr, for example, emphasized that "nature," where it could "express itself freely and without restraint," namely in dreams, "proceeds punctually and exactly according to the prescription of the new school" of symbolist "rebus literature."[9] With Freud, dream interpretation presupposes cutting apart any continuous series of images before syllables or words can substitute for them. It is no accident that the rebus Freud describes or makes up contains a running figure whose head has been conjured away. Only a cripple without a head yields an unconscious, and only the dismembered phenomena of the dream yield readable script. The poem of the picket fence divides syllables by the space between them in exactly the same way; and in exactly the same way the film camera cuts up continuous movement. The fact that *The Interpretation of Dreams* ignores the phenomenon of the dream is the first step toward deciphering dreams. Transpositions liquidate the medium from which they proceed. Every syllable and word of Freud's requirement that one substitute for every image a syllable or word is to be taken literally. This is demonstrated in his treatment of hysterics, who are "for the most part visually oriented."

Once a picture has emerged from the patient's memory, we may hear him say that it becomes fragmentary and obscure in proportion as he proceeds with his description of it. *The patient is, as it were, getting rid of it by turning it into words.* We go on to examine the memory picture itself in order to discover the direction in which our work is to proceed. "Look at the picture once more. Has it disappeared?" "Most of it, yes, but I still see this detail." "Then this residue must still mean something. Either you will see something new in addition to it, or something will occur to you in connection with it." When this work has been accomplished, the patient's field of vision is once more free and we can conjure up another picture. On other occasions, however, a picture of this kind will remain obstinately before the patient's inward eye, in spite of his having described it; and this is an indication to me that he still has something important to tell me about the topic of the picture. As soon as this has been done the picture vanishes, like a ghost that has been laid.[10]

F. L. Goltz showed that *A Dog Without a Cerebrum* has no visual representations. Freud shows how one can eliminate images from a dream or memory without a scalpel (and attribute the elimination to the patients themselves). "Putting into words" blinds the "inner eye" in which Anselmus and Hoffmann delighted. Sensitive souls can repeat the fashionable condemnation that Freud burdened an economy of libidinal expenditure with an obsolete Mosaic ban on images.[11] But it was one of the few options left to writers in the discourse network of 1900. Up against a competition that could replace substitutive sensuality with the real flow of data, the administrators of words swore by the phrase "Look at the image again. Has it disappeared?" The flood of images is literally exhausted, that is, taken apart element by element in such paradoxical questions. When even the most imaginative hysterics lose their store of images on the couch, they also learn the renunciation that writers completed and announced circa 1900: "Without the word, no thing can be."[12]

> Und weinen dass die bilder immer fliehen
> Die in schöner finsternis gediehen—
> Wann der klare kalte morgen droht.
>
> And weep because the visions which assail
> In exultant darkness always pale
> When the clear and cold of dawn return.[13]

George wrote it down, and Schönberg's music made it unforgettable . . .

But what spirit has been laid to rest once the hysteric's flood of images has been transposed into words? It is impossible to identify with certainty, but there are indices. The images appear before an inner eye; they appear in a malady that, by contrast to imageless obsessional neurosis, most commonly affects women; they illustrate a love that is obedience to the nuclear family. Could the spirit that Freud drives out not be simply the classical function of the feminine reader? The hystericizing of women circa 1800, after all, consisted in teaching them to read in such a way that poetic content was translated, through enjoyment and hallucination, into signifieds. What was brought to light on the couch may thus have been only a historical sediment,[14] at the moment when it became dysfunctional, in order to teach another kind of reading, the literal, of everyday experience. Psychoanalysis would have stood at the spot of a "bifurcation" that from 1900 on divided high and popular cultures according to the "phrase, book or picture; there is no third choice."[15] Women, children, and the insane, instead of continuing to dream images in books, discovered the unconscious of the movie house; the science of psychoanalysis, by contrast, discovered in women, children, and the insane, in order to inscribe it into them, an elite unconscious of secret scriptural codes.[16] At the end of her cure, one of Freud's famous hysterics dreamed that even she was reading calmly in a "big book."[17]

Immediately after the initial showing of the first German art film, Otto Rank began to psychoanalyze it. One of his assumptions was "that representation in the movies, which is suggestive of dream technique in more than one respect, expresses in clear and sensual picture language certain psychological conditions and connections that the Poet cannot always grasp with words."[18] Instead of pursuing such associations, Rank transposed the film sequences of *The Student of Prague* serially into the lexicon of literary doppelgänger motifs and this lexicon in turn into the analytic theory of narcissism. Professional readers overlook the fact that the doppelgänger motif films the act of filming itself. The movies are only the "actual psychic surface," the "arbitrary and banal starting point for broaching extensive psychological problems."[19] Rank is thus quite convinced of the manifest-latent distinction—not only for the psychic apparatus, but for the connection between the technical and literary.

And Freud? In 1883, directly continuing the work of Muybridge, Albert Londe built an electrical "short-exposure series" camera, and two years later Charcot used it to film his hysteric patients in the Salpêtrière. The young neurologist Freud was watching.[20] But for him, as well, film recordings—that is, the cutting up of the great hysterical curve—were only an arbitrary and banal starting point. His approach to hysterics broached the completely different problem of exhausting the flood of images. Movies aren't mentioned in *The Interpretation of Dreams*. Uwe Gaube's fine study *Film and Dreams* fills this gap by citing American psychologists, who read the manifest dream-content cinematographically.[21] Philologically and historically speaking, however, it remains a fact that Freud did not even ignore the Other of his decoding. The filmlike, presentative symbolism of the dream images vanished in the rhetorical-scriptural domain instituted by psychoanalysis. Whatever "visual forms of the flight of ideas" haunted unfolding dreams were excluded.[22] As with Saussure, whose linguistics could begin only after the mythical separation of firmament and water,[23] of thoughts and sound, of anything hallucinatory and undifferentiated, the movie pleasures of viewers like Rönne and Pinthus remained a limit concept on the system's edge. "The unity of this world appears to me to be something obvious, unworthy of emphasis. What interests me is the dissection and division of something that would otherwise be lost in the primal soup."[24]

The soup is thus not denied, but circumvented. That was the professional path, by contrast to mystical and philosophical contemporaries.

Rudolf Steiner made into a secret doctrine Benedict's discovery that those saved from death had seen their lives pass before them as in a time-lapse film.[25] Henri Bergson denounced, in favor of his *Creative Evolution*, the "cinematographic mechanism of consciousness," which was unable to process the continuous flow of the *durée* and was limited to discrete images.[26] The philosophy of life thus became a kind of movie that would have sacrificed its working principle, the cutting of images, to what was only a cunningly produced illusion in the viewer. Freud, however, persisted, like the researcher on the tachistoscope, in investigating a mechanics of dreamwork that was accomplished not by an illusory consciousness but by the unconscious itself.

The fact that psychoanalysis, given the options of cinematic dream and the tachistoscope, chose the symbolic method is indicative of its place in the system of sciences in 1900. This place had nothing to do with a "scientific self-misunderstanding" and for that reason also had little to do with the human sciences.[27] In his admirable uncertainty about whether the return of language circa 1900 represented the last moraine of transcendental knowledge or a new beginning, Foucault placed psychoanalysis, ethnology, and structural linguistics in a position where the human sciences' inner perspective on Man was transversed by language as an exterior element. The uncertainty arose because Foucault conceived discursive rules as comprehensible and therefore overlooked technologies. But innovations in the technology of information are what produced the specificity of the discourse network of 1900, separating it from transcendental knowledge and thus separating psychoanalysis from all human sciences.

Freud's early work *On Aphasia* was a brilliant, immediately acclaimed critique of brain physiology and its relation to language. Without doing any original experiments or dissections, the neurologist demonstrated to his colleagues that their all too localized language centers did not take into account the primacy of function. The critic maintained his allegiance to all the assumptions of that theory of language; he drew conclusions from deficiencies and isolated discursive functions, although not primarily in an anatomical sense. His *Project for a Scientific Psychology* consequently contains a topical model of isolated functions (consciousness and the unconscious), whose positions remain strictly functional. The *Project* provided the very model of contemporary models; the soul became a black box. One need only compare the hypothetical pathways, discharges, cathexes, and (of course discrete) neurones of Freud's text with statements about the material of brain physiology, which, since Sigmund Exner, had described the brain as a "street system" with more or less deeply engraved "driving tracks," [28] or as a network of telegraphic "relay stations" with more or less prompt connections. [29] Freud's mental apparatus, which has recently been interpreted as protostructuralist, merely conforms to the scientific standards of its day. [30] The sole difference, though one fraught with consequences, between it and neurophysiology is its lack of anatomical localization. Psychoanalysis, not content with looking forward to "filling in this gap" in a distant future, [31] undertook another kind of localization.

Freud's study of aphasia inherited all the material on speech deficits and defects that doctors had obtained by distinguishing and localizing individual aphasias. "'Quill pen' instead of 'pencil,' 'butter' [*Butter*] for 'mother' [*Mutter*], 'Fother' for 'father' and 'mother'" [32] are only selected examples, and their oddly Freudian quality is not just an effect of the context they appear in. *The Psychopathology of Everyday Life* thankfully made use of the parapraxes in speaking, reading, and writing that the Indogermanic linguist Rudolf Meringer and the psychiatrist Karl Mayer had gathered from colleagues and patients, in their attempt to demonstrate, first, that parapraxes were not a matter of free "subjectivity" [33] and, second, that they could be localized in an anatomically conceived system of language rules. Freud thus had an immense store of nonsense at his disposal, material that had been statistically ordered by doctors and linguists so as to provide inferences from the known deficiencies to brain functions and from those to language as a system. But anyone who attacks localization breaks the only thread holding together the statistics and lists. The collection of nonsense became a mere aggregate. That was reason enough to reverse the sorting procedure. Instead of ordering the data of countless speakers in columns until the rules of language emerged, psychoanalysis assembled the linguistic errors of one speaker into a text in which the rules of his individual speech came to light.

There were sound psychophysical premises for such a methodological shift. The psychoanalytic distinctions of condensation and displacement, metaphor and metonymy, on the one hand, and the structural linguistic distinction of the paradigmatic and syntagmatic on the other, are only transpositions of the fundamental principle of associationist psychology. Ziehen established that all associations play only on similarity or contiguity, on the paradigmatic or syntagmatic axes. [34]

Scientific discretion led Meringer and Mayer to indicate only parenthetically and with abbreviations which colleagues or patients committed particular solecisms; they recorded the fine specimen "Freuer-Breudian method" [35] under the rubric initial-consonant-syllabic confusion, or according to rules of similarity. Freud had only to leaf through the contiguity of their pages to find the same speaker committing another distortion of *Freud*—and the Breuer-Freudian method could suppose, quite unlinguistically, that the particular academic "was a colleague and not particularly delighted with this method."[36] Nothing could be easier. The experimental or statistical jumble of syllables is given another location on paper. Rather than placing *fother*, the word combined from *father* and *mother*, under the heading of general paraphrase, as would have been done in the early days of neurology, the analyst Freud reads it, in the context of all the others provided by the same patient, as part of a single rebus. Of course, father-and-mother *is* this context.

The same shift in method also brought Jung to psychoanalysis. His first efforts in psychiatry carried on the statistical experiments in association and flight of ideas of investigators like Emil Kraepelin, Ziehen, and Stransky, although his subjects were limited to the patients in Eugen Bleuler's institute in Burghölzli. From report to report the statistics diminished and the space devoted to particular cases increased. Just two associations of a hysteric woman, read together, "demonstrate beautifully" that "the conscious ego is merely a marionette that dances on the stage of a hidden automatic mechanism."[37] Thus one day Jung reversed the sorting procedure and worked exhaustively with a single schizophrenic patient. All the patient's neologisms were recorded and spoken back to her, until "all associations" of each "stimulus word" were produced and could in turn be used to produce associations, and so on, to the point where even hieroglyphs provided material for psychoanalytic decoding.[38] But Jung was unable to hear that he had himself become a telephonic instrument of torture. "Her suffering had no rhyme or reason for her, it was a 'hieroglyphic' illness. The fact that she had been locked up for fourteen years, so that 'not even [her] breath could escape,' seemed to be nothing more than an exaggerated declaration of her forced institutionalization. The suffering through 'mouthpieces that are held in from the outside,' seems to refer to the 'telephone,' or voices."[39]

Psychoanalysis does not cut across the human sciences from an outside called language; it traverses the field of psychophysics, working with the latter's premises and material. The shift of focus from language as system to speech does not imply that individuality has become the object of investigations. "No one makes an arbitrary error in speech"—this already-established fact in anatomical and linguistic systems is brought to bear on the singular system of the unconscious.[40] The individual falls in the crossfire between psychophysics and psychoanalysis; in its place is an empty point of intersection constituted by statistical generality and unconscious singularity. As an instance of initial-consonant-syllabic confusion *and* of Freud repression, a particular colleague is fully classified.

Whereas individuals consisted of matured and unified speech and writing, individual cases are specified by the scattered debris of their language use. Uniqueness in the discourse network of 1900 is always a result of the decomposition of anonymous, mass-produced products. According to Rilke, two "completely similar" knives bought by two schoolboys on the same day are only "remotely similar" a week later.[41] To use therefore means to wear down: out of industrially guaranteed similarity come broken, but singular things. Because these things, only a little the worse for wear, gather together whole case histories at once, the detectives Holmes and Freud carry the day. Dr. Watson doesn't have a chance when he attempts to foil his master with the following challenge: " 'I have heard you say that it is difficult for a man to have any object in daily use without leaving the impress of his individuality upon it in such a way that a trained observer might read it. Now, I have here a watch which has recently come into my possession . . .' "[42] The scratches on the watch provide the cocaine user Holmes with the welcome opportunity to turn page after page in the secret family history of his constant companion. As Bleuler recognized, the sciences of gathering evidence "certainly have a future." From handwriting, from "its style, indeed from the wear of a pair of shoes," it is possible to deduce the whole person.[43] Bleuler's assistant, Jung, investigated the psychotic wear and tear on the finished product of language.

The cocaine user Freud, however, in his great small-mindedness, would begin an analysis by considering a neurotic misuse of the finished product that is the alphabet. A twenty-four-year-old patient on the couch in the Berggasse told "the following story from the fifth year of his childhood": "He is sitting in the garden of a summer villa, on a small chair beside his aunt, who is teaching him the letters of the alphabet. He is in difficulties over the difference between m and n, and he asks his aunt to tell him how to know one from the other. His aunt points out to him that the m has a whole piece more than the n—the third stroke."[44] The patient sees this as a romantic childhood scene, one that brings back summer and the historical happiness of being alphabetized by the Mother's Mouth. The analyst does not dispute the reliability of the memory, but does question its imaginary significance. Had he done the former, Freud would have been like the physiologists of reading, who never encountered any confusion between m and n (only confusion between n and r, and m and w). Because he was concerned more with the differences between letters than with letters, and more with letters than with significance, Freud transposed the intervals in a language to the intervals in speech. At the very place where Stephani's mothers' mouths slid lustfully and continuously from m to n, Freud confirms a harsh binary opposition. The opposition between m and n stands in as a "symbolic representation" for another opposition that can and must be written as the patient's rebus. "For just as at that time he wanted to know the difference between *m* and *n*, so later he was anxious to find out the difference between boys and girls, and would have been very willing for this particular aunt to be the one to teach him. He also discovered then that the difference was a similar one—that the boy, too, has a whole piece more than the girl." [45]

An inscription as meaningless as it is unforgettable can thus be decoded. The triumph of the Freudian transposition of media is to have made it possible to solve singular problems of differentiation with an individual experimental subject. Psychophysicists had certainly recognized that small letters at x-height "are most often subject to confusion"; [46] but no one had asked why individual subjects (themselves as well) produced one kind of mistake and no other. Ebbinghaus was only surprised that nonsense exhibited "very significant and nearly incomprehensible differences" in what people retained (as the twenty-four-year-old demonstrated). Gutzmann was led only as far as "the discovery of certain suspected trains of thought" by the "phonographic tests" he conducted, in that experimental subjects automatically and suspiciously heard or wrote nonsense as meaningful words. [47] But any aspects of test material that could not be evaluated physiologically or typographically were discarded. The discarded material was so copious and so literal that no one, including the twenty-four-year-old, could approach it save as a novice. This is the reason for psychoanalysis. Material discarded by psychophysics can be resorted and then decoded. Freud's discourse was a response not to individual miseries but to a discourse network that exhaustively records nonsense, its purpose being to inscribe people with the network's logic of the signifier.

Psychoanalysis made into something significant—indeed, into the signifier itself—the nonsensical attribution of nonsense to the fact that someone confused precisely the letters *m* and *n*. An opposition of letters yields the minimal signifier of a sexualized body. From this point on, the patient knows that alphabetization was only a screen for his sexuality and that sexuality is only a metaphor for the elementary opposition. What is scandalous in Freud is not pansexuality, but the return to a lucid and tangible play of letters of an eroticism that, as Spirit and Nature, had pervaded the so-called world circa 1800. The phallus is as nonsensical and block-letter-like as the small mark that the *m* has and the *n* does not have. No handwriting of a continuous individual can get around the latter difference, nor can any illusion in the war between the sexes survive the former difference. What the boy's aunt began as pedagogical education ends in a system of notation that abolishes pedagogy and the soul.

What must be said, with Aristotle, is that it is not the soul that speaks, but man who speaks by means of his soul—as long as we take into account that he has received this language, and that in order to sustain it he throws in much more than his soul: even his instincts, whose ground resonates in the depths only to send back the echo of the signifier. It is such that when the echo returns the speaker is delighted and responds with the praise of an eternal romanticism. "When the soul *speaks*, then" . . . the soul does speak, that is, . . . "oh! it is no longer the *soul* that speaks." You can hear it; the illusion will not last long.[48]

All of Freud's case histories demonstrate that the romanticism of the soul has yielded to a materialism of written signs. When a patient "decorates his writing and notes with an *S*," it is only because *S* is "the first letter of his mother's name" (and not, say, an abbreviation of authorship).[49] When the Wolf-Man, recounting a dream, says *Espe* rather than the hallucinated *Wespe* ["wasp"], the amputation of the initial letter represents a castration complex that is typographic, and the rebus word *Espe* is the abbreviation S.P., or the proper name of the Wolf-Man.[50] Precisely because they do not occur in nature, letters are the keys to the unconscious. They cancel out conscious intention and hermeneutic understanding in order to expose people to their subjection to language. But methodologically this means that Freud (to use a pervasive metaphor of 1900) was a proofreader. Instead of reading over mistakes because of his complete alphabetization, he seeks out mistakes.[51] In line with such professionalism, in the Berggasse mistakes such as (*W*)*Espe* are neither produced nor recorded in writing. The patients speak; as a good interview psychologist, the doctor avoids taking notes during the session. Otherwise he would only disturb the flow of speech, make "a detrimental," that is, meaningful, "selection" and distract his free-floating attention with bureaucratic tasks.[52] Psychoanalysis provides the singular example of a discourse network that has writing as its object but writing's complete opposite as method. Even this rebus can be solved.

Just as the patient must relate everything that his self-observation can detect, and keep back all the logical and affective objections that seek to induce him to make a selection from among them, so the doctor must put himself in a position to make use of everything he is told for the purposes of interpretation . . . without substituting a censorship of his own for the selection that the patient has forgone. To put it in a formula, he must turn his own unconscious like a receptive organ towards the transmitting unconscious of the patient. He must adjust himself to the patient as a telephone receiver is adjusted to the transmitting microphone. Just as the receiver converts back into sound-waves the electric oscillations in the telephone line which were set up by sound waves, so the doctor's unconscious is able, from the derivatives of the unconsciousness which are communicated to him, to reconstruct that unconscious, which has determined the patient's free associations.[53]

The paradox of writing without script can only be solved with technological media. Freud, determined to sacrifice his knowing subjectivity, produces a transposition of media onto himself: his ears become a telephone receiver. As it is written, men have ears only in order not to hear (and to transform everything into sense). Only the connection between electroacoustical transducers guarantees the reception of a full spectrum of noise, one that is informative to the degree that it is white. Once more, the word is "Listen to the Sacred Vibrations." All conscious "communicating" between the two counts only as a keyed rebus transmitted from one unconscious to the other. Its manifest sense is nonsense; Freud the telephone receiver picks out the parapraxes that would be mere debris under a postulate of sense.

In order to be able to fish m/n or $S./P.$ as telltale, interspersed signifiers out of a flow of speech that is merely the intimidation and resistance, the seduction and distortion, of a consciousness, the doctor must have recorded them in advance. Freud's telephone analogy does not go far enough. Although it avoids the traditional recording device of writing, psychoanalysis works like a phonograph that in its developed form couples electroacoustical transducers with memory. Only sound recorders can register spoken typographic errors (an oxymoronic concept in itself).

Benjamin synchronized psychoanalysis and film with the argument that the former "isolated and made analyzable things which had heretofore floated along unnoticed in the broad stream of perception," whereas the other "for the entire spectrum of optical, and now also acoustical, perception . . . has brought about a similar deepening of apperception." [54] That doesn't quite do justice to the facts. Technologies and sciences of media transposition do not simply extend human capacities; they determine recording thresholds. In the physiology of the senses these thresholds cannot be determined too exactly. Freud's treatment of dream and memory images is not the first or only instance of his exclusion of the whole optical realm. The fact that the doctor and hysteric patient are not allowed to look at one another means that the couch (in the best Nietzschean manner) is a pure realm of hearing. Both people are in the same room, so that eye and other forms of contact would be expected. But because mouths and ears have become electroacoustical transducers, the session remains a simulated long-distance call between two psychic apparatuses (in Freud's fine phrase). Psychoanalysis has no vague parallels to film; it has much more precisely learned the lesson of technological sound recorders. Its phonography of unconscious sound waves fishes, not in the wide stream of perception, but only among acoustical data.

The catch is restricted to discrete elements. Not only the imaginary significance, but also the real aspects of discourse are excluded. Freud had as little to do with the physiology of speech (precisely, that studied by his teacher, E. W. Brücke) as he did with escaping to the images in the movies. Female hysterics, those born starlets, could run through, instead of the single "oh," the many real pleasures and pains of speech on the couch—from spastic halting to stuttering, clicking the tongue, gasping, or muteness—but the supposedly filterless receiver filtered them all out. Freud's inimitably forthright justification: he "could not," unlike any boy on the street, "imitate" these real aspects of speech.[55] The one who once diagnosed his own "motoric aphasia" recorded, in a complete reversal of Berliner's gramophone, the letters of sound—everything that was already written, but only that, in the flow of speech.[56]

Movies and the gramophone remain the unconscious of the unconscious. Psychoanalysis, the science born with them, confronts sequences of images with a primal repression and sequences of sound with their distortion into chains of signifiers. Only the day when psychoanalysis becomes psychochemistry—Freud's dream and the nightmare of others[57]—might witness the repression of this repression as well.

A transposition of media that transposes images and sounds into letters does not stop there. By the force of its own logic it finally transferred the letters into books. This is the relation between analytic practice and theory. What would have disturbed free-floating attention during the session later occurs after all: Freud reaches for his pen. As Walter Muschg recognized early on, Freud belonged "to the modern movement of German letters."[58]

Writing circa 1900 means being without voice and writing with the alphabet. Fundamentally, psychoanalysts must know when to remain silent vis-à-vis their word-jumble generators. Not only for "persons with hysterical mutism" did writing become a "vicarious" means of expression;[59] the motoric aphasic behind the couch did not suffer from agraphia, either. Written case histories made a "talking cure" into—literature. The expression itself shows how this happened. Freud had no such striking expression for his invention; his first patient, Anna O. (alias Bertha von Pappenheim), gave her "new type of treatment the name 'talking cure' [in English]."[60] The writer in Freud had only to put the foreign words on paper and honor them by his definition.

But this relationship between speech and writing, prompter and author, so fundamental between Freud and his hysteric patients, does not make him a Schlegel or Anselmus, or Pappenheim a Dorothea or Serpentina. The simple fact that Anna O. "during this period of her illness remarkably spoke and understood only English,"[61] separated her from a Mother's Mouth that could whisper even Sanskrit texts in High German.

The discourse network of 1900 determined that Freud would not once put the expression "talking cure" into German. Psychoanalysis is not a translating universalization that makes the speech of many women into the originary language of One Woman. In practice as in theory, in listening as in recording, psychoanalysis remained the feedback of data that circumscribed an individual case. "If" Freud's famous hysteric patient should "by chance" come to read the *Fragment* of her analysis, she would read nothing that she and only she did not "already know." But because or in spite of this, an "embarrassment" awaits her: [62] the parts of her speech that have found their way into print are not the expressions of a naïve lay philosophy of the sort that Schlegel ascribed to women, but of the organs and functions of her sexuality.

The meticulous Freud calls his activity the "written record" and "accordingly not absolutely—phonographically—faithful." But in this explicit competition it has such a "high degree of dependability" that Wildenbruch would for once be made nervous by literature. [63] Every medium that brings the hidden to the light of day and forces the past to speak contributes, by gathering evidence, to the death of Man. This distinguishes psychoanalytic case-study novels from the classical-romantic epic form. When Goethe put together his heroines from the different individual features of different women, inviting all feminine readers to identify themselves with the Woman, the models, although they may have seen themselves robbed of eyes, hair, or mouths, hardly had the fear or pleasure of being publicly recognized. The discourse network of 1800 had no need of formal, legal guidelines about authorial discretion, because it voluntarily, or philosophically, saw the individual as genus. Not until the current century did popular literature begin by disclaiming any similarity between fictional heroes and living models. One popular novelist, Thomas Mann, was drawn into an exemplary trial in 1905 and had to defend *Buddenbrooks* against the charge of being a roman à clef by stressing the transposition of media as his artistic achievement. [64] In the same year, another novel "Fragment" began: "I am aware that—in this city, at least—there are many physicians who (revolting though it may seem) choose to read a case history of this kind not as a contribution to the psychopathology of neuroses, but as a roman à clef designed for their private delectation. I can assure readers of this species that every case history that I have occasion to publish in the future will be secured against their perspicacity by similar guarantees of secrecy, even though this resolution is bound to put quite extraordinary restrictions upon my choice of material." [65]

The novelist Freud thus does not rule out the novelistic reading of his case histories. He simply disapproves. It is possible, but distasteful, to decode psychoanalytic decodings of individual cases. Such are the intimidation tactics of one who turned the subject index in Mayringer-Merer, excuse me, Meringer-Mayer, into a secret-person index. Such is the protection of data records, which are exhaustive only because he, the discreet doctor, in a move of fine symmetry, forbade his patients to have any discretion. Freud broke off the analysis of "a high official who was bound by his oath of office not to communicate certain things because they were state secrets."[66] The shift from bureaucratic ethos to psychophysics, from an oath of office to the exhausting of material, could hardly occur more drastically. Writing circa 1900 necessarily conflicted with rules of discretion—simply because it was no longer the imagination that dictated. Freud would sooner renounce writing books than subject signifiers to the kind of distortions that once translated recognizable, bourgeois Veronicas into the pure signified of a Serpentina.

If the distortions are slight, they fail in their object of protecting the patient from indiscreet curiosity; while if they go beyond this they require too great a sacrifice, for they destroy the intelligibility of the material, which depends for its coherence precisely upon the small details of real life. And from this latter circumstance follows the paradoxical truth that it is far easier to divulge the patient's most intimate secrets than the most innocent and trivial facts about him; for, whereas the former would not throw any light on his identity, the latter, by which he is generally recognized, would make it obvious to everyone.[67]

What distinguishes case histories from Poetry is the fact that the depths of the soul do not betray the identities of the persons described to readers addicted to decoding. That Freud did not advance as far as the phonograph, which with particulars like the voice or breath would have betrayed persons' identities to even the most naïve media consumers, is the very structure of writing. Only small, factual details remain as indices, which as people's symbolic aspect inscribe them in public networks of discourse. Certainly Freud's novels leave "no name standing which could put a lay reader onto the right track."[68] But because psychoanalysis is concerned with gathering evidence of the letter, names remain essential. Without the play of signifiers, whose differences are as incomprehensible as they are important, unconscious connections would be destroyed.

Under the hesitantly established heading, "The Presentation of Man" in Freud, Muschg writes of the "remarkably anonymous characters that occupy his writings."[69] It is indeed a strange anonymity that consists of indices and names. Obsessional neurotics appear as the Rat-Man or Wolf-Man,[70] hysterics as Anna O., Frau Emmy v. N., Dora, Fräulein Elizabeth v. R. For these figures the texts develop neither imaginative images nor novels of *Bildung*—none of the representations of man in the Spirit of 1800, in other words. Only a mass of spoken material is presented, through which unconscious inscriptions run their jagged, telltale course. The rebus is written down as rebus. Because Freud's own texts will be scrutinized by distasteful colleagues, the texts encode each rebus a second time according to the rules of media transposition. Thus wherever a rebus appears to be solved, another one begins (along with yet another book on Freud). Anyone who can decipher the initials of the Wolf-Man in the castrated word (W)*Espe*, just as the formidable Sherlock Holmes discovered the place name *Ballarat* in the ordinary word *rat*,[71] has still not fixed upon a referent, to say nothing of a man behind the words. Simmel's objective interpretation allows for solutions quite other than those of the author; Freud permitted and practices "Constructions in Analysis,"[72] which beyond psychoanalytic practice determined the constructions of his writing as well. The surname of the Wolf-Man has only recently been revealed. For seventy years it was anyone's guess as to whether the initials S. P. corresponded to the Wolf-Man's passport or whether they were the discreet fiction of a writer who had encoded a solved rebus a second time.

Small facts like initials or abbreviated names are thus quite literally the contact surface on which two discourses oppose *and* touch one another: on one side the speech of the patients, on the other side the writing vocation of their doctor. It is finally impossible to determine which of the two one might be reading at any given moment, simply because inscriptions on one side trace through to the reverse side. The contact surface—as is only proper in a discourse network that does justice to the material aspects of media—consists simply of paper. Whether in Freud's sense or not, his paper is and remains the place where the discourse network of 1900 comes into contact with people. Either the patients really spoke as if speech were a masquerade for the rebus, or psychoanalysis selected from the flow of the voice only what it could transpose into signifiers and then transpose a second time to foil roman à clef readers. In any case, psychoanalysis occupies the systemic position taken by Poetry in the discourse network of 1800. The position consists in the place of initiation. If voices and dream images are to be grounded in the logic of the signifier, they must first cross the threshold of psychoanalysis; if, in return, any rituals of the sign or psychophysics are to be inscribed on individual bodies, they must first cross the threshold of psychoanalysis. The discourse network of 1900 places all discourse against the background of white noise; the primal soup itself appears in psychoanalysis, but only to be articulated and thus sublimated via writing proper.[73]

There is nothing further to say about the wider effects of such a strategy. The only nontrivial problem is one of method. If Freud's technique consists in transposing optical and acoustical streams of data into words and words into the signifier script of his own texts, then his universal science confronts only one superfluity or impossibility: data that have already assumed written form. Wherever articulation has already occurred, "the dissection and division of something that would otherwise be lost in the primal soup" is unnecessary. Thus Freud granted texts, regardless of who their authors were, a special status. Whether or not the texts were distinguished by literary honors was secondary to a certain testimonial function.[74]

The pact between Freud and the people who believed that dreams could be read, despite the objections of all philosophers, would have had no discursive support if the spoken dream stories of patients had not been media-transposed by literary dream texts and confirmed by the ordinary documentary means of pen and paper. The mere written existence of Jensen's *Gradiva*, a novella about mania and dreams, was sufficient to defend Freud against attack. That it is not of particularly enduring value, that its author "refused his co-operation"[75] when approached and thus would not personally authorize its transposition into the medium of psychoanalysis, is insignificant. Objective interpretation can do without authorial assent. Freud thus reached the following conclusion on the relationship between writers and analysts: "We probably draw from the same source and work upon the same object, each of us by another method. And the agreement of our results seems to guarantee that we have both worked correctly. Our procedure consists in the conscious observation of abnormal mental processes in other people so as to be able to elicit and announce their laws. The author no doubt proceeds differently. He directs his attention to the unconscious in his own mind, he listens to its possible developments and lends them artistic expression instead of suppressing them by conscious criticism. Thus he experiences from himself what we learn from others—the laws which the activities of this unconscious must obey. But he need not state these laws, nor even be clearly aware of them; as a result of the tolerance of his intelligence, they are incorporated within his creations."[76]

The same source, the same object, the same result—writers and psychoanalysts moved into a proximity equal to that which joined the Thinkers and Poets of 1800. Yet the reverse conclusion is equally possible and logical: namely, that writers end up on the side of the patients. If Freud's patients and the hero of the novella share the same dreams, paranoid structures, and hysterias, then these must belong to the writer's unconscious as well. There is one small difference, however: hysteria speaks, but Jensen publishes. *Mania and Dreams* can no longer be attributed to an individual case. The material already present in the medium that supports the psychoanalyst has achieved "artistic expression." Rather than proceeding according to the rules of hermeneutics and assuming that fictional heroes naturally dream the dreams of their authors, Freud finds in *Gradiva* written dreams "that have never been dreamt at all, that were invented by a writer and attributed to fictional characters in the context of a story."[77] Therefore, there is no need to portion out statistically distributed nonsense to individual cases. Jensen, no different in this from Freud, is separated by a thin but impermeable piece of paper from its reverse side, from mania and dreams, and is above the suspicion of being their referent. His relation to the primal soup is not one of participation, but simulation. For invented individuals he invents dreams that in spite of this squared fiction "contain in embodied form" all the "laws" of the unconscious. Laws, let us note, and not, say (as one often prefers to read) contents. With its central metaphor, the burial of Pompeii under lava and ash, Jensen's novella does not symbolize this or that repressed content, but rather provides a "parable" of the metapsychological process of repression itself. "There really is no better analogy."[78]

In distinction from the doctor (Freud once more leaves out the mystery of his self-analysis), the writer does not extrapolate the laws of the unconscious from others' mouths, which are unable to say why their sense becomes nonsense and their nonsense sense. A strange listening in on his own mental processes gives him not only their repressed contents but beyond that their signifying logic. Once again, then, the writer seeks out a norn-like authority, which administers the rules of all writing. but because they are rules, it remains unnecessary and impossible to "pronounce" the unconscious laws that have been discovered. It is enough that they have been given a material location: paper, on which discursive rules such as repression are "embodied."

In written material, therefore, the localization that defines psychoanalysis in the discourse network of 1900 is left out—because it has already occurred. If the diverse local centers of the brain-physiological localization doctrine are linked together in the typewriter, psychoanalysis—mysteriously true to its neurophysiological beginnings—reverses the founding relationship. Its textual theory replaces that body with a typewriterly corpus.

The text as embodied psychoanalysis does not distinguish the literary or even the classical. It is simply the effect of a medium that governs the analyst himself, first when he reads the flow of the voice as a rebus, and second when he writes. In order to achieve this effect, it is sufficient for a mania, rather than flood Freud's senses with hysterical visuality and the spoken façade of dreams, to have been written down. If and because a work called *Memoirs of My Nervous Illness* is present in the form of a book, psychoanalysis treats it very differently than it would a mentally ill person on the couch.

Freud's "Psycho-analytic Notes on an Autobiographical Account of a Case of Paranoia" seems at first to be a compromise solution arrived at in an attempt to extend his practice to cases who, in contrast to neurotics, cannot wander around freely and so (if they have not lost language altogether) can only send out messages in bottles. Paranoiacs cannot be analyzed; they "cannot be compelled to overcome their internal resistances, and . . . in any case they only say what they choose to say." Such, however, ever since Pilate's ὃ γέγραφα γέγραφα ("What I have written I have written"; John 19:22), is the very definition of a text. Which is why "precisely" in the case of a paranoiac "a written report or a printed case history can take the place of personal acquaintance with the patient" (read: his spoken story).[79]

So much for the introduction to and justification for the analytic act. By the end everything reads much differently. Schreber's book, instead of simply replacing the flow of the hysteric's voice, attains all the honors of theory, in that the *Memoirs of My Nervous Illness* also contains what is indeed memorable: the embodied laws of the unconscious. As with Jensen, the writer Freud greets as a colleague, albeit one who was at the time a patient in the Sonnenstein asylum in Pirna.

Since I neither fear the criticism of others nor shrink from criticizing myself, I have no motive for avoiding the mention of a similarity which may possibly damage our libido theory in the estimation of many of my readers. Schreber's "rays of God," which are made up of a condensation of the sun's rays, of nerve-fibres, and of spermatazoa, are in reality nothing else than a concrete representation and projection outwards of libidinal cathexes; and they thus lend his delusions a striking conformity with our theory. . . . these and many other details of Schreber's delusional structure sound almost like endopsychic perceptions of the processes whose existence I have assumed in these pages as the basis of our explanation of paranoia. I can nevertheless call a friend and fellow-specialist to witness that I had developed my theory of paranoia before I became acquainted with the contents of Schreber's book. It remains for the future to decide whether there is more delusion in my theory than I should like to admit, or whether there is more truth in Schreber's delusion than other people are as yet prepared to believe.[80]

After seventy-five pages of interpretation, Freud proclaims that interpretation has hardly been necessary. He finds the basic assumptions of his libido theory in Schreber also. There could be no clearer literary testimony from one author to another. Here psychoanalysis runs into legal difficulties quite different from those encountered in writing case histories: in case histories, the analyst must protect the identities of those described, but here the author must protect his copyright. In Schreber's case "the object of the analysis is not actually a person, but rather a book produced by that person," and so "the problem of professional discretion does not enter in."[81] Yet a more serious problem raises its head. In order to present Schreber as a mere witness and not cede him the psychoanalytic copyright, Freud has to call another witness to the stand. A psychiatrist friend will swear to the fact that the patient and his analyst (in the terms customary for fictional disclaimers) arrived independently at the same results.

Psychoanalytic discourse itself must be at stake if its founder moves to head off charges of plagiarism. In fact, Schreber's mania archives as body and text the libido theory that psychoanalysis reached only through the long detours of interpretation. Schreber's relation to the theory is that of all writers. Jensen, according to Freud, could register and write down processes occurring "in his own mind"; Schreber, according to Freud, does this with "endopsychic perceptions." The *Memoirs* depicts a nerve-diseased body as the theater for whole theomachies, where divine nerve rays invade and retreat, destroy organs and extract brain fiber, lay down lines of communication and transmit information—a psychic information system that Freud takes at its word rather than as mania. Freud is not so believing at other points, as, for example, when the paranoiac accuses his psychiatrist, Flechsig, of persecutorial intent; behind this image of his colleague Freud senses only the patient's father. In describing the mind as information system, however, the psychotic text, which describes the system throughout its four hundred pages, is said to be the unmetaphoric truth.

There are grounds for this methodological distinction. The Oedipus complex is the nucleus of the neuroses, but the mental apparatus is coextensive with psychoanalysis itself. Only by "assuming the existence of a spatially extended, advantageously constructed apparatus developed in meeting the exigencies of life," can Freud build his science "on a basis similar to that of other natural sciences." But these bases are not available for experimental verification. One can only infer them with the help of "artificial aids," because "'reality' will always remain 'unknowable.'"[82] Accordingly, "reality" would be a necessary *and* impossible limit concept on the edge of the system, were it not for Schreber's endopsychic perceptions, which without doubt describe a body, his own, as a spatially extended mental apparatus. The corpus of the psychotic text provides psychoanalysis with its indispensable but undiscoverable basis: a body. A body is the piece of evidence without which psychoanalysis, by contemporary standards, would have remained empty speculation.

From the first, aphasia studies had made brain localization into a methodological space; psychoanalysis becomes the destination of the long route that traverses this space. Schreber's mania guarantees that there is "not more mania contained" in analytic theory than its inventor would "wish." Processes that allow endopsychic perceptions in an experimental subject, however delirious, cannot not exist from a psychophysical standpoint. Schreber's body is the verso of the pages Freud filled with writing.

The Doctor of Law Daniel Paul Schreber (1842–1911), son of the widely known inventor of the Schreber garden, which is still cultivated on the edge of German cities, entered the Leipzig University Nerve Clinic of Dr. Paul Emil Flechsig in 1884 as a failed candidate for the Reichstag, was released in 1885, was appointed in 1893 to the second highest judicial position in the Kingdom of Saxony, the Presidency of the Senate of the Supreme Court, immediately thereafter entered Flechsig's clinic once more, was transferred several times, was released in 1902, and in 1907 was finally institutionalized until his death. The *Memoirs* appeared in a private edition in 1903 with the declared intention of allowing "expert examination of my body and observation of my personal fate during my lifetime."[83]

Freud's "Psycho-analytic Notes" thus appeared just at the moment to fill out and cash this blank check.[84] In 1911, whoever gave his body over to science would get a response posthaste. Not only is the mental apparatus, as described by the psychotic and psychoanalytic corpus, a single, highly complex information system; the two corpora in tandem constitute this system a second time. Tidings of the impossible reality reach the symbolic, via media transposition. Freud receives what Schreber sends; Schreber sends what Freud receives. All that remains unsaid is why the whole discourse network worked so promptly and precisely around one individual body. Freud was much too concerned with the testimonial value of the received messages to investigate the logic of the channels. What Schreber writes, what writers write—everything became for Freud an anticipation of psychoanalysis. And he is not alone in this. Schreber too grants poets like Wagner occasional anticipations of his neuro-theology.[85] In the competition for corporeal knowledge, then, the question about which channels of knowledge constitute the body is left out. The discourse network of 1900 withholds its proper name.

The *Memoirs* constitutes an "exhaustion"[86] of Schreber's body while he was still alive. The transposition of a body into a corpus was just as necessary—namely, as necessary for survival—as was the fictional composer Lindner's transposition of letter to note values. After Schreber has published his book (against the wishes of his family and the medical establishment), the natural sciences of the mind have only to open it—and

Schreber's person is "*offer*[*ed*] . . . *as an object of scientific observation for the judgment of experts.*" Otherwise, "at some future time" the experts could only confirm "such peculiarities of my nervous system . . . by *dissection of my body*," for "I am informed that it is extremely difficult to make such observations on the living body."[87]

Schreber as writer or Schreber as anatomical preparation—these are the only alternatives in the discourse network of 1900. Like all writers of the epoch, he plays the role of the "victim of his own writing,"[88] in order to be able, in place of his autopsy, to prepare refuse, a bodily substitute, a text. Only thus can his case remain "soul murder"[89] and not descend to the postmortem examination of those peculiarities that make people with nervous diseases so attractive to their psychiatrists. The patient dissects his own organs and notes their modifications while he is still alive, with a positivism that honors psychophysics and comes close to correcting factually Kraepelin's *Psychiatry* (on the subject of hallucinations). Schreber thus practiced, as if to realize Nietzsche's assertion "for there is no soul," preventative soul murder.

But "soul murder"—in Schreber's divine "primary-" or "nerve-language" an autonym for the neurophysiological relationship between him and God—is also a chapter title in Ellen Key's *The Century of the Child*. Schreber could once more confront his blind exegetes and their multiple associations on the phrase, with the extent of his reading of contemporary works, which aside from Kraepelin, Du Prel, and Haeckel, also included her. What is called divine nerve-language in divine nerve-language and not accidentally contains many "expressions *which would never have occurred to*" Schreber, namely expressions "of a scientific, and particularly medical nature,"[90] is simply the code of the epoch. In 1903 it did not take private religious illuminations to reduce, in the first sentence of one's book, the soul to nervous tissue and to the language of nervous tissue, or in the final sentences to see one's own mental illness "*in the sense of a nervous illness*," although not in its ordinary sense.[91]

But if the soul has only neurophysiological reality, university nerve clinics are more likely than Ellen Key's schools to be responsible for soul murder. A book that does not bear the title *Memoirs of My Nervous Illness* was unable to use the words *nervous illness* without the epithet *so-called*, and set forth from the beginning the doctrine that there are "no independent illnesses of the mind without those of the body."[92] The book is Paul Flechsig's inaugural lecture as the second professor of psychiatry in the history of the University of Leipzig. The first was named Johann Heinroth and was faithful to Hoffbauer and Reil in teaching the "mistaken doctrine" of mental cures. A "chasm" thus "gaped" between him and his successor Flechsig, one "no less deep and wide than the chasm between medieval medicine" and modern medicine.[93] In "the age of Flechsig and Wernicke," (Benn's term),[94] souls became nerve information systems, and cures became experiments. The "'localization of nervous diseases'" entered "a new epoch" (as Freud says)[95] with Flechsig, who posed for his festschrift photograph in front of the picture of a massive, cut-open brain. Only the individual case created difficulties, relative ones, in the Leipzig University Nerve Clinic; only curing such a case created absolute difficulties. On the one hand, the brain contains "the key to every natural conception of mental activity" and a fortiori to those of mental disturbances.[96] On the other, "the protected position of the brain" means that the substratum of the psychoses, namely, chemical and physical nerve damage, "can be detected *in the living* only through more or less composite inferences." Thus the psychiatrist Flechsig was impelled onto a royal diagnostic road that was simultaneously a therapeutic dead end: "the emphasis on postmortem examination."[97]

No sooner said than done. The corpse of Hölderlin, an insane or, in other words, not bureaucratically employed teacher, was among the first to enter the new order of things via the dissection table.[98] The corpse of Schreber, a judicial bureaucrat who had gone over into the new order, suffered the same, now foreseeable, fate (without the feared or hoped-for modifications in nervous tissue being found).[99]

And yet, what was said had already been done. After Flechsig decreed postmortem examination to be the psychiatric royal road, Schreber's discreet, anonymous reference to having "been informed" about the difficulties of in vivo diagnosis of insanity is superfluous. In Schreber's case, the situation of the text leaves no doubt: the imaginative copyright to the patient's theology, developed from the notion of the epistemological advantages of being a corpse, belongs to Paul Flechsig.[100]

The above picture of the nature of God and the continued existence of the human soul after death differs markedly in some respects from the Christian views on these matters. It seems to me that a comparison between the two can only favour the former. God was not *omniscient* and *omnipresent* in the sense that He *continuously* saw inside every individual living person, perceived every feeling of his nerves, that is to say at all times "tried his heart and reins." But there was no need for this because after death the nerves of human beings with all the impressions they had received during life lay bare before God's eye, so that an unfailingly just judgment could be reached as to whether they were worthy of being received into the realms of heaven.[101]

The precision of this image of God is equaled only by Flechsig's festschrift photograph. Everything runs according to the plan set out in Flechsig's inaugural lecture, *Brain and Soul*. That God can discipline his still-living victims with mental cures or psychological introspection is an age-old fallacy. The soul consists of nervous tissue, which makes in vivo investigation impossible, but the nerves are perfect data recorders and for that reason will yield all their secrets to the clinical eye at the moment of dissection. In other words: according to this theology, "*within the Order of the World, God did not really understand the living human being* and had no need to understand him, because, according to the Order of the World, He dealt only with corpses," until he initiated his world-order-defying relationship to Schreber.[102] The theology simply equates God with the professor. Psychophysics banned all introspection, and theology complied; Flechsig restricted all diagnoses to corpses, and pious Schreber, performing the written dissection of his nerves, could only accommodate him. With that Schreber fabricated, to the joy of Freud, once a neurologist, the impossible piece of evidence for psychoanalysis: endopsychic perceptions of brain functions.

Channels of information are indeed intimately linked. Schreber's case, rather than being an independent and indubitable piece of evidence for a libido theory, demonstrates the nexus between psychophysics and psychoanalysis. As reader and writer, Freud walked blindly into the discourse network to which he himself belonged. The *Project for a Scientific Psychology* and the *Memoirs of My Nervous Illness* are two continuations of a single discourse. No wonder they ran into the plagiarism problem of being reverse sides of one another.

Just where Freud could have resolved the imaginary rivalry, his keen intellect failed before the discourse of the Other. Although he cannot not have noticed that the language of Schreber's nerves and delirium *is* the language of the experimental neurologist Flechsig,[103] his interpretation systematically replaces the name *Flechsig* with that of the inventor of the Schreber Garden. All the patient's sentences concerning his doctor and "God Flechsig"[104] are treated only as the displacement of a homosexual libido directed at the father. With this, Freud founded the boundless Schreber literature that anchors all the sufferings of Schreber *fils* in the wild childrearing methods of Daniel Gottlieb Moritz Schreber. The head bandages or orthopedic bed invented by Schreber senior and mentioned in passing in the *Memoirs* are then declared the "true background of Schreber's conception of God as One Who knows man only as a *corpse.*"[105] Flechsig's message of the death of man, more hidden than Nietzsche's, has not reached the exegetes. Again and again the attempt is made to explain the second industrial revolution by the first: Schreber as information system is related to orthopedic mechanics, the writing machine in Kafka's "Penal Colony" to frieze heads and planers. But nerve-language remains nerve-language, and typewriters with their own specially constructed means of making script visible are Underwood models.[106] The system of 1900 could spare itself the effort to spare muscular energy because it undertook to create substitutions for the central nervous system itself. Beyond mechanical head bandages, Schreber's paranoia followed the lead of an insane neurophysiologist. His book begins (running the risk of libel suits) with an open letter to Flechsig, asking the distinguished privy counselor to put aside his anger for once, as the undersigned has done, and answer the rigorous scientific query whether he possibly

like so many doctors, could not completely resist the temptation of using a patient in your care *as an object for scientific experiments* apart from the real purpose of cure, when by chance matters of the highest scientific interest arose. One might even raise the question whether perhaps all the talk of voices about somebody having committed soul murder can be explained by the souls (rays) deeming it impermissible that a person's nervous system should be influenced by another's to the extent of imprisoning his will power, such as occurs during hypnosis.[107]

The professor in Leipzig never answered this open letter (which appeared in Leipzig). Whereas Schreber could embroil his later psychiatrists in expert-testimony disputes, which his legal understanding helped him to win, the soul murderer maintained a silence that even today puts exegetes on the wrong track. All the interest in Schreber's so-called father problems substitutes consanguinity for enmity, causality for war. But the classical pedagogic power of Schreber senior can only be equated with the extremely efficient disposition of power in 1900.[108] The nerve-language at the basis of the new disposition states that "an educative influence directed outwards" has been played out.[109] Because God or psychiatrists, according to the world order, can only know corpses, a temptation to conduct psychophysical experiments arises. "The miracles directed against my *head and the nerves of my head*"[110] inscribe themselves into the nervous system without a pedagogic detour and substitute an experimental arrangement for the impossible cure for paranoia. The practical consequence is that anything identifiable as *"influences on my nervous system emanating from your* [Flechsig's] *nervous system"* breaks down in the discourse of the doctor or experimenter into "mere 'hallucinations'" of his patient.[111]

If psychophysics can explain its effects out of existence, then experimental subjects have no choice but open warfare and thus publication. Schreber writes to Flechsig in Flechsig's language in order to demonstrate in the latter's own territory that Schreber's purported hallucinations are facts effectuated by the discourse of the Other. The *Memoirs* stand and fight in the war of two discourse networks. They constitute a small discourse network with the single purpose of demonstrating the dark reality of another, hostile one.

The mentioned writing-down-system is extraordinarily difficult to explain to other people even vaguely. . . .

Books or other notes are kept in which for years have been *written-down* all my thoughts, all my phrases, all my necessaries, all the articles in my possession or around me, all persons with whom I come into contact, etc. I cannot say with certainty who does the writing down. As I cannot imagine God's omnipotence lacks all intelligence, I presume that the writing down is done by creatures given human shape on distant celestial bodies . . . but lacking all intelligence; their hands are led automatically, as it were, by passing rays for the purpose of making them write down, so that later rays can again look at what has been written.

To illuminate the purpose of this whole system I must enlarge further.[112]

Enlarging somewhat further, it first of all should be explained that rays are nerve-language information channels that maintain a psychotechnical, material link between Schreber and Flechsig (or his incarnation as God), very much counter to the conditions of the world order. Rather than manifesting Himself only to corpses, God occupies Schreber's nervous system by innervating all local language centers with the exception of the external speech apparatus; that is, like a good aphasia researcher, he stimulates only sensory and motoric word *images*.[113] No wonder, then, that the nerve-language appears to be hallucinated, no wonder that it can also bridge cosmic distances. According to Flechsig, who wrote an influential monograph on nerve tracts, "the greatest part of the human cerebrum" consists "in nothing more than millions of well-isolated circuits, measuring thousands of kilometers."[114] All the data on Schreber wanders through such interwoven cables to its destination on distant planets. The information comes in, is registered, and can be reread by other rays, which are preparing to move in the opposite direction. The neurologist-god of 1900 is a single discourse network. Whether he (like the gods of Rousseau or the Apocalypse) still uses the book as a storage bank no longer matters. All books are discourse networks, but not all discourse networks are books. If the recording occurs mechanically and without any *Geist*, the probability of its being a purely technical procedure is greater. "It is presumably a phenomenon like telephoning."[115] There is, for example, the appearance of a writing angel in the trademark of a gramophone company.

It is no accident that the neurotheological discourse network stores particulars, and stores them exhaustively. Not one of Schreber's thoughts, sentences, or personal possessions is left out. The paranoid machine operates like an integrated system of all the data-storage devices that revolutionized recording circa 1900. And because its strategy was aimed not at statistical series but at exhausting the arbitrary case of Schreber, it also exemplifies the methodological project at the basis of psychoanalysis.

In 1882 Stanley Hall began, in what was still a very statistical procedure, to gather material for a study entitled *The Contents of Children's Minds*. Soon thereafter the investigation also included individual cases, as when the vocabulary and neologistic creations of two thirteen-year-old girls were inventoried.[116] Consequently, Erdmann could define even a poetic vocabulary as a denumerable group of words. And consequently Freud, in his case histories, could develop a "neurosis inventory," which included all the thoughts, turns of phrase, and significant persons in the lives of his patients. The feeble-minded discourse network around Schreber is thus (as if to demonstrate Freud's remark on the incalculable proximity between mania and theory) *the* discourse network of 1900. Only delirious memoirs betray the actual purpose of the immense effort at recording and storage, which "has increased to such an extent that it now includes almost all the words used in the human language."[117]

Exhaustion links individual cases to the discourse network of 1900. The material taken from Schreber's nerves and stored on distant suns is explicitly intended for inscription. Because it "seems to lie in the nature of the rays that they must *speak* as soon as they are in motion," they grant their victim, by virtue of an appropriate autonymity, this "law"[118] and then further the words for everything that Schreber coincidentally happens to be doing. It is thus made certain that his nerves do not constitute an exception to the law, but rather serve up a verbal stew with compulsive automatism. The rays have "the boundless impudence—I can use no other expression—to demand that I should express this falsified nonsense in spoken words as if it were my own thoughts."[119] As with Pameelen, the discourse network dictates nonsense, which, however, does not remain in the no man's land of psychophysical experiments, but demands Schreber's signature. It is not enough that he suffer the compulsive need to speak, which robs him of sleep and "not-thinking-of-anything-thought,"[120] those basic rights of man, but he must also say that *he* is the speaker of all the nonsense. This is inscription as coupling.

The sudden, direct link between data-storage machines and individual cases liquidates a basic concept of 1800: the ownership of discourses. That Schreber is forced to sign the nonsense forced upon him logically reverses the storage procedures that ensnared him and his contemporaries. God in his ignorance of Man countenances what by the bureaucratic norm is the "completely mistaken view" that when Schreber, "for example, reads a book or newspaper, . . . the thoughts contained therein are my own thoughts." The patient threatened with soul murder need only quite accidentally sing a few notes from the revenge aria in the *Magic Flute*, and immediately his brain fills with whispering voices "which presume that . . . I am actually in the grip of despair." [121] Data-storage machines are much too accurate to make the classical distinctions between intention and citation, independent thought and the mere repetition of something already said. They register discursive events without regard for so-called persons. Thus the pretext of being able to distinguish between mental ownership, citation, and parapraxes became as superfluous as in psychoanalysis.[122] To attribute each and every *flatus vocis* to a speaker as his mental property means to divest him of everything and drive him into insanity—an unparalleled trick indeed.

> The writing-down also serves as another peculiar trick which again is based on a total misunderstanding of human thinking. It was believed that my store of thoughts could be exhausted by being written-down, so that eventually the time would come when new ideas could no longer appear in me. . . . This was the trick: as soon as an idea I had had before and which was (already) written-down, recurred—such a recurrence is of course quite unavoidable in the case of many thoughts, for instance the thought in the morning "Now I will wash" or when playing the piano the thought "This is a beautiful passage," etc.—as soon as such a budding thought was spotted in me, the approaching rays were sent down with the phrase "We have already got this," *scil.* written-down.[123]

It makes no difference, then, whether the heavenly secretaries inscribe sentences or describe things as they occur. At one moment Schreber has to subscribe to the view that the imbecility forced on him is natural to him, at another that what is natural to him is imbecility. As precisely as Ebbinghaus sorted out previously learned nonsense, the nerves note all of Schreber's previously spoken sentences, so that he is subject to the recurrence of recurrence itself. In triumphant Saxon accents, the nerves mock the correct High German faith of the bureaucrat on leave, according to which thinking and speaking are the nature of Man. With the eternal recurrence of "We already have't; we already have't" [*hammirschon hammirschon*] eternal recurrence triumphs over original genius, as does psychophysics over Absolute Spirit. In order to make someone an imbecile, it suffices to impute to him an exhaustible supply of possible thoughts. Every discursive manipulation produces whatever claims it happens to make. It is not for nothing that the beings in charge of recording have no need for minds; their imbecilic inventorying drives Schreber out of his. The psychiatric insight that lists, address books, inventories, and a fortiori discourse networks are fundamentally examples of the flight of ideas, becomes practice. The case of Schreber verifies once more Stransky's observation that the flight of ideas can have pathological grounds as easily as it can have experimental grounds.

But when experiment and pathology coincide and the experimenter indeed does drive the experimental subject crazy, the remaining problem is self-defense. All the gods that pursue Schreber announce their plan as "We want to destroy your reason"; against all such pursuit Schreber attempts "my allotted task of at all times convincing God . . . of my undiminished powers of reason." [124] To this end he not only reads newspapers and books, but also cultivates the "notion" that "human thinking is inexhaustible; for instance reading a book or a newspaper always stimulates new thoughts." [125] The basic principles of the classical discourse network have thus deteriorated into being the defensive weapons of a mental patient. In the crossfire of psychophysics, the last bureaucrat is left with only the sediment of his education, whose norms, however, are taken apart bit by bit. Inexhaustibility, this *signum* of great works, becomes in Schreber's desperation an attribute of newspapers as well. Poems suffer a similar fate. Among the "methods of defense" that make "even the most drawn-out voices finally perish," Schreber included reciting verses learned by heart, "particularly Schiller's ballads." But he then had to realize that "however insignificant the rhymes, even obscene verses" did just as well as his classical poet. "As mental nourishment" obscene verses are "worth their weight in gold . . . compared with the terrible nonsense my nerves are otherwise forced to listen to." [126]

Newspaper rather than oeuvre, memorization rather than understanding, bawdy verse rather than Schiller—the President of the Judicial Senate (on leave) himself takes apart the education that should have provided a defense against his neurologist-tormentor. The old bureaucratic race of the Schrebers must pay for the fact that Flechsig's plot denied Schreber "choice of those professions which would lead to closer relations with God such as that of a nerve specialist." [127] Only countering one medium with another can save one from psychophysics, and only mimicry can save one from voices that level all discourses to the stratum of their materiality. "There had been times when I could not help myself but speak aloud or make some noise, in order to drown the senseless and shameless twaddle of the voices." [128] That this tactic, despite every refinement, "appeared as raving madness to the physicians who did not know the true reason" simply demonstrates once more how indistinguishable pathology and experiment are. [129] God makes an imbecile of someone who resists the onslaught with imbecility. The voices generate "more or less senseless and partly offensive phrases, vulgar terms of abuse, etc."; [130] Schreber combines Schiller and bawdy verse, poetry and noise. As in every war, the defensive forces have to learn from the attacking side. The case of Schreber is "the unheard-of event," as Goethe defined the proper material of the novella, of responding to Flechsig's psychophysics with a psychophysical nonsense.

And that, if it is not madness, is at least literature. In the Sonnenstein asylum high above the Elbe, a solitary and unrecognized experimenter practiced the apotropaic techniques that twelve years later would win fame and a public for the Zurich Dadaists in the Café Voltaire. On March 29, 1916, Richard Huelsenbeck, Tristan Tzara, and Emil von Janko appeared

in the performance of a *poème simultan*. This is a contrapuntal recitative, in which three or more voices speak, sing, whistle, and so on simultaneously, so that their encounters constitute the elegaic, comic, or bizarre context of the thing. The obstinacy of the voice is starkly expressed in such simultaneous poems, and so too is the determining effect of accompaniment. The noises (an *rrr* drawn out for minutes, banging sounds or the wail of a siren, and so on) have an existence whose energy surpasses that of the human voice. The *poème simultan* deals with the value of the voice. The human voice represents the soul, the individuality in its errant journey accompanied by demonic guides. The noises provide the background—the inarticulate, the fatal, the determining. The poem attempts to expose man's entanglement in mechanistic processes. With typical abbreviation it shows the conflict of the *vox humana* with a world that threatens, strangles, and destroys, whose speed and noise are inescapable.[131]

The insane asylum and the artists' cafe witness performances too similar to require comment. Only Hugo Ball's commentary requires comment, in that it abandons its own insight into the determining importance of indeterminate and unarticulated elements. Schreber too wandered between demonic guides and mechanistic processes, but he did not employ the *vox humana* (which is an organ register, not Nature) in order to assert individuality. He simulated—as Huelsenbeck, Tzara, and Janko also did—noises whose energy surpassed that of his own voice. He took the side of the unarticulated, which is the background of all modern media. Those who roar, howl, or whistle are not presenting lachrymose theories of Man in a technological world; rather, they aim at discursive effects against definite and hostile discourses. The inhuman discourse network of 1900 is as inescapable as Gertrude Stein's dark oracle, but precisely its inhumanity allows one to escape from the imperative of sense. Like the audience in the coffee house, Schreber is released from all "effort" to "distinguish single words in the confusion of voices,"[132] just as in the coffee house words drown in the noise of the self-produced confusion of four artists' voices. When power rescinds its classical imperative of establishing only signifieds, even the victims gain new pleasure. The rays are by nature flighty and forgetful; thus Schreber too can indulge his beloved thoughts-thinking-nothing. God, the neurological mutant, places physical pleasure above all morality; thus Schreber too is permitted enjoyment on consistent grounds: "On the other hand God demands *constant enjoyment*, as the normal mode of existence for souls within the Order of

the World. It is my duty to provide Him with it in the form of highly developed soul-voluptuousness. . . . If I can get a little sensuous pleasure in
this process, I feel I am entitled to it as a small compensation for the excess of suffering and privation that has been mine for many years past." [133]

Wherever sense ends, enjoyment begins: a pleasure in the margins that
a discourse network of pure signifiers leaves to its victims. Recollection
and the establishment of sense, work and the deferral of drives may once
have been the tasks of an individual, judicial bureaucrat—but the nerves
and their slave practice a Nietzschean or "natural tendency . . . to forget"
that "would soon have erased any . . . impressions" [134] and knows only
the many present moments of voluptuousness. Because there is already an
exhaustive comprehension of data, data-storage machines need not be
implanted in people as well, thus giving each a soul. The discourse network around Schreber is more merciful than Lindhorst's archive. Roaring, forgetful, suffering flight of ideas, the Senate President on leave can
enjoy a freedom this side of bureaucratic and human dignity. That freedom has been the definition of a subject since 1900. Schreber, because
Flechsig's psychophysics used or misused him in experiments counter to
the world order, became singular as only used pencils, knives, and watches
could be. In opposition to the productive individual, he is allowed simply
to consume whatever "falls off" chains of signifiers in the way of "sensual
pleasure." The subject of the unconscious is literally a "residuum." [135]

Individual differences drop onto the position of the subject. Whether
the arbitrary case is called Schreber or Nietzsche means little. Assistant
physician Dr. Ziehen said of his patient, Nietzsche: "He speaks rapidly,
loudly, and without coherence, often for many hours. His mood is mor-
bidly cheerful and exalted." [136] Dr. Weber, director of the Sonnenstein insane asylum, said of Schreber, his guest at the family dinner table: "Obviously it often requires his greatest energy not to utter the 'bellowing
noises,' and as soon as the table is cleared while he is still on his way to
his room one can hear his inarticulate sounds." [137] The "howling monkey"
Nietzsche produced just such howls or "miraculous bellows" before the
daughters of the desert. But whereas Nietzsche still appeared as a European who found the perfect "sign amnesia" [138] only in the envied opposition of two women, Schreber took the flight of ideas so far as to forget his
gender. If "my whole body is filled with nerves of voluptuousness from
the top of my head to the soles of my feet, such as is the case only in the
adult female body, whereas in the case of a man, so far as I know, nerves
of voluptuousness are only found in and immediately around the sexual
organs," [139] then this body *is* "a woman."

Not the Woman, who does not exist, but a woman with the great
privilege from which drive deferment and bureaucratic duties have kept

her: "succumbing to intercourse."[140] Any man who becomes a neurophysiological case can no longer be a man. In repeated petitions addressed to his
doctor, as formal as they were pressing, a Senate President requested an
experimental test of his proposition that he was a woman with nerves of
voluptuousness interpenetrating his body from head to toe.

Thus the neurologist's strategy to extract Schreber's brain tissue failed
due to its success.[141] Sensual pleasure is gained by killing off Man and the
male. Schreber enjoyed the becoming-a-woman that threatened him; he
used the discourse network that emptied him. Although the *Memoirs of
My Nervous Illness* no sooner promises than forgets to provide an "anthology"[142] of all the senseless, insulting, common, and obscene discourses that the discourse network has stored and mobilized in making
Schreber an imbecile—the bulk of its four hundred pages is just this anthology. In the *Memoirs* a choice anthology of sexual descriptions that
the bureaucrat Schreber would never have uttered or put on paper can
and must be written down. The moral and legal measures Schreber could
have taken to ensure an author's mental ownership fail when it comes to
writing down a discourse network.[143] Having become a woman in order
to take the dictation of a neurologist God, having become a taker of dictation in order to be permitted to write the voluptuousness of being a
woman, Schreber is free. *Schreber as Writer* [*Schreber als Schreiber*][144]
writes up what has written him off. Without originality, mechanically,
like nothing so much as those mindless beings who attend to the task of
recording, he put Flechsig's neurophysiology or imbecilic nonsense on
paper. Nothing and no one could hinder him in so doing. "For all miracles are powerless to prevent the expression of ideas in writing."[145]

A Simulacrum of Madness

In the eyes of I don't know which,—perhaps a very near culture we will be the
ones who brought two sentences into the closest proximity, sentences that are both
as contradictory and as impossible as the famous "I am lying," and that both designate the same empty autoreferentiality: "I am writing" and "I am mad."[1]

Literature in the discourse network of 1900 is a simulacrum of madness. As long and insofar as someone writes, his delirium is protected
from the loss of the word. Distinguished from madness by a nothing
named simulacrum, by a foil named paper, writing traverses the free
space of eternal recurrence. Literary writing is its own justification precisely in its empty self-referentiality.[2] Whereas the claim of not being delirious necessarily leads, under the discursive conditions of brain physiology, to the delirium of originality and authorship, the reverse claim

achieves discursive reality. A delirium written down coincides with what sciences and media themselves were doing.

The simulation of madness presupposes that the sciences of nonsense have become possible and dominant. Only when there is psychophysics to serve as a random generator and psychoanalysis to ensure the exhaustion of nonsense will a UTILIZATION OF REFUSE [*Abfallverwertung*], as nonsensical as it is indisputable, finally take effect. Even after Flechsig has extracted all the nervous tissue from the brain and Freud has decoded all the libidinous cathexes of an arbitrary case, something remains: the fact of a delirious memoir. All experimental measures or miracles are powerless against texts that do not pretend to make sense but rather insist on their purely written character. The nonsense of writing down nonsense is as powerful and indisputable as Wilhelm Jensen's undertaking to supply invented persons with invented manias. "Every nonsense carried to extremes destroys itself in the end" wrote the sharp-witted Schreber (or the God that dictated to him).[3] When that has happened, there is one more literary text.

Today "in the place of Lancelot we have Judge Schreber."[4] Delirious texts entered the realm of literature when literature began to simulate madness. Schreber makes delirium into literature when he describes every hallucination as a fact of the nerve-language rather than underwriting each with an authorial name, and when in defense against the imbecility forced on him he occasionally simulated the imbecile. These were recording measures and simulations that, in all justice to the material and aside from any psychology, necessarily lead to masses of words. The rebus does not end with its psychoanalytic decoding; victims and simulators of madness remain to tinker "with words instead of things."[5] Not only the "nerve-language" itself, but also the enormous quantity of names and idioms, dialect words and obscenities, that the language, through its neurological short cut, inscribed in Schreber's brain is simply a discursive event. Words that did not exist in Kraepelin or even in Bleuler were put down on paper.

Such is also the practice of a literature that "seeks new words for new moods."[6] It is only a step from the memorable productions of Schreber's nerve-language to "Nasobēm," which does not occur in Alfred Brehm and Meyer because it first saw the light of day in Morgenstern's work.[7] If the madness of 1900 is allowed to seep beyond the poetic freedom of dramatic monologues and overflow lexicon, syntax, and orthography as well,[8] then literature is its simulation. Nasobēms counter "a concept of the linguistic expression" in which "it is appropriate to have a meaning." The insane and their simulators instead produce pure signifiers or "anything at all which appears and claims to be an expression, whereas when one looks more closely, this is not the case." [9] With Morgenstern, this simulation occurs on the surface of scientific-lexical storage; with Hugo Ball, it occurs on the surface of psychiatry itself. Among Ball's *Seven Schizophrenic Sonnets*, "The Green King" stands out with its claim of imperial proportions.

> Wir, Johann, Amadeus Adelgreif,
> Fürst von Saprunt und beiderlei Smeraldis,
> Erzkaiser über allen Unterschleif
> Und Obersäckelmeister von Schmalkaldis,
>
> Erheben unsern grimmen Löwenschweif
> Und dekretieren vor den leeren Saldis:
> "Ihr Räuberhorden, eure Zeit ist reif.
> Die Hahnenfedern ab, ihr Garibaldis!
>
> Mann sammle alle Blätter unserer Wälder
> Und stanze Gold daraus, soviel man mag.
> Das ausgedehnte Land braucht neue Gelder.
>
> Und eine Hungersnot liegt klar am Tag.
> Sofort versehe man die Schatzbehälter
> Mit Blattgold aus dem nächsten Buchenschlag."
>
> We, Johann Amadeus Noblegripp,
> Prince of Saprunt and of both Smeraldis,
> Emperor of all the raff and riff
> And Chief Sack Master of Schmalkaldis,
>
> Lift up our terrible lion's mane
> And decree before the empty Saldis:
> "You robber hordes, your time has come.
> Down with your cockfeathers, you Garibaldis!
>
> Collect all the leaves from the forests' trees
> And fashion coin from them, as many as you may.
> The extended nation needs new rupees.
>
> And starvation is as clear as day.
> So fill right up the treasury shieves
> With beech-leaf coin without delay." [10]

The poem preserves the forms of the sonnet and of the decree only in order to make a delirious claim in its empty interior. It proclaims a power without referent, which confirms the diagnostic criteria of schizophrenia in the self-referentiality of the act of writing. A prince whose entire empire consists in the neologisms of his title raves deliriously as he writes. With the inexorability of imperial messages, that vanishing point of Kafka's writing, his decree establishes the monetary value of puns. All shortages vanish thanks to a word of power, which, as in Freud's insight, works "with words instead of things."

Of course, this procedure affects above all words themselves. Schreber's imbecilic voices rhyme without any regard for "sense," simply according to the "similarity of the sounds," as in such distant signifiers as "'Santiago' or 'Cathargo,'" "'Ariman' or 'Ackermann.'"[11] Ball has his Green King add a few strange examples to this list. Such rhymes have nothing to do with the orality and echo effects of a whispering Mother Nature. They constitute a mimicry of madness and are thus naked dictation. The writer does not invent, but only simulates an insane person who in turn has not invented the rhymes but rather, "in an actual rhyming mania," "had to construct verses without any regard for the nonsense that resulted."[12]

The seriousness of such simulations is not diminished in the least by being "limited to linguistic phenomena, that is, to only *one* symptom among many."[13] Contemporary psychiatrists did not proceed any differently. "Simply because most of one's acts in higher cultural life are not concrete actions but spoken or written words, language in itself" offers writers "the same possibility of portraying mental illness that a person's speech allows us"—that is, psychiatrists—"the possibility of making an unbiased diagnosis of mental illness."[14] Psychiatrists and writers are thus remarkably in accord about restricting the range of possible data to the symbolic. The former compile and order whole archives of psychotic speech errors, which are then at the disposal of the latter. Only when sciences localize madness in "language in itself" does its literary simulation become possible and important. Psychiatric discourse provides monographs on psychotic neologisms, rhyme manias, and special languages, to which writers, seeking information from competent sources, need only help themselves. The necessary consequence is a writing that has no referent outside of psychiatry and of which Bölsche provided an early and exact description. If literature "rightly despises" its secular support in philosophers such as Hegel or Schopenhauer, in order to exploit instead the details amassed by psychiatry and pathology, it can only be a simulacrum of madness.

A number of careful minds, particularly practicing writers, rightfully despise this shaky bridge and have boldly confronted amassed details of objective knowledge. The success reveals a serious danger in this undertaking as well. Scientific psychology and physiology are constrained, by conditions familiar to all, to conduct their studies mainly with the diseased organism, and so they coincide almost entirely with psychiatry and pathology. Now the writer who in a justified thirst for knowledge intends to gain instruction from these disciplines, finds himself unintentionally drawn more and more into the atmosphere of the clinic. He begins to turn his attention away from his rightful object, from healthy, universal human life, toward the abnormal, and in the intention of observing the premises of his realistic art, he unwittingly fills his pages with the premises of his premises, with the observed material itself, from which he should be drawing conclusions. Then there arises a literature of man as sick, of mental illnesses, of difficult child births, of the arthritic—in short, of what not a few ignorant people imagine to be realism itself.[15]

Bölsche describes what literature does in the discourse network of 1900: it utilizes refuse from the nonsense stored by psychophysics. The delirious discourses that gain entry to the scientific archives only on the condition of making no sense lose even this referent in literary simulation. Anyone who fills page after page with the premises of his premises speaks neither of the world or of Man. As a simulacrum of madness, literature loses its classical distinction of springing immediately from Nature or the Soul and of subsequently having this naturalness certified by philosophical interpreters. It becomes secondary literature in the strictest sense of the word. Its discourse, cut off from "universal human life," deals with other discourses, which it can only transpose. Because media transpositions render useless such concepts as authenticity and primacy,[16] any vestige of extradiscursive verification is lost. Literature does not reveal phenomena or determine facts; its field is a madness that, as Münsterberg realized, exists only on paper.

Many fictional presentations of abnormal mental states are taken to be sensitive psychological portraits precisely in areas where the scientifically trained observer would recognize an impossibility. If persons were actually to behave in the manner the writer has them act and speak in these novelistic mental disturbances, the doctor would have to conclude that they were simulating.[17]

"Novelistic mental disturbances" accordingly occur in a no man's land, which can be verified neither by immediately accessible mental truths nor by controlled experiments. Its name is simulacrum. Writers who simulate being psychiatrically informed describe persons who, viewed from the standpoint of psychiatry, are simply simulators. But that is the point. Simulation without reference dissolves the old connection between madness and illness in order to establish an entirely different connection: between madness and writing.[18]

Novelistic mental disturbances, which occurred in more than novels in 1900, did not renew the affiliation of artists and the insane against a philistine bourgeoisie. The appearance of expressionist "young artists" was not necessary "to obtain the provocative possibility of concretely representing their opposition to the ruling norms and notions of value" by the revised and positive valuation of madness.[19] This transvaluation occurred when positivistic sciences began determining cultural technologies from deficits and defects and thus liquidated classical norms. The myths of the young and of provocation only obscure the complete extent of the young provocateurs' dependence on the discourse network of their period.[20]

Something completely different is at stake when psychophysics and literature collide. Illusory political-moral struggles, in which writers purportedly are the first to discover madness, are superfluous; the struggle concerns only the use of the same discourse. Whereas psychophysics held on to the connection between madness and illness, literature constructed a completely different connection between madness and writing. Its simulation created individual cases that speak and write out of standardized collections of symptoms. And so they appeared, accidental and singular as only dilettantes of the miracle could be: "The Madman" (Georg Heym), "The Imbecile" (Ball), "The Visionnut" [*Der Visionarr*] (Jakob van Hoddis), "The Idiot" (Huelsenbeck, Zech, Johannes Becher). They appear and begin their nonsensical speech: the "Song of the Escapees" (Johannes Urzidil), "The Idiot's Song" (Rilke), not to forget "The Song of the Crazy Women" (Paul Adler).

As if to name the discursive status of these songs, the young Breton wrote, across the barrier erected by the First World War:

> Démence précoce, paranoia, états crépusculaires.
> O poésie allemande, Freud et Kraepelin!
>
> Dementia praecox, paranoia, twilight states
> Oh German poetry, Freud and Kraepelin![21]

No one could say more clearly that literature utilizes the discarded material of contemporary psychiatry. Dementia praecox is, of course, "in its contemporary form" Kraepelin's "new creation."[22] And so the glory of literature was reflected onto psychiatry. Psychiatry's archives became rough drafts of poetry and provided material and methods for pure writing. Of course, classical and romantic writers learned from the psychic cures of their Reils and Hoffbauers,[23] but the Occident remained the predominant theme and archive. Meaning always came from Above; nonsense, by contrast, cannot be invented, it can only be transcribed and written down. Thus a "German poetry" of Freud and Kraepelin took over the systemic position occupied by Poetry in the classical-romantic discourse network, and literature moved from second to third place in the new order of discourse. The third place is (just as for Schreber) the site of sensual pleasure. A remainder of nonsense, of no further use to even the sciences of nonsense, is left over for games.

Because it cuts the old bond between madness and illness, the game of the simulated delirium makes the distinction between doctors and patients somewhat tenuous. Münsterberg was probably right to suspect that simulators of medical science actually describe simulators of madness. In 1893 a four-part work appeared in Berlin entitled *Body, Brain,*

Mind, God, a work that (with the exception of God) cataloged in its title the basic problems of 1900 and identified its author as a "practicing doctor."[24] Its intent is true psychophysics: Karl Gehrmann brings case history after case history to bear on the problem of relating diverse physical symptoms to neural centers in the brain. But the place names on this brain atlas outdo one another in their poetry, the recorded dreams of countless patients become more and more beautiful and flowery, until after two thousand pages there is no longer any doubt that all the neural centers, case histories, and recorded dreams can only refer to a single subject, the institutionalized writer. Doctors, proceeding like the institutionalized Schreber toward exhausting the contents of the brain, end up in madness themselves.

One need only write down psychophysics to produce "German poetry." That is exactly what the young assistant doctor Benn does when he lets a, or his, professor speak for himself.

PROFESSOR: And now, gentlemen, I have in conclusion a very special surprise for you. As you can see, I have colored the pyramidal cells from the hippocampus of the left hemisphere of the cerebrum taken from a fourteen-day-old rat of the Katull variety. Now observe: the cells are not red, but pink, with a light brownish-violet coloration that shades into green. This is indeed most interesting. You are aware that lately a paper came out of the Graz Institute that disputes this fact, despite my thorough investigations of the matter. I will not say anything about the Graz Institute in general, but I must say that this paper struck me as premature. As you see, I now have the proof at hand. This does have enormous implications. It would be possible to distinguish rats with long black fur and dark eyes from those with short rough fur and light eyes through this fine difference in cell color, as long as the rats are of the same age, have been fed with candy, have played for half an hour daily with a small puma, and have spontaneously defecated two times in the evening with the temperature at 37 or 36 degrees centigrade.[25]

The utilization of discarded material from psychophysics is as concrete as it is perilous. During his training with famous psychiatrists and pathologists, Benn published scientific work *and* texts that ridiculed brain research, notably works with the same titles and contents as his own.[26] The montage of its senseless accumulation of fact made psychophysics into the mental disturbance it was investigating, and made the pink brain cells of the rat into phenomena as magnificent as those found in Gehrmann. In the literary publication of his lectures, Benn's professor takes his rightful place alongside the Flechsig of the *Memoirs* (assistant doctor Rönne threatened to sue the professor "because of brain damage").[27] Most likely, only because Ziehen and Karl Bonhoeffer did not read the materials their assistant Benn published in marginal avant-garde journals was Benn saved from the compromising situations of Gehrmann or

Schreber.[28] For Hoffmann, the bureacratic-poetic double life was a useful arrangement because it betrayed the secret unity of both functions; Benn was confronted with double-entry bookkeeping, in which one hand continued to write statistics and the other exploited a singular delirium.

Along with Ernst Mach and Mauthner, those philosophic sources for most research on expressionism, Ziehen taught that the unity of the ego was a fiction when compared with the reality of the association of ideas.[29] Benn and Rönne had only to put their boss's theory into practice in writing. It was an irreconcilable but permissible use of psychiatric discourse to turn it on one's own accidental case. Exactly that happened when Benn's report on his last year as a psychiatrist, 1913, produced the psychiatric diagnosis of the irreconcilability of writing and treatment.

I attempted to find out for myself what I was suffering from. The manuals on psychiatry that I consulted led me to modern psychological works, some quite remarkable, particularly in the French school; I immersed myself in the descriptions of the condition designated as depersonalization . . . I began to see the ego as an entity that strove, with a force compared to which gravity would be the touch of a snowflake, for a condition in which nothing that modern culture designated as intellectual gifts played any part.[30]

The writer as insane—not a mythic conflict between artists and the bourgeoisie, but the semi-official doctrine of psychiatric textbooks creates the connection. Benn and Rönne are psychiatrists who become incapable of "taking interest in a newly arrived case or observing the old cases with constant individualizing attention,"[31] which according to Ziehen and the rules of data exhaustion, would be their professional obligation.[32] Instead, Rönne, lying motionless in the doctor's office, simulates the catatonic, and Benn simulates a situation in which he is the newly arrived case in need of constant observation. But a doctor who transfers the latest diagnoses, such as depersonalization, from his patients onto himself, uses Janet or Ribot no differently from how Schreber used Kraepelin's textbook. Education or "intellectual gifts" have no role in either case.

But by isolating psychophysical results, literature simulated only what distinguished psychoanalysis in the discourse network of 1900. Biographically, first of all, there is Freud's self-analysis, the mythic origin of his new science, which proceeds by the same inversion of roles. As Benn would later discover his psychotic depersonalization, so Freud found the basic complex of his neurotic patients "in my own case too."[33] Methodologically, psychoanalysis singularized statistical material: it does not order the collected nonsense into nosological entitites, but attributes the material to unconscious subjects. Finally, in a literary sense, this organization of the material appears in the case histories, which count as "modern German letters" or "German poetry."

Like the Poets and Thinkers one hundred years earlier, writers and analysts came into "close and fruitful contact."[34] As early as 1887 the philosopher Dilthey deplored a new "misology" among artists, who hated thinking, aesthetics, and culture [*Bildung*].[35] One friendship was over (even if other critics did not have Dilthey's keen ear for the announcement), and another, just as perilous, could begin. What Goethe had said about philosophers—that he could never do without them and yet could never come to terms with them—from 1900 on was addressed to Freud: although or because, according to Kafka, there was "of course" a great deal of Freud in "The Judgment," his literary writing obeyed the imperative "No more psychology!"[36] The solidarity of solidarity and competition, once the fate of Poets and Thinkers, became the fate of writers and analysts.

Of course, it was no longer a question of meaning and its interpretation. Writers and psychoanalysts did not constitute a state-supporting community of interpreters in which there was a mutual exchange of certificates validating the creation of eternal values. Their mutual relationship was supported by the existence, at the basis of all cultural technologies, of bodies and their nonsense. These bodies, however, were only accessible to psychophysical experiments at the price of silence and death. But on the couch, where "alas, everything is different," "nothing takes place . . . but an interchange of words."[37] In literature, where even such exchange is lacking, nothing occurs but intransitive writing. Psychoanalysis must thus focus on the nonsense in speech until it can gather a linked set of indices that closes around an inaccessible reality. Literature must purify pieces of paper of everything readable until the body of its words coincides with the other body in an instantaneous shortcircuit. As such, however, the two discourses compete with one another. There is a reality inaccessible to both, and two mutually exclusive detours: decoding and the shortcircuit.

Freud did not ever claim to be able to explain the fact that literature exists. In spite or because of this, writers have done their utmost to keep him from any such explanation. Given the alternatives of laying their bodies on the couch or setting down bodies of words, almost all opted for pure writing as against a "(possibly unproductive) life."[38] So the relationship between writers and analysts became all kinds of things—dialogue, reading, greetings addressed even without an accompanying chalice—but it did not become practice.

"At one time I did consider psychiatric treatment," he said, "but dropped the idea just in time."

For a long time he actually had believed that his salvation lay in psychoanalysis. His beloved, Lou Andreas-Salomé, was an avid follower of Freud and his circle and had urged Rilke to lay himself on the famous couch. For years before the war Rilke considered the pros and cons but finally, at the last moment, drew back. "I won't have anyone poking around in my brain," he said to me, "I'd rather keep my complexes."

Later he did meet Freud personally, but said nothing about his problems. After that he avoided Freud whenever they encountered one another. The panic fear of being picked apart and sucked dry constantly pursued him.[39]

As paranoid as Schreber, who also lived in fear of a brain-pillaging doctor, Rilke took the opposite course. One gave his body over to a science that was hardly capable of demonstrating itself worthy of such a gift. The other withdrew his body from a science that had neither the intention nor the capability of poking around in his brain, because of course it dealt only in the exchange of words. The rage of simulated paranoia is worse than that of the clinical variety. The fact that psychoanalysis transferred psychophysical methods to individual cases unleashed the phantasm of trephination. The writer's brain became the mythic vanishing point of all attempts to ground discourse neurologically. Writing circa 1900 therefore means: this brain, its clinical or simulated madness notwithstanding, shall be immediately transposed into texts and protected from any medical soundings. This transposition of media had to pass through that other vanishing point, the endopsychic perception of brain functions. What Gehrmann and Schreber began, issued into literature.

Shortly after Apollinaire received his head wound in the trenches at Aisne, he issued a challenge to his critics, the admirers of Boileau and Ben Akiba: "But is there nothing new under the sun? It remains to be seen. What! My head has been x-rayed. I have seen, while I live, my own cranium, and that would be nothing new?"[40] A "new spirit," then, as the title of the essay promises, inspires the poet. No last words are pronounced on the life-threatening wound to the head, in that it opens up the much more exciting possibility of endopsychic perception. Dr. Bardel's x-rays and trephination of Apollinaire made literal truth of what Flechsig and his clever student expected only of the postmortem examination. It is only logical, therefore, that Apollinaire should immediately appeal to writers to approach the great novelty under the sun and connect their writing with technological media like film and the phonograph.

Brains—the title of Benn's early collection of novellas—designates an entire writing project. Rönne, the hero, was originally a psychiatrist and brain researcher, who "in these hands had held hundreds or even thousands" of brains,[41] not merely those of rats. But when he makes the transition from doctor to patient, all of his research interests shrink to a single enigma. Rönne constantly performs a gesture "as if he were breaking open a soft, large fruit, or as if he were unfolding something"[42]—a rebus that adoring nurses are finally able to decode as the opening of his own brain. It stands, like Rönne's association with brain damage, for a new writing project: literary impulses are to be fed on the vivisected fruit of his own brain. That is why the hero procures himself a journal and a pencil.[43]

And as if to take Rönne's decision at its word, Flake, an admirer of Benn, made an entire novel out of the latter's laconic novellas; out of *Brains*, that is, came an entire *City of the Brain*. The hero, Lauda, has, of course, studied medicine and for three semesters has "always begun again hesitantly with the opening cut": "sometimes into the up-turned hemispheres, the gelatinous site of conscious throught, which can be modified, sometimes into the base, the more defined, differentiated, architectonic portion."[44] He has thus already been to school with Rönne, when years later, after leaving the office and secretary, he happens to read a paper on neurology. It describes the brain as an endlessly complex "cross network" consisting of transmitters/receivers of "electrical waves." The reader instantly decides "to construct a model of the world from this." Because models of the world in 1900 consist in "words, perhaps only words," Lauda begins a "metaphysical journal" that by means of "psycho-physiology" derives his own thought apparatus from "nerve tracts" and describes his brain as "a city of pathways that I laid down according to individual acts and now must travel forever." Having sunk to being the knowing slave of his "thought paths," Lauda therefore falls asleep, only to return to the impossible place of such reflections. Rönne's gesture becomes a dream act. Lauda stays in a scientifically "read-in" city of the brain until the next morning brings the realization or renunciation that is decisive for writers: "A physical residence in the city of the brain is impossible, only the allegorical is possible." Because the impossible wishes tell the truth, the renunciation reveals the character of literature in the discourse network of 1900: Lauda henceforth intends only to "scream walk write" [*schrein schreiten schreiben*].[45] The novel itself becomes an allegorical residence in the brain, a deciphering of neurophysiological engrams.

Marcel, the narrator, dawdles in his pursuit of *The Remembrance of Things Past* as long as he fails to realize that the goal of his search lies simply in the "storehouse" of his own brain and is stored only there. The fact that he, like Gehrmann or Lauda, will have to transcribe nerve tracts is simultaneously and immediately also the fear that a "head accident" could make him forget all the stored traces, indeed make him forget the forgetting of them.[46] Thus Marcel began to write just in time, driven by the furies of an eventual aphasia, which was, not coincidentally, a subject on which the physician Dr. Adrien Proust, the writer's father, had published.[47]

But enough demonstration. The puzzling question common to neurologists and the insane, to psychoanalysts and writers circa 1900 is summed up in the title *Brain and Language*.[48] The doctors (who take precedence in formulating the problem) pose the theme; the writers work it through. Their writing stands exactly at the place or takes the place of the brain vivisection that all psychophysics must dream of *and* do without. Rilke fled psychoanalysis because his own "work" was for him "actually nothing other than that sort of self-treatment."[49] Thus he fled not merely because Freud or Viktor Gebsattel would poke around in his brain, but to be able to compete with the vivisectors. The underlying mutuality of the two discourses excluded any overlap. In the discourse network of 1900, writers are people who in the analysis—that is, the decomposition—of their psychic apparatus prefer to go it alone.

With his mute gesture, Rönne turns his own brain hemispheres inside out in order to reach the source of his thought; Lauda visits the city of his brain in the metaphor of the dream; but there was one who, widely decried as a dreamer and maker of images, took on the impossible task common to them all, and did it technologically, without images. However, he was a poet and hated the approximate. In order to define the status of literature, Rilke, in his "notebook" *Primal Sound* [*Ur-Geräusch*], chose a model that since 1900 has designated all inscription and decoding: the phonograph.

Fourteen or fifteen years after an unforgotten day in school on which he constructed a phonograph out of cardboard and parchment paper, candle wax and the bristles of a clothes brush,[50] Rilke attended anatomy lectures at the Ecole des Beaux-Arts in Paris. Among all the medical samples, what "enchanted" the writer was a "special housing closed against all worldly space"—the skull. Rilke acquired a skull and spent the evenings studying it—with the result that his childhood memory was completely rewritten. If it once seemed that "this autonomous sound [would] remain unforgettable, apart from us, preserved outside," the student of anatomy learned that not the sounds "from the funnel," but "those markings traced on the cylinder of the phonograph"[51] were much more essential. But the *sutura coronalis* effects the shift from reproduction to inscription, from reading to writing in the technological age. "In the peculiarly vigilant and demanding light of the candle the cranial suture was quite evident and I soon realized what it reminded me of: those unforgotten lines that were once scratched onto a little wax roll by the point of a bristle!"[52]

The suture that divides the two cranial hemispheres like a sagittal incision designates the status of all script for a writer of 1900. Only a scratch or cut into the flesh of forgetfulness itself can be unforgettable. What Nietzsche learned investigating the genealogy of morals, what Kafka's explorer learned in the penal colony,[53] Rilke was able to learn from anatomy. If ever an initiation did justice to the material, then this was it. The cranial suture functions as the left-over trace of a writing energy or art that, instead of "making variations or imitating," "had its joy in the dance of existences," in a "dictatorial art that presents dispositions of energy." A "consciousness of an ethical nature,"[54] of the kind evoked in the titles of Nietzsche and Kafka, can add nothing to this. Technology and physiology are responsible for material inscription.

More exactly, a system composed of technology and physiology is responsible. That is what the skull for years had "suggested again and again" to Rilke the writer.

The coronal suture of the skull (this would first have to be investigated) has—let us assume— a certain similarity to the closely woven line which the needle of the phonograph engraves on the receiving, rotating cylinder of the apparatus. What if one changed the needle and directed it on its return journey along a tracing which was not derived from the graphic translation of sound, but existed of itself naturally—well: to put it plainly, along the coronal suture, for example. What would happen? A sound would necessarily result, a series of sounds, music . . .

Feelings—which? Incredulity, timidity, fear, awe—which of all the feelings here possible prevents me from suggesting a name for the primal sound which would then have made its appearance in the world . . .[55]

Unlike poets such as Shakespeare or Gottfried Keller, who throw their heroes into the traditional melancholy associations at the sight of a skull, the writer is an experimenter. He suggests, more radically than technicians and physiologists—and in a language that maintains a wonderful balance between precision and caution—a phonographic test of human body parts. The insight of information science, that recording and playback devices are essentially convertible,[56] allows the decoding of a track that no one had ever encoded. But the fact that nature has thrown away the keys to its secrets is no reason, in 1900, to leave the rebus untouched. Let deranged people like Gehrmann attempt to solve it with mere books, but "we," the art-physiologists and artists, "inevitably think of a process similar to Edison's *phonograph* when it comes to the molecules and nerve tracts in the brain."[57] Simmel's objective interpretation, Freud's analytic construction, Rilke's apparatus—all can track traces without a subject. A writing without the writer, then, records the impossible reality at the basis of all media: white noise, primal sound.

That is only logical. Certainly "it" has been making noise from time immemorial, as long as there has been Brownian motion. But for any distinction between noise and information to be possible, the real must be able to move through technological channels. Printing errors occur in the book as medium, but there is no primal sound. The phonographic reproduction of a groove "that is not the graphic translation of a sound" mocks translatability and universal equivalents. Setting gramophone needles onto coronal sutures is only possible in a culture that gives free reign to all discursive manipulations. And of course anything that "exists naturally," like the skull, thereby loses its distinctiveness. At such extremes the transposition of media creates only unconscious programs out of so-called nature. Otto Flake and Proust dreamed of making literal reproductions of the inscribed pathways in their brains; Rilke made technological suggestions for the technological realization of their dreams. Yet Rilke reserves this realization for writers. It was not for the "Poets," who, according to Rilke's historically exact insight, "were overwhelmed" by "almost only" one sense, the visual, whereas "the contribution made by an inattentive sense of hearing" was practically nil. Rilke had in mind an artistic practice that "contributes more decisively than anyone else to an extension of the several sense fields," that is, with more determination than even "the work of research." [58]

Writers and analysts of the mental apparatus thus engaged in open, unrelenting competition. The very Rilke who fled psychoanalytic vivisectors programmed, as the writer's only task, the transposition of coronal sutures. Even his enigmatic "inner-world space" was only another name for the engram stored in the brain and transcribed by writers. The evidence is that Rilke called the skull a "special housing closed against all worldly space" and thereby restated the physiologist's insight that, for such a housing, "our own body is the external world." [59] Interpreters who read "inner-world space," this technological and physiological system, philosophically, thus remain as far behind the state of the art, as belated as their totemic animal, the proverbial owl.

More than one hundred pages on aphasia research and phonographs, psychoanalysis and paranoia, will perhaps not have been wasted if they make it possible to spell out for the first time, and not merely to understand, *The Notebooks of Malte Laurids Brigge.*

Spelling in the *Notebooks* is taken over by psychiatrists (whereas philosophers do not appear at all). Doctors in the Salpêtrière are the ones who make *a-v-a-n-t* out of *avant*, which Brigge (as the title of the book indicates) has only to note down. The question is why this twenty-eight-year-old, who is not in the Salpêtrière to gather racy material on doctor-patient relationships, [60] shows up in the insane asylum instead of sticking to anatomy lectures and the Ecole des Beaux-Arts. The answer is that Brigge, like his novelist, "had once considered psychiatric treatment, but dropped the idea just in time."

He enters the Salpêtrière, explains his case, is registered for electro-shock therapy, is questioned briefly by a couple of assistant doctors, and is sent back to the waiting room. While Brigge is waiting for the promised or threatened electrical shocks, the discursive event occurs: his ears catch a hot, flaccid stuttering "*a-v-a-n-t*." Psychophysical decomposition of language becomes the secret code of an initiation. Just like the word DADA, which occurs in a child's "babbling phase" and reminds people "of their honorably dirtied diapers and of the cry that is now supposed to delight the world,"[61] the "*a-v-a-n-t*" also leads to a short circuit between experiment and primal sound, psychophysics and children's language.

And, then, as I listened to the hot, flaccid stuttering on the other side of the parti-tion, then for the first time in many, many years it was there again. That which had struck into me my first, profound terror, when as a child I lay ill with fever: the Big Thing. Yes, that was what I had always called it, when they all stood around my bed and felt my pulse and asked what had frightened me: the Big Thing. And when they got the doctor and he came and spoke to me, I begged him only to make the Big Thing go away, nothing else mattered. But he was like the rest. He could not take it away, though I was so small then and might easily have been helped. And now it was there again. . . . Now it grew out of me like a tu-mor, like a second head, and was a part of me, though it could not belong to me at all, because it was so big. . . . But the Big Thing swelled and grew over my face like a warm bluish boil and grew over my mouth, and already the shadow of its edge lay upon my remaining eye.[62]

At precisely the place or precisely in place of a psychiatric treatment that does not occur, because Brigge flees the Big Thing and the Salpêtrière in one and the same movement, what does occur is the return of his child-hood. To drop the idea of psychoanalysis just in time thus means to walk the royal road alone and lift infantile amnesias. But lower abdominal play is not what returns with the repressed; it is the debris of a horror that could not be spoken and for which "the Big Thing" is still a euphemism. What appears is something real that cannot be spoken in any language because the very act of introducing it into language filters it out. Only the primal sound of the overheard psychiatrist is capable of evoking it, whereas the pleas of Brigge the child and Brigge the twenty-eight-year-old to his doctors can do nothing.

The law governing delirium and hallucination determines that what has not entered the daylight of the symbolic appears in the real. The de-lirious Brigge becomes the debris of the debris that pours from his head. A second head, larger than the feverish one, blocks his eyes and mouth. Everything happens, then, as if Rönne's impossible gesture were possible.

The brain, this warm bluish boil, turns itself inside out and encloses the external world. Because no one and nothing can introduce the material substratum of language into language, the shadow of neurophysiology falls on Brigge's mouth.

What occurs in the place of this eclipse is—writing. "I have taken action against fear. I have sat all night and written,"[63] Brigge writes of the fear that drove him in and then out of the Salpêtrière. Writing therefore means: to put the exploded "inner-world space," the tumescent brain, down on paper, rather than have the explosion or tumor treated by the appropriate scientific methods. From then on Brigge spends his days reading in the Bibliothèque nationale and his nights writing on the sixth floor of his hotel. Rilke once told Gebsattel that one cannot live without the couch, but one could "read and write and endure";[64] Brigge uncouples his writing from speech and communication: he notes down whatever makes him mute, and when he writes letters they are never sent. There is no longer any question, then, of a life in poetry, led simultaneously in Atlantis and Dresden, on paper and in loving embraces. The medium of script reveals its coldness; it is purely archiving. Therefore it cannot replace, represent, or be life, but only remember, repeat, and work through. To do something against fear means to write down the fear itself.

The objects of writing are neighbors who somehow come within hearing, who creep out, and in some cases reach the brain to multiply and thrive there like pneumococci. The objects of writing are insane kings whose flesh has become indistinguishable from the amulets that cover it and the worms that devour it. The objects of writing are the dead heaped over battlefields, intertwined like a monstrous brain, and the dying, all of whose accumulated meanings vanish and for whom a large tumor rises in the brain—like a sun that transforms the world for them.

There is thus only one object of writing: the primal soup of brain physiology. What interests Freud is its organization; what interests Brigge is noting it down.

Better perhaps to have remained in the darkness, and your unconfined heart would have sought to be the heavy heart of all that is indistinguishable. . . .

O night without objects. O obtuse window outward, o carefully closed doors; arrangements from long ago, taken over, accredited, never quite understood. O stillness in the staircase, stillness from adjoining rooms, stillness high up against the ceiling. O mother: o you only one, who shut out all this stillness, long ago in childhood. . . . You strike a light, and already the noise is you. And you hold the light before you and say: it is I; don't be afraid.[65]

The fact that there is articulation at all becomes the enigma of a writing that inevitably articulates. Because Brigge (unlike Freud) does not raise the standards of his medium to norms of the real, it remains a question whether they are "better" than primal soup. But thus his simple description correlates with psychophysical results.

It is wrong to assume that originally (as soon as the sense organs function) there were nothing but particular impressions out of which secondary connections among impressions were then formed. . . . The original situation should rather be thought of as a diffuse, whole sensibility. For example, when we lie daydreaming on the sofa with closed eyes, we do not notice anything particular in the brightness that penetrates our eyelids, in the distant noise on the street, in the pressure of our clothing, or in the temperature of the room, but rather fuse all these things in the totality of our receptivity. Such—though much more vague and muffled— is how we must first think of the sensibility of the infant. Before we investigate the associations between particular impressions, we must first ask how the child manages to isolate a particular phenomenon out of this confused, whole state.[66]

As anticipatory as ever, Ebbinghaus addressed this question to his colleague, Stern, and isolated infantile isolation.

A very young child looked from a particular position into a particular room. He received a diffuse, hardly differentiated impression. Now his mother pulls him in his wagon into an adjoining room; for the most part another whole impression replaces the first. But the mother and the wagon have remained the same. The optical stimuli they produce thus find the material disposable to them as well as their mental effects somewhat prepared in advance, and in addition they reinforce one another through mutual association; the other, modified stimuli do not have this double advantage. . . . The impression derived from the sight [of the mother] forms more and more easily on the one hand, and on the other hand it differentiates itself more and more from the various diffuse backgrounds in which it was originally dissolved: the sight of the mother becomes a progressively more independent part of the given whole impression.[67]

When one isolates the perceptual isolation of the child rigorously enough, it is no longer that of the child. The construction of articulated environments proceeds through the first human contacts. What Ebbinghaus describes coincides with what Brigge calls the shutting out of the indistinguishable. The *Notebooks*, or the *Remembrance of Things Past*, critically decried as "mystical" or "oedipal" whenever they evoke childhood and the mother, simply inquire into the elemental relation, circa 1900, between particular and background, sign and primal soup, language and primal sound. The answer to this inquiry can only be that discrete signs arise from sheer iteration. The mother (in Ebbinghaus) must return in order to be distinguished from the diffuse backgrounds; the mother (in the *Notebooks*) must say, "It is I, don't be afraid." Behind all identities and selections lurks the endless region of darkness.

"We know not what the imagination would be without darkness, its great school."[68] reads the first empirical, child-psychological study of its kind, *A Study of Fears*. Eleven years before the *Notebooks*, in his case histories Stanley Hall archived all the childhood fears of Brigge: aside from mirrors, needles, and masks, there was also the moment that played such a key role for Malte and Marcel.

28. F., 18. The great shadow over all her early life was the dread of the moment her mother should kiss her good night and leave her alone in the dark; she lay tense and rigid, held her breath to listen with open mouth, smothered herself under the clothes, with which her head must always be covered, fancied forms bending over her, often awoke with her heart pounding and a sense of dropping through the air, flying or falling backward, feeling quivery for hours; she now vows "I will always put my whole foot on the stairs."[69]

The fact that Otto Rank's book on incest picked out the corresponding fear of Brigge, and only that one, as if to apprehend one more oedipal suspect,[70] betrays the competition between literature and psychoanalysis. Childhood fears were copiously noted down in the discourse network of 1900. Psychophysics provided the theoretical and statistical framework; psychoanalysis and literature made texts of fitting individual cases, until the system was complete. None of the three discourses had solid points of reference in the two others; there is only a network of the three.

The object or abject caught in the net, however, was the child. None of the three discourses has any further concern for what mothers do and say, for the kind of love or education they instill in their children. Instead of minimal signifieds of a first love, all that counts are the first signifiers on an indistinguishable background. The archiving of first signs, even if they are as vague as "the Big Thing" or as babbled as the "o-o-o-o-/*da*," that is, "*fort*/*da*" of Freud's grandson became a communal task.[71] The iteration and opposition of minimal signifiers provided material enough for constructing a system. And systems exist to be written down.

One winter evening the child Brigge is drawing. A red pencil rolls off the table and onto the carpet. The child, "accustomed to the brightness above and all inspired with the colors on the white paper," cannot find the pencil in the "blackness" under the table: *da*/*fort*. Instead, he sees his own searching hands as strange, blind creatures. Much has been written about this depersonalization, but not about the pencil, paper and blackness, these three necessary and sufficient conditions for a medium, of which interpretations themselves are a part. And the pencil returns years later, as if it came back from *Beyond the Pleasure Principle*, only to designate itself as the sign of a sign. A little gray woman turns it over endlessly in her miserable hands, until Brigge realizes that "it was a sign, a sign for the initiated," and senses "that there actually existed a certain compact" with the woman.[72]

Pencils are produced in order to make signs, not to be signs. But right before Brigge's eyes the woman transposes the writing instrument into special contexts that cut across the literary-alphabetic code. The pencil, once lost in the signless darkness of the carpet, as if in a jungle, returns as "the Big Thing" to reduce all writing to one code among others. Precisely the fact that it is "old," if not a piece of debris, makes it significant. In the *Notebooks* newspapers are sold by a blind man, who cannot read them.[73] Writing materials come to be misused by sign-giving analphabets. And so it goes in a discourse network that measures cultural technologies by their deficiencies and particular things by their degree of wear and tear. The pretty pictures produced prior to its disappearance by Brigge's pencil under the gaze of a reading governess do not count; for they are only the Basedow raisins of an alphabetizing power. What counts and is therefore put down on paper is the analphabetic adventure with writing material and paper. Freud's patient, the one who confused *m* and *n*, knew this story well.

The discourse network of 1800 had archived the way in which children autonomously reproduced the engrained alphabet. But it did not begin to comprehend other children with other pleasures/fears. The discourse network of 1900 cut apart the pedagogic feedback loop and directed children to write down their analphabetism. It was a paradoxical and impossible role that could only be taken on as simulacrum.

Brigge fills pages about an old pencil; the art-education movement had essays written on "The Rusty Pen." Packed together with 144 other similar pens in industrial boxes three weeks previously, it is finally "good for nothing else" than to be thrown in the waste basket. But because only use singularizes, the useless pen becomes the subject of a writer. His semi-official name is the happy child; his empirical name is Heinrich Scharrelmann—a high school teacher who, in the place of pens and pupils that don't write, wrote a book entitled *Happy Children*.[74]

As it is in little things, so it is in big ones. At the convention of the art-education movement in Weimar, which dealt with German language and literature from October 9 to 11, 1903, laymen were in attendance along with thirty-four educational bureaucrats. One of the nonteachers, Dr. Heinrich Hart, clarified his status at the beginning of his address.

When my friend, Caesar Flaischgen, asked me to speak about the choice of literature for schools at the art-education conference, I was seized by a slight fear. How could I possibly presume to speak about educational matters! I have never—I must admit to my shame—stood at the lectern, and any educational talent I possess barely suffices to educate myself. (*Laughter.*) I intended to decline the invitation at once, when it occurred to me that I have indeed had a relationship to schools in one respect, and how would it be if I presented myself to the gathering of distinguished art educators not as a colleague, but as a pupil. . . .

The three combined words, "Education, School, Poetry," do not resound with inspiring harmony in my poor pupil's soul. I will not go into further detail about what I suffered and endured during the years that I was taught, infused with, and force-fed poetry. "I don't want your pity." I will only say, if you will pardon me this, that for a time I placed poetry in the same category as cod-liver oil and medicine.[75]

With this bitter pill for educational bureaucrats, the pupil himself speaks up. But what would have been a scandal in the discourse network of 1800 produces only hearty laughter among the art educators. The mythic pupil can say that medicine is the shadow side of pedagogy. He can say that he is neither educated nor an educator, simply because the highest alphabetization (reading the Poets) never reached him. Instead, Dr. Hart became (as he is listed in the program of speakers) a "writer." After Nietzsche, the career path of makers of words presupposes not being able to read. Anyone who "still has nightmares"[76] about reading Horace in school is a walking archive of childhood fears, perfectly suited to the sciences of nonsense. "The analysis of material from pupils," reads one questionnaire that queried prominent people concerning their *years as pupils*, "is a necessity that cannot be sufficiently stressed."[77] And observe: the most bitter and derisive items in this material come from "poets and writers."[78] Indeed, among people who could speak it was considered fashionable in 1912 "to view the tragedies of youth and school children, which had been portrayed in a few fine stories of the period, as something that was almost obvious and obligatory."[79]

That is only logical in a discourse network that needs someone for the impossible role of the writing analphabet. Writers are thus commissioned to simulate the pupil or the madman. Children who in searching for lost pencils fail to recognize their own hands are no less delirious than children whose reading of Horace still gives them nightmares decades later. When the art-education convention puts writers on the program in order to draw all their plans for reform from the "poor pupil's soul," the simulacrum of madness receives semi-official recognition. Ellen Key's "school of the future," in which first of all the analphabets "pronounce their judgment" on teachers and lesson plans found its beginning.[80]

But the tragically isolated Poet is the most cherished illusion of interpreters. One overlooks the system-immanent function of literature. Texts written to order for a new pedagogy were at best credited as portrayals of the "suffering imposed by the social order."

The hero of Meyrink's *Golem* "repeats" words so often and so "spasmodically, that they suddenly appear nakedly as meaningless, frightening sounds from a barbaric, prehistorical past"—above all, the word *b-o-o-k*. His grand plan is to "take on the alphabet in the primer in reverse order from *Z* to *A*, in order finally to arrive at the spot where [he] began to learn in school."[81] *A* as in ape—that is the null point at which Kafka's "A

Report to an Academy" begins. The leap out of a speechless and analphabetic ape-truth to the alphabetization of the report itself becomes the
subject of a story that links the acquisition of language with a tootling
gramophone and alcoholism.[82] It is a force-feeding like Hart's, by whose
analysis future academies and culturization campaigns will profit.

Literary texts of 1900 record how an alphabetic culture is to be defined from an analphabetic outside. Brigge's notebooks (to keep to the
story) are also written with the child's vanished pencil. "The infinite reality" of being a child, in which it is certain "that it would never end," determines every sentence on reading and writing. Brigge never stops writing down the endlessness of agraphia and alexia.

It is well simply to recognize certain things that will never change, without de-
ploring the facts or even judging them. Thus it became clear to me that I never
was a real reader. In childhood I considered reading a profession one would take
upon oneself, later some time, when all the professions came along, one after the
other. . . .
    Until the beginning of such changes I postponed reading too. One would then
treat books as one treated friends, there would be time for them, a definite time
that would pass regularly, complaisantly, just so much of it as happened to suit
one. . . . But that one's hair should become untidy and dishevelled, as if one had
been lying on it, that one should get burning ears and hands as cold as metal, that
a long candle beside one should burn right down into its holder, that, thank God,
would then be entirely excluded. . . .
    Of what I so often felt later, I now somehow had a premonition: that one had
no right to open a book at all, unless one pledged oneself to read them all. With
every line one broke off a bit of the world. Before books it was intact and perhaps
it would be again after them. But how could I, who was unable to read, cope with
them all?[83]

If being alphabetized means being able to translate immeasurable
heaps of letters and books into the miniature model of meaning, then it is
and remains a norm of the others, beyond Brigge as only the Beyond can
be. A historical system departs from the earth to disintegrate in beauty
and nothingness.[84] In this world, to which Brigge remains true, there are
only bodies, burning ears, and cold hands. These bodies can either not
read at all or, when they sit in the Bibliothèque nationale, are completely
strange bodies, without eyes and ears and with "the hair of someone
sleeping." Everything looks, then, as if professional readers were more
analphabetic than a child, who at least still believes in the illusion of
being able to read in the future. Instead, those who frequent the library—
who for the first time in the history of German writing are described from
the outside—have indeed learned something, but at the price of their disappearance. "One is not aware of them. They are in the books."[85]

In 1799 the warning was issued to undertake all reading "in the work-
place of our inner selves" and "not to forget ourselves" over what we are

reading. Otherwise we would "lose our presence of mind and become insane through distraction." [86] In 1910 it makes no difference whether one can read or not: madness overtakes one anyway. Because there is no synthetic function capable of selecting among the enumerable masses of data with the eventual aim of establishing meaning, books continue to pile up beyond any possible comprehension. According to Brigge, reading would only be possible and permissible if it could accommodate all books. Thus in reading an impossible exhaustion takes the place of transcendental apperception.

In 1803 one could assure that the healthy mind "seeks to establish unity everywhere in the manifold, and processes all given material according to its organization. In the consciousness of self it winds the immeasurable thread of time into a ball, reproduces dead centuries, and gathers the infinitely extended limbs of space, mountain ranges, forests, and the stars cast over the firmament into the miniature portrait of an idea." [87] The poetic screenplays of 1800 and their ability to gather up space and time could not be more beautifully described. Space shrank for cultured writers/readers until the world fit into the box of the *New Melusine*, or the whole earth, in a poetic dream of flight, "looked only like a golden bowl with the finest engraving." Time shrank for cultured writers/ readers until "the longest stories" were "pulled together in short, brilliant minutes," [88] or the immeasurable threads of one's own life came together into the yarn of a briefly leafed-through book of Provençal poetry. Such miracles become impossible under the law of exhaustion. Certainly technical devices are extraordinarily capable of expanding or contracting time and space. But a device is not a mind and establishes no unity in whatever dispersion it encounters. It is of no help to people. In their bodily forgetfulness, agraphia, and alexia, they can only work through serial data (to borrow once more the apt language of programmers) in real-time analysis.

The twenty-four hours in the life of Leopold Bloom undergo a real-time analysis. Real-time analysis threatens to become *la recherche du temps perdu*. Only a real-time analysis can "achieve" (in the Rilkean sense) childhood. But the rule of remembering, repeating, and working through does not govern only biographies and psychoanalyses. Without "choice or refusal," [89] Brigge's notebooks also present what every hermeneutics has avoided: power. "For whatever of torment and horror has happened on places of execution, in torture-chambers, madhouses, operating theatres, under the vaults of bridges in late autumn: all this has a tough imperishability, all this subsists in its own right . . . and clings to its own frightful reality. People would like to be allowed to forget much of this; sleep gently files over such grooves in their brains." But just as "dreams . . . trace the designs again,"[90] so do the *Notebooks*. That is, they intentionally refuse to provide a miniature portrait, as Reil quite rightly characterized it, in the spirit of German classicism; rather, they provide real-time analysis of engrams. It is a procedure as "fateful" as only pre-Gutenberg technologies could be. For what moved and delighted a certain insane king of France in passion plays was "that they continually added to and extended themselves, growing to tens of thousands of verses, so that ultimately the time in them was the actual time; somewhat as if one were to make a globe on the scale of the earth."[91]

A globe on the scale 1 : 1; Brigge could erect no finer monument to commemorate his descriptive procedure. He only needs to take care that nothing exceptional creeps into the process, even something as minimal as the act of writing itself. Yet as a twenty-eight-year-old, when he reads Baudelaire or the book of Job, Brigge is still not completely alphabetized. Because "an alphabetic individual thinks only in particulars,"[92] his dealings with texts remain a Passion Mystery.

There it lies before me in my own handwriting, what I have prayed, evening after evening. I transcribed it from the books in which I found it, so that it might be very near me, sprung from my hand like something of my own. And now I want to write it once again, kneeling here before my table I want to write it; for in this way I have it longer than when I read it, and every word is sustained and has time to die away.[93]

Thus Brigge, in his personal book, despite Gutenberg and Anselmus, writes as if he were a simple monk-copyist. But if reading is choice and refusal, then models of texts, too, can only be permitted on the scale of 1 : 1. Writing becomes, rather than miniatures of meaning, an exhaustion that endlessly refuses to end. For if Brigge has transcribed the passages (which of course are not disfigured with authorial names) from Baudelaire and Job, the effect is still as if he had never done it. He must, he intends to, "write it once again," so that each word can function in the real time of its being written down. "Transcribing is superior to reading and spelling in that the motoric representation of writing is immediately linked to the sensory representation of writing and to the motoric representation of language."[94] And so it goes. The *Notebooks* actually contain two pages that Brigge transcribes from his transcription, that the publisher Rilke transcribes from this transcription of a transcription, and that the printing press transcribes countless times (throughout which Baudelaire's French of course remains untranslated).

"How do we raise the level of performance in German?," asked an art educator the year the *Notebooks* appeared. His answer: through "transcription exercises,"[95] the subroutine that psychophysics had so rigorously isolated. Under the pressure of competition from other media, writing once again became what it had been before universal alphabetiza-tion—a professional specialty—while ceasing to be indivisibly and auto-matically coupled with reading. Because writing requires manual craft, transcription replaced reading among the practitioners of high literature. Dealing with texts thus became the *One Way Street* at whose junction Benjamin (a pupil of art-education) recognized the despotic traffic sign of the signifier. His observation that "the reader follows the movement of his ego in the free space of revery," whereas "the transcriber" lets this movement be "commanded"[96] could have been transcribed from the *Notebooks*.

The discourse network of 1900 rescinds the freedom of the writing imagination. No one who picks up a pen, from a child in school to a writer, is better positioned than the professional typists who with each "hand movement . . . follow the instructions *literally*, that is, *do nothing more* than what they stipulate."[97] There is a method to exercises in writ-ing and transcribing. The age of engineers demands technically exact re-productions of technical processes.

Brigge's father had stipulated in his will that the doctors should per-form a perforation of his heart. The son explains why, rather than avoid-ing such a horrible sight, he reproduced it as a literary witness. "No, no, nothing in the world can one imagine beforehand, not the least thing. Everything is made up of so many unique particulars that cannot be fore-seen. In imagination one passes over them and does not notice that they are lacking, hasty as one is. But the realities are slow and indescribably detailed."[98] The sentences practice the insight they contain. They them-selves owe nothing to imagination, but are rather transcriptions of art-pedagogical method. Heinrich Scharrelmann had pointed to a fundamen-tal unimaginability years before Brigge.

It is unbelievable how little we adults see, how inexactly we observe things around us. . . . How many bicycles the city dweller sees rush by every day. If one is not the owner of a bicycle, who knows all its parts very well, one might try to sit down and draw it. The most incredible sketches would be produced, because memory fails the drawer and he doesn't know where the pedals are attached, whether the chain is linked to the front or back wheel, where the seat is, and so forth. One need only attempt to make a mental sketch of any everyday object to be struck by the poverty and inexactness of our notion of that object.[99]

One need only read the perforation of the heart and the bicycle in paral-lel, as examples of literary and pedagogical practice, to determine that they are not examples at all. Writing circa 1900 necessarily addresses operations and apparatuses as the only two approaches to the real. In fact, there can be no miniature portraits of the real, as they were cher-ished by inwardness and produced by the imagination. Circumstances that "are composed of many individual details" escape the grasp of any hermeneutics; they have to be scored up and denumerated. The reason is simple: there are only constructed facts or circumstances. Programs, diagrams, and numbers exist in order to encode the real. Thus the philosopher Alain, continuing in the line of Scharrelmann and Brigge, summed up all the criticism of the poetics of Kant and Hegel in the terse observation that one cannot count the columns of an imagined Pantheon.[100]

The fundamental unimaginability of the real calls for autopsies in which its discrete elements are specified one after another. That is what Brigge does in Paris when (avoiding the Pantheon) he makes torn-down houses, blind newspaper sellers, hospital waiting rooms, and moribund patients the subject of a writing that proceeds exhaustively, like technological media. Poets who hate the approximate belong in a culture of doctors and engineers. Torn-down houses still count in technology, as do hopeless cases in medicine. The writer takes pleasure in making use of discarded material—and therefore broken-down walls take the place of the Hall of Fame. Engineers and doctors make particular things that function; Brigge's writing does the reverse when it "makes" the accidental and singular newspaper seller "the way one makes a dead man."[101] It changes nothing in the logic of construction.

It changes nothing, not even if the construction seems to be imaginary. Before Scharrelmann and thus long before Brigge, Daniel Paul Schreber, "in the unending monotony of my dreary life," trained himself in a kind of "drawing" that consisted in establishing representations, without pencil and paper, of landscapes and women's breasts "in such surprising faithfulness and true color" that Schreber himself and the divine rays "have almost the exact impression of the landscapes I want to see again as if they were actually there." The solitary man at Sonnenstein thus imagined, but with such precision that the imagination could go hand in hand with physiology. "In the same way as rays throw on to my nerves pictures they would like to see . . . I too can in turn produce pictures for the rays which I want them to see."[102] Nothing distinguishes nerve rays thus impressed from the angel to whom Rilke, beginning with the *Duino Elegies*, showed the simplicities and details of the earth.

But those who have no dealings with nerves or angels are forced to develop techniques of material reproduction. In contrast to the inexactness that adults betray in drawing bicycles, Scharrelmann's pupils practice gestural simulation.

When I next asked, "How does the knife sharpener work?," many children were at once prepared to imitate the movements of the sharpener. They imitated not only the pumping of the foot on the pedal and the hands holding the knife, but they also mimicked the bent back, the head thrust forward, the shifting glances to check the edge, brushing off dust, and so on, so naturalistically, carefully, and completely that I was astounded at the accuracy and certainty of the children's ability to observe. I myself have sometimes learned to observe carefully some adult action by first watching children imitate it.[103]

This, too, is a method for raising the level of achievement in German. Instead of writing interpretations and thoughtful essays, the pupils engage in a bodily reproduction of technical processes, a reproduction that teaches observation and description. One need only trade the knife sharpener for an epileptic (which is more appropriate for the literary use of discarded material), and one has "The Portrayal of the So-Called Jerk-Tic by Rainer Maria Rilke." As a psychiatrist showed in a study with that title, the *Notebooks* provide a clinically exact picture of the illness, completely in keeping with the conception of it in contemporary medical science.[104] It is not a question of the so-called jerk-tic's portrayal by Rainer Maria Rilke, however, but of its simulation by Malte Laurids Brigge: in the description, Brigge follows his mad subject, takes on his anxieties and gestures, and only thus encounters something real that would remain closed to empathy or hermeneutics. When a man with jerk-tic and another man who simulates him as naturalistically, carefully, and completely as Scharrelmann's class simulated the knife sharpener, when these two walk down the Boulevard Saint-Michel, one after the other, then an allegory walks through Paris: the writer as simulator of madness.

The Notebooks of Malte Laurids Brigge could perhaps better be called *Memoirs of My Simulations of Nervous Illness.* Just as the rule of exhaustion that governs all Brigge's descriptions returns in the writing itself, so also does the procedure of simulation. A key passage shows that Brigge's hands as well as his feet follow the tracks of madness. After he has noted how all prearranged meanings vanish at the moment of death and how a tumor in the brain becomes the sun of a new world, there is a note that describes his own note taking. "For a while yet I can write all this down and express it. But there will come a day when my hand will be far from me, and when I bid it write, it will write words I do not mean. The time of that other interpretation will dawn, when not one word will remain upon another, and all meaning will dissolve like clouds and fall down like rain."[105]

Anyone who, as occult medium, predicts the end of hermeneutics and the victory of occult media, has a right not to be subjected to hermeneutics. No commentary, then, only further evidence for "the time of that other interpretation."

In the century of the child, there was a reform movement for free essay writing. The free essay was the opposite practice of the rereading that classical-romantic times established as the rule of the German essay—

whether as interpretation that presented another reading of the work or as the thoughtful essay that promoted thoughtful, writing hands. In the free essay, that the pupil does not "reread" anything, that "his pencil flies across the table," is "just right." [106] "To produce means to give the creative power free reign over the treasure chests of our brains." [107] The pupils are thus permitted to write what is inscribed in their brains, not what they believe their teacher believes they ought to be thinking. This freedom is "not at all easy" to bring about: "They always insist they aren't allowed to write 'that kind of thing.'" [108] The reason: for a century the pedagogic essay stood under the sign or title "Our School Essay as Disguised Dime Novelist." Pupils have "had eight years of instruction in essay writing, have written 'good' essays every week; every sentence has been scrutinized, filed down, and propped up." They have "had to analyze characters in *William Tell* and write reports about deep-sea fauna." Because a logic of the signified stood over the whole process, the essay "was charged with the task of unifying all preceding exercises (orthographic, grammatical, etc.) into a whole." [109]

The free essay, by contrast, uncouples the subroutines whose imaginary unity has been called German. It is pure writing: writing minus grammar, orthography, and the norm of the high idiom. But that can only occur when rereading is no longer practiced, by teachers as well as pupils, when essays no longer return censored in red ink. The self-imposed censorship that forbids writing "that kind of thing" is the "feed forward" command of a discourse carried on with the Other. A number of uncounted voices circa 1900 demanded an end to the red marks in the essay's margin, [110] until an elementary school teacher in Leipzig came out with a monograph on the subject. Paul Georg Münch's polemic *Around the Red Inkwell* corrects essay corrections with probably the best-proven means that psychophysics can muster against the presumptions of sense. "These strange distorted pictures between the lines! These ugly red checks, needles, squiggles, claws, thorns, snakes . . . ! And everything conscientiously registered once more on the margin! Doesn't this edge really look like the ragged flag of Chinese marauders? Turn the essay upside down and just let the image of burn marks and black ink sink in: you'd think you were in the company of the mummies of tattooed south-sea islanders!" [111] A class of signs breaks apart under ethnological observation until nothing remains but a naked, Nietzschean power of inscription. Münch uses turning upside down (the technique Ebbinghaus and Morgenstern recommended for newspapers and the contents of images) [112] to urge his colleagues in the educational bureaucracy to forget their forebear Lindhorst and to read, not the essays, but their own corrections as squiggles and ink marks.

Teachers without red ink necessarily become experimenters, and free-essay-writing pupils become their subjects. "The nature of pedagogical problems" is identical to "the question of the localization of mental operations in the brain. In both cases experiments are required."[113] If Ziehen's association tests with school children in Jena had the theoretical effect of freeing psychology "from the unnatural, but until now unshaken patronage of logic," then the free essay had the effect, which puzzled Ziehen, of being able "to construct in a practical way—*sit venia verbo*—instruction in association."[114] It provides "immensely important documentation in empirical pedagogy" and gives "the scientists" among the teaching staff "findings in experimental psychology."[115] Thus one should not be taken in by the attribute of freedom. What is at stake when pupils free associate on topics of their own choosing has nothing to do with the autonomous child's mind of 1800. What applied, rather, was the fundamental psychoanalytic rule that an uncontrolled flow of speech liberates the fatality of the unconscious. Experimental psychology is nothing without evidence, data—which is why uncorrected essays provide an opportunity for teachers to trade in their obsolete red ink for a more scientific variety of marker, one that can be used in statistical tests and evaluations of *The Evidence of Hearsay in Children*.[116] Literary bohemians, however, who could not be suspected of favoring disciplinary measures, supported these methods. For Peter Hille, any adults who perpetuate the irresponsible "old-style education" have "no business with children." Their new privilege was to "oversee this beautiful, fresh young world."[117]

There is no such thing as a document that documents nothing but its author. Automatic writing, psychoanalytic association, the free essay—all provide evidence of powers that reduce the writer to a medium. Even impressionistic essay exercises necessarily issue in dictation.

I conduct impressionistic exercises daily with my nine- and ten-year-olds. I have six or eight of them come up to the classroom windows with pencil and paper and have them observe things in their environment in the natural light, rather than in the lighting of the classroom, and then write about what they see. They are to name the simplest things on the street and should see how the moment brings these things together. Their thoughts can then be embodied in words without constraint, their senses can dictate their experiences into writing without delay, and this proceeds without any thought being given as to whether the sentences might yield a "good" essay or not.[118]

In Münch's experiment, then, the senses dictate, and these in turn take dictation from whatever occurs on the street. It is no accident that his book ends with an emphatic reference to the new *Exercise-Program for the Infantry*, which appeared in 1906 and also programmed the immediacy of stimulus and response.[119] Whether it is a pencil or rifle, then, the hands that hold it are unencumbered by an ego (or, in the end, a teacher) and its intentions. Consequences other than depersonalization would contradict a discursive rule that stipulates "the avoidance of orthography, punctuation, as well as words and phrases not based in sensation" [120] and that applies to children as well as the insane. The free essay in German was an experiment in coupling the two impossible sentences, *I am writing* and *I am delirious*.

This linkage is quite clear in the experiment set up by Oskar Ostermai, a teacher in Dresden. One year before Brigge, the serious *Journal of German Instruction* reported unheard-of news to its readers.

I had a seventh form. The children were used to writing free essays on their experiences and did this with enthusiasm and joy. One day a child arrived at nine o'clock instead of at eight. The child had a letter from his father, which stated that the child had become sick the previous evening, but had insisted that he be allowed to go to school at nine o'clock at least so that he could write his essay. And what did the child want to write? "How I got a fever last night." At ten o'clock the child had to return home and was then absent for several days. [121]

Thus, a child with a fever writes how he got the fever. The senses that dictate their data into writing without delay are delirious. But only a father still calls the delirium an illness; the child and the teacher take it as a necessary and sufficient ground for essays in which the act of writing guarantees what is written. For a single school hour the child appears out of the indistinguishable ground of all media and articulates this ground, before it again becomes all powerful. Hall's *A Study of Fears* continues its experimental course, and madness circa 1900 radically dissolves its old affinity with illness and finds a place far from pathology—in discourse itself. "There will come a day when my hand will be far from me, and when I bid it write, it will write words I do not mean. The time of that other interpretation will dawn, when not one word will remain upon another, and all meaning will dissolve like clouds and fall down like rain."

Writers appear in the place of the feverish child that writes down his fever. At twenty-eight Brigge is still unable to understand how he "managed wholly to return from the world" of his childhood, speechless fevers. [122] Because he does not understand, the fever's recurrence in the insane asylum is no reason to wait for the doctor in the next room. "Like one who hears a glorious language and feverishly conceives plans to write, to create in it," [123] Brigge leaves and runs to his desk. There he notes down what fever is, freed from the tutelage of logic and the high idiom— namely, not fever at all, not a nosological entity, but "the Big Thing." Only words from a child's language could adequately represent the Thing in (to use the jargon of German teachers) "form and content."

Brigge writes free essays. His *Notebooks* do not parallel the art-education movement in the history of ideas; they carry out that movement's program. Informed contemporaries, such as the experimental psychologist Ernst Meumann, saw that the free essay provoked "the outgrowth of expressionism and futurism" as well as of "modern lyric poetry." Indeed, it taught "future generations . . . linguistic confusion and undisciplined thinking." [124] Germanists, however, when confronted with a meaning that falls like rain, have little inkling of "the other interpretation." They have searched meticulously for the artistic symmetries, arrangements, and unifying laws in Brigge's serial notes and have attempted to weaken the suspicion of Angelloz that such things don't exist. One must suspend the interpretive disposition in writing a free essay, or else the essay will become "memorandum stuff, slogan provisions, dressings for skeletal intentions." [125] Like Münch's pupils, Brigge notes the simplest occurrences with the simplest aleatory method: "how the moment brings these things together."

When Rilke, with Brigge, opts for writing and against psychoanalysis, he sounds like Münch: "Piety keeps me from allowing this intrusion, this great cleaning and straightening up that life does not do—from this correction of a written page of life, which I imagine as thoroughly marked with red improvements—a foolish image and certainly a completely false one." [126] Foolish images do demonstrate something, then—namely, that literature circa 1900 joined the struggle around the red inkwell. Rilke's image is false only in its judgment of a science that would do as little to restore proper form and meaning to errors in language as would literature, and would instead use them to trace unconscious signifiers. In any case, Rilke's renunciation of psychoanalysis makes clear that *The Notebooks of Malte Laurids Brigge* indeed *are* the written page of life in uncorrected rough form.

Georg Heym, writer and doctoral candidate at the University of Würzburg, received the following response from one of its committees: "The law and political science faculty has decided not to accept the work submitted by you in its present form, in that it does not meet the faculty's requirements. According to the report, the work contains so many typographical errors and deficiencies in sentence structure that it obviously has not been proofread after having been typed." [127] This officially determines what is not a work and who is not an author. In the discourse network of 1800, to which faculties continue to belong, rereading established a corpus out of heaps of paper and an imaginary body called the author out of people. But someone like Carl Einstein's Bebuquin, who prays for the sickness and dissociation of his limbs, in order to attain another kind of writing through "metamorphosis" or "dissolution," [128] someone like Brigge or Heym, who deliver uncorrected pages, whose hands write independently of the ego, functions differently. Authors are not needed for utilizing discarded psychophysical nonsense. Arbitrary individual cases are necessary and sufficient; they count as discarded material to be utilized. The pencil in the woman's hands, which do not use it at all, signals something quite simple to Brigge the observer: he, the writer, is one of those whom his notebooks so exhaustively record—"refuse" or "husks of humanity that fate has spewed out." [129]

Intransitive writing, practiced by writers as well as children, whom the discourse network of 1900 "places side by side," [130] is an anonymous and arbitrary function. Now that children no longer perform the brilliant feats brought about by premature alphabetization, in which letters immediately became hallucinations, the recruitment of well-known authors no longer takes place. Arbitrary individual cases that for one reason or another have acquired paper (perhaps given to them outright by members of the art-education movement) just gather aleatory data. "If I give three eight- or nine-year-old boys a few cents for spending money and send them to the fair in Leipzig, then two of the three will certainly buy themselves a notebook. And it doesn't matter how tempting . . . the roller coaster or Turkish gingerbread are: two of the three will still buy notebooks!" [131] So much for the initial situation from the point of view of the experimenter. Now for the experimental confirmation from the point of view of the experimental subject.

If I had a notebook at hand, or if there were any other opportunity, I would write down what occurs to me. Something is always occurring to me. So I incur a major occurrence, which I'd like to record with incurred innocence.

It's not all too hot; blue floods through the sky, humid and blown up from the coast; each house is next to roses, some are completely sunk in them. I want to buy a book and a pencil; I want to write down as much as possible now, so that it won't all flow away. I lived for so many years, and it has all sunk. When I began, did I still have it? I no longer know.

But if all this is possible—has even no more than a semblance of possibility—then surely, for all the world's sake, something must happen. The first comer, he who has had this disturbing thought, must begin to do some of the things that have been neglected; even if he is just anybody, by no means the most suitable person: there is no one else at hand. This young, insignificant foreigner, Brigge, will have to sit down in his room five flights up and write, day and night: yes, he will have to write; that is how it will end. [132]

It is a precarious and arbitrary practice, the writing of these interchangeable individual cases. But at least it realizes, materially, manifestly, the impossible sentence *I am writing*. Otto Erich Hartleben, civil servant, candidate for the high court, and subsequently a writer, first demonstrated that "the activity of the court apprentice is certainly one of the most noble of all human activities, because it can never be replaced or rendered superfluous by any machine. . . . The court apprentice effortlessly defies the inventors of the cheapest and best typewriters. As little as a typewriter might cost, he costs even less: he is gratis." From this, it follows that Hartleben's period of candidacy fulfilled a childhood dream:

Writing! To be able to write, perhaps to become a real writer. This wish had essentially been fulfilled. I was allowed to write, I could write, indeed I had to write. And if for the time being I was not putting my own thoughts and figures down on paper, but mostly dictated reports, I could at least console myself with the thought that not everything could happen at once. In any case: I had attained what was manifest, material, in my wish: I was writing.[133]

Writing is the *acte gratuit* itself. It makes neither an author famous nor a reader happy, because the act of writing is nothing beyond its materiality. The peculiar people who practice this act simply replace writing machines. Because technologies and pathologies are convertible circa 1900, the bachelor machines known as writers have to be pretty much crazy in order to have any pleasure in the *acte gratuit*. No one promises them a silver taler or the daughter of a Lindhorst, but only the mystical union of writing and delirium.

The beginning of writing will thus, to follow Brigge's lead, always be its end. What Ball's Laurentius Tenderenda "would like to record with incurred innocence" slips out of others' hands. Karl Tubutsch, the hero of a novella by Ehrenstein, watches two flies drown in his inkwell, in consequence trades his pen (lacking a typewriter) for a pencil, and finally does not write at all.[134] It is not necessary, then, for one's own black heart to drown first in the inkwell, as with Nietzky; even two dead flies can stop an act as precarious and delirious as writing. "What keeps me from making an end to everything, from finding eternal rest in some lake and inkwell or solving the question What God gone mad or demon does the inkwell belong to, the one in which we live and die? and To whom in turn does this God gone mad belong?"[135]

Poetic works of 1800 belonged in the Kingdom of God. An Absolute Spirit, in which no member was sober, consumed all authors and works at the end of their earthly cycles. The authors turned in their civic names at the chalice of this realm of spirits, but only in order to attain the infinity of interpretation and the immortality of meaning.

A completely different God stands over the discourse network of 1900 and its inkwells. He has gone mad. In him the simulators of madness have their master. When the insane God drinks, it is not in order to sublate fantasies in a threefold sense. Where in 1800 there was a function of philosophical consumption, one hundred years later there is bare annihilation. Writers who drown in the inkwell of the insane God do not achieve the immortality of an author's name; they simply replace anonymous and paradoxical analphabets who are capable of writing down a whole discourse network from the outside. For that reason there are no authors and works, but only writers and writings.

Titles like *The Notebooks of Malte Laurids Brigge* are not approximations. They designate a denumerable collection of letters in their materiality and an arbitrary writer—"this young, insignificant foreigner, Brigge"—in his singularity. In Ehrenstein's story, one sees the same thing. The first sentence is: "My name is Tubutsch, Karl Tubutsch. I mention that only because I possess very little other than my name." And the last is: "But I possess nothing, nothing at all that could make me glad in my heart of hearts. I possess nothing except as mentioned—my name is Tubutsch, Karl Tubutsch." [136]

Brigge, Tubutsch, Rönne, Pameelen—the names do not vanish in a *Phenomenology of the Spirit*, which is Spirit itself and therefore nameless. But the fact that these names remain behind demonstrates only their nullity. All the bare last names paraphrase Nietzsche's phrase that there is as little to makers of words as to words. An insane God rules over makers of words, and this God, lacking omnipotence, is ruled by other powers. It is not hard to guess their names. The fact that after the fly accident someone recommends to Tubutsch that he buy a typewriter reduces the demonology of the inkwell to the nothingness it is under technical-physiological conditions. These other powers have no need for literature. Technology and physiology survive without the Interpretation of the Poet, which in the discourse network of 1800 was created by chairs in philosophy. After the toasts between Goethe and Hegel became obsolete, there was no longer an address at the university for anything that makers of words produced. Having fallen to the third and last place of the discourse network, literature became the debris it described.

In 1900 there is no universal educational bureaucrat to legitimize poetic works, because they legitimize the bureaucrat. The practice-oriented educational bureaucrats became experimenters and conducted media transpositions, not interpretations, with literary texts.[137] The philosophy professors left texts to the professors of literature, who had become one type of media professional among others.[138] Where the discourse network of 1800 enthroned Man or the Bureaucrat as the king of all knowledge, there was left a gaping hole. Therefore writers could only simulate children and the insane, the subjects of psychophysics; apart from simulation, there was the reality, the act, of becoming a functionary. "They were given the choice of becoming kings or king's messengers. Like children, they all wanted to be messengers. Therefore there are nothing but messengers; they race through the world and, because there are no kings, call out their messages, which have become meaningless in the meantime, to each other. They would gladly quit this miserable existence, but don't dare to because of their oath of office." [139]

Such is the comment, still nicely metaphorical, of the bureaucrat Kafka on the professional position of writers once the king's position has been done away with. The same phenomenon was described with deadly seriousness by a technical illustrator who entered the Silesian insane asylum, Troppau. The conspiracy described in minute detail by Anton Wenzel Gross operates without any central, commanding figure. All it takes to drive him insane is a group composed of "supposed mailmen, court clerks, policemen, guards," and, above all, "lithographers, book printers, typesetters, die makers, stamp cutters, chemists, pharmacists, technicians." [140] They are all discursive functionaries, then, with the technical competence to block channels of information or postal contacts at crucial points, or, in the guise of professional benevolence, to falsify documents and reports that would have rehabilitated Gross. As such they are identical to the mindless beings who, with mechanical precision, carried out the task of driving a bureaucrat by the name of Schreber out of his mind. The discourse network at Sonnenstein also stored only the falsified nonsense that other and equally subaltern nerve messengers shouted into Schreber's ears.

Man or the Bureaucrat was the universal memory of all the products of the mind, but discursive functionaries constitute a disparate group with particular and circumscribed responsibilities. None stores everything, but together they obliterate the monopoly on books and meaning that had been incorporated under the name of Spirit. Whether they are called messengers by Kafka, letter carriers by Gross, or writing powers by Schreber—a physiologist's axiom applies to them all.

In physiology the distinction of partial memories is a familiar truth; but in psychology the method of "faculties" has so long forced the recognition of memory as an entity that the existence of partial memories has been wholly ignored, or, at the most, regarded as anomalous. It is time that this misconception was done away with, and that the fact of special, or, as some authors prefer, *local* memories, was clearly recognized. This last term we accept willingly on the condition that it is interpreted as a disseminated localization. . . . The memory has often been compared to a store-house where every fact is preserved in its proper place. If this metaphor is to be retained, it must be presented in a more active form; we may compare each particular memory, for instance, with a contingent of clerks charged with a special and exclusive service. Any one of these departments might be abolished without serious detriment to the rest of the work. [141]

Dispersed localization, operated by bureaucrats who can be dismissed and who are thus more like functionaries—this is a brain physiology that also describes the factual discursive arrangements of 1900. If the faculty of all faculties, the Mind or Spirit, does not exist, then there are only the specialized functions of specified carriers of information. For this reason so many of Kafka's texts deal with the materiality of channels of information: the channels bleed into one another ("My Neighbor"); they function with dead or delay times ("An Imperial Message"); they are not thoroughly interconnected (*The Castle*); and whatever they transmit has no meaning beyond the statement that they exist ("Before the Law").

But the fact that messages become meaningless when there is no king at the origin and destination of discourses is only one, albeit thoroughly described, side of the contemporary discourse network. Technology makes it possible for the first time to record single and accidental messages. It is no longer possible for a philosopher to walk in and reduce protocol sentences to categories, or spoken words to written truth. Anything expressed remains undisputed and indisputable as it is, because specialized memory functions appear for the oddest bits of speech. In *Diagnostic Studies of Association*, which the great psychiatrist Bleuler left for his assistants at Berghölzli to finish, one of the four hundred stimulus words, in exact reprise of the *Phenomenology*, is the stimulus word *dark*. And one of the sixty-five experimental subjects, a "thirty-eight-year-old idiot," actually reproduced the unforgettable protocol sentence of sense certainty. "Dark: that is now."[142] But this did not move assistant doctors Jung, Riklin, and Wehrlin to repeat the experiment twelve hours later or to show the thirty-eight-year-old idiot, with speculative finesse, the idiocy of his conception of "now." Translations into the native land of the signified are not the prerogative of functionaries, but of the Discourse of the Master. Bleuler, meanwhile, did not derive even one philosopheme from the 14,400 recorded associations, but instead wrote a preface to them in which he described the omnipotence of unconscious associations with the example of "when I, for instance, write about associations." Thus "Dark: that is now" returns once more, but in the act of writing. The idiot and the director of the experiment are in the end only the marionettes of their "bodily sensations."[143]

An entire *Phenomenology* resulted from the refutation of the sentence, "The now is night." The entire discourse network of 1900 is fed by the return of an opaque thisness. The rough material for an essay that Ostermai's pupil handed in at ten o'clock, before his bodily sensations took him back home, probably also said only, "*Fever, that is now.*" That, at least, is what the parallel passage of the simulated madman Brigge suggests: "Now it," namely the Big Thing, "had returned." None of these instances of thisness has an address; none has a meaning. Dispersed specialized or local memories call out meaningless messages to one another.

With that, however, the sheer Now, or that which incessantly ceases, is halted for the first recorded time.

Recorders that record thisnesses become thisnesses themselves. That makes every instance of archiving into a discursive event. The less purpose a discourse in the discourse network of 1900 has, the more impossible it becomes to neutralize it. It follows that incomprehensible debris, that is, literature, incessantly does not cease. (Valéry's entire poetics deals with this.) A literature that writes down thisnesses exclusively or that appears as thisness in its words and typography occupies all storage equipment and so drives out the type of poetry about which "the name 'philosophical lyric' already says enough." The fact that Schiller, "an extremely learned poet," treated themes such as *Nature* or the *Walk* as "thought-out things . . . that are accomplished through abstractions and syntheses, and thus through logical rather than real or natural processes," disqualifies him and the entire conspiracy between Poets and Thinkers.[144] The vacated regal position then can and must be filled with many particular points of the present: recorders as singular as whatever they record. Whole series of chapters in *A rebours* and *Dorian Gray* list the most priceless objects— jewels, carpets, spices. But who reads such lists? Does anyone at all?

There are two possible answers to these questions, one esoteric and the other the opposite. Both are options in the same realm. The esoteric answer says that what is stored is what is stored, whether people take note of it or not.[145] Oscar Wilde, composer of one of the longest inventories of precious objects, unabashedly traced the creation of an excellent modern poetry in England to the fact that no one read and therefore corrupted it.[146] Thus Zarathustra's maxim of doing nothing for the reader is put into practice. The journal *Pages for Art* was devoted, it announced, to "a closed and member-invited circle of readers." Such scarcity-producing techniques, which program discursive events, have, of course, excited horror and contempt in upstanding citizens. But their attacks glance off a logic against which even critical theory, in order to raise any objection at all, is for once forced to believe in the People.[147] The esoteric Hofmannsthal, for instance, based his disinterest in everything "that one usually refers to as the social question" in an unassailable nominalism. "One never encounters it as anything real: and probably no one knows what it 'really' is, neither those who are in it nor even the 'upper classes.' I have never met the People. I don't think the People exists; here, at least, there are only folks."[148]

The impossible real that dominates all recording and memory circa 1900 thus becomes a kind of pragmatic linguistics. A literature in which only particulars are written down will recognize, among its readers or nonreaders, only particular readers. The vernacular expression *folks* has no philosophical or sociological status. It is a sign for the second possible answer, for stochastic dispersion, the white noise over and against which media are what they are.

It makes little difference, then, whether literature deals with decadence or with what has sunk to the level of debris, whether it simulates aristocracy or psychosis. On the unattainable reverse side there will always be stochastic dispersion, especially in the option opposed to esotericism. With his beginnings in Prague, Rilke first adopted Wilde's posture, as when in his lecture on modern lyric poetry he thanked the German public for its notorious disinterest. Modern poetry can be because people let it be.[149] Yet Rilke personally distributed collections of his and others' poetry. "I've sent a number of copies to civic organizations and guilds, to bookstores and hospitals, etc., and have distributed *Chicory* myself in several areas. Whether they will really reach 'the people'—who knows? . . . I'm counting on chance to see that a copy here and there will arrive among the people and find its way into a solitary room."[150] This mode of distribution solves the social question in that it puts *the people* between quotation marks and establishes only individual cases. Rilke's strange wanderings through Prague seek out the "folks" that for the esoteric Hofmannsthal solely constitute the real. But "people" can no longer be sought out, because there are no longer any multipliers and hence no longer any methods for the distribution of poetry. Rilke's project avoided schools, the only institution that produces readers as such. And the hospitals and guilds he included function less as multipliers than as the letter-drops used in espionage. The writer, fallen to the level of functionary, lets his *Chicory* (as the plant name indicates) fall on the biblical stones by the side of the road. All he "counts" on is "chance." And one cannot calculate chance without using statistics. Whether literature since 1900 reaches anyone at all remains a question for empirical social research.

The only philological evidence available is the way in which impossible addresses to particular readers, or measures adopted in order *not* to reach the educated individual enter textuality. Only a mode of dealing with debris counts as a mode of distributing texts that constitute the debris of a discourse network. In this, literature opposes the classical-romantic program of proliferating Poetry.

A final word on Hoffmann and Lindhorst. Young men and feminine readers were caught in the classical-romantic manner with very finely woven nets. The well-known bureaucrat and secret Poet commissioned a judge and Poet to function as a poetic multiplier. This secondary Poet then brought a young man into the picture, who learned hermeneutic reading so perfectly that he became capable of writing Poetry. Feminine readers were then able to puzzle endlessly over which woman was the true object of the Poet's love, and young but poetic bureaucrats, faithful disciples of Anselmus, learned to read the image of Woman with sufficient hallucinatory vividness to be able to find the image again in so-called life. Nothing in this program survived the turning point of 1900. The eradication of the ambiguous name, which could designate author-individuals like Anselmus or Amadeus *and* bureaucrats like Heerbrand or Hoffmann, was enough to ensure the break. Even though Rilke scholars continue to make friends with Malte, Malte Laurids Brigge nonetheless remains the "young, insignificant foreigner, Brigge." The name as pure signifier excludes imaginary identification. Kafka's "K." and "Joseph K." allow only the kind of game that Freud played with his anonymous personnel of Emmy v. N's and Anna O.'s. Such bare and dismembered family names cannot support a continuous history of *Bildung* and thus alphabetization. Heroes that labor under agraphia or alexia can never represent the Author.

"Biography no longer counts. Names don't matter," as it was once put in the telegraphic style of 1912.[151] The name that in the discourse network of 1800 was or became "sound and smoke" ("Schall und Rauch"; *Faust*, l. 3457) was of course that of the Master—HErr. After its eradication, authors' names could fill its place, and their poetic biographies could inspire readers to write and feminine readers to love. But the despotic signifier that stands over the discourse network of 1900 orders soul murder or the twilight of mankind. Thus authors' names disappear, some into the nullity of individual cases, others into a factual anonymity. "He who knows the reader, does nothing further for the reader"—so, according to Nietzsche, he provides no information on his own spiritual history and the "probable further course of his development." Döblin the doctor, for instance, gave this psychoanalytic comment on Döblin the writer: "I have nothing to say concerning my mental development; as a psychoanalyst, I know how false any self-disclosure is. In psychic self-relation I'm a touch-me-not, and approach myself only through the distance of epic narration."[152] Rubiner, for instance, took the anthology title *Twilight of Mankind* literally and refused the publisher's traditional request for biographical information. "Ludwig Rubiner requested that no biography be included. He believes that the recounting not only of acts but also of lists of works and dates derives from a vain error of the past, that of the individualistic grand-artist. His conviction is that only anonymous, creative membership in community has any importance for the present or future."[153]

The writers who beginning in 1912 contributed to a journal with the significant title *The Loose Bird* [i.e., "a loose fellow"]—such as Max

Brod, Robert Musil, Ernst Stadler, Robert Walser, and Franz Werfel—carried the project to factual anonymity. Rubiner explains what the loose bird means:

Anonymity is the rule in this journal published by Demeter. Is it possible to conceive of a word that would give the least indication of this shake-up, of the bliss of this realized utopia? What must be made clear is that a century whose function was to give us mess tins, single-sized boots, and scores by Wagner no longer exists as a hindrance for the mind. . . . Anonymity is again the rule in a new journal: that is, after a century there is once again commitment and relation.

The day that *one person* really had the courage to think the concept of anonymity through to its end is the day that belongs to the creative period of contemporary history.[154]

The anonymity of loose birds is thus an intentional break with classical-romantic writing, a discursive event intended to make discursive events possible. In the elite space of the cult of the letter that the discourse network of 1900 left to makers of words, an earlier, widespread practice is taken up "again."[155] This "relinquishing of the author" can be psychiatrically conceptualized as depersonalization"[156] or celebrated as the creative act of "the mind"—in each case anonymity guarantees words the effects of radical foreignness. "The mind leaps into the stone-walled space of the objective. A word, a sentence is left to resound in the world."[157]

But beware: the *one person* who "really had the courage to think the concept of anonymity through to its end" could be named George. When in the last issues of *Pages for Art* "authors' names were omitted as nonessential elements," Rubiner, the upright leftist without name or biography, was alarmed. Then the one, despotic signifier, without betraying names, issued the call to World War I. Words were left to resound in the world and could not be neutralized by ordinary legal procedures.[158] And it became terrifyingly clear what "loose bird" means.

UN COUP DE DÉS JAMAIS N'ABOLIRA LE HASARD.

Artists who no more sign their works than "the earth signs the grass that grows out of it,"[159] who leave their *Chicory* on corners at workers' pubs, who issue their right- or left-wing calls to battle without the civic attributability of names, all perched on stochastic dispersion and operated in the strategic field. The discourse network of 1900 created the conditions of possibility for a genuine sociology of literature. The combined program announced in Gustave Lanson's title *Literary History and Sociology* follows the loose birds and depersonalized writing hands that have flown across paper since 1900. The fact that writers write words that an ego neither intends nor answers for makes the book a social fact. "The book, therefore, is an evolving social phenomenon. Once it is published, the author no longer possesses it; it no longer signifies the thought of the author, but the thought of the public, the thought of the publics that succeed one another in turn." [160]

Here, what divides theory from practice is that Lanson writes about thoughts, whereas for a long time signifiers had not only not signified an author's thoughts, but not signified anything at all. Whatever factual readers do with the social fact of the book can be done entirely without thinking. When a school library opened its *Poetic Treasure* to ten-year-old Hans Carossa in 1888, he "did not understand a tenth of what [he] read," but was "gripped and formed by the sound and rhythm of the poems." Orders are always more effective when nothing or no one neutralizes them. Where Reiser, Karl Friedrich von Klöden, *e tutti quanti* were offended by incomprehensible letters, Carossa was bewitched, as if by magical incantations. What offended him was just the opposite. "I was a little disturbed in the beginning by the names that stood beneath each poem and did not belong there; at least I could not imagine what such funny words as *Klopstock, Rückert, Mörike, Goethe,* or *Kopisch* had to do with that intimate music." [161]

A young man like Carossa is incapable of letting his anger issue into acts and eradicating funny names like *Goethe.* The wrath of a mature woman is required. This woman's name is Abelone and she is unable to sit by when a man named Brigge unsuspectingly reads around in *Goethe's Correspondence with a Young Girl.*

"If you would at least read aloud, bookworm," said Abelone after a little. That did not sound nearly so quarrelsome, and since I thought it high time for a reconciliation, I promptly read aloud, going right on to the end of the section, and on again to the next heading: To Bettina.

"No, not the answers," Abelone interrupted. . . . Then she laughed at the way I was looking at her.

"My goodness, Malte, how badly you've been reading."

Then I had to admit that not for one moment had my mind been on what I was doing. "I read simply to get you to interrupt me," I confessed, and grew hot and turned back the pages till I came to the title of the book. Only then did I know what it was. "And why not the answers?" I asked with curiosity.

Abelone seemed not to have heard me. She sat there in her bright dress, as though she were growing dark all over inside, as her eyes were now.

"Give it to me," she said suddenly, as if in anger, taking the book out of my hand and opening it right at the page she wanted. And then she read one of Bettina's letters.

I don't know how much of it I took in, but it was as though a solemn promise were being given me that one day I should understand it all. [162]

Lanson's law is rigorous. Books circa 1900 are social phenomena, possessed by no one, not even their original author. Historical change makes

Goethe's Correspondence with a Young Girl into the correspondence of a woman with no one—because a second woman interrupts every time Goethe, in the name of his name, puts off a loving admirer. A century later, his name is gone; Brigge has to look back at the title for it, and Abelone (like the *Notebooks* as a whole) does not even pronounce it.

Discursive manipulations are incisions. Topologically speaking, mapped onto the discourse network of 1900 a correspondence carried on during the years 1807 to 1812 is no longer equivalent to its earlier self. Proximities in a book (between love letters and replies) are destroyed, and other proximities (between love and love and love) are established. The transposition of media creates a new corpus, the corpus Bettina Brentano. "Just now, Bettina, you still *were*; I understand you. Is not the earth still warm with you, and do not the birds still leave room for your voice? The dew is different, but the stars are still the stars of your nights. Or is not the whole world of your making?"[163] The corpus of Bettina Brentano, also called the world, appears in the place of authorship and of the dominance of the work. Where the creator named Goethe is absent, space fills with the voices of birds and women. A letter writer who was quite happy to be insignificant does not become an author posthumously. But what she wrote into the wind ceases, in the absence of authorship, to cease. Precisely because it does nothing but eternally repeat a love, this writing is suddenly timely. It is timely when the eternal recurrence of opaque thisness defines all writing.

Each discourse network alters corpora of the past. The anonymous or pseudonymous women who remained at the margins of writing circa 1800 now move into the center of the system, because the authors or men in whose work they perished were perishing in turn. *Women in Eighteenth- and Nineteenth-Century German Intellectual Life*—whether in statistics or in increasing singularity, women were honored in such monographs circa 1900.[164] Goethe's mother, with her orthographically catastrophic letters, provided a model for the free essay.[165] Rahel Varnhagen is taken to be a "great power" of the classical period.[166] George dedicated a poem to the shore of the Rhein where Karoline von Günderode threw herself in. Bettina Brentano, finally, marked the limit and failure of Goethe. When intransitive writing becomes the sign of literature, unheard-of women, writers of letters, prefigure the new act of writing, whereas texts written in authorial code and thus familiar to the general world of readers become anathema. Brigge writes to Bettina Brentano:

You yourself knew the worth of your love; you recited it aloud to your greatest poet, so that he should make it human; for it was still element. But he, in writing to you, dissuaded people from it. They have all read his answers and believe them rather, because the poet is clearer to them than nature. But perhaps it will someday appear that here lay the limit of his greatness. This lover was imposed upon him, and he was not equal to her. What does it signify that he could not respond? Such love needs no response, itself contains both the mating-call and the reply; it answers its own prayers.[167]

Significantly, it was not Brigge who achieved this transvaluation of all values. By reading Goethe's answers he would have cancelled out the intransitive love once more, if he had not read so badly and for the sole purpose of being interrupted. If there is to be an *écriture féminine*, one must put an end to *alphabêtise*. Instead of progressing continuously toward his own authorship by reading Goethe, Brigge exposes his reading to an interruption that functions like the Geneva stop of film or the tachistoscope of psychophysics. When Abelone takes up the book and reads, she does not substitute good reading for bad. For the first time, she reveals (as Larisch might say) the "between" of Goethe's answers. Her listener does not gain hermeneutic understanding, only the promise that "one day" he "should understand it all."

A woman who reads out loud the unheard-of (in both senses of the word) love letters of a woman closes a circle around both sexes that excludes male hermeneutics. Because there is no author to suggest to feminine readers that his soul is the cryptic word of their love, Abelone is released from the obligation of close reading. The functions that defined the sexes in the discourse network of 1800, the productive continuation of texts and pure consumption, both fall away. Brigge is not Anselmus and Abelone is not Veronika. He hands the book to her and she does what she likes with it. One hundred years later, then, what was impossible between Bettina Brentano and Goethe occurs. "But he should have humbled himself before her in all his splendor and written what she dictated, with both hands, like John on Patmos, kneeling. There was no choice for him before this voice which 'fulfilled the angels' function.'"[168] Reading aloud in a voice that continues to amplify because it feeds back into another woman, Abelone dictates all of Brigge's future insights. She dictates what Bettina Brentano was unable to dictate under the conditions of classical discourse. The function of angels is of course to announce a death. Dictations are always the death of the author. Whereas Goethe "left empty" the "dark myth" that a woman's voice had prepared for his death,[169] the writer of the *Notebooks* assumes this myth. The era of the other interpretation means being without the honorable title of author and being subject to the dictates of others. Kneeling, as Goethe failed to, Brigge transcribes. With that, however, the promise that emanated from Abelone's incomprehensibility "is still being fulfilled."[170]

Everything written about women in the *Notebooks* is dictated by a resounding voice, at once Abelone and Bettina: that, for instance, there is nothing to say about her, "because only wrong is done in the telling"; [171] that there is no question of writing letters to her, only drafts of letters that Brigge does not send; that all attempts to rise to the level of an author by writing for young ladies (as Goethe might have put it) come to nothing against the will of women "to remove from [their] love all that was transitive"; [172] and that an intransitive love can only consist in a kind of writing that circa 1900 is incorporated as literature. What does it mean that women, according to Rilke, "for centuries now . . . have performed the whole of love; they have always played the full dialogue, both parts"? [173] As in Adelbert von Hanstein or Ellen Key, it outlines an alternative literary history consisting of unanswered and intransitive calls of love—of Bettina Brentano, Sappho, Heloïse, Gaspara Stampa, Elisa Mercoeur, Clara d'Anduze, Louise Labbé, Marceline Desbordes-Valmore, Julie Lespinasse, Marie-Anne de Clermont, and so many others. [174]

Where the divinity of the author disappeared, women who write appeared, as irreducible as they are unread. Because their texts exist, their writers cannot be confounded with the One Mother who has made someone an author (as Goethe confounded even Bettina Brentano). The discourse network of 1900 obeyed the rule of impossible exhaustion nowhere more rigorously than in the field of sexual difference. Not only are Schillerian abstractions such as "Nature" or "*The* Walk" impossible, but so are all discourses that unify the sexes. Such is the insight that Brigge receives in dictation from his impossible beloved.

Is it possible that one knows nothing of young girls, who nonetheless live? Is it possible that one says "women," "children," "boys," not guessing (despite all one's culture, not guessing) that these words have long since had no plural, but only countless singulars?

Yes, it is possible . . .

But if all this is possible—has even more than a semblance of possibility—then surely, for all the world's sake, something must happen. The first comer, he who has had this disturbing thought, must begin to do some of the things that have been neglected; even if he is just anybody, by no means the most suitable person: there is no one else at hand. This young, indifferent foreigner, Brigge, will have to sit down in his room five flights up and write, day and night: yes, he will have to write; that is how it will end. [175]

Queen's Sacrifice

La femme n'éxiste pas. Women in the discourse network of 1900 are enumerable singulars, irreducible to the One Woman or Nature. All the media and the sciences that support the network compete in a queen's sacrifice.

Technical engineers make the first move. The Hungarian chess master Rezsö Charousek, immortalized in Gustav Meyrink's *Golem*, immortalized himself through a queen's sacrifice. And Edison, as celebrated by Villiers de l'Isle-Adam, betrayed the secret of his profession. "By the way, I'd like to be introduced to that great lady 'Nature' some day, because everybody talks about her and nobody has ever seen her."[1]

The novel *Tomorrow's Eve* unfolds this aphorism across its entire plot. An English lord has fallen helplessly in love with a woman whose beauty (as if to confirm the physiologist Paul Möbius) is surpassed only by the imbecility of everything she says. The father of the phonograph then decides to furnish his despairing friend with a love object that has no troublesome aspects. He reconstructs the man's beloved electromechanically in all her corporeality, but exchanges for her mind that of the Woman. Tomorrow's Eve—as Edison's automaton is called—"replaces *an* intelligence with Intelligence itself."[2] A "*copy* of Nature" is created, which is more perfect than the original in both mind and body, and which will thus "bury" nature.[3] Not only is the flesh of the Android imperishable, but the cultural technologies built into her surpass all the possible desires of any lover. Instead of lungs she has two electrical phonographs—far ahead of the then-current state of research—which contain the most beautiful words of love ever spoken by Poets and Thinkers. Lord Ewald has only to switch from one woman to the Woman and speak to the Android, and the two phonographs will spit out, according to the method of Ebbinghaus, the vocabulary fed into them. They are capable of producing different replies to tender words of love for sixty hours, as a mechanism plays through all possible combinations of the material.

Of course Lord Ewald, to whom Edison explains everything in technical detail, is shaken at first. He cannot think of loving an automaton's limited vocabulary and repertoire of gestures, until the engineer demonstrates that love is always only this litany. Whereas women in plurality (as the case of Abelone shows) say things entirely different from what men would like to hear, the Woman pleases with each of her automatic words. Edison showed before Erdmann, then, that not only every professional language but all everyday language makes do with a modest store of signifiers, and that, finally, in matters of love as well "the great kaleidoscope of human words" is best left to automatized female media-professionals.[4]

The programmed outcome occurs; Lord Ewald falls madly in love with the One Woman or Love; and Edison is able to bring a century of "ah's," "oh's," and Olympias to a close. "This must be the first time that Science showed it could cure a man, even of love."[5] Only the spear can heal the wound it has made. The technological substitute perfects *and* liquidates all the characteristics attributed to the imaginary image of Woman by Poets and Thinkers. Spallanzani's Olympia could utter the one primal sigh; Edison's mechanical Eve talks for sixty hours. The great lady Nature whom everyone talks about and no one has seen dies of perfect simulation—*Tomorrow's Eve*, or the negative proof that Mother Nature does not exist. In consequence, only women in plurality remain after Edison's experiment, as discarded experimental material, to be sure, but nonetheless real.

After the technologists come the theoreticians. If the phantasm of Woman arose in the distribution of form and matter, spirit and nature, writing and reading, production and consumption, to the two sexes, a new discourse network cancelled the polarity. As long as women too have an "innate, ineradicable, blindly striving formative principle" that "seizes mental material,"[6] the complementarity of form and matter, man and woman, is irretrievably lost. Henceforth there are Ariadnes, Bettinas, Abelones, and thus women's discourses. To formulate "the essential difference between the sexes" in "terms such as 'productivity' and 'receptivity'" is mere "parochialism in the age of modern psychology."[7] Instead of establishing one sole difference between the sexes, modern psychology, through observation and experiment, discovers differential differences that are dependent variables or respectively applied standards.[8] Even philosophers like Otto Weininger—who used psychophysical data and measured brain weight in an attempt to develop an ideal of each sex—concede that "in actual experience neither men nor women exist," but only the mixed relationships or differential differences to which quantitative description alone does justice.[9] Weininger's less speculative colleagues did not even attempt to define ideals. The title of an essay by Ernst Simmel, "On the Psychology of Women," written long before Brigge's *Notebooks*, clearly indicates that it is impossible to speak of members of a sex except in the plural.[10]

The many women established in the discourse network of 1900 were looked at in every light save that of love. *Tomorrow's Eve* shows, after all, that the necessary *and* sufficient condition for love is the Woman as simulacrum. Empirical individual females, unburdened of the ideal, took on other roles. They could speak and write, deviating from the classical polarity of the sexes. Franziska von Reventlow does not mention her child's Name-of-the-Father anywhere in her writing. Accordingly, "we" are confronted, in an anthology entitled *Love Songs of Modern Women*, "not simply with the normal course of a woman's love life," but with "its demonic and pathological aberrations" as well.[11]

Since 1896 the word and deed of psychoanalysis have existed to accommodate these demons and pathologies. The other illness for which Freud provided a cure—obsessional neurosis, the scourge of men—is "only a dialect of the language of hysteria,"[12] or of women's language. Freud was faced with the radical new task of listening to women for thirty years and gathering everything they said under the enigmatic question "What does a woman want?" The fact that the question remained unanswered, as Freud finally confessed, not gratuitously, to a woman who had been his student,[13] is one more piece of evidence for the nonexistence of the Woman. Her one "ah!" and the one way in which it might be cured, according to a classical therapist by the name of Mephisto, disappear together. The place left vacant is filled by enumerable words, which Freud registers, as if at the bidding of Edison in Villiers's novel. Gramophonics commands that one no longer read Holy Writ, but that one listen to divine vibrations—especially since hysteria, although a complete language, has as many dialects and variations as Morgenstern's Weather-Wendish. Only by offering no response to the love of his female patients could Freud draw out the peculiar vibrations of female sexuality. This rule of nonresponsiveness established as part of psychoanalytic method what Brigge learned from Bettina and Abelone: there is no longer desire when satisfied by the other sex. When Freud once gave in to temptation and, following all the rules of transference, identified the desire of a female hysteric with a certain "Mr. K." and this "K." with himself, the cure failed. To the "complete confusion" of the beginner Freud, "the homosexual (gynecophilic) love for Mrs. K." was "the strongest unconscious current" of Dora's love life.[14]

One of Lacan's mathemes states that psychoanalytic discourse exists as the transposition of hysterical discourse. This implies that women are no longer excluded from knowledge. The nonexistent beloved of all men yields to drives and their vicissitudes, among which genital love is now only an accident—it is even taboo in the consulting room in the Berggasse. There was no Poetry to feed the enigmatic knowledge unknowingly transported by female hysterics, or to translate it into love for Freud, to his greater glory as author. Women's knowledge remained knowledge and was transmitted to women—which indeed "would ruin any chance . . . of success at a University"[15]—as the science of psychoanalysis. Marie Bonaparte, to whom Freud divulged his question about the question of women, was only one of many women students; Lou Andreas-Salomé was another (to say nothing of Freud's daughter).

"Ladies and Gentlemen"—so begins the *Introductory Lectures on Psychoanalysis*, delivered at the University of Vienna during the winter semesters from 1915 to 1917. A discourse based on women's discourse can and must, even under academic conditions, return to women. This distinguishes it from the Discourse of the University, which from 1800 on systematically excluded women so that countless bureaucrats could conduct their dance around the alma mater. Only a Great Mother could make possible the hero so necessary for subjects of the university to utter any knowledge: the author.[16] A masculine discourse on and from the Mother fed university discourse, just as hysteric discourse fed psychoanalytic discourse. In 1897, immediately before the only university reform that has ever been worthy of the name, when Arthur Kirchhoff gathered his *Judgments of Prominent University Professors, Teachers, and Writers on the Aptitude of Women for University Study*, the university subject Dr. Hajim Steinthal opined that women should not attend the university, for "in the uncertain hope of producing another Goethe, I could only regret the certainty of losing a mother-of-Goethe."[17]

Lectures to "Ladies and Gentlemen" thus eliminate, along with "Frau Rat," the necessary preconditions of authorship, even if they produce a great many women writers and analysts. Either there is an alma mater on one side and on the other young men to whom (excluding such impossible women as Günderode) an authorial God's Kingdom is revealed, or the whole interpreter's game between man and the world comes apart. If man and woman, author and mother, can no longer be added up—and the synthesis of form and matter, spirit and world, was man in a psychological sense and the world in a philosophical sense—it was because on August 18, 1908, a forty-year war for the admission of women to universities finally led to victory, even in Prussia. It then became impossible to lead male and only male students around by the nose in the Faustian manner—during the lectures they had so many Cleopatra's noses right before their eyes.

The university reform was a radical turning point in the relationship between sexuality and truth. What disappeared was "the particular character of German students" and that "unbridled student atmosphere" known from the Auerbach's Keller (in Goethe's *Faust*). For the first time, women talked about sexuality and thus "cast off the ideal that Germans fortunately still demand from a woman." [18] In other words, only Eve or the One Woman can satisfy the desires of professors and male students, whereas the plurality of women students enter a domain of discourse that, since Edison, no longer knows love. "Having both sexes in the classroom" necessarily means "putting no emphasis whatsoever on sexual difference" and "confronting the phenomena of intellectual-historical life soberly and objectively" rather than in fantasies of love. [19]

No sooner said than done. Immediately before he delivers the good news to the ladies among the ladies and gentlemen present that, anatomically, they also have a phallus, and that in dreams they have the symbols wood, paper, and books, Freud states that he owes an account of his treatment of primary sexual characteristics. [20] His response matches the principles of coeducation just cited. "As there can be no science *in usum Delphini*, there can be none for schoolgirls; and the ladies among you have made it clear by their presence in this lecture-room that they wish to be treated on an equality with men." [21]

Now that is equal rights. Nothing stands in the way of writing for women, who, first, *have* a phallus or stylus and who, second, *are* wood, paper, or books—least of all a determination of the human race that differentiated authors as engravers and women as the writing tablets of nature. If both sexes can be found on both sides of the difference, they are ready for a writing apparatus that can do without a subject and a stylus. There was a time when needles in the hands of women wove cloth, when pens in the hands of authors wove another cloth called text. But that time is past. "Machines everywhere, wherever one looks! There is a replacement for the countless tasks that man performed with an able hand, a replacement and one with such power and speed. . . . It was only to be expected that after the engineer had taken the very symbol of feminine skill out of women's hands a colleague would come up with the idea of replacing the pen as well, the symbol of masculine intellectual production, with a machine." [22]

Machines do away with polar sexual difference and its symbols. An apparatus that can replace Man or the symbol of masculine production is also accessible to women. Apart from Freud, it was Remington who "granted the female sex access to the office." [23] A writing apparatus that does not represent an erotic union of script and voice, Anselmus and Serpentina, Spirit and Nature, is made to order for coeducational purposes. The typewriter brought about (Foucault's *Order of Things* overlooks such trivialities) "a completely new order of things." [24]

Whereas the first generation of women students, described in Marianne Weber's *The Changing Image of University Women*, "consciously renounced the garland of feminine grace," another type soon appeared. This type discovered "an infinite variety of new kinds of human contact in the previously unavailable possibilities of intellectual exchange with young men: comradeship, friendship, love." Unsurprisingly, this type also "finds ready encouragement from most professors." [25] Mrs. Förster-Nietzsche was told by a professor in Zurich that "the emancipated women of the earlier period are gradually becoming more charming," and they "are highly valued as secretaries and assistants at universities and libraries." [26] She could have heard the same thing from an ex-professor of Basel who went half-blind and had to alternate between using secretaries and typewriters.

"It is better to become the amanuensis of a scholar than to do scientific work at one's own cost"—such was Ellen Key's advice to working women. [27] They found a place in the university mid-way between being slaves at the typewriter and research assistants. As the example of Felice Bauer shows, the situation was the same in office work. Employed by a firm that happened to manufacture phonographs, Kafka's fiancée was promoted from a secretarial to a managerial position in just a few years, simply because she was a good typist. Certainly "office work, whether keeping the books, handling accounts, or typing, gives a woman little opportunity to make her special, most characteristic contribution." [28] Yet despite or because of this *The Entrance of Women into Male Professions*, as one title put it, occurred in the field of text production. Women have the admirable ability "to sink to the level of mere writing machines." Whereas men, with the commendable exception of a writers' elite and the Stefan George script, continued to depend on their classically formed handwriting and thereby blindly, without resistance, left a market position unoccupied, young women "with the worst handwriting" advanced "to operating a typewriter"—as if, from the pedagogue's point of view, "one were building a church tower in thin air, having forgotten the foundation walls." [29]

That is just it. Foundation walls no longer count. Remington typewriters turned the systematic handicap of women, their insufficient education, into a historical opportunity. The sales division of the firm just cited had only to discover, in 1881, the masses of unemployed women—and out of an unprofitable innovation came the typewriter as mass-produced product.[30] A two-week intensive course with a rented typewriter made the long classical education required for the secretary Anselmus and his fundamentally male colleagues in the nineteenth century unnecessary. "The so-called 'emancipation' of women"[31] *was* their taking hold of the machine that did away with pedagogical authority over discourse. Office work, in Germany and elsewhere, became the front line in the war between the sexes because it was "not a profession protected by entrance and selective examinations."[32]

Jonathan Harker, a lawyer in an English notary office, keeps a diary while traveling to Transylvania with documents to be delivered to Count Dracula. The notebook is his salvation from the strange pleasures that overcome the Count night after night. Harker, like Brigge, Rönne, Lauda, and all the others, notes: "As I must do something or go mad, I write this diary."[33] Harker has learned stenography, but even so notebook writers still gain identifiability, coherence, and thus individuality from their handwriting.

Meanwhile Harker's fiancée sits longingly at the typewriter back in Exeter. Whereas her betrothed will one day simply inherit the notary practice on the death of his employer, Mina Murray is sorely in need of new discursive technologies. She is an assistant schoolmistress but, not content with pedagogic half-emancipation, she dreams of doing "what I see lady journalists do." So she diligently practices typing and stenography in order to be able "to take down what he wants to say" after her marriage to Jonathan.[34] However (as Lily Braun had so rightly seen), the "disintegration of the old family structure" sets in "precisely where one thought oneself quite conservative":[35] for office girls, even if they have other dreams, there is no "return to any sort of position in the family."[36] The typewriter and office technology can never be contained in the closed space of motherhood. Their function is always that of the interface between branching and specified streams of data. This becomes clear as Stoker's novel develops.

Instead of simply taking dictation from Jonathan, now her husband, Mina Harker is forced to become the central relay station of an immense information network. For the Count has arrived secretly in England and is leaving scattered and fearful signs of his presence. One is a madman in whose brain the psychiatrist, Dr. Seward, discovers new and dreadful nerve paths; he immediately has the verbal traces of these paths spoken into his phonograph. Another is Mina's friend, Lucy Westenra; two small wounds appear on her throat and she becomes increasingly somnambulant, anemic, and (to put it briefly) hysterical. Finally, there is a Dutch physician, who "has revolutionized therapeutics by his discovery of the continuous evolution of brain-matter."[37] This allows him to discover what is actually behind the scattered evidence of the horror. But his insight would remain a gray theory of vampirism if Mina Harker did not undertake the task of exhaustive evidence gathering. She who dreamed of doing what she saw lady journalists do uses her typewriter to transcribe every diary entry, every phonograph roll, every relevant newspaper clipping and telegram, every document and log book. She makes copies of her transcriptions; she delivers these daily to all the investigators, and so on and on.[38]

The Count, had he any idea of what was occurring, might have exclaimed in the words of Schreber: "For years they have been keeping *books or other notations*, in which all my thoughts, my verbal expres-

sions, my personal articles, all objects in my possession or anywhere near me, all people I come into contact with, etc., are *written down*."

It is not always easy for a woman to incorporate into a text every shred of evidence of a perverse desire. Seward's (not to say Stransky's) phonographic roll turns faster than a typist's hands would like. The "wonderful machine" is also so "cruelly true" that the transcribing Mina perceives the beating of tormented hearts "in its very tones."[39] But a discourse functionary does not give in, simply because she has become a discourse functionary. Her friend, however, like so many hysterics since Eugène Azam and Richard Wagner, suddenly manifests a second personality at night: while still wretched and docile, she refuses medication, draws her gums back from her eyeteeth, and speaks in an uncharacteristically soft, salacious voice. It is as if Kundry in the first act of *Parsifal* had become Kundry in the magic garden.

"What does a woman want?" In the discourse network of 1900 the alternatives are no longer motherhood or hysteria, but the machine or destruction. Mina Harker types, whereas Lucy Westenra's second personality is the will willed by a despotic signifier. On the one hand, a desexualization permits the most intimate diaries and most perverse sexualities to be textualized; on the other hand, there is the truth. Indeed, precisely the truth corresponds to Freud's original insight and was simultaneously being publicized by an extended juristic-journalistic dragnet: the fact that hysteria consists in having been seduced by a despot. Lucy's sleepwalking does not arise from her own soul, but from her paternal inheritance.[40] The dreams of wolves and the bites from eyeteeth are no fantasies; they are the Count's engrams in brain and throat. Whereas Mina types, her friend ends up on the nocturnal side of machine writing. Two tiny bite wounds on the throat materialize Beyerlen's law that eyeteeth or a piece of type, through a single, brief application of pressure, place the entire engram in the proper position on skin or paper. "The spot that should be seen is always visible, except at the moment when visibility is necessary or is believed to be necessary." For blind acts of writing, only after-the-fact decoding is possible. But someone who, like Lucy's Dutch physician, is deeply immersed in Charcot's theory of hysteria can take the wounds and dreams of a hysteric for the sexuality they signify and hunt down the dream wolf (at the risk of becoming hysterical oneself) by the light of day.

No despot can survive when a whole multimedia system of psycho-analysis and textual technologies goes after him. The special forces have "scientific experience," whereas Dracula has only his "child's brain" with engrams dating back to the battle of Mohács (1526).[41] He does have an inkling of the power about to bring him down, for otherwise he would not throw the phonographic rolls and typescripts he finds into the fire. But the hunters have Mina and "thank God there is the other copy in the safe."[42] Under the conditions of information technology, the old-European despot disintegrates into the limit value of Brownian motion, which is the noise in all channels.[43]

A stab to the heart turns the Undead to dust. Dracula's salaciously whis-pering bride, the resurrected vampire Lucy, is put to death a second time, and finally, on the threshold of his homeland, so is he. A multimedia sys-tem, filmed over twenty times, attacks with typescript copies and tele-grams, newspaper clippings and wax rolls (as these different sorts of dis-course are neatly labeled). The great bird no longer flies over Transylvania.

"They pluck in their terror handfuls of plumes from the imperial Eagle, and with no greater credit in consequence than that they face, keeping their equipoise, the awful bloody beak that turns upon them . . . Everyone looks haggard, and our only wonder is that they succeed in looking at all."[44] It is always the same story in the discourse network of 1900. The last lines of Henry James, before the agony began, were pre-served by a typewriter. And the enigma of their meaning is the prehistory of this materiality.

The writer James, famous for his compact yet overarticulated style, turned to dictation before 1900 in order to move from style to "free, un-answered speech," thus to "diffusion" or flight of ideas. In 1907 Theo-dora Bosanquet, an employee in a London typing service who was at the time busy typing the *Report of the Royal Commission on Coast Erosion*, was ordered to report to James, who in the initial interview appeared as a "benevolent Napoleon." Thus began Bosanquet's "job, as alarming as it was fascinating, of serving as medium between the spoken and machined word." Alarming, because Bosanquet was of course only the will of the dictator's will, who in his dreams again and again appeared as Napoleon. Fascinating, because she became indispensable: whenever the pink noise of the Remington ceased, James would have no more ideas.[45]

Gertrude Stein's dark oracle predicted everything, all of it, even that an oracle was incapable of warning anyone. The writer who engaged a medium in 1907 in order to shift his style to "Remingtonese" was felled by a stroke in 1915. Sheer facts of literary history realize an epoch's wildest phantasm. The blood clot in the brain did not deprive James of clear diction, but it did claim all prearranged meanings. Paralysis and asymbolia know only the real. And this real is a machine. The Remington, together with its medium, were ordered to the deathbed in order to take three dictations from a delirious brain. Two are composed as if the emperor of the French, that great artist of dictation, had issued and signed them; the third notes that the imperial eagle is bleeding to death and why it is bleeding.

Nothing is more unthinkable, but nothing is clearer: a machine registers itself.

When King David was old and of many days, he asked for a beautiful young woman to warm him. And they gave him Abigail of Sunem. The writer does not ask for Theodora Bosanquet, but for her typewriter. And the queen's sacrifice is complete.

In the discourse network of 1900—this is its open secret—there is no sexual relation between the sexes. Apparent exceptions do not alter the fact. If Maupassant, who probably for the same venereal-opthalmological reasons as Nietzsche occasionally dictated to a secretary, could not refrain from sleeping with her, it was only as preparation for a full-stage separation comedy.[46] The comedies of unification, by contrast, are left to the media and their literary ancillary industries. According to a fine tautology, men and women, who are linked together by media, come together in media. Thus the entertainment industry daily creates new phantasms out of the open secret of 1900. After Dracula's black heart has bled dry, the powerless hero Harker and his typist are able to have a child after all. As long as there are gramophones and secretaries, every boss and wordsmith is smiling.

"My Honey Wants to Take Me Sailing on Sunday," runs a song from 1929, which sings out the industrial secret of its fiction in the first verse.

Träumend an der Schreibmaschin'
saß die kleine Josephin',
die Sehnsucht des Herzens, die führte die Hand.
Der Chef kam und las es und staunte, da stand:

"Am Sonntag will mein Süßer
mit mir segeln gehn,
sofern die Winde wehn,
das wär' doch wunderschön!
Am Sonntag will mein Süßer . . ."

At the typewriter in a dream
There sat little Josephine
Her longing heart played with her hands
The boss came and read it but didn't understand:

"My honey wants to take me
sailing on Sunday
we'll sail away
and that will be so lovely!
My honey wants to take me . . ."[47]

The Lyre and the Typewriter, a 1913 screenplay that was unfortunately never filmed, promises to take up Anselmus's and Serpentina's dreams of Atlantis. It is included in Pinthus's *Movie Book*, and it links movies, the typewriter, and writing in a perfect picture of the times, in which only a gramophone and sound track are lacking. Richard A. Bermann's technological Atlantis begins when a swarthy typist comes home from the movies, which she loves to distraction, and tells her boyfriend everything promised in the silent film. The film within the film, however, begins with the opposite: a young writer of verses chews on his pen in vain and tears up sheets of paper after writing one line. "Ce vide papier que sa blancheur défend" inspires writers after Mallarmé only with the wish to flee.[48] The writer runs out and is soon following a woman, but she is not one of those who do it for money, and finally she closes her door in his face. Only then does the sign on her door, her promise, become readable.[49]

MINNIE TIPP

Typing Service

Transcription of Literary Works

Dictation

The writer rings the bell, is admitted, assumes a dictating pose and says: "Miss, I love you!" And Minnie—just like her namesake in Stoker, who also no longer knew anything as private—simply types it out on her machine.[50] The next day the bill arrives in the mail. When messengers without kings and discourse functionaries without bureaucrats transport messages from medium to medium, messages containing meaning or love do not arrive. Money, the most annihilating signifier of all, standardizes them. (In 1898 one thousand typed words cost 10 Pf.)[51]

If this were not enough, Bermann's screenplay stipulates that the typed line "Miss, I love you!" appear on the "white screen." Even if the woman had been sitting at a typewriter on which it was not possible to see the typescript, film would make amorous whispering mute, visible, and ridiculous. A discourse network of rigorous evidence gathering does not ignore the soul; it confronts it with mechanical devices and women who go to the movies. Bermann's screen reverses Demeny's phonoscope, which combined experimental phonetics and serial photography to divide the two seconds it takes a man's mouth to pronounce the sound series "JE V OUS AI ME" into twenty still shots of the mouth's successive positions.[52]

But of course men grow in front of machines. Afterwards, the young writer is able to write poems about his love that Minnie Tipp finds readable and, through her copies, is able to turn into "several hundred perfectly transcribed manuscripts," which literary critics can read. With typewritten copy "one secures and increases one's market."[53] Thus the book goes to press and the divinely comic day arrives when the two, the man with the lyre and the woman with the typewriter, "no longer typed."[54] End of the film within the film. Francesca and Paolo, Serpentina and Anselmus in the age of the film screen.

The two lovers in the frame story, however, are not brought together. The swarthy movie-goer and typist sees in the film the triumph of the feminine power of reeducation in even the most outdated of male professions. To her friend, who believes in works written with the pen, the story means that the typewriter turns high literature into mass literature and makes women frigid. Whereupon the woman laughs.

Twenty-four years later this laughter will have infected the revue girls who dance across the keyboard of a giant typewriter in Billy Wilder's film *Ready, Willing, and Able.*

Yet *The Lyre and the Typewriter*, a year before it was written, *was* filmed—in the real. In 1912 the writer Kafka met Felice Bauer one evening at the house of Max Brod, immediately after the typist had been granted the head clerkship of her parlograph and dictation-machine firm

JE

V

OUS   *AI*

ME

or, in other words, had attained a power opposed to her previous position: she was allowed to sign *Carl Lindström A. G.* Kafka spent the following weeks in his office at a typewriter, which he was not accustomed to use and which he misused to write the initial love letters.[55] These letters revolve around a spoken word "which so amazed me that I banged the table. You actually said you enjoyed copying manuscripts, that you had also been copying manuscripts in Berlin for some gentleman (curse the sound of that word when unaccompanied by name and explanation!) and you asked Max to send you some manuscripts."[56]

Thunder and lightning, or the knock on the table. Jealousy of a nameless man in Berlin (who also dictates to Minnie Tipp, to the horror of the film hero),[57] jealousy of his friend (who worked in the telephone division of the Prague Postal Service)—jealousy of the entire media network, then, teaches the writer to love. This means that it is not love at all. Mr. K. and Felice B. (to speak with Freud and Mallarmé) will never be a single mummy under happy palms, even if they were only the palms in a library like Lindhorst's.

That evening defies description: Kafka and Brod are going through Kafka's still-unpublished manuscripts and selecting those that will eventually be published by Rowohlt. Also present is Felice, stopping over during a trip, who happens to mention that she enjoys typing manuscripts. She omits the fact that such work also pays—which distinguishes her from Minnie Tipp. But Kafka is already burning with love. He is able to type himself; there is even someone in his office whose job is to type for him, and Kafka's "principal task" as well as "happiness" consists "in being able to dictate to a living person."[58] But this functionary is a man and has never declared that Kafka's happiness is his as well. Office work remains the one-sided pleasure of a pervert who, in spite of his bureaucratic position, constantly reverts to cunning measures à la George. As Kafka writes to Felice Bauer: "I could never work as independently as you seem to; I slither out of responsibility like a snake; I have to sign many things, but every evaded signature seems like a gain; I also sign everything (though I really shouldn't) with FK only, as though that could exonerate me; for this reason I also feel drawn toward the typewriter in anything concerning the office, because its work, especially when executed at the hands of the typist, is so impersonal."[59]

A woman who can type *and* sign documents is made to order for someone who systematically avoids signatures and yet, when switching from the office to his own desk every evening, is always betrayed by his handwriting. FK's double-entry bookkeeping, which registers the flow of documents in bureaucratic anonymity during the day and in literary manuscripts during the night, seems to have found a "happy ending." With a typist as wife, the unknown writer would have "the operational means of the printing press at his disposal" right at his desk.[60] It would be literally true that the typewriter "arrives as the liberator of those dedicated to the demanding service of the pen."[61]

But Felice Bauer's self-advertisement (not to say "the sign on her door") is directed to Brod, and the man whose texts she transcribes is a professor in Berlin. Bauer's professional independence does not rule out, but rather stipulates, that her literary taste, such as it is, places any number of writers above Kafka. The gloominess of intransitive writing hardly charms women. The composer of love letters therefore fabricated texts, even without Minnie Tipp's adornments, that would be readable, indeed media-appropriate for typists. As if the feminine power of reeducation had taken root, Kafka showed intense interest in Carl Lindström's company catalogs—because, like a second Wildenbruch, he considered gramophonics "a threat."[62] As if subaltern bureaucrats were more independent than female managers, Kafka made plans for a massive media network in the name of that very company. Lindström was to develop parlographs that could be connected to typewriters, to juke boxes, to telephone booths, and finally to that fearful recorder of real data, the gramophone.[63] This gigantic project could appropriately have been called Project Dracula, and, in the seventy years since it was written down, it has been realized. But Ms. Bauer (as far as one can judge from her side of the correspondence, which was destroyed) did not take up the suggestion.

Dracula appears once more, just where the marriage between the lyre and the typewriter does not take place. "Writing" in Kafka's sense "is a deep sleep, and thus death, and just as one will and cannot pull a dead man out of his grave, so it is with me at my desk at night."[64] From the site of this grave or desk the writer not only fantasized about the massive media network of a company whose strategy was the coupling and mass production of recording devices,[65] but he put such a network together, if only by using or misusing available technologies.

For twenty-four weeks he sent up three letters per day, but did not take a train, which would have brought him to Berlin in a couple of hours, and he did not answer the telephone. . . . The correspondence shows how it is possible to touch, chain, torture, dominate, and destroy another person, simply through the systematic and total use of the mail and telephone.

First, Kafka established an exact schedule of all mail pick-ups in Prague and of all deliveries in Berlin. Second, he plotted Felice's movements between home and office by the hour, so he would know what time of day she would receive a letter, depending on whether it was addressed to her office or residence. Third, he determined the exact path each letter would take, through which hands it would pass, at home (concierge, mother and sisters of the unfortunate) and at the office (mailroom, orderlies, secretaries). Fourth, he noted the time and distance taken by a normal letter on the one hand, and by an express letter on the other. Fifth, he noted the time it would take a telegram to reach her. . . . If one considers that Kafka not only put the words he had just written into envelopes, but also made mysterious references to letters he had written but not sent and likewise stuck in, whenever they fit, recriminations that he had formulated weeks before; if one considers that, in extreme cases, he put the ten to twelve pages of a single letter, written at different times, into as many different envelopes and mailboxes, one must admit that Kafka maximized the dispatch of all modalities and schedules of the mail in order, with this collective firepower, to force Felice to surrender.[66]

Cournot's brilliant analysis shows that in Kafka's stories the modalities of the technological channels of information—cross-talk and delay, networks and noise-levels—served no uncertain purpose. The love letters that Erich Heller celebrates as "the work of an unknown minnesinger from the first half of the twentieth century" break all technical records.[67] The anonymity of an FK has nothing to do with the namelessness of a minnesinger. It simply makes very clear that no love is to be given to women employed in discursive functions. The concentrated firepower of letters, express mail, and telegrams stands where cultured women or simple feminine readers once would willingly have been all eyes and ears. But the possibility of effortlessly recruiting feminine readers disappears along with the "meaning" that neither the writer Kafka nor the reader Bauer can find in "The Judgment."[68] The reason Rilke distributed his *Chicory* so awkwardly, by hand, was that no one was asking for it. The fact that Kafka vied for an arbitrary individual with an empty face rather than for a public changes nothing in the lack of demand. Only the dead need technically calculate their love letters.

If writers in the discourse network of 1900 are the discarded material that they write down, then nothing can take place beyond writing itself. "I have the definite feeling that through marriage, *through the union, through the dissolution of this nothingness* that I am, I shall perish."[69] There is no chance on either side of the Kafka-Bauer correspondence of words reaching through to a soul. On one side is writing that occupies the place of madness and incessantly dissolves into its nothingness.[70] On the other side, the processing of texts begins, which is no less transitory, only a medium among media.

The Technical Manifesto of Futurist Literature proclaims the motto that masses of molecules and spinning electrons are more exciting than the smile or tears of a woman (*di una donna*).[71] Rilke reported that one woman identified his cranial-suture-phonographic expansion of the five senses with "presence of mind and grace of love." The writer, however, disagreed. Love "would not serve the poet, for individual variety must be constantly present to him, he is compelled to use the sense sectors to their full extent."[72] That means, as in Kafka's letter strategies and plans for the Lindström company, the creation of unheard-of media-network connections, such as those between coronal sutures and writing.

At the same time, the media-network amateurs Rilke and Kafka still politely formulated their queen's sacrifice: in gentle qualifications and love letters that were machine written and thus not love letters. But the expressionists had bad manners. "Get out with your love!" cries Ehrenstein's Tubutsch.[73] Döblin demanded, in a single sentence, "the self-loss [*Entselbstung*], the exteriorization of the author" and the end of literary "eroticism." The dissolution of the function of authorship drove all love out of books: love described as well as the constitutive love that joined the Poet and feminine readers in empathy. Material equality on paper guarantees quite "naturally" that "the novel has as little to do with love as painting has to do with man or woman."[74] When the imagination and "feeling" no longer react, then "love, woman, and so on" disappear from "a literature for discriminating bachelors."[75]

So much for programmatic declarations from the founding period. To conclude, consider later, confirming evidence from two exact literary historians, who have registered the central fact and its preconditions. Benn and Valéry demonstrate in theory and practice that the new order of things, founded by the typewriter, is the space of contemporary writing. "Circa 1900," the union of love disappears from paper.

Art is a truth that does not yet exist. In the most significant novels since 1900, women are ranged in categories: in the ethnic-geographic (Conrad), the artistic (*Die Göttinnen*), and the aesthetic (*Dorian Gray*). In part they are brought in aphoristically, serving a purpose of ovation and reminiscence rather than determining structure, and thus speaking a foreign language: in *The Magic Mountain*. In the most serious instance, love is a test faced by a newly developing typological principle.[76]

Taking stock of things in this way has consequences for paper itself.

A celebration for Dionysus, for wine rather than corn, for Bacchus rather than Demeter, for phallic congestion rather than the nine-month's magic, for the aphorism rather than the historical novel! One has worked on a piece, with paper and typewriter, thoughts, sentences, it sits on the desk. One returns from other spheres, from acquaintances, professional circles, overloadings of the brain with circumstances, overflows, repressions of every flight and dream—after hours of it one returns and sees the white streaks on the desk. What is it? A lifeless something, vague worlds, something painfully, effortfully put together, thought together, grouped, tested, improved, a pathetic remainder, loose, unproven, weak—tinder, decadent nothing. The whole of it an absurdity, an illness of the race, a black mark, a confusion of all relation? There comes Pallas, unerring, always with the helmet, never fertile, the slim childless goddess, born of her father, sexless.[77]

A literature that only arranges women and even despises the Woman or Mother, a literature for discriminating bachelors, has bitter need of a Pallas as tutelary goddess. Whatever bachelor machines produce with "paper and typewriter" remains refuse as long as there is no one to clean up the desk and magically transform refuse into art.

Little has changed, then, since the days of Nietzsche. In a typewritten letter to Overbeck, the half-blind man complains that his Malling Hansen is as "skittish as a young dog," and makes for "little entertainment" and "much trouble." He is looking for young people to relieve his writing difficulties and would "for this purpose even agree to a two-year marriage."[78] Benn realized Nietzsche's subjunctive in his "marriage of comradeship."[79] In 1937, six years before the panegyric for the virginal Athena, a longtime woman friend of Benn's received a letter concerning his marriage plans: it clearly lays out the code for *Pallas*.

So a little relationship has developed here; it brings some warmth and illumination into my existence and I intend to nourish it. Just so that you know. There are, first, *external* reasons. Outwardly I'm completely falling apart. Things broken down, a mess everywhere, unfinished letters. . . . The bed sheets are torn up; the bed lies unmade all week; I have to do my own shopping. Heating also, sometimes. I don't answer letters anymore because I have no one to write for me. I can't work because I have no time, peace, and no one to take dictation. I make coffee at 3:30 in the afternoon, and that's the one event of my life. At 9 in the evening I go to bed and that's the other. Like a beast. . . .

Nonetheless, I must make another attempt to construct a serious human relationship and with its help try to pull myself out of this mire. Morchen, I'll tell you everything, but only you. And now if I tell you what sort of person this is, the one who will probably become unhappy, you'll probably be surprised.

Quite a bit younger than I am, just thirty years old. Not at all attractive like Elida and Elisabeth Arden. Very good figure, but the face is negroid. From a very good family. No money. Job similar to that of Helga, well paid, types 200 syllables, an expert typist. By our standards, that is, by the standards of our generation, uneducated.[80]

The end of love does not exclude, it includes marriage. Literary utilizers of discarded material are educated, but unable to straighten out the discarded files known as their desks. Thus they marry women who, like Felice Bauer, are neither beautiful nor educated, but who with their 200 typewritten syllables per minute are nearly record-setters.[81] The name of the Pallas who comes to rescue and redeem the decadent paper tinder on the desk could be, rather than Herta von Wedemeyer, Minnie Tipp. For the helmet she never lays aside is her machine, which takes dictation. This is the way that pathetic remainders, loose, unproven, weak, which lie on the desk like white streaks, become a truth that does not yet exist— become art.

In 1916 Valéry noted: "Love is, no doubt, worth making . . . but as an occupation of the intellect, as a subject of novels and studies, it is traditional and tedious."[82] In 1940, between Benn's marriage of comradeship and *Pallas*, Valéry put his literary-historical statement to the test: he wrote '*My Faust.*' Whereas the second half of the dramatic fragment introduces a nameless Nietzsche, who greets Goethe's hero as "trash" and discards him as trash, the first half revolves around a Demoiselle Luste. This pretty person with the pretty name is as able as the hermit of Sils to characterize the irretrievable past of German Poetry. Only Mephisto, who still thinks in terms of major, decisive actions, of Spirit and Nature, can imagine that Faust loves the Demoiselle. But the devil is just a poor devil and, like Dracula, brainless. The developments of modern science and technology have passed him by.[83] Faust, by contrast, stands at the height of an experiment that, as the "rediscovery of ancient chaos in the body," makes all discourses into secondary phenomena. Therefore his relationship to Luste cannot be love, but only an experiment in media connection.

Me, Valéry, the books: let us sum it all up.

First Faust reads everything that has been written about him in literature and interpretation. He begins with an autobibliographical exhaustion, whose completeness, however, cannot be guaranteed. The second step is to transfer everything that has been stored into a discourse network called the *Mémoires*. Here are the title and the opening sentences.

"The Memoirs of My Self, by Professor Doctor Faustus, Member of the Academy of Dead Sciences, etc. . . . Hero of several literary works of repute . . ." So much has been written about me that I no longer know who I am. True, I have not read all the many works in question, and doubtless there are many more than one whose existence has not been made known to me. But those with which I am acquainted are enough to give me a singularly rich and complex idea of myself and my destiny. Thus I can choose freely among a variety of dates and places for my birth, all equally attested by irrefutable documents and proofs, put forth and discussed by critics of equal eminence.[84]

The memoirs of the classical founding hero exceed the discourse network he inaugurated. As the rules stipulate, an author has arisen in the media network of poetic works and interpretations, and that author has all the attributes of literary fame. But precisely for that reason, mathematical combinatorics replaces the organic autobiography. Countless books about books about Faust cancel one another out. What remains is white noise, from which the memoir writer can extract arbitrary selections. Whoever no longer knows who he is and writes his memoirs with the declared intention of disappearing as an I is no longer an author.

Faust, having become the empty intersection of countless discourses, rescinds Goethe's *Poetry and Truth*. This means that, practically speaking, he dictates other things and otherwise than the Ur-author did. John, Johann Christian Schuchardt, Friedrich Theodor Kräuter, Johann Peter Eckermann, Friedrich Wilhelm Riemer, or even Geist—so runs the list of the names of men who would have been able to sign Goethe's truths and fictions if the rules in operation had been those of the materiality of writing rather than the Discourse of the Master. Male secretaries were on the one side, and on the other were first a mother, who could hardly write one word correctly, then a wife, who provided for Goethe's "domestic peace and marital happiness" simply by never desiring "fame as a woman writer" and properly eschewing any "mixing in official and literary matters."[85] Such were the parameters of a practice of writing, which led to the conception of an ideal in feminine form, or in the form of a woman. To dictate to the subaltern men present what the One, Only, and Absent Feminine has whispered—writing Poetry is nothing else. Even when Professor Abnossah Pschorr, one hundred years later, built his phonograph in the study of the Goethe House, the roll still registered men's voices: the Author as he whispers his words of wisdom to Eckermann.[86]

Valéry's 'My Faust' is a systematic reversal of all classical writing practices. He too dictates, but not as a bureaucrat who ends up with the state-supporting pact of his own signature. "The mere fact of knowing how to sign my name cost me dear once"—thus "I never write now,"[87] but instead he dictates toward the vanishing point designated by Kafka's avoidance of the signature. These dictations doubly oppose the Goethean variety. First, they set no life or ideal of woman into writing, but only the sentences that poets and interpreters have written about an impossible real. Second, this book of books is being written by a woman, not a man. The fact that Demoiselle Luste has been with Faust for eight days is simply explained by her taking dictation. Mephisto can suspect whatever he likes, but what takes place at the end of the idea of Faust is a bargain sale of all poetic-hermeneutic discourse to a woman's ear. The ear is small and magical, as one could have predicted of an admirer of Nietzsche and Mallarmé, and it is by no means there to understand anything.[88] Luste's ear is to take dictation with phonographic accuracy, clean off what was dictated at the beginning of the next day, and otherwise, otherwise be a not unattractive sight for the flight of ideas.[89]

Luste, a second Pallas, brings order into the combinatory chaos of the last Faust. The writer of the memoir neither has nor desires to have an overview of a life that too many books have described. With or without the help of the devil, who once in a while brings by an insidious text, his desk is a heap of refuse. But there is Luste, that is, the "modest but honorable part of the thing that discreetly helps to oil the machinery of your thought."[90] A woman who knows nothing of the thought or life of the one who dictates takes up the chaos of memoirs with clever ears and crystalline logic. That is why Faust hired her. For phonographic accuracy means doing away with the constitutive repressions in discourses. When Faust for once is not interested in dictating and instead talks about the evening sun and his desire for a little flirtation, Luste, just like Minnie, puts that too onto the mute page. When he risks a physiological definition of laughter, which (as abstraction or parapraxis) applies just as well to orgasm, Luste responds with an endless laugh. When in his finest philosophical style he styles his "relations with men and things" as the theme of the memoirs, Luste questions the ambiguous word *men*, and Faust must be more specific and add that he also had dealings with women. Thus the simple presence of a secretary decomposes the unity of mankind and leaves everywhere only two divided sexes. Faust can no longer play Fichte-Schelling-Luden's representative of all mankind because his words strike a clever woman's ear.

Again and again in the war between the sexes, one leads the other around by the nose. The memoir writer tries this with his secretary, using delicate bits of memory. But the beautiful willing widows of autobiography, whether they are (with Faust) fiction or (with Mephisto) truth, remain women in plurality. The myth of life sources and Nature's breasts has it otherwise. Ever since European universities have included female secretaries as well as Faust, M.A., and his assistant Wagner, the myth risks provoking only laughter. Luste is Wagner, Luste is Gretchen, Luste is therefore neither one nor the other. The comedy *Luste* begins with her laughter, and it ends with her "no" to love. Women in plurality, laughing and writing, make affairs like that with Gretchen utterly impossible (as Faust explains to the devil). Because discourses are of secondary importance under conditions of advanced technology, one need not say what has replaced love and sighs. Signifiers are unambiguous and dumb. The one who laughs is Luste.

Afterword to the Second Printing

Quod est inferius, est sicut quod est superius.
Tabula Smaragdina

The term *discourse network*, as God revealed it to the paranoid cognition of Senate President Schreber, can also designate the network of technologies and institutions that allow a given culture to select, store, and process relevant data. Technologies like that of book printing and the institutions coupled to it, such as literature and the university, thus constituted a historically very powerful formation, which in the Europe of the age of Goethe became the condition of possibility for literary criticism.

In order to describe such systems as systems, that is, to describe them from the outside and not merely from a position of interpretive immanence, Foucault developed discourse analysis as a reconstruction of the rules by which the actual discourses of an epoch would have to have been organized in order not to be excluded as was, for example, insanity. His concept of the archive—synonymous with the library in Foucault's research methods, if not in his theory[1]—designates a historical a priori of written sentences. Hence discourse-analytic studies had trouble only with periods whose data-processing methods destroyed the alphabetic storage and transmission monopoly, that old-European basis of power.[2] Foucault's historical research did not progress much beyond 1850.

All libraries are discourse networks, but all discourse networks are not books. In the second industrial revolution, with its automation of the streams of information, the analysis of discourses has yet to exhaust the forms of knowledge and power. Archeologies of the present must also take into account data storage, transmission, and calculation in technological media. Literary criticism can learn from an information theory that has formalized the current state of technical knowledge, and thus made measurable the performance or limits of information systems. After the destruction of the monopoly of writing, it becomes possible to draw up an account of its functioning.

Traditional literary criticism, probably because it originated in a particular practice of writing, has investigated everything about books except their data processing. Meaning as the fundamental concept of hermeneutics and labor as the fundamental concept of the sociology of literature both bypass writing as a channel of information and those institutions, whether schools or universities, that connect books with people. Hermeneutics did not deal with the literal materiality of the letter, but with works and traditions, because only these were said to be historical and capable of producing history. Contemporary sociology of literature takes the opposite approach and reads texts as reflections of relations of production, whose paradigm is energy or labor rather than information. Steam engines and looms (in Goethe also) became topics, but typewriters did not.

Discourse analyses, by contrast, have to integrate into their materialism the standards of the second industrial revolution. An elementary datum is the fact that literature (whatever else it might mean to readers) processes, stores, and transmits data, and that such operations in the age-old medium of the alphabet have the same technical positivity as they do in computers. Printed laments over the death of Man or the subject always arrive too late.

What remain to be distinguished, therefore, are not emotional dispositions but systems. Information networks can be described only when they are contrasted with one another. The source, sender, channel, receiver, and drain of streams of information, Shannon's five functions, in other words,[3] can be occupied or left vacant by various agents: by men or women, rhetoricians or writers, philosophers or psychoanalysts, universities or technical institutes. Whereas interpretation works with constants, the comparison between systems introduces variables. If the latter pursues historical investigations, then "at least *two* limiting events" are indispensable, for which either systemic differentiation or communicational technique can be considered criteria.[4]

Universal alphabetization circa 1800 and technological data storage circa 1900 constitute just such turning points, for which there is sufficient evidence within about fifteen years. Whether data, addresses, and commands circulate among pedagogy, Poetry, and philosophy, or among media technologies, psychophysics, and literature, the difference changes the place value of each word. In describing such feedback systems of senders, channels, and receivers, the instantaneous exposures or snapshots of a single moment can be of more help than intellectual histories. According to Heidegger, the nineteenth and "most ambiguous" century can "never be understood by means of a description of the chronological succession of its periods. It must be demarcated and approached simultaneously from two sides."[5]

The examination rules of the new philologies had little to do with demarcating borders. The literary history of the smallest increments or distinctions functions almost like "devices that cannot distinguish a pseudo-random sequence from a real random sequence, when the length of a period" (determined by an "easy-to-fill condition") "is larger than its capacity for storage."[6] By contrast, system comparisons like that between the age of Goethe and the turn of the century need to seek minimal auto-correlation functions whose periods can be counted in centuries. What intellectual history conjures up as the nonsimultaneity of the simultaneous, and hermeneutics as the infinite number of possible contexts thus shrinks to options or erratic values. A belief in inexhaustible works is simply an unwillingness to allow holy writ to be joined by its long forgotten siblings. Discourse analyses, however, even if they cannot establish any ἅπαξ λεγόμενον, at least have the advantage of Occam's razor: data that have not been multiplied beyond necessity can be transmitted under the conditions of high technology—as books into other media and as homes into other countries.

Meanwhile, *Discourse Networks 1800/1900* has become part of an information network that describes literature as an information network. Avital Ronell deciphers Goethe's authorship as dictation to his Eckermanns and psychoanalysts. Klaus Theweleit tells of the women and media from whom books have emerged in Freud, Benn, or Céline. Wolfgang Scherer applies the historical breaks of alphabetization and media technologies to the history of music and its criticism; Bernhard Siegert and Frank Haase establish the postal system as a universal transmission medium. The irretrievable effects of film on autobiographies and theoretical constructions of modernity have been discussed by Manfred Schneider and Thorsten Lorenz. And finally, Hans Ulrich Gumbrecht and Karl Ludwig Pfeiffer reconstruct a space of communicative materialities that have granted literature its origin and end.

Literary texts can thus be read as a methodological, but only a methodological, center of *Discourse Networks*, in contexts that explode the two-cultures schema of our academic departments. Information technology is always already strategy or war. "And that means: pessimism all the way down the line. Mistrust in the fate of literature, mistrust in the fate of freedom, mistrust in the fate of European humanity, but above all mistrust, mistrust, and more mistrust in all understanding: between the classes, between peoples, between individuals. And unlimited trust only in I. G. Farben and the satisfactory perfection of the air force."[7]

Under conditions of high technology, the work of putting things in order (this structural activity) becomes as old-fashioned as it is inescapable. Putting things in order, although it is not a sublation [*Aufheben*], does not lag far behind in ambiguity. Hegel's project of determining the nature of the discourse network in the age of Goethe resulted in the judgment that "art, considered in its highest vocation, is and remains for us a thing of the past."[8] Works that put things in order do not furnish any judgments or even oracles, but they "dispossess" people of "that discourse in which they wish to be able to say immediately and directly what they think, believe, or imagine."[9]

At the beginning of *Discourse Networks 1800/1900* stood the Fugs with their song "Exorcizing the Evil Spirits out of the Pentagon." At the end stand words that have brought other words onto a screen.

There is no end to the writing of books, wrote the preacher. Even books written to bring about the end of books and of their ordering submit to this pronouncement.

Reference Matter

Notes

Full authors' names, titles, and publication data for works given in short form below may be found in Works Cited, pp. 419–47.

The following abbreviations have been used in the notes. Because of the frequent repetition of similar titles in German editions, these abbreviations represent *titles* or substantial parts of titles, not works per se. Thus one will find, for example, both Goethe, *SW*, and Pestalozzi, *SW*, representing the different complete editions of these respective authors. In the list below, the authors for whom each abbreviation is used are given after each title.

AL	*Aufsätze zur Literatur* (Döblin)	*K*	*Kampfzeiten* (H. Lange)
B	*Briefwechsel* (Hoffmann, Hofmannsthal, Nietzsche)	*KA*	*Kritische Ausgabe* (F. Schlegel)
		KS	*Kritische Schriften* (A. Schlegel)
CE	*Critical Essays* (Barthes)	*LCMP*	*Language, Counter-Memory, Practice* (Foucault)
G	*Gesamtausgabe* (J. Fichte)		
GAW	*Gesamt-Ausgabe der Werke* (George)	*OC*	*Oeuvres complètes* (Mallarmé)
GS	*Gesammelte Schriften* (Benjamin, Dilthey, Wagner)	*PS*	*Pädagogische Schriften* (Schleiermacher)
		S	*Schriften* (Hardenberg, Tieck)
GW	*Gesammelte Werke* (Benn, Einstein, Morgenstern)	*SE*	Standard Edition (Freud)

SS	*Sämtliche Schriften* (Goethe)	W	*Werke* (C. Brentano, Goethe, Nietzsche,
SW	*Sämtliche Werke* (J. Fichte, Goethe, Herder, Pestalozzi, Rilke)	WB	J. P. Richter) *Werke und Briefe* (B. Brentano, Nietzsche)

The Scholar's Tragedy

NOTE: We are grateful to Stanley Corngold for allowing us to draw on his personal translation of this chapter. [Trans.]

1. Goethe, *Faust*, ll. 354–57. The German text is from Goethe, *SW*; the translation is by Walter Kaufmann, copyright © 1961 by Walter Kaufmann (used by permission of Doubleday, a division of Bantam, Doubleday, Dell Publishing Group, Inc.). The opening monologue of Goethe's *Faust* is written in Knittelverse, an irregular meter of four feet used by the sixteenth-century poet Hans Sachs. This and all following translations have very occasionally been adapted from the published sources given in the Works Cited where this was necessary to highlight aspects of the original under discussion. [Trans.]

2. Schiller, *SW* (1963), I: 313. In German, the title of Schiller's distich is "Sprache" ("Language"). Note that the German word contains and transforms the "ach!" of the soul's sigh, thereby enacting the alienation of the soul in language that the distich states thematically. [Trans.]

3. See Lacan, *Encore*, p. 55.   4. Foucault, *Order*, p. 206.

5. Rickert, *Goethes Faust*, p. 156.   6. Luther, IV: 3.

7. See the speech-act analysis in Gessinger (*Sprache*, pp. 38–43), whose depreciatory categories demonstrate how contemporary concepts of language persist in rewriting Faust and how they can describe other orders of discourse only as terror.

8. Tiedemann, *Untersuchungen*, III: 359.

9. Lacan, "The Agency of the Letter in the Unconscious or Reason since Freud," *Ecrits* (New York), p. 174.

10. Foucault, *Order*, p. 41.

11. Foucault, "Language to Infinity," in *LCMP*, pp. 66–67.

12. See Derrida, *Grammatology*, pp. 20–21.

13. Cited in Herbertz, p. 559.

14. In Faust's time, Herder did so, and was then able only to write out the unspeakable Johannine polysemy. "*Word*! but the German 'word' does not say what this primary concept says," namely, "*concept* and *expression, primary concept* and *first cause, idea* and *imprint, thought* and *word*." (Herder, "'Johannes,'" in *SW*, VII: 320.)

15. Derrida, "Structure, Sign, and Play," in *Writing and Difference*, p. 279.

16. For the terminology, see Barthes, "The Imagination of the Sign," in *CE*, pp. 206–8. On the interpretation, see Wilkinson, "Faust," pp. 119–23, which, referring to Saussure, attributes an awareness of the paradigmatic to Faust. His various Germanizations are said to be choices "between alternatives that were available since the beginning of Biblical interpretation"; consequently, they provide "an impression of the dangers, heresies, and violence that belonged to the traditional accompaniments of the exegesis of the word *logos*." That is hermeneutically correct but untenable from the perspective of discourse analysis, be-

cause Faust's own discursive violence dispenses with all reference to traditions.

17. Barthes, "The Imagination of the Sign," in *CE*, p. 205.

18. Nietzsche, *WB*, III: 367.

19. Bielschowsky, II: 635.

20. Hegel, *Aesthetics*, II: 967–68; see also Turk, "Hegel," p. 132.

21. Spinoza, p. 172.   22. Ibid., p. 161.

23. See L. Strauss, pp. 179–86.   24. Rickert, p. 158.

25. Goethe, *Über Philostrats Gemählde*, in W, XLIX, 1, p. 142.

26. Derrida, "Freud and the Scene of Writing," in *Writing and Difference*, p. 226.

27. This "here I am" of the Spirit was grasped at once by Hegelian interpreters of *Faust*: Faust, "instead of proceeding to the sign of the macrocosmos and microcosmos, now opens the sacred Original, which, because it belongs to the manifestation of divine truth, he does not consider merely word and letter, but which, because he cannot possibly esteem the word so highly, he raises with the help of the Spirit to the level of living Spirit." (Hinrichs, p. 97.)

28. Nietzsche, *Zarathustra*, I, 11 ("On the New Idol"), pp. 160–63.

29. Nietzsche, W, III, 2, p. 231f. On the concrete form of such supervision—namely, in the state examinations for teachers—see Prahl, p. 248f.

30. "It should be remembered that the 'Word' in John represents Christ, and so Faust's disparagement of the 'Word' also implies an indictment of the Savior whom it symbolizes in the Bible. It is not a mere word, but a specific reference to Christ that Faust is here attempting to excise from the Bible." (Durrani, p. 61.)

31. Baumgart, "Gelehrte," p. 58. See also McClelland, p. 79.

32. Paulsen, *Deutschen Universitäten*, p. 77.

33. Paulsen, *Geschichte*, II: 93.

34. *Allgemeines Landrecht*, II, 12, §1; p. 584. See also II, 13, §3; p. 589.

35. Jeismann, p. 23.

36. Gedike, "Einige Gedanken über Schulbücher und Kinderschriften," in *Gesammelte Schulschriften*, I: 438–40.

37. J. P. Richter, "Das Kampaner Tal oder über die Unsterblichkeit der Seele," in W, IV: 649.

38. "Hähnische Litteralmethode," p. 94f. Katharina Rutschky carries coals to the Newcastle of reform pedagogues when she characterizes Hähn's old-fashioned literal method as the "destruction of the world through instruction." (Rutschky, *Schwarze Pädagogik*, pp. 563–67.)

39. See Goethe, *Aus meinem Leben: Dichtung und Wahrheit*, in SW, XXII: 149.

40. Bünger, p. 231.

41. Schmack, p. 55.

42. Such was the diagnosis of the polemical Catholic von Hammerstein, pp. 230–36.

43. F. Schlegel, *Athenäums-Fragmente*, in *KA*, II: 182.

44. See Deleuze/Guattari, *Thousand Plateaus*, pp. 75–85, on the "order-word."

45. See, e.g., Durrani, p. 60.

46. *Code Napoléon*, §4, 1807: 2. See Seebohm, *Kritik*, p. 13f.

47. Hintze, p. 11. The final scene of *Faust* concerns the difference between "life-long" and "indissoluble."

48. Cited in Bradish, p. 200.

49. Ibid., p. 18f.

50. Goethe, document of November 1785, in *SS*, I: 420. See Curtius, p. 113.
51. Bradish, p. 18.
52. Foucault, *Discipline*, pp. 29, 30.
53. Penzenkuffer, p. 92.
54. Ibid., p. 96.
55. Baumgart, "Faust," p. 94.

The Mother's Mouth

1. The capitalized and crossed-out article is a Lacanian notation indicating that woman does not exist as One in that women, as they exist, exist in a plurality and thus cannot be inscribed in the phallic function (universality). See Lacan, *Encore*, passim; in relation to classical-romantic poetry, see Schreiber, "*Zeichen der Liebe*," pp. 276–83.
2. Tobler, in Goethe, *SW*, XXXIV: 5.
3. Lacan, *Encore*, p. 90.
4. See Kaiser, *Wandrer und Idylle*, p. 106.
5. See Geissler, pp. 35–37.
6. Nietzsche, *Human, All Too Human*, vol. II, pt. 2, 124, p. 340.
7. See F. Kittler, "Autorschaft und Liebe," pp. 155–59.
8. Hinrichs, p. 152f.
9. See Hamacher, pp. 116–24.
10. Brandes, *Betrachtungen*, pp. 108, 183. On the recrudescence of the familiar form of address, see Wolke, p. 89; also Goethe, *SW*, XXII: 269.
11. Brandes, *Betrachtungen*, p. 108.
12. See Donzelot, *Policing*, p. 20.

Learning to Read in 1800

1. J. A. Huber, p. 28.
2. J. P. Richter, *Leben Fibels, des Verfassers der Bienrodischen Fibel* (vordatiert 1812), in *W*, VI: 426.
3. Hobrecker, p. 7.
4. Buno, cited in Helmers, p. 40.
5. Freud, *Interpretation of Dreams*, in *SE*, IV: 312.
6. Goethe, *Aus meinem Leben. Zweiter Abteilung erster und zweiter Band* (*Italienische Reise*), in *SW*, XXVII: 184.
7. Splittegarb, pp. 5f.　　8. Olivier, pp. 15, 24.
9. J. H. Campe, p. 73.　　10. Basedow, I: 17–19.
11. See Olivier, p. 58; and Niethammer, "Bedürfniss," p. 239. For the early European history of edible letters, see Dornseiff, p. 17f.
12. Niemeyer, p. 242.
13. Basedow, I: 27.
14. Schleiermacher, "Katechismus der Vernunft für edle Frauen," in *PS*, V: 239.
15. For a detailed discussion, see F. Kittler, "Lullaby," pp. 10–13.
16. See Pestalozzi, *Über den Sinn des Gehörs, in Hinsicht auf Menschenbildung durch Ton und Sprache*, in *SW*, XVI: 290.
17. See Kehr, pp. 385–89.
18. Stephani, *Beschreibung*, p. 3.
19. See Kehr, p. 390f, and Meumann, *Vorlesungen*, III: 450.

20. Stephani, *Beschreibung*, pp. 16–18.

21. Foucault, *Order*, p. 286; see also Liede, II: 223f.

22. For a description of how autobiographers of 1800 related their experience with their spelling-method instructors, see Hardach-Pinke and Hardach, pp. 115, 152.

23. Stephani, *Beschreibung*, p. 12f. On equating letters and musical notation, see also Olivier, p. 95; on the collaboration of voice and German teachers at a school in Leipzig, see von Türk, p. 174ff.

24. Stephani, *Beschreibung*, p. 18.

25. See Basedow, I: 21; and Bünger, pp. 83, 239.

26. Stephani, *Beschreibung*, pp. 24–26. See also von Türk, p. 188, on the phonetic method of Johann Friedrich Adolph Krug in Leipzig.

27. Stephani, *Beschreibung*, p. 33f.

28. C. Brentano, *W*, II: 613.

29. Stephani, *Beschreibung*, p. 10. Stephani claimed that his method "would make reading one of the most enjoyable of entertainments. You, noble mother, will find that you have to break off reading with your young ones more often than you like."

30. Ibid., p. 25; see also F. Kittler, "Erziehung," pp. 121–27.

31. Stephani, *Beschreibung*, p. 7.

32. Ibid., pp. 26, 32.

33. Ibid., p. 7.

34. Von Türk, p. 176; see also Petrat, p. 76f.

35. See Gessinger, *Schriftspracherwerb*, pp. 93–101.

36. Hardenberg, "Monolog," in *S*, II: 672.

37. Goethe, *Aus meinem Leben: Dichtung und Wahrheit*, in *SW*, XXIII: 44. For an overview, see Blackall.

38. See Chapuis and Gelis, II: 202–6.

39. Olivier, p. 99.   40. Ibid., pp. 95, 101.

41. See ibid., p. 91.   42. H. J. Frank, p. 309.

43. Herder, *Von der Ausbildung der Schüler in Rede und Sprache. Schulrede Weimar*, in *SW*, XXX: 217f. Von Türk's diagnosis and therapy program for the Leipzig dialect was quite similar (perhaps even more severe because it involved his own accent); see von Türk, p. 56f.

44. See Foucault, *Order*, p. 297f.   45. Herrmann, p. 116.

46. Stephani, *Beschreibung*, p. 51f.   47. *Erstes Lesebüchlein.*

48. Grüssbeutel, A^{V}IV and BII.   49. Jordan, A^{V}IV.

50. Kehr, pp. 364–68; this mistake is repeated by all historians of ABC books.

51. See Foucault, *Order*, pp. 19–20.

52. "The beginner can consider any animal and, by imitating its voice, will naturally pronounce the letters." One will find similar comments in Comenius (1659), cited in E. Schwartz, p. 61.

53. See Bünger, p. 29.

54. Herder, *Ueber die neuere Deutsche Litteratur*, in *W*, I: 401.

55. See Giesecke, p. 61.   56. Herder, "Origin," p. 116.

57. Lohmann, p. 66.   58. Herder, "Origin," p. 117.

59. This is the view of Grob, pp. 5–29.

60. Herder, "Origin," p. 87.

61. See ibid., p. 90.

62. Ibid., p. 91. Of Rousseau's analogous anthropological language, Starobinski writes: "Rousseau would have us consider what precedes the human order

of speech. Of course, he asserts that there is discourse, but he does so to reveal a *voice* that begins before all discourse. . . . By definition, the voice of nature must precede any speech" (p. 283).

63. Noted by Lohmann, p. 67.

64. Herder, "Origin," pp. 90–91.

65. Hippel, *Lebensläufe*, III: 1.

66. See the interpretation of Milch, pp. 156–59.

67. Hoffmann, "The Sandman," in *Tales*, p. 103.

68. Ibid., p. 115.

69. Wolke, p. 150; such definitions seem so self-evident to Germans that they can be ridiculed as a German metaphysics of language. See Parain, *Untersuchungen*, pp. 151–54.

70. Hoffmann, "The Sandman," in *Tales*, p. 118.

71. Bosse, "Herder," p. 82.

72. Niethammer, "Bedürfnis," p. 221f.

73. Hegel, *Philosophy of Subjective Spirit*, III: 181; see also Bernhardi, II: 260ff.

74. A. W. Schlegel, *KS*, I: 141.

75. See T. Meyer, p. 161.

76. Foucault, *Order*, p. 286.

77. Hegel, *Philosophy of Subjective Spirit*, III: 179.

78. Bernhardi, I: 61–71.   79. Herder, "Origins," p. 94.

80. Ibid., p. 90.   81. Von Loeben, p. 62.

82. See the detailed discussion in Wyss, pp. 156–60.

83. Von Türk, p. 181.   84. Olivier, p. 84f.

85. Liscov, III: 103f.   86. Grüssbeutel, A, II^r.

87. Ickelsamer, C, IV^r.

88. See Herder, *Buchstaben- und Lesebuch*, in W, XXX: 297; Splittegarb, p. 15; *ABC*, p. 4.

89. Bünger, p. 27; see also J. P. Richter, *Leben Fibels*, in W, IV: 430, 550.

90. Niemeyer, p. 243; see also Basedow, I: 17–19.

91. Niemeyer, p. 243.

92. Tillich, p. 1.

93. See Hegel, *Logic*, p. 82. "Perhaps," suggested Novalis, "the ultimate book is like an ABC book" (Hardenberg, fragment of 1798, in *S*, II: 610).

94. See Zwirner, p. 33.

95. See Bünger, p. 316, on this unavailable edition.

96. See Foucault, *Discipline*, p. 159–60.

97. Pestalozzi, "Wie Gertrud ihre Kinder lehrt; ein Versuch, den Müttern Anleitung zu geben, ihre Kinder selbst zu unterrichten," in *SW*, XIII: 194f.

98. Pestalozzi, "Pestalozzi's Brief an einen Freund über seinen Aufenthalt in Stanz," in *SW*, XIII: 27.

99. Herder, *Lesebuch*, in W, XXX: 293.

100. Moritz, *Anton Reiser*, p. 15.

101. Paulsen, *Geschichte*, II: 166.

102. Lacan, letter of January 5, 1980.

103. See Fritzsch, p. 497, for the historical context of Tiedemann's work.

104. Tiedemann, *Beobachtungen*, pp. 23, 27.

105. Ibid., p. 27.

106. See Stern, *Psychologie*, p. 88f.

107. See Chapuis and Gelis, II: 208–12.

108. Stephani, *Fibel*, p. 4f.

109. Wolke, p. 65. On the immediate pedagogic exploitation of the newly discovered phenomenon of deprivation, see also Basedow, I: 202.

110. Stephani, *Beschreibung*, p. 65f.

111. Rousseau, p. 19f.

112. Von Lang, p. 10; see also Schenda, p. 50.

113. See G. Stephan, p. 67.

114. See Melchers, p. 28f.

115. See Benjamin, "Alte vergessene Kinderbücher," *GS*, III: 12–22.

116. Hempel, p. ix.

117. Köpke, I: 14.

118. Tieck, *Der blonde Eckbert*, in *S*, IV: 154. The following anticipates any
commentary on this typical plot line in Tieck fairy tales: "Many people are so
attached to nature because they grew up afraid of their fathers and took refuge
with their mothers" (Hardenberg, fragment of 1798–99, in *S*, III: 360).

Motherliness and Civil Service

1. Pestalozzi, "Wie Gertrud ihre Kinder lehrt; ein Versuch, den Müttern Anleitung zu geben, ihre Kinder selbst zu unterrichten," in *SW*, XIII: 326.

2. Pestalozzi, *Das Buch der Mütter, oder Anleitung für Mütter, ihre Kinder
bemerken und reden zu lehren*, in *SW*, XV: 350.

3. On the conceptual pair εἶδος/ὕλη as representation *and* veiling of sexual
difference, see Lacan, *Encore*, p. 76.

4. See F. Kittler, "Lullaby," pp. 5–19.

5. See G. A. Kittler, p. 314.

6. Humboldt, X: 213; see also W. T. Krug, *Staat und Schule*, pp. 128–30.

7. Derrida, "Nietzsches Otobiographie," p. 94 (a summary of Nietzsche's
words).

8. For details see Paulsen, *Geschichte*, II: 279–82.

9. Holst, p. 175.

10. See Wychgram, pp. 262, 291; as a decoding of Napoleon's orders, consider the lines by Pink Floyd, "Mother, will they put me in the firin' line? Mother,
isn't it just a waste of time?"

11. Von Türk, p. 156f; see also Blochmann, p. 56f.

12. Holst, p. 167.

13. Gleim, II: 150; see also Hippel, *Nachlass über weibliche Bildung*, in *SW*,
VII: 14f.

14. Holst, p. 58f. Thus someone directly involved contradicts the sociologist's
supposition that the defined gender roles of 1800 served "without doubt to secure
ideologically the dominance of patriarchy" (Hausen, p. 375).

15. See Wychgram, p. 225 (on Vives).

16. See Foucault, *History of Sexuality*, p. 117.

17. Holst, p. 55.

18. Pestalozzi, "Weltweib und Mutter," in *SW*, XVI: 347–54.

19. Holst, p. 175.

20. See Hardenberg, "Glauben und Liebe oder Der König und die Königin,"
in *S*, II: 491–94.

21. Articles 3 and 30, cited in Blochmann, p. 114; see also Schwarz, p. 262f.,
and von Türk, p. 139 (the teacher and "poetess Carolina Rudolphi" was "a
tender mother" to all her students in Heidelberg).

22. Voss, I: 429f.

23. Hippel, *Bürgerliche Verbesserung*, p. 129: "Truly, in order to reorient ourselves we ought to prefer women for service in the state; they have an undeniable, God-given talent for such service, something that most of our good-for-nothings in high office conspicuously lack."

24. Holst, p. 5f.

25. Voss, I: 419.

26. Hardenberg, fragment of 1799–1800, in S, III: 568.

27. Gleim, I: 104f.

28. Goethe, *Die Wahlverwandtschaften*, in SW, XXI: 205. For Goethe's stipulation that the male servants are servants of the state, see F. Kittler, "Ottilie Hauptmann," p. 262.

29. Heydenreich, p. 99.

30. Ibid., pp. 99, 98.

31. See Hattenhauer, p. 174 (on civil service law and the state idol).

32. Hardenberg, "König und die Königin," in S, II: 489.

33. See von Westphalen, p. 9.

34. Dilthey and Heubaum, p. 246.

35. Humboldt, document of July 8, 1809, in ibid., p. 253. On demand for the general civil service exam, see Hattenhauer, p. 177.

36. Stephani, *Grundriss*, pp. 80, 74.

37. Roessler, p. 266.

38. Jeismann, p. 100.

39. *Allgemeines Landrecht*, II, §§ 66 and 73; p. 587.

40. Süvern, 1817, cited in Heinemann, p. 344.

41. Penzenkuffer, pp. 91f., 271. See also W. T. Krug, *Staat und Schule*, p. 97. The historical differentiation of systems of power that Foucault entitles *Discipline and Punish* was already accomplished (during the moment of differentiation itself, one might say,) by Penzenkuffer: in the earlier period, when the state had its foundation in bureaucrats who dispensed justice, the state remained despotic; it became a free and moral state only in 1800 when its foundation shifted to educational bureaucrats.

42. Von Westphalen, p. 118.

43. Schleiermacher, lecture of 1826, in PS, V: 238.

44. See, e.g., Niethammer, p. 197f. One of the first sentences that one primer dictates to a child's writing hand reads: "I call myself a human being" (Herrmann, p. 70).

45. Hausen, p. 385.

46. One pedagogue, however, said that the mother-child nexus was "nowhere more visible than in the classes that conduct the business of the state" (Schwarz, p. 4).

47. Kleist, *Prinz Friedrich von Homburg*, I: 677. The sentence is a partial plot summary of Kleist's play; see Act 3, scene 5. [Trans.]

48. See Hausen, pp. 283–87.   49. Donzelot, *Policing*, p. 18.

50. Holst, p. 106.   51. See Oppermann, p. 106.

52. See Jeismann, p. 112.

53. Schleiermacher, document of December 14, 1810, in P. Schwartz, p. 195.

54. Matthias, p. 218. Matthias has counted the following old-European certificates: examination in theology; formal written application; trial lesson; master's or doctoral degree; certificate of seminar completion; entrance examination.

55. Von Westphalen, p. 122.

56. K. Marx, I: 253. Marx, of course, is citing Hegel.

57. Gleim, I: 105; see also Bäumer, p. 22.

58. Cited in Blochmann, p. 116.

59. Goethe, *Wahlverwandtschaften*, in *SW*, XXI: 31.

60. Gleim, I: 106f.

61. Niethammer, p. 245; see also F. Kittler, "Ottilie Hauptmann," p. 264.

62. See Schreiber, "Zeichen," p. 293f.

63. See Leporin, p. 130f., and von Hanstein, I: 167.

64. Leporin, p. 142. Johann Christoph Gottsched was of the same opinion: see Wychgram, p. 224f. See also Boehm, pp. 301–23.

65. See von Hanstein, II: 348–53. Those who consider the poetic incest of Odoardo and Emilia Galotti to be interpretation run wild should reflect on the bridal dress the girl is wearing. See Act V of Lessing's *Emilia Galotti*.

66. See Busshoff, pp. 15–21.

67. See Stephani, *Grundriss*, pp. 77–81. Similarly, see W. T. Krug, *Staat und Schule*, p. 76.

68. F. Schlegel, *Über die Philosophie. An Dorothea*, in *KA*, VIII: 42.

69. Hintze, pp. 7, 39.

70. Hegel, *Logic*, p. 50.

71. See Lacan, *Encore*, p. 33. "Ontology is what has foregrounded in language the usage of the copula, isolating it as a signifier. . . . To exorcize it, it would perhaps suffice to propose that, when one says of anything at all that it is what it is, nothing obligates us in any way to isolate the verb *to be* [*être*]. It is pronounced *it is what it is* [*c'est ce que c'est*], and it could just as easily be written *idiswadidis* [*seskece*]. In this usage one would miss the copula completely. One would miss it completely if a discourse, which is the discourse of the master, of "being-to-me" [*m'être*], did not put the accent on the verb to be. . . . The entire dimension of being is produced in the current of the discourse of the master, of he who, uttering the signifier, expects of it that which is one of its effects as link, not to be overlooked, and whose condition of existence is that the signifier command. The signifier is first of all imperative." In the original French, the phrase "being-to-me" plays on the homophony of *m'être* and *maître*—"to be" with a first-person object pronoun, and "master." *Etre* is also the standard French translation of the Heideggerian *Sein* ("Being"). [Trans.] (Translation courtesy of Daniel Katz.)

72. Hegel, *Subjective Spirit*, III: 191. See also Reil, p. 416; and Hoffbauer, II: 99f.

73. Von Türk, p. 176.

74. F. Schlegel, *Philosophie*, in *KA*, VIII: 45.

75. Ibid., p. 46.

76. Ibid., p. 45.

77. Brandes, I: 53.

78. F. Schlegel, *Philosophie*, in *KA*, VIII: 61.

79. Tobler, in Goethe, *SW*, XXXIX: 6.

80. F. Schlegel, *Philosophie*, in *KA*, VIII: 48.

Language Channels

1. F. Schlegel, "Georg Forster. Fragment einer Charakteristik der deutschen Klassiker," in *KA*, I: 99; see also Hardenberg, "Dialogen," in *S*, II: 661–63.

2. Stephani, *Grundriss*, p. 54.
3. F. Schlegel, "Forster," in *KA*, I: 99.
4. Bergk, *Bücher*, p. 170.

The Im-possibility of Translations

1. F. Schlegel, *KA*, XVIII: 203.
2. Heinz Schlaffer, *Faust*, p. 135.
3. Goethe, letter of Sept. 7, 1821, in *W*, IV: 35, 75.
4. Goethe, *Aus meinem Leben: Dichtung und Wahrheit*, in *SW*, XXIV: 56f.
5. Goethe, *Wilhelm Meisters Lehrjahre*, in *SW*, XVII: 166.
6. Hegel, speech of Sept. 29, 1809, cited in Thaulow, III: 191f. According to Hegel, translated works of the ancients "taste like flat Rhine wine"—fine evidence for reading as oral consumption.
7. Hegel, *Aesthetics*, II: 964.
8. Bernhardi, II: 398, 422.
9. Foucault, *Order*, p. 283.
10. Hardenberg, letter of Nov. 30, 1797, in *S*, IV: 237.
11. F. Schlegel, "Forster," in *KA*, I: 99.
12. McLuhan, p. 206.
13. Goethe, "German Romance," in *SW*, XXXVIII: 142.
14. See Hegener.
15. Hardenberg, letter of Nov. 30, 1797, in *S*, IV: 237.
16. F. Schlegel, "Gespräch über die Poesie," in *KA*, II: 303.
17. Hardenberg, "Heinrich von Ofterdingen," in *S*, I: 287. Von Loeben's *Guido*, a mediocre imitation of *Ofterdingen*, provides the plain text for such a metaphysics: "The princess often seemed to have forgotten that she was speechless; for her father did not miss a single one of her words" (p. 13).
18. Herder, "Ueber die Wirkung der Dichtkunst auf die Sitten der Völker in alten und neuen Zeiten," in *SW*, VIII: 339; see also Bergk, *Bücher*, p. 109.
19. Heidegger, *Language*, pp. 118, 119.
20. See Giesebrecht, p. 118f.
21. See Bosse, "Dichter," pp. 117–25.
22. Moritz, *Anton Reiser*, p. 15.
23. See Moritz, "Erinnerungen," pp. 65–70.
24. Moritz, *Anton Reiser*, p. 176. A book of essay topics for young students begins with a corresponding pedagogic "fiction." It concerns an orphan day-laborer named Karl who "can hardly earn his keep." Thus, "his favorite pastime was to collect any piece of paper that had something written or printed on it and read it during the evening. Finally, he had the idea of sacrificing until he could afford to buy new paper. An old inkwell of his father's and a few quill pens that he found amounted to his greatest wealth; with these he wrote down his first thoughts about himself." (Dolz, p. 95f.) This is classical-romantic acculturation in a nutshell.

25. Moritz, *Anton Reiser*, p. 15f.
26. Ibid., p. 415.
27. Ibid., p. 222.
28. Stenzel, p. 36.
29. Moritz, *Anton Reiser*, p. 416.
30. For a detailed discussion, see Herrlitz, p. 81.
31. Hegel, *Aesthetics*, I: 593.
32. Kaiser, *Keller*, p. 31; see also p. 24.
33. Moritz, *Anton Reiser*, p. 30f.

34. Hoffmann, "Nachrichten von den neuesten Schicksalen des Hundes Berganza," in *Nachtstücke*, p. 139.

"The Golden Pot"

1. Hoffmann, "The Golden Pot," in *Tales*, p. 15.
2. Ibid., p. 38.
3. Ibid., pp. 26, 17.
4. Ibid., p. 18.
5. See Wagner, *My Life*, pp. 32 and 549. The allusion, of course, is to the opening of *Das Rheingold*. [Trans.]
6. Wagner actually constructed his "Wagalaweia" according to Grimm's rules of root meanings; see R. M. Meyer, p. 92.
7. Tillich, p. 27.
8. Hoffmann, "Golden Pot," in *Tales*, p. 18.
9. Ibid., p. 35.
10. On Goethe's poem "Erlkönig," see Zons, p. 127; on Hoffmann, see Schmidt, p. 168f.
11. Hoffmann, "Golden Pot," in *Tales*, p. 37.
12. Ibid., p. 49. A report from an elementary school in Dessau demonstrates that English cursive script was the pedagogical standard: "I saw several samples of the boys' writing taken from the latest public examination. They are a credit to the writing master. Several of the samples equal the finest English cursive" (von Türk, p. 19). A sample of a writing test (from 1743) can be found in Degering, p. 98.
13. Hoffmann, "Golden Pot," in *Tales*, pp. 49–50.
14. Ibid., p. 67.
15. Hardenberg, *Heinrich von Ofterdingen*, in *S*, I: 295. See F. Kittler, "Irrwege," pp. 442–48.
16. See Hoffmann, "Das fremde Kind," in *Serapions-Brüder*, pp. 472–510.
17. See the summary in Hey, pp. 26–30.
18. Stephani, *Schreibmethode*, p. 3f.
19. Ibid., p. 8; see also Schmack, p. 105.
20. Pöhlmann, p. xiv.
21. Stephani, *Schreibmethode*, p. 27f.
22. Ibid., p. 74.
23. Ibid., p. 44.
24. Pöhlmann, p. 121.
25. See Hey, pp. 35, 95, on this "reformer" from Döbeln.
26. Rühm, p. 278.
27. Stephani, *Schreibmethode*, pp. 43, 72–75.
28. Ibid., p. 41.
29. Hegel, *Phenomenology*, p. 344.
30. Stephani, *Schreibmethode*, p. 26.
31. Gleim, II: 57. Today's pedagogues did not invent the phrase "learning to learn" of which they are so proud.
32. Hippel, *Verbesserung*, p. 166.
33. See F. Kittler, "Sozialisation," pp. 99–115.
34. Charlotte tried to make Ottilie write, indeed, "to lead her toward a freer line in handwriting" in *Elective Affinities* (Goethe, *SW*, XXI: 51). The attempt failed and is thus the exception that proves the rule of writing in the classical pe-

riod: women, particularly ideal mothers like Ottilie, exist to make others speak, not to write; women, in particular real mothers like Charlotte, are not to teach writing. Ottilie, with her "stiff" handwriting, ends up copying the handwriting of a man, Eduard, who is far from perfect.

35. Hoffmann, "Golden Pot," in *Tales*, p. 60.

36. Montandon, p. 12.

37. Hoffmann, "Golden Pot," in *Tales*, p. 59.

38. Hardenberg, "Die Lehrlinge zu Sais," in *S*, I: 79.

39. Von Loeben, p. 338; see also p. 237.

40. Gedike, "Einige Gedanken über die Ordnung und Folge der Gegenstände des jugendlichen Unterrichts," in *Gesammelte Schulschriften*, II: 148f.

41. Hoffmann, "Johannes Kreislers Lehrbrief," in *Nachtstücke*, p. 323. See also Jaffé, pp. 153–55.

42. Hoffmann, "Golden Pot," in *Tales*, p. 51.

43. Ibid., pp. 33, 47.

44. Ibid., pp. 36, 52.

45. See Lacan, *Ecrits* (New York), pp. 321–24.

46. Olivier, p. 78.

47. See Hoffmann, "Golden Pot," in *Tales*, pp. 51, 58–59.

48. Basedow, II: 68.

49. Hufeland, *Guter Rat*, p. 64.

50. Stephani, *Schreibmethode*, p. 36.

51. Brandes, *Betrachtungen*, p. 108.

52. For Novalis, see F. Kittler, "Irrwege," p. 445.

53. Nietzsche, *The Gay Science*, V, pp. 348–49, 290–92.

54. Hoffmann, "Golden Pot," in *Tales*, p. 28.

55. Ibid., p. 66.   56. Ibid., p. 29.

57. Ibid., p. 45.   58. Ibid., pp. 26–27.

59. Hoffmann, "The Sandman," in *Tales*, pp. 94–99; see the discussion in F. Kittler, "Phantom," pp. 140–59.

60. See Ehrenreich and English, pp. 9–27; and Donzelot, pp. 16–18.

61. "Dark and unspeakable" because the Lindhorst-Rauerin or salamander-snake pair is incestuous. But in romanticism incest was the rule (rather than the exception) for family structure.

62. See Hoffmann, "Golden Pot," in *Tales*, pp. 45, 79.

63. Ibid., p. 42.

64. See Aschoff, p. 415f; and Geistbeck, p. 2f.

65. See Jaffé, p. 322f.

66. Hoffmann, "Golden Pot," in *Tales*, p. 63.

67. Foucault, "Fantasia of the Library," in *LCMP*, p. 90.

68. Hoffmann, "Golden Pot," in *Tales*, p. 63.

69. Menzel, I: 17.

70. See Paulsen, *Universitäten*, p. 79.

71. Paulsen, *Geschichte*, II: 222f.

72. Hoffmann, "Golden Pot," in *Tales*, p. 30.

73. Ibid., pp. 63–64.

74. Stephani, *Beschreibung*, p. 68; on "effort" see Hoffmann, "Golden Pot," in *Tales*, pp. 50–51.

75. Hoffmann, "Golden Pot," in *Tales*, p. 231.

76. See Bolz, p. 79f.

77. See Nietzsche, *Beyond Good and Evil*, V, 192, p. 105.
78. Lichtenberg, I: 814.
79. See D. Richter, p. 219.
80. Oest and Campe, 1787, cited in Rutschky, p. 314.
81. Schneider, p. 116.
82. See Foucault, *History of Sexuality*, pp. 41–42.
83. Hoffmann, "Golden Pot," in *Tales*, p. 91.
84. J. P. Richter, *Leben des Quintus Fixlein, aus fünfzehn Zettelkästen gezogen*, in *W*, IV: 74f.
85. The view of Schenda.
86. Hoffmann, "Golden Pot," in *Tales*, p. 68.
87. Furet and Ozouf, I: 90.
88. Niemeyer, p. 242.
89. Stephani, *Beschreibung*, p. 13.
90. Niemeyer, p. 247; see also Basedow, I: 61.
91. Trapp, p. 361.
92. The view of Engelsing, *Analphabetentum*, p. 126; but see Kehr, pp. 403–9.
93. Hoffmann, "Golden Pot," in *Tales*, p. 25.
94. Ibid., p. 92.
95. Tieck, "Die Gemälde," in *S*, XVII: 70; see M. Frank, *Allgemeine*, p. 351.
96. Stephani, *Schreibmethode*, pp. 6, 12.
97. Ibid., p. 4.
98. Hoffmann, "Golden Pot," in *Tales*, p. 38.
99. The words come from an academic report, prepared according to then recently established guidelines, on the new judge Ernst Theodor Wilhelm Hoffmann (document of July 18, 1795, in Hoffmann, *B*, I: p. 64). See also Heinemann, p. 68. [Ernst Theodor Wilhelm was Hoffmann's given name—Trans.]
100. Hoffmann, "Golden Pot," in *Tales*, p. 30.
101. See Hoffbauer, I: 168f.; and Reil, pp. 173–78.
102. See Maass, p. 296; and comments by Foucault, *Histoire de la folie*, Trans. as *Wahnsinn und Gesellschaft*, p. 507.
103. Hoffmann, "Golden Pot," in *Tales*, p. 23. An early reviewer of "The Golden Pot" visited Court Councilor Heerbrand and his wife Veronica in Dresden and while there had several long conversations with Heerbrand about "the invention of the high art of writing, . . . a certain authority possessed by the Fraktur script," and "the controversial question as to whether the Greeks used writing sand and blotter paper" (Anonymous, 1817, in Hoffmann, *B*, III: 62). The technological basis of the writing system of 1800 was thus administered by state bureaucrats, whereas by 1817 the poet Anselmus had long since disappeared with Serpentina to Atlantis. From this transcendental position, however, distant from all writing, Anselmus creates the possibility that readings or reviews of "The Golden Pot" can take place as visits with characters in the novella.
104. On the function of coffee, see Schivelbusch, pp. 50–52.
105. Hahnemann, "Striche," II: 244.
106. For more on the contrast between the two types of handwriting, see Gedike, "Ordnung," in *Gesammelte Schulschriften*, II: 150f.
107. Herder, "Vitae, non scholae discendum. Schulrede Weimar," in *SW*, XXX: 267.
108. Foucault, "La Folie," p. 128.
109. R. Campe, pp. 142, 154.

110. Hoffbauer, II: 100.

111. Hoffmann, "Golden Pot," in *Tales*, p. 70.

112. Ibid., p. 75.

113. Lichtenberg, I: 655.

114. Goethe, *Die Wahlverwandtschaften*, in *SW*, XXI: 21.

115. For a humorous and precise discussion, see Fühmann, pp. 78–80.

116. See Lacan, "The Deconstruction of the Drives," in *Four Fundamental Concepts*, p. 167.

117. Hoffmann, "Golden Pot," in *Tales*, p. 73.

118. See Foucault, "La Folie," p. 128.

119. Hoffmann, "Golden Pot," in *Tales*, p. 251.

120. Grävell, p. 5.

121. Document of Feb. 21, 1802, in Hoffmann, *B*, III: 109.

122. Grävell, p. 37.

123. Hoffmann, "Golden Pot," in *Tales*, p. 88.

124. Ibid., p. 67.

125. Ibid., p. 89.

126. Brandes, *Betrachtungen*, II: 440.

127. Pöhlmann, p. 38.

128. Why arrack, rather than something from the elder tree? To anticipate a possible book on intoxication and speech, Hoffmann's autobiographical explanation, that arrack was "the favorite drink" of "his friend, the conductor Johann Kreisler" ("Golden Pot," in *Tales*, p. 89) is tautological. More relevant is the fact that, at least in Ceylon, southern Arabia, and Persia, arrack was made with fermented palm juice. Lindhorst's library is, of course, lined with palm trees and his genealogical manuscript is made of palm leaves. The use of arrack therefore obeys a strict rule of symmetry: the same plants that, transformed into Serpentina, create the romantic intoxication of the hero create, when distilled, the alcoholic intoxication of the fairy tale's author.

129. See Elling, p. 27.

130. Hoffmann, "Golden Pot," in *Tales*, p. 91. One psychiatrist could not resist stressing the accuracy of this diagnostic description. It is indeed characteristic that the delirium of habitual drinkers "is not a hallucination concentrated in a single sense, but a *combined* occurrence across all the senses" (Klinke, p. 233).

131. Hoffmann, "Golden Pot," in *Tales*, p. 91.

132. Villaume, p. 62. Compare also Karl Philipp Moritz's new concept of style.

133. See the interpretation of the end of "The Golden Pot" by Apel, p. 206.

134. Hoffmann, "Golden Pot," in *Tales*, p. 92.

Authors, Readers, Authors

1. Furet and Ozouf, I: 90.

2. Pestalozzi, *Wie Gertrud ihre Kinder lehrt; ein Versuch, den Müttern Anleitung zu geben, ihre Kinder selbst zu unterrichten*, in *SW*, XIII: 306f.

3. Hoffmann, *Serapions-Brüder*, p. 26. Important comments on pseudo-Serapion arguments can be found in Hoffbauer, II: 65.

4. Spiess, p. 56.

5. Tieck, "Der Runenberg," in *S*, IV: 224; see Lindemann, p. 269f.

6. Arnold, II: 210; see also the overview provided by Leibbrand and Wettley, p. 349f.

7. J. P. Richter, *Leben des Quintus Fixlein, aus fünfzehn Zettelkästen gezogen*, in *W*, IV: 11.
8. Hoffmann, *Serapions-Brüder*, p. 22.
9. Hardenberg, *Heinrich von Ofterdingen*, in *S*, I: 312.
10. Tiedemann, *Untersuchungen*, III: 267.
11. J. P. Richter, *Leben Fibels, des Verfassers der Bienrodischen Fibel (vordatiert 1812)*, in *W*, IV: 417, 426f.
12. Brandes, *Betrachtungen*, III: 20.
13. Goethe, *Aus meinem Leben: Dichtung und Wahrheit*, in *SW*, XXV: 10.
14. Foucault, "What Is an Author?," in *LCMP*, pp. 113–38.
15. Bermann, in Pinthus, *Kinobuch*, p. 29.
16. J. P. Richter, *Leben Fibels*, in *W*, VI: 369.
17. Ibid., p. 435f.
18. A. W. Schlegel, *S*, II: 225.
19. Hegel, *Aesthetics*, II: 626–27; see also Hardenberg, *Ofterdingen*, in *S*, I: 209f.
20. Hegel, *Aesthetics*, II: 627.
21. Ibid., II: 967.
22. Hardenberg, fragment of 1798, in *S*, II: 650.
23. Goethe, *Wilhelm Meisters Wanderjahre oder Die Entsagenden*, in *SW*, XX: 15; see also Hannelore Schlaffer, *Wilhelm Meister*, p. 144f.
24. Lessing, *Laocoön*, p. 75.
25. Hoffmann, "Golden Pot," in *Tales*, pp. 55–56.
26. Hoffmann, "The Sandman," in *Tales*, pp. 104–5; see F. Kittler, "Phantom," pp. 162–64.
27. Hoffmann, *Serapions-Brüder*, p. 531.
28. Von Klöden, pp. 46, 72, 79, 89, 104.
29. K. M. Michel, p. 20.
30. Herrmann, p. 107.
31. Moritz, *Anton Reiser*, p. 176; see Wuthenow, p. 90.
32. Persuasively argued by K. M. Michel, p. 20.
33. See Arnheim, p. 27f.
34. Wagner, "Das Kunstwerk der Zukunft," in *GS*, III: 105f.
35. Spiess, p. 56.
36. Tieck, "Runenberg," in *S*, VI: 224.
37. For the theological interpretation, see M. Frank, *Allgemeine*, p. 267. Contemporary psychiatric cures provided contrary technical evidence. To cure fixed ideas, Reil used an almost theatrical method consisting in "an uninterrupted series of objects, like the images of the magic lamp, [which] passed before the senses of the mental patients" (Reil, p. 199).
38. Von Matt, p. 169.
39. Hoffmann, "Der Kampf der Sänger," in *Serapions-Brüder*, p. 274.
40. Von Matt, p. 171.
41. See Eisner, p. 105f.; exceptions in literary criticism are Bloom, pp. 36–52, and McConnell.
42. Hegel, letter of Nov. 13, 1797, in *B*, I: 55.
43. F. Schlegel, "Eisenfeile," in *KA*, II: 399.
44. Hardenberg, fragment of 1798, in *S*, III: 377.
45. Hardenberg, *Ofterdingen*, in *S*, I: 264.

46. Eichendorff, II: 55.

47. Hardenberg, *Ofterdingen*, in *S*, I: 264f.

48. Ibid., p. 345.

49. In *Wilhelm Meister's Apprenticeship*, the recruitment scenario during the initiation in the tower already shows signs of time-lapse photography. However, the four images from Meister's biography lack the transitiveness that constitutes the hallucinatory quality in *Ofterdingen*.

50. Goethe, conversation of 1806, cited in Riemer, p. 261.

51. See Freud, "Group Psychology and the Analysis of the Ego," in *SE*, XVIII: 106.

52. See Derrida, "Nietzsche's Otobiographie," pp. 33–36.

53. Von Loeben, p. 38f.

54. Ibid., p. 338.

55. On the *figuram implere*, see Auerbach, p. 66; applied to *Ofterdingen*, see Heftrich, p. 82.

56. Hardenberg, fragment of 1798, in *S*, II: 563.

57. Hardenberg, *Ofterdingen*, in *S*, I: 265.

58. See Haym, p. 378: "In the guise of mythology, in the generalization of metaphysics, the poem encapsulates the inner history, the poeticized life history of the poet himself. . . . This might seem to be an allegorical excess—but the poet, the hero of the apotheosis, is Hardenberg himself!"

59. Foucault, "What Is an Author?," in *LCMP*, p. 125.

60. Ibid., loc. cit. For Germany, see Bosse, "Autorisieren."

61. Lempicki, pp. 261f., 290.

62. Hoffmann, "*Kampf der Sänger*," in *Serapions-Brüder*, p. 278.

63. Hoffmann, "Ritter Gluck," in *Nachtstücke*, p. 22f.

The Toast

Function: Feminine Reader . . .

1. Hegel, manuscript of 1799–1800, in "Der Geist des Christentums," p. 466.

2. F. Schlegel, "Über die Philosophie. An Dorothea," in *KA*, VIII: 48.

3. Even Basedow, in order to give direction to the "idle gossip" of women, planned "a whole program for women's visits and social gatherings": it consisted in reading poetry (Wychgram, p. 240f).

4. Brandes, *Betrachtungen*, II: 466.

5. Schwarz; see also Blochmann, p. 66.

6. F. Schlegel, "Philosophie," in *KA*, VIII: 45; see Brandes, *Betrachtungen*, II: 281.

7. T. Huber, in L. F. Huber, pt. 3, vol. 3.

8. D. Schlegel, letter of Feb. 14, 1800, in *Briefwechsel*, I: 31.

9. Schlegel's editing of *Florentin* put the novel into the high or literary idiom—it contains almost none of the dative-accusative confusions that were the agrammatical rule in women's discourse circa 1800. Compare Deibel, p. 65.

10. Deibel, p. 1; for more perspective see Hannelore Schlaffer, "Frauen als Einlösung," p. 287.

11. T. Huber, in L. F. Huber, pt. 3, vol. 3.

12. Ibid., pt. 4, vol. 5. See also Riemer, pp. 164–66, on Goethe's marriage: Christiane was to "facilitate his more complete devotion to art, science, and offi-

cial duty by taking over onerous tasks.—Such was the only type of feminine creature he needed for free and relatively unhindered self-development. The type of woman concerned with rank and titles, who frequents learned society, and perhaps even has literary ambition herself, would never have been helpful or have provided for his domestic happiness."

13. Schwarz, p. 179.

14. T. Huber, in L. F. Huber, pt. 3, vol. 4.

15. See Strecker, pp. 9f.   16. B. Brentano, I: 300.

17. Ibid., p. 279.   18. Ibid., p. 254.

19. Ibid., p. 479; see F. Kittler, "Writing into the Wind," pp. 33–37.

20. C. Brentano, in B. Brentano, I: 19.

21. C. Brentano, in Steig, pp. 262–74.

22. L. F. Huber, 1802, cited in Kluckhohn, p. 276.

23. B. Brentano, II: 370. Bettina's identification with Mignon met with the author's approval. See Goethe, *Gespräche*, III: 224.

24. B. Brentano, II: 222, on Goethe's Ottilie.

25. Bergk, *Bücher zu lesen*, pp. 61, 64.

26. Brandes, *Betrachtungen*, II: 468.

27. Lacan, *Encore*, p. 71.

28. D. Schlegel, letter of Nov. 18, 1799, in *Briefwechsel*, I: 23.

29. Varnhagen, letter of Aug. 20, 1815, in *Briefwechsel*, IV: 266f; see Bürger, pp. 94–97.

30. Varnhagen, cited in Key, *Rahel*, p. 142.

31. Varnhagen, letter of Oct. 30, 1808, in *Briefwechsel*, I: 88.

32. Goethe, *Tasso*, 11. 1084–86; the German text is cited from Goethe, *SW*. Subsequent line numbers will be given in the text. We are grateful to Suhrkamp Publishers for permission to cite the translation by Michael Hamburger. [Trans.]

33. B. Brentano, II: 354 (about Goethe).

34. Goethe, conversation of Nov. 24, 1809, reported in Riemer, p. 313f; see Schreiber, "Zeichen der Liebe," p. 283.

35. Goethe, *Aus meinem Leben. Dichtung und Wahrheit*, in *SW*, XXIV: 176.

36. The quoted words of the Princess are "to say the least, ambiguous. In view of the sentiments Tasso has expressed throughout the scene, the effect upon him of the Princess's words is only to be expected. He interprets these lines as encouragement, which her final speech of the scene only strengthens. When Tasso is overcome with ecstasy, she can hardly be said to rebuff him" (Waldeck, p. 18).

37. See Lacan, "The Function and Field of Speech and Language in Psychoanalysis," in *Ecrits* (New York), p. 69.

38. B. Brentano, II: 163.

39. Goethe, conversation of 1807, in Riemer, p. 266.

40. Tieck, "Der Runenberg," in *S*, IV: 243.

41. Tieck, "Phantasus. Eine Sammlung von Mährchen, Erzählungen, Schauspielen und Novellen," in *S*, IV: 244.

42. Hoffmann, "The Golden Pot," in *Tales*, p. 38.

43. Hoffmann, "Golden Pot," in *Tales*, p. 16f; see Hoffbauer, II: 97–100.

44. Hoffmann, "Golden Pot," in *Tales*, p. 40; Councilor Heerbrand reacts with the same cry of "romantic rot!" when in 1817, during a visit from the reviewer, he finds his wife Veronica reading "The Golden Pot" (Anonymous, in Hoffmann, *B*, III: 63).

45. Hoffmann, "Golden Pot," in *Tales*, p. 41.

46. See Clément, pp. 148–54.

47. Hoffmann, "Golden Pot," in *Tales*, p. 73.

48. Ibid., p. 40.

49. Theweleit and Langbein, p. 144.

50. Hoffmann, "Golden Pot," in *Tales*, p. 86. The reviewer of 1817 also comes up with this interpretation (Anonymous, 1817, in Hoffmann, *B*, III: 63).

51. Hoffmann, "Golden Pot," in *Tales*, p. 86.

52. Friedrich Schleiermacher, "Katechismus der Vernunft für edle Frauen," in F. Schlegel, *Prosaischen Jugendschriften*, II: 267.

53. For a preliminary reading see Schmidt, pp. 165–76.

54. Goethe, conversations of Dec. 6 and 10, 1809, in Riemer, p. 236.

55. Goethe, conversation of 1809, in *Gespräche*, II: 474. See the ironic comments by Brandes, *Betrachtungen*, II: 460.

56. Alewyn, "Klopstocks Leser," p. 115.

57. Kaiser, *Wandrer*, p. 201. See also Gleim's contemporary formulation, II: 110.

58. F. Schlegel, *Ideen*, in *KA*, II: 267.

59. Menzel, I: 2.

60. Goethe, conversations of 1806 and Jan. 29, 1804, in Riemer, pp. 260, 247.

61. See Erning, p. 69.

62. Anonymous, cited in Schenda, p. 60.

63. Gessinger, *Schriftspracherwerb*, p. 39.

64. Hoche, p. 68.

65. Beyer, p. 23.

66. Hence the law "bars and lending libraries are not tolerated here" in the American constitution of *Wilhelm Meister's Travels*. (Goethe, *Wilhelm Meisters Wanderjahre oder Die Entsagenden*," in *SW*, XX: 164). See Hannelore Schlaffer, p. 141.

67. Beyer, p. 27. "They" are, of course, the worthless books and not, as Beyer's failure might imply, the scholars.

68. See I. H. Fichte, I: 6f.

69. J. G. Fichte, "Die Grundzüge des gegenwärtigen Zeitalters," in *W*, VII: 111.

70. Bergk, *Bücher zu lesen*, pp. 411–13.

71. Ibid., p. 64.

72. Ibid., p. 339; see also Bergk, *zu Denken*, p. 16.

73. Bergk, *Bücher zu lesen*, p. 409.   74. Ibid., p. 34.

75. Ibid., p. 199.   76. See Graubner, pp. 72–75.

77. J. P. Richter, "Kleine Nachschule zur ästhetischen Vorschuler," in *W*, V: 509–11.

78. Niethammer, *Der Streit*, pp. 144–49.

79. Hegel, letter of Nov. 13, 1797, in *Briefe*, I: 55f. The credit for calling attention to these lines belongs to Derrida, *Glas*, p. 174.

80. Schwarz, p. 191.

81. Niethammer, "Bedürfniss," cited in Goethe, *W*, XL: 402.

82. The view of Helmers, p. 194.

83. Bünger, p. 293.

84. Gleim, cited in H. J. Frank, p. 295. For a discussion of Betty Gleim, see Zimmermann.

85. See Blochmann, pp. 71, 99–112. Further, and in part underestimated evi-

dence from girls' schools and related programs can be found in Wychgram, pp. 246–55, above all p. 255 (on reading as therapy for reading mania).

86. Gleim, II: 110.

87. Sartorius, in Goethe, conversation of Oct. 16, 1808, in *Gespräche*, II: 375. Similar statements can be found in Kluckhohn, p. 283.

88. Blochmann, p. 71.

89. This phrase is in English in the original book. [Trans.]

90. Hoffmann, "Klein Zaches," p. 33.

91. Schwarz, p. 173; see also Blochmann, p. 66.

. . . and the Kingdom of God

1. Niethammer, "Bedürfniss," in Goethe, *W*, XL: 2, p. 401.

2. Niethammer, letter of Feb. 3, 1809, in Goethe, *W*, XL: 2, p. 410.

3. See Kesting, pp. 420–36.

4. Niethammer, "Bedürfniss," in Goethe, *W*, XL: 2, p. 405.

5. Ibid., p. 405f.

6. Ibid., p. 407f.

7. Niethammer, letter of June 28, 1808, in Goethe, *W*, XL: 2, p. 398.

8. Lacan, *Encore*, p. 51.

9. Herrlitz, pp. 95–96, provides evidence from Goethe's papers.

10. Ludwig, p. 57.

11. Niethammer, "Bedürfniss," cited in Goethe, *W*, XL: 2, p. 402.

12. For a discussion of Lacan's terms *le discours du maître* and *le discours universitaire*, see Hass, pp. 9–34.

13. See Herrlitz, p. 75.

14. Niethammer, cited in Herrlitz, p. 97.

15. See Matthias, pp. 403, 211.

16. Thiersch, I: 340. Gedike had similar ideas, see "Einige Gedanken über deutsche Sprach- und Stilübungen auf Schulen," in *Gesammelte Schulschriften*, II: 236f.

17. Matthias, p. 186; see Jäger, "Deutschunterricht," p. 144f.

18. Giesebrecht, p. 126.

19. Schleiermacher, document of Dec. 14, 1810, in P. Schwartz, p. 196.

20. Bernhardi, document of 1810, in P. Schwartz, p. 171.

21. Schleiermacher, document of Dec. 14, 1810, in P. Schwartz, p. 196.

22. Giesebrecht, p. 129.

23. See H. J. Frank, p. 260f.

24. P. Schwartz, p. 187.

25. See the figures in L. von Wiese, I: 33, 41, 404f.

26. The view of Brandes, *Betrachtungen*, III: 31f.

27. See Gessinger, *Sprache*, p. 79.

28. Schleiermacher, document of Dec. 14, 1810, in P. Schwartz, p. 173.

29. F. Schlegel, *Ideen*, in *KA*, II: 261.

30. Niethammer, *Der Streit*, p. 257; see also Heinemann, p. 198. The same criterion for the formation of bureaucrats can be found in J. G. Fichte, "Ueber das Wesen des Gelehrten, und seine Erscheinung im Gebiete der Freiheit. In öffentlichen Vorlesungen, gehalten zu Erlangen im Sommer-Halbjahre 1805," in *SW*, VI: 354.

31. Süvern, document of 1816, in Budde, I: 72.

32. Penzenkuffer, p. 62f, n.

33. See Turk and Kittler, pp. 9–20.

34. Voss, II: 326.

35. K. Fricke, p. 16. Indeed, only a teacher would have been capable of such a singularly clear formulation.

36. Hinrichs, p. 69f.

37. J. G. Fichte, *Die Grundlage der gesammten Wissenschaftslehre*, in *G*, I: 415.

38. Ibid., p. 415n.

39. See Vietta, *Sprache*, p. 25f, on Hardenberg's reception of Fichte's ideas.

40. J. G. Fichte, *Plan anzustellender Rede-Uebungen*, in *G*, II: 130. With these words, the tutor Fichte offered his services, immediately after the establishment of the *Abitur* and the inclusive German essay, as director of a private, but publicly funded, essay-writing institute. The institute was not established, but German Poetry was.

41. McLuhan, *Understanding Media*, p. 173.

42. J. G. Fichte, *Deducirter Plan einer zu Berlin zu errichtenden höheren Lehranstalt*, in *SW*, VIII: 98; see Engelsing, *Der literarische Arbeiter*, p. 103f.

43. See I. H. Fichte, I: 195. Humboldt also gave theoretical consecration to this style of lecturing. See McClelland, p. 124.

44. J. G. Fichte, letter of June 21, 1794, in *G*, III: 143.

45. See Schiller's explanation (XVI: 52f) of why *Don Carlos* cannot have textual coherence in the conventional sense; also consider Fichte's disdainful reply to Schiller's charges of incoherence: "The discovery that everything I write is in such dire need of revision has made me, as it should, quite attentive" (J. G. Fichte, letter of June 26, 1795, in *G*, III: 340).

46. Schiller, letter of Aug. 3–4, 1795, in I. H. Fichte, II: 388.

47. See J. G. Fichte, letter of June 27, 1795, in I. H. Fichte, II: 380.

48. See B. von Wiese, pp. 487, 447.

49. Goethe, letter of April 13, 1821, in Hegel, *Briefe*, II: 258. See also Löwith, pp. 17–28.

50. Hinrichs, p. 8.

51. See F. Kittler, "Vergessen," pp. 202–9.

52. Lukács, p. 541.

53. Ibid.

54. Hegel, *Aesthetics*, II: 1224.

55. On Hinrichs, see Weimar, pp. 307–12; note his dictum, "German literary criticism, as an applied aesthetic, was born in the Hegelian school" (p. 312).

56. Blumenberg, p. 93.

57. Wellek and Warren, p. 120f.

58. Derrida, "Titel (noch zu bestimmen)," p. 25f.

59. Bürger; for a general commentary, see McClelland, p. 16: "How ironic that the German universities have for generations taught their students to look with an open and critical eye upon every matter except the institution of the university."

60. Holborn, p. 365.

61. See Reinhardt, "Die klassische Walpurgisnacht. Entstehung und Bedeutung." in *Von Werken*, pp. 384–90.

62. Hegel, *Phenomenology*, p. 493.

63. Ibid., p. 492.

64. Baggesen, 1795, cited in Léon, I: 436f. Consider above all the refrain of this "drinking doctrine": "I am an I, who drank the not-I, sitting in my cups: / Hallelujah!"

65. Hegel, letter of Aug. 2, 1821, in *Briefe*, II: 275.

66. Hegel, *Phenomenology*, pp. 65, 27.

67. F. Schlegel, letter of June, 1793, in *Briefe*, I: 97.

68. J. G. Fichte, *Die Grundzüge des gegenwärtigen Zeitalters*, in *SW*, VII: 109. See Bosse, "Autorisieren," p. 130f.

69. Hegel, *Phenomenology*, p. 218.   70. See ibid., p. 16.

71. Ibid., pp. 218–19.   72. Ibid., p. 221.

73. Hinrichs, p. 136.   74. See Lacan, *Encore*, p. 78.

75. Hegel, *Phenomenology*, p. 59.   76. Ibid., p. 9.

77. Hegel, *Aesthetics*, II: 1218.

78. Von Rochow, 1776, cited in Gessinger, "Schriftspracherwerb," p. 26. For parallels in other primers of the period, see Schenda, p. 51f.

79. See, alone among all interpreters of Hegel, Neumann, p. 385f.

80. On the signature and date in general, see Derrida, "Signature Event Context," in *Margins*, pp. 309–30.

81. Stephani, *Beschreibung*, p. 66.

82. See Hegel, *Phenomenology*, pp. 38–41.

83. Ibid., p. 39; note the same claim or arrogance in Schopenhauer, I: xiii.

84. See F. Kittler, "Vergessen," p. 210.

85. Hegel, *Phenomenology*, p. 66.

86. Garfinkel, *Common Sense*, I: 210.

87. Hegel, "Wie der gemeine Menschenverstand die Philosophie nehme,— dargestellt an den Werken des Herrn Krug's," in *GW*: IV: 178.

88. Ibid., p. 179.

89. Henrich, p. 160.

90. Hegel, *System der Philosophie*, in *SW*, IX: 63n.

91. W. T. Krug, *Lebensreise*, p. 5f.

92. Ibid., pp. 114–21.

93. Ibid., pp. 122–26.

94. Hegel, "Wie der gemeine Menschenverstand," in *GW*, IV: 180.

95. See Derrida, *Glas*, pp. 108–87 (on Nanette Endel, Maria von Tucher, and above all Hegel's sister Christiane, who vanished from an insane asylum in Zwiefalten into the water of the Nagold—an Antigone in the Real).

96. Hegel, *System der Philosophie*, in *SW*, X: 355.

97. Goethe, letter of June 24, 1794, in J. G. Fichte, *G*, III: 145.

98. See Rohde, p. vi.

99. See Creuzer, "Das Studium," pp. 1–22.

100. Rohde, p. v.

101. Creuzer, letters of June 30, 1806, and May 17, 1805, in *Liebe*, pp. 259, 95.

102. Ibid., pp. 277, 197.

103. Ibid., p. 142.

104. See Rohde, p. 50.

105. See Creuzer, letters of Nov. 7, 1804, and Dec. 19, 1805, in *Liebe*, pp. 33, 202.

106. Ibid., p. 292f.

Nietzsche: Incipit Tragoedia

1. Benn, *Roman des Phänotyp. Landsberger Fragment*, in *GW*, II: 169. Nietzsche's *Foreword* appeared the year Benn was born, 1886.

2. Benn, speech in Knokke, in *GW*, I: 543.

3. Hofmannsthal, *Buch*, p. 61.

4. Meier-Graefe, II: 733. The distinction made here by two proper names elsewhere came together as Shiva.

5. Nietzsche, *Zarathustra*, I, "On Reading and Writing," p. 152.

6. Villaume, p. 67.

7. Nietzsche, *Beyond Good and Evil*, V, 192, p. 105.

8. Schenda, p. 444. According to Schenda's cautious estimates, the percentages of the central-European population over the age of six that had been alphabetized were: 25 percent in 1800; 40 percent in 1830; 75 percent in 1870; and 90 percent in 1900.

9. Nietzsche, *Untimely Meditations*, II, 5, p. 87.

10. "We absorb all previous culture only to entomb it in paper once more. We pay for the books we read with those that we write." (Menzel, I: 4).

11. Nietzsche, *Human*, Vol. II, I, 156, p. 248.

12. Nietzsche, *Untimely Meditations*, II, 5, p. 87.

13. Nietzsche, fragment of 1887, in *W*, VIII, 2, p. 218.

14. Kirchner, p. 14; see Hellpach, "Psychopathologisches," p. 199.

15. See Nietzsche, diary entry for Dec. 8, 1859, in *WB*, I: 188.

16. Klossowski, p. 323.

17. Nietzsche, lecture of 1872, in *W*, III, 2, p. 170f. "The pinnacle of public-school education" is a literal quote from the pedagogue Deinhardt. See also Jäger, *Schule*, p. 41.

18. See Jensen and Lamszus, pp. 20–67, 142.

19. Nietzsche, "Über die Zukunft unserer Bildungs-Anstalten," *W*, III, 2, p. 171.

20. Nietzsche, letter of Oct. 19, 1861, in *WB*, II: 1–5.

21. Nietzsche, fragment of 1868–69, in ibid., V: 254.

22. Nietzsche, fragment of 1862, in ibid., II: 71.

23. Franziska Nietzsche, letter of Aug. 3, 1889, cited in Gilman, "Nietzsche's 'Niederschriften,'" p. 323.

24. See the discussion in Gilman, p. 342.

25. Rupp, "Der 'ungeheure Consensus,'" p. 191.

26. Foucault, *Order*, p. 300.

27. Nietzsche, fragment of 1868–69, in *WB*, V: 205.

28. See, e.g., Reil, p. 417: "The patient hears a wild noise, but nothing comprehensible; he is incapable of extracting any sound from the manifold and tracing it to its cause, and thus cannot determine its meaning."

29. Ibid., p. 136.

30. Nietzsche, fragment of 1864, in *WB*, II: 408.

31. Nietzsche, *Ecce Homo*, "Why I Am So Clever," 10, p. 258.

32. Ziehen, document of May 18, 1889, in Podach, p. 1453.

33. Nietzsche, *Nietzsche contra Wagner*, "Where I Offer Objections," p. 664.

34. Nietzsche, fragment of 1884–85, in *W*, VII, 3, p. 59.

35. Valéry, "Poetry and Abstract Thought," p. 63.

36. Mallarmé, "Crise de vers," in *OC*, p. 366.

37. See Bridgwater, "Sources," p. 32 (on Mauthner, Holz, Walden, and the *Sturm* poets); see also the documents in Pörtner, pp. 395–461.

38. See Valéry, diary entry for Oct. 10, 1891, in *Oeuvres*, I: 1723 (on Mallarmé).

39. See Matthias, pp. 253f, 350f.

40. Lehmann, cited in Paulsen, *Geschichte*, II: 710.

41. Jensen and Lamszus, p. 147.

42. Hackenberg, p. 70.

43. See Stern, *Psychologie*, p. 88, and Ament, p. 80.

44. Barthes, "Preface," in *CE*, pp. xiv–xv.

45. See F. Kittler, "Wie man abschaft," pp. 152–54.

46. Nietzsche, "Ueber Wahrheit und Lüge im aussermoralischen Sinne," *W*, III, 2, p. 371.

47. Ibid., p. 373.

48. See also Mallarmé, "Crise de vers," in *OC*, p. 363f.

49. See F. Kittler, "Nietzsche," p. 192.

50. Nietzsche, *Untimely Meditations*, IV, 5, p. 249.

51. Nietzsche, *Beyond Good and Evil*, VIII, 255, p. 195. See F. Kittler, "Pink Floyd, Brain Damage," p. 474f.

52. Nietzsche, *Birth of Tragedy*, 9, p. 67.

53. Arnheim, p. 27.

54. Nietzsche, *Birth of Tragedy*, 9, p. 67.

55. For the basics of film, see Hein and Herzogenrath, p. 31f.

56. For the similarity of such music to the subsequent sound techniques, see Schlüpmann, pp. 104f, 127.

57. Nietzsche, *Untimely Meditations*, IV, 10, p. 249.

58. Nietzsche, fragment of 1868, in *WB*, V: 268.

59. Rupp, *Rhetorische Strukturen*, p. 95.

60. Nietzsche, *Twilight*, "What I Owe to the Ancients," I, p. 557.

61. Nietzsche, letter of Feb. 2, 1884, in *WB*, II: 575.

62. Nietzsche, *Genealogy*, Preface, 8, p. 23.

63. Sarkowski, p. 18.

64. See Jean Paul Richter, *Leben des Quintus Fixlein aus fünfzehn Zettel-kästen gezogen*, in *W*, IV: 81f.

65. See Mallarmé, "La Littérature. Doctrine," in *OC*, p. 850.

66. Nietzsche, letter of Nov. 5, 1879, in *Briefe*, IV: 28.

67. Kohlschmidt, p. 47.

68. See the discussion in Geistbeck, pp. 43f, 155f; for an insightful discussion of the literary consequences, see O'Brien, pp. 464–72.

69. Stramm, p. 26.

70. Ibid., p. 62.

71. Nietzsche, *Ecce Homo*, "Human, All-Too-Human," 4, pp. 287–88.

72. Ibid., "Why I Am So Clever," 8, p. 253.

73. Mallarmé, "L'Action restreinte," in *OC*, p. 370. This and following Mallarmé translations courtesy of Marian Sugano. [Trans.]

74. Nietzsche, *Ecce Homo*, "Why I Am So Clever," 9, p. 254.

75. Nietzsche, letter of Aug. 14, 1881, in *Briefe*, IV: 71f. Nietzsche's plan dates back to the "year of blindness," 1879; see the letter of Aug. 14, 1879, in *B*, II, 5, p. 435.

76. Janz, II: 95.

77. Nietzsche, letter of March 1882, in *Briefwechsel mit Overbeck*, p. 170. Another invalid among Germany's pioneers of the typewriter, the forgotten officer and feuilletonist Dagobert von Gerhardt, didn't explain why he got a typewriter: a war wound in his arm left him physically and psychically crippled (see von Gerhardt). This much, at any rate, is clear: Hoffmann's captain, also suffering from an arm wound, was saved in 1813 by a wise woman; the officer of 1870–71 is saved by technology.

78. Burghagen, p. 22f.

79. Burghagen, p. 119f; also see Scholz, p. 9. But even with the Remington, one ophthalmologist found that the decisive aspect of "progress was that one could write with the eyes closed" (Cohn, p. 371). Thus Sherlock Holmes erred in supposing that nearsightedness should hinder typewriting (Conan Doyle, p. 192).

80. Janz, II: 95, 81.

81. Burghagen, p. 120.

82. Herbertz, p. 560.

83. See Lacan, "Agency of the Letter in the Unconscious," in *Ecrits* (New York), p. 150f.

84. Burghagen, p. 49. See the discussion in Richards, p. 24.

85. Mallarmé, "La littérature. Doctrine," in *OC*, p. 850.

86. See the discussion in Scholz, p. 12f.

87. Cited in Herbertz, p. 559; see also Münsterberg, *Grundzüge*, p. 386.

88. Nietzsche, letter of Feb., 1882, in *Briefe*, IV: 97.

89. Nietzsche, *Genealogy*, II, 3, p. 61.

90. Ibid., 7, p. 68.

91. Reinhardt, "Nietzsches Klage der Ariadne," in *Von Werken*, p. 477.

92. Nietzsche, *Dionysos-Dithyramben*, W, VI, 3, pp. 396–99.

93. Nietzsche, *Ecce Homo*, "Thus Spoke Zarathustra," 8, p. 308.

94. Nietzsche, *Beyond Good and Evil*, IX, 295, p. 234.

95. Nietzsche, *Twilight*, "Skirmishes of an Untimely Man," 19, p. 526.

96. Nietzsche, *Ecce Homo*, "Why I Write Such Good Books," 5, p. 267.

97. Nietzsche, *Beyond Good and Evil*, IX, 269.

98. H. Lange, "Wie lernen Frauen die Politik verstehen?," in *K*, II: 101.

99. H. Lange, "Weltanschauung und Frauenbewegung," in *K*, I: 252.

100. Schreiber, "Die Ordnung," p. 229.

101. See Nietzsche, *Zarathustra*, I, "Zarathustra's Prologue," 7, pp. 132–33.

102. Nietzsche, *The Gay Science*, II, 84, p. 138; see also Du Prel, p. 67.

103. Scholz, p. 15; see also Richards, p. 1.

104. Nietzsche, letter of July 23, 1885, in Janz, II: 393.

105. Förster-Nietzsche, p. 138.

106. For an overview, see Braun, p. 139.

107. See Nietzsche, letter of April, 1884, in Förster-Nietzsche, p. 202: "As to topics for fine dissertations, my *The Dawn* is rich material. I encourage you to read it, as well as *The Gay Science*—both books are also introductions and commentaries to my *Zarathustra*."

108. The author of a monograph entitled *Nietzsche and Women* finds the "grotesqueness of this fact" something "not worthy of further emphasis" (Brann, p. 170f).

109. Nietzsche, letter of Oct. 22, 1884, in *Briefe*, V, 2, p. 571.

110. Janz, II: 398.

111. Nietzsche, letter of July 19, 1887, in Janz, II: 354.

112. See Nietzsche, *Twilight,* "Skirmishes of an Untimely Man," 19, p. 526.

113. Druskowitz, *Pessimistische Kardinalsätze,* p. 18f. (The date of publication for this work is uncertain—biographies sometimes make it difficult to establish bibliographies.)

114. Nietzsche, *Human,* I, 7, no. 409, p. 153.

115. Nietzsche, fragment, in *W,* VII, 1, pp. 540–44.

116. See Nietzsche, *Untimely Meditations,* 1–3, and the discussion in F. Kittler, "Nietzsche," pp. 159–97.

117. Ziehen, document of Jan. 19, 1889, in Podach, p. 1453.

The Great Lalulā

Psychophysics

1. See Lacan, "Lituraterre," p. 10.

2. Ebbinghaus, *Memory,* p. 25.

3. Ibid., p. 5.

4. On the history of this research, see Manis, p. 27.

5. Kvale, p. 240.

6. Ebbinghaus, *Memory,* p. 28.

7. Ibid., p. 55.

8. "Die Hähnische Litteralmethode," p. 94.

9. Thus a text of "art physiology" (!) distinguishes the "psychological age of the doctrine of memory" ("memory as an aid to consciousness") from the physiological age, in which only storage techniques count (Hirth, p. 327f).

10. On Nietzsche, see Foucault, "Nietzsche, Genealogy, History," in *LCMP,* pp. 162–64.

11. The prerequisite for any psychophysics, according to Bölsche, p. 16.

12. Ebbinghaus, *Memory,* p. 25.   13. Ibid., p. 23.

14. Ibid. See also Ogden, p. 187.   15. Ebbinghaus, *Memory,* p. 23.

16. Hatvani, p. 210.   17. Ebbinghaus, *Memory,* p. 22.

18. See Ebbinghaus, *Grundzüge,* I: 676.

19. Ebbinghaus, *Memory,* p. 23.

20. For a definition, see Lacan, "Subversion of the Subject and Dialectic of Desire," in *Ecrits* (New York), p. 298.

21. Such is Turk's critical interpretation of Foucault's history of language in "Das 'Klassische Zeitalter.'"

22. Ebbinghaus, *Memory,* p. 22.

23. Ibid., p. 101.

24. See R. Stephan, p. 59f.

25. Morgenstern, "Der Gingganz," in *Galgenlieder,* p. 319.

26. See Derrida, *Grammatology,* pp. 8–26.

27. Morgenstern, "Epigramme und Sprücher," in *GW,* p. 330.

28. See Spitzer, pp. 104–6.

29. C. Brentano, "Aus der Chronika eines fahrenden Schülers," in *W,* II: 684.

30. Kvale, p. 241 (on Ebbinghaus).

31. Morgenstern, "Stufen," in *GW,* p. 392.

32. Liede, I: 6.

33. Alewyn, "Morgenstern," p. 401.

34. Spitzer, p. 90.

35. The view of the romantic, Bernhardi, II: 422.

36. Ebbinghaus, *Memory*, p. 51.   37. Solomons and Stein, p. 508f.

38. Hatvani, p. 210.   39. Zeitler, p. 443.

40. "It is remarkable that pedagogy has concerned itself so little with investigating such laws. One would think that it would attend to a child's actual behavior before it proceeded to try to improve performance." So say Jensen and Lamszus (p. 16) of their classical predecessors. Similar thoughts are expressed by Ostermai, p. 51f.

41. See Berger, p. 172.

42. Ebbinghaus, *Grundzüge*, I: 709.

43. See Preyer, p. 36, and Goldscheider, p. 505.

44. Ebbinghaus, *Grundzüge*, I: 728.

45. Tarde, p. 350.

46. Preyer, p. 7.

47. Stern, *Psychologie*, p. 157.

48. Kussmaul, p. 182 (on clinical and experimental work).

49. For a history of the relevant research, see the summary in Hécaen and Angelergues, pp. 25–50.

50. Durr, in Ebbinghaus, *Grundzüge*, II: 730.

51. Ziehen, "Aphasie," p. 670 (conceivably a precise enumeration of literary possibilities since 1900).

52. Von Kieseritzky, p. 53.

53. A certain Gowers located it in the right-brain correlate of the Broca position.

54. See Saussure, p. 66. The "sound-image," which is rigorously distinguished from the motoric image, corresponds to the "word-sound image" of physiology (Ziehen, "Aphasie," p. 665f), which abbreviates the following formulation: "activity in the audible region corresponding to previous excitation of this center by an external stimulus" (Sachs, p. 3).

55. Freud, "The Unconscious," in *SE*, XIV: 201f.

56. Lindner, p. 191. See also Münsterberg, *Grundzüge*, p. 247f.

57. See Philipp, p. 126f.

58. Hofmannsthal, "Chandos," p. 130.

59. Ibid., p. 138.

60. Von Monakow, p. 416f. On the inability to read whole words, see also Lay, p. 81. Interpretations based on Hofmannsthal's attendance at university lectures in Vienna are one-sided in their treatment of the language-deficiency theme; only Ernst Mach's epistemology is considered relevant (see Wunberg).

61. Ziehen, "Aphasie," p. 675.

62. Hofmannsthal, "Chandos," pp. 133, 144.

63. See Lindner, p. 193f, and R. Lange, pp. 76–78.

64. Hofmannsthal, "Chandos," p. 135.

65. Von Monakow, p. 522; see also Kussmaul, p. 176f.

66. Ebbinghaus, *Grundzüge*, I: 675f.

67. Gutzmann, p. 484.

68. Sachs, p. 70.

69. Klinke, p. 202.

70. Ibid., p. 100f. On sources of noise, see also Ziehen, *Leitfaden*, p. 182; R. M. Meyer, p. 255, and Schreber, p. 229.

71. See the general discussion in Heidegger, "Rimbaud," p. 17.
72. Schreber, pp. 168—69.
73. Ziehen, *Leitfaden*, p. 145f. See also Jung and Riklin, p. 63.
74. Liede, I: 8.
75. On the poetry of train noise, see Breucker, p. 323f.
76. See Ach, pp. 196—210.
77. George, *Zwei Träume*. In *GAW*, XVII: 30f.
78. Nietzsche, *Genealogy*, I, 5, p. 29.
79. Ziehen, "Aphasie," p. 685.
80. Freud and Josef Breuer, *Studies on Hysteria*, in *SE*, II: 55, 179.
81. Rilke, *Brigge*, p. 58.   82. Wundt, I, 1, 569.
83. See Erdmann and Dodge, p. 9.   84. Zeitler, p. 403.
85. Erdmann and Dodge, p. 1.   86. Hoffbauer, II: 286f.
87. Filippo Marinetti, *Futurist Manifesto*, cited in Baumgarth, *Geschichte*, p. 169.
88. Zeitler, p. 401. See also Wernicke, p. 511.
89. Messmer, p. 288; see also p. 273f.
90. Bahr, p. 9.
91. Ibid., p. 28.
92. Holz, X: 574.
93. Ibid.; see also Schulz, pp. 71—83. Of course, one wonders why Holz didn't carry his idea through to its logical conclusion:

> If this note were not part of a scholarly work,
> then this type of positioning alone,
> more than any central axis,
> would minimize the ophthalmokinetic return path.

94. Spengler, I: 41.
95. Swift, p. 302.
96. See Ellenberger, I: 177, and the already-historical historical summary in Janet, pp. 376—404.
97. Solomons and Stein, p. 503.
98. Ibid., p. 504.
99. Ibid., p. 505.
100. Freud, "Recommendations to Physicians Practising Psycho-analysis," in *SE*, XII: 115.
101. See Foucault, "Revolutionary Action: 'Until Now,'" in *LCMP*, pp. 218—33.
102. See biographical material in Brinnin, p. 29.
103. See Solomons and Stein, pp. 500, 506.
104. Stein, cited in Brinnin, p. 30.
105. Stein, p. 295.
106. On Gertrude Stein, see Skinner, pp. 50—57; on women who write and the university in general, see Maschke, p. 12.
107. Solomons and Stein, pp. 508, 498.
108. Breton, *Manifesto*, pp. 29—30.
109. Preyer, p. 12.
110. Hegel, *System der Philosophie (Encyclopädie)*, in *SW*, X: 351.
111. Solomons and Stein, p. 506.

Technological Media

1. Solomons and Stein, p. 506.
2. Ibid., p. 506f.
3. See, e.g., Villiers, p. 38, and, by contrast, Read and Welsh, pp. 2-6.
4. Villiers, p. 13. Perhaps because he despised phonographs, H. H. Ewers translated the final sentence into German with virtuoso repression, putting "words" for "vibrations"; Hugo Ball's "oscillating of divine cadences," by contrast, matches Villiers' fine phrase, even though it is not a translation (cited in Philipp, p. 127).
5. Villiers, p. 10. For the scientific approximation of such novelistic utopias, see Hornborstel and Abraham, p. 223f.
6. Friedlaender, p. 159.
7. Ibid., p. 159f.
8. Cros, p. 136. Translation by Daniel Katz. [Trans.]
9. See Chew, p. 3, and Read and Welsh, p. 17.
10. See Bruch, p. 26.
11. See Villiers, p. 17, and Kittler, "Pink Floyd," p. 470.
12. Key, Das Jahrhundert, pp. 219-49.
13. See Bruch, pp. 31, and (on the illustration) 69.
14. The situation is like that alleged in a parody of Arno Holz's concept of art: "In such a view the history of art would be the history of artistic techniques!" (cited in Holz, X: 191).
15. See Gutzmann, pp. 493-99.
16. Surkamp, p. 13.
17. Ibid., p. 30; see also Parzer-Mühlbacher, p. 106.
18. Rilke, "Primal Sound," p. 52.
19. Surkamp, p. 14.
20. Hackenberg, p. 70f, also Scharrelmann, Weg, p. 90.
21. See Morgenstern, Galgenlieder, p. 280, and Steiner, p. 262. According to Steiner, gramophones are a "shadow of the spiritual" from which—were mankind ever to love it—only the gods could save us.
22. Morgenstern, Galgenlieder, p. 123. Translation by Michael Metteer. [Trans.]
23. Hall, Contents, p. 31. See comments in Meumann, Vorlesungen, I: 348.
24. Alewyn, "Morgenstern," p. 399.
25. See Liede, I: 287-91.
26. Wildenbruch, cited in Bruch, p. 20.
27. Herder, Rezension: Klopstocks Werke, in SW, XX: 322f.
28. Döblin, "Futuristische Worttechnik," in AL, p. 10.
29. Tarde, p. 363; see also Preyer, p. 60.
30. Lichtenberg, fragment of 1778, cited in Hegel, Phenomenology of Spirit, p. 191.
31. See Ginzburg, p. 7.
32. "New Phonograph," p. 422.
33. Stern, "Sammelbericht," p. 432.
34. Stern, Psychologie, p. 14.
35. Stransky, "Amentia," pp. 7, 18. Anticipations of the technique can be found as early as 1890, in Blodgett, p. 43.

36. See, for comparison, Stoker, chap. 24, pp. 374–75, and Ach, p. 18.
37. Stransky, "Amentia," p. 17f.
38. Ibid., p. 96.
39. Ibid., p. 45.
40. See Wittgenstein, 4.461–64, p. 131.
41. "The noblest product of needful humanity, the state . . . would be difficult" were it not for the role of language in the formation of individualities and
totalities: an insight of romantic thought on language (Bernhardi, I: 4f). The political correlate of flight of ideas, by contrast, is "anarchy" (Liepmann, p. 82).
42. Stransky, "Amentia," pp. 81–83.
43. Mauthner, *Wörterbuch*, II: 398. Ellen Key's "soul murder" in the school
has thus founded a school of thought.
44. Kafka, *Description*, pp. 80–81.
45. Stransky, "Amentia," p. 4.
46. Liepmann, p. 74, see also p. 59f.
47. Ufer, 1890. Under the conditions of classical education or culture, only a
Bettina Brentano could have such an insight. See B. Brentano, *WB*, I: 290, and
comments by F. Kittler, "Writing," p. 41f.
48. Stransky, "Amentia," p. 96.
49. Benn, "Der Vermessungsdirigent," in *GS*, II: 324.
50. The painter Titorelli does the same thing; see Kafka, *Trial*, chap. 7, p. 204.
51. Three desiderata in Pameelen's obsolete concept of communication.
52. Benn, "Der Vermessungsdirigent," II: 324–26.
53. Wehrlin, p. 115.
54. Hellpach, "Psychopathologisches," p. 144.
55. Ziehen, *Ideenassoziation*, I: 12f.
56. Ibid., p. 6.
57. Benn, *Die Reise*, in *GW*, II: 33.
58. Ibid., p. 43.
59. Such is Rönne's diagnosis in Irle, p. 101.
60. Benn, *Gehirne*, in *GW*, II: 18f.
61. Benn, *Die Reise*, in *GW*, II: 34.
62. Ibid., p. 35f.
63. See Sellmann, p. 54: "The cinematograph can only do one thing, as its
name implies, and that is to record movement."
64. See the general thesis in Morin, p. 139: "The viewer reacts to the screen as
if to an external retina tele-relayed to his brain."
65. See Guattari, p. 99f.
66. Sartre, p. 122.
67. Ibid., p. 120. A movie house in Mannheim advertised with the slogan,
"Come on in, our theater is the darkest in the whole city!" (cited in Vietta, "Literatur und Film," p. 295).
68. Sartre, pp. 124–25.
69. Ibid., p. 119.
70. Egon Friedell, "Prolog vor dem Film" (1912), in Kaes, ed., *Kino-Debatte*,
p. 45. See the pertinent remarks of Koebner, pp. 17–19.
71. Hans-Heinz Ewers, letter of Oct. 8, 1912, in Zglinicki, p. 375.
72. See Münsterberg, *Film*, pp. 18–48, 84–87.
73. McLuhan, pp. 192–93.

74. Pinthus, *Kinobuch*, p. 22.

75. An anthropological theory of film (in opposition to the accumulation of technical data) can be found in Morin, pp. 31–53.

76. Pinthus, *Kinobuch*, p. 23. See also Kaes, ed., *Kino-Debatte*, p. 23–29.

77. Pinthus, *Kinobuch*, pp. 21–23.

78. See Schanze, "Literaturgeschichte," p. 133.

79. Pinthus, *Kinobuch*, pp. 13, 16. See Zglinicki, pp. 364–86.

80. Sellmann, p. 54f.

81. Benn, letter of Aug. 28, 1935, in *B*, I: 63.

82. See Lindau, pp. 86, 81f. The copy I cite once belonged to the Royal Police Department of Munich.

83. Pinthus, *Kinobuch*, p. 23.

84. As is the case in Sasse, p. 226.

85. Hofmannsthal, "Poesie," pp. 316–18. See also Holz, X: 187–90, as well as the many unordered bits of evidence in Daniels, ed.

86. Dilthey, "Die Entstehung der Hermeneutik," in *GS*, V: 318f.

87. Schanze, "Literaturgeschichte," p. 133.

88. According to the same Schanze, *Medienkunde*, p. 52. For historical evidence, see the demarcation of film and theater in Münsterberg, *Film*, p. 73ff.

89. Sasse, p. 226.

90. Mallarmé, "Sur le livre illustré," *OC*, p. 878.

91. Kafka, letter of Oct. 25, 1915, cited in Sarkowski, p. 71. See also George, letter of Aug., 1903, in George and Hofmannsthal, p. 195; on the unrepresentability of Morgenstern's poems, see Spitzer, p. 91.

92. Wolters, p. 320; see also Scharffenberg, p. 72f.

93. Schleiermacher, *Pädagogische Schriften*, p. 580. For further examples of such bans, see Liede, II: 65, 102, 199f.

94. Apollinaire, p. 228.

95. Ebbinghaus, *Grundzüge*, II: 2f; see also Wundt, I: 577.

96. Kaes, ed., *Kino-Debatte*, p. 10.

97. Kussmaul, p. 5.

98. See Ballet, p. 30, and comments by Hécaen and Angelergues, p. 35.

99. Kussmaul, pp. 126, 128. The literary echo of such concepts can be seen in Maupassant, XVIII: 30.

100. Erdmann and Dodge, p. 165.

101. Ibid., pp. 187, 161. Mallarmé's experimental "A Dice Throw" is correspondingly a poem "having no novelty but for the spacing out of what is to be read. The white spaces, indeed, take on importance, are striking at first" (Mallarmé, "Un coup de dés jamais n'abolira le hasard," *OC*, p. 455.)

102. See Zeitler, p. 391. Graphology had only to copy down such research results, according to Klages, *Handschrift*, p. 53.

103. Zeitler, p. 403.

104. Lindner, p. 196.

105. Saussure, p. 131.

106. See Derrida, *Grammatology*, pp. 87–90.

107. Saussure, p. 119.

108. Such is the thesis of M. Frank, *Das individuelle Allgemeine*, pp. 170–75.

109. Soennecken, p. 12.

110. See Meumann, *Über Ökonomie.*

111. Meumann, *Vorlesungen*, III: 608.

112. Soennecken, p. 39. See also Burgerstein, p. 33, as well as the "80 binary combinations," from which Preyer (pp. 49–52) attempted to construct *any* conceivable script.

113. See G. R. Lange, p. 231.

114. Soennecken, p. 41.

115. Von Larisch, pp. 97, 109.

116. See graphic material in Riegger-Baurmann, pp. 209–57.

117. See Soennecken, pp. 39–41 (the graphic on p. 39).

118. Von Larisch, p. 11.

119. Ibid., p. 102f.

120. Morgenstern, *Galgenlieder*, p. 59; *Gallows Songs*, p. 17. The translation, © Max E. Knight, is reprinted courtesy of the University of California Press. [Trans.]

121. Spitzer, p. 6of.

122. Ibid., p. 65.

123. Liede, I: 292.

124. Morgenstern, *Galgenlieder*, p. 31.

125. Burghagen, p. 193.

126. See Scharffenberg, p. 75.

127. Von Larisch, p. 106. On the personal book, see also Schur, p. 138f, as well as Tarde, p. 347.

128. Von Larisch, pp. 9, 114.   129. McLuhan, p. 260.

130. Burghagen, p. 120.   131. Just, p. 229.

132. Schur, pp. 228, 231.

133. Rilke, letter of Oct. 2, 1901, in Scharffenberg, p. 177.

134. Meumann, *Vorlesungen*, III: 605f, 614.

135. See Burgerstein, p. 39.

136. Messmer, pp. 218, 224f.

137. Münsterberg, *Grundzüge*, p. 252. For literary-critical confirmation, see the clear propositions in H. Fricke, pp. 17–22.

138. Mattenklott, p. 209.   139. See Burgerstein, p. 39.

140. Preyer, p. 128.   141. Forrer, p. 521.

142. Mallarmé, "Sur la graphologie," in *OC*, p. 878.

143. See George, *GAW*, VI-VII: 215.

144. Klages, pp. 91–95.

145. Bondi, p. 13.

146. Tarde, p. 350. See also Preyer, p. 86: "It is difficult to find definite characteristics of natural handwriting when one uses block letters. Therefore, anyone who does not want to be immediately recognized by his handwriting on the address of a letter can use block letters, as long as he does not mind the effort involved and does not prefer the typewriter."

Block letters or the typewriter—aside from writers who write bad checks, criminals take such advice to heart. A certain Mr. Windibank, who deceives his stepdaughter, a typist, with love letters, types even the signature for safety's sake. And it is this truly George-like bit of cunning that inspires Sherlock Holmes, the successful opposing technician, to write the first monograph entitled "On the Typewriter and Its Relation to Crime" (Doyle, *Complete Sherlock Holmes*, pp.

197–99). The detective is once more ahead of his time. Not until much later did comparable scientific monographs appear, as, e.g., Streicher, "The Criminological Use of Typescript" (1919).

147. See Foucault, *Order*, pp. 366–67.

148. George, *GAW*, IX: 134 (orig. pub. 1919); *Works*, p. 408. Translation by Olga Marx and Max Morwitz © The University of North Carolina Studies in the Germanic Languages and Literatures, 1974, reprinted courtesy of the University of North Carolina Press. [Trans.]

Rebus

Untranslatability and the Transposition of Media

1. Rilke, "Primal Sound," p. 55.

2. For the technical details, see McLuhan, *Understanding Media*, pp. 56–61.

3. See Blumner, cited in Daniels, ed., pp. 251–54.

4. See Heidegger, *Being and Time*, pp. 102–7 (on non-readiness-to-hand), and in connection to "The Word," Heidegger, *Language*, pp. 60–61.

5. Mattenklott, p. 179f.

6. R. M. Meyer, p. 55.

7. Heidegger, *Language*, p. 65.

8. George, *GAW*, VI-VII: 150; *Works*, p. 281. For this and following George poems, translation by Olga Marx and Max Morwitz © The University of North Carolina Studies in the Germanic Languages and Literatures, 1974, reprinted courtesy of the University of North Carolina Press. [Trans.]

9. Heidegger, *Language*, p. 62.

10. Morgenstern, *Mensch Wanderer*, p. 164. "Geist ist nur Heissen; Heisst, so schrieb sich besser Geist. / Der Heisst heisst alle Ding (doch Ding ist auch nur Heisst)."

11. Waetzoldt, p. 255f. See also R. Lange, pp. 110–14.

12. Dilthey, "Dichterische Einbildungskraft und Wahnsinn," *GS*, VI: 158. See also G. T. Fechner, I: 51.

13. On the topos, see, e.g., Cumont, pp. 87, 240, 295. On the new fashion, see George, *GAW*, XVII: 53; Klages, *Rhythmen*, p. 474; Ball, *Die Flucht*, pp. 92–96; Freud, *Introductory Lectures on Psychoanalysis*, in *SE*, XV: 17–18. In 1922 Valéry gave the title *Charmes* to a volume of his poetry.

14. Morgenstern, letter of 1911, in Spitzer, p. 107.

15. G. Meyer, p. 40.

16. See Rouge, p. 21 (on George, Volapük, Ido, and Esperanto).

17. George, *GAW*, VI-VII: 128–29; *Works*, p. 271. See comments in Boehringer, "*Über hersagen*," p. 19, and the general discussion in Forster, p. 87.

18. See David, p. 16.

19. See R. M. Meyer, p. 269.

20. Liede, II: 239.

21. Nietzsche, fragment of 1873, in *W*, III, 4, p. 318 (on "Poetry").

22. Bahr, p. 28f.

23. Simmel, "Vom Wesen," pp. 18, and (on machines) 19.

24. E. Strauss, p. 197f.

25. Ibid., p. 122.

26. Kussmaul, p. 27. See also A. Proust, p. 310; Baumann, p. 12f, and Sachs, p. 122.

27. E. Strauss, pp. 133–42. In 1885 Paulhan "observed that the sound of a waterfall or of a train made the conception of a melody considerably easier for him" (Ballet, p. 31). Gertrude Stein preferred to write in the presence of distracting noises (see Skinner, p. 54); one of Otto Flake's heroes wrote to the sound of gas pipes (Flake, p. 205). Rilke is, as usual, the most precise; see "On the Young Poet" and the sources of his inspiration: "Who will name all of you, co-contributors to inspiration, you who are nothing more than noises, or bells that have ceased ringing, or miraculous new bird calls in neglected woods?" (Rilke, "Über den jungen Dichter," SW, VI: 1054). In spectral analysis, bells do in fact have the highest proportion of noise (in the technical sense) of all sounds.

28. Morgenstern, *Galgenlieder*, p. 13.

29. Morgenstern, "Über die Galgenlieder," in GW, p. 226.

30. Boehringer, *Über hersagen*, pp. 77–88.

31. Maier-Smits, pp. 158–61 (recollections of the first female pupil).

32. See the minute wiring plan in Villiers, p. 129f.

33. For details, see von Zglinicki, pp. 277–94.

34. Pinthus, *Kinobuch*, p. 9. See comments in Münsterberg, *Film*, pp. 84–87.

Psychoanalysis and Its Shadow

1. See Freud, *The Interpretation of Dreams*, in SE, IV: 55.

2. Ibid., pp. 96–98.

3. Ibid., pp. 277–78.

4. As an expressionist puts it: "So much of victory is in simple position, be it that of armies or sentences" (Hatvani, p. 210).

5. Freud, *Interpretation of Dreams*, in SE, IV: 303.

6. Ibid., p. 99.

7. Muschg, pp. 315, 306.

8. Freud, *Interpretation of Dreams*, in SE, IV: 297.

9. Bahr, p. 30 (in relation to the internal-stimulus theory of dreams).

10. Freud, *Studies on Hysteria*, in SE, II: 280–81.

11. As does Lyotard, *Des dispositifs*, p. 77.

12. Mattenklott (p. 309f) turns this homology between literature and psychoanalysis into its opposite.

13. George, *GAW*, III: 106; "Evening of Peace," in *Works*, p. 107.

14. See Foucault, *Mental Illness and Psychology*, pp. 76–88.

15. Langbehn, p. 8 (coined for science and art).

16. See Guattari, p. 102f.

17. Freud, *Studies on Hysteria*, in SE, VII: 110. See comments in Foucault, "Dream," p. 57.

18. Rank, *Der Doppelgänger*, p. 7f. Todorov (*Fantastic*, p. 160) takes only a half truth from such interpretive claims, namely that "psychoanalysis has replaced fantastic literature (and thus rendered it superfluous)." But the divide between the book and the image simultaneously made for the resurrection of all imaginary mirror images on another, popular level, in the real of the film screen.

19. Rank, *Der Doppelgänger*, p. 7.   20. See Farges, p. 89.

21. See Gaube, p. 42.   22. Jung and Riklin, p. 63.

23. See Saussure, p. 112.

24. Freud, letter of July 30, 1915, in Freud and Andreas-Salomé, p. 36.

25. See Steiner, "Initiationserkenntnis," pp. 96–98.

26. Bergson, p. 330f.

27. The view of Habermas, pp. 300–31.
28. Bölsche, p. 15. See also Flechsig, *Hirnlehre*, p. 41.
29. Kussmaul, p. 34.
30. On Helmholtz and Brücke, see Bernfeld, pp. 435–55.
31. Freud, "The Unconscious," in *SE*, XIV: 174–75.
32. Freud, *On Aphasia*, p. 22. On *"Butter/Mutter"* [butter/mother], see Kussmaul, p. 188.
33. Meringer and Mayer, p. vi. See also Freud, *The Psychopathology of Everyday Life*, in *SE*, VI: 53–60. Collections of parapraxes are as old as psychophysics itself. See G. T. Fechner, I: 225f.
34. See Ziehen, *Leitfaden*, p. 144, as well as comments by Liepmann, p. 20.
35. Meringer and Mayer, p. 20, see also p. 38.
36. Freud, *Psychopathology*, in *SE*, VI: 84.
37. Jung, "Beitrag," p. 19.
38. Jung, *Dementia praecox*, p. 130.
39. Ibid., p. 146f.   40. Meringer and Mayer, p. 9.
41. Rilke, *Brigge*, p. 29.   42. Conan Doyle, p. 92.
43. Bleuler, p. 52.
44. Freud, *Psychopathology*, in *SE*, VI: 48.
45. Ibid.
46. Zeitler, p. 391.
47. Gutzmann, p. 499. See also Münsterberg, *Grundzüge*, p. 708.
48. Lacan, *Ecrits* (Paris), p. 469.
49. Freud, *Psychopathology*, *SE*, VI: 214.
50. Freud, "From the History of an Infantile Neurosis," in *SE*, XVII: 94.
51. See Freud, *Interpretation of Dreams*, *SE*, V: 499. The same image can be found in Villiers, *Tomorrow's Eve*, p. 206; Meringer and Mayer, p. 100; Hirth, p. 535f.; Sachs, p. 37; Münch, p. 87; Münsterberg, *Grundzüge*, pp. 28, 708f. In the discourse network of 1800 there was reason to warn against the proofreader's eye and its forgetting of "sense" as if against an "idiosyncrasy," which should "remain within the norm" (Reil, p. 102). In 1910, this idiosyncrasy defined the poet, as when Brigge "copies down" a biographical note on the dramatist Alexis-Félix Arvers: "He was dying in a gentle and unruffled way, and the nun perhaps thought he had gone further with it than in reality he had. Quite loudly she called out an indication where such and such was to be found. She was a rather uneducated nun; the word 'corridor,' which at that moment was not to be avoided, she had never seen written; so it was that she said 'collidor,' thinking that was the word. At that Arvers postponed dying. It seemed to him necessary to put this right first. He became perfectly lucid and explained to her that it should be 'corridor.' Then he died. He was a poet and hated the approximate" (Rilke, *Brigge*, p. 146).
52. Freud, "Recommendations to Physicians Practising Psycho-analysis," in *SE*, XII: 113.
53. Ibid., pp. 115–16.
54. Benjamin, "Work of Art," p. 235.
55. See Freud, *Studies on Hysteria*, in *SE*, II: 49f.
56. Freud, "An Autobiographical Study," in *SE*, XX: 12.
57. See Habermas, p. 302 (there are the nightmares, too).
58. Muschg, p. 333.
59. Freud, "Fragment of an Analysis of a Case of Hysteria," in *SE*, VII: 39.
60. Freud, *Five Lectures on Psycho-analysis*, in *SE*, XI: 13.

61. Ibid.
62. Freud, "Fragment," in *SE*, VII: 8.
63. Ibid., p. 10.
64. "If I have made a sentence out of something—what does that something have to do with the sentence?" (Mann, p. 24). See comments in Carstensen, pp. 175–79.
65. Freud, "Fragment," in *SE*, VII: 9.
66. Freud, "On Beginning the Treatment," in *SE*, XII: 136. Compare the precarious, but not completely impossible relationship between the Royal Privy Archivarius Lindhorst and his poet.
67. Freud, "Notes upon a Case of Obsessional Neurosis," in *SE*, X: 156.
68. Freud, "Fragment," in *SE*, VII: 8.
69. Muschg, p. 322f.
70. On the mythic sense of these names, see Turk and Kittler, p. 42.
71. See Conan Doyle, p. 214, and, on Freud and Holmes, the testimony of the Wolf-Man, in Gardiner, ed., p. 146.
72. See Freud, "Constructions in Analysis," *SE*, XXIII: 255–70.
73. See Muschg, p. 316.
74. On this and the following, see Kittler, *Der Traum*, pp. 319–23.
75. Freud, *Delusions and Dreams in Jensen's 'Gradiva,'* in *SE*, IX: 94.
76. Ibid., p. 92.
77. Ibid., p. 7.
78. Ibid., p. 40.
79. Freud, "Psycho-analytic Notes on an Autobiographical Account of a Case of Paranoia (Dementia Paranoides)," in *SE*, XII: 9.
80. Ibid., pp. 78–79.
81. Freud, "Fragment," in *SE*, VII: 14 (footnote added by Freud in 1923).
82. Freud, *Outline*, in *SE*, XXIII: 196.
83. Schreber, p. 31.
84. Freud, "Psycho-analytic Notes," in *SE*, XII: 10.
85. See Schreber, pp. 46n, 48, 52n.
86. Lacan, "L'Etourdit," p. 16.
87. Schreber, p. 251.
88. Foucault, "What Is an Author?," p. 117.
89. Schreber, pp. 54–61.
90. Ibid., p. 49n.
91. Ibid., pp. 45 and 286; see also p. 200n.
92. Flechsig, *Grundlagen*, p. 21. See, above all, Schreber, p. 243.
93. Flechsig, *Grundlagen*, p. 3f.
94. Benn, *Der Aufbau der Persönlichkeit*, in *GW*, I: 92.
95. Freud, "Charcot," in *SE*, III: 15. For which Flechsig thanked him . . .
96. Flechsig, *Gehirn*, p. 18.
97. Flechsig, *Grundlagen*, pp. 9, 11.
98. On the dissection of Hölderlin, see Fichtner, p. 54f.
99. On the dissection of Schreber, see Baumann, p. 522.
100. And, after having used up so much typewriter ribbon, I too see that the intellectual achievement of describing the discursive network Flechsig-Schreber-Freud belongs first to Roberto Calasso. His admirable human science fiction has already drawn on all sources to recreate the vicissitudes of German "nerve-theology." The only thing Calasso overlooked is Flechsig's stark imperative of

weighing postmortem evidence, which he replaced with a philosophical notion that cannot have motivated Schreber's anxiety and writing. See Calasso, *Die geheime Geschichte*, p. 61.

101. Schreber, p. 54.

102. Ibid., p. 75.

103. Mannoni's insight, p. 91. On possible grounds for Freud's complicity, see Calasso, *Die geheime Geschichte*, p. 22f.

104. Schreber, p. 91.

105. S. M. Weber, p. 490.

106. See Kafka, "Penal Colony," p. 164, and the commentary by Wagenbach, p. 70f. Neumann, pp. 396–401, however, links "writing machines" in Kafka and Schreber.

107. Schreber, pp. 34–35.

108. An equation made most decisively by Schatzman.

109. Schreber, p. 155.

110. Ibid., p. 135.

111. Ibid., p. 34.

112. Ibid., p. 119. On "rays," see the "audible rays" and the "primary visual rays" in Flechsig, *Hirnlehre*, p. 20.

113. See the physiological details in Schreber, p. 69.

114. Flechsig, *Gehirn*, p. 26. Compare the echo in Schreber, p. 118.

115. Schreber, p. 229. See also p. 113n (on light-telegraphics).

116. See Chamberlain, p. 263.

117. Schreber, p. 222.

118. Ibid., p. 121. See comments by Lacan, "On a Question Preliminary to Any Possible Treatment in Psychosis," in *Ecrits* (New York), p. 184f.

119. Schreber, p. 121.

120. Ibid., p. 144.

121. Ibid., p. 197.

122. In an exemplary analysis, Freud deduces all the erotic troubles of a travel acquaintance from an incorrectly cited verse of *The Aeneid* (Freud, *Psychopathology*, in *SE*, VI: 8–11.

123. Schreber, p. 122.

124. Ibid., pp. 166n and 146.

125. Ibid., p. 122.

126. Ibid., p. 176.

127. Ibid., p. 57.

128. Ibid., p. 123n.

129. Ibid. But see Kussmaul, p. 217, where the actual state of affairs is entirely clear to a psychiatrist.

130. Schreber, p. 122.

131. Ball, *Die Flucht*, p. 79f.

132. Schreber, p. 226.

133. Ibid., p. 209.

134. Ibid., p. 52.

135. See Deleuze/Guattari, *Anti-Oedipus*, p. 17 (on Schreber).

136. Ziehen, letter of Jan. 26, 1889, in Gilman, p. 337.

137. G. Weber, document of Nov. 28, 1900, in Schreber, p. 280.

138. A concept of Ribot, p. 15.

139. Schreber, p. 204.

140. Ibid., p. 63.

141. Ibid., p. 135.

142. Ibid., p. 122.

143. See comments in Mannoni, p. 80f.

144. Mannoni's title.

145. Schreber, p. 298. See comments in S. M. Weber, pp. 37, 47.

A *Simulacrum of Madness*

1. Foucault, "La folie," p. 128.
2. On Gertrude Stein, see Skinner, p. 55.
3. Schreber, p. 226.
4. Foucault, *Discipline*, p. 194.
5. Freud, "The Unconscious," *SE*, XIV: 204.
6. Mauthner, *Beiträge*, I: 122.
7. See Morgenstern, *Galgenlieder*, p. 79; *Gallows Songs*, pp. 74–75.
8. See Herzfelde, p. 297.
9. Husserl, II, 1, 54. Husserl's example, as if to confirm the incantation-fashion of 1900, is "Abracadabra."
10. Ball, *Gedichte*, p. 34. Translation by David E. Wellberg. [Trans.] See also Rilke, "Madness," from "The Book of Images," in Rilke, *Selected Poems*, pp. 22–23.
11. Schreber, p. 168.
12. The testimony of a sufferer of acute mania, whose rhyming has been exhaustively collected. See Forel, p. 974.
13. Cardinal, p. 315; on the most famous and extensive simulation of madness, see Breton and Eluard's "Immaculée Conception" of 1930.
14. Hellpach, "Psychopathologisches," p. 140. Scheerer, *Studien*, p. 144, an otherwise precise investigation of surrealistic simulations of madness, demonstrates the exact correspondences between discourses and diagnosed illnesses ca. 1900 on the basis of information mailed from a regional clinic in 1970.
15. Bölsche, p. 9f.
16. See comments in Enzensberger, p. 183.
17. Münsterberg, *Grundzüge*, p. 665. Similarly, see Cardinal, p. 315.
18. See Foucault, "La Folie," p. 128f.
19. Anz, p. 151.
20. Ott, pp. 371–98.
21. Breton, letter of Sept. 25, 1916, cited in Bonnet, p. 99.
22. Stransky, "Amentia," p. 158.
23. On Goethe, see, e.g., Diener.
24. See Gehrmann, and comments in Benjamin, "Einbahnstrasse," in *GS*, IV, 2, p. 618f.
25. Benn, *Ithaka*, in *GW*, II: 293f.
26. Ibid., p. 295f, and comments by Rübe, in Benn, *Medizinische Schriften*, p. 96f.
27. Benn, *Ithaka*, in *GW*, II: 298 (thus another soul murder).
28. "A wide readership in lay circles . . . could create confusion, despite the clear condition of the case," reads a psychiatric review of Schreber's book (Pfeiffer, p. 353). That is a fortiori true of a wide readership for experiments on rat brains.
29. See Ziehen, *Leitfaden*, p. 172f.
30. Benn, *Epilog*, in *GW*, IV: 9.
31. Ibid.
32. See Ziehen, *Die Geisteskrankheiten*, III: 126.
33. Freud, letter of Oct. 15, 1897, *Letters to Fliess*, p. 272.
34. Hesse, p. 47.
35. Dilthey, "Dichterische Einbildungskraft und Wahnsinn," in *GS*, VI: 195f.

36. On Kafka's comments, see Ryan and Seidler.
37. Freud, *Introductory Lectures on Psycho-analysis*, in *SE*, XV: 17.
38. Rilke, letter of Jan. 24, 1912, in *Letters*, p. 51.
39. Goll, p. 65.   40. Apollinaire, p. 232.
41. Benn, *Gehirne*, in *GW*, II: 18.   42. Ibid., p. 16.
43. Ibid., p. 13.   44. Flake, p. 267.
45. Ibid., pp. 273–84.
46. M. Proust, III: 1092. On *The Remembrance* as a gigantic evidence-gathering project, see Ginzburg, p. 33.
47. See A. Proust, and comments by Bariéty, p. 575, and Le Masle, p. 55 (further work by the student of Broca and Charcot on paralysis in the area of the lips, tongue, and jaws, on brain localization, and on trephination). Biographers of Proust, however, bring in only Adrian Proust's measures against cholera, which have no relevance for *The Remembrance*.
48. Sachs's title, *Brain and Language*.
49. Rilke, letter of Jan. 14, 1912, in *Letters*, p. 52.
50. Rilke, "Primal Sound," p. 51. That such ordinary materials suffice is the reason for the then-current misconception that the phonograph could have been invented centuries ago, as in Villiers, *Tomorrow's Eve*, p. 20.
51. Rilke, "Primal Sound," p. 52.
52. Ibid., p. 53. On the cranial suture in ontogenesis, see Rilke, *Brigge*, p. 184.
53. See Bridgwater (*Kafka and Nietzsche*, pp. 104–11) on the homology of these two texts.
54. Flake, pp. 284, 282; see also p. 95.
55. Rilke, "Primal Sound," p. 53.
56. See comments in Enzensberger, p. 160.
57. Hirth, p. 38.
58. Rilke, "Primal Sound," pp. 54–56.
59. Sachs, p. 4.
60. As does Clarétie, in his piquant *Les Amours d'un interne*.
61. Huelsenbeck, p. 23. See also Ball, *Die Flucht*, p. 88.
62. Rilke, *Notebooks*, pp. 58–59.
63. Ibid., p. 23.
64. Rilke, letter of Jan. 24, 1912, in *Briefe*, IV: 184.
65. Rilke, *Notebooks*, pp. 69–70.
66. Stern, *Psychologie*, p. 58f. See also the early childhood "Heniden" in Weininger, p. 121f.
67. Ebbinghaus, *Gründzuge*, II: 15.
68. Hall, *Study of Fears*, p. 188.
69. Ibid., p. 184. See related passages in M. Proust, *Remembrance*, I: 3–15.
70. See Rank, *Das Inzest-Motiv*, p. 671f.
71. Freud, *Beyond the Pleasure Principle*, in *SE*, XVIII: 14–15.
72. Rilke, *Notebooks*, pp. 84, 42.
73. See Bradley, p. 52.
74. See Scharrelmann, *Weg*, pp. 139–43.
75. Hart, p. 122f.
76. Ibid., p. 126.
77. Graf, p. 7.
78. See Hermann Bahr, Hans Bethke, Alfred Kerr, Carl Spitteler, in Graf,

pp. 181f, 201, 256. On the whole issue, see Rilke, "Rezension: Ellen Key, 'Das Jahrhundert des Kindes," in *SW*, V: 588.

79. Heuss, p. 67.

80. Key, *Das Jahrhundert*, p. 299.

81. Meyrink, pp. 180, 94.

82. Kafka, "A Report to the Academy," in *Complete Stories*, pp. 256–57.

83. Rilke, *Notebooks*, pp. 169–72.

84. Ibid., p. 201.

85. Ibid., p. 40. Brigge simply objectifies what then-contemporary psychology (also using the example of reading) describes as the selectivity of all attention: "While the attended impression becomes more vivid, all other impressions become less vivid, less clear, less distinct, less detailed. They fade away. We no longer notice them. They have no hold on our mind; they disappear. If we are fully absorbed in our book, we do not hear what is said around us, and we do not see the room; we forget everything. Our attention to the page of the book brings with it our lack of attention to everything else" (Münsterberg, *Film*, p. 36).

86. Bergk, *Bücher zu lesen*, p. 339.

87. Reil, p. 55.

88. Hardenberg, *Heinrich von Ofterdingen*, in *S*, I: 202, 325. According to Goethe, "true poetry" is altogether a "bird's-eye perspective" on the earth (Goethe, *Aus meinem Leben. Dichtung und Wahrheit*, in *SW*, XXIV: 161).

89. Rilke, *Notebooks*, p. 67; see also Liepmann, p. 57.

90. Rilke, *Notebooks*, p. 68.

91. Ibid., p. 187; see also Borges, *Historia universal de la infamia*, in *Obras completas*, III: 131f.

92. Ferrier, p. 322.

93. Rilke, *Notebooks*, p. 52.

94. Lay, p. 176.

95. R. Lange, pp. 61–63; see also Scharrelmann, *Weg*, p. 89.

96. Benjamin, "Einbahnstrasse," in *GS*, IV, 1, 90.

97. Burghagen, p. 211; see also Key, *Jahrhundert*, p. 38.

98. Rilke, *Notebooks*, p. 138.

99. Scharrelmann, *Weg*, p. 71.

100. See Alain, *Système*, p. xxx.

101. Rilke, *Notebooks*, p. 177.

102. Schreber, p. 181.

103. Scharrelmann, *Weg*, p. 18.

104. See Müller, p. 272f.

105. Rilke, *Brigge*, p. 52.

106. Scharrelmann, *Kinder*, p. 85.

107. Scharrelmann, *Weg*, p. 44.

108. R. Lange, *Leistungen*, p. 98.

109. Münch, pp. 3, 26.

110. See Key, *Das Jahrhundert*, p. 280; E. Strauss, p. 115; Wolgast, "Jugendschrift," p. 113; Ostermai, p. 68f; R. Lange, *Leistungen*, p. 103. For comments on the historical period, see H. J. Frank, pp. 365–67.

111. Münch, p. 73.

112. See Ebbinghaus, *Grundzüge*, II: 13, and Morgenstern, *Gallows Songs*, pp. 162–63.

113. Dilthey, "Schulreformen und Schulstuben," in *GS*, VI: 89.

114. Ziehen, *Ideenassoziation*, I: 65f.

115. Münch, p. 42; see also Scharrelmann, *Weg*, pp. 160–65.

116. See O. H. Michel, p. 421, and Ostermai, p. 55.

117. Hille, II: 104; see the same argument in Benjamin, "Die Schulreform, eine Kulturbewegung," in *GS*, II, 1, p. 15.

118. Münch, p. 97.

119. See the important comments in Hirth, p. 364f, on the identity of training maneuvers, weapons technique, and art psychology.

120. Herzfelde, p. 297. See Scharrelmann, *Kinder*, p. 85.

121. Ostermai, p. 54.

122. Rilke, *Brigge*, p. 89. As evidence that seventy years have changed nothing in the discourse rules, consider this transcription of a verse from Pink Floyd: "When I was a child I had a fever. / My hands felt just like two balloons. / Now I've got that feeling once again. / I can't explain, you would not understand." (The lines, of course, are addressed to a doctor.)

123. Rilke, *Brigge*, p. 214.

124. Meumann, *Vorlesungen*, III: 826. Among Rilke scholars, only Storck shares this view; he has vigorously stressed the presence of Ellen Key and the free schools in Rilke's work (J. W. Storck, pp. 257–66). His question concerning emancipation, however, evades the point that interests Meumann, which is really an aspect of the school.

125. Münch, p. 28.

126. Rilke, letter of Jan. 14, 1912, in *Letters*, pp. 42–43.

127. Cited in Heym, III: 256.

128. Einstein, "Bebuquin oder Die Dilettanten des Wunders," in *GW*, p. 234.

129. Rilke, *Brigge*, p. 42.

130. Rilke, "Rezension," in *SW*, V: 591.

131. Münch, p. 98f.

132. Ball, *Tenderenda*, p. 115; Benn, *Gehirne*, in *GW*, II: 13; Rilke, *Brigge*, p. 30.

133. Hartleben, II: 147f.   134. See Ehrenstein, pp. 17–19.

135. Ibid., p. 48.   136. Ibid., pp. 8, 54.

137. Otto Karstadt's "Working poetry hours," for example, used texts as pretexts for role playing, children's drawings, and confabulations. See comments in H. J. Frank, p. 369f.

138. See Langenbucher, p. 57. A journalist and President of the Republic says of his first semester as a student in Munich, the winter semester of 1902: "I didn't have any visiting cards printed, but I did write on small cards: 'student of neophil.' The usual 'Ph.' appeared to me, after an admittedly short taste of it, too old-fashioned" (Heuss, p. 217).

139. Kafka, fragment of 1917–18, in *Hochzeitsvorbereitungen*, p. 44.

140. Anton Wenzel Gross, cited in Bose and Brinkmann, p. 34. Franz Jung, another simulator of madness, used these notes for his novella *The Telepathics*.

141. Ribot, pp. 141–42. See Maupassant, XVIII: 29.

142. Wehrlin, p. 119.   143. Bleuler, p. 52.

144. Wehnert, p. 473.   145. See Mallarmé, *OC*, p. 230.

146. See Wilde, *Soul of Man*, p. 248.

147. See Mattenklott, p. 12.

148. Hofmannsthal, letter of June 18, 1895, in Hofmannsthal and Bebenburg, *B*, p. 80.

149. See Rilke, speech of 1898, in *SW*, V: 364.

150. Rilke, letter of Feb. 1, 1896, in *Briefe*, I: 12f. See also Rosenhaupt, p. 239.

151. Rubiner, "Die Anonymen," p. 302.

152. Döblin, "Autobiographische Skizze," in *AL*, p. 21.

153. Pinthus, *Menschheitsdämmerung*, p. 357.
154. Rubiner, "Die Anonymen," p. 300.
155. On medieval anonymity as a model, see Mauthner, *Wörterbuch*, I: xviii.
156. Döblin, "Bemerkungen zum Roman," in *AL*, p. 18.
157. Rubiner, "Die Anonymen," p. 302.
158. See Rubiner, "Rezension," p. 214 (on the war poems of the George circle).
159. Hans Arp, cited in Goll, p. 45.
160. Lanson, p. 631.
161. Carossa, p. 134. For the theory of such reading technique, consider Stern (*Psychologie*, p. 157): "Further, the analysis of early childhood learning reveals that the sense and significance of the learning material do not play nearly so great a role as they do later. For grade-school pupils it is considered important—rightly so—that material be significant and age appropriate; a text that such a pupil cannot comprehend has no actual educative value and demands incomparably more time and energy in learning than a more comprehensible text of equal length. Early childhood, by contrast, is really the more appropriate phase for rote memory. If, as we have seen, the child repeats words for the simple pleasure of their sound and this process leads to unintentional memorizing, the effect is hardly diminished by the fact that the child almost never understands the short verses in their entirety—often such understanding is confused and partial. But it would be unnecessary pedantry to insist that understanding be brought about through long and tiresome explanations, or to exclude poems that cannot be completely understood."
162. Rilke, *Notebooks*, p. 173–74.
163. Ibid., p. 175.
164. See von Hanstein.
165. Ostermai, p. 69.
166. Key, *Das Jahrhundert*, p. 57; see also Key, *Rahel*, passim.

167. Rilke, *Brigge*, pp. 175–76.	168. Ibid., p. 176.
169. Ibid.	170. Ibid., p. 174.
171. Ibid., p. 111.	172. Ibid., p. 208.
173. Ibid., p. 119.	174. Ibid., pp. 198, 87, 210–16.
175. Ibid., p. 30.	

Queen's Sacrifice

1. Villiers, p. 60.	2. Ibid., p. 131.
3. Ibid., p. 60.	4. Ibid., p. 133.

5. Ibid., p. 217.
6. H. Lange, "Organisches oder mechanisches Prinzip in der Mädchenbildung?," in *Kampfzeiten*, II: 67.
7. Gaudig, p. 232.
8. See, e.g., Stern, *Psychologie*, pp. 25–27.
9. Weininger, p. 10f.
10. Simmel, *Zur Psychologie*, p. 16.
11. Grabein, p. ix.
12. Freud, "Notes upon a Case of Obsessional Neurosis," in *SE*, X: 157.
13. Freud, cited in Jones, II: 421.
14. Freud, "Fragment of an Analysis of a Case of Hysteria," in *SE*, VII: 120.

15. Freud, *Introductory Lectures on Psychoanalysis*, in *SE*, XV: 16.

16. Lacan, "Radiophonie," p. 97. "In the discourse of the university, it is the gap produced in which the subject vanishes for having to suppose that knowledge has an author."

17. H. Steinthal, cited in Kirchhoff, *Die akademische Frau*, p. 216.

18. J. Scheiner, cited in Kirchhoff, ed., p. 264.

19. H. Lange, "Organisches," in *Kampfzeiten*, II: 73.

20. See Freud, *Introductory Lectures*, in *SE*, XV: 154.

21. Ibid.

22. "Schreiben mit der Maschine," p. 863. On sewing machines and typewriters, see also Burghagen, p. 31.

23. Scholz, p. 15.

24. Burghagen, p. 1.

25. M. Weber, pp. 3, 5.

26. Förster-Nietzsche, p. 136.

27. Key, *Das Jahrhundert*, p. 56.

28. Krukenberg, p. 38.

29. Schwabe, p. 6f.

30. See Bliven, pp. 3–16, 69–79, for amusing historical details and the laconic sentence, "There are more women working at typing than at anything else."

31. Richards, p. 1.

32. Krukenberg, p. 38. See also the international statistics in Braun, p. 178f.

33. Stoker, p. 344. Compare pp. 49–50.

34. Ibid., p. 70. On women journalists, see Maschke, p. 26f.

35. Braun, p. 197.

36. Schwabe, p. 21.

37. Stoker, p. 292.

38. This ideal portrait of Mina Harker was taken from Chew, p. 27.

39. Stoker, p. 266.

40. See Stoker, p. 91, as well as Freud, letter of Sept. 21, 1897, in *Letters to Fliess*, pp. 264–65.

41. See Stoker, pp. 360, 405f, and 42.

42. Ibid., p. 340.

43. Ibid., p. 372.

44. Henry James, cited in Hyde, p. 277.

45. Bosanquet, pp. 243–48; see McLuhan, pp. 227–32.

46. See details in Lumbroso, p. 620f.

47. Gilbert and Profes, in L. W. Wolff, ed., p. 59.

48. See Mallarmé, OC, p. 38.

49. Bermann, in Pinthus, *Kinobuch*, p. 30.

50. Such scenes were mass produced. "In the early fiction written with secretaries for heroines, the hero (a rising young executive in the firm) was usually so impressed by his secretary's decorum that he didn't dare even to propose; in one story after another he called her in and dictated a proposal, building to the climax in which she, her eyes brimming with tears, asked 'And to whom, Sir, is this missive to be addressed?'" (Bliven, p. 12).

51. See Burghagen, p. 28.

52. The photos of Georges Demeny, who was of course at once experimenter and subject, were taken from Maréchal, p. 406.

53. Burghagen, p. 28.

54. Bermann, in Pinthus, *Kinobuch*, pp. 31–33.

55. Kafka could have read in Conan Doyle that typed love letters are not love letters. See Conan Doyle, p. 194, and comments in Bliven, pp. 71, 148.

56. Kafka, letter of Oct. 27, 1912, in *Letters to Felice*, p. 16.

57. See Bermann, in Pinthus, *Kinobuch*, p. 33.

58. Kafka, letter of Nov. 2, 1912, in *Letters to Felice*, p. 23.

59. Kafka, letter of Dec. 21, 1912, in ibid., p. 115.

60. McLuhan, *Understanding Media*, p. 260; also Burghagen, p. 22.

61. Burghagen, p. 25.

62. Kafka, letter of Nov. 27, 1912, in *Letters to Felice*, p. 70; see also p. 149.

63. See this fascinating passage in Kafka, letter of Jan. 22–23, 1913, in *Letters to Felice*, pp. 167–68.

64. Kafka, letter of June 26, 1913, in ibid., p. 279.

65. For the sake of Kafka scholarship, which is not exactly well informed about information technology, the following data is supplied: "The Deutsche Grammophon Aktiengesellschaft (DGA), came to occupy in Germany much the same position as its British parent, the Gramophone Company. It dominated the quality market. . . . Its arch-enemy in the marketplace and in the courts was the firm of Carl Lindström, which, by a series of amalgamations, built up an enormous local and foreign trade in instruments and motors and, by 1913, controlled the sale of Beka, Dacapo, Favorite, Fonotipa, Homophon, Lyrophon, Jumbo, and Odeon records as well as its own Parlophones. . . . In the period 1903–14 German ingenuity was concentrated aggressively on the techniques of mass production" (Chew, p. 38). Founded in 1896, the Lindström company, like many others, vanished after the introduction of the electrical gramophone.

66. Cournot, p. 60f.

67. Heller, "Introduction," in Kafka, *Letters to Felice*, p. vii.

68. Kafka, letter of June 2, 1913, in ibid., p. 265.

69. Kafka, letter of July 10, 1913, in ibid., p. 288.

70. Kafka, letter of July 13, 1913, in ibid., p. 289.

71. Marinetti, *Manifesto*, in Baumgarth, p. 168.

72. Rilke, "Primal Sound," p. 55.

73. Ehrenstein, p. 34.

74. Döblin, "Bemerkungen zum Roman," in *AL*, p. 23.

75. Einstein, "Anmerkungen zum Roman," in *GW*, p. 54.

76. Benn, *Roman des Phänotyp*, in *GW*, II: 198.

77. Benn, *Pallas*, in *GW*, I: 366.

78. Nietzsche, letter of March 1882, in *Briefwechsel mit Overbeck*, p. 169f.

79. Benn, letter of Feb. 6, 1937, in *Den Trauem*, p. 192.

80. Benn, letter of Jan. 10, 1937, in *Den Trauem*, pp. 184–86.

81. See Burghagen, p. 21.

82. Valéry, *Cahiers*, IV: 44. Translation by Daniel Katz. [Trans.]

83. See Blüher, p. 48f. 84. Valéry, 'My Faust,' pp. 13, 14.

85. Riemer, pp. 164, 166. 86. See Friedlaender, pp. 169–75.

87. Valéry, 'My Faust,' p. 54. 88. Ibid., p. 18.

89. Ibid., p. 10. 90. Ibid., pp. 10–11.

Afterword

1. Foucault, *Archeology*, pp. 126–31.

2. See Innis.

3. Shannon and Weaver, pp. 33–35.

4. Luhmann, p. 11; see also pp. 19–21.

5. Heidegger, *Nietzsche*, I: 102.
6. Tietze and Schenk, p. 510.
7. Walter Benjamin, "Der Surrealismus. Die letzte Momentaufnahme der europaischen Intelligenz," in *GS*, II: 308.
8. Hegel, *Aesthetics*, I: 11.
9. Foucault, *Archeology*, p. 211.

Works Cited

ABC oder Namenbüchlein, zum Gebrauche der Schulen nach dem Wiener Exemplar. Koblenz, 1778.

Ach, Narziss. *Über die Willenstätigkeit und das Denken. Eine experimentelle Untersuchung mit einem Anhange. Über das Hippsche Chronoskop*. Göttingen, 1905.

Alain (Emile Auguste Chartier). *Les arts et les dieux*. Ed. Georges Beneze. Paris, 1958.

———. *Système des beaux-arts*. 2d ed. Paris, 1920.

Alewyn, Richard. "Christian Morgenstern." In his *Probleme und Gestalten: Essays* (Frankfurt a. M., 1974), pp. 397–401.

———. "Klopstocks Leser." In Bernhard Fabian, ed., *Festschrift für Rainer Gruenter* (Heidelberg, 1978), pp. 100–21.

Allgemeines Landrecht für die Preussischen Staaten. Ed. Hans Hattenhauer. Frankfurt a. M., 1970. Orig. issued 1794.

Ament, Wilhelm. "Fortschritte der Kinderpsychologie 1895 bis 1903." *Archiv für die gesamte Psychologie* 2 (1904): 69–136.

"An den Verfasser der *Fantasiestücke in Callot's 'Manier'*." N. p., 1817.

Anz, Thomas, ed. *Phantasien über den Wahnsinn. Expressionistische Texte*. Munich, 1980.

Apel, Friedmar. *Die Zaubergärten der Phantasie. Zur Theorie und Geschichte des Kunstmärchens*. Heidelberg, 1978.

Arnheim, Rudolf. "Systematik der frühen kinematographischen Erfindungen." In his *Kritiken und Aufsätze zum Film*, ed. Helmut H. Dieterichs (Munich, 1977).

Arnold, Thomas. *Observations on the Nature, Kinds, Causes and Prevention of Insanity, Lunacy or Madness*. Leicester, 1782.

Aschoff, Volker. "Die elektrische Nachrichtentechnik im 19. Jahrhundert." *Technikgeschichte* 33 (1966): 402–19.

Auerbach, Erich. "Figura." In his *Gesammelte Aufsätze zur romanischen Philologie* (Bern and Munich, 1967), pp. 55–92.

Bahr, Hermann. *Studien zur Kritik der Moderne*. Frankfurt a. M., 1894.

Ball, Hugo. *Die Flucht aus der Zeit*. Lucerne, 1946.

———. *Gesammelte Gedichte*. Zurich, 1963.

———. *Tenderenda der Phantast*. In his *Roman*. Zurich, 1914–20.

Ballet, Gilbert. *Le langage intérieur et les diverses formes de l'aphasie*. Paris, 1886.

Bariéty, Maurice. "Eloge d'Adrien Proust." *Bulletin de l'Académie nationale de médecine* 153 (1969): 574–82.

Barthes, Roland. *Critical Essays*. Trans. Richard Howard. Evanston, Ill., 1972.

Basedow, Johann Bernhard. *Elementarwerk*. Ed. Theodor Fritzsch. Leipzig, 1909. (Orig. pub. 1785.)

Baumann, Julius. *Über Willens- und Charakterbildung auf physiologisch-psychologischer Grundlage*. Berlin, 1897.

Bäumer, Gertrud. "Die Geschichte der Frauenbewegung in Deutschland." In Helene Lange und Gertrud Bäumer, eds., *Handbuch der Frauenbewegung*. Part I: "Die Geschichte der Frauenbewegung in den Kulturländern" (Berlin, 1901).

Baumeyer, Franz. "Der Fall Schreber." *Psyche* 9 (1955–56): 513–36.

Baumgart, Wolfgang. "Faust, lesend." In Rainer Gruenter, ed., *Leser und Lesen im 18. Jahrhundert* (Heidelberg, 1977). pp. 92–97.

———. "Der Gelehrte als Herrscher: Fausts griechischer Traum." In Bernhard Fabian, ed., *Festschrift für Rainer Gruenter* (Heidelberg, 1978). pp. 58–69.

Baumgarth, Christa. *Geschichte des Futurismus*. Reinbek, 1966.

Benjamin, Walter. *Gesammelte Schriften*. Ed. Rolf Tiedemann and Hermann Schweppenhäuser. Frankfurt a. M., 1972.

———. "The Work of Art in the Age of Mechanical Reproduction." In Hannah Arendt, ed., *Illuminations*, trans. Harry Zohn (New York, 1969).

Benn, Gottfried. *Briefe*. Vol. I: *Briefe an F. W. Oelze*. Ed. Harald Steinhagen and Jürgen Schröder. 3 vols. Wiesbaden, 1977–80.

———. *Gesammelte Werke*. Ed. Dieter Wellershoff. Wiesbaden, 1959–61.

———. *Medizinische Schriften*. Ed. Werner Rube. Wiesbaden, 1965.

———. "Pallas." In his *Prose, Essays, Poems*, ed. Volkmar Sander, trans. Ernst Kaiser and Eithne Wilkins. New York, 1987.

———. *Den Traum alleine Tragen: Neue Texte, Briefe, Dokumente*. Ed. Paul Raabe and Max Niedermeyer. Munich, 1969.

Berger, G. O. "Ueber den Einfluss der Uebung auf geistige Vorgänge." *Philosophische Studien* 5 (1889): 170–78.

Bergk, Johann Adam. *Die Kunst, Bücher zu lesen, nebst Bemerkungen über Schriften und Schriftsteller*. Jena, 1799.

———. *Die Kunst zu denken. Ein Seitenstück zur Kunst, Bücher zu lesen*. Leipzig, 1802.

Bergson, Henri. *L'Evolution créatrice*, 26th ed. Paris, 1923. (Orig. pub. 1907.)

Berlioz, Hector. *Symphonie fantastique*. London, 1830.

Bermann, Richard A. *Leier und Schreibmaschine*. In Kurt Pinthus, ed., *Kinobuch*. Zurich, 1963. (Orig. pub. 1913.)

Bernfeld, Siegfried. "Freuds früheste Theorien und die Helmholtz-Schule." *Psyche* 35 (1981): 435–55. (Orig. pub. as "Freud's Earliest Theories and the School of Helmholtz," 1944.)

Bernhardi, August Ferdinand. *Sprachlehre*. 2 parts. 2d ed. Berlin, 1801–3.

Beyer, Johann Rudolph Gottlieb. *Ueber das Bücherlesen, in so fern es zum Luxus unsrer Zeiten gehört.* Acta Academiae Electoralis Moguntinae Scientiarum Utilium quae Erfurti est. Erfurt, 1796.

Bielschowsky, Albert. *Goethe. Sein Leben und seine Werke.* 2 vols. 12th ed. Munich, 1907.

Blackall, Eric A. *The Emergence of German as a Literary Language (1700–1755).* Cambridge, 1959.

Bleuler, Eugen. "Diagnostische Assoziationsstudien. Vorwort: Über die Bedeutung von Assoziationsstudien." *Journal für Psychologie und Neurologie* 3 (1904): 49–54.

Bliven, Bruce, Jr. *The Wonderful Writing Machine.* New York, 1954.

Blochmann, Elisabeth. *Das "Frauenzimmer" und die "Gelehrsamkeit." Eine Studie über die Anfänge des Mädchenschulwesens in Deutschland.* Heidelberg, 1966.

Blodgett, A. D. "A New Use for the Phonograph." *Science* 15 (1890): 43.

Bloom, Harold. "Visionary Cinema of Romantic Poetry." In his *The Ringers in the Tower: Studies in the Romantic Tradition* (Chicago, 1971). pp. 36–52.

Blüher, Karl Alfred. *Strategien des Geistes. Paul Valérys Faust.* Frankfurt a. M., 1971.

Blumenberg, Hans. *Arbeit am Mythos.* Frankfurt a. M., 1979.

Boehm, Laetitia. "Von den Anfängen des akademischen Frauenstudiums in Deutschland. Zugleich ein Kapitel aus der Geschichte der Ludwig-Maximilians-Universität München." *Historisches Jahrbuch* 77 (1958): 298–327.

Boehringer, Robert. *Mein Bild von Stefan George.* Munich, 1951.

———. "Über hersagen von gedichten." *Jahrbuch für die geistige Bewegung* 2 (1911): 77–88.

Bölsche, Wilhelm. *Die naturwissenschaftlichen Grundlagen der Poesie. Prolegomena einer realistischen Ästhetik.* Ed. Johannes J. Braakenberg. Munich, 1976. (Orig. pub. 1887.)

Bolz, Norbert W. "Der Geist und die Buchstaben. Friedrich Schlegels hermeneutische Postulate." In Ulrich Nassen, ed., *Texthermeneutik: Aktualität, Geschichte, Kritik* (Paderborn, 1979), pp. 79–112.

Bondi, Georg. *Erinnerungen an Stefan George.* Berlin, 1934.

Bonnet, Marguerite. *André Breton: Naissance de l'aventure surréaliste.* Paris, 1975.

Borges, Jorge Luis. *Obras completas.* Buenos Aires, 1964–66.

Bosanquet, Theodora. *Henry James at Work.* The Hogarth Essays. London, 1924.

Bose, Günter, and Erich Brinkmann, eds. *Grosz/Jung/Grosz.* Berlin, 1980.

Bosse, Heinrich. "Autorisieren. Ein Essay über Entwicklungen heute und seit dem 18. Jahrhundert." *Zeitschrift für Literaturwissenschaft und Linguistik* 11 (1981): 120–34.

———. *Autorschaft ist Werkherrschaft. Über die Entstehung des Urheberrechts aus dem Geist der Goethezeit.* Paderborn, 1981.

———. "'Dichter kann man nicht bilden.' Zur Veränderung der Schulrhetorik nach 1770." *Jahrbuch für Internationale Germanistik* 10 (1979): 80–125.

———. "Herder." In Horst Turk, ed., *Klassiker der Literaturtheorie* (Munich, 1979), pp. 78–91.

Bradish, Joseph A. von. *Goethes Beamtenlaufbahn.* New York, 1937.

Bradley, Brigitte L. *Zu Rilkes 'Malte Laurids Brigge.'* Bern, 1980.

Brandes, Ernst. *Betrachtungen über das weibliche Geschlecht und dessen Ausbildung in dem geselligen Leben.* 3 parts. Hanover, 1802.

————. *Ueber das Du und Du zwischen Eltern und Kindern.* Hanover, 1809.

Brann, Henry Walter. *Nietzsche und die Frauen.* 2d ed. Bonn, 1978.

Braun, Lily. *Die Frauenfrage, ihre geschichtliche Entwicklung und wirtschaftliche Seite.* Leipzig, 1901.

Brentano, Bettina. *Bettina von Arnim, Werke und Briefe.* Ed. Gustav Konrad. Frechen, 1959–63.

Brentano, Clemens. *Werke.* Ed. Friedholm Kemp. Munich, 1963–68.

Breton, André. "Manifesto of Surrealism." In *Manifestoes of Surrealism,* trans. Richard Seaver and Helen R. Lane (Ann Arbor, 1969), pp. 1–47.

————, and Eluard, Paul. *Die unbefleckte Empfängnis. L'Immaculée Conception.* Bilingual ed. Munich, 1974.

Breucker, Fritz. "Die Eisenbahn in der Dichtung." *Zeitschrift für den deutschen Unterricht* 25 (1911): 305–24.

Bridgwater, Patrick. *Kafka und Nietzsche.* Bonn, 1974.

————. "The Sources of Stramm's Originality." In Jeremy D. Adler and John H. White, eds., *August Stramm: Kritische Essays und unveröffentlichtes Quellenmaterial aus dem Nachlass des Dichters* (Berlin, 1979). pp. 31–46.

Brinnin, John Malcolm. *The Third Rose: Gertrude Stein and Her World.* London, 1960.

Bruch, Walter. "Von der Tonwalze zur Bildplatte: 100 Jahre Ton- und Bildspeicherung." *Die Funkschau.* Special issue, 1979.

Budde, Gerhard August. *Die Pädagogik der preussischen höh. Knabenschulen unter dem Einflusse der pädagogischen Zeitströmungen vom Anfange des 19. Jahrhunderts bis auf die Gegenwart.* 2 vols. Langensalza, 1910.

Bünger, Ferdinand. *Entwickelungsgeschichte des Volksschullesebuches.* Leipzig, 1898.

Bürger, Christa. *Der Ursprung der bürgerlichen Institution Kunst. Literatursoziologische Untersuchungen zum klassischen Goethe.* Frankfurt a. M., 1977.

Burgerstein, Leo. *Die Weltletter.* Vienna, 1889.

Burghagen, Otto. *Die Schreibmaschine. Illustrierte Beschreibung aller gangbaren Schreibmaschinen nebst gründlicher Anleitung zum Arbeiten auf sämtlichen Systemen.* Hamburg, 1898.

Busshoff, Heinrich. *Politikwissenschaft und Pädagogik. Studien über den Zusammenhang von Politik und Pädagogik.* Berlin, 1968.

Calasso, Roberto. *Die geheime Geschichte des Senatspräsidenten Dr. Daniel Paul Schreber.* Frankfurt a. M., 1980. (Orig. pub. as *L'impuro folle* [Milan, 1974]).

Campe, Johann Heinrich. *Neues Bilder Abeze.* Ed. Dietrich Leube. Frankfurt a. M., 1975. (Orig. pub. 1807.)

Campe, Rüdiger. "Schreibstunden in Jean Pauls Idyllen *Fugen.*" *Deutsch-französisches Jahrbuch für Text-Analytik* 1 (1980): 132–70.

Cardinal, Roger. "André Breton. Wahnsinn und Poesie." In Bernd Urban and Winfred Kudszus, eds., *Psychoanalytische und psychopathologische Literaturinterpretation* (Darmstadt, 1981), pp. 300–20.

Carossa, Hans. *Verwandlungen einer Jugend.* In his *Sämtliche Werke,* vol. 2 (Frankfurt a. M., 1962), pp. 109–261.

Carstensen, Jens. "Bilse und Thomas Mann." *Der Junge Buchhandel* 24 (1971): 175–79.

Chamberlain, Alexander. *The Child and Childhood in Folkthought.* London, 1896.

Chapuis, Alfred, and Gélis, Edouard. *Le monde des automates. Etude historique et technique.* 2 vols. Paris, 1928.

Chew, Victor Kenneth. *Talking Machines 1877–1914: Some Aspects of the Early History of the Gramophone.* London, 1967.

Clarétie, Jules. *Les Amours d'un interne.* Paris, 1881.

Clément, Cathérine. "Hexe und Hysterikerin." *Die Alternative* 19 (1976): 148–54.

Code Napoléon. Nouvelle édition conforme à l'édition de l'Imprimerie Impériale. Paris, 1807.

Cohn, Hermann. "Das Auge und die Handschrift. Vom Fels zum Meer. *Speemann's Illustrirte Zeitschrift für das Deutsche Haus* 1 (1881): 356–72.

Conan Doyle, Sir Arthur. *The Complete Sherlock Holmes.* Pref. by Christopher Morley. New York, 1930.

Cournot, Michel. "'Toi qui as de si grandes dents . . .': Franz Kafka, lettres à Félice." *Le Nouvel Observateur,* March 17, 1972, pp. 59–61.

Creuzer, Friedrich. *Die Liebe der Günderode. Friedrich Creuzers Briefe an Caroline v. Günderode.* Ed. Karl Preisendanz. Munich, 1912.

——. "Das Studium der Alten, als Vorbereitung zur Philosophie." *Studien* 1 (1805): 1–22.

Cros, Charles. *Le Collier des griffes.* In Louis Forestier and Pascal Pia, eds., *Oeuvres completes* (Paris, 1964).

Cumont, Franz. *Les Religions orientales dans le paganisme romain.* 4th ed. Paris, 1924.

Curtius, Ernst Robert. "Goethes Aktenführung." *Die Neue Rundschau* 62 (1951): 110–21.

Daniels, Karlheinz, ed. *Über die Sprache. Erfahrungen und Erkenntnisse deutscher Dichter und Schriftsteller des 20. Jahrhunderts. Eine Anthologie.* Bremen, 1966.

David, Claude. *Stefan George: Son Oeuvre poétique.* Lyon, 1952.

Degering, Hermann. *Die Schrift. Atlas der Schriftformen des Abendlandes vom Altertum bis zum Ausgang des 18. Jahrhunderts.* Berlin, 1929.

Deibel, Franz. *Dorothea Schlegel als Schriftsteller im Zusammenhang mit der romantischen Schule.* Berlin, 1905.

Deleuze, Gilles, and Guattari, Felix. *Anti-Oedipus: Capitalism and Schizophrenia.* Trans. Robert Hurley, Mark Seem, and Helen R. Lane. Minneapolis, 1983. (Orig. pub. 1977.)

——. *A Thousand Plateaus: Capitalism and Schizophrenia.* Trans. Brian Massumi. Minneapolis, 1987.

Derrida, Jacques. *Glas.* Trans. John P. Leavey, Jr., and Richard Rand. Lincoln, Nebraska, 1986.

——. *Margins of Philosophy.* Trans. Alan Bass. Chicago, 1982.

——. "Nietzsches Otobiographie oder Politik des Eigennamens. Fugen." *Deutsche-französisches Jahrbuch für Text-Analytik* 1 (1980): 64–98.

——. *Of Grammatology.* Trans. Gayatri Chakravorty Spivak. Baltimore, 1976.

——. *Writing and Difference.* Trans. Alan Bass. Chicago, 1978.

——. "Titel (noch zu bestimmen)." In Friedrich A. Kittler, ed., *Austreibung des Geistes aus den Geisteswissenschaften. Programme des Poststrukturalismus* (Paderborn, 1980), pp. 15–37.

Diener, Gottfried. *Goethes 'Lila.' Heilung eines "Wahnsinns" durch "psychische*

Kur." Vergleichende Interpretation der drei Fassungen. Mit ungedruckten Texten und Noten und einem Anhang über psychische Kuren der Goethezeit und das Psychodrama. Frankfurt a. M., 1971.

Dilthey, Wilhelm. *Gesammelte Schriften.* Leipzig, 1914–58.

———, and Heubaum, Alfred. "Ein Gutachten Wilhelm von Humboldts über die Staatsprüfung des höheren Verwaltungsbeamten." *Jahrbuch für Gesetzgebung, Verwaltung und Volkswirtschaft im Deutschen Reich* 23 (1899): 1455–71.

Döblin, Alfred. *Aufsätze zur Literatur: Ausgewählte Werke in Einzelbänden.* Ed. Anthony W. Riley. Olten, 1963.

Dolz, Johann Christian. *Praktische Anleitung zu schriftlichen Aufsätzen über Gegenstände des gemeinen Lebens, besonders für Bürgerschulen.* 2d ed. Reutlingen, 1811.

Donzelot, Jacques. *The Policing of Families.* Trans. Robert Hurley. New York, 1979.

Dornseiff, Franz. *Das Alphabet im Mystik und Magie.* Leipzig, 1922.

Druskowitz, Helene. *Moderne Versuche eines Religionsersatzes. Ein philosophischer Essay.* Heidelberg, 1886.

———. *Pessimistische Kardinalsätze. Ein Vademekum für die freiesten Geister.* Wittenberg, ca. 1900.

———. *Zur neuen Lehre. Betrachtungen.* Heidelberg, 1888.

Durrani, Osman. *Faust and the Bible: A Study of Goethe's Use of Scriptural Allusions and Christian Religious Motifs in 'Faust' I and II.* Bern, 1977.

Ebbinghaus, Hermann. *Grundzüge der Psychologie.* Vol. 1, 2d ed. Leipzig, 1905. Vol. 2 (completed by Ernst Durr). Leipzig, 1913.

———. *Memory: A Contribution to Experimental Psychology.* Trans. Henry A. Ruger. New York, 1913.

Ehrenreich, Barbara, and English, Deirdre. *Hexen, Hebammen, und Krankenschwestern.* Munich, 1976.

Ehrenstein, Albert. *Tubutsch.* Leipzig, 1919.

Eichendorff, Joseph, Freiherr von. "Ahnung und Gegenwart." In Gerhart Baumann, ed., *Neue Gesamtausgabe der Werke und Schriften.* Stuttgart, 1957–58.

Einstein, Carl. *Gesammelte Werke.* Ed. Ernst Nef. Wiesbaden, 1962.

Eisner, Lotte H. *Die dämonische Leinwand.* Ed. Hilmar Hoffmann and Walter Schobert. Reinbeck, 1975.

Ellenberger, Henry F. *Die Entdeckung des Unbewussten.* 2 vols. Bern, 1973.

Elling, Barbara. *Leserintegration im Werk E. T. A. Hoffmanns.* Bern, 1973.

Engelsing, Rolf. *Analphabetentum und Lektüre. Zur Sozialgeschichte des Lesens in Deutschland zwischen feudaler und industrieller Gesellschaft.* Stuttgart, 1973.

———. *Der literarische Arbeiter.* Vol. 1. *Arbeit, Zeit und Werk im literarischen Beruf.* Göttingen, 1976.

Enzensberger, Hans Magnus. "Baukasten zu einer Theorie der Medien." *Kursbuch* 20 (1970): 159–86.

Erdmann, Benno, and Dodge, Raymond. *Psychologische Untersuchungen über das Lesen auf experimenteller Grundlage.* Halle, 1898.

Erning, Günter. *Das Lesen und die Lesewelt. Beiträge zur Frage der Lesergeschichte: dargestellt am Beispiel der schwäbischen Provinz.* Bad Heilbrunn, 1974.

Erstes Lesebüchlein für die lieben Kleinen in den deutschen katholischen Schulen des Grossherzogthums Baden. 4th ed. Rastatt, 1811.

Exerzier-Reglement für die Infanterie. Vom 29. Mai 1906. Neuabdruck mit Einfügung der bis August 1909 ergangenen Änderungen. Berlin, 1909.

Fargers, Joël. "L'image d'un corps." *Communications,* no. 23 (Psychanalyse et cinéma), 1975, pp. 88–95.

Fauth, Franz. *Das Gedächtnis.* Berlin, 1898.

Fechner, Gustav Theodor. *Vorschule der Ästhetik.* 2 pts. Leipzig, 1876.

Fechner, Heinrich. "Geschichte des Volksschul-Lesebuches." In Carl Kehr, ed., *Geschichte der Methodik des deutschen Volksschulunterrichtes* (Gotha, 1877–82), II: 439–519.

Ferrier, Sir David. *The Functions of the Brain.* London, 1876. Trans. as *Die Functionen des Gehirns.* Braunschweig, 1879.

Fichte, Immanuel Hermann. *Johann Gottlieb Fichte's Leben und literarischer Briefwechsel.* 2 vols., 2d ed. Leipzig, 1862.

Fichte, Johann Gottlieb. *Gesamtausgabe.* Ed. Reinhard Lauth and Hans Jacob. Stuttgart, 1962.

———. *Sämmtliche Werke.* Ed. I. H. Fichte. N. p., 1845.

Fichtner, Gerhard. "Psychiatrie zur Zeit Hölderlins." "Ausstellung anlässlich der 12. Jahresversammlung der Hölderlin-Gesellschaft in Tübingen im Evangelischen Stift," June 9–11, 1972. (Typescript.)

Flake, Otto. *Die Stadt des Hirns.* Berlin, 1919.

Flechsig, Paul. *Gehirn und Seele.* 2d ed. Leipzig, 1896.

———. *Die körperlichen Grundlagen der Geistesstörungen.* Leipzig, 1882.

———. *Meine myelogenetische Hirnlehre mit biographischer Einleitung.* Berlin, 1927.

Förster-Nietzsche, Elisabeth. *Friedrich Nietzsche und die Frauen seiner Zeit.* Munich, 1935.

Forel, August. "Selbst-Biographie eines Falles von Mania acuta." *Archiv für Psychiatrie und Nervenkrankheiten* 34 (1901): 960–97.

Forrer, R. "Handschriften Irrsinniger." *Vom Fels zum Meer: Spemann's Illustrirte Zeitschrift für das deutsche Haus* 2 (1888): 515–22.

Forster, Leonhard. *Dichten in fremden Sprachen. Vielsprachigkeit in der Literatur.* Munich, 1974.

Foucault, Michel. *The Archaeology of Knowledge and the Discourse on Language.* Trans. A. M. Sheridan Smith. New York, 1972.

———. *Discipline and Punish: The Birth of the Prison.* Trans. Alan Sheridan. New York, 1979.

———. "Dream, Imagination, and Existence: An Introduction to Ludwig Binswanger's 'Dream and Existence.'" Trans. Forrest Williams. *Review of Existential Psychology and Psychiatry* 19 (1986): 31–78.

———. "La Folie, l'absence d'oeuvre." Trans. in Foucault, *Schriften zur Literatur.* Munich, 1974.

———. *Histoire de la folie à l'âge classique.* Paris, 1961. Trans. as *Wahnsinn und Gesellschaft: Eine Geschichte des Wahns im Zeitalter der Vernunft* (Frankfurt a. M., 1969).

———. *The History of Sexuality.* Vol. I: *An Introduction.* Trans. Robert Hurley. New York, 1980.

———. *Language, Counter-Memory, Practice.* Ed. Donald F. Bouchard. Ithaca, N. Y., 1977.

———. *Mental Illness and Psychology.* Trans. Alan Sheridan. New York, 1976.

——. *The Order of Things: An Archaeology of the Human Sciences.* New York, 1973.

——. *Von der Subversion des Wissens.* Ed. Walter Seitter. Munich, 1974.

Frank, Horst Joachim. *Geschichte des Deutschunterrichts. Von den Anfängen bis 1945.* Munich, 1977.

Frank, Manfred. *Das individuelle Allgemeine: Textstrukturierung und -interpretation nach Schleiermacher.* Frankfurt a. M., 1977.

——, ed. *Das kalte Herz und andere Texte der Romantik.* Frankfurt a. M., 1978.

Freud, Sigmund. *The Complete Letters of Sigmund Freud to Wilhelm Fliess. 1887–1904.* Trans. and ed. Jeffrey Moussaieff Masson. Cambridge, Mass., 1985.

——. *On Aphasia: A Critical Study.* Trans. E. Stengel. New York, 1953.

——. *The Standard Edition of the Complete Psychological Works of Sigmund Freud.* Ed. and trans. James Strachey. 23 vols. London, 1962.

——, and Lou Andreas-Salomé. *Briefwechsel.* Ed. Ernst Pfeiffer. Frankfurt a. M., 1966.

Fricke, Harald. *Norm und Abweichung. Eine Philosophie der Literatur.* Munich, 1903.

Fricke, K. "Die geschichtliche Entwicklung des Lehramts an den höheren Schulen." In K. Fricke and K. Eulenburg, *Beiträge zur Oberlehrerfrage.* Leipzig, 1903.

Friedlaender, Salomo (Mynona). "Goethe spricht in den Phonographen." In *Das Nachthemd am Wegweiser und andere höchst merkwürdige Geschichten des Dr. Salomo Friedlaender* (Berlin, 1980). pp. 159–78. (Orig. pub. 1916.)

Fritzsch, Theodor. "Zur Geschichte der Kinderforschung und Kinderbeobachtung." *Zeitschrift für Philosophie und Pädagogik* 13 (1906): 497–506.

Fühmann, Franz. *Fräulein Veronika Paulmann aus der Pirnaer Vorstadt oder Etwas über das Schauerliche bei E. T. A. Hoffmann.* Rostock, 1979.

Furet, François, and Ozouf, Jacques. *Lire et écrire: L'Alphabétisation des Français de Calvin à Jules Ferry.* 2 vols. Paris, 1977.

Gardiner, Muriel, ed. *The Wolf-Man.* New York, 1971.

Garfinkel, Harold. "Common Sense Knowledge of Social Structures: The Documentary Method of Interpretation in Lay and Professional Fact Finding" and "Das Alltagswissen über soziale und innerhalb sozialer Strukturen." In Bielefeld Sociological Study Group, ed., *Alltagswissen, Interaktion und gesellschaftliche Wirklichkeit* (Reinbek, 1973), I: 189–262.

Gaube, Uwe. *Film und Traum. Zum präsentativen Symbolismus.* Munich, 1978.

Gaudig, Hugo. "Zum Bildungsideal der deutschen Frau." *Zeitschrift für pädagogische Psychologie* 11 (1910): 225–37.

Gedike, Friedrich. *Gesammelte Schulschriften.* 2 vols. Berlin, 1789–95.

Gehrmann, Carl. *Körper, Gehirn, Seele, Gott.* 3 vols. Berlin, 1893.

Geissler, Horst Wolfram, ed. *Gestaltungen des Faust. Die bedeutendsten Werke der Faustdichtung seit 1587.* Vol. 1: *Die vorgoethische Zeit.* Munich, 1927.

Geistbeck, Michael. *Der Weltverkehr. Telegraphie und Post, Eisenbahnen und Schiffahrt in ihrer Entwicklung dargestellt.* Freiburg, 1887.

George, Stefan. *Gesamt-Ausgabe der Werke.* Berlin, 1927–34.

——. *The Works of Stefan George.* Trans. Olga Marx and Max Morwitz. 2d ed. Studies in the Germanic Languages and Literatures, no. 78. Chapel Hill, N.C., 1974.

——, and Hofmannsthal, Hugo von. *Der Briefwechsel zwischen George und Hofmannsthal.* Berlin, 1938.

Gerhardt, Dagobert von (Amyntor). *Skizzenbuch meines Lebens*. 2 vols. Breslau, 1893–98.

Gessinger, Joachim. "Schriftspracherwerb im 18. Jahrhundert: Kulturelle Verelendung und politische Herrschaft." *Osnabrücker Beiträge zur Sprachtheorie* 11 (1979): 26–47.

———. *Sprache und Bürgertum. Sozialgeschichte sprachlicher Verkehrsformen im 18. Jahrhundert in Deutschland*. Stuttgart, 1980.

Giesebrecht, Ludwig. "Der deutsche Aufsatz in Prima. Eine geschichtliche Untersuchung." *Zeitschrift für das Gymnasialwesen*, 1856, pp. 113–52.

Giesecke, Michael. "Schriftspracherwerb und Erstlesedidaktik in der Zeit des 'gemein teutsch'—eine sprachhistorische Interpretation der Lehrbücher Valentin Ickelsamers." *Osnabrücker Beiträge zur Sprachtheorie* 11 (1979): 48–72.

Gilman, Sander L. "Friedrich Nietzsche's 'Niederschriften aus der spätesten Zeit' (1890–1897) and the Conversation Notebooks." In Bernd Urban and Winfried Kudszus, eds., *Psychoanalytische und psychopathologische Literaturinterpretation* (Darmstadt, 1981), pp. 321–46.

Ginzburg, Carlo. "Spurensicherung: Der Jäger entziffert die Fährte, Sherlock Holmes nimmt die Lupe, Freud liest Morelli—die Wissenschaft auf der Suche nach sich selbst." *Freibeuter* (1980), no. 3, pp. 7–17, and no. 4, pp. 11–36.

Gleim, Betty. *Erziehung und Unterricht des Weiblichen Geschlechts: Ein Buch für Eltern und Erzieher*. 2 vols. Leipzig, 1810.

Goethe, Johann Wolfgang von. *Gespräche: Aufgrund der Ausgabe und des Nachlasses von Flodoard Freiherrn von Biedermann*. Ed. Wolfgang Herwig. Zurich, 1965–72.

———. *Goethe's Faust*. Trans. and introd. Walter Kaufmann. New York, 1963.

———. *Sämtliche Schriften*. Ed. Willy Flach. Weimar, 1950–72.

———. *Sämtliche Werke*. Jubilee ed. Ed. Eduard von den Hellen. Stuttgart, 1904–5.

———. *Torquato Tasso*. Trans. Michael Hamburger. In Goethe, *Verse Plays and Epic*, ed. Cyrus Hamlin and Frank Ryder (New York, 1987), pp. 55–140.

———. *Werke*. Ed. by commission of Sophie, Grand Duchess of Saxony. Weimar, 1887–1919.

Goldscheider, Alfred. "Zur Physiologie und Pathologie der Handschrift." *Archiv für Psychiatrie und Nervenkrankheiten* 24 (1892): 503–25.

Goll, Claire. *La Poursuite du vent*. Paris, 1976. Trans. as *Ich verzeihe keinem. Eine literarische Chronique scandaleuse unserer Zeit*. Munich, 1980.

Grabein, Paul, ed. *Liebeslieder moderner Frauen*. Berlin, 1902.

Graf, Alfred, ed. *Schülerjahre: Erlebnisse und Urteile namhafter Zeitgenossen*. Berlin, 1912.

Graubner, Hans. "'Mitteilbarkeit' und 'Lebensgefühl' in Kants 'Kritik der Urteilskraft': Zur kommunikativen Bedeutung des Ästhetischen." In Friedrich A. Kittler and Horst Turk, eds., *Urszenen: Literaturwissenschaft als Diskursanalyse und Diskurskritik* (Frankfurt a. M., 1977), pp. 53–75.

Grävell, Max Friedrich Karl Wilhelm. *Der Staatsbeamte als Schriftsteller oder der Schriftsteller als Staatsbeamte im Preussischen: Aktenmässig dargethan*. Stuttgart, 1820.

Grob, Karl. *Ursprung und Utopie. Aporien des Textes*. Bonn, 1976.

Grüssbeutel, Jacob. *Eyn besonder fast nützlich stymen büchlein mit figuren*. In Heinrich Fechner, ed., *Vier seltene Schriften des 16. Jahrhunderts*. Berlin, 1882. (Orig. pub. 1534.)

Guattari, Félix. "Le divan du pauvre." *Communications*, no. 23 (Psychanalyse et cinéma), 1975, pp. 96–103.

Gutzmann, Hermann. "Über Hören und Verstehen." *Zeitschrift für angewandte Psychologie und psychologische Sammelforschung* 1 (1908): 483–503.

Hass, Norbert. "Exposé zu Lacans Diskursmathemen." *Der Wunderblock*, no. 5/6, 1980, pp. 9–34.

Habermas, Jürgen. *Erkenntnis und Interesse*. Frankfurt a. M., 1968.

Hackenberg, Albert. "Der mündliche Ausdruck." In *Kunsterziehung. Ergebnisse und Anregungen des zweiten Kunsterziehungstages in Weimar am 9., 10., 11. Oktober 1903*. Deutsche Sprache und Dichtung (Leipzig, 1904), pp. 64–75.

Hahnemann, Samuel. *Handbuch für Mütter, oder Grundsätze der ersten Erziehung der Kinder (nach den Prinzipien des J. J. Rousseau)*. Leipzig, 1796.

———. "Striche zur Schilderung Klockenbrings während seines Trübsinns." In Ernst Stapf, ed., *Kleine medizinische Schriften* (Leipzig, 1829), II: 239–46. (Orig. pub. 1796.)

"Die Hähnische Litteralmethode." In Carl Philipp Moritz, ed., *Gnothi sauton oder Magazin zur Erfahrungsseelenkunde als ein Lesebuch für Gelehrte und Ungelehrte* (1805), pt. 1, vol. II, pp. 94–95. (Document dated 1783.)

Hall, G. Stanley. *Contents of Children's Minds on Entering School*. New York, 1893.

———. "A Study of Fears." *The American Journal of Psychology* 8 (1896–97): 147–249.

Hamacher, Werner. "Hermeneutische Ellipsen: Schrift und Zirkel bei Schleiermacher." In Ulrich Nassen, ed., *Texthermeneutik: Aktualität, Geschichte, Kritik* (Paderborn, 1979), pp. 113–48.

Hammerstein, Ludwig von. *Das Preussische Schulmonopol mit besonderer Rücksicht auf die Gymnasien*. Freiburg, 1893.

Hanstein, Adalbert von. *Die Frauen in der Geschichte des Deutschen Geisteslebens des 18. und 19. Jahrhunderts*. 2 vols. Leipzig, 1899–1900.

Hardach-Pinke, Irene, and Hardach, Gerd. *Deutsche Kindheiten: Autobiographische Zeugnisse 1700–1900*. Frankfurt, 1978.

Hardenberg, Friedrich von. *Schriften*. Ed. Paul Kluckhohn and Richard Samuel. Stuttgart, 1960.

Hart, Heinrich. "Das dichterische Kunstwerk in der Schule (Seine Auswahl)." In *Kunsterziehung: Ergebnisse und Anregungen des zweiten Kunsterziehungstages in Weimar am 9., 10., 11. Oktober 1903*. Deutsche Sprache und Dichtung. Leipzig, 1904.

Hartleben, Otto Erich. "Der Einhornapotheker." In Franz Ferdinand Heitmueller, ed., *Ausgewählte Werke in drei Banden*. Berlin, 1920.

Hattenhauer, Hans. *Geschichte des Beamtentums*. Vol. I: *Handbuch des öffentlichen Dienstes*. Cologne, 1980.

Hatvani, Paul. "Spracherotik," *Der Sturm* 3 (1912): 210.

Hausen, Karin. "Die Polarisierung der 'Geschlechtscharaktere'—Eine Spiegelung der Dissoziation von Erwerbs- und Familienleben." In Werner Conze, ed., *Sozialgeschichte der Familie in der Neuzeit Europas* (Stuttgart, 1976), pp. 363–93.

Haym, Rudolf. *Die romantische Schule: Ein Beitrag zur Geschichte des deutschen Geistes*. Berlin, 1870.

Hécaen, Henry, and Angelergues, René. *Pathologie du langage: L'Aphasie*. Paris, 1965.

Heftrich, Eckhardt. *Novalis: Vom Logos der Poesie.* Frankfurt, 1969.

Hegel, Georg Wilhelm Friedrich. *Aesthetics: Lectures on Fine Arts.* Trans. T. M. Knox. 2 vols. Oxford, Clarendon, 1975.

———. *Briefe von und an Hegel.* Ed. Johannes Hoffmeister. Hamburg, 1961.

———. *"Der Geist des Christentums": Schriften 1796 bis 1800.* Ed. Werner Hamacher. Frankfurt, 1978.

———. *Gesammelte Werke.* Ed. by commission of the German Research Society. Hamburg, 1968–.

———. *Hegel's Philosophy of Subjective Spirit.* Ed. and trans. M. J. Petry. 3 vols. Dortrecht, 1978.

———. *Hegel's Science of Logic.* Trans. A. V. Miller. New York, 1976.

———. *Phenomenology of Spirit.* Trans. A. V. Miller, with a Foreword by J. N. Findley. Oxford, Clarendon, 1977.

———. *Sämtliche Werke.* Ed. Hermann Glockner. Stuttgart, 1927–40.

Hegener, Johannes. Die Poetisierung der Wissenschaften bei Novalis: Studie zum Problem enzyklopädischen Welterfahrens. Bonn, 1975.

Heidegger, Martin. "Antwort auf die Enquête Rimbaud." *Archives des lettres modernes* 8 (1976): 12–17.

———. *Being and Time.* Trans. John Macquarrie and Edward Robinson. New York, 1962.

———. *Nietzsche.* Pfullingen, 1961.

———. *On the Way to Language.* Trans. Peter D. Hertz. New York, 1971.

Hein, Birgit, and Wulf Herzogenrath. *Film als Film. 1910 bis heute. Vom Animationsfilm der zwanziger zum Filmenvironment der siebziger Jahre.* Stuttgart, 1978.

Heinemann, Manfred. *Schule im Vorfeld der Verwandlung. Die Entwicklung der preussischen Unterrichtsverwaltung von 1771–1800. Studien zum Wandel von Gesellschaft und Bildung im 19. Jahrhundert.* Göttingen, 1974.

Hellpach, Willy. *Erzogene über Erziehung. Dokumente von Berufenen.* Heidelberg, 1954.

———. "Psychopathologisches in moderner Kunst und Literatur." In *Vierter Internationaler Kongress zur Fürsorge für Geisteskranke (Berlin 1910),* (Halle, 1911), pp. 131–58.

Helmers, Hermann. *Geschichte des deutschen Lesebuches in Grundzügen.* Stuttgart, 1970.

Hempel, Friedrich. *Nachtgedanken über das A-B-C-Buch von Spiritus Asper, für alle, welche buchstabiren können.* 2 vols. Leipzig, 1809.

Henrich, Dieter. "Hegels Theorie über den Zufall." In his *Hegel im Kontext* (Frankfurt a. M., 1967).

Herbertz, Richard. "Zur Psychologie des Maschinenschreibens." *Zeitschrift für angewandte Psychologie* 2 (1909): 551–61.

Herder, Johann Gottfried von. "On the Origin of Language." In *'On the Origin of Language': Two Essays by Jean-Jacques Rousseau and Johann Gottfried Herder,* trans. John H. Moran and Alexander Gode (New York, 1966), pp. 87–176.

———. *Sämtliche Werke.* Ed. Bernhard Suphan. Berlin, 1877–1913.

Hermann, Friedrich. *Neue Fibel für Kinder oder methodischer Elementarunterricht im Lesen und Abstrahiren nach Pestalozzi, Olivier und eignen Ideen.* Leipzig, 1804.

Herrlitz, Hans-Georg. *Der Lektüre-Kanon des Deutschunterrichts im Gym-*

nasium. Ein Beitrag zur Geschichte der müttersprachlichen Schulliteratur.
Heidelberg, 1964.

Herzfelde, Wieland. "Die Ethik der Geisteskranken." *Die Aktion* 4 (1914):
298–302.

Hesse, Hermann. "Künstler und Psychoanalyse." In *Gesammelte Werke* (Frankfurt a. M., 1970), X: 47–53.

Heuss, Theodor. *Vorspiele des Lebens. Jugenderinnerungen.* Tübingen, 1953.

Hey, C. "Die Methodik des Schreibunterrichtes." In Carl Kehr, ed., *Geschichte der Methodik des deutschen Volksschulunterrichtes* (Gotha, 1879), II: 1–178.

Heydenreich, Karl Heinrich. *Mann und Weib. Ein Beitrag zur Philosophie über die Geschlechter.* Leipzig, 1798.

Heym, Georg. *Dichtungen und Schriften. Gesamtausgabe.* Ed. Karl Ludwig Schneider. 3 vols. Hamburg, 1960–64.

Hille, Peter. "Das Recht der Kindheit. Ein Mahnwort." In *Gesammelte Werke,* vol. II (Berlin, 1904).

Hinrichs, Hermann Friedrich Wilhelm. *Aesthetische Vorlesungen über Goethe's Faust als Beitrag zur Anerkennung wissenschaftlicher Kunstbeurteilung.* Halle, 1825.

Hintze, Otto. *Der Beamtenstand.* Vorträge der Gehe-Stiftung zu Dresden, vol. 3. Leipzig, 1911.

Hippel, Theodor Gottlieb von. *Lebensläufe nach aufsteigender Linie nebst Beilagen A, B, C.* In *Sämmtliche Werke.* Berlin, 1828–35.

———. "Nachlass über weibliche Bildung." In *Sämmtliche Werke.* Berlin, 1828–35.

———. *Über die bürgerliche Verbesserung der Weiber.* Ed. Ralph-Rainer Wuthenow. Frankfurt a. M., 1977. Orig. pub. 1793.

Hirth, Georg. *Aufgaben der Kunstphysiologie.* 2d ed. Munich, 1897.

Hobrecker, Karl. *Alte vergessene Kinderbücher.* Berlin, 1924.

Hoche, Johann Georg. *Vertraute Briefe über die jetzige abentheuerliche Lesesucht und über den Einfluss derselben auf die Verminderung des häuslichen und öffentlichen Glücks.* Hanover, 1794.

Hoffbauer, Johann Christoph. *Untersuchungen über die Krankheiten der Seele und die verwandten Zustände.* 3 vols. Halle, 1802–7.

Hoffmann, Ernst Theodor Amadeus. *Briefwechsel.* Ed. Friedrich Schnapp. 3 vols. Darmstadt, 1967–69.

———. *Fantasie- und Nachtstücke.* Ed. Walter Müller-Seidel. Munich, 1976.

———. "Klein Zaches genannt Zinnober: Ein Märchen." In Walter Müller-Seidel, ed., *Späte Werke.* Munich, 1969.

———. *Die Serapions-Brüder.* Ed. Walter Müller-Seidel. Munich, 1963.

———. *Tales of E. T. A. Hoffmann.* Ed. and trans. Leonard J. Kent and Elizabeth C. Knight. Chicago, 1969.

Hofmannsthal, Hugo von. "Buch der Freunde." In Herbert Steiner, ed., *Aufzeichnungen: Gesammelte Werke in Einzelausgaben.* Frankfurt a. M., 1959.

———. "Letter of Lord Chandos." In *Selected Prose,* trans. Mary Hottingen, Tania Stern, and James Stern (New York, 1952).

———. "Poesie und Leben." In Rudolf Hirsch, ed., *Ausgewählte Werke,* 2 vols., Frankfurt a. M., 1957.

———, and Edgar Karg von Bebenburg. *Briefwechsel.* Ed. Mary E. Gilbert. Frankfurt a. M., 1966.

Holborn, Hajo. "Der deutsche Idealismus in sozialgeschichtlicher Beleuchtung." *Historische Zeitschrift* 174 (1952): 359–84.

Holst, Amalie. *Ueber die Bestimmung des Weibes zur höhern Geistesbildung.* Berlin, 1802.

Holz, Arno. *Das Werk.* Berlin, 1924–25.

Hornbostel, Erich Moritz von, and Otto Abraham. "Über die Bedeutung des Phonographen für vergleichende Musikwissenschaft." *Zeitschrift für Ethnologie* 36 (1904): 222–36.

Huber, Johann Albert. *Ueber den Nutzen der Felbigerschen Lehrart in den kaiserlich-königlichen Normalschulen für beyde Geschlechter. Eine Rede in einer Versammlung von verschiedenen Klosterfrauen aus den vorderösterreichischen Landen.* Freiburg, 1774.

Huber, Ludwig Ferdinand. *Sämmtliche Werke.* 4 parts. Tübingen, 1806–19.

Huelsenbeck, Richard. *En avant Dada. Die Geschichte des Dadaismus.* Berlin, 1978. (Orig. pub. 1920.)

Hufeland, Christoph Wilhelm. *Guter Rat an Mütter über die wichtigsten Punkte der physischen Erziehung der Kinder in den ersten Jahren.* Berlin, 1799.

———. "Vorsorge für die Augen in Hinsicht auf den Druck und das Papier der Bücher." In Immanuel Kant, *Von der Macht des Gemüths durch den blossen Vorsatz, seiner krankhaften Gefühle Meister zu sein,* ed. C. W. Hufeland (Minden, 1873).

Humboldt, Wilhelm von. "Bericht der Sektion des Kultus und Unterrichts an den König." In Preussische Akademie der Wissenschaften, ed., *Gesammelte Schriften.* Berlin, 1903–36.

Husserl, Edmund. *Logische Untersuchungen.* Tübingen, 1968.

Hyde, H. Montgomery. *Henry James at Home.* London, 1969.

Ickelsamer, Valentin. *Die rechte weis auffs kürtzist lesen zu lernen.* In Heinrich Fechner, ed., *Vier seltene Schriften des 16. Jahrhunderts.* Berlin, 1882. (Orig. pub. 1534.)

———. *Ein Teütsche Grammatica.* In Heinrich Fechner, ed., *Vier seltene Schriften des 16. Jahrhunderts.* Berlin, 1882. (Orig. pub. 1533.)

Innis, Harold Adam. *Empire and Communications.* Oxford, Clarendon, 1950.

Irle, Gerhard. *Der psychiatrische Roman.* Stuttgart, 1965.

Jaffé, Aniela. *Bilder und Symbole aus E. T. A. Hoffmanns Märchen "Der Goldene Topf."* 2d ed. Hildesheim, 1978.

Jäger, Georg. "Der Deutschunterricht auf Gymnasien 1750 bis 1850." *Deutsche Vierteljahrsschrift für Literaturwissenschaft und Geistesgeschichte* 47 (1973): 120–47.

———. *Schule und literarische Kultur.* Vol. I: *Sozialgeschichte des deutschen Unterrichts an höheren Schulen von der Spätaufklärung bis zum Vormärz.* Stuttgart, 1981.

Janet, Pierre. *L'Automatisme psychologique: Essai de psychologie expérimentale sur les formes inférieures de l'activité humaine.* Paris, 1889.

Janz, Kurt Paul. *Friedrich Nietzsche: Biographie.* 2 vols. Munich, 1978–79.

Jeismann, Karl-Ernst. *Das preussische Gymnasium in Staat und Gesellschaft: Die Entstehung des Gymnasiums als Schule des Staates und der Gebildeten.* Industrielle Welt. Schriftenreihe des Arbeitskreises für moderne Sozialgeschichte, Vol. XV. Stuttgart, 1974.

Jensen, Adolf, and Lamszus, Wilhelm. *Unser Schulaufsatz ein verkappter Schund-*

literat. Ein Versuch zur Neugründung des deutschen Schulaufsatzes für Volks-schule und Gymnasium. Hamburg, 1910.

Jones, Ernest. *The Life and Work of Sigmund Freud.* 3 vols. New York, 1953.

Jordan, Peter. *Leyenschul.* In Heinrich Fechner, ed., *Vier seltene Schriften des 16. Jahrhunderts.* Berlin, 1882. (Orig. pub. 1533.)

Jung, Carl Gustav. "Beitrag: Über das Verhalten der Reaktionszeit beim Assozia-tionsexperimente. Diagnostische Assoziationsstudien, IV." *Journal für Psy-chologie und Neurologie* 6 (1905): 1–36.

———. *Ueber die Psychologie der Dementia praecox: Ein Versuch. Frühe Schriften II.* Olten, 1972. (Orig. pub. 1907.)

———. "Über Simulation von Geistesstörungen." *Journal für Psychologie und Neurologie* 2 (1903): 181–202.

———, and Franz Riklin. "Experimentelle Untersuchungen über Assoziationen Gesunder. Diagnostische Assoziationsstudien, II." *Journal für Psychologie und Neurologie* 3 (1904): 55–83, 145–64, 193–215, 283–308; and 4: 24–67.

Just, Klaus Günther. "Asthetizismus und technische Welt: Zur Lyrik Karl Gustav Vollmoellers." *Zeitschrift für deutsche Philologie* 82 (1963): 211–31.

Kaes, Anton, ed. *Kino-Debatte: Texte zum Verhältnis von Literatur und Film 1909–1929.* Munich, 1978.

Kafka, Franz. *The Complete Stories.* Ed. Nahum N. Glatzer. New York, 1976.

———. *Description of a Struggle.* Trans. Tania and James Stern. New York, 1958.

———. *Hochzeitsvorbereitungen auf dem Lande.* In Max Brod, ed., *Gesammelte Werke.* New York, 1953.

———. *Letters to Felice.* Ed. Erich Heller and Jurgen Born. Trans. James Stern and Elisabeth Duckworth. New York, 1971.

———. *Letters to Friends, Family, and Editors.* Trans. Richard and Clara Win-ston. New York, 1977.

———. *The Trial.* Trans. Willa and Edwin Muir, rev. E. M. Butler. New York (Modern Library), 1956.

Kaiser, Gerhard. *Gottfried Keller: Das gedichtete Leben.* Frankfurt a. M., 1981.

———. "Mutter Nacht—Mutter Natur. Anlässlich einer Bildkomposition von Asmus Jacob Carstens." In Friedrich Kittler, ed., *Austreibung des Geistes aus den Geisteswissenschaften: Programme des Poststrukturalismus* (Paderborn, 1980), pp. 87–141.

———. *Wandrer und Idylle. Goethe und die Phänomenologie der Natur in der deutschen Dichtung von Gessner bis Gottfried Keller.* Göttingen, 1977.

Karstädt, Otto. *Dem Dichter nach.* Part 1: *Schaffende Poesiestunden.* 7th ed. Berlin, 1930.

Keiver Smith, Margaret. "Rhythmus und Arbeit." *Philosophische Studien* 16 (1900): 197–305.

Kehr, Carl. "Die Geschichte des Leseunterrichtes." In Carl Kehr, ed., *Geschichte der Methodik des deutschen Volkschulunterrichtes* (Gotha, 1879).

Kesting, Marianne. "Aspekte des absoluten Buches bei Novalis und Mallarmé." *Euphorion* 68 (1974): 420–36.

Key, Ellen. *Das Jahrhundert des Kindes. Studien.* Berlin, 1902.

———. *Missbrauchte Frauenkraft. Ein Essay.* Berlin, 1904.

———. *Rahel. Eine biographische Skizze.* Leipzig, 1908.

———. *Seelen und Werke. Essays.* Berlin, 1911.

Kieseritzky, Ingomar von. *Die ungeheuerliche Ohrfeige oder Szenen aus der Geschichte der Vernunft*. Stuttgart, 1981.

Kirchhoff, Arthur, ed. *Die akademische Frau. Gutachten hervorragender Universitätsprofessoren, Frauenlehrer und Schriftsteller über die Befähigung der Frau zum wissenschaftlichen Studium und Berufe*. Berlin, 1897.

Kirchner, Carl. *Die Landesschule Pforta in ihrer geschichtlichen Entwickelung seit dem Anfange des XIX. Jahrhunderts bis auf die Gegenwart*. Einladungsschrift zur dritten Säcularfeier ihrer Stiftung den 21. Mai 1843. Naumberg, 1843.

Kittler, Friedrich A. "Autorschaft und Liebe." In Friedrich Kittler, ed., *Austreibung des Geistes aus den Geisteswissenschaften: Programme des Poststrukturalismus* (Paderborn, 1980), pp. 142–73.

———. "'Erziehung ist Offenbarung': Zur Struktur der Familie in Lessings Dramen." *Jahrbuch der deutschen Schillergesellschaft* 21 (1977): 111–37.

———. "Die Irrwege des Eros und die 'absolute Familie.'" In Bernd Urban und Winfried Kudszus, eds., *Psychoanalytische und psychopathologische Literaturinterpretation* (Darmstadt, 1981), pp. 421–70.

———. "Lullaby of Birdland: Der Wunderblock." *Zeitschrift für Psychoanalyse* 3 (1979): 5–19.

———. "Nietzsche." In Horst Turk, ed., *Klassiker der Literaturtheorie* (Munich, 1979), pp. 191–205.

———. "Ottilie Hauptmann." In Norbert W. Bolz, ed., *Goethes Wahlverwandtschaften: Kritische Modelle und Diskursanalysen* (Hildesheim, 1981), pp. 260–75.

———. "'Das Phantom unseres Ichs' und die Literaturpsychologie: E. T. A. Hoffmann—Freud—Lacan." In Friedrich Kittler and Horst Turk, eds., *Urszenen: Literaturwissenschaft als Diskursanalyse und Diskurskritik*. Frankfurt a. M., 1977, pp. 139–66.

———. "Pink Floyd, Brain Damage." In Klaus Lindemann, ed., *europaLyrik 1775 bis heute. Gedichte und Interpretationen* (Paderborn, 1982), pp. 467–77.

———. *Der Traum und die Rede: Eine Analyse der Kommunikationssituation C. F. Meyers*. Bern, 1977.

———. "Über die Sozialisation Wilhelm Meisters." In Gerhard Kaiser and Friedrich Kittler, *Dichtung als Sozialisationspiel: Studien zu Goethe und Gottfried Keller* (Göttingen, 1978), pp. 12–124.

———. "Vergessen." In Ulrich Nassen, ed., *Texthermeneutik: Aktualität, Geschichte, Kritik*. Paderborn, 1979.

———. "Wie man abschafft, wovon man spricht: Der Autor von Ecce homo." In *Literaturmagazin*, no. 12, *Nietzsche* (Reinbeck, 1980), pp. 153–87.

———. "Writing into the Wind, Bettina." *Glyph* 7 (1980): 32–69.

Kittler, Gustav-Adolf. "Der Oberamtskanzler Karl Gottfried Herrmann und seine Mitwirkung bei der Organisation des Volkschul- und Seminarwesens der Oberlausitz." *Neues Lausitzisches Magazin der Zeitschrift der Oberlausitzischen Gesellschaft der Wissenschaften* 104 (1928): 305–78.

Klages, Ludwig. *Handschrift und Charakter. Gemeinverständlicher Abriss der graphologischen Technik*. 1st ed. Leipzig, 1917.

———. *Rhythmen und Rumen*. Leipzig, 1944.

Klein, Carl August, ed. *Die Blätter für die Kunst*. 1892–1919.

Kleist, Heinrich von. *Prinz Friedrich von Homburg. Ein Schauspiel*. In Helmut Sembdner, ed., *Sämtliche Werke und Briefe*. Darmstadt, 1962.

Klinke, Otto. *E. T. A. Hoffmanns Leben und Werk. Vom Standpunkte eines Irrenarztes.* Braunschweig, 1902.

Klöden, Karl Friedrich von. *Jugenderinnerungen, Hrsg. und durch einen Umriss seines Weiterlebens vervollständigt von Max Jähne.* Leipzig, 1874.

Klossowski, Pierre. *Nietzsche et le cercle vicieux.* Paris, 1969.

Kluckhohn, Paul. *Die Auffassung der Liebe in der Literatur des 18. Jahrhunderts und in der deutschen Romantik.* 1st ed. Halle, 1922.

Koebner, Thomas. "Der Film als neue Kunst: Frühe Filmtheorien der Schriftsteller (1911–1924)." In Helmut Kreuzer, ed., *Literaturwissenschaft—Medienwissenschaft* (Heidelberg, 1977), pp. 1–31.

Kohlschmidt, Werner. "Zu den soziologischen Voraussetzungen des literarischen Expressionismus in Deutschland." In Karl Rüdinger, ed. *Literatur—Sprache—Gesellschaft* (Munich, 1970), pp. 31–49.

Köpke, Rudolf. *Ludwig Tieck: Erinnerungen aus dem Leben des Dichters nach dessen mündlichen und schriftlichen Mittheilungen.* 2 vols. Leipzig, 1855.

Kraepelin, Emil. *Psychiatrie: Ein Lehrbuch für Studirende und Ärzte.* 5th rev. ed. Leipzig, 1896.

Krug, Johann Friedrich Adolph. *Ausführliche Anweisung die hochdeutsche Sprache recht aussprechen, lesen und recht schreiben zu lehren. Nach seiner in der Bürgerschule zu Leipzig betriebenen Lehrart.* Leipzig, 1808.

Krug, Wilhelm Traugott. *Meine Lebensreise. In sechs Stazionen zur Belehrung der Jugend und zur Unterhaltung des Alters beschrieben von Urceus.* Leipzig, 1825.

———. *Der Staat und die Schule. Oder Politik und Pädagogik in ihrem gegenseitigen Verhältnisse zur Begründung einer Staatspädagogik dargestellt.* Leipzig, 1810.

Krukenberg, Elisabeth. *Über das Eindringen der Frauen in männliche Berufe.* Essen, 1906.

Kunne-Ibsch, Elrud. *Die Stellung Nietzsches in der Entwicklung der modernen Literaturwissenschaft.* Tübingen, 1972.

Kussmaul, Adolf. *Die Störungen der Sprache. Versuch einer Pathologie der Sprache.* 2d ed. Handbuch der speciellen Pathologie und Therapie, ed. H. v. Ziemessen. Vol. 12, Supplement. Leipzig, 1881.

Kvale, Steinar. "Gedächtnis und Dialektik: Einige Überlegungen zu Ebbinghaus und Mao Tse-Tung." In Klaus F. Riegel, ed., *Zur Ontogenese dialektischer Operationen* (Frankfurt, 1978), pp. 239–65.

Lacan, Jacques. *Ecrits.* Paris, 1966.

———. *Ecrits: A Selection.* Trans. Alan Sheridan. New York, 1977.

———. *Encore.* Bk. 20 of *Le Séminaire de Jacques Lacan.* Paris, 1975.

———. "L'Etourdit." *Scilicet,* no. 4, 1973, pp. 5–52.

———. *The Four Fundamental Concepts of Psychoanalysis.* Ed. Jacques-Alain Miller. Trans. Alan Sheridan. New York, 1981.

———. "Lituraterre." *Littérature,* no. 3, 1971, pp. 3–10.

———. "Radiophonie." *Scilicet,* no. 2–3, 1970, pp. 55–99.

Lang, Karl Heinrich Ritter von. *Die Memoiren, 1764–1835.* Ed. Hans Haussherr. Stuttgart, 1975. (Orig. pub. 1842.)

Langbehn, Julius. *Rembrandt als Erzieher. Vom einem Deutschen.* Leipzig, 1890.

Lange, Günter Richard. "Über die psychologischen Hintergründe der heutigen Grotesk-Mode." *Imprimatur: Ein Jahrbuch für Bücherfreunde,* no. 2 (1958–59–60): 230–34.

Lange, Helene. *Kampfzeiten: Aufsätze und Reden aus vier Jahrzehnten.* 2 vols. Berlin, 1928.

Lange, Richard. *Wie steigern wir die Leistungen im Deutschen?* Leipzig, 1910.

Langenbucher, Wolfgang R. "Das Publikum im literarischen Leben des 19. Jahrhunderts." In *Der Leser als Teil des literarischen Lebens.* (Bonn, 1971), pp. 52–84.

Lanson, Gustave. "L'Histoire littéraire et la sociologie." *Revue de métaphysique et de morale.* 12 (1904): 621–42.

Larisch, Rudolf von. *Unterricht in ornamentaler Schrift.* 8th ed., Vienna, 1922. (Orig. pub. 1905.)

Lay, Wilhelm August. *Führer durch den Rechtschreib-Unterricht. Neues, naturgemässes Lehrverfahren gegründet auf psychologische Versuche und angeschlossen an die Entwickelungsgeschichte des Rechtschreibunterrichts.* Karlsruhe, 1897.

Leibbrand, Werner, and Annemarie Wettley. *Der Wahnsinn. Geschichte der abendländischen Psychopathologie.* Freiburg, 1961.

Le Masle, Robert Charles Achille. "Le Professeur Adrien Proust (1834–1903)." Medical dissertation, Paris, 1935.

Lempicki, Sigmund von. *Geschichte der deutschen Literaturwissenschaft bis zum Ende des 18. Jahrhunderts.* 2d ed. Göttingen, 1968.

Léon, Xavier. *Fichte et son temps.* Paris, 1954–58.

Leporin, Dorothea Christina. *Gründliche Untersuchung der Ursachen, die das Weibliche Geschlecht vom Studiren abhalten, Darin die Unerheblichkeit gezeiget, und wie möglich, nöthig und nützlich es sey, Dass dieses Geschlecht der Gelahrsamkeit sich befleisse.* Hildesheim, 1975. (Orig. pub. Berlin, 1742.)

Lessing, Gotthold Ephraim. *Gesammelte Werke.* Ed. Paul Rilla. Berlin, 1968–74.

——. *Laocoon: An Essay on the Limits of Painting and Poetry.* Trans. Edward Allen McCormic. Baltimore, 1984.

Lichtenberg, Georg Christoph. *Schriften und Briefe.* Ed. Wolfgang Promies. Munich, 1968–74.

Liede, Alfred. *Dichtung als Spiel. Studien zur Unsinnspoesie an den Grenzen der Sprache.* 2 vols. Berlin, 1963.

Liepmann, Hugo Karl. *Über Ideenflucht. Begriffsbestimmung und psychologische Analyse.* Sammlung zwangloser Abhandlungen aus dem Gebiete der Nerven- und Geisteskrankheiten. Vol. 4, no. 2, Halle, 1904.

Lindau, Paul. *Der Andere. Ein Schauspiel.* Leipzig, 1906.

Lindemann, Klaus. *Geistlicher Stand und religiöses Mittlertum. Ein Beitrag zur Religionsauffassung der Frühromantik in Dichtung und Philosophie.* Frankfurt a. M., 1971.

Lindner, Rudolf. "Die Einführung in die Schriftsprache." *Zeitschrift für pädagogische Psychologie* 11 (1910): 177–203.

Liscov, Christian Ludwig. "Die Vortrefflichkeit und Nohtwendigkeit der elenden Scribenten." In Carl Müchler, ed., *Schriften* (Berlin, 1806), III: 3–138. (Orig. pub. 1736.)

Loeben, Ferdinand August Otto Heinrich Graf von. *Guido.* Mannheim, 1808.

Löwith, Karl. *Von Hegel zu Nietzsche. Der revolutionäre Bruch im Denken des 19. Jahrhunderts.* 2d ed. Stuttgart, 1950.

Lohmann, Johannes. *Philosophie und Sprachwissenschaft.* Berlin, 1965.

Lotmann, Jurij M. *Probleme der Kinoästhetik. Einführung in die Semiotik des Films*. Frankfurt a. M., 1977.

Ludwig, Albert. "Schiller und die Schule." *Mitteilungen der Gesellschaft für deutsche Erziehungs- und Schulgeschichte* 20 (1910): 55–95.

Luhmann, Niklas. "Das Problem der Epochenbildung und die Evolutionstheorie." In Hans Ulrich Gumbrecht and Ursula Link-Heer, eds, *Epochenschwellen und Epochenstrukturen im Diskurs der Litteratur- und Sprachhistorie*. Frankfurt a. M., 1985.

Lukács, Georg. "Faust-Studien." In *Gesamtausgabe*, vol. VI: *Probleme des Realismus III*. Neuwied, 1965.

Lumbroso, Albert. *Souvenirs sur Maupassant, sa dernière maladie, sa mort*. Paris, 1905.

Luther, Martin. "Der grosse Katechismus." In Otto Clemen, ed., *Werke in Auswahl* (Bonn, 1912–13), Vol. IV.

Lyotard, Jean-François. *Des dispositifs pulsionnels*. Paris, 1973. Trans. as *Intensitäten*. Berlin, 1980.

Maass, Johann Gebhard Ehrenreich. *Versuch über die Einbildungskraft*. 2d ed. Halle, 1797.

McClelland, Charles E. *State, Society, and University in Germany, 1700–1914*. Cambridge, 1980.

McConnell, Frank. *The Spoken Seen: Film and the Romantic Imagination*. Baltimore, 1971.

McLuhan, Marshall. *Understanding Media*. New York, 1964.

Maier-Smits, Lory. "Die Anfänge der Eurhythmie." In *Wir erlebten Rudolph Steiner: Erinnerungen seiner Schüler*. 3d ed. (Stuttgart, 1967), pp. 147–68.

Mallarmé, Stéphane. *Oeuvres complètes*. Ed. Henri Mondor and G. Jean-Aubury. Paris, 1945.

Manis, Melvin. *An Introduction to Cognitive Psychology*. Belmont, Calif., 1971.

Mann, Thomas. *Bilse und ich*. 4th ed. Munich, 1910. (Orig. pub. 1906.)

Mannoni, Octave. "Schreber als Schreiber." In his *Clefs pour l'Imaginaire* (Paris, 1969), pp. 75–99.

Maréchal, G. "Photographie de la parole." *L'Illustration*, no. 2543, Nov. 21, 1891, p. 406.

Marinetti, Filippo Tommaso. *Manifesto tecnico della letteratura futurista*. May 11, 1912.

Marx, Karl. "Zur Kritik des Hegelschen Staatsrechts." In Karl Marx and Friedrich Engels, *Werke* (Berlin, 1967–73), I: 201–333.

Marx, Werner. *Absolute Reflexion und Sprache*. Frankfurt, 1967.

Maschke, Marie. *Die Schriftstellerin. Forderungen, Leistungen, Aussichten in diesem Berufe*. 2d ed. 1902. (Orig. pub. 1899.)

Matt, Peter von. *Die Augen der Automaten. E. T. A. Hoffmanns Imaginationslehre als Prinzip seiner Erzählkunst*. Tübingen, 1971.

Mattenklott, Gert. *Bilderdienst. Ästhetische Opposition bei Beardsley und George*. Munich, 1970.

Matthias, Adolf. *Geschichte des deutschen Unterrichts*. Vol. 1, no. 1 of his *Handbuch des deutschen Unterrichts an höheren Schulen*. Munich, 1907.

Maupassant, Guy de. "Le Horla," in *Oeuvres complètes*. Paris, 1925–47.

Mauthner, Fritz. *Beiträge zu einer Kritik der Sprache*. Stuttgart Wörterbuch der Philosophie, Neue Beiträge zu einer Kritik der Sprache. Stuttgart, 1901–2.

———. *Wörterbuch der Philosophie. Neue Beiträge zu einer Kritik der Sprache.* 2 vols. Zurich, 1980. (Orig. pub. 1910–11.)

Meier-Graefe, Julius. *Entwicklungsgeschichte der modernen Kunst. Vergleichende Betrachtung der bildenden Künste als Beitrag zu einer neuen Ästhetik.* 2 vols. Stuttgart, 1904.

Melchers, Wilhelm. "Die bürgerliche Familie des 19. Jahrhunderts als Erziehungs- und Bildungsfaktor. Auf Grund autobiographischer Literatur." Ph.D. dissertation, Cologne, 1929.

Mensch, Ella. *Die Frau in der modernen Literatur. Ein Beitrag zur Geschichte der Gefühle.* Berlin, 1898.

Menzel, Wolfgang. *Die deutsche Literatur.* Stuttgart, 1828.

Meringer, Rudolf, and Karl Mayer. *Versprechen und Verlesen. Eine psychologisch-linguistische Studie.* Vienna, 1895.

Messmer, Oskar. "Zur Psychologie des Lesens bei Kindern und Erwachsenen." *Archiv für die gesamte Psychologie* 2 (1904): 190–298.

Meumann, Ernst. *Über Ökonomie und Technik des Lernens.* Leipzig, 1903.

———. *Vorlesungen zur Einführung in die experimentelle Pädagogik und ihre psychologischen Grundlagen.* 2d ed. 3 vols. Leipzig, 1911–14.

Meyer, Gustav. "Weltsprache und Weltsprachen. In his *Essays und Studien zur Sprachgeschichte und Volkskunde* (Strasbourg, 1893), II: 23–46.

Meyer, Richard M. "Künstliche Sprachen." *Indogermanische Forschungen* 12 (1901): 33–92, 242–318.

Meyer, Theo. *Kunstproblematik und Wortkombinatorik bei Gottfried Benn.* Cologne, 1971.

Meyrink, Gustav. *Der Golem. Ein Roman.* Leipzig, 1915.

Michel, Karl Markus. "Schön sinnlich. Über den Teufel und seinesgleichen, das Fummeln, Schnüffeln und anderen Kitzel." *Kursbuch* 49 (1977): 1–35.

Michel, O. H. "Über das Zeugnis von Hörensagen bei Kindern." *Zeitschrift für angewandte Psychologie* 1 (1908): 421–25.

Milch, Werner. "Das zweifache 'Ach' der Alkmene." In Gerhard Burkhardt, ed., *Kleine Schriften zur Literatur- und Geistesgeschichte* (Heidelberg, 1957), pp. 156–59.

Möbius, Paul Julius. *Über den physiologischen Schwachsinn des Weibes.* Sammlung zwangloser Abhandlungen aus dem Gebiete der Nerven- und Geisteskrankheiten, vol. 3, no. 3. Halle, 1900.

Monakow, Constantin von. "Über den gegenwärtigen Stand der Frage nach der Lokalisation im Grosshirn." *Ergebnisse der Physiologie* 6 (1907): 334–605.

Montandon, Alain. "Ecriture et folie chez E. T. A. Hoffmann." *Romantisme* 24 (1979): 7–28.

Morgenstern, Christian. *Alle Galgenlieder.* Wiesbaden, 1956.

———. *The Gallows Songs: Christian Morgenstern's 'Galgenlieder,' a Selection.* Trans. Max Knight. Berkeley, 1963.

———. *Gesammelte Werke in einem Band.* Ed. Margareta Morgenstern. N.p., 1965.

———. *Mensch Wanderer: Gedichte aus den Jahren 1887–1914. Sämtliche Gedichte,* Section II, vol. 12. Basel, 1976.

Morin, Edgar. *Le cinéma ou l'homme imaginaire: Essai d'anthropologie sociologique.* Paris, 1956.

Moritz, Carl Philipp. *Anton Reiser. Ein psychologischer Roman.* 2d ed. Leipzig, 1959. (Rpt. of 1785–90 ed.)

————. "Erinnerungen aus den frühesten Jahren der Kindheit." *Gnothi sauton, oder Magazin zur Erfahrungsseelenkunde als ein Lesebuch für Gelehrte und Ungelehrte,* 2d ed. (Berlin, 1805), I, 65–70.

Müller, Dagobert. "Über die Schilderung eines sog. Spring-Tics durch Rainer Maria Rilke." *Psychiatrie, Neurologie und medizinische Psychologie* 10 (1958): 270–77.

Münch, Paul Georg. *Rund ums rote Tintenfass.* Leipzig, 1909.

Münsterberg, Hugo. *Grundzüge der Psychotechnik.* Leipzig, 1914.

————. *The Photoplay: A Psychological Study.* Reissued as *The Film: A Psychological Study: The Silent Photoplay in 1916.* Ed. Richard Griffith. New York, 1970. (Orig. pub. 1916.)

Muschg, Walter. "Freud als Schriftsteller," in his *Die Zerstörung der deutschen Literatur* (Bern, 1956), pp. 303–47. (Orig. pub. 1930.)

Neumann, Gerhard. "Schreibschrein und Strafapparat: Erwägungen zur Topographie des Schreibens." In Günter Schnitzler, ed., *Bild und Gedanke: Festschrift für Gerhart Baumann zum 60. Geburtstag* (Munich, 1980), pp. 385–401.

"The New Phonograph." *Scientific American* 57 (1887): 421–22.

Niemeyer, August Hermann. *Grundsätze der Erziehung und des Unterrichts für Eltern, Hauslehrer und Erzieher.* Ed. Hans-Hermann Groothoff and Ulrich Herrmann. Paderborn, 1970. (Orig. pub. 1796.)

Niethammer, Friedrich Immanuel. "Das Bedürfniss eines Nationalbuches, als Grundlage der allgemeinen Bildung der Nation betr." Document of June 22, 1808.

————. *Der Streit des Philanthropinismus und Humanismus in der Theorie des Erziehungs-Unterrichts unserer Zeit.* Jena, 1808. Rpt. in his *Philanthropinismus—Humanismus: Texte zur Schulreform,* ed. Werner Hillebrecht, (Weinheim, 1968), pp. 81–445.

Nietzsche, Friedrich. *Beyond Good and Evil.* Trans. Walter Kaufmann. New York, 1966.

————. *The Birth of Tragedy.* Trans. Walter Kaufmann. New York, 1967.

————. *Briefe.* Ed. Elisabeth Förster-Nietzsche and Peter Gast. Berlin, 1902–9.

————. *Briefwechsel: Kritische Gesamtausgabe.* Ed. Giorgio Colli and Mazzino Montinari. Berlin, 1975–.

————. *Briefwechsel mit Franz Overbeck.* Ed. Richard Oehler and Carl Albrecht Bernoulli. Leipzig, 1916.

————. *Ecce Homo.* Trans. Walter Kaufmann and R. J. Hollingdale. New York, 1967.

————. *The Gay Science.* Trans. Walter Kaufmann. New York, 1974.

————. *The Genealogy of Morals.* Trans. Walter Kaufmann and R. J. Hollingdale. New York, 1967.

————. *Human, All Too Human.* Trans. R. J. Hollingdale. London, 1986.

————. *Nietzsche contra Wagner.* Trans. Walter Kaufmann. In *The Portable Nietzsche* (New York, 1954), pp. 661–83.

————. *Thus Spoke Zarathustra.* Trans. Walter Kaufmann. In *The Portable Nietzsche* (New York, 1954), pp. 103–439.

————. *Twilight of the Idols.* Trans. Walter Kaufmann. In *The Portable Nietzsche* (New York, 1954), pp. 463–563.

————. *Untimely Meditations.* Trans. R. J. Hollingdale. Cambridge, 1983.

————. *Werke: Kritische Gesamtausgabe.* Ed. Giorgio Colli and Mazzino Montinari. Berlin, 1975–.

————. *Werke und Briefe: Historisch-kritische Ausgabe.* Ed. Karl Schlechte and Hans Joachim Mette. Munich, 1933–42.

O'Brien, Robert Lincoln. "Machinery and English Style," *The Atlantic Monthly* 94 (1904): 464–72.

Ogden, Robert Morris. "Untersuchungen über den Einfluss der Geschwindigkeit des lauten Lesens auf das Erlernen und Behalten von sinnlosen und sinnvollen Stoffen." *Archiv für die gesamte Psychologie* 2 (1903): 93–189.

Olivier, Ferdinand. *Die Kunst lesen und rechtschreiben zu lernen auf ihr einzig wahres, höchst einfaches und untrügliches Grundprincip zurückgeführt. Eine glückliche, in jeder Sprache anwendbare Entdeckung und Erfindung.* Rev. ed. Leipzig, 1803.

Oppermann, Thomas. *Kulturverwaltungsrecht. Bildung—Wissenschaft—Kunst.* Tübingen, 1969.

Ostermai, Oskar. "Vom Aufsatzunterrichte in der Volksschule." *Zeitschrift für den deutschen Unterricht* 23 (1909): 50–70.

Ott, Karl August. "Die wissenschaftlichen Ursprünge des Futurismus und Surrealismus." *Poetica* 2 (1968): 371–98.

Parain, Brice. *Recherches sur la nature et les fonctions du langage.* Paris, 1942. Trans. as *Untersuchungen über Natur und Funktion der Sprache.* Stuttgart, 1969.

Parzer-Mühlbacher, Alfred. *Die modernen Sprechmaschinen (Phonograph, Graphophon und Grammophon), deren Behandlung und Anwendung. Praktische Ratschläge für Interessenten.* Vienna, 1902.

Paulsen, Friedrich. *Die deutschen Universitäten und das Universitätsstudium.* Berlin, 1902.

————. *Geschichte des gelehrten Unterrichts auf den deutschen Schulen und Universitäten vom Ausgange des Mittelalters bis zur Gegenwart. Mit besonderer Rücksicht auf den klassischen Unterricht.* 3d, expanded ed. Ed. Rudolf Lehmann. Berlin, 1919–21.

Penzenkuffer, Christian Wilhelm Friedrich. *Vertheidigung der in dem obersten Staatszwecke begründeten Rechte und Ansprüche der gelehrten Schullehrer meines Vaterlandes.* Nuremberg, 1805.

Pestalozzi, Johann Heinrich. *Sämtliche Werke.* Ed. Artur Buchenau, Eduard Spranger, and Hans Stettbacher. Berlin, 1927–76.

Petrat, Gerhardt. *Schulunterricht. Seine Sozialgeschichte in Deutschland 1750–1850.* Munich, 1979.

Pfeiffer, R. "Rezension: Denkwürdigkeiten eines Nervenkranken." *Deutsche Zeitschrift für Nervenheilkunde* 27 (1904): 352–53.

Philipp, Eckhard. *Dadismus. Einführung in den literarischen Dadaismus und die Wortkunst des "Sturm"-Kreises.* Munich, 1980.

Pinthus, Kurt, ed. *Kinobuch.* Leipzig, 1963. (Orig. pub. 1914.)

————. *Menschheitsdämmerung.* 1920. Reissued as *Menschheitsdämmerung. Ein Dokument des Expressionismus.* Ed. Kurt Pinthus. Reinbeck, 1959.

Podach, Erich. "Nietzsches Krankengeschichte." *Die medizinische Welt* 4 (1930): 1452–54.

Pöhlmann, Johann Paulus. *Meine Scheibelectionen, oder praktische Anweisung für Schullehrer, welche den ersten Unterricht im Schönschreiben zugleich als Verstandesübung benützen wollen.* Fürth, 1803.

Pörtner, Paul, ed. *Literatur-Revolution 1910–1925. Dokumente. Manifeste. Programme.* Vol. 1: *Zur Aesthetik und Poetik.* Neuwied, 1960.

Prahl, Hans-Werner. *Sozialgeschichte des Hochschulwesens.* Munich, 1978.

Prel, Carl Freiherr Du. *Psychologie der Lyrik. Beiträge zur Analyse der dichterischen Phantasie.* Leipzig, 1880.

Preyer, Wilhelm. *Zur Psychologie des Schreibens.* Hamburg, 1895.

Proust, Adrien. "De l'aphasie." *Archives générales de médecine* 129 (1872): 147–66, 303–18, 653–85.

Proust, Marcel. *The Remembrance of Things Past.* 3 vols. Trans. C. K. Scott Moncrieff, Terence Kilmartin, and Andreas Mayer. New York, 1981.

Rank, Otto. *Der Doppelgänger. Eine psychoanalytische Studie.* Leipzig, 1925. (Orig. pub. 1914.)

———. *Das Inzest-Motiv in Dichtung und Sage: Grundzüge einer Psychologie des dichterischen Schaffens.* Leipzig, 1912.

Read, Oliver, and Walter L. Welsh. *From Tin Foil to Stereo: The Evolution of the Phonograph.* Indianapolis, 1959.

Reil, Johann Christian. *Rhapsodieen über die Anwendung der psychischen Curmethode auf Geisteszerrüttungen.* Halle, 1803.

Reinhardt, Karl. *Von Werken und Formen. Vorträge und Aufsätze.* Godesberg, 1948.

Ribot, Théodule. *Diseases of Memory, Diseases of Personality, Diseases of the Will. Significant Contributions to the History of Psychology,* vol. 1. Ed. Daniel N. Robinson. Washington, D.C., 1977.

Richards, George Tilghman. *The History and Development of Typewriters.* 2d ed. London, 1964.

Richter, Dieter. "Die Leser und die Lehrer. Bilder auf der Geschichte der literarischen Sozialisation." In Dietmar Larcher and Christine Spiess, eds., *Lesebilder. Geschichten und Gedanken zur literarischen Sozialisation. Lektürebiographien und Leseerfahrungen* (Reinbeck, 1980), pp. 201–22.

Richter, Jean Paul. *Werke,* ed. Norbert Miller. Munich, 1959–67.

Rickert, Heinrich. *Goethes Faust. Die dramatische Einheit der Dichtung.* Tübingen, 1932.

Riegger-Baurmann, Roswitha. "Schrift im Jugendstil in Deutschland." In Jost Hermand, ed., *Jugendstil* (Darmstadt, 1971), pp. 209–57.

Riemer, Friedrich Wilhelm. *Mitteilungen über Goethe. Aufgrund der Ausgabe von 1814 und des handschriftlichen Nachlasses.* Ed. Arthur Pollmer. Leipzig, 1921. (Orig. pub. 1841.)

Rilke, Rainer Maria. *Briefe.* Ed. Ruth Sieber-Rilke and Carl Sieber. 5 vols. Leipzig, 1933–39.

———. *Fifty Selected Poems.* Trans. C. F. MacIntyre. Berkeley, Calif., 1940.

———. *Letters of Rainer Maria Rilke.* Trans. Jane Bannard Greene and M. D. Herter Norton. New York, 1947.

———. *The Notebooks of Malte Laurids Brigge.* Trans. M. D. Herter Norton. New York, 1964.

———. "Primal Sound," in *Selected Works,* vol. 1. Trans. C. Craig Houston. London, 1960.

———. *Sämtliche Werke.* Ed. Ernst Zinn. N.p. 1955–66.

Roessler, Wilhelm. *Die Entstehung des modernen Erziehungswesens in Deutschland.* Stuttgart, 1961.

Rohde, Erwin. *Friedrich Creuzer und Karoline von Günderode. Briefe und Dichtungen.* Heidelberg, 1896.

Rosenhaupt, Hans Wilhelm. *Der deutsche Dichter um die Jahrhundertwende und seine Abgelöstheit von der Gesellschaft.* Berlin, 1939.

Rouge, Carl. "Schulerinnerungen an den Dichter Stefan George." *Volk und Scholle. Heimatblätter für beide Hessen* 8 (1930): 20–25.

Rousseau, Jean-Jacques. *The Confessions.* Trans. J. M. Cohen. London, 1953.

Rubiner, Ludwig. "Die Anonymen." *Die Aktion* 2 (1912): 299–302.

———. "Rezension: Die Blätter für die Kunst." In Klaus Schuhmann, ed., *Der Dichter greift in die Politik. Ausgewählte Werke 1908–1919.* Frankfurt a. M., 1976.

Rühm, Gerhard. *Gesammelte Gedichte und visuelle Texte.* Reinbeck, 1970.

Rupp, Gerhard. *Rhetorische Strukturen und kommunikative Determinanz—Studien zur Textkonstitution des philosophischen Diskurses im Werk Friedrich Nietzsches.* Ph.D. diss., Frankfurt a. M., 1976.

———. "Der 'ungeheure Consensus der Menschen über die Dinge' oder Das gesellschaftlich wirksame Rhetorische. Zum Nietzsche des Philosophenbuches." In *Literaturmagazin,* no. 12, Nietzsche (Reinbeck, 1980), pp. 179–203.

Rutschky, Katharina. *Schwarze Pädagogik. Quellen zur Naturgeschichte der bürgerlichen Erziehung.* Frankfurt a. M., 1977.

Ryan, Lawrence. "'Zum letztenmal Psychologie!' Zur psychologischen Deutbarkeit der Werke Franz Kafkas." In Wolfgang Paulsen, ed., *Psychologie in der Literaturwissenschaft* (Heidelberg, 1970), pp. 157–73.

Sachs, Heinrich. *Gehirn und Sprache.* Grenzfragen des Nerven- und Seelenlebens, no. 36. Wiesbaden, 1905.

Sarkowski, Heinz. *Wenn Sie ein Herz für mich und mein Geisteskind haben. Dichterbriefe zur Buchgestaltung.* Frankfurt a. M., 1965.

Sartre, Jean-Paul. *The Words.* Trans. Bernard Frechtman. New York, 1964.

Sasse, Günther. *Sprache und Kritik. Untersuchungen zur Sprachkritik der Moderne.* Göttingen, 1977.

Saussure, Ferdinand de. *Course in General Linguistics.* New York, 1966.

Schanze, Helmut. "Literaturgeschichte als 'Mediengeschichte'?" In Helmut Kreuzer, ed., *Literaturwissenschaft—Medienwissenschaft* (Heidelberg, 1977), pp. 131–44.

———. *Medienkunde für Literaturwissenschaftler. Einführung und Bibliographie.* Munich, 1974.

Scharffenberg, Renate. "Der Beitrag des Dichters zum Formwandel in der äusseren Gestalt des Buches um die Wende von 19. zum 20. Jahrhundert." Ph.D. diss. Marburg, 1953.

Scharrelmann, Heinrich. *Fröhliche Kinder. Ratschläge für die geistige Gesundheit unserer Kinder.* Hamburg, 1906.

———. *Weg zur Kraft.* Prt. II of *Des "Herzhaften Unterrichts."* Braunschweig, 1920.

Schatzman, Morton. *Soul Murder: Persecution in the Family.* London, 1973.

Scheerer, Thomas M. *Textanalytische Studien zur "écriture automatique."* Bonn, 1974.

Schenda, Rudolf. *Volk ohne Buch. Studien zur Sozialgeschichte der populären Lesestoffe 1770 bis 1910.* Frankfurt a. M., 1970.

Schiller, Friedrich von. "Briefe über Don Carlos." In his *Sämtliche Werke. Säkular-Ausgabe,* ed. Eduard von der Hellen. Stuttgart, 1904–5.

———. *Sämtliche Werke.* Ed. Gerhard Fricke and Herbert G. Göpfert. Munich, 1963.

Schivelbusch, Wolfgang. *Das Paradies, der Geschmack und die Vernunft. Eine Geschichte der Genussmittel.* Munich, 1980.

Schlaffer, Hannelore. "Frauen als Einlösung der frühromantischen Kunsttheorie." *Jahrbuch der deutschen Schillergesellschaft* 21 (1977): 274–96.

———. *Wilhelm Meister. Das Ende der Kunst und die Wiederkehr des Mythos.* Stuttgart, 1980.

Schlaffer, Heinz. *Faust zweiter Teil. Die Allegorie des 19. Jahrhunderts.* Stuttgart, 1981.

Schlegel, August Wilhelm von. *Kritische Schriften und Briefe.* Ed. Edgar Lohner. Stuttgart, 1962–67.

Schlegel, Dorothea. *Dorothea v. Schlegel geb. Mendelssohn und deren Söhne Johannes und Philipp Veit. Briefwechsel.* Ed. Johann Michael Raich. 2 vols. Mainz, 1881.

Schlegel, Friedrich von. *Briefe an seinen Bruder August Wilhelm.* Ed. Oskar F. Walzel. Berlin, 1890.

———. *Friedrich Schlegel 1794–1802. Seine prosaischen Jugendschriften.* Ed. Jakob Minor. 2 vols. Vienna, 1882.

———. *Kritische Friedrich-Schlegel-Ausgabe.* Ed. Ernst Behler. Munich, 1958–.

Schleiermacher, Friedrich. *Gutachten der wissenschaftliche Deputation zu Berlin über die Abiturientenprüfungen.* Document of December 14, 1810.

———. *Pädagogische Schriften.* Ed. C. Platz. 2d ed. Langensalza, 1876.

Schlüpmann, Heide. *Friedrich Nietzsches ästhetische Opposition. Der Zusammenhang von Sprache, Natur und Kultur in seinen Schriften 1869–1876.* Stuttgart, 1977.

Schmack, Ernst. "Der Gestaltwandel der Fibel in vier Jahrhunderten." Ph.D. diss. Cologne, 1958.

Schmidt, Jochen. "'Der goldne Topf' als Entwicklungsgeschichte." In Jochen Schmidt, ed., *E. T. A. Hoffmann, "Der goldne Topf"* (Frankfurt a. M., 1981), pp. 145–76.

Schneider, Manfred. "Lichtenbergs ungeschriebene Autobiographie. Eine Interpretation." *Fugen. Deutsch-französisches Jahrbuch für Text-Analytik* 1 (1980): 114–24.

Scholz, Hermann. *Die Schreibmaschine und das Maschinenschreiben.* Leipzig, 1923.

Schopenhauer, Arthur. *The World as Will and Representation.* 2 vols. Trans. E. F. J. Payne. New York, 1958.

Schreber, Daniel Paul. *Memoirs of My Nervous Illness.* Ed. and trans. Ida Macalpine and Richard A. Hunter. London, 1955. (Orig. pub. 1903.)

"Schreiben mit der Maschine. Vom Fels zum Meer." *Spemann's Illustrirte Zeitschrift für das Deutsche Haus,* 1889, pp. 863–64.

Schreiber, Jens. "Die Ordnung des Geniessens. Nietzsche mit Lacan." In *Literaturmagazin,* no. 12, *Nietzsche* (Reinbeck, 1980), pp. 204–34.

———. "Die Zeichen der Liebe." In Norbert W. Bolz, ed., *Goethes Wahlverwandtschaften. Kritische Modelle und Diskursanalysen zum Mythos Literatur* (Hildesheim, 1981), pp. 276–307.

Schulz, Gerhard. *Arno Holz. Dilemma eines bürgerlichen Dichters.* Munich, 1974.

Schur, Ernst. "Ziele für die innere Ausstattung des Buches." *Zeitschrift für Bücherfreunde* 2 (1898–99): 32–34, 137–41, 227–32.

Schwabe, Jenny. *Kontoristin. Forderungen, Leistungen, Aussichten in diesem Berufe.* 2d ed. Leipzig, 1902.

Schwartz, Erwin. *Der Leseunterricht.* Vol. 1: *Wie Kinder lesen lernen. Beiträge zur Geschichte und Theorie des Erstleseunterrichts.* Braunschweig, 1964.

Schwartz, Paul. "Die Gründung der Universität Berlin und der Anfang der Reform der höheren Schulen im Jahre 1810." *Mitteilungen der Gesellschaft für deutsche Erziehungs- und Schulgeschichte* 20 (1910): 153–208.

Schwarz, Friedrich Henrich Christian. *Grundriss einer Theorie der Mädchenerziehung in Hinsicht auf die mittleren Stände.* Jena, 1792.

Seebohm, Thomas M. *Zur Kritik der hermeneutischen Vernunft.* Bonn, 1972.

Seidler, Ingo. "Das Urteil: 'Freud natürlich'? Zum Problem der Multivalenz bei Kafka." In Wolfgang Paulsen, ed., *Psychologie in der Literaturwissenschaft* (Heidelberg, 1970), pp. 174–90.

Sellmann, Adolf. "Kinematograph, Literatur und deutsche Sprache." *Zeitschrift für den deutschen Unterricht* 26 (1912): 54–56.

Shannon, Claude E., and Warren Weaver. *The Mathematical Theory of Communication.* Urbana, Ill., 1967.

Simmel, Georg. "Vom Wesen des historischen Verstehens." In *Geschichtliche Abende. Zehn Vorträge im Zentralinstitut für Erziehung und Unterricht.* Berlin, 1918.

———. "Zur Psychologie der Frauen." *Zeitschrift für Völkerpsychologie und Sprachwissenschaft* 20 (1890): 6–46.

Skinner, B. F. "Has Gertrude Stein a Secret?" *The Atlantic Monthly*, January 1934, pp. 50–57.

Soennecken, Friedrich. *Fraktur oder Antiqua im ersten Unterricht? (Ist für Schulneulinge im allgemeinen und Hilfsschüler im besonderen Fraktur oder Antiqua zunächst geeignet?)* Bonn, 1913.

Solomons, Leon M., and Gertrude Stein. "Normal Motor Automatism." *Psychological Review* 3 (1896): 492–512.

Spengler, Oswald. *The Decline of the West: Form and Actuality.* 2 vols. Trans. Charles Francis Atkinson. New York, 1950.

Spiess, Christian Heinrich. *Biographien der Wahnsinnigen.* Ed. Wolfgang Promies. Neuwied-Berlin, 1966.

Spinoza, Baruch [Benedict] de. *A Theologico-Political Treatise and a Political Treatise.* Trans. R. H. M. Elwes. New York, 1951. (Orig. ed. 1883; orig. pub. in Latin, 1670.)

Spitzer, Leo. *Die groteske Gestaltungs- und Sprachkunst Christian Morgensterns. Motiv und Wort. Studien zur Literatur- und Sprachpsychologie.* Leipzig, 1918.

Splittegarb, Carl Friedrich. *Neues Bilder ABC. Eine Anleitung zum Lesen, dergleichen es bisher noch nicht gab.* Berlin, 1787.

Starobinski, Jean. "Rousseau et l'origine des langues." In *Europäische Aufklärung, Herbert Dieckmann zum 60. Geburtstag* (Munich, 1967), pp. 281–300.

Steig, Reinhold. "Bettina." *Deutsche Rundschau* 72 (1892): 262–74.

Stein, Gertrude. "Cultivated Motor Automatism: A Study of Character and Its Relation to Attention." *Psychological Review* 5 (1898): 295–306.

Steiner, Rudolf. "Initiationserkenntnis." In Verein für erweitertes Heilwesen, ed., *Mit Kindern leben.* Stuttgart, 1979. (Orig. pub. 1923.)

———. *Theosophie. Einführung in übersinnliche Welterkenntnis und Menschenbestimmung.* 28th ed. Stuttgart, 1955. (Orig. ed. 1910.)

Stenzel, Jürgen. *Zeichensetzung. Stiluntersuchungen an deutschen Prosadichtungen.* Göttingen, 1966.

Stephan, Gustav. *Die häusliche Erziehung in Deutschland während des 18. Jahrhunderts.* Wiesbaden, 1891.

Stephan, Rudolf. *Neue Musik. Versuch einer kritischen Einführung.* Göttingen, 1958.

Stephani, Heinrich. *Ausführliche Beschreibung der genetischen Schreibmethode für Volksschulen.* Erlangen, 1815.

————. *Beschreibung meiner einfachen Lesemethode für Mütter.* Erlangen, 1807.

————. *Fibel für Kinder von edler Erziehung, nebst einer genauen Beschreibung meiner Methode für Mütter, welche sich die Freude verschaffen wollen, ihre Kinder selbst in kurzer Zeit lesen zu lehren.* Erlangen, 1807.

————. *Grundriss der Staats-Erziehungs-Wissenschaft.* Weissenfels, 1797.

Stern, William. *Psychologie der Kindheit bis zum sechsten Lebensjahre. Mit Benutzung ungedruckter Tagebücher von Clara Stern.* Leipzig, 1914.

————. "Sammelbericht über Psychologie der Aussage." *Zeitschrift für angewandte Psychologie* 1 (1908): 429–50.

Stoker, Bram. *Dracula.* Harmondsworth, Middlesex, 1979.

Storck, Joachim W. "Emanzipatorische Aspekte im Werk und Leben Rilkes." In Ingeborn H. Solbrig and Joachim W. Storck, eds., *Rilke heute. Beziehungen und Wirkungen* (Frankfurt a. M., 1975), pp. 247–85.

Stramm, August. "Historische, kritische und finanzpolitische Untersuchungen über die Briefpostgebühren des Weltpostvereins und ihre Grundlagen." Ph.D. diss. Halle, 1909.

Stransky, Erwin. *Über Sprachverwirrtheit. Beiträge zur Kenntnis derselben bei Geisteskranken und Geistesgesunden.* Sammlung zwangloser Abhandlungen aus dem Gebiete der Nerven- und Geisteskrankheiten, no. 6. Halle, 1905.

————. "Zur Lehre von der Amentia." *Journal für Psychologie und Neurologie,* 1904–5, no. 4, pp. 158–71; no. 5, pp. 18–36; no. 6, pp. 37–83, 155–91.

Strauss, Emil. *Freund Hein. Eine Lebensgeschichte.* 32d–36th ed. Berlin, 1925. (Orig. pub. 1902.)

Strauss, Leo. *Persecution and the Art of Writing.* Glencoe, Ill., 1952.

Strecker, Gabriele. *Frauenträume Frauentränen. Über den deutschen Frauenroman.* Weilheim, 1969.

Surkamp, Ernst. *Die Sprechmaschine als Hilfsmittel für Unterricht und Studium der neuern Sprachen.* Stuttgart, 1913.

Swift, Edgar J. "The Acquisition of Skill in Type-Writing." *The Psychological Bulletin* 1 (1904): 295–305.

Tarde, Gabriel de. "La graphologie." *Revue philosophique* 44 (1897): 337–63.

Thaulow, Gustav. *Hegel's Ansichten über Erziehung und Unterricht. Als Fermente für wissenschaftliche Pädagogik.* In 3 parts. Kiel, 1853.

Theweleit, Klaus, and Martin Langbein. "Wenn der Kopf sich abmüht und das Herz bleibt kalt." In Rochus Herz, ed., *Heimlichkeiten der Männer* (Munich, 1977), pp. 139–214.

Thiersch, Friedrich. *Ueber gelehrte Schulen, mit besonderer Rücksicht auf Bayern.* 3 vols. Stuttgart, 1826–37.

Tieck, Ludwig. *Schriften.* Berlin, 1828–54.

Tiedemann, Dietrich. *Beobachtungen über die Entwicklung der Seelenfähigkeiten bei Kindern.* Ed. Christian Ufer. Altenberg, 1897. (Orig. pub. 1787.)

————. *Untersuchungen über den Menschen.* 3 vols. Leipzig, 1777–78.

Tietze, Ulrich, and Christian Schenk. *Halbleiter-Schaltungstechnik.* 5th ed. Berlin, 1980.

Tillich, Ernst. *Erstes Lesebuch für Kinder.* 2d rev. ed. Leipzig, 1809.

Tobler, Johann Christoph. "Fragment über die Natur." See Goethe, *Sämtliche Werke,* Jubilee ed.

Todorov, Tzvetan. *The Fantastic: A Structural Approach to a Literary Genre.* Trans. Richard Howard. Ithaca, N. Y., 1975.

Trapp, Ernst Christian. *Versuch einer Pädagogik.* Berlin, 1780.

Turk, Horst. "Hegel." In Horst Turk, ed., *Klassiker der Literaturtheorie* (Munich, 1979), pp. 122–32.

———. "Das 'Klassische Zeitalter.' Zur geschichtsphilosophischen Begründung der Weimarer Klassik." In Wolfgang Haubrichs, ed., *Probleme der Literaturgeschichtsschreibung* (Göttingen, 1979), pp. 155–74.

———, and Kittler, Friedrich. "Einleitung." In Horst Turk and Friedrich Kittler, eds., *Urszenen. Literaturwissenschaft als Diskursanalyse und Diskurskritik* (Frankfurt a. M., 1977), pp. 9–43.

Türk, Karl Wilhelm Christian Ritter von. *Beiträge zur Kenntniss einiger deutscher Elementar-Schulanstalten, namentlich der zu Dessau, Leipzig, Heidelberg, Frankfurt am Mayn und Berlin.* Leipzig, 1806.

Ufer, Christian. *Nervosität und Mädchenerziehung in Haus und Schule.* Wiesbaden, 1890.

———. *Das Wesen des Schwachsinns.* Vol. 1 of Christian Ufer, ed., *Beiträge zur pädagogischen Psychopathologie.* Langensalza, 1893.

Valéry, Paul. *Cahiers.* Paris, 1957–61.

———. *'My Faust.'* Trans. David Paul and Robert Fitzgerald. In *Collected Works,* Vol. III, *Plays* (New York, 1960).

———. *Oeuvres.* Ed. Jean Hytier. Paris, 1957–61.

———. "Poetry and Abstract Thought." In *The Art of Poetry,* trans. Denise Folliot (New York, 1961), pp. 52–81.

Varnhagen, Rahel. *Briefwechsel zwischen Varnhagen und Rahel.* 6 vols. Leipzig, 1874–75.

Vietta, Sylvio. "Expressionistische Literatur und Film. Einige Thesen zum wechselseitigen Einfluss ihrer Darstellung und Wirkung." *Mannheimer Berichte* 10 (1975): 294–99.

———. *Sprache und Sprachreflexion in der modernen Lyrik.* Bad Homburg, 1970.

Villaume, Peter. *Methode jungen Leuten zu der Fertigkeit zu verhelfen, ihre Gedanken schriftlich auszudrücken.* N.p., 1786.

Villiers de l'Isle-Adam, Philippe Auguste Mathias, Comte de. *Tomorrow's Eve.* Trans. Robert Martin Evans. Urbana, Ill., 1982.

Voss, Christian Daniel. *Versuch über die Erziehung für den Staat als Bedürfnis unserer Zeit, zur Beförderung des Bürgerwohls und der Regenten-Sicherheit.* 2 parts. Halle, 1799–1800.

Waetzoldt, Stephan. "Der Deutsche und seine Muttersprache." In *Kunsterziehung. Ergebnisse und Anregungen des zweiten Kunsterziehungstages in Weimar am 9., 10., 11. Oktober 1903.* Deutsche Sprache und Dichtung (Leipzig, 1904): pp. 250–65.

Wagenbach, Klaus, ed. *Franz Kafka, "In der Strafkolonie." Eine Geschichte aus dem Jahre 1914.* Berlin, 1975.

Wagner, Richard. *Gesammelte Schriften und Dichtungen.* 4th ed. Leipzig, 1907.

———. *My Life.* Ed. May Whittal. Trans. Andrew Gray. Cambridge, 1983.

Waldeck, Marie-Louise. "The Princess in 'Torquato Tasso': Further Reflections on an Enigma." *Oxford German Studies* 5 (1970): 14–37.

Weber, Marianne. *Vom Typenwandel der studierenden Frau.* Berlin, 1918.

Weber, Samuel M. "Die Parabel." In Daniel P. Schreber, *Denkwürdigkeiten eines Nervenkranken,* ed. Samuel M. Weber. Frankfurt a. M., 1973.

Wedag, Friedrich Wilhelm. *Handbuch über die frühere sittliche Erziehung zunächst zum Gebrauche für Mütter in Briefen abgefasst.* Leipzig, 1795.

Wehnert, Bruno. "Der Spaziergang. Ein Beitrag zu Schillers Verhältnis zur Natur." *Zeitschrift für den deutschen Unterricht* 23 (1909): 473–91.

Wehrlin, K. "Diagnostische Assoziationsstudien, II. Beitrag. Über die Assoziationen von Imbezillen und Idioten." *Journal für Psychologie und Neurologie* 4 (1904): 109–23, 129–43.

Weimar, Klaus. "Zur Geschichte der Literaturwissenschaft. Forschungsbericht." *Deutsche Vierteljahresschrift für Literaturwissenschaft und Geistesgeschichte* 50 (1976): 298–364.

Weininger, Otto. *Geschlecht und Charakter. Eine prinzipielle Untersuchung.* 19th ed. Leipzig, 1920. (Orig. pub. 1903.)

Wellek, René, and Austin Warren. *Theory of Literature.* New York, 1956.

Wernicke, Carl. "Der aphasische Symptomencomplex." In Ernst von Leyden and Felix Klemperer, eds., *Die deutsche Klinik am Eingange des zwanzigsten Jahrhunderts in akademischen Vorlesungen* (Berlin, 1906), 6: 487–556.

Westphalen, Raban Graf von. *Akademisches Privileg und demokratischer Staat. Ein Beitrag zur Geschichte und bildungsgeschichtlichen Problematik des Laufbahnwesens in Deutschland.* Stuttgart, 1979.

Wiese, Benno von. *Friedrich Schiller.* 3d ed. Stuttgart, 1963.

Wiese, Ludwig von. *Verordnungen und Gesetze für die höheren Schulen in Preussen. Erste Abtheilung: Die Schule; zweite Abtheilung: Das Lehramt und die Lehrer.* Berlin, 1867–68.

Wilde, Oscar. "The Soul of Man under Socialism." In *The Soul of Man under Socialism and Other Essays,* intro. Philip Rieff (New York, 1970), pp. 227–71.

Wilkinson, Elizabeth M. "Faust in der Logosszene—willkürlicher Übersetzer oder geschulter Exeget? Wie, zu welchem Ende—und für wen—schreibt man heutzutage einen Kommentar?" In Victor Lange and Hans-Gert Roloff, eds., *Dichtung, Sprache, Gesellschaft. Akten des IV. Internationalen Germanisten-Kongresses 1970 in Princeton* (Frankfurt a. M., 1971), pp. 115–24.

Wittgenstein, Ludwig. *Prototractatus.* Trans. D. F. Pears and B. F. McGuinness. Ithaca, N. Y., 1971.

Wolff, Gustav. "Zur Pathologie des Lesens und Schreibens." *Allgemeine Zeitschrift für Psychiatrie und psychisch-gerichtliche Medicin* 60 (1903): 509–33.

Wolff, Lutz-W., ed. *Puppchen, du bist mein Augenstern. Deutsche Schlager aus vier Jahrzehnten.* Munich, 1981.

Wolgast, Heinrich. *Ganze Menschen! Ein sozialpädagogischer Versuch.* Berlin, 1910.

———. "Jugendschrift, Schülerbibliothek, das billige Buch." In *Kunsterziehung. Ergebnisse und Anregungen des zweiten Kunsterziehungstages in Weimar am 9., 10., 11. Oktober 1903: Deutsche Sprache und Dichtung* (Leipzig, 1904), pp. 182–93.

Wolke, Christian Friedrich. *Kurze Erziehungslehre oder Anweisung zur körperlichen, verständlichen und sittlichen Erziehung anwendbar für Mütter und Lehrer in den ersten Jahren der Kinder. In Verbindung mit dessen Anweisung für Mütter und Kinderlehrer zur Mittheilung der allerersten Sprachkenntnisse und Begriffe von der Geburt des Kindes an bis zur Zeit des Lesenlernens.* Leipzig, 1805.

Wolters, Friedrich. *Stefan George und die Blätter für die Kunst. Deutsche Geistesgeschichte seit 1890.* Berlin, 1930.

Wunberg, Gotthard. *Der frühe Hofmannsthal. Schizophrenie als dichterische Struktur.* Stuttgart, 1965.

Wundt, Wilhelm. *Völkerpsychologie. Eine Untersuchung der Entwichlungsgesetze von Sprache, Mythos und Sitte.* Vol. 1 (2 parts): *Die Sprache.* Leipzig, 1904.

Wuthenow, Ralph-Rainer. *Im Buch die Bücher oder Der Held als Leser.* Frankfurt a. M., 1980.

Wychgram, Jakob. "Geschichte des höheren Mädchenschulwesens in Deutschland und Frankreich." In Karl Adolf Schmid, ed., *Geschichte der Erziehung vom Anfang an bis auf unsere Zeit* (Stuttgart, 1901), 5: 222–97.

Wyss, Ulrich. *Die wilde Philologie. Jacob Grimm und der Historismus.* Munich, 1979.

Zeitler, Julius. "Tachistoskopische Untersuchungen über das Lesen." *Philosophische Studien* 16 (1900): 380–463.

Zglinicki, Friedrich von. *Der Weg des Films. Die Geschichte der Kinematographie und ihrer Vorläufer.* Berlin, 1956.

Ziehen, Theodor. "Aphasie." In Albert Eulenburg, ed., *Real-Encyclopädie der gesamten Heilkunde.* 4th ed. (Berlin, 1907), 1: 664–88.

———. *Die Geisteskrankheiten des Kindesalters mit besonderer Berücksichtigung des schulpflichtigen Alters.* Sammlung von Abhandlungen aus dem Gebiete der pädagogischen Psychologie und Physiologie, vols. 5, 7, 9. Berlin, 1902–6.

———. *Die Ideenassoziation des Kindes.* Sammlung von Abhandlungen aus dem Gebiete der pädagogischen Psychologie und Physiologie. Berlin, 1898–1900.

———. *Leitfaden der Physiologischen Psychologie in 15 Vorlesungen.* 2d ed. Jena, 1893.

Zimmermann, Josefine. "Betty Gleim (1781–1827) und ihre Bedeutung für die Geschichte des Mädchenbildungswesens." Ph.D. diss., Cologne, 1926.

Zons, Raimar St. "Ein Familienzentrum: Goethes 'Erlkönig.'" *Fugen. Deutschfranzösisches Jahrbuch für Text-Analytik* 1 (1980): 125–31.

Zwirner, Eberhard. "Bemerkungen über die Dehnbarkeit der deutschen Silben bei Karl Philipp Moritz und in Goethes 'Italienischer Reise.'" *Archiv für Vergleichende Phonetik* 5 (1941): 33–36.

Index of Persons

The index lists persons from the two time periods covered, together with, as far as possible, their biographical dates and their roles in the discourse network.

Library of Congress Cataloging-in-Publication Data

Kittler, Friedrich A.
[Aufschreibesysteme 1800/1900. English]
  Discourse networks 1800/1900 / Friedrich A. Kittler; translated
by Michael Metteer, with Chris Cullens; foreword by David E.
Wellbery.
        p.   cm.
Translation of: Aufschreibesysteme 1800/1900.
Includes bibliographical references.
ISBN 0-8047-1616-1 (cl.):   ISBN 0-8047-2099-1 (pbk.)
  1. German literature—19th century—History and criticism.
2. German literature—20th century—History and criticism.   3. Books
and reading in literature.   4. Authorship.   5. Books and reading—
Germany—History—19th century.   6. Books and reading—Germany—
History—20th century.   7. Literature and society—Germany—
History—19th century.   8. Literature and society—Germany—
History—20th century.   I. Title.
PT345.K5813   1990   89-26291
830.9'357—dc20   CIP

⊗   This book is printed on acid-free paper